Reconstruction

Post-War, the destroyed South struggled to survive while under the occupation of a cruel and alien enemy.

"The War to Survive" by artist Jerry McWilliams

Reconstruction

Destroying a Republic
and Creating an Empire

James Ronald Kennedy

Reconstruction: Destroying a Republic and Creating an Empire

Copyright© 2024 by James Ronald Kennedy

ALL RIGHTS RESERVED. No part of this publication may be reproduced, distributed, or transmitted in any form or by any means, including photocopying, recording, or other electronic or mechanical methods, or by any information storage and retrieval system without the prior written permission of the publisher, except in the case of very brief quotations embodied in critical reviews and certain other non-commercial uses permitted by copyright law.

Produced in the Republic of South Carolina by

SHOTWELL PUBLISHING LLC

Post Office Box 2592

Columbia, So. Carolina 29202

www.ShotwellPublishing.com

Cover: Adapted from public domain photo. 'The "Strong" government 1869-1877—The "weak" government 1877-1881' / J.A. Wales, 1880. Courtesy of loc.gov.

ISBN 978-1-963506-13-6

FIRST EDITION

10 9 8 7 6 5 4 3 2

Contents

Foreword ix
Reconstruction via Deconstruction

Chapter 1: 1
What Could Have Been—
A Biracial Moral and Ethical Society

Chapter 2: 21
Reconstruction—Tyranny and Racial Hatred
—Then and Now

Chapter 3: 35
The Republican Party's Goal for Reconstruction

Chapter 4: 51
The South's Five Strategic Failures

Chapter 5: 85
Slander: Justifying Invasion, Conquest, and
Domination of the South

Chapter 6: 103
The Constitutional Origins of Reconstruction

Chapter 7: 121
Race Relations Before Lincoln's War and
Republican Reconstruction

Chapter 8: 135
Divide & Rule—Republicans Use Racial Hatred
to Gain Political Power

Chapter 9: 149
The Southern People's Right of Self-Determination

Chapter 10: 157
The South's Post-War Social, Economic, and Political Situation

Chapter 11: 175
Lincoln's Ten Percent Reconstruction Plan

Chapter 12: 197
Republicans Reconstruct the Constitution
—Republic to Empire

Chapter 13: 217
Active Reconstruction—1866-77

Chapter 14: 273
Alabama Endures Republican Reconstruction

Chapter 15: 285
Arkansas Endures Republican Reconstruction

Chapter 16: 293
Reconstruction in Florida

Chapter 17: 301
Georgia Under Republican Reconstruction

Chapter 18: 317
Kentucky Punished With Reconstruction

Chapter 19: 325
Louisiana—Yankee Tyranny in the Bayou State

Chapter 20: 337
Maryland Reconstructed Since 1861

Chapter 21: 353
Mississippi Suffers the Wrath of Reconstruction

Chapter 22: 379
Reconstruction in Missouri

Chapter 23: 387
North Carolina-Reconstruction and The Klan-Kirk War

Chapter 24: 411
South Carolina—
Reconstruction in the Cradle of Secession

Chapter 25: 427
Tennessee—Lincoln's and Brownlow's Reconstruction

Chapter 26: 445
Texas—Independent Nation to Sovereign State to Puppet State

Chapter 27: 459
Virginia—Reconstruction in the Old Dominion

Chapter 28: 475
West Virginia—The Hypocrisy of Reconstructing a Loyal State

Chapter 29: 485
Passive Reconstruction, The Gilded Age,
and The Progressive Era

Chapter 30: 511
Modern Era Reconstruction Post 1965

Chapter 31: 521
Modern Era Southern Resistance Movement

Chapter 32: 529
Timeline for Lincoln's Secret War Conspiracy

Bibliography 539

Index 547

About the Author 549

Foreword

RECONSTRUCTION VIA DECONSTRUCTION

> *Reconstruction was the continuation of the Civil War into a new phase, in which the revolution passed from the stage of armed conflict into primarily a political struggle which sought to consolidate the Northern triumph.*
> —James S. Allen, Marxist historian, and member of the Communist Party USA

ESTABLISHMENT HISTORIANS are quick to praise the Reconstruction era as the high watermark of American civil liberty and justice for all. Establishment historians, those who embrace the victor's view about the War for Southern Independence, and others who pay homage to the victor's view, seldom allow "the rest of the story" about that war and the Reconstruction era to be given an honest hearing. With the publication of this book, the hidden story is at last fully detailed.

This book exposes many hidden stories about Reconstruction. These otherwise hidden stories will include subjects such as the last slave state to be admitted to the Union was under the direction of Lincoln and the Republican Party; Maryland was the first Southern state to feel the heavy hand of Reconstruction; former Confederate officials advocating education and civil rights for former slaves; the use of racial division by the Republican Party to prevent their loss of power in Washington; Union League violence that incited the formation of the Klan; the Southern resistance movement was more about unsound government and heavy taxation than race; the Union before the War is NOT the same Union that was created after the War; and, how the action of the Republican Party made the creation of today's Deep State not only possible but inevitable. Currently, conservatives and Republicans loudly complain about Democrats who are "weaponizing" the Federal Government and using the Federal Government to attack the Democratic administration's conservative opponents. Yet, as will be documented herein, Lincoln and the Republican Party began the weaponization process.

The author skillfully destroys the incessant demands of Critical Race Theory advocates that the South was responsible for slavery and is the center of racism in America today. He informs the reader that the South led the way in ending the nefarious African slave-trade, advocating gradual emancipation, educating, and training slaves to become productive members of society while embracing a strong family network based upon Christian values. These efforts were destroyed by Northern Radical Abolitionists who sought to promote a Haitian-styled slave uprising with all its attendant horrors. Think about how different this nation would be today if the South's high road of emancipation was taken instead of the Republican Party's low road. It was a peaceful, just, and fair society that *could have been*.

At the time of this writing, October 2023, Hamas terrorists have instituted a wide-scale attack upon Israel, killing not just Israeli soldiers but non-combatant men, women, *and* children. Terror swept the nation of Israel, not just the population along the borders where these acts are taking place, but the entire nation. This was the type of fear that swept the South in 1860. This sense of fear for innocent family and friends in Israel in 2023, is the same sense of fear faced by all Southerners, non-slaveholders (80%) as well as slave-holders (20%) in 1860. It was a fear created by Northern-supported Radical Abolitionist's efforts to promote Nat Turner and John Brown slave uprisings in the South. Is it any wonder that when Lincoln was elected president with only 39.6% of the popular vote, the South no longer felt secure in that government?

Other reasons for fearing for the safety of Southern families were that the Republican Party was so unpopular that it was not on the ballot in one-third of the States of the country, and another was the Republican Party's friendly attitude toward the Radical Abolitionist's cause. As a result, the South no longer felt safe in that government. As James Madison points out in *Federalist Papers* Number 43, "the safety and happiness of society are the objects at which all political institutions must be sacrificed." The "safety and happiness" of the Southern people trumped Mr. Lincoln's Union.

Unlike other books about Reconstruction, this book explains that although the South was the primary focus of Reconstruction, it was the Federal Government and therefore, these United States that were being reconstructed. As pointed out in the following pages, without Lincoln and the Republican Party's destruction of America's original Constitutional Union, Deep State Federal tyranny would not be possible. Before Lincoln and the GOP's war on States' Rights, the Federal Government did not possess the ability to close churches, shut down private businesses, use its unlawful power to censor political thought or forcefully medicate its subjects. None of this is new! It began with Lincoln and the Republican Party in 1861.

If the reader doubts that the War to Prevent Southern Independence was not a war upon real States' Rights, consider these 21st-century actions of the Federal Government: When Arizona began enforcing Federal laws against illegal immigration, the Federal Government forced Arizona to "cease and desist" from enforcing Federal law and when Alabama placed copies of the Ten Commandments in Alabama State Courthouses, a Republican President sent Federal marshals into Alabama courthouses and forcefully removed the Ten Commandments. These are but two of countless acts of the Federal Government dictating what is and is not permissible for a state to do. Remember, before 1861, all States were acknowledged to be free and sovereign States, but today they are mere servants of the Federal Government. Where now are your vaunted States' Rights? States' Rights have been replaced with States' privileges, privileges that the Federal Government will determine if, when, and how long a state can exercise said privilege.

The author of this book begins his review of Reconstruction not after the end of the War, but by reviewing *what could have been* if the North allowed the South to follow the high road to emancipation. He then explains the great change in the Federal Government since 1861. As he points out, the great change in the nature of the Federal Government was established not by the act of *consent* but by the act of *conquest*. It is impossible to compare the nature of the two Federal Governments, the one before Reconstruction, and the current Federal Government. These two Federal Governments can only be contrasted, not compared. By revealing the facts about the true nature of the original Federal Government created for "We the People" of the Sovereign States by the Founding Fathers, the author has a starting point to demonstrate just how tyrannical the present "reconstructed" Federal Government has become.

Throughout this book, one is reminded that, according to the Declaration of Independence, the only *legitimate* government is the one that is based upon the *consent* of the governed. As the author so correctly points out, when the consent of the governed is replaced by coercion of the governed, tyranny abounds—at that point, the government is *illegitimate*. The act of the United States invading the Confederate States and forcing the people thereof into a government, not of their free choice, is a blatant, un-American act if one holds to the principles of the Declaration of Independence. Lincoln's invasion of the South was an act of treason to the principles of the Declaration of Independence. Under the current political *status quo*, no state of these United States can "alter or abolish" a government they no longer feel safe living under and "institute new Government...in such form, as to them shall seem most likely to affect their Safety and Happiness." These concepts come directly from the Declaration of Independence, yet no people of any state can exercise these ideas. As has often been stated, "If you can't leave, you are not free." As a result of the invasion and conquest of the Confederate States of America by the United States of America, Reconstruction was imposed upon all Americans. Indeed, Reconstruction sounded the death knell for the America of Thomas Jefferson, James Madison, Patrick Henry, and the majority of America's Founding Fathers.

The facts demonstrated within this book challenge the current neo-Marxist's woke view about Reconstruction. Yet, during an earlier era when leftist ideology and emotions did not trump facts, the truth about the horrors committed against the people of the South during Reconstruction was acknowledged by Americans. This was demonstrated in 1929, when an Indiana native, Claude Bowers, published one of the most complete and shocking revelations about the horrors of Reconstruction in his book titled *The Tragic Era*. Today, neo-Marxists condemn Bowers's book, but his book was given a glowing review in the September 1929 issue of *Wings*, the official journal of The Literary Guild of America published in New York. Dr. Carl Van Doren, editor of *Wings*, noted that Reconstruction was part of an American revolution. Van Doren stated that Bowers was "engaged in explaining why and how this revolution came about." Bowers book on Reconstruction was highly recommended by a New York journal associated with numerous well-known literary and social leaders in American society, (including people such as Mrs. Franklin D. Roosevelt). Such high praise for Bowers's book underscores the reality that the views expressed by Bowers and others of that era were at one time widely accepted by Americans.

In the following pages, the reader will discover many hidden facts that will challenge the reader to rethink the so-called "accepted" version of the War and Reconstruction. As the Communist historian James S. Allen noted, Reconstruction was part of a "revolution" designed to turn Federal military victory into a "political struggle which sought to consolidate the Northern triumph." Currently, the revolution Allen describes continues its attack upon all traditional American values. As the author so succinctly and appropriately points out, Americans do not have to accept the Reconstruction destruction of American freedom. The means of overturning the Marxist revolution that was set loose upon these United States by Lincoln and the Republican Party in 1861 is plainly described. The only question is, "Are Americans courageous enough to engage in a real fight for victory over big government tyranny?"

Deo Vindice

Walter D. (Donnie) Kennedy
Louisiana, CSA, (occupied)

GENERAL NATHAN BEDFORD FORREST, CSA

"We were born on the same soil, breathe the same air, live in the same land, and why should we not be brothers and sisters...I want you to do as I do—go to the polls and select the best men to vote for....Although we differ in color, we should not differ in sentiment....Do Your duty as citizens, and if any are oppressed, I will be your friend," Nathan Bedford Forrest speaking to a group of black voters. This is an example of what could have been.

Chapter 1:

WHAT COULD HAVE BEEN— A BIRACIAL MORAL AND ETHICAL SOCIETY

"The slave must be made fit for his freedom by education and discipline and thus be made unfit for slavery." —Jefferson Davis[1]

THE STORY TOLD by Northern propagandists[2] about the Southern resistance to Reconstruction is that the resistance movement was motivated by hatred for blacks. One of the South's many failures, from 1776 to today, is that it never developed an efficient mechanism to challenge the North's narrative about "We the People" of the South. From the colonial era to 1860, Southerners working privately as individuals attempted to find a peaceful way to emancipate, at their own expense, a significant part of their population. As Jefferson Davis said in Congress, if allowed, the day will come when slave owners can complete the journey on the high

---

1   Jefferson Davis, cited in Kennedy & Kennedy, *The South Was Right!* 3rd edition (Columbia, SC: Shotwell Publishing, 2020), 141.

2   Northern propagandists in the nineteenth and early twentieth centuries were yellow dog newspapers and public orators of the New England school. These propagandists promoted Northern dominance of the Federal Government by spreading vicious, slanderous, anti-South stories about evil, slave-beating Southerners. Such "stories" were picked-up by European papers and printed as factual. Thus, not only the North but the entire world was told and began to believe that Southerners were evil "slave-whippers," racists, and inhuman haters of human liberty. The purpose of the aggressor's propaganda is to separate the targeted people from the community of acceptable humanity. After that, it is easy to "morally" justify exterminating such human vermin.

road to emancipation.³ The question for most Southerners, slave owners, and non-slave owners, was not if slavery should end but how and when it should end. Patrick Henry understood the need to find a solution to the difficult question of slavery. He declared:

> Slavery is detested. We feel its fatal effects. We deplore it with all the pity of our humanity. I would rejoice my very soul if every one of my fellow human beings was emancipated.... But is it practicable, by any human means, to liberate them without producing the most dreadful and ruinous consequences?
>
> We ought to soften, as much as possible, the rigor of their unhappy fate. I know that in a variety of particular instances the legislature [Virginia] listening to complaints, have admitted their emancipation.⁴

The high road to emancipation was seen as a time to prepare a race of people who never created a democratic society for full membership in a free and prosperous Southern society. This was a Southern society that *could have been*, a society in which both blacks and whites could continue to live together in friendship and produce a peaceful, prosperous, Christian society. Confederate General Bradley T. Johnson described what *could have been* in a speech delivered on February 22, 1896:

> If the institution of slavery had been left to work itself out under the influence of Christianity and civilization, the unjust and cruel incidents would have been eliminated....Institutions and society change by the operation of the law of justice and love, of right and charity, and by its influence the

---

3   Kennedy & Kennedy, *Jefferson Davis: Highroad to Emancipation and Constitutional Government* (Columbia, SC: Shotwell Publishing, 2022).

4   Patrick Henry cited in John Remington Graham's *Principles of Confederacy* (Salt Lake City, UT: Northwest Publishing, 1990), 574-5; Graham cites Virginia Convention, June 24, 1788, in *Elliot's Debates, vol. 3,* 590-591.

negro would have been trained and educated in habits of industry, of self-reliance, of self-denial, of moral self-government, until in due time he would have gone into the world to make his struggle for survivorship on fair terms.[5]

After the War former Confederate Vice President Alexander Stephens told the Georgia legislature that white Southerners owe a debt of gratitude to black Southerners. Numerous, but untold, are the stories of slaves protecting their "white folks" during the War. Fred Ardis was Captain Isac Ardis's slave. While the Captain was visiting home during the closing days of the War, Fred noticed a group of deserters who were planning to kill the Captain. Fred warned Captain Ardis who managed to flee out a back door. Fred then went to the slave quarters, gathered several men who armed themselves with axes and placed themselves as guards around the house. Fred then told Mrs. Ardis, "Now, Miss Lizabeth, you go to sleep. If anybody gets in this house tonight, they have got to kill us first."[6] The white South's debt of gratitude could have been the foundation for a mutually beneficial biracial Southern society, but Yankee invasion and occupation destroyed the potential.

Conditions immediately after the end of the War gave evidence of what "could have been." What *could have been* if the Yankee Empire had not destroyed the high road to emancipation and imposed Lincoln's low road to emancipation. The impoverishment, malnutrition, disease, and death rate of post-War black and white sharecroppers (a new form of slavery) that resulted from Lincoln's low road to emancipation are well documented.[7]

---

5 General Bradley T. Johnson, *Confederate Veteran*, Vol. V., No. 10, Oct. 1897, republished in *The Confederate Veteran Magazine* Vol. V (Harrisburg, PA: The National Historical Society, 1987), 509.

6 *Confederate Veteran* Vol. IX, No. 1, Jan. 1901, republished in *The Confederate Veteran Magazine* Volume IX (Harrisburg, PA: The National Historical Society, 1987), 36.

7 Kennedy & Kennedy, *Punished with Poverty-The Suffering South*, 2nd ed. (Columbia, SC: Shotwell Publishing, 2020).

Black and white Southerners, immediately after the end of the War, understood the need to begin rebuilding their society. W.H. Trescott of South Carolina, in *DeBow's Review,* wrote the following about black Southerners a year after emancipation:

> ... [there] was no impatience, no insubordination, no violence. They have received their freedom quietly and soberly. They remained pretty steadily on the farms of their [former] masters, a very general disposition being manifested to adjust the terms of compensation on a reasonable basis."[8]

This reflects the potential that the high road to emancipation held—a peaceful and prosperous potential that was violently denied to "We the People" of the South. Lincoln's low road to emancipation meant immediate emancipation without preparation and training for the mostly illiterate black Southern population. It was a recipe for social disaster but a recipe that worked to the advantage of the victorious Republican Party in Congress.

The Republican Party was aware that, with the end of chattel slavery, blacks would be counted as a full person in the census instead of three-fifths. This would mean that the South would gain between 11 to 15 new representatives in Congress! If black and white Southerners worked together, they and Northern Democrats would force the Republican Party into the position of a minority, sectional Party. To prevent this, the Republican Party initiated their divide-and-rule efforts to separate black and white Southerners.

The willingness of whites and blacks to work together for their mutual benefit is demonstrated by the account of what Benjamin Hill of Georgia found when he returned to his plantation after the War. When former Confederate Senator Benjamin Harvey Hill of Georgia returned to his home, the La Grange plantation, he found that not one of his slaves deserted or betrayed him, even though Georgia was full of Yankees. In a speech delivered in Atlanta denouncing the Republican Reconstruction Plan, he paid special

---

8   Henry, Robert Selph, *The Story of Reconstruction* (New York: Konecky & Konecky, 1938), 29.

attention to the evil perpetrated upon freedmen by those claiming to be their new friends:

> Oh, I pity the colored people who have never been taught what an oath is or what the Constitution means. They are drawn up by a selfish conclave of traitors to inflict a death-blow on the Republic by swearing them into a falsehood. They are to begin their political life with perjury to accomplish treason.... They are neither legally nor morally responsible—it is you, educated, designing white men, who thus devote yourselves to the unholy work, who are the guilty parties.... Ye hypocrites! Ye whited sepulchers! Ye mean in your hearts to deceive him and buy up the negro vote for your own benefit.[9]

Then Hill continued by addressing the freedmen in the audience directly:

> They tell you they are your friends—it is false. They tell you they set you free—it is false. These vile creatures never went with the Army except to steal spoons, jewelry, and gold watches. They are too low to be brave. They are dirty spawn, cast out from decent society, who come down here to see and to use you to further their own base purposes.... Improve yourselves; learn to read and write; be industrious; lay up your means; acquire homes; love in peace with your neighbors; drive off as you would a serpent the miserable dirty adventurers who come among you... and seek to foment among you hatred of the decent portion of the white race. [10]

---

9 Bowers, Claude, *The Tragic Era* (New York: Halcyon House, 1929), 211.

10 Note that Hill encourages blacks not to learn to hate "the decent portion of the white race." In this, he acknowledges that there are some "indecent" whites just as there are some "indecent" people in all races. See Bowers, Claude, *The Tragic Era*, 212.

Hill understood what pacified Southerners and conservatives of today refuse to recognize: "the ultimate but complete change of all American government from the principle of consent to the rule of force and a war of races."[11] Hill's stinging but truthful words struck the ears of the occupying Yankees like canister shot. Shortly after Hill's speech, Union General Pope wrote to General Grant insisting that such Southern spokesmen should be banished from their state—like the way President Lincoln banished Ohio Representative Vallandigham from the United States due to Vallandigham's criticism of Lincoln's unconstitutional war.[12]

In the early days of the Freedmen's Bureau, when it was non-political, the Bureau acted in a fair manner, seeking to help the freedmen. In Georgia, Bureau agents hired two hundred and forty-four agents from the local population. Note the fact that they hired from the "local population." It was openly acknowledged that these local agents "did not encounter the prejudice felt against officers of the Army, or agents from the North, and were thereby enabled more readily to secure justice to the freedmen, and to build up and foster a healthy public opinion."[13] This is another example of what "could have been" had the South been allowed to follow the high road to emancipation.[14] White Southerners were not filled with animosity against the newly freed slaves. There existed a sense of community between the races in the pre-War and post-War South. Even after four long years of war, there was still a "well of friendship" between black and white Southerners.[15] But, as has been well documented, "freeing the slaves" and "helping oppressed blacks" was not the Yankee Empire's fundamental motive for waging aggressive war.

---

11 Ibid., 213.

12 DiLorenzo, Dr. Thomas J., *The Real Lincoln* (New York: Three Rivers Press, 2002), 154-5.

13 Henry, Robert Selph, *The Story of Reconstruction* (New York: Konecky & Konecky, 1938), 148.

14 Kennedy & Kennedy, *Jefferson Davis: High Road to Emancipation and Constitutional Government*, 267-91.

15 African American Louisianian, Dr. Leonard Haynes quoted in Kennedy & Kennedy, *Punished With Poverty-The Suffering South* 2nd ed., 155-6.

Black and White Southerners Working Together

Shortly after the end of the War, General P.G.T. Beauregard of Louisiana urged his fellow white conservatives to accept the circumstances and make the best out of a bad situation. Beauregard was an early Southern champion of black suffrage.

> In Negro suffrage he saw an element of strength for the South in the future and a possibility of defeating the radicals with their own weapon.[16]

He openly declared a general understanding of all white Southerners when he stated, "The Negro is Southern born; with a little education and some property qualifications he can be made to take sufficient interests in the affairs and prosperity of the South to ensure an intelligent vote."[17] This attitude was also expressed by General Nathan Bedford Forrest who addressed a meeting of blacks in Memphis and declared:

> We were born on the same soil, we breathe the same air, live in the same land, and why should we not be brothers and sisters.... I want you to do as I do—go to the polls and select the best men to vote for.... Although we differ in color, we should not differ in sentiment.[18]

Former Vice President of the Confederacy, Alexander Stephens, addressed the Georgia legislature lamenting the fact that the newly freed slaves were, through no fault of their own, "poor, untutored, uninformed, liable to be imposed upon..." and urged the legislature to secure for the freedmen "ample and full protection... so that they may stand equal before the law in the possession and enjoyment

---

16 Beauregard cited in Williams, T. Harry, *P.G.T. Beauregard: Napoleon in Gray* (Baton Rouge, LA: LSU Press, 1955), 266.

17 *Ibid.*

18 Forrest cited in Kennedy & Kennedy's *Punished With Poverty-The Suffering South* 2nd ed., 147.

of all the rights of person, liberty, and property."[19] From these statements of former military and civil officers of the Confederacy, it can be seen that there was no overwhelming animosity toward the newly freed slaves. As former Vice President Stephens said in his address to the Georgia legislature, "we owe these people a debt of gratitude." Gratitude and continuing friendship were the attitudes of post-War white Southerners toward black Southerners at the advent of carpetbaggers and the Union League.

Perhaps the best examples of the closeness between black and white Southerners were demonstrated by the way the returning Confederate veterans were treated by the former slaves—now free but remaining home with "their" white folks. Sergeant James W. Nicholson, 12th Louisiana Infantry is typical of the Plain Folk of the old South who made up approximately 80% of the Confederate Army. Upon returning home to the family farm (not a plantation), he was met by his sisters and father—his mother passed away during the War. This is his account of his return:

> The darkies politely stood aloof until the salutations of the whites had somewhat abated. Good Old Uncle Nathan, unable to restrain himself longer, burst in, and seizing me by the arms, exclaimed, "Bless de Lawd fur all his mercies; de boy is cum back to us er man." Aunt Callie, my old nurse, came next, and grasping my hand she sobbed, "My dear baby boy! What fur yu stay so long? Yo Callie ben waiting, watching, and praying fur yu all dese years. My! What a big un my baby is got to be!" To her hand I held fast for the very comfort to be had from that living contact.[20]

---

19 Alexander Stephens cited in Henry, Robert Selph, *The Story of Reconstruction*, 149.

20 Nicholson, James W., *Stories of Dixie* (1915, Toccoa, GA: The Confederate Reprint Co., 2015), 163-4.

Postmodern[21] propagandists masquerading as historians discount such examples as being nothing more than an attempt of defeated Southerners to justify their treason against the good ole USA. However, numerous Yankee sources support the truth represented by such examples. Union officer and Radical Republican Carl Schurz reported the post-War congenial relations between former slaves and former masters in a report to Congress. He reported:

> Instances of the most touching attachment of freedmen to their old masters and mistresses have come to my notice. To a white man whom they believe to be sincerely their friend they cling with greater affection even than to one of their own race.... Centuries of slavery have not been sufficient to make them the enemies of the white race.[22]

This observation was made by a Yankee Radical who saw in it the potential for cooperation between former slaves and well-meaning white Southerners. Such cooperation in the political realm would spell doom for the local and national Republican Party. The great irony of American history is that what centuries of slavery could not accomplish, that is, teaching blacks to hate whites, the Republican Party accomplished in a decade of Active Reconstruction.

The friendship between the races even during the early stages of "Jim Crow" segregation is demonstrated by the continuing comradery between black and white Confederate veterans. Confeder-

---

21 Postmodernists seek to "deconstruct" or "debunk" traditional Western European/American values. They are politically leftists who challenge traditional truth and reality because they believe that Western society used traditional values of truth and reason to establish an oppressive society. They assert that the oppression of women, racial or sexual minorities is part of a Western society that must be destroyed. "The inspirational and philosophical source of postmodernism… the philosophy of Marxism." Hicks, Stephen R.C., *Explaining Postmodernism-Skepticism and Socialism from Rousseau to Foucault* 2nd ed. (Ockham's Razor Publishing: 2011), 2-5.

22 *A Just and Lasting Peace: A Documentary History of Reconstruction*, ed. John David Smith (New York: Signet Classics, 2013), 140.

ate Veteran, Robert E. Houston from Aberdeen, Mississippi wrote in June 1902 concerning the status of state pensions for Confederate Veterans, "We have quite a number of colored servants who deserve and receive pensions."[23]

Race was not the reason post-War white Southerners objected to granting the privilege of voting to the newly freed slaves. Race is always the knee-jerk emotional response of anti-South leftist propagandists. Post-War whites objected because most of the freedmen, through no fault of their own, lacked the social and political skill necessary to be an informed voter. Their civil deficiency made them easy tools for unscrupulous men (carpetbaggers and scallywags) seeking to use (exploit) illiterate voters for their personal gain. This could have been avoided had the South been allowed to follow the high road to emancipation. But allowing black and white Southerners to work out the mutually beneficial parameters of a new and free Southern society would have cost the Republican Party and its financial and commercial elites their positions of power and control. Instead, black and white people of the South were forced, at bayonet point, down Lincoln's and the Republican Party's low road to emancipation. The evil thus done carried through Active Reconstruction (1866-1877), into Passive Reconstruction (1877-1965), and continues with a vengeance today during Modern Era Reconstruction (post-1965).

From the Mississippi legislature, we can find examples of the respect and political cooperation between white and black Southerners after the end of Active Reconstruction and into Passive Reconstruction. It demonstrates what "could have been," it demonstrates how black and white Southern politicians worked together even though they belonged to different political parties. Both Republicans and Democrats joined in presenting a watch to Representative John R. Lynch, a black Republican. The Democrats offered a resolution praising Representative Lynch for his "ability, courtesy, and impartiality" as speaker of the Mississippi House of

---

23 *Confederate Veteran* Vol. X, No. 8, Aug. 1902. Republished in *The Confederate Veteran Magazine* Volume X (Harrisburg, PA: The National Historical Society, 1987), 355.

Representatives.[24] Another black member of the Mississippi legislature during this time stated on the floor of the State House of Representatives that:

> I was born in Mississippi but raised in a Northern State; associations there led me to regard the Southern white man as dire foes to the Negroes but receiving such cordial and unprejudiced association upon this floor [Mississippi House of Representatives] by the entire Democratic party here these suspicions have been eliminated from the bosoms of this feeble six [he and his fellow black representatives] and for them I am authorized to speak. You are our best friends....[25]

Where is the intrinsic racial animosity that Yankee propagandists constantly claim exists down South? Even after the War and Reconstruction, there remained a sense of community between black and white Southerners. Even at that late stage, this sense of community could have been used to develop a mutually agreeable Southern society, but the opportunity was cruelly denied. As one contemporary Southern historian noted, it "could have been" a Southern-based emancipation without war.[26]

Mississippi not only provides an excellent example of why the Southern resistance to Reconstruction arose but also why blacks who owned property were willing to cooperate with their white friends and neighbors. By 1874, the Republican city government of Vicksburg, Mississippi, virtually spent the city into bankruptcy. The city's debt grew from $13,000.00 to $1,400,000.00 in just five years of Republican rule! The city officials were elected by the mass of mostly illiterate, non-taxpaying voters. In the election of 1874, the city Republicans nominated for mayor a white man with twen-

---

24 Henry, Robert Selph, *The Story of Reconstruction*, 456-7.

25 Representative More cited in Kennedy & Kennedy, *The South Was Right!* 3rd ed., 147.

26 Livingston, Donald W, "Confederate Emancipation Without War," *To Live and Die In Dixie*, ed. Frank Powell, III (Columbia, TN: Sons of Confederate Veterans, 2014), 455-89.

ty-three indictments against him and for alderman one illiterate white and seven illiterate or of "low moral standards" freedmen. An uprising began to brew among the white and around fifty black taxpayers. Included in the uprising were two Republicans, Union General C.E. Furlong, and George McKee who represented the district in Congress. The peaceful "uprising" was a success and on August 4, 1874, the old city government was replaced with a new one that represented the interests of the taxpayers—both black and white.[27] This demonstrates the willingness of whites to work with blacks to elect officials who would not abuse their offices.

In the Mississippi elections of 1875, many property-owning blacks voted for the Democratic ticket even though this brought upon them severe social ostracism among their fellow blacks. But their votes, just like the votes of whites, were not based on race but on the need to remedy the oppressive tax load created by the Republican Party that controlled the state legislature. Hiram Revels, the first black man to serve as a US Senator, wrote to President Grant explaining the 1875 vote rejecting Republican rule in Mississippi. He explained that: "At the late election men, irrespective of race, color, or party affiliation, united and voted together against men known to be incompetent and dishonest...."[28]

When Mississippi's black Lt. Governor, Alexander Kelso Davis, was impeached by the state's House of Representatives and tried in the state's Senate, the vote was overwhelming in favor of conviction. The vote in favor of conviction included one black Republican voting for conviction. Despite what Yankee propagandists claim, not everything is about race.[29] There were men of goodwill of both races who could have worked together to create a fair and just Southern society but what "could have been" was aborted by a North under the influence of radical abolitionists before the War and by Radical Republicans after the War.

---

27 Henry, Robert Selph, *The Story of Reconstruction*, 530.

28 Senator Revels in Robert Selph Henry's *The Story of Reconstruction*, 549.

29 Henry, Robert Selph, *The Story of Reconstruction*, 553.

Mississippi was not the only place where such friendship and cooperation between black and white Southerners occurred. Just before the North Carolina constitutional convention in 1865, "a convention of freedmen gathered in the African church in Raleigh to discuss the status of their race....The first political act of North Carolina Negroes, is notably conservative."[30] This is an example of what "could have been" possible if the South had been allowed to follow the high road to emancipation. Yankee-imposed cultural distortion via its divide-and-rule policy aborted this golden opportunity.

In Louisiana, the entire summer of 1872 was spent with five different groups hammering out a compromise between the various elements that wanted to reform the state government and make it a fair and efficient representative of the people. After much work and mutual compromises, the five groups were reduced to two groups both recognizing black voters and black candidates in the list of candidates.[31] Note, that the compromise position of the Louisiana conservatives was to recognize black voters and to include black candidates on the list of favorable candidates. Recall how General Beauregard was promoting a similar stance immediately after the end of the War. Southern whites were willing to work with their black friends and neighbors. This is something that, in 1872, would never have been tolerated in a Northern state!

In Louisiana during the 1876 election, future Governor Nicholls and his conservative followers made specific efforts to break the political color line that was created by the Republican Party's imposed Reconstruction. As in the other Southern States, the division of race was primarily in politics. This antagonistic division of the races down South was essential for the Republicans to hold the state in the Republican camp. Louisiana conservatives secured the support of many property-owning black citizens by an appeal to the mutual desire for honest government and fair taxation.[32]

---

30   Ibid., 92.

31   Ibid., 478.

32   Ibid., 560.

South Carolina's Republican Reconstruction legislature had a few black elected officials who could have been a major political contributor to society had the South been allowed to follow the slow but steady high road to emancipation. James S. Pike observed that even though the Reconstruction legislature was a "shocking burlesque upon legislative proceedings," there were some of the black members who conducted themselves with dignity and decorum. Pike noted that the black chaplain of the South Carolina House of Representatives was "in dignities and proprieties of his office, in what he says, and still better, in what he omits to say, he might be profitably studied as a model by the white political parsons who so often officiate in Congress."[33]

During Wade Hampton's campaign for governor of South Carolina, the white conservatives worked to mend the racial antagonism brought about by the Republican Party's divide-and-rule Reconstruction policy. Hampton declared: "I am in this fight to save South Carolina...to bring the two races in friendly relations together with equal and impartial justice."[34] Here we see a Southern Statesman attempting to undo the harm done by the Republican Party's divide-and-rule scheme to control the South. Such sentiment points toward what "could have been" if the South was left alone to correct its social issues without interference by power-hungry Northerners.

Approximately a year after emancipation, W.H. Trescott of South Carolina, in *DeBow's Review,* wrote of the following, "... [there] was no impatience, no insubordination, no violence. They have received their freedom quietly and soberly. They remained steadily on the farms of their [former] masters, a very general disposition being manifested to adjust the terms of compensation on a reasonable basis."[35] This reflects the potential that the high road to emancipation held for a peaceful and mutually respectful Southern society. It was a dream denied!

---

33 Ibid., 497.

34 Ibid., 566.

35 Ibid., 29.

Even in the circuses of Republican-controlled Southern state Constitutional Conventions, there were black members who demonstrated a gift for and a sincere desire to "do the right thing" for their state. The graft and corruption of these post-War Republican-led state Constitutional Conventions were done to serve the peculiar interest of the national Republican Party. As one Southern historian noted, the black members of these Conventions generally demonstrated better judgment and appreciation of the realities back home than the white carpetbaggers, scalawags, and other demagogues.[36]

These examples are evidence of what "could have been" (1) if before the War, Northern radical abolitionists had not destroyed the South's vibrant emancipation movement[37] and (2) if after the War, the Yankee Empire had not initiated its campaign to use divide-and-rule as a political technique to control the South.[38] The Republican Party needed black voters in the South to keep their Party in power in Washington. Creating mistrust and hatred between black and white Southerners via a policy of divide-and-rule was their solution. Today, during Modern Era Reconstruction (post-1965), the Democratic Party is following the example set by the Republican Party during Active Reconstruction. In the Yankee Empire, the more things change, the more they remain the same.

Pre-War, the South was making a slow but definite movement toward finding a safe, efficient, and humane way to end slavery. Before the 1830s, the South had more abolitionist societies than the North—this fact of Southern history is ignored by South-hating academics.[39] New England's radical abolitionists of the John Brown school were mainly responsible for cooling the South's movement

---

36   Bowers, Claude, *The Tragic Era* (New York: Halcyon House, 1929), 217-8, The author cites Walter F. Fleming's *Civil War and Reconstruction in Alabama*, 522-3.

37   Kennedy & Kennedy, *Yankee Empire: Aggressive Abroad and Despotic at Home* (Columbia, SC: Shotwell Publishing, 2018), 179-99.

38   Kennedy & Kennedy, *Punished with Poverty-The Suffering South* 2nd ed., 13, 56, 149, 152 footnote, 407. See also Kennedy & Kennedy, *Yankee Empire: Aggressive Abroad and Despotic at Home*, 115, 124-5, 195, 345.

39   Livingston, "Confederate Emancipation Without War," *To Live and Die in Dixie*, 468.

toward emancipation. Judge William Rawle from Pennsylvania, whose textbook on the Constitution was used at West Point, was an active abolitionist, but he disapproved of New England's radical abolitionists.[40] By the early 1830s, it became clear that "the New England intellectual climate became increasingly favorable to the agitator."[41]

POST-WAR LABOR ISSUES COULD HAVE BEEN AVOIDED

The sudden emancipation of the major portion of the South's labor force caused a great deal of issues for landowners seeking to return their land to productive use. Just as important, the newly freed slaves, most of whom had no concept of "free labor" with written work contracts, were not adequately prepared to support themselves and their families in a free labor system—see Jefferson Davis's quote at the beginning of this chapter. This confusion could have been avoided had the South been allowed to take the high road to emancipation. When Lincoln was asked how the slaves were to survive after immediate emancipation and the destruction of the plantation system, he replied, "Let them root hog or die."[42] It was not unexpected that confusion would reign under Lincoln's low road to emancipation. Such circumstances created the perfect storm to be exploited by unscrupulous Northerners (carpetbaggers) and Southerners (scallywags) seeking personal gain at the expense of newly freed slaves in the South's post-War society.

Before the Union League worked its cruel "magic" on black Southerners and early after the end of the War, there seemed to be an opportunity to establish a free labor system. J.H. Christy of Georgia noted that:

---

[40] Bauer, Elizabeth Kelley, *Commentaries on the Constitution 1790-1860* (New York: Columbia University Press, 1952), 64.

[41] Floan, Howard R., *The South in Northern Eyes-1831 to 1861* (New York: McGraw-Hill Book Co., 1958), 11.

[42] Lincoln cited in Alexander H. Stephens's, *Constitutional View of the Late War Between the States* (1870, Harrisonburg, VA: Sprinkle Publications, 1994), Vol. II, 617.

> Generally, the Negroes work better than I supposed they would. A great many of them acquire property. I suppose there are from sixty to seventy-five in my town who have houses and lots. They are industrious.[43]

Again, this shows the potential of what "could have been." It represents a peaceful nonviolent and mutually agreeable potential that "could have been; if the pre-War South was allowed to follow the gradual and privately sponsored high road to emancipation.

The potential of free labor was beginning to express itself even under the dreadful economic, political, and social conditions in the South during the early post-War years. In 1868, the Little Rock, Arkansas, *Gazette* noted: "The wages paid to Negro laborers in the cotton fields of Arkansas far exceed the wages ever before paid to labor anywhere, except in California during the few years after the first discovery of gold."[44] A fact that is ignored by Yankee propagandists is that not all blacks in the South were "field hands." Many became skilled craftsmen while slaves on "their" plantation. Modern, fair-minded scholars documented that while slavery limited opportunities for bondsmen, still "over 25 percent of male slaves were managers, professionals, craftsmen, and semi-skilled workers."[45] It was only when greedy and aggressive Northerners brought politics into the social relations between white and black Southerners that a division along racial lines occurred. Edward King of Middlefield, Massachusetts, traveled the South during the post-War period. In his book *The Southern States of North America*, he wrote, "the same negro who will bitterly oppose his old master politically, will implicitly follow his advice in matters of labor and investment."[46] If this much social and economic good could be accomplished during the bad times of Reconstruction,

---

43 Henry, Robert Selph, *The Story of Reconstruction*, 362.

44 Ibid., 364.

45 Fogel & Engerman, *Time On The Cross: The Economics of American Negro Slavery* (New York: Little, Brown, and Company, 1974), 40.

46 Henry, Robert Selph, *The Story of Reconstruction*, 365.

one can only imagine what "could have been" accomplished if the South was allowed to follow the high road to emancipation.

President Johnson Endorses The Slow Road to Full Citizenship For Blacks

President Johnson presents a sad picture of a principled but confused man attempting to work within a system of "Constitutional" government that, post-War, existed only in his imagination. To a limited extent and without his own understanding, he represented the last shadow of the high road to emancipation. He advised that the freedom of blacks in the South should be safeguarded, especially their property rights and their right to engage in free labor contracts and in the enjoyment of the fruits of their labor. As a Southerner, he, unlike many Northerners, believed that black and white Southerners could "live side by side in a state of mutual benefit and goodwill." But the President warned post-War Northerners about being too hasty in moving former slaves into full citizenship. Like Jefferson Davis's high road to emancipation, President Johnson took a long, slow, and steady approach to bring the mostly illiterate black population into full citizenship. He admonished his critics that "time is always an element in reform." [47] But time was not on the agenda of a power-hungry Republican Party full of bloodlust for their conquered foe and an unquenchable passion for political power.

What Could Have Been

The South's resistance movement against the cruel and tyrannical oppressions imposed upon "We the People" of the once free and sovereign States is slandered by postmodern[48] Yankee propagandists as evidence of intrinsic Southern racism. It will be demon-

---

47   *Ibid.*, 138.

48   Postmodernists, neo-Marxists, and leftists in general do not want tools that aid in understanding, they want weapons to destroy their opponents. Truth, facts, and logic will never win against an opponent who has an emotional argument combined with a vast media to promote their emotional argument while censoring or slandering our counter argument. Conservatives have yet to learn that the truth can also be presented as an emotional appeal if we have a media to present our emotional but true argument to the public.

strated throughout this book that the Southern Resistance Movement that arose during Active Reconstruction was an effort by all conservatives, mostly white but many blacks as well, to regain control of their state and local governments. The Southern Resistance Movement was an effort to establish a system of government that honored the American principle of "No taxation without representation." Before Lincoln's war,[49] the issue of slavery—which was the emotional issue used by the North to justify an aggressive and unconstitutional war—could have been resolved by private individuals in the South following the high road to emancipation. Post-War black and white Southerners of goodwill could have established a fair, just, and mutually beneficial society. However, allowing such things would not have allowed the aggressive North to establish a supreme Federal Government that they would control. It would not allow them to foist upon "We the People" a new system of American government that would provide unlimited perks, privileges, and power to Northern ruling elites and their cronies.[50]

The people of the South were denied the opportunity to develop a just and fair biracial society. Such a society had never been accomplished. Yet, the South was making slow progress as it slowly traveled down the high road to emancipation. The South "could have been" a part of the country where black and white Southerners shared the responsibilities and benefits of their society. The antebellum South "could have been" a place where slaves were slowly granted their freedom in a manner that allowed them to immediately become a successful and prosperous part of Southern society. It "could have been" a community of friends and neighbors who judged each other by the content of their character. It "could have been," but we will never know if such a social experiment would have worked. The opportunity was denied by Lincoln's war and the Republican Party's Active Reconstruction—a denial that continues today.

---

49 The justification for the term "Lincoln's war" is documented in Chapter 32, "Timeline Lincoln's Secret War Conspiracy."

50 During Modern Era Reconstruction (post-1965) international Globalists became a part of America's ruling elite.

The Consequences of Lincoln's War

Southern scholar, Dr. M.E. Bradford (1934-1993) succinctly summarized the lasting impact that Lincoln had upon America:

> That this kind of politics would destroy the Union did not worry Mr. Lincoln.... But once he was finished in this career, he had left behind him a trail of blood, an emancipation under the worst possible circumstances, and a political example which continues to injure the Republic which he did so much to undermine. It is at our peril that we continue to reverence his name.[51]

In the next chapter, we will review the modern-day impact of Reconstruction. Throughout this book, it is demonstrated that Reconstruction never ended but continued into the post-1965 Modern Era Reconstruction. The so-called "Deep State" with its anti-conservative, weaponized Federal bureaucracy was impossible before Lincoln's war and the Republican Party's Active Reconstruction (1866-1877).

---

51 Bradford, Dr. M.E., *Against the Barbarians and Other reflections on Familiar Themes* (Columbia, MO: University of Missouri Press, 1992), 245.

Chapter 2:

RECONSTRUCTION—TYRANNY AND RACIAL HATRED—THEN AND NOW

"That the Southern people literally were put to the torture is vaguely understood, but even historians have shrunk from the unhappy task of showing us the torture chambers" —Claude Bowers[52]

YANKEE GENERAL SHERMAN'S admissions about his war crimes committed during the War is the best example of the North's pure hatred for the Southern people. General Sherman admitted that 80% of the physical destruction his Army inflicted upon the South's civilian population was unnecessary as a war strategy. He said that only 20% of the war's destruction "has inured to our advantage, and the remainder is simple waste and destruction."[53] The valuation of Southern private property by the end of the War, excluding capital investments in slave property, was 59% of what it was in 1860[54] and increased to only 63% by 1870. In 1880, the value of farms in the eleven Confederate States was only 67% of the 1860 value. The value of farm implements was only 45% of the value of such implements in 1860.[55] The

---

52 Bowers, Claude, *The Tragic Era* (New York: Halcyon House, 1929), vi.

53 Johnson, Dr. Ludwell H., *The North Against the South: The American Iliad 1848-1877* (1978, Columbia, SC: The Foundation for American Education, 1993), 187.

54 The 59% number drops to 37% when you include the capital investment in slaves. The North never inflicted uncompensated emancipation on Northern slave owners.

55 Johnson, Dr. Ludwell H., *The North Against the South: The American Iliad 1848-1877*, 189.

CULTURAL GENOCIDE PRACTICED BY AMERICA'S NEO-MARXIST POLITICAL ESTABLISHMENT

THE REMOVAL OF GENERAL LEE'S MONUMENT IN RICHMOND, VA

The destruction of our honorable Southern Heritage is justified by the outpouring of vicious anti-South fake history and other neo-Marxist propaganda. It merely proves that Reconstruction never ended. Cultural Genocide is used by tyrants to remove from the minds of an occupied people the memory of past glories and days of freedom. Monuments to past heroes are a vivid reminder to the occupied people of the possibility of regaining their lost freedom—therefore, tyrants (or their agents) will attempt to eradicate all such heroic symbols of past freedom.

Monuments matter:

destruction of the South was so great that, by 1900, the South had barely reached the same level of economic development it achieved in 1860. The prior data represents only the property/economic damage inflicted on a people who only asked to be left alone to govern themselves and resolve their social issues in a manner that would benefit all its citizens—free and slave.[56] But far greater than property and economic damage was the human cost of the Yankee Empire's illegitimate invasion and conquest of the once free and self-governing people of the South. But worse was to come. The Republican Party's Reconstruction came after Lincoln's war.[57]

Reconstruction was not a time of rebuilding the destroyed South. It was a time in which the conquered and occupied people of the Confederate States of America were forced, at the point of bloody Yankee bayonets, into a political torture chamber. Most white Southerners were disfranchised and turned into political vassals of the supreme Federal Government controlled by the Republican Party. Illiterate former slaves were placed in positions over experienced and educated local Southern political leaders. Uneducated and ill-prepared former slaves were manipulated by local scallywags and Northern carpetbaggers to establish a system of fraud, corruption, and lawlessness unheard of in Western Christian civilization. Those who had little, or no taxable property were given the ability to set the tax rates on those who had taxable property, while those with taxable property were not represented in the government that imposed confiscatory taxes. The 1776 war cry of the American Colonies—*No Taxation Without Representation*—became the complaint of black and white Southern property owners. It was a time in which a spontaneous Southern resistance movement developed.

Unlike the false narrative of the Yankee Empire's postmodern propagandists, the post-War Southern resistance movement was not directed at the newly freed slaves. It was a resistance movement

---

56   Kennedy & Kennedy, *Jefferson Davis: High Road to Emancipation and Constitutional Government* (Columbia, SC: Shotwell Publishing, 2022), 5-14. 57-9.

57   The justification for the term "Lincoln's war" is documented in Chapter 32, "Timeline Lincoln's Secret War Conspiracy."

that was, in essence, a tax revolt and a revolt against lawlessness and the political enslavement of formerly free people. It was a torture chamber that no American, other than Southerners, ever endured. It was a time of vicious anti-South slander—a ruthless slander that the South, then and now, was prevented from adequately answering. The evil inflicted upon "We the People" of the South continues today and is used as an excuse to inflict the latest stages of the Yankee Empire's campaign of anti-South cultural genocide during Modern Era Reconstruction (post-1965).[58]

RECONSTRUCTION, THE FEDERAL GOVERNMENT'S NEVER-ENDING OPPRESSION OF THE SOUTH

Judge John H. Reagan described the purpose of Reconstruction as:

> The plan adopted for the restoration of the Union and the *pacification* of the Southern people was to deprive them of all political rights...[59] [Emphasis added].

Reconstruction never ended. It continues in cities and States not only in the South but, today, its impact is felt in every state of America's centralized, all-powerful, tyrannical "indivisible" Union. Key elements of Active Reconstruction (1866-77) included themes that are familiar to conservative Americans at the beginning of the 21st century. During Republican-enforced Congressional Reconstruction (herein referred to as Active Reconstruction), the South suffered from out-of-control taxation, fraudulent elections, normalized and accepted fraud/corruption among elected officials, and the use of racial hatred to exploit blacks for the political benefit of party politicians. A glance at today's news headlines will demonstrate that these key elements are currently at work in the South and throughout these United States.

---

58 Government-sponsored, anti-South, cultural genocide: Pulling down ancient monuments to Southern heroes, banning display of Confederate flags, removing Southern symbols from the US Capitol, renaming military bases once named for Southern heroes, destroying the North/South Reconciliation monument in Arlington National Cemetery, and using social terror to silence anyone who dares to speak up for their Southern heritage.

59 Judge Reagan, *Confederate Veteran* Vol. V, No. 7, July 1897. Republished in *The Confederate Veteran Magazine* Vol. V (Harrisburg, PA: The National Historical Society, 1987), 346.

To the average conservative American, the era referred to as "Reconstruction" was a time of rebuilding the South after the so-called "Civil War." To the average liberal, it was a time of glorious experimentation for social equality—an effort that was destroyed by hateful, evil, racist, white Southerners. The latter is the description of Reconstruction taught by America's postmodern (neo-Marxist) educational system. America's ruling elites in government, Globalist financial elites, postmodernist academia, and the mainline media benefit from their monopoly of "facts" about the War (the so-called Civil War) and Reconstruction.[60] Reconstruction continues today. It began as Active Reconstruction (1866-77), the post Active Reconstruction era referred to herein as Passive Reconstruction (1877-1965), and Reconstruction in the Modern Era (post-1965). In the following pages, we will *not* explain the *causes* of the War, but we will explain the *consequences* of the War and subsequent Active, Passive, and Modern Era Reconstruction. The unacknowledged consequence of Lincoln's war and the Republican Party's Reconstruction Plan was the destruction of America's original Republic of Sovereign States and the illegitimate construction of the current unconstitutional supreme Federal Government—also referred to herein as the political *status quo* or the Yankee Empire.

Before Lincoln's war and Republican-enforced Active Reconstruction, the United States government as designed by the Founding Fathers was a constitutionally limited Republic of Sovereign States. It was a system of government in which "We the People," through our sovereign States were the ultimate decision-makers regarding matters that affected our local communities and families. After Lincoln's war and the Republican Party's imposed Active Reconstruction, the Federal Government unconstitutionally morphed into America's centralized, supreme government holding the final authority to determine the limits, if any, of its powers. It became a government that could violate the First Amendment's guarantee of Freedom of Religion by simply declaring a crisis. It

---

60 The more accurate title for the American conflict of 1861-1865 is the War for Southern Independence. Throughout this book it is referred to as "the War" or "War" as in post-War.

evolved into a government that could deny the Biblical admonition that children are a gift from God to parents by declaring that children belong to the government. Republican-created Active Reconstruction continues, in its modern form, today!

Reconstruction is divided into three eras of American history. Active Reconstruction (1866 to 1877) was the time in which the Republican-controlled Congress used military occupation, bayonet rule, and slanderous anti-South propaganda to control its newly conquered Southern territories (formerly the Sovereign States composing the conquered and occupied sovereign nation, the Confederate States of America). Passive Reconstruction, part of which, includes a time referred to as the Progressive Era. Passive Reconstruction (1878-1965) was a time in which the ruling elites in Washington (political, financial, and social) enacted Federal legislation to gain control of America's banking system via the establishment of the Federal Reserve, expanding Federal powers via Federal Supreme Court decisions, and "Progressive" legislation ending with the passage of the 1964-5 Civil Rights Acts. During Passive Reconstruction, the South suffered widespread poverty which was intentionally imposed upon the South.[61] Modern Era Reconstruction (post-1965) is a time in which the ruling elites found it politically advantageous to break the post-War North/South bargain for reconciliation[62] and imposed a modern-day version of Active Reconstruction on not just the South but on all of America. The recent destruction of the Reconciliation Monument in Arlington National Cemetery is a good example. Designed by Moses Ezekiel, a Confederate veteran, the monument was proposed by Union veteran and President William McKinley. It was an attempt to heal old wounds and unite the country. Its destruction is a reflection of our times; when government elitists hire Woke radical leftists to promote malice, hatred, antagonism, bitterness, and resentment. What message is being sent when

---

[61] See Kennedy & Kennedy, *Punished with Poverty-the Suffering South* 2nd ed. (Columbia, SC: Shotwell Publishing, 2020).

[62] "The Bargain is Broken," Chapter 18, Kennedy & Kennedy, *The South Was Right!* 3rd ed. (Columbia, SC: Shotwell Publishing, 2020), 412-20.

monuments meant to heal are destroyed? America must regain its senses and bring back to the fore the shared values derived from our Christian Western heritage.

The story of Reconstruction is the story of the intentional destruction of America's original Constitution and its replacement with a "living" Constitution that, as Thomas Jefferson warned, can be "molded like a lump of clay" to any shape that today best supports the progressive, liberal, neo-Marxist agenda. This new Constitution can be used to support the latest social fad advocated by social justice warriors in Washington's political and bureaucratic Deep State and its sycophants (propagandists) in academia and the mainline/digital media. Before Lincoln and the Republican Party's Active Reconstruction, the idea of using the Federal Government to harass parents complaining about the teaching of Critical Race Theory or Drag Queens in local schools was impossible. Yet, in the Modern Era Reconstruction (post-1965), such use of the FBI or armed IRS agents is not only possible—it is occurring. In Modern Era Reconstruction, the citizen's right to privacy as declared in the Fourth Amendment is routinely violated by Federal agencies such as the National Security Agency (NSA).[63] Reconstruction that was imposed upon the defeated and occupied South by the Republican-controlled Congress set the stage for the ultimate destruction of local self-government and the rise of an empire—the Yankee Empire.[64] As predicted by General Robert E. Lee in 1870 with the destruction of States' Rights, the Federal Government has become "aggressive abroad and despotic at home."

How did the United States of America get to the point where leftist (neo-Marxists/postmodernist) activists masquerading as social, political, or judicial experts violate with impunity the most basic principles in the Constitution? They routinely violate constitutional rights if it serves their purpose of advancing their postmodernist, neo-Marxist, progressive agenda. Thomas Jefferson warned about the impending consolidation of ultimate political

---

63   Morgan, Sean. "19 Recent Deep State Surveillance Abuses," *Breitbart News* (Breitbart.com), 20 December 2023. (Accessed 12/21/2023) www.bit.ly/xdeepstate.

64   See Kennedy & Kennedy, *Yankee Empire: Aggressive Abroad and Despotic at Home*.

power in the Federal Government, "The judiciary branch is the instrument which, working like gravity, without intermission, is to press us at last into one consolidated mass."[65] Jefferson's warning came early in American history, long before Lincoln's war. After the War, General Lee was asked by Lord Acton what would become of America with the defeat of the South, the destruction of States' Rights, and the concentration of political power in Washington. Lee predicted that, with the destruction of States' Rights, the United States would become "aggressive abroad and despotic at home."[66]

As General Lee predicted, America's unconstitutional supreme Federal Government, created by Lincoln and a Congress controlled by the Republican Party during Active Reconstruction, became "oppressive at home." News headlines in the 2020s are vivid evidence of this truth:

- FBI Whistleblower Claims DOJ Used Counterterrorism Tools against Parents in Response to School-Board Memo[67]
- States' Lawsuit Reveals Feds Pushed Censorship Tools to Big Tech[68]
- Biden Military Vaccine Mandate Was a Way to Purge Patriots[69]

---

65   Thomas Jefferson cited in Quirk & Bridwell's *Judicial Dictatorship* (New Brunswick & London: Transaction Publishers, 1995), 18.

66   Robert E. Lee cited in Kennedy & Kennedy, *Yankee Empire: Aggressive Abroad and Despotic at Home*, 65.

67   Evans, Zachory, "FBI Whistleblower Claims DOJ Used Counterterrorism Tools against Parents in Response to School-Board Memo," *National Review* (nationalreview.com) 16 November 2021 (Accessed 25 May 2023), www.bit.ly/xWhistle

68   Bokhari, Allum, "States' Lawsuit Reveals Feds Pushed Censorship Tools to Big Tech," *Breitbart News* (Breitbart.com), 20 December 2023. (Accessed 04 April 2023), www.bit.ly/xPushFed.

69   Poor, Jeff, "GOP Rep. Moore: Biden Military Vaccine Mandate 'Was a Way to Purge Patriots,'" *Breitbart News* (Breitbart.com), 28 January 2023. (Accessed 28 Jan 2023). wwwbit.ly/xMilPurge.

- Transgender Federal Assistant Secretary of Health supports normalizing transgenderism[70]
- Biden's Department of Justice raids home of Christian pro-life advocate[71]

None of the above-listed transgressions of basic constitutional rights was possible before Lincoln's war and the Republican Party's Active Reconstruction. For instance, in 1793, the Federal Supreme Court attempted to compel the Sovereign State of Georgia to appear in Federal Court to defend itself against a suit filed by a citizen of another state. Before this, during the debates on whether to ratify the Constitution (1787-8), the Anti-Federalists expressed concern about the possible expansion of the Federal Courts powers and their potential to overrule the rights of a State. High Federalist Alexander Hamilton assured those who were concerned about the possibility of the proposed Supreme Court claiming jurisdiction over a Sovereign State that such a thing was unthinkable. He wrote in *Federalist Number 81*: "I hope that no gentleman will think that a State will be called at the bar of the Federal court... It is not rational to suppose that the sovereign power should be dragged before a court." Despite the plain language of Hamilton's (insincere?) promise in 1793, four short years after the ratification of the Constitution, the sovereign state of Georgia was called to defend itself before the Federal court! The legislature of Georgia was so enraged that it passed a resolution declaring that any Federal official who attempted to enforce the Federal court order would be "hung by the neck without benefit of clergy." Did President George Washington call for seventy thousand soldiers to march into Georgia, making Georgia howl, burning, pillaging, and raping to enforce the Federal Court's order? No! In a matter of a few months, Georgia's sister States passed the Eleventh Amendment prohibiting the Supreme Court from hearing suits of private citizens against a sovereign state. Georgia nullified the oppressive

---

70   Lindquist, Spencer, "Rachel Levine Calls on Doctors to Become 'Ambassadors' to Normalize Transgenderism," *Breitbart News* (Breitbart.com), 05 December 2022. (Accessed 05 December 2022), wwwbit.ly/xRachelCalling.

71   O'Connor, Aidan, "Catholic Pro-Life Home Raid.", ChurchMilitant.com, 25 September 2022 (Accessed 26 September 2022), wwwbit.ly/xRaid-PL-Home.

and unconstitutional Federal Court order, and her sister States endorsed Georgia's right of nullification by ratifying the Eleventh Amendment.[72] This was the way "We the People" protected our rights against an oppressive Federal Government before Lincoln's war and the Republican Party sponsored Active Reconstruction.

RECONSTRUCTION ALLOWED PAGANISM TO BECOME AMERICA'S UNOFFICIAL RELIGION

"With no more than five exceptions, they [the Founding Fathers] were orthodox members of one of the established Christian Communions. An internal transformation of American society in the direction of a secularized egalitarian state was the furthest thing from the minds of these men."[73] As Dr. Bradford so succinctly points out, America was originally founded on Christian social and moral principles. Yet today, we are no longer a "nation under God," at least not the one true God of the Holy Bible. Secular humanism in its numerous wicked forms is the only god recognized and worshiped by America's social and political ruling elites. American culture that originally espoused the virtues of freedom, self-reliance, and Biblical morality has morphed into a hedonistic pagan model that espouses fraud, corruption, sexual perversion, political censorship, and intolerance for traditional conservative moral and political views. It is as if America has rejected the God of the Old and New Testaments and embraced the ancient gods of paganism. One author noted the similarity between America's politically correct, woke society and ancient societies that worshiped the pagan god Ishtar, (Ishtar wore a rainbow necklace):

---

72 The very next day after the Supreme Court handed down its demand to Georgia, Massachusetts Representative Theodore Sedgwick denounced the Supreme Court's action as an attack upon state sovereignty. Upon the floor of the House of Representatives, he declared, "I rise to protest in the name of Massachusetts against this decision. It reduces free and independent sovereignties to the rank of mere provinces." Sedgwick then suggested a resolution be passed to amend the Constitution to prevent such unconstitutional actions, said resolution became the Eleventh Amendment to the Constitution. See Kennedy and Benson, *Lincoln, Marx, and the GOP* (Columbia, SC: Shotwell Publishing, 2023), 275-6.

73 Bradford, Dr. M.E., *Founding Fathers: Brief Lives of the Framers of the United States Constitution* (Lawrence, KS: University Press of Kansas, 1981), xvi.

Anyone who refused to pay her homage, anyone refusing to go along with her altering of sexuality, marriage, and gender, would suffer the unleashing of her fury. She would vilify them, portray them as haters, incite the culture against them, and seek to deprive them of their livelihood, their speech, and their freedom.[74]

America's march toward the hedonism and perversions of Gomorrah was made possible by the concentration of power in Washington, DC. How else could they[75] have ejected God, the Bible, and prayer from "our" public schools? Their monopolistic control of the digital and mainline media is made possible by the concentration of power in Washington, DC. The bankrupting of America via non-stop accumulation of trillions of dollars of debt (not to mention the hundreds of trillions of dollars of unfunded mandates) is made possible by the concentration of power in Washington, DC. The financial deterioration of America's once burgeoning middle class is made possible by the concentration of power in Washington, DC. The surrender of America's national sovereignty to financial Globalist elites is made possible by the concentration of power in Washington, DC. Conservative States being repopulated with illegals crossing "open borders" is made possible by the concentration of power in Washington, DC. None of this concentration of power would have occurred without Lincoln's war and the Republican Party's reconstruction of America's original Constitution and its Republic of Sovereign States—all done by America's first Republican President and a post-War Congress controlled by the Republican Party.

---

74 Cahn, Jonathan, *The Return of the Gods* (Lake Mary, FL: FrontLine, 2022), 223.

75 "They" include a whole host of individuals describing themselves as liberals, socialists, atheists, postmodernists, progressives, social justice warriors, Globalists, and neo-Marxists—just to name a few of the labels they apply to themselves.

Reconstruction—The South's Resistance Movement

The Yankee Empire's propagandists insist that the efforts of conservative, primarily white, Southerners to overturn the Reconstruction regimes imposed upon the Southern States by the Republican Party was essentially a campaign of terror against blacks motivated by racial hatred. For example, Wikipedia, the digital source of "knowledge" for many Americans, claims that Reconstruction was a time in which white Southerners were:

> Fighting against suffrage and full rights for freedmen, and in favor of giving the returning Southern States relatively free rein over former slaves, were the white "Redeemers"; Southern Bourbon Democrats; and especially the Ku Klux Klan, which intimidated, terrorized, and murdered freedmen and Republicans, ...throughout the former Confederacy.[76]

This type of explanation is the principal leftist "talking points" when discussing Reconstruction. The truth is that it was the Republican-sponsored Union League that "drew first blood" by initiating a reign of terror across the South with its secret meetings, hate-filled speeches, barn burnings, and armed and insolent black militias. As noted by a modern-day Southern scholar:

> Armed black mobs (officially designated militia) led by Carpetbaggers roamed around intimidating, stealing, harassing, and murdering. They deliberately provoked violent response...the Union League used the methods of the Ku Klux Klan before the Klan came into existence.[77]

The Southern resistance movement was an effort to reclaim the right to vote that was denied to most white Southerners, establish

---

[76] "Reconstruction Era," Wikipedia.com, n.d. (Accessed 30 June 2023) . www.bit.ly/wReconstruct.

[77] Wilson, Clyde N., Forward to John Chodes's *Washington's KKK: The Union League During Southern Reconstruction* (Columbia, SC: Shotwell Publishing, 2016), viii.

a fair and functional legal system, restore law and order, and remove the confiscatory taxation imposed upon white and black property owners. During the War, the Federal Government was very creative in its efforts to prevent opponents of the War from voting. In Maryland:

> The Federal government placed posters at polling booths instructing everyone to point out any peace activists to soldiers so they could be arrested... ballots were made of different colors so that the soldiers could throw out the Peace Party votes. Many who attempted to vote for the Peace ticket in Baltimore were arrested for carrying a ballot of the wrong color. The charge against these men was simply polluting the ballot box.[78]

If Lincoln and his co-conspirators were willing to do this to their own citizens who opposed their agenda, it should be no surprise that they were willing to do much more to prevent white Southerners from voting. The fact that most property-owning whites were not allowed to vote caused a return to the 1776 cry of "No taxation without representation." The Southern resistance movement was primarily a tax revolt that was supported by property owners regardless of skin color.

The post-War Southern resistance movement was similar to the French resistance movement that developed naturally after the Nazi invasion and occupation of France in the beginning of World War II. The post-War Southern resistance was a movement against criminality in high places, against oppressive, even confiscatory taxation, against the breakdown of law and order, all imposed upon an occupied, defenseless, intentionally impoverished, but formerly free, self-governing Southern people. Postmodern "intellectuals" ignore the fact that the Yankee Empire, by waging aggressive war, deprived "We the People" of the South of the right to live under a government based upon the consent of the

---

78 DiLorenzo, Dr. Thomas J., *The Real Lincoln* (NY: Three Rivers Press, 2002), 143.

governed—a formerly cherished American political principle. Then, during Active Reconstruction, the Republican Party denied the right of local self-government to a population that had for over 75 years freely governed themselves. The tyranny of Northern Congressional leaders was sanctioned by Northern votes but as Thomas Jefferson declared, legislatures can become tyrants as easily as Kings. Jefferson also noted that "An elective despotism was not the government we fought for."[79] Yet, an elective despotism in the form of state *puppet governments* was imposed upon "We the People" of the South, and it remains in place today![80]

THE SOUTH'S FIVE STRATEGIC FAILURES

While it has been customary for conservative Southerners to blame the North for Reconstruction, this is not the whole story. Reconstruction is the result of five strategic failures made by Southerners from the very beginning of these United States down to this day. Failure to recognize these strategic failures assures the continuation of Modern Era Reconstruction. These failures will be explained in Chapter 4. But first, let us investigate the Republican Party's primary goal for Reconstruction.

---

79   Thomas Jefferson cited in Trevor Colbourn's *The Lamp of Experience* (1965, Indianapolis, IN: Liberty Fund, 1998), 200, 210.

80   Some Southern conservatives may object to labeling the South's current state governments as "puppet governments." General Stephen D. Lee writing in 1899 labeled States "organized and sustained by the military forces of the United States, not by the free will of its citizens," as "bogus governments." See *Confederate Military History*, Vol. XII (1899, Harrisburg, PA: The Archives Society, 1994), 277.

Chapter 3:

THE REPUBLICAN PARTY'S GOAL FOR RECONSTRUCTION

"I was not educated in the school of passive obedience. I will not maintain the Union when the Constitution is overthrown. Obedience to such a Union is treason to the Constitution"
—Robert Toombs[81]

THE MODERN-DAY JUSTIFICATION for Reconstruction is based upon three slanderous lies about Lincoln's war of invasion and extermination.[82] These Yankee lies hide the fact that Lincoln's war was waged against the people of a sovereign nation—The Confederate States of America. America's ruling elite, who control the current political *status quo*, must maintain these anti-South, slanderous lies to prevent Southerners, as well as the rest of conservative America, from questioning the legitimacy of the current political *status quo*. These three lies are:

1. The North fought to preserve the Union,
2. The North fought to free the slaves, and
3. The North sought to use Reconstruction to establish civil rights for blacks.

---

81 Robert Toombs cited in Dr. M.E. Bradford's *A Better Guide Than Reason: Federalists & Anti-Federalists* (1979, New Brunswick & London: Transaction Publishers, 1994), 160.

82 The justification for the term "Lincoln's war" is documented in Chapter 32, "Timeline Lincoln's Secret War Conspiracy."

RADICAL REPUBLICAN
REPRESENTATIVE THADDEUS STEVENS (R-PA)

"Our generals have a sword in one hand and shackles in the other... The South must be punished under the rules of war, its land confiscated.... These offending States were out of the Union and in the role of a belligerent nation to be dealt with by the laws of war and conquest," Rep. Thaddeus Stevens. The United States' sword was used to deny the people of the South the right of self-government, the shackles are used to make political slaves of the people in the Union's newly conquered territories. As the Romans would declare to its newly conquered people, Vae Victis—Woe to the vanquished.

The slanderous implication in each of these lies is that the South fought to destroy the Union, fought to keep slavery as a permanent labor system, and the South's resistance to Reconstruction was based on race hatred and a desire to deny blacks an opportunity to participate as free men and women in society. The Northern victor writes and enforces his version of history while censoring efforts of the conquered people to "tell their side of the story." The result is that, for over a century and a half, most Americans have only heard the victor's excuses for its illegal invasion of the South. The invader used these slanderous lies to justify its cruel war to deny the Southern people the right of self-determination—a human right boldly proclaimed in America's Declaration of Independence.

Southern Truth vs Yankee Lies

The fact that the Union did not dissolve when the Southern States seceded demonstrates the total fabrication of the first lie. This first lie was and remains an effective emotional propaganda tool to rally misguided patriots into unquestioning support for an all-powerful Federal Government. The Federal Union was in no more danger of dissolving when the Southern States seceded in 1861 than was Great Britain in 1776, after the Thirteen American Colonies seceded from their union with Great Britain.[83] In both cases, the only danger for these central governments was the loss of control of a large geographical area and its population which was providing the central government with tremendous resources. For both central governments (empires) the contest was not over the principle of liberty but their potential loss of profits!

The second lie, that the North was fighting to free the slaves, is easy to destroy if facts mean anything in modern America.[84] The simple fact is that after most Southern States withdrew their representatives and senators from the US Congress—meaning

---

83 In May of 1776, Virginia declared that the "union" between Virginia and Great Britian was "totally dissolved." See Kennedy & Kennedy, *Jefferson Davis: High Road to Emancipation and Constitutional Government*, 343.

84 Unfortunately, truth and facts mean nothing in postmodern America. See "Yankee Empire: Where Truth No Longer Matters," Addendum XI, Kennedy & Kennedy, *The South Was Right!* 3rd ed., 471-7.

the North had complete control of Congress—the remaining Northern States and two Border States voted for and sent to the States for state ratification the Corwin Amendment. Republican Senator Corwin from Ohio authored, and Lincoln supported, the Corwin Amendment. This proposed constitutional amendment would "forever prevent the federal government from interfering with slavery in the States where it existed."[85] Lincoln was more than willing to tolerate slavery if the Southern States would return to the Union and allow the Federal tax collectors to collect tariff revenue in Southern ports—Yankee profits were at risk.

Lincoln and the Republican Party's war did not end slavery—it merely set the stage for a labor system far worse than Southern chattel slavery. After "emancipation," blacks and poor whites were reduced to a new form of slavery—sharecropping.[86] After the War, the formerly prosperous white plain folk of the old South were reduced to America's new class of peasants.[87] Lincoln's low road to emancipation led millions of black and white Southerners into a system of economic serfdom—the opposite of the alluring but false promise of Yankee freedom.

The third lie, that Republicans were earnestly seeking a system of government that would guarantee civil rights for freed slaves, will be explored and exposed in subsequent chapters. The exposure of these three lies which is so essential for the establishment and maintenance of the unconstitutional (illegitimate) supreme Federal Government leads to an important question—a question that the current political *status quo* is determined to prevent from ever being asked! "What was the motivating factor causing the Republican Party to impose Radical Reconstruction on the South?" The South suffered and continues to suffer, but eventually, the polit-

---

85 Mitcham, Jr., Dr. Samuel W., *It Wasn't About Slavery: Exposing the Great Lie of the Civil War* (Washington, DC: Regnery History, 2020), 127.

86 Kennedy & Kennedy, *Punished With Poverty: the Suffering South*.

87 McDonald, Dr. Forrest & McWhiney, Dr. Grady, "The South from Self-Sufficiency to Peonage: An Interpretation," *The American Historical Review*, Vol. 85, No. 5, (Dec. 1980).

ical *status quo*[88] that arose after Active Reconstruction imposed Reconstruction on all of America in the post-1965 Modern Era Reconstruction. The impact of Modern Era Reconstruction in America today demonstrates the truthfulness of Confederate Vice President Stephens's words, who, after the War, declared, "The cause of the South is now the cause of all."[89]

The Yankee Empire's propagandists confidently informed gullible Americans[90] that the North generously and magnanimously instituted Reconstruction to rebuild a destroyed South and establish a permanent reconciliation between the North and the South. This, of course, is nothing but propagandists' lies used as a smoke-screen behind which they hide their nefarious intentions.

REPUBLICANS IMPOSED MILITARY DICTATORSHIP AND RACIAL HATRED ON THE SOUTH

The goal of the post-War Republican-controlled Congress was to make the South a permanent economic and political vassal of the Republican Party. The Republican Party became anxious for its political future early in 1866 when it saw former Union men who were not Radical Republicans sent to Congress by Southern States. These Southern States were "reconstructed" under Lincoln's Ten Percent Reconstruction Plan. The Republican Party foresaw the possible combining of old-line Southern Unionists with National Democrats. Such a combination would end the Republican Party's control of Congress and its vision of a greater American Empire controlled by Republican elites.[91] In his 1879 novel, *A Fool's Errand by One of the Fools*, Union officer Albion Tourgee wrote that the drive for Republican-sponsored Radical Reconstruction

---

88 America's political *status quo* includes both national political parties, Washington's Deep State, the military-industrial-complex, business, and financial cronies, and Globalists—all of whom subscribe in varying degrees to postmodern, leftist, "Woke" ideology.

89 Stephens, Alexander H., *Constitutional View of the Late War Between the States* Vol. II (1870, Harrisonburg, VA: Sprinkle Publications, 1994), 666.

90 Purposefully made gullible by America's left-of-center education system controlled by postmodern (neo-Marxists) "intellectuals" in academia.

91 Henry, Robert Selph, *The Story of Reconstruction* (New York: Konecky & Konecky, 1938), 134.

did not come from the people of the North but "from its politicians." Tourgee noted that the purpose of Republican Reconstruction was to assure Republican "political victory and party ascendency."[92]

Republicans such as Secretary of War Edwin M. Stanton saw the North's victory over the Confederate States of America not as an opportunity for North/South reconciliation but as an opportunity to impose revenge upon the white people in the Yankee Empire's newly conquered territory. He saw it as an opportunity to extract retribution upon sinful white Southerners.[93] Republican Senator Charles Sumner declared that all these seceding States committed "state suicide." At the same time, the infamous Thaddeus Stevens (R-Pennsylvania) opined that the seceding States were nothing more than conquered provinces held and "governed by the will and at the pleasure of their conquerors, without any weak talk of rights of rebels, ex-rebels, or rebel States."[94] The Roman Empire used the phrase *Vae victis* (woe to the vanquished) when discussing what to do with the people of a newly conquered territory. This was, in practice, the motto of the Republican Party when dealing with the people of the conquered and occupied South—woe to the conquered.

Representative Thaddeus Stevens (R- Pennsylvania) made clear the intentions of the Radical Republicans in Congress in a speech delivered three days before Lincoln's assassination, declaring he favored a Congressional Reconstruction policy that would allow the confiscation of "every foot of ground they [the people of the South] pretend to own."[95] This was the attitude of a conquering empire as it began to exploit the resources and people from its newly conquered and occupied territory. Lincoln's unconstitutional war

---

92 Tourgee, Albion W., *A Fool's Errand* (1879, Cambridge, Massachusetts: The Belknap Press, 1961), 237-8.

93 Henry, Robert Selph, *The Story of Reconstruction*, 2-3.

94 Sumner and Stevens cited in Robert Selph Henry's *The Story of Reconstruction* (New York: Konecky & Konecky, 1938), 9.

95 Bowers, Claude, *The Tragic Era*, 6, The author cites the *Lancaster Intelligencer*, March 21, 1867.

and the Republican Party's unconstitutional and tyrannical Active Reconstruction set the stage for the emergence of the Yankee Empire.[96]

While promoting one of his Reconstruction bills, Thaddeus Stevens, speaking on the House floor, declared he looked forward to the day that "every rebel who shed the blood of loyal men should be prevented from exercising any power in this government." He was interrupted by the question of whether he would turn the South into a penitentiary large enough to hold eight million people—Stevens responded, "Yes, a penitentiary which is built at the point of the bayonet down below, and if they undertake to come here, we will shoot them down."[97] This hatred was the mentality of the men who controlled the United States government. These leaders were eagerly inflicting the Federal Government's tyrannical rule over "We the People" of the former independent Confederate States of America. Before 1861, these Southerners were citizens of the free, independent, and sovereign States of these United States of America.

During the War, the Radicals in the Republican Party opposed Lincoln's less radical Reconstruction Plan. Lincoln's plan called for a state's readmission to the Union as soon as ten percent of the state's citizens who were registered to vote in the 1860 election declared their loyalty and registered to vote. Their state would then be readmitted to the Union. The controlling element of the Republican Party, led by Thaddeus Stevens (R- Pennsylvania), opposed Lincoln's Ten Percent Reconstruction Plan for the readmission of Southern States. The Radical Republicans were determined to keep the bleeding wounds of war open until they (the Republicans in Congress) could remake the authority of the Federal Government to "...secure perpetual ascendency to the party of the Union," meaning, of course, the Republican Party.[98]

---

96 Kennedy & Kennedy, *Yankee Empire: Aggressive Abroad and Despotic at Home*, 75-131.
97 Bowers, Claude, *The Tragic Era*, 113. The author cites the *Congressional Globe*, May 10, 1866.
98 Henry, Robert Selph, *The Story of Reconstruction*, 132.

One of the great ironies of post-War Washington politics was that the Republican Party needed the South to maintain political control of Congress. They knew they could not rely on the traditionally conservative white Southerner to vote Republican. The answer was to maintain military dictatorship throughout the South and disfranchise "disloyal" white Southerners (anyone who supported the Confederacy) while enfranchising illiterate freedmen whose votes could be controlled by the Republican Party. The leaders of the Republican Party sought to enjoy the prospect of humiliating the South by establishing a new government that would legislate protective tariffs to assure profits for the more highly industrialized and prosperous States of the North. General Bradley T. Johnson perceptively noted, "...the Northern society, which was and is based on the idea of profit and loss."[99] This meant *their* new Federal Government must control the newly created puppet States in the South to ensure they consistently voted Republican. Gideon Wells, Lincoln's Secretary of the Navy, asked Senator Sumner of Massachusetts, "Do you really think that Massachusetts could govern Georgia better than Georgia could govern herself?" Senator Sumner's reply was, "That is Massachusetts' mission!"[100] To achieve its goal of controlling the South and creating puppet Republican state governments in the South, the Republican-controlled Congress used the ancient technique that all empires used to control the people in its newly conquered territory—Divide-and-Rule.[101]

---

99 General Bradley Johnson in *Confederate Veteran* Vol. V, No. 10, October 1897. Republished in *The Confederate Veteran Magazine* Vol. V (Harrisburg, PA: The National Historical Society, 1987), 507.

100 Henry, Robert Selph, *The Story of Reconstruction*, 133.

101 Kennedy & Kennedy, *Yankee Empire: Aggressive Abroad and Despotic at Home*, 115, 124, 345.

Divide and Rule—Yankee-Imposed Racial Hatred

Encouraging racial hatred and fear as weapons, agents of the Republican Party produced a division between black and white Southerners.[102] A vital part of the Republican Party's divide-and-rule strategy was to persecute and humiliate the disarmed white Southerners to the point of open rebellion against Federal authority. This, of course, would give the Republican-controlled Congress the perfect excuse to maintain the military occupation of the South for years to come.[103] One technique was to station undisciplined, armed black "militia" throughout the South near the homes of widows and crippled veterans. As one author noted:

> Nothing short of stupendous ignorance, or brutal malignity, can explain the arming and uniforming of former slaves and setting them as guardians over the white men and their families.[104]

Black troops routinely marched four abreast in the streets and sidewalks of towns and cities across the South, purposely forcing whites into the ditches or off the street. It was not unusual to see black "troops" dressed in new, bright blue uniforms, challenging, and harassing old crippled and hungry men wearing the only clothing they had—their tattered gray uniform. In Chester, South Carolina, black troops clubbed and bayoneted an old man; in Abbeville, South Carolina, black troops ordered all whites off the sidewalks; in Charleston, South Carolina, black troops forced their way into homes and demanded that the women of the house feed them; in one such case, a guardian of the lady of the house challenged the black soldier for his insult of the lady. The black

---

102 Republican agents included the Union League, the Freedman's Bureau, the occupying military, newly organized and armed black militias, carpetbaggers, and local scallywags.

103 The direct military occupation of the South was necessary only until the North could admit new Northern States carved out of the lands taken from the American Indians in the West. Once these new Northern States were admitted to the Union, the Republican party lost interest in black voters in the South. See Clark & Kirwan, *The South Since Appomattox* (New York: Oxford University Press, 1967), 67; Johnson, Dr. Ludwell H., *The North Against the South: The American Iliad 1848-1877*, 206.

104 Bowers, Claude, *The Tragic Era*, 52.

militiamen dragged the white defender to their camp, murdered him, and danced upon his grave. With similar barbaric outrages occurring across the South and with no reliable legal system in place to arrest and prosecute the offenders, it would be irrational to think that some form of vigilante activity would not take place. Vigilantism occurs even in the modern era when the legal system refuses to protect the innocent from the criminal elements of society.[105]

For over 85 years since the signing of the Declaration of Independence, the white people of the South were a free and self-governing people. This incredible heritage of liberty and self-government was destroyed by Lincoln's aggressive war and the Republican Party's Reconstruction. Immediately post-War, the generally friendly relations between former slaves and former masters surprised the occupying forces of the North. For example, upon returning from the War, General Gideon J. Pillow borrowed money from one of his former slaves.[106] Former Union officer, socialist, and Republican politician Carl Schurz issued a report on the conditions down South on December 19, 1865, in which he noted his surprise:

> Centuries of slavery have not been sufficient to make them the enemies of the white race… Instances of the most touching attachment of freedmen to their old masters and mistresses have come to my notice. To a white man whom they believe to be sincerely their friend they cling with greater affection even than to one of their own race.[107]

---

105   See Nolte, John, "When Democrats Stop Enforcing the Law-You Get Vigilantes" *Breitbart News* (www.breitbart.com) 04 May 2023. (Accessed 05 May 2023) www.bit.ly/xVigilantes

106   *Confederate Veteran 1893* Vol. I, No. 11. Republished in *The Confederate Veteran Magazine* Vol. I, 330.

107   Schurz, Carl cited in *A Just and Lasting Peace: A Documentary History of Reconstruction*, ed. John David Smith (New York: Signet Classics, NY: 2013), 140.

But that would soon change with Republican Reconstruction and the political exploitation of newly freed slaves registered as Republican voters. The *New York Herald* described how the Union League managed black votes:

> The voter got his ticket from the captain, the captain had it from the colonel, and he from the general, and the general of course had it from the owners and managers in Washington of the grand scheme to secure political supremacy."[108]

The Union League successfully hid most of its political activities in the South through secrecy. Before a newly freed slave could become a Republican voter, he was required to join the League. The initiation was full of mysterious ceremony, held at night, and designed to intimidate the suspicious freedman. The final ritual was performed before a fire on an altar. "Then the candidates placed their hands upon the flag and took the oath of allegiance to the United States. Then, 'right hand to Heaven, thumb and third finger touching their ends over palms, say Loyal. Hand and finger on chests, other thumb in waistband, say League.'"[109] And all of this was done while the Federal Government denied "rebel" whites the right to vote.

The political power of the Union League and the black militia was demonstrated during the 1868 Presidential election. General Grant carried every Southern state with a strong Union League backed by a black militia. Grant did not carry the States of Louisiana and Georgia, where there was no strong Union League backed by a black militia.[110] Across the South, secret meetings were held with the newly freed slaves and men claiming to represent the Federal Government. Acts of local terror were encouraged, such as

---

108 Bowers, Claude, *The Tragic Era*, 219, The author cites Water F. Fleming's *Documentary History of Reconstruction*, 514-16.

109 Chodes, John, *Washington's KKK: The Union League During Southern Reconstruction* (Columbia, SC: Shotwell Publishing, 2016), 12; *Sewanee Review*, Vol. 20 (1912), 491.

110 Chodes, John, *Washington's KKK*, 22.

barn burnings and intimidation of blacks who maintained friendly relations with local whites. The Union League drew first blood and became the Federal Government's secret society that promoted terror against black and white Southern conservatives. With no way to effectively challenge the alien powers that controlled their state and local governments, "We the People" of the South began forming a resistance movement.

To secure its political dominance in Washington, the Republican Party placed the South under military dictatorship enforced by bayonet rule. Most of those federal bayonets were in the hands of the mostly illiterate, poorly trained, and undisciplined black militia. This was done purposely by Republican-controlled Congress to drive a wedge of mistrust and racial hatred between black and white Southerners. Postmodern "historians" and academic "intellectuals" claim that Republican Reconstruction efforts were motivated by a desire to help blacks. But even liberal academics admit that brotherly love was not the motive.

> The black-white alliance within the Republican party was at best an uneasy one...most white Republicans believed in white supremacy.[111]

The Republican Party's post-War aim was not civil rights for blacks in the South but political power for the Republican Party in Washington, DC.

REPLACING THE FOUNDER'S REPUBLIC WITH AN EMPIRE

Under America's original and legitimate Constitution, the sovereign States authorized the creation of a Republic of Sovereign States. The Constitution was ratified and, therefore, given its legitimate authority, by the individual sovereign States, each acting upon its authority and free of compulsion outside that sovereign state. No state or group of States could force another state to secede from the Union created by the Articles of Confederation and ac-

---

[111] Cruden, Robert, *The Negro in Reconstruction* (Englewood Cliffs, New Jersey: Prentice-Hall, Inc., 1969), 88.

ceded to (join) the new Union created by the original Constitution. The act of a Sovereign State acceding to the new Union, according to Article VII of the Constitution, demonstrated who created the Federal Government. It also established who was the ultimate authority regarding the powers delegated—not surrendered—to the Federal Government under the Constitution. This was the fundamental understanding of States' Rights outlined in the Kentucky and Virginia Resolutions of 1798, authored by Thomas Jefferson and James Madison, and passed by the legislatures of Kentucky and Virginia.[112] For 85 years this was the understanding of the Constitution. As one scholar and authority on the origins and meaning of the Constitution noted:

> The Constitution meets that definition of law, except that its commands and prohibitions apply not to private individuals, not to the citizenry, not to the people, but to government. It is, in other words, law that governs government.[113]

In the original Republic of Sovereign States, before Lincoln's war and the Republican Party's Reconstruction, the Constitution consisted of prohibitions against the Federal Government. Words such as "Congress shall not" were the hallmark of the original Constitution. In addition to limiting what the Federal Government was authorized to do, the Constitution established the procedure for establishing and outlining the legitimate departments and functions of the Federal Government. The Constitution was not intended to be a list of rights the government grants its subjects. The Ninth and Tenth Amendments make this very clear, especially the Ninth, which declares that there is a vast reservoir of *unenumerated* rights that belong to "We the People," and said

---

112 Kennedy & Kennedy, *Jefferson Davis: High Road to Emancipation and Constitutional Government*, 371-6.

113 McDonald, Dr. Forrest, *A Constitutional History of the United States* (Malabar, FL: Robert E. Krieger Publishing Co., 1982), 27.

rights shall not be encumbered or encroached upon by the Federal Government merely because they are not specifically listed in the Constitution.[114]

According to the Kentucky and Virginia Resolutions of 1798, the sovereign state retains the right to interpose its authority between an oppressive Federal Government and the people of the sovereign state. In 1859, the state of Wisconsin did precisely that when it nullified the fugitive slave clause of the Federal Constitution[115] by passing its personal liberty laws. This is the function of a sovereign state within a republic of sovereign States. This States' Rights principle stood in the way of the Republican Party's dream of empire and had to be destroyed. A former Union Army officer, socialist, and Republican politician declared, "The great stumbling block, the great obstruction in Lincoln's way and in the way of thousands, was the old doctrine of States' Rights."[116] It is impossible to establish an empire without a strong central government controlled by a small group of elites. Hitler knew this and expressed it in his book, outlining the nefarious philosophy of his new centralized government.[117] And so it was with the post-War Republican Party—the old decentralized American government had to be reconstructed into a centralized, supreme Federal Government controlled by Northern political, financial, and social elites.

---

[114] Rights that exist even though they are not specifically mentioned or listed in the Constitution. The right of a man and woman to get married exists even though it is not mentioned in the Constitution. The original, and therefore, legitimate, Constitution is a document created to limit the power of the Federal Government not to grant certain rights to the people or to solve social issues that are better handled locally not by some bureaucrat or politician in faraway Washington, DC.

[115] Article V, Section 2 of the US Constitution—removed in 1865 by the States' ratification of the Thirteenth Amendment prohibiting slavery in the USA. The first fugitive slave law was passed by the United Colonies of New England, Massachusetts, being the largest colony of that union.

[116] Ingersoll cited in Kennedy & Kennedy, *Yankee Empire: Aggressive Abroad and Despotic at Home*, 116.

[117] Kennedy and Benson, *Lincoln, Marx, and the GOP*, 68-82.

Lincoln's war destroyed the spirit of the original Constitution. Still, the letter of the law—the old Constitution—remained and potentially hindered future Republican dreams of an economic, commercial, and political empire. The Republican Party used its illegal and unconstitutional control of the Federal Congress to destroy the letter of the law by forcing, via bloody bayonets, new amendments to the Constitution. Following the illegal enactments of the Fourteenth and Fifteenth Amendments[118] during the so-called Progressive Era, the Supreme Court would convert the meaning of the "Bill of Rights" from its original prohibition against the Federal Government into prohibitions against the once sovereign States. As pointed out by a progressive, constitutional "scholar" of the modern era, "The Bill of Rights did not limit the powers of the States until this century.... Ratification of the Fourteenth Amendment in 1868, however, changed the constitutional landscape and laid a new basis for applying the Bill of Rights to the States."[119] These new prohibitions against the once sovereign States would subsequently be enforced by the supreme Federal Government.[120]

Lincoln's war and Republican Active Reconstruction destroyed America's original, legitimate, and Constitutionally limited Republic of Sovereign States. In place of the legitimate Federal Government, there arose an all-powerful, *illegitimate*, supreme, Federal Government. The destruction of America's legitimate (pre-1860) government was accomplished in an unconstitutional, political *coup d'é·tat*. Its establishment and continuation are a direct result of five strategic Southern failures discussed in the next chapter.

---

118   Kennedy & Kennedy, *The South Was Right!* 3rd ed., 232-54.

119   O'Brien, David M., *Constitutional Law and Politics* Vol. 2, 2nd ed. (New York: Norton & Company, 1991), 302.

120   Under the original Constitution, the "Bill of Rights" were applied only against the Federal Government, i.e., "Congress shall not." After the Republican Party forced at bayonet point the enactment of the 14th and 15th Amendments, the Court slowly began to "incorporate" the "Bill of Rights" into its authority to control the once sovereign States. It was a slow process, but by 1925 it was completed in the case *Gitlow v. New York*. See *The Oxford Companion to the Supreme Court*, ed. Kermit L. Hall (New York: Oxford University Press, 1992), 191, 426-7.

Chapter 4:

The South's Five Strategic Failures

> "Another great failure, and one for which people cannot be readily forgiven, is the surrender of initiative. I believe there is at bottom a consciousness of failure. Probably the decision of 1865 has been interpreted too literally"
> —Richard Weaver[121]

WHEN FACED WITH FAILURE, humans tend to blame others or make excuses for their failures. When faced with failure, we tend to shift the blame away from ourselves. The problem this causes is that it prevents an honest—and sometimes painful—analysis of our failure. Seeking the "why" of failure is a bitter process people often attempt to avoid. But failing to understand the "why" of failure greatly increases the potential for future failures. Southerners often overlook the South's part in bringing about the conditions that set the stage for Reconstruction in the first place as well as Reconstruction's continuation into the modern era.

The South made five critical strategic mistakes (failures) from the beginning of these United States, during the period leading up to the War, during the War, during the post Active Reconstruction era, referred to as Passive Reconstruction, and today in the 21st century, referred to as Modern Era Reconstruction. In this chapter, we will consider these strategic failures. In Chapter 1, **What**

---

121 Weaver, Richard M., *The Southern Tradition at Bay* (New Rochelle, NY: Arlington House, 1968), 390.

Could Have Been, we used historical reflection to see how different things *could have been* had the South recognized its strategic failure and changed its approach to the political and social controversy Southerners faced then and now.

A short explanation of the establishment of America's original constitutionally limited Republic of Sovereign States is necessary before reviewing the South's five strategic failures. The founding principles of America's original Republic play an essential role in four of the five strategic Southern failures. These essential American political principles are virtually unknown or only vaguely understood by most Southern conservatives today—let alone Americans in general. This general lack of public knowledge about America's essential founding principles has been a godsend for the neo-Marxists[122] who dominate America's educational, entertainment, media, economic, and political society. This vast monopoly on the public exchange of ideas turned the average American into the ruling elite's political slave. America's masters, the ruling elite, control the political *status quo* and use it for their ideological and financial benefit. Americans in the modern era live under a system of governmental tyranny that could not have occurred if the South avoided Reconstruction.

Modern-day conservatives are passionate about the need to "return" to the Constitution. Unfortunately, most conservatives are not aware that the current system of supreme Federalism is vastly different from the Federal Government proposed[123] by the

---

122 The term "neo-Marxists" refers to those individuals who have abandoned the basic principles of Western Christian civilization and traditional American principles of Christian morality, individual responsibility, limited, and unintrusive government. They see the Constitution as a living document to be molded by unelected judges into any form that will advance their leftist, postmodern ideology. They use the force of government to destroy traditional values and to establish their vision of an equitable society. Neo-Marxists have abandoned classical Marxism of capital vs. labor and adopted group conflict such as minority groups vs. the patriarchy (meaning white males). They sometimes refer to themselves as liberals, social justice warriors, Woke/politically correct Americans, socialists, atheists, or postmodernists.

123 The new Federal Government was only proposed by the Constitutional Convention. It did not receive its legitimacy until it was established after receiving the ratification by nine Sovereign States and then its authority extended only over those Sovereign States that elected to ratify the proposed Constitution.

original Constitution and given its legal authority by the ratification of the Constitution by the Sovereign States. The current supreme Federal Government is a near replica of the Federal Government specifically and emphatically *rejected* by our Founding Fathers. "We the People" today are ruled by an oppressive, unconstitutional, and therefore illegitimate Federal Government made possible by Lincoln's war and the Republican Party's Active Reconstruction (1866-1877).

ORIGINS OF STATE SOVEREIGNTY

America's original Federal Government was created by the sovereign States under the Articles of Confederation (1781-1789). At that time, the primary concern was that the various States, some very large and others very small—as measured by population or geography—did not want to create another centralized tyranny to rule over them like the one in London from which they had recently seceded. Each sovereign state was very jealous of its "sovereignty, freedom, and independence" and declared so in Article II of the Articles of Confederation. This "sovereignty, freedom, and independence" was recognized by Great Britain in the Treaty of Paris in 1783. By this treaty, Great Britain acknowledged to the entire world that these former colonies were now thirteen sovereign States—not one solitary, centralized, unitary government known as the United States of America, but each colony was recognized by name as an independent state. These independent thirteen States were leagued together, as the United States of America, for self-defense and other purposes better accomplished together than by each separate state. The word "state" used here and in the Treaty of Paris means *nation*. In the Treaty of Paris, Great Britain is referred to as "the state of Great Britain." These newly free and sovereign States (nations) leagued together for common defense as the United States of America (note plural States) were unwilling to voluntarily relinquish their hard-won sovereignty. As a matter of historical fact, they never relinquished their hard-won sovereignty—at least not voluntarily!

The Declaration of Independence (1776) was more than a joint declaration of freedom for thirteen American colonies. It also marked the beginning of the end of the age of absolute monarchy. Before the Declaration of Independence, sovereignty in the Western world was presumed to be granted from God to a Royal Monarch.[124] Americans declared otherwise when they withdrew their allegiance to the British Crown. The Declaration of Independence announced to the world that sovereignty did not reside in the person of a Royal Monarch commissioned by God to rule the people. In the American system of government, sovereignty came from God to the people. The people, not a king nor a central (or Federal) government, but the people are sovereign. The Declaration of Independence made it clear that the people are "endowed by their Creator with certain unalienable rights" and that among these rights is the right to live under a government that derives its "just powers from the consent of the governed." And most importantly, "whenever any Form of Government becomes destructive of these ends, it is the Right of the People to alter or to abolish it, and to institute new Government."

In America, sovereign authority to form, alter, or abolish governments resides not with the Royal Court, a monarch, a Supreme Court, or a central government of any type—it belongs to "We the People." But equally as important—indeed more important for Americans—is that such sovereign authority belongs not to "We the People" in the aggregate (as in "We the People" of the United States of America *en masse*) but to "We the People" within our separate sovereign States! The American States were "sovereign, free, and independent," as acknowledged by the British Crown in the Treaty of Paris (1783) and specifically noted in Article II of the Articles of Confederation. Therefore, government authority flowed from the people to their specific state and then via these individual sovereign States to the Federal Government. Thus,

---

124 It was not the first. On July 26, 1581, the Dutch issued a declaration against the Spanish Crown in their Act of Abjuration. Many think that Thomas Jefferson used it as a blueprint for the Declaration of Independence. See *The Act of Abjuration*, eds. Paul Brood & Raymond Kubben (The Hague: Tilburg University, 2011).

original sovereignty—or the authority to form, modify, control, or leave the Federal Government—resides with "We the People" within our separate and sovereign States.[125]

A MORE PERFECT UNION VS
A COMMERCIAL AND POLITICAL EMPIRE

It soon became apparent that the loose confederation created by the Articles of Confederation was not meeting all the needs of the new republic. Many people in various States felt that the Federal Government needed a more reliable system of funding, a better way to facilitate national defense, and they wished to encourage the free flow of commerce between the States—the original North American Free Trade Zone. In 1787, most Americans within each state would have been satisfied with merely modifying the Articles of Confederation to rectify these problems. However, when the Constitutional Convention met in 1787 it became apparent very early in the discussions that others came to the convention not to provide a more perfect union of sovereign States, but essentially to dissolve the States and create a vast, centralized, all-powerful, supreme Federal Government. These High Federalists were shrewd enough to keep their plans to themselves. If their intentions to create an all-powerful Federal Government that would dissolve the sovereignty of the States became public knowledge before the convention very few if any States would have sent delegates to the Constitutional Convention. The Constitutional Convention was not a group suicide convention of Sovereign States.

The term "a more perfect union" found in the preamble of the Constitution is erroneously assumed by many people, suffering from a postmodern education,[126] to mean a consolidated, monolithic, supreme national government or, simply put, a supreme

---

125   Rawle, William, *A View of the Constitution*, 1825, edited and annotated by Kennedy & Kennedy in *A View of the Constitution: Secession as Taught at West Point* (Wake Forest, NC: The Scuppernong Press, 2020), 251-63.

126   Postmodernists do not seek educational tools that aid in understanding, they want weapons to destroy their opponents. See Hicks, Stephen R.C., *Explaining Postmodernism-Skepticism and Socialism from Rousseau to Foucault* 2nd ed. (Ockham's Razor Publishing: 2011), 17, 177.

Federal Government. It is commonly understood in law that the preamble, title, or chapter heading of a contract or law has no enforceable authority. It merely serves an illustrative purpose—the wording of the contract or law itself is the only authoritative part of the law or contract. Many Americans are misled (propagandized) by the government's postmodern educational system and, therefore, assume that the term "more perfect union" in the preamble of the Constitution is meant to convey the fact that the Constitution created a consolidated, supreme, indivisible, Union, or central government. What, then, does the phrase "more perfect union" mean?

It may be shocking to some conservatives, but the true meaning of the phrase, "a more perfect union," is the opposite of what it is presumed to mean today. The union created by the Articles of Confederation was an association, freely entered by equals—thirteen sovereign American States (nations). Many Americans at the time did not believe the old union (Federal Government) under the Articles of Confederation adequately provided for national defense, and it did not allow for the free flow of commerce between the thirteen sovereign States. The Founding Fathers at the Constitutional Convention designed a new Federal Government or Union. But to ratify the proposed constitution and create a new Federal Government, the States making up the original Federal Government under the Articles of Confederation, each independent of the other, *seceded* from the original union and formed a new "more perfect" union under the Constitution. Note, that it only required the accession of nine sovereign States to form the new union. But this new union would have authority *only* over those sovereign States that freely elected to leave (secede from) the old union and join (accede to) the new union.[127] Some States were very reluctant to join the new union. For a short while, the States of Rhode Island and North Carolina stood outside the

---

127 Kennedy & Kennedy, *Jefferson Davis: High Road to Emancipation and Constitutional Government*, 224-6.

new union as sovereign, free, and independent States (nations) until they freely elected to join the new union as per Article VII of the US Constitution.

A union is a free and voluntary association of equals, each member having the right to join or leave at will—indeed if a member of the union cannot leave, then that member is not free! A prison is a union of sorts, but not the type of union that the Founding Fathers sought to create under the original Constitution. The hawk's talons and a dove's breast may form a union of sorts as well as a wolf's jaw and a lamb's throat, but these are not symbolic of the political union of sovereign, free, and independent States. Such bloody unions are emblematic of political tyranny! Never forget that if a member of a union cannot leave, that member is not free! Only empires are indivisible.[128] The more perfect union created by the original Constitution was not designed to be an ironclad union controlled by ruling elites who wield the power of a supreme Federal Government. It was a union held together by mutual respect and mutual benefit. The Founding Fathers did not create a union that would be pinned together by bloody bayonets. Even though the High Federalists wanted a supreme Federal Government, they did not have the support in the Constitutional Convention to create their desired system of Federal supremacy.

High Federalists—
Early Advocates of Federal Supremacy

High Federalist is the term used to describe those post-colonial political leaders who wanted to create a supreme Federal Government. They wanted an energetic Federal Government in which the States would no longer be sovereign and could be forced to yield ultimate political decision-making authority (sovereignty) to the Federal Government. Of the two key High Federalists at the Constitutional Convention, Alexander Hamilton was by far the most ardent advocate of a supreme Federal Government. In the Constitutional Convention, he proclaimed that he was "…a friend

---

128 Kennedy & Kennedy, *The South Was Right!* 3rd ed., 258-66.

to a vigorous Government."[129] Hamilton considered the States merely "imaginary" things—political bodies having no organic reality and no essential connection to the concepts of individual liberty and sovereignty. Hamilton was different from most of the other delegates in that he was a relatively recent immigrant to America—he did not come of age and mature in a particular state. He had no "roots" in the vibrant political society of a native state. He had no kinship or cultural connection to a local community of fellow citizens. In his view, the States in America were no different than provinces in a European nation. He envisioned American States as mere subservient political subdivisions answerable to a central government.

Early in the Convention, before all the delegates arrived, Hamilton proposed a new, more powerful—sometimes referred to as an "energetic"—Federal Government. Specifically, he advocated a Federal chief executive who would hold office for life and would hold absolute veto powers (similar to the power of a king); a senate composed of individuals holding office for life (similar to the House of Lords); a Federal supreme court that would have complete jurisdiction over all cases—including state cases; and governors of the various States who would be appointed by the Federal Government. No wonder Thomas Jefferson—Hamilton's arch nemesis—referred to Hamilton as a "monarchist." Hamilton's dream of a supreme Federal Government was too radical for even his fellow High Federalists. Hamilton's dream of a supreme Federal Government would have to wait for the arrival of Lincoln and the Republican Party.

Much to the surprise of many conservatives, the second-ranking High Federalist at the Constitutional Convention was none other than James Madison! Madison came to the Convention with his vision of an "energetic" Federal Government. He came with great personal expectations and ambitions, but he left a humbler and more conservative advocate of a limited Federal Government. He

---

129   Hamilton cited in James Madison's *The Debates in the Federal Convention of 1787 Which Framed the Constitution of the United States of America* (Union, New Jersey: The Lawbook Exchange, 1999), 538.

soon realized that the Convention's job was to design a government that the people of the sovereign States would accept and, therefore, as sovereign States, ratify. Unlike Hamilton, Madison was able to learn from the elder statesmen at the Constitutional Convention. The main lesson he learned was that he was part of a community of Virginians. His fellow Virginians were his kith and kin. Folks who understood the necessity of a strong Virginia to counteract any tyrannical tendencies that might arise from a faraway central government. As William Samuel Johnson of Connecticut declared, "the States do exist as political societies...[and] must be armed with some power of self-defense."[130]

While still a High Federalist, James Madison presented his plan for an energetic Federal Government at the Convention. He presented his plan at the beginning of the Convention before the arrival of all the delegates. He called his plan the "Virginia Plan." His strategy was to be the first to offer specific details for a new Federal Government and thereby set the agenda and ensure that he and other High Federalists would control and direct the debate and eventual outcome of the Convention. The most important points of Madison's plan for a new Federal Government were:

- State representation in the Federal Congress would be determined by population.
- The Federal Congress would have veto power over laws enacted by the States.
- The Federal Congress would have the power "to legislate in all cases to which the separate States are incompetent or in which the harmony of the United States may be interrupted by the exercise of individual legislation."

While Madison's Virginia Plan had fewer attributes of British monarchy than Hamilton's vision of a new energetic Federal Government, both were typical of the dreams of High Federalists. High Federalists were determined to create a supreme national government in which sovereign authority ultimately resided with

---

[130] Bradford, M.E., *Original Intentions: On the Making and Ratification of the United States Constitution* (Athens, GA: University of Georgia Press, 1993), 9.

the Federal Government. In their system of government, the States composing the "more perfect union" would be no different than the local provincial governments in Europe. European provinces were nothing more than mere administrative districts of their central government. Instead of the sovereign States creating, via the Constitution, a Federal Government to be the agent of the States, the High Federalists sought to dissolve the States and create a Federal Government that would be served by its administrative districts—the once sovereign States!

FOUNDING FATHERS REJECT THE PROPOSED SUPREME FEDERAL GOVERNMENT

When all delegates were seated at the Constitutional Convention, Madison's Virginia Plan was quickly recognized as a recipe for centralized mass democracy—something that most of the Founding Fathers viewed with great skepticism. Madison's plan was so unacceptable to most delegates that its very offering almost caused the Convention to close before it began its work. Caleb Strong of Massachusetts described the Convention as "nearly at an end."[131] Roger Sherman of Connecticut complained that "we are at full stop." Hugh Williamson of North Carolina thought that "our business must soon be concluded." The day was saved when Benjamin Franklin suggested public prayer. Elder statesmen, such as Oliver Ellsworth from Connecticut, came forward to guide the workings of the Convention. Ellsworth viewed the business at hand as not one of "razing the foundations of the building when they need only repair the roof." John Dickinson of Delaware lectured James Madison and declared to Madison, "You see the consequence of pushing things too far?" On July 16, with all the delegates to the Constitutional Convention seated, Madison's plan was rejected! On the following day, the Convention voted seven States to three to remove Madison from the responsibility of drafting the final version of the new Constitution. The Convention turned the task over to the conservative John Rutledge of South Carolina.

---

131 This and following citations from Bradford's *Original Intentions: On the Making and Ratification of the United States Constitution*.

Madison came to the Convention expecting to be the great lawgiver of a strong, centralized, supreme Federal Government, but he quickly became a humbled student of organic American political philosophy. The politically immature Madison came to the Convention with wild dreams of a strong central government served by weak States (essentially provinces). He was unprepared for the energized reaction from the delegates of the sovereign States assembled. Gouverneur Morris of Pennsylvania described the High Federalists' vision as being "terrible to the States;" John Lansing of New York described the plan for a supreme Federal Government as being "more injurious" than the British government's rule over the colonies; and men such as George Mason of Virginia, Luther Martin of Maryland, and John Dickinson of Delaware warned the Convention of the danger in any system of Federalism that did not allow enough capacity for the States to protect their reserved rights. Pierce Butler of Pennsylvania declared his concern that the delegates may be "running into an extreme in taking away the powers of the States." Madison came to the convention as a supporter of the Hamiltonian vision of an energetic supreme Federal Government. He left the Convention as a humbled moderate Federalist with a new understanding of the importance of the sovereign States in this proposed "more perfect union." Eventually, he became one of Thomas Jefferson's strongest allies in the continuing fight for real States' Rights. Real States' Rights including the rights of state nullification and secession. Without the rights of nullification and secession, the constitutional principle of States' Rights devolves into nothing more than States' Privileges—privileges allowed at the permission of an all-powerful supreme Federal Government. Under such a system, the once-free citizen becomes a mere subject of the all-powerful government.

A Federal Government the People Would Accept

The main work of the Constitutional Convention, as Madison and Hamilton learned, was to create a "more perfect union," one that the people of at least nine of the thirteen States would ratify. To find out what kind of government the people of the States would accept, we need to look *not* at the arguments surrounding the Constitutional Convention but at the debates and discussions surrounding the ratification within each distinct and separate sovereign state. The majority within most States were hesitant to accept the new "more perfect union" proposed by the Constitutional Convention. The moderate Federalists answered these concerns in what is now known as *The Federalist Papers*, written by John Jay of New York, Alexander Hamilton of New York, and James Madison of Virginia.

In *The Federalist Papers*, Hamilton, Madison, and Jay advocated the moderate Federalist position. The moderate Federalist position was that the Constitution proposed a very limited Federal Government with the vast residuary of rights reserved to the sovereign States. Even Hamilton, the High Federalist, argued that the sovereign States would be completely safe in the proposed "more perfect union." In *Federalist Paper* number 28, he promised that "it may safely be received as an axiom in our political system, that the State governments will, in all possible contingencies, afford complete security against invasions of the public liberty by the national authority." Then again, in *Federalist Paper* number 85, he attempted to calm the anti-Federalist fears in the States when he declared, "We may safely rely on the disposition of the State Legislatures to erect barriers against the encroachment of national authority." Here, we see examples of how even a High Federalist such as Alexander Hamilton was forced to admit to his fellow countrymen that the Federal Government proposed under the Constitution would *not* be a supreme government but that the Constitution contemplated that the States would act as a barrier, a check, or counterbalance against unconstitutional acts of the newly created Federal Government.

James Madison provides conclusive proof regarding the status of the sovereign States vis-à-vis the newly proposed Federal Government under the Constitution. In *Federalist Paper* number 40, Madison asked the following rhetorical question of the Anti-Federalists who were skeptical regarding the new powers being proposed for the Federal Government and the potential impact on the powers of the sovereign States: "Do they require that, in the establishment of the Constitution, the States should be regarded as distinct and independent sovereigns?" In the following sentence, he answered his question: "They are so regarded by the Constitution proposed." Madison recognized that the proposed "more perfect union" was not a new and all-powerful Federal Government. It was merely an adjustment to the limited powers already held by the Federal Government created under the Articles of Confederation. The two governments, one under the Articles of Confederation and the other under the Constitution, were different in degrees, but they were not different in principles of limited Federalism and state sovereignty. In the same paper, Madison explained this fact by noting, "The truth is, that the great principle of the Constitution proposed by the convention may be considered less as absolutely new, than as the expansion of principles which are found in the Articles of Confederation." We see now that High Federalist Hamilton and Moderate Federalist Madison agreed that the States under the proposed constitution were sovereign and maintained the sovereign, free, and independent authority that they, as individual States (nations), acquired in the Treaty of Paris of 1783 and boldly proclaimed in Article II of the Articles of Confederation.

STRATEGIC FAILURE 1: FAILURE TO FOLLOW THE ADVICE OF THE ANTI-FEDERALISTS—1787-8

The chief political advantage the Anti-Federalists held over their Federalists opponents was that the Anti-Federalists could see beyond the immediate commercial and national defense benefit offered by the new "more perfect union." The Anti-Federalists could see the latent genesis of tyranny in the proposed constitution. Their concern centered not so much on the document but on the fact that the proposed constitution would, after all, be administered by men whose personal interests would naturally and eventually overwhelm their dedication to the spirit of limited Federalism. This, of course, assumes that Federalists had such dedication to limited Federalism in the first place! The Anti-Federalists understood that the proposed Constitution was a mere paper barricade. It was a paper barricade that could be easily overwhelmed by unprincipled men who had a special interest in gaining and using Federal power to improve themselves financially or politically at the expense of the unorganized masses.

Patrick Henry of Virginia was a leading anti-Federalist who quickly diagnosed the fatal flaw in the proposed "more perfect union." He realized the new taxing authority proposed for Congress would become an open invitation for the powerful to exploit those with less power. He saw very quickly that the commercial interests of the Northern States, so often championed by Alexander Hamilton, would hold a voting advantage in Congress over the agricultural interests of the Southern States. He succinctly warned, "I am sure that the dangers of this system are real when those who have no similar interests with the people of this country [Virginia] are to legislate for us—when our dearest interests are to be left in the hands of those whose advantage it will be to infringe them."[132] Patrick Henry read the tea leaves of the South's political destiny correctly. While the moderate Federalists were looking to gain more national security and commercial prowess—even if it created a potential risk to liberty—Patrick Henry was looking to America's legacy of liberty: "The first thing I have at heart is American *liberty*, the second thing is American Union."[133]

Anti-Federalists understood that man tended toward evil,[134] and therefore, they felt that men should not be tempted by unchecked governmental power. Men such as Virginian John Taylor of Caroline were so distrustful of government that they had little faith in a written constitution or any system to check the

---

132   Patrick Henry cited in Kennedy & Kennedy, *Punished With Poverty-The Suffering South*, 2nd ed., 34; Henry, William Wirt, *Patrick Henry: Life, Correspondence and Speeches*, Vol. III (1891, Harrisonburg, VA: Sprinkle Publications, 1993), 520.

133   Patrick Henry cited in Kennedy & Kennedy's *Yankee Empire: Aggressive Abroad and Despotic at Home*, 201; Henry, William Wirt, *Patrick Henry: Life, Correspondence and Speeches*, Vol. III, 449.

134   The Anti-Federalists embraced the Christian doctrine of man as a fallen creature with an inherently sinful nature. Dr. Robert L. Dabney claimed that the Founding Fathers (Federalists) did not properly account for the natural depravity within man and that any system of free government they devised would therefore be unable to stand the test of time. See Weaver, Richard, *The Southern Tradition at Bay* (New Rochelle, NY: Arlington House, 1968), 144.

abuse of power of government because, as he stated, "Great power should never be granted in the first place."[135] Thomas Jefferson and James Madison noted that men were not "angels" and could not be trusted with the administration of an unlimited government. In a letter to Spencer Roane, Jefferson, at age seventy-five, expressed a similar attitude toward the danger of government: "[It is] an axiom of eternal truth in politics, that whatever power in any government is independent [unchecked], is absolute also: in theory only, at first, while the spirit of the people is up, but in practice, as fast as that relaxes." Patrick Henry made it clear that the Sovereign State was the ultimate check on Federal tyranny when he declared, "If there be a real check intended to be left on Congress, it must be left in the State governments."[136] The ultimate check on an abusive Federal Government is real States' Rights, inclusive of the rights of state nullification and secession. Deny these rights (nullification and secession) and "States' Rights" become state privileges exercised only if the supreme Federal Government gives its permission.

The great fear of Anti-Federalists and many moderate Federalists was that the Federal Government would become an "unchecked," supreme, centralized power. Jefferson and the Anti-Federalists warned that the paper barricade of the Constitution would not withstand the onslaught of special interests. They warned that there was great danger that the rights reserved to "We the People" of the sovereign States under the Constitution would eventually be nullified by a supreme Federal Government. They foresaw the potential of an aggressive Federal Government controlled by those whose interest it would be to violate the spirit and letter of the Constitution. They foresaw that rights reserved to "We the People" would one day be usurped, as Patrick Henry warned, by "those whose advantage it will be to infringe them." Current (Modern Age Reconstruction) American politics has unquestioningly established that the Anti-Federalists were right!

---

135 Taylor, John, *News Views and An Inquiry into the Principles and Policy of the Government of the United States* (1814: New Haven: Yale University Press, 1950), xvii.

136 Henry, William Wirt, *Patrick Henry: Life, Correspondence and Speeches*, Vol. III, 500.

Additional Anti-Federalists Warnings

- The National Legislature with such a power may enslave the States. Such an idea will never be accepted....[137]
- This consolidation of the States has been the object of several men in this country for some time past. Whether such a change can ever be attained in any manner: whether it can be effected without convulsions and civil wars; and whether such a change will not totally destroy the liberties of their country time can only determine.[138]
- The eight Northern States have an interest different from the five Southern States....The Southern States had therefore grounds for their suspicions.[139]
- The regulation of trade is to be given to the General Government, they [the Southern States] will be nothing more than overseers for the Northern States.[140]
- Mr. Charles Pinkney of South Carolina laid before the house the draught of a federal Government which he had prepared, to be agreed upon between the free and independent States of America.[141]

The State of New York, in its cautious ratification of the Constitution, formerly asserted:

> We the Delegates of the People of the State of New York.... Do declare and make known....That the

---

[137] Kennedy & Kennedy, *Yankee Empire: Aggressive Abroad and Despotic at Home*, 276. The Anti-Federalist Papers and the Constitutional Convention Debates, 60.

[138] Kennedy & Kennedy, *Yankee Empire: Aggressive Abroad and Despotic at Home*, 277. The Anti-Federalist Papers and the Constitutional Convention Debates, 260.

[139] George Mason of Virginia cited in Kennedy & Kennedy, *Yankee Empire: Aggressive Abroad and Despotic at Home*, 157.

[140] Charles Pickney of South Carolina cited in Kennedy & Kennedy's *Yankee Empire: Aggressive Abroad and Despotic at Home*, 157.

[141] Madison, James, *The Debates in the Federal Convention of 1787 Which Framed the Constitution of the United States of America*, 26.

Powers of Government may be reassumed by the People, whensoever it shall become necessary to their Happiness; that every Power, Jurisdiction, and right, which is not by the said Constitution clearly delegated to the Congress of the United States, or the departments of the Government thereof, remains to the People of the several States, or to their respective State Governments....[142]

The South's first and greatest strategic failure was to ignore the Anti-Federalists' warnings. Southern Moderate Federalists were gentlemen who assumed that they were dealing with other gentlemen. Southerners entered the constitutional compact with the assurances and expectations that gentlemen of the North would keep their word. Patrick Henry had a different view of Northerners. During the 1788 Virginia convention, he "...plainly indicated the distrust of the Northern States which their conduct had engendered in his bosom."[143] Unfortunately, most Southerners were too naive to understand that honesty to the Northern merchants was a policy—"honesty is the best policy." But, when a business policy harms profits, a good Yankee merchant would change that policy to enhance profits. Southerners viewed honesty not as a policy but as a principle. Principles never change regardless of actual or threatened personal harm.[144] The first great Southern strategic failure was to ignore anti-Federalist warnings and enter a political compact/union with people grossly dissimilar in character, morals, and principles. This strategic failure set the stage for the political, social, and economic disasters awaiting the South. In retrospect, conservative Southerners can confidently say, "The Anti-Federalists were Right!"

---

142 *Ibid.*, 665-6.

143 Henry, William Wirt, *Patrick Henry: Life, Correspondence and Speeches*, Vol. II, 301.

144 Weaver, Richard, *The Southern Tradition at Bay*, 115, 149, 154, 228-9.

STRATEGIC FAILURE 2: DEFENDING SLAVERY ON CONSTITUTIONAL GROUNDS INSTEAD OF DEMANDING THE RIGHT TO FOLLOW THE HIGH ROAD TO EMANCIPATION

By 1850, it was apparent that the North was determined to destroy the approximate equality of representation between the North and the South in Congress. The North was following their prior efforts to prevent Southern States, such as Louisiana and Texas, from joining the Union. They objected to these new States because it would increase the South's voting power in Congress—a Congress in which the North was the numerical majority from the inception of the United States. This was one of the primary reasons Patrick Henry opposed the ratification of the Constitution. He foresaw the day the North would use its numerical majority in Congress to tax the agricultural (primarily Southern) States for the benefit of Northern commerce.[145]

The primary issue used by the North to "fence-in" the South and make sure the Southern States remained a minor section of the expanding Union was the emotional issue of slavery. Northern politicians and their media propagandists continually made the erroneous claim that the South aimed to extend slavery to every state in the Union and to maintain slavery as a labor system permanently. This emotional allegation, though not supported by facts, was nonetheless effective. Southerners, such as Jefferson Davis, favored solving the problem of slavery, but such attitudes were never broadcast to the North or internationally. Davis advocated that slavery should be used as an "institution for the preparation of that race for civil liberty and social enjoyment." He urged the North to "leave natural causes to their full effect, and when the time shall arrive at which emancipation is proper, those most interested will be most anxious to effect it."[146] The South made the strategic mistake of answering the North's emotional allegations with constitutional facts. Just as today, conservative Southerners never realize that when dealing with the

---

145 Henry, William Wirt, *Patrick Henry: Life, Correspondence and Speeches*, Vol. II, 447.

146 Davis cited in Eli N. Evans's *Judah P. Benjamin-The Jewish Confederate* (New York: The Free Press, 1988), 72.

public, emotional arguments always prevail over truth, facts, and evidence.[147] By 1850, Southern political leaders could see the South being boxed into its current geographic area while the North was free to establish new States in the West. A convention of Southern leaders was held in Nashville, Tennessee, June 3-11, 1850, to discuss how to respond to the efforts of the North to limit the western expansion of Southern States. The Nashville Convention was a tactical victory of sorts, but it was a strategic disaster.[148]

The 1850 Nashville Convention comprised 176 delegates from Alabama, Arkansas, Florida, Georgia, Mississippi, South Carolina, Tennessee, Texas, and Virginia. The delegates denounced the attempt of the North to ban slavery in the new territories acquired by the Louisiana Purchase and the Mexican-American War. This, of course, was propaganda fodder for Northern anti-South politicians and newspapers. The people of the North were instructed by their politicians and newspapers that the South was determined to turn the United States into a slave-owning nation. The Nashville Convention is one example of how Southern leaders, relying on facts, truth, and the Constitution, would be overpowered by their Northern adversaries who relied on emotional arguments. It was made to appear to the Northern population that the South was using the Constitution and States' Rights to advance slavery. And to make matters worse, this was the message that European audiences were receiving. This would work to the South's detriment when seeking European recognition for the Confederate States of America. Instead of a minor tactical victory the Nashville

---

147 Recall that the media produced national hysteria over the death of a drugged, black man, with a criminal record, who resisted lawful orders of the police. Emotions produced the desired leftist political impact, while the facts of the case were irrelevant. The emotions remain long after the news cycle is over. In a mass democracy, emotions trump facts and logic—a fact that conservatives in general and Southerners specifically are, seemingly, incapable of recognizing.

148 The Nashville Convention delegates proposed a slave/non-slave States dividing line by extending the Missouri Compromise of 1820 to the Pacific Coast. The US Congress enacted the Compromise of 1850, which only gave the anti-South advocates more *emotional* ammunition to use against the South. Soon, speeches would be heard proclaiming that a house divided could not stand. Meaning that part of the "house" had to be reconstructed.

Convention could have been a strategic victory. This failure was recognized by a Southern author in the 1930s:

> ...the Nashville Convention of 1850....The Southern States did not heed his warning, for *their strong emotional attachment to the Union* clouded the force of Calhoun's logic. He could not teach them that the purpose of the Union was to sustain their independence, and that this was now possible only in a Southern Union, since the commercial and industrial States had upset the balance of power in their [the North's] favor.[149] [Emphasis added by author].

The Nashville Convention was a strategic failure because their efforts were aimed at maintaining the political *status quo* instead of setting the stage for independence by removing the issue of slavery via the high road to emancipation. Their "emotional attachment to the Union" prevented them from obtaining freedom for "We the People" of the South. It set the stage for Federal tyranny during all three phases of Reconstruction. They forgot or rejected Patrick Henry's admonition: "The first thing I have at heart is American liberty, the second is American union." This type of "conservative" leadership would continue to haunt the thinking of the "pitiful service [of] the inept Southern politicians."[150]

During Passive Reconstruction (1877-1965), the South became so "patriotic" and enamored with the "one nation indivisible," that they forgot that as far as the South was concerned, this one nation indivisible did not allow for "liberty and justice for all." The conservatism of the South's elected leaders was simply to give hot speeches about the glorious Constitution, pretending that the original Constitution still existed. In addition, they tacitly agreed to forgo anything that might appear to be an attempt to encourage

---

149 Lytle, Andrew Nelson, *Bedford Forrest and His Critter Company* (1931, Nashville, TN: J.S. Sanders & Company, 1992), 30.

150 John Crowe Ransom, "Reconstructed But Unregenerate," *I'll Take My Stand*, (1930, Baton Rouge, LA: LSU Press, 1983), 26.

a peaceful revolutionary movement to restore America's original Republic of Sovereign States. Southern political and social leaders could not bring themselves to take audacious steps to redeem America's original Federalism, in which the Constitution was enforced by real States' Rights, including the rights of nullification and secession. The Nashville Convention made it appear to the world that preserving slavery was all that concerned the South. Once again, Southerners played into the hands of vile Yankee propagandists whose political currency was emotions, not facts, truth, or logic. "The South possesses an inheritance which it has imperfectly understood and little used. It is in the curious position of having been right without realizing the grounds of its rightness."[151]

The South had a long history of resisting the nefarious slave trade carried on by English and New England merchants. During the Colonial era, Southern colonies attempted to prohibit the slave trade, but the King and Parliament nullified their legislative efforts.

> Among the imports were African slaves in large numbers. This wicked traffic was the subject of protests by the colonies, time and again, and ...Virginia, which went so far as to pass an act prohibiting it. But ... a large share of the enormous profits made by the traders went into the coffers of the British sovereigns, and the laws interfering with the traffic were disapproved and annulled by them.[152]

Until the rise of New England's Radical Abolitionists of the John Brown school who were promoting a slave uprising and the resultant massacre of whites, circa 1830s, there were more abolitionist societies in the South than in the North.[153] By 1860, Southern slave owners had, at their own expense, granted freedom

---

[151] Weaver, *The Southern Tradition at Bay*, 388.

[152] Henry, , *Patrick Henry: Life, Correspondence and Speeches*, Vol. II, 54.

[153] Livingston, Donald W., "Confederate Emancipation Without War," *To Live and Die In Dixie*, ed. Frank Powell, III (Sons of Confederate Veterans, 2014), 468.

to multiple thousands of former slaves. Southern leaders, such as John Randolph of Virginia and Jefferson Davis of Mississippi, followed the high road to emancipation by providing freedom (John Randolph) and education (Jefferson Davis) for their slaves. Jefferson Davis spoke of the high road to emancipation in Congress. He put his principles into practice by establishing schools for his slaves on all his plantations. His goal was to prepare a people who never in their history established a democratic government for the day in which they would be a free and productive part of society.[154]

The facts about the abolition efforts in the South should have been turned into an emotional appeal to the North and transmitted to European nations. The emotional argument would be that the South demanded to be left alone as it moved along the high road to emancipation. A definite future date on which slavery would be ended within each Southern state would be established by each Southern State. As the Southern States moved into the West, the South would develop natural allies with the agricultural communities in the West who were also harmed by New England's demand for protective tariffs. Even if the North rejected this offer, it would take away the emotional issue of slavery and reduce Northern popular support for Lincoln's invasion of the South. It would have also encouraged European nations to recognize and possibly support the South's independence. The South depended upon Constitutional facts and the truth about the rights reserved by the Sovereign States. But the North depended upon emotions. The South, even to this day, never recognized it as an unfair battle that it was destined to lose.

Emotions always trump facts when dealing with the public—especially in a mass democracy such as today's America.[155] South-

---

[154] Kennedy & Kennedy, *Jefferson Davis: High Road to Emancipation and Constitutional Government*, 5-14, 56-9.

[155] "Crowds are only powerful for destruction. Their rule is always tantamount to a barbarian phase.... A civilization involves fixed rules, discipline, a passing from the instinctive to the rational state, forethought for the future, an elevated degree of culture—all of them conditions that crowds, left to themselves, have invariably shown themselves incapable of realizing." See Le Bon, Gustave, *The Crowd: A Study of the Popular Mind* (1896, London: T. Fisher Unwin, 1910), 19.

ern scholar Dr. M.E. Bradford (1934-1993) described the dangers of emotional ideological thinking. "We reason at our best when we keep dialectics to a minimum and treat no artifact made of words as if it were a dish served up to the gods."[156] Bradford defended tradition against the isms of in-vogue but temporary ideas that often descend from that New England "City on a Hill" to afflict "We the People."

STRATEGIC FAILURE 3: THE BATTLE OF FIRST MANASSAS—MISSED OPPORTUNITY FOR A STRATEGIC VICTORY

The First Battle of Manassas is an excellent study of how not to win a war. It demonstrates the danger of being satisfied with a tactical victory instead of moving immediately, even at great risk, to create a strategic victory. The rout of the invader's Army presented the South with an excellent opportunity to pursue and destroy the invader's Army and to follow the fleeing enemy into Washington, dictate the terms of surrender, or at least, if Lincoln and his Republican government fled the capitol, establish the rationale for foreign recognition of the Confederacy.

When President Davis arrived at Beauregard's headquarters, he was surprised the pursuit had stopped. It was late and the battle was hard fought all day, but President Davis asked if the pursuit could be renewed. Indecision reigned, and, at last, it was decided to renew the pursuit the following morning. President Davis understood it would be a full-scale pursuit, but Beauregard understood it to be a reconnaissance in force. By the morning, rain had turned the roads into mud, and no pursuit was possible.[157] As a non-West Point Confederate military genius (General Nathan Bedford Forrest) would say, "Put the scare on and keep the scare on." The failure to "keep the scare on" the fleeing Yankee invaders resulted in substituting a strategic victory for a mere tactical victory—a victory that, in the long run, meant nothing as far as

---

156 Bradford, M.E., *Against the Barbarians and Other reflections on Familiar Themes* (Columbia, MO: University of Missouri Press, 1992), 14, 19.

157 Williams, T. Harry, *P.G.T. Beauregard: Napoleon in Gray* (Baton Rouge, LA: LSU Press, 1955), 89-90.

securing the independence of the Confederate States of America. The War presented the Southern people with two choices: to gain self-government via Southern independence or become vassals in the newly emerging Yankee Empire. The strategic failure at First Manassas set the South on the road to Republican-initiated Active Reconstruction—the South would become and remains today the Yankee Empire's economic, social, and political vassal.

The pattern of settling for a tactical victory instead of planning and maneuvering for a strategic victory—a victory that will make a *fundamental* difference—continues to be followed by Southern conservatives today. When Antifa, BLM, NAACP, and other social justice warriors began to tear down Confederate monuments, the typical Southern response was to hire an expensive lawyer and "sue the bastards!" Even if the conservative effort is successful, which few such lawsuits are, it is only a tactical victory. Conservatives are satisfied with a temporary local victory that results in no *fundamental* change in the political *status quo*. It is the political *status quo* that not only allowed but encouraged the destruction of traditional American values and heroes in the first place. American conservatives refused to recognize that the attack on traditional American values and heroes is a part of a worldwide neo-Marxist attack against Western Christian civilization. In the late 1940s, English moral philosopher C.S. Lewis warned that anti-Christian actors are engaged in efforts to "debunk traditional values."[158] Their strategic goal is to replace Western civilization based on Christian values with a neo-Marxist society based on postmodern, neo-Marxist values. While modern-day Southerners may criticize Generals Beauregard, Johnston, and President Davis for not seeking a strategic victory at Manassas, these same contemporary Southerners are following a similar pattern of avoiding audacious action that would bring about a strategic victory while settling for a hoped-for tactical victory.

The South's failure to turn a tactical victory at Manassas into a strategic victory resulted in the South's eventual surrender at

---

158 Lewis, C.S., *The Abolition of Man* (1944, New York: Harper Collins, 2001), 51. 65.

Appomattox. Appomattox was the death-knell of the Constitution. Two postmodern historians joyfully declared, the conservative theory of strict interpretation of the Constitution "died at Gettysburg and Appomattox."[159]

STRATEGIC FAILURE 4: FAILURE TO CONTINUE THE STRUGGLE FOR SOUTHERN INDEPENDENCE AFTER THE END OF ACTIVE RECONSTRUCTION

Post-War, the conquered and occupied Southern States were at the mercy of their conquerors. The South was treated the same as any nation that suffered invasion, conquest, and foreign occupation by an aggressive empire. As the Romans would say, *Vae Victis*—woe to the vanquished. As will be documented in subsequent chapters, the victorious North under the political leadership of the Republican Party was seething with hatred for the South. Northern political leaders, their sycophants in the media, and a large majority of the Northern people were motivated by a passionate desire for revenge against Southern whites. They were eager to foist upon the defeated South a hideous, corrupt, and tyrannical form of state government that Northerners would not have accepted for themselves—yet they happily inflicted it upon the whites in the defeated Southern States.

The North's Republican political leaders and its allied business interests were eager to exploit politically and economically their newly acquired Southern territories. Exploitation of newly conquered people is what all empires do with their conquest. While Americans today ignore or repress this sad part of American history, it was recognized by foreign journalists at the time. The London *Telegraph* in 1866 observed that, while the United States "may remain a republic in name, but some eight million of the people are subjects, not citizens."[160] The London *Times* recognized

---

159 Hyman and Wiecek, *Equal Justice Under Law: Constitutional Development, 1835-1875* (New York: Harper and Row, 1982), 552. Bradford's *Original Intentions: On the Making and Ratification of the United States Constitution*, 156, footnote, 18.

160 Bowers, Claude, *The Tragic Era*, 146-7. Author quotes the *New York World*, November 24, 1866.

the Republican Party's tendency toward political tyranny in their September 13, 1862, edition, "Republicans put empire above liberty, and resorted to political oppression and war rather than suffer any abatement of national power....[national power] was upheld, like any other Empire, by force of arms." It was evident that the old American Jeffersonian Republic was dead. Active Reconstruction (1866-1877) was a time in which millions of former self-governing Americans (Southerners) were held under military dictatorship with no rights that the United States government was required to respect. Republican Thaddeus Stevens of Pennsylvania declared the Republican-controlled Congress would treat the South as "an outside, conquered people, they can be refused admission to the Union unless they voluntarily *do what we demand.*"[161] Under the Republican-controlled Congress, white Southerners were treated similarly to the way American Indians of the Western Plains were treated—the Federal Government's ultimate aim was to exterminate those people who stood in the way of their expanding empire. During the War, Union officers and officials openly announced their desire to exterminate Southern men, women, and children.[162] Failing to exterminate the South as a people with a common culture, political and social values, and traditions, they were at least successful in exterminating the South as a political barrier to the creation of a Northern-controlled supreme Federal Government.

The South's struggle against Active Reconstruction was a resistance movement like the French Resistance against their German occupiers during World War II. It was a resistance movement aimed at overturning Republican-initiated Active Reconstruction and regaining some form of local political and social "normality." Each Southern State had its own unique resistance movement. Each state's resistance movement will be discussed in chapters 14 through 28. One of the main points of this book is to

---

161 Bowers, Claude, *The Tragic Era*, 18. Author cites Stevens's speech reported in the *Lancaster Intelligencer*, September 13, 1865.

162 See, Chapter 7, "The War To Exterminate Black and White Southerners" in Kennedy & Kennedy, *Punished With Poverty* 2nd ed., 77-96.

document that Reconstruction did not end in 1877. While Yankee troops were removed and the Southern States were allowed the *appearance* of self-government, the reality was that a new form of Reconstruction emerged—Passive Reconstruction (1877-1965). During Passive Reconstruction, a tacit North/South Bargain was established. The South would, under duress, swear allegiance to the newly created supreme and indivisible Federal Government,[163] abandon all claims to Southern independence, never question the origins or legitimacy of the new supreme Federal Government, and patriotically support the new but illegitimate and unconstitutional government.[164] This new patriotism is best demonstrated by the number of Southerners serving in the US military beginning with the Spanish-American War and continuing in every war down to the twenty-first century. It was a time of North/South reconciliation—it was a time when it was cool to be a rebel.[165] But it brought with it another major Southern strategic failure—a failure that haunts freedom-loving Americans today.

History offers numerous examples of conquered nations and people who managed to endure their conquerors' oppressive rule and eventually gain their freedom or at least gain protection for their unique cultural values and heritage. Scotland and Quebec are modern-day examples of how a people maintained their cultural uniqueness even when occupied by an empire.[166] They did this by peacefully maintaining their right to independence. Their resistance efforts included ballot initiatives on independence. The empire was forced to compromise with the occupied people to prevent a successful independence vote. The *valid* threat of secession gave the occupied people a bargaining leverage they would not have had otherwise. Even though Quebec and Scotland lost

---

163 James Iredell of North Carolina during the debates on ratification of the Constitution (circa 1787) declared that no oath of allegiance to a prince is binding if it is not consistent with the safety and liberties of the people. See Bradford, M.E., *Original Intentions: On the Making and Ratification of the United States Constitution*, 26.

164 Kennedy & Kennedy, *The South Was Right!* 3rd ed., 331-2.

165 See Chapter 1, "When Rebel Was Cool," in Kennedy & Kennedy, *The South Was Right* 3rd ed., 1-19.

166 Kennedy, James Ronald, *Dixie Rising-Rules for Rebels*, 2nd ed.(Columbia, SC: Shotwell Publishing., 2021), 112-14, 108-10.

their recent votes for independence, they still won major political and social advantages. The *valid* threat of secession was used to at least gain protection for their unique standing as a people with their own culture and heritage. The Federal Government of Canada would not dare to pull down monuments in Quebec honoring French heroes, nor would the British government dare to initiate a new campaign of cultural genocide in Scotland. In both cases, the narrow defeat of the independence vote would suddenly change if the occupying government attacked the right of the people to protect their culture and heritage. Such anti-Quebec or anti-Scottish acts by the central government would create a public demand for independence, and the following vote for independence would be successful. The *valid* threat of secession is often enough to keep the wolves of tyranny at bay.

Instead of fostering and encouraging in each generation of Southerners the dream of eventual Southern independence, the pacified South took another route following the end of Active Reconstruction. During Passive Reconstruction, Southerners were primarily concerned with avoiding any acts or words that would give the Yankee Empire an excuse for reinstating Active Reconstruction. The fear of a renewal of Active Reconstruction was not an irrational fear. As late as 1890, Congressman Henry Cabot Lodge, Sr. (R-Massachusetts) introduced a bill calling for what amounted to a return to Active Reconstruction-type of control of Southern elections.[167] The political and social horrors the South endured during Active Reconstruction created a permanent fear of Republican-sponsored black rule in the South. To avoid provoking the Yankee Empire's ruling elite, Southern leaders abandoned even the discussion of Southern independence and "swallowed the dog"[168] by swearing allegiance to Lincoln's and the Republican Party's newly created "indivisible" Federal Government (the Yankee Empire).

---

167 Clark & Kirwan, *The South Since Appomattox* (New York: Oxford University Press, 1967), 71.

168 "Swallowing the dog" was a term used by Confederate veterans who were required to take an oath of allegiance to the United States as a prerequisite for receiving Yankee "pardon." Some Southerners, such as Judah P. Benjamin's brother Joseph, refused to swear allegiances to the new Union and fled the country, taking up residence in Honduras—When Judah P.

This was the price of peaceful subjugation. It was the price that had to be paid if Southerners were allowed even the *semblance*, façade, or pretense of self-government. The legitimate American political principle of States' Rights in which the Constitution was enforced by "We the People" within our sovereign state was dead. As Supreme Court Justice Chase joyfully announced in the 1869 case *White vs. Texas*, "The North's victory killed State sovereignty."[169] The American constitutional principle of States' Rights was replaced with the reality of States' Privileges, privileges that are allowed to be exercised by the Yankee Empire's subjects if *and only if* they have the permission of their ultimate master, the supreme Federal Government. For example, in 2008 the people of California voted for and passed Proposition 8, a ballot initiative defining marriage as between one man and one woman. Yet, the Federal Government intervened and nullified the democratically expressed will of "We the People" of that once sovereign state. Bloody bayonets were used via war and Active Reconstruction to compel "We the People" to accept a form of government that the Founding Fathers specifically rejected!

America's Constitution was changed from a document that limited the power of the Federal Government into a document that limited the right and ability of "We the People" within our sovereign States to protect ourselves from an oppressive Federal Government.[170] The emerging Yankee Empire created this new, illegitimate, and unconstitutional government. Lincoln and the post-War Republican Party created it with the use of massed bloody bayonets. As Jefferson Davis predicted, consent was replaced with coercion. Post-War during Active Reconstruction, the South was

---

Benjamin, Confederate Secretary of Treasury, was asked where he was going, he replied, "To the farthest place from the United States, if it takes me to the middle of China." He fled to England.

169 Kilpatrick, James Jackson, *The Sovereign States* (Chicago: Henry Regnery Co., 1957), 222; *Texas vs. White*, 7 Wallace 700 (1869).

170 The American principle of States' Rights was upheld and explained in the Kentucky and Virginia Resolutions of 1798, authored by Thomas Jefferson and James Madison. See Kennedy & Kennedy, *Jefferson Davis: High Road to Emancipation and Constitutional Government*, 371-6.

forced to accept its assigned position as a colonial province of the Yankee Empire.[171] This was a major post-War Southern strategic failure. The Yankee Empire's ruling elite were free to enact any number of oppressive laws, rules, regulations, issue oppressive court orders, and vastly increase direct taxation, indirect taxation via inflation, public debt, and open borders without fear of a Southern-led popular revolt. Southerners surrendered the right of *effective* resistance to Federal tyranny and learned to accept and even love its federal chains—while vainly repeating "one nation indivisible."[172] Henceforth, the South's elected leaders in the national Congress would make hot speeches for home consumption while diligently working in Washington to maintain their position in the Yankee Empire's political *status quo*. All seemed to be working well for the South's pacified politicians during Passive Reconstruction, the time when it was cool to be a rebel, but that time came to a crashing halt. The failure of the South to effectively maintain its dream and demand for independence by demonstrating a valid threat of secession allowed and encouraged the Yankee Empire's ruling elite to end Passive Reconstruction and initiate Modern Era Reconstruction (post-1965).

Instead of being a leader in the effort to restore America's legitimate constitutionally limited Republic of Sovereign States, the South became an active supporter of the current unconstitutional supreme Federal Government. The South could have been a leader in national efforts to limit the authority of the Federal Government to force God out of public schools or efforts to limit the Federal Government from weaponizing the FBI against parents protesting the radical leftist indoctrination and grooming of their children in public schools. The modern-day resistance to Federal tyranny

---

171   Kennedy & Kennedy, *Punished With Poverty* 2nd ed., 170-1, 217, 221-3, 226-7.

172   The political term "one nation indivisible" was promoted by Karl Marx and Frederick Engels. At the request of the Communist Party of Germany in 1848, Karl Marx and Fredrick Engles wrote the *Seventeen Points of German Communism*. The very first point Marx and Engles announced was to make the German Federal Republic "one nation indivisible." This is the rationale of all tyrants vis-a-vis States of a Federal Republic. See, Kennedy, Walter D., *Lincoln, the Non-Christian: Exposing the Myth* (Columbia, SC: Shotwell Publishing, 2023), 52-56.

could have been accomplished if there was a political force demanding such limitations. For example, a South-wide ballot initiative, demanding the submission to the States of an amendment to the Constitution acknowledging the States' Rights of nullification and secession, would encourage non-Southern States to join the fight to limit an out-of-control Federal Government. But such audacious acts are beyond the thinking of the South's pacified elected leaders. Today's bureaucratic or Deep State with its allegiance to Globalist financial interests demonstrates the detrimental national impact that the South's strategic failure allowed. The South's strategic failure to maintain its dream of independence supported by a *valid* threat of secession gave the enemies of traditional American values a free hand in their war to deconstruct (or debunk) all traditional American values.

STRATEGIC FAILURE 5: FAILURE TO UNDERSTAND THAT THE CURRENT POLITICAL SYSTEM IS UNCONSTITUTIONAL AND THEREFORE ILLEGITIMATE[173] THIS FAILURE ALLOWED FOR THE INITIATION OF RECONSTRUCTION IN THE MODERN ERA BEGINNING IN 1965

Before an addict can be cured of his addiction, he must first admit to himself that he has an addiction problem. The same is true for American conservatives who are constantly complaining about high taxation, inflation, open borders, the destruction of traditional moral values via government rules, regulations, court orders, etc. The typical conservative solution is to "elect good conservatives." But when elected, these "good conservatives" become part of the political *status quo*.[174] The twentieth century was a century of steady conservative retreat before the forces of big gov-

---

173 Throughout this book, the current political *status quo*—the supreme Federal Government—is branded as unconstitutional and therefore illegitimate. The only legitimate way to correct this is to form a political pressure group demanding a return to America's original Republic of Sovereign States. It cannot be accomplished by armed insurrection. Violence committed by adherents to Quebec nationalism almost destroyed the entire movement. Any attempt to restore constitutional liberty must be done via non-violent political actions.

174 Kennedy, James Ronald, *Nullification: Why and How*, 17-22. Free downloadable copy at www.bit.ly/Kennedys_freePDF.

ernment (progressives, liberals, socialists, etc.).[175] The problem is that, regardless of who is elected president or who is elected to Congress, they are compelled to work within the political *status quo*. If the Federal Government is accepted as the final judge to the extent of its own power, there will be no real conservative reforms, conservative "contracts with America," or effective conservative "draining of the swamp." Even Mr. Conservative Ronald Reagan with two terms as President could not produce a *fundamental* change in America's political *status quo*. When President Clinton was compelled to declare that the day of big government is over, conservatives celebrated, but nothing really happened except big government eventually renewed its growth and its tyrannical grasp on power. This is another example of a "conservative" tactical victory but a strategic defeat, just like the Battle of First Manassas.

The political and social leadership of the South (which includes the South's religious leaders) should be leading a popular, non-violent, political revolt demanding a *fundamental* change in America's political system.[176] The South should be leading the discussions about how to restore America's original constitutionally limited Republic of Sovereign States—an American government in which the ultimate authority for enforcing the constitutional limitation on the Federal Government resides not with the Federal Supreme Court but with "We the People" within our respective sovereign state(s). The South made a strategic failure by failing to recognize and declare publicly that the current political system—the political *status quo*—is unconstitutional, illegitimate, and therefore must be replaced. This strategic failure left Southerners as well as all conservative Americans in the position of political slaves to America's Woke, politically correct, leftist, political and social establishment.

The conservative South's refusal to declare to its own people and the people of its sister States in the North and West that the

---

175 See Chapter 1, "Conservatism: A Century of Failure," in James Ronald Kennedy's *Reclaiming Liberty* (Gretna, LA: Pelican Publishing Co., 2005), 15-43.

176 Such a revolt could be accomplished by using the technique of irregular political warfare. See James Ronald Kennedy's *Dixie Rising-Rules for Rebels* 2nd ed., 19-34.

current system of government is unconstitutional and must be replaced with America's original, legitimate Republic of Sovereign States had a pernicious impact on American liberty. It turned "conservatives" into docile political slaves of America's Woke, Globalist ruling elite. It is the South's final strategic failure—a failure that prevents a popular demand for a *fundamental* change in America's current left-of-center Federal Government.

The North's powerful anti-South centers of propaganda were a major factor in the ability of the North to inflict Active Reconstruction upon the South and then to replace the legitimate Republic of Sovereign States with an all-powerful Federal Government controlled by Northern political and financial elites. In the following chapter, the history of the propaganda methods used by the North to destroy the South and change America's original Republic of Sovereign States into an all-powerful supreme Federal Government—the Yankee Empire—will be explained.

Chapter 5:

SLANDER: JUSTIFYING INVASION, CONQUEST, AND DOMINATION OF THE SOUTH

"An old Russian saying is that the Czar's power is more far-reaching than God's, for God makes only the future, while the Czar remakes the past."
—Theodore Dalrymple[177]

THE CONQUERED AND OCCUPIED South, with its puppet state governments firmly established and accepted, is no longer "kept in its place" by bloody Yankee bayonets. The military occupation of the South is no longer needed. Today, the Yankee Empire keeps the Southern people in their assigned place upon the "stools of everlasting repentance"[178] not with physical force but with psychological force. Military force was replaced with vicious and unanswered anti-South slander and fake history. The post-War Republican emotional appeal to Northerners constantly reminded them that Southerners killed Northern men, and only by voting Republican could the "rebels" be controlled. This emotional appeal is referred to as waving the bloody shirt. Waving the bloody shirt, so effectively used by the Yankee press during Active Reconstruction, was replaced in Modern Era Reconstruction with slanderous, anti-South fake news and fake history. American

---

177   Dalrymple, Theodore, *Our Culture, What's Left of It* (Chicago, Ill: Ivan R. Dee Publishers, 2005), 172.

178   Owsley, Frank Lawrence, "The Irrepressible Conflict," *I'll Take My Stand* (1930, Baton Rouge, LA: LSU Press, 1983), 63.

founding father John Taylor of Caroline correctly noted, "Tyranny is wonderfully ingenious in the art of inventing specious phrases to spread over its nefarious designs."[179]

The Yankee Empire's leftist propagandists in the media and academia are responsible for creating psychological pressure on traditional Southerners and especially Southern political "leaders."

> But what pitiful service have the inept Southern politicians for many years been rendering to the cause! Their Southern loyalty at Washington has rarely had any more imaginative manifestation than to scramble vigorously for a Southern share in the federal pie. They will have to be miraculously enlightened.[180]

This psychological pressure intimidates spineless Southern politicians while compelling rank-and-file Southerners to self-censor[181] themselves and meekly accept their assigned second-class social, political, and economic status in America's politically correct, Woke society. A postmodern, neo-Marxist, Dartmouth history professor explained their intentions when he labeled all who opposed leftist extremists as "fascists." He admitted they aimed to make "everyday fascists fearful of leaving their homes, and to make their views recede into hiding."[182] America's political *status quo* and its sycophants in the digital media, mainline media, postmodern academia, and Woke social justice warriors have silenced all national voices defending traditional conservative Southern values and heritage. Southerners have no effective voice in today's Woke America. "We the People" of Dixie are second-class citizens in this "one nation indivisible," and the promise of

---

179 Taylor, John, *Tyranny Unmasked* (1822: Indianapolis: Liberty Fund, 1992), 78.

180 Ransom, John Crowe, "Reconstructed But Unregenerate," *I'll Take My Stand*, 26.

181 Ekins, Emily, "Poll: 62% of Americans Say They Have Political Views They're Afraid to Share," Cato Institute (Cato.org), 22 July 2020. (Accessed 27 July 2020) www.bit.ly/62scared

182 Posobiec, Jack, *The ANTIFA: Stories from Inside the Bloc* (Washington, DC: The Calamo Press, 2021), 198.

"liberty and justice for all" is a lie when dealing with the South and our traditional conservative political and moral values.

During Active, Passive, and Modern Era Reconstruction, the South became the ruling elites' whipping boy.[183] Using the slanderous but emotionally effective "bloody shirt" in the form of anti-South lies allows the ruling elite to shift responsibility away from the disaster their corrupt actions brought on America. Using the "bloody shirt" during Active Reconstruction allowed the Northern ruling elites to rally votes necessary to maintain control of the political *status quo*. Slandering the South was the mainstay of Northern propaganda since the early 1830s. It was aggressively used during Active Reconstruction and continues today. As Southern comedian Lewis Grizzard said, "The more outlandish a thing that is said about the South, the more likely a Yankee is to believe it."

The attitude of Yankees toward Southerners before and after the War is virtually identical to the view of Englishmen toward the conquered Celts of Ireland, Wales, and Scotland. It was the attitude of arrogant superiority felt by the conqueror over the conquered. Arrogant New Englanders followed the example of their English fathers. One arrogant Yankee declared, "I believe that the great conception of a Christian society, which was in the minds of the Pilgrims of the Mayflower....is to displace and blot out the foul [South] ....with all its heaven-offending enormities." Another Yankee was more specific regarding how to cure the Yankee-diagnosed evils down South, "I would exterminate them root and branch."[184]

Shortly after the Confederate victory at the Battle of First Manassas, Yankee newspapers reported that Confederate General

---

183 A whipping boy was a commoner boy and companion of a prince (or boy monarch) in Europe who received corporal punishment for the prince's misdeeds. The prince was not punished because he was in a unique situation as a royal. An evil prince could take advantage of this arrangement because he could do anything he wanted without fear of punishment for his misdeeds.

184 Cited in Drs. McWhiney & Jamieson, *Attack and Die: Civil War Military Tactics and the Southern Heritage* (The Tuscaloosa, AL: University of Alabama Press, 1982), 182.

Beauregard was seen riding around the battlefield on a headless horse!185 Outlandish, yes, but believable if you are a Yankee who, for generations, eagerly consumed such outlandish stories about the South in your local newspaper. As Admiral Raphael Semmes, CSN, noted, "Northerners, who never hesitated to use the most unblushing falsehoods, if they thought these would serve their purposes better than the truth."186 The April 8, 1861, edition of the Philadelphia *Inquirer* carried a report of a mail bag from Florida in which two venomous snakes were found. The report did not mention any nefarious intentions related to the snakes. The next day, on April 9, the Lowell *Daily Courier* carried the story with a few changes. By April 15, the story reached New England, where the New Hampshire *Sentinel* carried the story stating that the snakes were mailed to President Lincoln to assassinate the President.187 Such "Yellow Journalism" was standard fare for many Northern newspapers from the early days of radical abolitionism. Similar outlandish stories about "rebel outrages" would be used by the Republican Party's propagandists in the media to convince the Northern public to support the Republican Party's punitive and unconstitutional Reconstruction policies.

William Lloyd Garrison, owner of a radical anti-South newspaper, the *Liberator*, was typical of radical abolitionists who spewed slanderous lies about the South. He fictionalized an evil narrative to describe any way of life that was not the same as his New England lifestyle. He hated slavery and the slave owner. He refused to distinguish between Southern slave owners and Southern non-slave owners. Yet, Southern non-slave owners composed nearly 80% of the South's white population. He used his paper to describe Southerners as "ruffians who insult, pollute and lacerate helpless women and ...conspire against the lives and liberties of

---

185 Williams, T. Harry, *P.G.T. Beauregard Napoleon in Gray* (Baton Rouge, LA: LSU Press, 1955), 91.

186 Semmes, Admiral Raphael, *Memoirs of Service Afloat* (1868, Secaucus, NJ: The Blue & Grey Press, 1987), 214.

187 White, D. Jonathan, "Copperheads: History and Historiography," *Northern Opposition to Mr. Lincoln's War* (McClellenville, SC: Abbeville Institute Press, 2014), 76-7.

New England citizens."[188] This is the type of Radical Abolitionist that attacked the South, threatening and encouraging bloody slave revolts. Even Daniel Webster of Massachusetts admitted that Northern abolitionists prevented the growth of the Southern abolition movement.[189] Numerous Southerners acknowledged that slavery was not a permanent labor system and, in their own way, were promoting the high road to emancipation. In 1856, Robert E. Lee wrote to his wife, "In this enlightened age, there are few, I believe, but what will acknowledge, that slavery as an institution, is a moral and political evil in any country."[190] President Jefferson Davis wrote to his wife, admitting that regardless of how the War turns out, the system of slavery would end.[191]

Radical Abolitionists could broadcast their hatred from the safety of the North, protected by Northern state governments and the knowledge that if their nefarious plan for a slave uprising did occur, their families would be safe because there were almost no blacks in their lily-white States. A historian who did a study on Northern pre-War anti-South propagandists' attitudes about Southerners observed: "Theirs was a propaganda of hatred and fear... [they] committed themselves, in the final analysis, to the ugly business of creating for the popular imagination a villain whom the people of the North would soon be quite willing to meet in battle."[192] Northern newspapers at the outbreak of the War demonstrated the malicious impact that generations of slanderous anti-South propaganda had on the Northern public (an effect that continues today). The New York *Tribune* looked forward to seeing the "hanging of traitors is sure to begin before one month is over." The New York *Times* wanted to send 25,000 Yankee troops

---

188 Floan, Howard R., *The South in Northern Eyes-1831 to 1861* (New York: McGraw-Hill Book Co., 1958), 6.

189 Johnson, Ludwell H., *North Against the South: The American Iliad 1848-1877* (1978, Columbia, SC: The Foundation of American Education, 1993), 179.

190 *Ibid.*, 179.

191 Kennedy & Kennedy, *Jefferson Davis: High Road to Emancipation and Constitutional Government* (Columbia, SC: Shotwell Publishing, 2020), 110.

192 Floan, Howard R., *The South in Northern Eyes-1831 to 1861*, 1958), 50.

"to Richmond and burn out the rats there." The Philadelphia *Press* described Southerners as "The rebels, a mere band of ragamuffins [who] will fly, like a chaff before the wind, on our approach."[193] Notice how these Northern propagandists characterized Southerners as "traitors," "rats," and a gang of "ragamuffins." It is a well-practiced propagandists' tactic that, before a tyrant can exterminate his enemy, he must first dehumanize them. Once the tyrant's propaganda has effectively removed the targeted group from the society of decent people, then the targeted people can be permanently removed from society. This is what the North did, and the political *status quo* continues to do to "We the People" of Dixie.

During the War, Northern military and political leaders often declared the need to "exterminate" Southerners.[194] For generations before the War, Northern extremists kept up a steady drumbeat of slanderous anti-South propaganda. The anti-South slander became an avalanche during Republican-imposed Active Reconstruction (1866-1877). The Republican-controlled Congress used it to push through punitive, oppressive, and unconstitutional legislation. Slanderous Yankee propaganda became a smoke-screen behind which the Republican Party could hide while it worked feverishly to control the state governments down South. In Washington, the Republican Party successfully worked to destroy America's original Republic of Sovereign States. The unconstitutional methods used to enact the Republican Party's Reconstruction legislation could not have occurred without the aid of slanderous anti-South propaganda. The various Republican-sponsored Reconstruction Acts were necessary for the Republican Party to maintain its grip on the post-War American government. The bloody shirt is a far more appropriate logo for the Republican Party than the elephant!

Senator Andrew Johnson (D-Tennessee), no friend of the South's plantation aristocracy and Lincoln's future Vice President, warned the North about their unprincipled attacks upon the

---

193   Pollard, E.A., *Southern History of the War*, Vol. I (1866, Secaucus, NJ: Crown Publishers: 1977), 76-7.

194   Kennedy & Kennedy, *Punished with Poverty* 2nd ed. (Shotwell Publishing Co., Columbia, SC: 2020), 63, 77-96.

South. Speaking in the Senate shortly after the New England-sponsored radical abolitionist John Brown's October 16, 1859, raid on Harper's Ferry, Virginia, Senator Johnson proclaimed, "The time has arrived when these things ought to be stopped; when encroachments on the institutions of the South ought to cease;...when the Southern States and their institutions should be let alone; ...when you must either preserve the Constitution or you must destroy the Union."[195] Unfortunately, the New England Radical Abolitionists already declared the Constitution a "Covenant with death and an agreement with Hell."[196] The choice for Republicans was simple—to gain and maintain political power, the original Constitution was ignored and eventually replaced with one that provided for a supreme Federal Government controlled by Northern political, financial, and social elites. Northern support for Radical Abolitionists such as John Brown, support that was manufactured by generations of slanderous anti-South propaganda, was pushing the South toward secession. This was recognized by pro-Union men such as Andrew Johnson, who would eventually become President upon Lincoln's death.[197]

During the War, Lincoln established his "Ten Percent Reconstruction Plan" for returning the Southern States to his new Union. His plan did not require an iron-clad oath—an oath affirming that the individual never supported the Confederacy. Under Lincoln's Plan, once ten percent of voters eligible to vote in the 1860 election were registered, after swearing current and *future* allegiance to the new Union, an election of the new state government would

---

[195] Bowers, Claude, *The Tragic Era* (New York: Halcyon House, 1929), 32-3. Author quotes from the *Congressional Globe*, 12 December 1859.

[196] "A Covenant with Death and an Agreement with Hell," Massachusetts Historical Society (masshist.org), July 2005. (Accessed 04 May 2023) www.bit.ly/MHS-hell

[197] Andrew Johnson is a study of political pragmatism and how it can destroy an otherwise sympathetic man. He hated rich plantation owners even though he owned slaves until 1863. He turned his back on his fellow Southerners and embraced the Northern political majority who eventually turned on him when he, as President, attempted to uphold the old Constitution that the Republicans had already destroyed. He holds the honor of being the last President who tried to uphold the spirit of the original Constitution, even though he never realized the role he played in its destruction.

be held. Even during the War, the Radical Republicans opposed Lincoln's Ten Percent Reconstruction Plan.

Under the Radical Republican's Reconstruction Plan, a Southern state could re-enter the Union only if the state government was elected by "loyal" men who took the iron-clad oath affirming loyalty, *past* and future. This would disfranchise every Confederate in the South. The iron-clad oath below was intentionally used to humiliate and disfranchise white Southerners.

> I have never voluntarily borne arms against the United States... I have voluntarily given no aid, countenance, counsel or encouragement to persons engaged in armed hostility thereto; I have not yielded a voluntary support to any pretended government, authority, power, or constitution within the United States, hostile or inimical thereto.[198]

The Lincoln Oath of December 8, 1863, unlike the iron-clad oath, looked to the future. Its most essential word was "henceforth." The Radical Republican Davis-Wade oath looked backward to the past. Only those who could and would swear to these things were allowed to take part in the restored government of a Southern state. Disfranchising white Southerners, while enfranchising mostly illiterate black Southerners, was the Republican Party's plan for controlling both the South and Washington.[199] It cannot be overemphasized that, for the Republican Party, controlling the South was synonymous with controlling Washington's perks, privileges, and power.

President Lincoln pocket-vetoed the Davis-Wade Bill and, on July 8, 1864, promptly issued a proclamation telling why he did not intend to force the undoing of the start already made in Arkansas and Louisiana under his Ten Percent Reconstruction

---

198 Henry, Robert Selph, *The Story of Reconstruction* (Konecky & Konecky, New York: 1938), 10.

199 *Ibid.*

Plan.[200] Lincoln's pocket-veto outraged Radical Republicans in Congress, who immediately responded. Representatives Wade and Davis published their Manifesto denouncing Lincoln's pocket veto. It was published in the New York *Tribune* on August 5, 1864. They charged that President Lincoln was bent on holding the "electoral votes of the rebel States at the dictation of his personal ambitions,"[201] which was most likely true.

After Lincoln's assassination, the Radical wing of the Republican Party took complete control of the Republican Party. This, and not Lincoln's election, was the beginning of the Republican Party as a national political force. The Republican Party needed an excuse to discard Lincoln's Ten Percent Reconstruction Plan and to substitute their anti-South, hate-inspired, and unconstitutional Reconstruction policy. The "reason" used to justify overturning Lincoln's plan was the claim that there were ongoing rebel outrages and rebellion against the Federal Government's authority down South. According to the Radicals, this "rebellion" or violent "outrages" necessitated the continuing use of the Yankee military to keep the unrepentant "rebels" in check. But men such as journalist Henry Watterson were publishing accounts of his tour of the South in which, instead of finding a spirit of rebellion or outrages against "loyal" citizens, he found "unmistakable evidence of a determination to renew in good faith their former relations" with the Federal Government.[202] The Republican Party needed a continuous stream of real or imaginary Southern outrages reported by a sympathetic Republican Yankee press to justify Congressional Republican Reconstruction. As Americans have seen in the modern era, a press in league with the political *status quo* can convince American citizens to violate any constitutional principle in the name of emergency, crisis, or necessity.

The bloody shirt was an effective propaganda technique used by the Republican Party and their sycophants to play upon unreasoned

---

200 *Ibid.*, 11.

201 *Ibid.*

202 Bowers, Claude, *The Tragic Era* (New York: Halcyon House, 1929), 55. Author cites *Doc. Hist.*, I, 51.

emotions to convince the Northern population that Southern whites were devoting themselves to killing inoffensive blacks. It was a form of confirmation bias in which the Northern people saw the confirmation of their biased anti-South attitudes—prejudices formed by generations of slanderous anti-South propaganda. Generations of Northerners eagerly consumed such outrageous anti-South propaganda. The more outlandish the slanderous anti-South stories became, the more likely Northerners were to believe these new stories of rebel outrages. Unsubstantiated emotional stories of Southern outrages always (even today) trump facts in the Yankee Empire's mass democracy. Bowers, in his 1929 book *The Tragic Era*, wrote:

> As part of the propaganda, petitions were sent... complaining of an alleged persecution and indictment of Union men for acts committed in the Union cause, and these were featured in the Northern press; the fact that an investigation disclosed but two indictments out of the fifty-six mentioned, and one of these for illegally selling liquor, was not permitted to reach the Northern people.[203]

Such slanderous anti-South propaganda became so common, widespread, and accepted by the Northern people that even Union General Wager Swayne (R-Ohio), who served as the military governor of Alabama from March 2, 1867, to July 14, 1868, was moved to denounce such stories. He wrote, "A man may travel in North Carolina with as much security as in any State of the Union. Cases of disturbance save in the chief towns are almost unheard of, and in the chief towns they are much less frequent than in your cities."[204]

Union Brigadier General John Tarbell testified that "These reports of outrages upon the colored people, of ill-treatment of the

---

203   *Ibid.*, 141. Author cites *The Correspondence of Jonathan Worth*, vol. I, 498.

204   *Ibid.*, 141. Again, author cites *The Correspondence of Jonathan Worth*, vol. I, 498.

Northern settlers, are quite exceptional cases and exaggerated, if not altogether false." He declared that he felt that:

> All these statements in the newspapers did the educated people of the South very great injustice.... I would as soon travel alone, unarmed, through the South as through the North. The South I left is not at all the South I hear and read about in the North. [205]

This was true then and continues to be true today. It will not change until the people of the South stand up and boldly defend the Cause of truth, honor, and America's original and legitimate Constitution.

This is why America's Founding Fathers sought to avoid creating a mass democracy. The danger of emotions used by unprincipled individuals in a mass democracy was pointed out during the Constitutional Convention in 1787. Mr. Elbridge Gerry of Massachusetts expressed this fear during the Constitutional Convention:

> The evils we experience flow from the excess of democracy. The people do not want virtue but are the dupes of pretended patriots. In Massachusetts it has been fully confirmed by experience that they are daily misled into the most baneful measures and opinions by the false reports circulated by designing men, and *which no one on the spot can refute.*[206] [Emphasis added by author.]

George Mason spoke of "the dangers of the majority oppressing the minority, and the mischievous influence of demagogues," and Patrick Henry warned that, under the influence of mass democracy,

---

205 General Tarbell cited in Henry, Robert Selph, *The Story of Reconstruction*, 120.

206 Mr. Elbridge Gerry, in Madison, James, *The Debates in the Federal Convention of 1787 Which Framed the Constitution of the United States of America*, eds. Hunt & Scott (Union, NJ: The Law Book Exchange, 1999), 32.

countries "have been enslaved by the hands of their own people."[207] Thomas Jefferson noted his fear of "mobocracy" when he declared that "the mobs of great cities add just so much to the support of free government, as sores do to the strength of the human body."[208] America's current mass democracy, where emotions rule, is the opposite of what America's Founding Fathers created—it is a form of government they specifically tried to prevent. America's current mass democracy is a direct result of Lincoln's war and the Republican Party's Active Reconstruction.

THE NORTH'S FASCINATION WITH THE BLOODY SHIRT

Why did these highly emotional, horrific, and mostly untrue stories about the South gain front-page headlines in Northern media? Such anti-South slander made (and still makes) good copy for those looking for evidence of unrepentant Southern animosity toward the Northern victor and the victor's ideology that underpins the Yankee Empire's unconstitutional, supreme Federal Government. Stories of post-War rebel outrages are examples of propagandists using confirmation bias. The Northern people tended to accept as truth the stories of rebel outrages because these new stories tended to confirm or strengthen their beliefs previously established by generations of biased reports about Southerners. Confirmation bias makes it very easy for a skillful propagandist to direct the thinking and actions of the target audience.[209]

The slanderous anti-South Yankee press was essential in keeping the anger and hatred toward the South burning fiercely in the hearts and minds of Northern voters. They did this by constantly waving the bloody shirt. Stories of Southern "outrages," some real but most pure hate-filled fantasy, were fed continuously to the Northern public, fueling their burning desire for vengeance. The

---

207 Patrick Henry cited in John Remington Graham's *Principles of Confederacy* (SLC, UT: Northwest Publishing, 1990), 35-6.

208 Thomas Jefferson cited in Trevor Colbourn's *The Lamp of Experience* (1965, Indianapolis, IN: Liberty Fund, 1998), 212.

209 "Propaganda tries to surround man by all possible routes, in the realm of feelings as well as ideas." Man needs to have a reason to sanction his ideas and actions. See Ellul, Jacques, *Propaganda: The Formation of Men's Attitudes* (New York: Alfred A. Knopf, 1965), 11.

New York Tribune described Southern outrages ongoing in rebel-controlled Arkansas, "the atrocious murder of thousands of good men, white and black with hundreds of unoffending blacks tied to trees, whipped unmercifully, and murdered. A reign of terror!"[210] Yet, when Colonel John Quincy Adams II of Massachusetts, son of Charles Francis Adams Sr., toured the South, he gave a different view while speaking in Charleston, South Carolina. He blamed the trouble between the races on the work of carpetbaggers.[211] As in all cases of the North against the South, emotions overruled facts and logic. Adams's speech was published in the North but had little to no impact on Northern blood lust. Again, it must be stressed that emotions always trump facts and logic in the mass democracy that America (the Yankee Empire) has become.

The slanderous anti-South Yankee propaganda published across the North concerning mostly fabricated Southern "outrages" against loyal blacks and whites had its desired impact. Waving the bloody shirt produced a Northern upsurge in the desire for revenge against the conquered South. The infamous New England abolitionist Wendell Phillips spoke at Steinway Hall in New York, demanding that the North "march thirty million men to the Gulf, irrespective of men, women, and children, and hang a few Generals."[212] He left the audience to decide what to do with the thirty million Southern men, women, and children once they were herded to the Gulf. This is the same Wendell Phillips who, before the War, insisted that "there could be no South until the North created one." Republican Active Reconstruction was the culmination of the North's eternal desire to destroy the old South and "create" a new South—a New South populated by pacified people who would henceforth be subservient to Northern ruling elites. Phillips is the same man who often looked hopefully for the day in which there would be an armed slave revolt in the South: "I can imagine the scenes of blood through which a rebellious

---

210   Bowers, Claude, *The Tragic Era*, 232. Author cites *New York Tribune*, 21 October 1868, "Letter from Little Rock."

211   *Ibid.*, 233, Author cites *New York Herald*, 19 October 1868.

212   *Ibid.*, 334. Author cites *New York Tribune*, 15 May 1871.

slave-population must march to their rights." Acknowledging the ghastly scene such a slave revolt would produce, he none-the-less endorsed it, declaring such a sight would seem "white as an angel's wing (when compared to) "the blackness of that darkness which has brooded over the Carolinas for two hundred years."[213]

By the 1830s, the fear of a Northern-instigated slave revolt destroyed the vibrant Southern abolitionist movement. This was the same Southern abolitionist movement that in 1808 voted to end the African slave trade, voted to deny the introduction of slavery into the Northwest Territory, and in Mississippi in 1820 and Virginia in 1830 condemned slavery and planned for its eventual abolition. The continuing threat of a Northern-instigated slave revolt was one of the primary reasons for the Lower South's secession in 1861.[214] The fear of a slave revolt was not exclusively a Southern fear. During the colonial era and up to the time of Independence, all American colonies were slave-holding colonies. The Northern colonies also feared the possibility of whites being massacred during a slave revolt. New York City experienced an attempted slave revolt in 1741. As explained by a Southern historian of the modern era:

> In 1741...investigations...uncovered the "Conspiracy of 1741," also known as the Negro Plot of 1741 or the Slave Insurrection of 1741.... More than two hundred people, including twenty poor whites, were jailed while more than a hundred were hanged, exiled, or burned at the stake. The two black leaders were gibbetted (i.e., hung in chains in a public display and left to die of exposure, thirst, and starvation).... At least thirty-eight slaves faced execution along

---

213 Floan, Howard R., *The South in Northern Eyes 1831 to 1861*, 13.

214 Kennedy & Kennedy, *Punished With Poverty* 2nd ed. (Columbia, SC: Shotwell Publishing, 2020), 48-54.

with several whites. Fourteen blacks were burned at the stake.[215]

Such stories are hidden from the public because they demonstrate the North's rank hypocrisy when it tries to present Yankees as paragons of racial love. It also supports the logic of the Deep South's secession from a people *actively encouraging slave revolts* in Southern States where slaves represented upwards of half the population.

During the War the Yankee Empire hoped for a general slave uprising that would bring the War to a quick end. A letter from Federal agent, Alexander S. Montgomery, was found in a mail pouch on a Federal steamer traveling between New Bern and Norfolk. The steamer was captured by the Confederates. The letter marked "Confidential" and dated "Washington, D.C., May 19, 1863, disclosed a Yankee plan for a general slave insurrection. Part of the letter admitted, "The main object of this letter is to state the time for the rising that it may be simultaneous over the whole South." The letter noted that it was "…sent to some generals in each Military Department in the seceded States, in order that they may act in concert and thus secure success."[216] The desire to see a massacre of innocent Southern men, women, and children via a slave uprising was first suggested by New England abolitionists and again during the War by the United States government and its military. The lower South was right to leave such a people and such a government.

Anti-South Propaganda Was Used To Support Military Rule In The South

The work of the anti-South, Yankee propagandists in the Northern media can be seen in their 1875 news report alleging that twenty-five hundred people were murdered in Louisiana since

---

215 Mitcham Jr., Dr. Samuel W., *It Wasn't About Slavery: Exposing the Great Lie of the Civil War* (Washington, DC: Regnery Publishing, 2020), 11.

216 *Confederate Veteran* Vol. XL, No. 12, Dec. 1932. Republished in *The Confederate Veteran Magazine* Vol. XL (Harrisburg, PA: The National Historical Society, 1987), 422. Citation of *Official Records*—Series 1, Vol. LI, Part II, Supplemental, 736.

1868. The purpose of this "report" was to justify the continued presence of the Yankee Empire's military in the state. The Yankee Empire's military was occupying the state to intimidate conservatives (primarily whites) and thereby maintain Republican carpetbag dictatorial rule. Businessmen from all parts of the United States met at the St. Charles Hotel in New Orleans and issued resolutions denouncing the "report" as unwarranted and untrue. An inquiry into the twenty-five hundred alleged murders determined that most of the murders occurred before 1868 and, of those, most were black-on-black crimes—imagine that! Who would have thought a radical upsurge in black-on-black crimes would occur once normal crime prevention is abolished?[217] Of the twenty-five hundred murders that made Northern headlines, whites killed only three blacks.[218] Some Northern papers were beginning to question the never-ending reports of "rebel outrages" down South. These "reports" seemed to magically appear during heated Southern elections in which the Republican carpetbag regimes feared losing the election. The *Nation*, in its January 21, 1875, edition, demanded proof of these constant allegations of outrages and commented that they were "somewhat incredulous about these appalling murders just before election."

The resistance in Mississippi was one of celebrations and restrained enthusiasm. It was something not seen since the early days of the Mississippi territory. Great masses of whites moved from place to place, attending rallies and barbeques and hearing speakers encouraging young and old alike to join the resistance movement and help redeem Mississippi. Some called it an uprising, while others countered that it was more; it was a peaceful insurrection—an effective resistance movement fighting for the right of self-government, law and order, and the removal of confiscatory taxation. Grand processions in towns with cannons fired from hilltops were commonplace. Speeches were made to

---

217 In the late 1950s, an elderly white gentleman shocked the Kennedy Twins when he told us that "If the white man does not control the blacks, they will not only kill us, but they will kill each other as well." The old white gentleman's father lived through Active Reconstruction.

218 Nordhoff, Charles, *The Cotton States in the Spring and Summer of 1875* (New York, 1875), 54.

motivate the people, but tones of demagoguery were absent in these speeches. These meetings, parades, and barbeques put fear in the carpetbag regime. The carpetbag/scallywag regime's only hope of maintaining their illegal grip on power was if violence broke out. Their Northern propaganda agents would then fill Northern papers with images of rebel outrages against innocent, loyal whites and blacks. But the leaders of Mississippi's resistance movement knew this and cautioned their followers to exercise restraint and beware of agent provocateurs paid by Republicans to foment violence.[219] A similar system of paid government "agent provocateurs" was believed to have been active during the so-called January 6, 2021 "insurrection." Modern Era Reconstruction is a replay of post-War Active Reconstruction.

    The Republican Party and its propagandists described the occupied South as full of rebels working against the Republican Party's newly created supreme Federal Government. They claimed the South was filled with ignorant, poor white trash. They claimed that white Southerners were full of racial hatred and committed outrages almost daily against the newly freed blacks. Republican anti-South propaganda described white Southerners as unrepentant murderers seeking every opportunity to commit the most violent outrages against blacks and "loyal" white citizens. According to Republican logic, the conquered South was a place that required the Federal military to control rebel savages no less than the need to control Native American "savages" out west. But when one considers the vast area of the former Confederate States, its relatively large population, the social disorder, and unsettled political conditions of the time, the number of "outrages" appear to be more occasional and sporadic than a general "uprising." And none of the Southern "riots" came close to the killings, lynchings, and destruction of property as did the anti-black draft riots in New York in 1863[220] or San Francisco during the anti-Chinese riots of 1877 In 1919, forty-two years after the end of Active Reconstruction, race riots broke out in the North, in Washington,

---

219   Smedes, Susan Dabney, *Memoirs of a Southern Planter* (Baltimore, 1888), 262.

220   Mitcham Jr., Dr. Samuel W., *It Wasn't About Slavery*, 164-66.

D.C. and Chicago, Illinois. These cities, unlike the devastated post-War Reconstruction South, were otherwise peaceful, with all public police, safety, and other services fully operational.[221] Yet, there was no cry from the political establishment for Federal troops to establish a military dictatorship in Northern States or cities. Yankee hypocrisy is all that Southerners can expect from a nation that falsely claims to offer "liberty and justice for all."

As described in Chapter 1, slanderous, anti-South propaganda derailed the South's effort to follow the high road to emancipation and left both black and white Southerners as economic and political vassals to an all-powerful Yankee Empire. It destroyed and prevented the development of a fair, just, and equitable Southern society. What *could have been,* but it was denied by a self-righteous and arrogant Northern majority.

The South, from the beginning of the Federal Government created by the original Constitution circa 1787, relied upon the paper barricade of the Constitution to protect its reserved rights. These reserved, unenumerated rights included the rights of nullification and secession—as per the Ninth and Tenth Amendments. While opponents of the South relied upon emotional, anti-South slander to advance its lust for political power and commercial profits, the South relied upon the Constitution. Unfortunately, this reliance set the stage for Lincoln's war and the Republican Party's Active Reconstruction. War was a necessary first stage because an unconstitutional, supreme Federal Government could not be created without violence. As admitted by leftist Herbert Croly, founding editor of the *New* Republic, the United States used violence "to cement their Union by waging a civil war."[222] In the next chapter, we will review the Constitutional origins of Reconstruction.

---

221 The 1919 Chicago race riots took the lives of 23 blacks and 15 whites, injured 537 individuals, and over 1,000 black families were made homeless as a result of the riots. See "Red Summer: The Race Riots of 1919" The National WWI Museum and Memorial (theworldwar.org), n.d., www.bit.ly/xRedSummer (Accessed 05 April 2023).

222 Croly cited in Jonah Goldberg's *Liberal Fascism* (New York: Double Day, 2007), 103.

Chapter 6:

THE CONSTITUTIONAL ORIGINS OF RECONSTRUCTION

"When this new Constitution should be adopted, the sun of the Southern States would set, never to rise again." —Rawlins Lowndes [223]

RECONSTRUCTION WAS NOT something that occurred spontaneously after the close of the War. It had its origins in the very founding of the Federal Government under the Constitution circa 1787-8. Modern-era Southern historian, Dr. Clyde N. Wilson, noted that, from the very beginning of these United States, New England Yankees "regarded the new Federal Government... as an instrument to be used for their own purposes."[224] While the new Constitution was being created, it became evident that certain individuals wanted to disband the concept of sovereign States and create an all-powerful, supreme, central government. These individuals were known as High Federalists. Their ideas were so repugnant to the Constitutional Convention delegates that it almost caused a break-up of the Convention. The contest between those wanting a strong central government and those wanting to pre-

---

223 Lowndes, Rawlins of South Carolina writing in 1787. Cited in Bradford, M.E., *Original Intentions: On the Making and Ratification of the United States Constitution* (Athens, GA: The University of Georgia Press, 1993), 66.

224 Clyde N. Wilson cited in Thomas J. DiLorenzo's, *Hamilton's Curse* (New York: Crown Forum, 2008), 12-3.

Reconstruction

These six men were John Brown's major financiers. They are indicative of the Northern radicals whose threat of a slave uprising pushed the lower South toward secession. The butchery of innocent white men, women, and children that would occur in a slave uprising made secession not a question of Constitutional principle but a question of survival.

serve the sovereignty and independence of the States was the first hint of a future war. The South was warned but chose to ignore the warnings—the South's strategic failure number one.

High Federalist is the term used to describe those post-colonial political leaders who wanted a supreme Federal Government. They wanted an energetic Federal Government[225] in which the States would **not** be sovereign and could be forced to yield ultimate political decision-making (sovereignty) to the Federal Government. Of the two key High Federalists at the Constitutional Convention, Alexander Hamilton was by far the most ardent advocate of a supreme Federal Government. Hamilton considered the States merely "imaginary" things—political bodies having no organic reality and no essential connection to the concepts of individual liberty and sovereignty. Hamilton was different from most of the other delegates in that he was a relatively recent immigrant to America. He had not come of age and matured in a particular state. He had no "roots" in the vibrant political society of a native state. He had no kinship or cultural connection to a local community of fellow citizens. In his view, the States in America were no different than provinces in a European nation. In Hamilton's view, the so-called States were mere subservient political subdivisions answerable to the central government. Early in the Convention, Hamilton proposed a new, more powerful—sometimes referred to as an "energetic"—government. Specifically, he advocated a Federal chief executive who would hold office for life and who would hold an absolute veto (similar to the power of a king); a senate composed of individuals holding office for life (similar to the House of Lords); a Federal Supreme Court that would have complete jurisdiction over all cases—including state cases; and governors of the various States who would be appointed by the Federal Government. No wonder Thomas Jefferson—Hamilton's arch nemesis—referred to Hamilton as a "monarchist, bottomed on corruption."[226]

---

225   DiLorenzo, Thomas J., *Hamilton's Curse*, 12.

226   Thomas Jefferson cited by C.C. Burr of Maine in Able P. Upshur's *The Federal Government: Its True Nature and Character* (1868, Houston, TX: St. Thomas Press, 1977), v, 21 footnote.

Hamilton's dream of a supreme Federal Government was too radical for even his fellow High Federalists. His dream eventually became the South's nightmare under Lincoln and the Republican Party. Much to the surprise of many modern-era conservatives, the second-ranking High Federalist at the Constitutional Convention was none other than Virginian James Madison! Madison came to the Convention with his own vision of an "energetic" Federal Government. He came with great personal expectations and ambitions but left a humbler and more conservative advocate of a limited Federal Government. In the *Federalist Papers*, he argued for a limited Federal Government, the only kind the people of the States would ratify. Unlike Hamilton, Madison was able to learn from the elder statesmen at the Convention. The main lesson he learned was that, as William Samuel Johnson of Connecticut declared, "the States do exist as political societies... [and] must be armed with some power of self-defense."[227] James Madison presented "his" plan for an energetic Federal Government at the beginning of the Convention before the arrival of all the delegates. He called his plan the Virginia Plan. His strategy was to be the first to offer specific details of a new Federal Government and, thereby, set the agenda and ensure that he and other High Federalists could control and direct the debate and eventual outcome of the Convention. The most essential points of Madison's plan for a new Federal Government were:

> 1. State representation in the Federal Congress would be determined by population.
>
> 2. The Federal Congress would have veto power over laws enacted by the States.
>
> 3. The Federal Congress would have the power "to legislate in all cases to which the separate States are incompetent or in which the harmony of the United States may be interrupted by the exercise of individual legislation."

---

[227] Bradford, Dr. M.E., *Original Intentions*, 9.

While Madison's Virginia Plan had fewer attributes of British monarchy than Hamilton's vision of a new energetic Federal Government, both were typical of the dreams of High Federalists. High Federalists envisioned a supreme national government in which sovereign authority ultimately resided with the Federal Government. In their system of government, the States composing the "more perfect union" would be no different than local provincial governments in Europe. European provinces were nothing more than mere administrative agents of the central government. Instead of the sovereign States creating via the Constitution a Federal Government to be the agent of the States, the High Federalists sought to dissolve the States and create a Federal Government that would be served by its administrative agents—the once sovereign States!

DID THE SOVEREIGN STATES COMMIT SUICIDE WHEN THEY RATIFIED THE CONSTITUTION?

The Founders' reactions to the suggestion of Federal supremacy demonstrate the true nature and original intentions of the Federal Government created under the Constitution. When all delegates were seated at the Constitutional Convention, Madison's Virginia Plan was quickly recognized as a recipe for centralized mass democracy—which most Founding Fathers viewed with great skepticism. Madison's plan was so unacceptable to most delegates that its very offering almost caused the Convention to close before it began its work. Caleb Strong of Massachusetts described the Convention as "nearly at an end." Roger Sherman of Connecticut complained that "we are at full stop." Hugh Williamson of North Carolina thought that "our business must soon be concluded." The day was saved when Benjamin Franklin suggested public prayer. Elder statesmen such as Oliver Ellsworth from Connecticut came forward to guide the workings of the Convention. Ellsworth viewed the business at hand as not one of "razing the foundations of the building when they need only repair the roof." John Dickinson of

Delaware lectured James Madison and declared to Madison, "You see the consequence of pushing things too far?"[228]

On July 16, with all the delegates to the Constitutional Convention seated, Madison's plan was rejected! The following day, the Convention voted seven States to three to remove the responsibility of drafting the final version of the new Constitution from Madison and turned the task over to the conservative John Rutledge of South Carolina. Madison came to the Convention expecting to be the great lawgiver of a strong, centralized Federal Government but quickly became a humbled student of organic American political philosophy. The politically immature Madison came to the Convention with unrealistic dreams of a strong central government served by weak States or, more accurately, provinces. He was unprepared for the energized reaction from the delegates of the sovereign States. Gouverneur Morris of Pennsylvania described the High Federalists' vision as being "terrible to the States;" John Lansing of New York described the plan for a supreme Federal Government as "more injurious" than the British government's rule over the colonies. Men such as George Mason of Virginia, Luther Martin of Maryland, and John Dickinson of Delaware, warned the Convention of the danger in any system of Federalism that did not allow enough capacity for the States. Pierce Butler of Pennsylvania declared his concern that the delegates may be "running into an extreme in taking away the powers of the States."

Madison came to the convention as a supporter of the Hamiltonian vision of an energetic supreme Federal Government. He left the Convention as a humbled, moderate Federalist with a new understanding of the importance of the sovereign States in this proposed "more perfect union." Eventually, he became one of Thomas Jefferson's strongest allies in the continuing fight for real State' Rights.

The primary task for the delegates to the Constitutional Convention was to create a Federal Government the people within their sovereign state would accept. The main work of the

---

228   *Ibid.*, 7.

Constitutional Convention, as Madison and Hamilton learned, was to create a "more perfect union," one that the people of at least nine of the thirteen "free, sovereign, and independent"[229] States would ratify. To understand what kind of government the people of the States would accept, we need to place more emphasis **not** on the arguments surrounding the Constitutional Convention, but we need to study the debates and discussions surrounding the ratification of the proposed Constitution within each distinct and sovereign state. *The Federalist Papers* were addressed in general to the American public but specifically to the delegates of each state's constitutional convention, debating the adoption or rejection of the proposed Constitution.

In *The Federalist Papers*, Alexander Hamilton, James Madison, and John Jay advocated the moderate Federalist position. The moderate Federalist position was that the Constitution proposed a limited Federal Government with the vast residuary of rights reserved to the sovereign States. Even Hamilton, the High Federalist, argued that the sovereign States would be completely safe in the proposed "more perfect union." In *Federalist Paper* number 28, he assured the Anti-Federalists who were opposed to the ratification of the Constitution that "[I]t may safely be received as an axiom in our political system, that the State governments will, in all possible contingencies, afford complete security against invasions of the public liberty by the national authority." Then again, in *Federalist Paper* number 85, he attempted to calm anti-Federalist fears when he declared, "We may safely rely on the disposition of the State Legislatures to erect barriers against the encroachment of national authority." Here are examples of how even a High Federalist such as Alexander Hamilton was forced to admit to his fellow countrymen that the Federal Government proposed under the Constitution would not be a supreme government but that the Constitution contemplated that the States would act as a barrier, a check, or counterbalance against unconstitutional acts of the newly created Federal Government. He was describing the act of state nullification or the principle of state interposi-

---

[229] As declared in Article Two of the Articles of Confederation.

tion to protect the rights of the people against an abusive Federal Government. The act of a sovereign state interposing its sovereign authority between the state and the Federal Government was used by "fourteen respected and honored Northern States" when they nullified the fugitive slave clause of the US Constitution by passing personal liberty laws.[230] States' Rights was a well-established American political doctrine before Lincoln's war and the Republican Party's Active Reconstruction.

James Madison provides conclusive proof regarding the status of the sovereign States vis-à-vis the newly proposed Federal Government under the Constitution. In *Federalist Paper* number 40, Madison asked the following rhetorical question of the Anti-Federalists who were skeptical regarding the new powers proposed for the Federal Government and the impact on the powers of the sovereign States: "Do they require that, in the establishment of the Constitution, the States should be regarded as distinct and independent sovereigns?" In the very next sentence, he answered his own question: "They are so regarded by the Constitution proposed." Madison recognized that the proposed "more perfect union" was not a new and all-powerful Federal Government but merely an adjustment to the limited powers already held by the Federal Government under the Articles of Confederation. The two governments (the Federal Government under the Articles of Confederation and the Federal Government under the proposed Constitution) differed in degrees. Still, they were not different in principle of limited Federalism and state sovereignty. In the same paper, Madison explained this fact by noting, "The truth is, that the great principle of the Constitution proposed by the convention may be considered less as absolutely new, than as the expansion of principles which are found in the Articles of Confederation." From these examples, we see that High Federalist Hamilton and moderate Federalist Madison agreed that the States under the proposed constitution maintained their sovereign, free, and

---

[230] The first fugitive slave law was passed by the United Colonies of New England circa 1643. The colony of Massachusetts was the major leader of this New England government or league. See Kilpatrick, James Jackson, *The Sovereign States: Notes of a Citizen of Virginia* (Chicago, IL: Henry Regnery Co., 1957), 204.

independent authority that was acknowledged in the Treaty of Paris of 1783 and proclaimed in Article II of the Articles of Confederation. This is overwhelming evidence that the sovereign States did not commit suicide when they individually seceded from the "perpetual" Union under the Articles of Confederation and individually acceded to the new Union created by the ratification of the proposed Constitution in 1787-8.[231]

ANTI-FEDERALISTS' WARNING—
DON'T TRUST BIG GOVERNMENT

The chief political advantage the Anti-Federalists held over their Federalist opponents was that the Anti-Federalists could see beyond the immediate commercial and national defense benefit offered by the new "more perfect union" and see the latent genesis of tyranny contained in the proposed constitution. This latent tendency of tyranny would eventually give birth to Lincoln's aggressive war, the Republican Party's Active Reconstruction, and the destruction of the original Constitution.

The concerns expressed by the Anti-Federalists centered not so much on the document but that the proposed constitution would, after all, be administered by men whose personal interests would naturally and eventually overwhelm their dedication to the spirit of limited Federalism. This assumes that Federalists had such dedication to limited Federalism in the first place! The Anti-Federalists understood that the Constitution was a mere paper barricade that could be easily overwhelmed when men who had special interests in gaining and using Federal power set about to improve themselves at the expense of the unorganized masses.

Patrick Henry was a leading anti-Federalist who quickly diagnosed the fatal flaw in the proposed "more perfect union." He realized that the new taxing authority proposed for Congress would become an open invitation for the powerful to exploit those with less power. He saw very quickly that the commercial interests of

---

[231] The Union under the Articles of Confederation was termed a "perpetual" union six times in the Articles of Confederation. The word "perpetual," so evident in the Articles, is conspicuous by its absence in the Constitution.

the Northern States, so often championed by High Federalists such as Alexander Hamilton would hold a voting advantage in Congress over the agricultural interests of the Southern States. He succinctly warned, "I am sure that the dangers of this system are real when those who have no similar interests with the people of this country [Virginia] are to legislate for us—when our dearest interests are to be left in the hands of those whose advantage it will be to infringe them."[232] Patrick Henry read the tea leaves of America's political destiny correctly. While the moderate Federalists looked to gain more national security and commercial prowess—risking liberty in the process—he was looking to America's legacy of liberty: "The first thing I have at heart is American liberty, the second thing is American Union."[233] Patrick Henry understood that liberty always trumps government, regardless of whether it is the government of a king, a parliament, or of the Union. Liberty always trumps government! "Liberty" is defined by the American principle that any people have the right to establish a government based upon the free and voluntary "consent of the governed" and to remove themselves from any government that violates that principle.[234]

Anti-Federalists understood that man tended toward evil,[235] and therefore, they felt that men should not be tempted by unchecked governmental power. Men such as Virginian John Taylor of Caroline were so distrustful of government that they had little faith in even a written constitution or any system to

---

232 Patrick Henry cited in Kennedy & Kennedy's *Punished With Poverty-The Suffering South* 2nd ed. (Columbia, SC: Shotwell Publishing, 2020), 34. Authors cite Henry, William Wirt, *Patrick Henry: Life, Correspondence and Speeches*, Vol. III (1891, Sprinkle Publications, Harrisonburg, VA: 1993), 520.

233 Patrick Henry cited in Kennedy & Kennedy, *Yankee Empire:*, 201. The authors again cite William Wirt, *Patrick Henry: Life, Correspondence and Speeches*, Vol. III, 449.

234 "[I]t is the Right of the People to alter or to abolish it [government], and to institute new Government" as per the Declaration of Independence. The Declaration made in 1776 by thirteen slave-holding American colonies.

235 This principle is part of Western Christian theology—man is a fallen creature. In the modern era, it was described by Russian dissident Aleksandr Solzhenitsyn in his internationally renowned book, *The Gulag Archipelago 1918-1956*, "The line separating good and evil passes not through States, nor between classes, nor between political parties either—but right through every human heart—and through all human hearts."

check the abuse of power of government because, as he stated, "Great power should never be granted in the first place." Thomas Jefferson and James Madison both noted that men were not "angels" and could not be trusted with the administration of an unlimited government.[236] In a letter to Spencer Roane, Jefferson, at age seventy-five, expressed a similar attitude toward the danger of government: "[It is] an axiom of eternal truth in politics, that whatever power in any government is independent [unchecked], it is absolute also: in theory only, at first, while the spirit of the people is up, but in practice, as fast as that relaxes." The great fear of Anti-Federalists and many moderate Federalists was that the Federal Government would become an "unchecked" centralized power.[237] Jefferson and the Anti-Federalists warned that the paper barricade of the Constitution would not withstand the onslaught of special interests. In the 1840s, Senator John C. Calhoun of South Carolina also warned Americans about the danger of special interests using the Federal Government for personal gain:

> Another of its effects [Federal supremacy] has been to engender the most corrupting, loathsome and dangerous disease, that can infect a popular government—I mean that known by the name of *"the Spoils."* It is a disease easily contracted under all forms of government—hard to prevent, and most difficult to cure, when contracted; but of all the forms of governments, it is, by far, the most fatal in those of a popular character.[238]

The Anti-Federalists warned that there was a great danger that the rights reserved to "We the People" of the sovereign States

---

236 Jefferson and Madison cited in Quirk & Bridwell, *Judicial Dictatorship* (New York: Transaction Publishers, 1995), 63, 76.

237 The Anti-Federalist's fear of the accumulation of big government power was expressed by John Taylor as follows: "Enormous political power invariably accumulates enormous wealth, and enormous wealth invariably accumulates enormous political power." See *Tyranny Unmasked* (1822: Indianapolis: Liberty Fund, 1992), 194.

238 Calhoun, John C., *On the Constitution and Government*, in *The Works of John C. Calhoun*, Vol I. (New York: Appleton & Co., New York, 1851), 347.

under the Constitution would one day be usurped by "those whose advantage it will be to infringe them." Some fifty years later, Senator Calhoun added his warning. With the passage of time and political activism, things only got worse. In the real world of modern-day American politics, it is self-evident that the Anti-Federalists were right!

AN EXPANDING FEDERAL GOVERNMENT BECOMES A DANGER TO THE SOVEREIGN STATES

The issue surrounding the Bank of the United States called into question whether there was Constitutional authority allowing the Federal Government to establish Federal Banks backed by the Federal Government and in competition with local state banks. States such as Indiana in 1816 and Illinois in 1818 sought to prevent the Federal Bank from operating within their States. The Supreme Court, under Chief Justice John Marshall, used a very liberal interpretation of the Constitutional phrase "necessary and proper" to justify Federal authority to do whatever was "necessary" to carry out the functions of the Federal Government. As one Southern author noted, Marshall's decision meant that:

> The States that had created the Constitution, and bound themselves by their mutual compact, were to have no effective voice in saying what the compact meant.[239]

The fight between the sovereign States and the Federal Government would continue even after John Marshall's Supreme Court decision declaring "banking" a necessary and proper role for the Federal Government. In 1821, the State of Ohio was engaged in a controversy with the Federal Bank. The people of Ohio were unwilling to accept the idea that the Federal Supreme Court—a department of the Federal Government—was entitled to decide how much power the Constitution grants to the Federal Government. The very idea that any government has the ultimate

---
[239] Kilpatrick, James Jackson, *The Sovereign States: Notes of a Citizen of Virginia* (Chicago, IL: Henry Regnery Co., 1957), 146.

authority to decide how much power it has is a recipe for tyranny. It means that the government, king, or dictator is the nation's ruler, not the people. Under these circumstances, the people become the government's subjects, not free, self-governing citizens. The people, whether they realize it or not, become political slaves of the governmental system that rules them.[240]

Ohio's House of Representatives issued a blistering denunciation of the Federal Bank and the Federal Supreme Court. Ohio's Senate concurred with the denunciation. The report declared:

> To acquiesce in such an encroachment upon the privileges and authority of the States, without an effort to defend them, would be an act of treachery to the State itself, and to all the States that compose the American Union.[241]

This report, plus the resolution endorsing it, expressly declared that the General Assembly of the State of Ohio approved the "Doctrine of '98," meaning the Kentucky and Virginia Resolutions of 1798. The battle between The Bank of the United States and local state banks was noted by French observer of early America, Alexis de Tocqueville:

> The bank's battle against its enemies is only one incident in the great American fight between the provinces [States] and the central power, between the spirit of independence and democracy, and the spirit of hierarchy and subordination...the attacks against the Bank of the United States are the result

---

240   Colonial Patriots denounced the King's efforts to turn Americans into political slaves. See Kennedy & Kennedy, Chapter 3, "The Founding Fathers Struggle Against Slavery," *Jefferson Davis: High Road to Emancipation and Constitutional Government* (Columbia, SC: Shotwell Publishing Co., 2022), 5-14.

241   Kilpatrick, James Jackson, *The Sovereign States: Notes of a Citizen of Virginia*, 152.

of the same instincts that militate against the federal government....²⁴²

By the mid-1800s, the South saw the sad fulfillment of Patrick Henry's and other Southern Anti-Federalists' predictions that the commercial North would use its power in Congress to exploit the agricultural South. Foreign observers and authors easily discerned this. General Sir James Marshall-Cornwall, in his book *Grant as a Military Commander*, observed that the real issue for the North's war against the South was fundamentally economic. He described the economic pressure coming from Northern commercial leaders to compel Congress to enact protective tariffs. The South resisted such efforts because it would significantly harm the free trade necessary for foreign exports of its agricultural products. Frenchman Alex de Tocqueville observed that:

> The parties that threaten the Union rely not on principles but on material interests.... Thus, recently we have seen the North contending for tariffs and the South taking up arms for free trade, simply because the North is industrial and the South agricultural, so that restrictions would profit the former and harm the latter.²⁴³

That the South would oppose Federal encumbrance on export/import trade is understandable. Anytime one nation establishes a tariff, the trading nations will retaliate with their own tariffs. The impact of Northern-sponsored protective tariffs is evident when looking at the volume of exports from the United States. In 1859, exports of cotton *alone* from the Southern States amounted to $161,434,923. The total exports of *all* products from the North in 1859 amounted to a mere $78,217,202. The North was fulfilling Patrick Henry's prediction of the North using their control of Congress to enrich themselves at the expense of the South.

---

242 Tocqueville, Alexis de, *Democracy in America* Vol. 1 (1848, Garden City, NY: Doubleday & Co.,), 389.

243 *Ibid.*, 177.

Senator William Grayson, one of Virginia's first United States Senators, expressed concern that the South would eventually become the "milch cow" (in modern parlance, "Cash Cow") of the Union. Shortly after the ratification of the Constitution, the Virginia legislature passed a resolution declaring that the North was attempting "the prostration of agriculture at the feet of commerce, and a change of the present form of federal government, fatal to the existence of American liberty." In 1828 Senator Thomas H. Benton declared:

> Before the Revolution [the South] was the seat of wealth...wealth has fled from the South and settled in regions north of the Potomac.... Under federal legislation, the exports of the South have been the basis of the Federal Revenue.... Virginia, the two Carolinas, and Georgia may be said to defray three-fourths, of the annual expense of supporting the Federal Government....This is the reason why wealth disappears from the South and rises up in the North. Federal legislation does all this.[244]

By 1860, it became evident that the South had two options: (1) It must accept its position as the "milch cow" of the Union while watching helplessly as Southern wealth was transferred to the elites of the North, or (2) It could do what the American Colonies did when faced with unfair taxation and exploitation by their central government in London—secede. But by 1860 it was too late! The North had the advantage in population (plus unlimited immigrants who would fill the depleted ranks of its Army), industrial resources, international recognition, an organized national government, and a standing Army and Navy. Added to this was the introduction in the mid-1850s of the rifled musket. This resulted in the battlefield fact that killing during a war would begin at a much greater distance.[245] That meant

---

244 Senator Benton cited in Kennedy & Kennedy's *The South Was Right!* 3rd ed., 60.

245 Drs. McWhiney & Jamieson, *Attack and Die: Civil War Military Tactics and the Southern Heritage* (Tuscaloosa, AL: University of Alabama Press, 1988), 48-9.

a prolonged war of attrition would favor the side with greater numbers, and the South was outnumbered nearly three to one.

The North, from 1788 until 1860, used the "love" of the Constitution to pacify the South while insidiously corrupting the Constitution to allow for the destruction of Southern political power. Men, such as John Marshall, Joseph Story, and Daniel Webster, warped the Constitution into an instrument of Northern political power.[246] The Federal Supreme Court played a major role under Chief Justice Marshall. Thomas Jefferson recognized this when, on January 19, 1821, he wrote to Archibald Thweatt: "The judiciary branch is the instrument which, working like gravity, without intermission, is to press us at last into one consolidated mass."[247] In *Federalist* 49, Madison sadly admitted the inability of parchment barricades to halt "... those encroachments which lead to a tyrannical concentration of all the powers of government in the same hands." In their Kentucky and Virginia Resolutions of 1798, Jefferson and Madison explained what else was needed—the Constitutional principles of real States' Rights, including the rights of nullification and secession. But the Northern powers arrayed against the South were sufficient to pervert the Constitution into an instrument of consolidation. It became an instrument ready-made for a tyrant to use against the conservative South. The sun of the South set not in 1865, but in 1787-8 when the South ignored the warnings of the Anti-Federalists. This was the South's first strategic failure.

The political leaders of the North had a love-hate attitude toward the Constitution. They loved it when it protected Yankee profits and hated it when it stood in the way of profits or Northern political power. Before the War, many Yankee politicians championed the States' Right of secession but after Lincoln initiated the War, they became virulent South-haters. In 1855 Ohio Senator B.F. Wade, speaking in the Senate declared, "Who is the judge in the last resort of the violation of the Constitution of

---

246 See Chapter 12, "The Character of President Davis's Accusers," in Kennedy & Kennedy, *Jefferson Davis: High Road to Emancipation and Constitutional Government*, 215-65.

247 Thomas Jefferson cited in Quirk & Bridwell, *Judicial Dictatorship*, 18.

the United States? Who is the final arbiter, the general government or the States in their Sovereignty? ...to yield up all the rights of the State to protect her own citizens, is to consolidate this government into a miserable despotism."[248] Yet, after Lincoln initiated the War, Senator Wade became a virulent hater of all things Southern including the original Constitution.

While the political forces of the North were busy perverting the Constitution, the Northern social forces were busy convincing the world that the South was populated by ignorant racists who hated blacks. The South stood on Constitutional principles, while the North attacked with emotional and slanderous propaganda. As previously noted, in mass democracies, emotion always trumps facts, truth, and logic. Post-War, the Republican Party used its propagandists in the media to convince the Northern people that the defeated white rebels were evil racists who hated blacks and took sadistic pleasure in mistreating blacks. In the next chapter, we will set the record straight regarding race relations in the pre-War South and, in so doing, destroy the North's justification for inflicting military dictatorship upon the post-War South.

---

248   Senator Wade cited in, *Confederate Veteran* Vol. XI, No. 9, Sept. 1903. Republished in *The Confederate Veteran Magazine* Vol. XI (Harrisburg, PA: The National Historical Society, 1987), 410.

Chapter 7:

RACE RELATIONS BEFORE LINCOLN'S WAR AND REPUBLICAN RECONSTRUCTION

"Race prejudice seems stronger in those States that have abolished slavery than in those where it still exists, and nowhere is it more intolerant than in those States where slavery was never known."
—Alexis de Tocqueville[249]

THE SLANDEROUS CHARGE that the South is the seat of racism, hatred, and intolerance was and continues to be used against the people of the South. In the modern era, it is virtually impossible to publicly challenge these charges for fear of social ridicule, shadow banning, and being branded as an evil white supremacist by leftist political figures including the current (2023) President. But what was the reality of race relations in the South before Lincoln's war?

Because the South was the last area of the country in which slavery existed, it carries the burden of "guilt" imposed on it by the North for the very existence of slavery. Part of the "guilt" for slavery is the allegation that slavery was possible in the South because Southerners are intrinsically racist haters of black people. Facts prove otherwise, but as pointed out in previous chapters, emotions outweigh facts and truth in America's mass democracy. The Southern colony of Virginia made upwards of 32 distinct

---

[249] Tocqueville, Alexis de, *Democracy in America* Vol. 1 (1848, Garden City, NY: Doubleday & Co., 1966), 343.

efforts in its Colonial Legislature to limit or prohibit the slave trade.[250] Yet, Northern propagandists give no credit to the South when they slanderously label the South as the land of slavery and racism. Leftist propagandists use the South as America's universal villain—America's whipping boy—responsible for slavery and racism. Quoting from *Basic Symbols*, Dr. Bradford notes that the Founding Fathers who wrote the Declaration of Independence rejected Thomas Jefferson's effort to include in the Declaration "the denunciation of slavery that Jefferson sought to include...."[251] It should be remembered that all the American Colonies in 1776 were slave-owning colonies. An act of Congress passed in 1808 with overwhelming support from the Senators and Representatives of the South ended the slave trade in the United States. The main opposition came from New Englanders who were actively engaged in the nefarious, yet very profitable, African slave trade. The Act took effect in 1808.[252] The North's slanderous charges against the South—upon which most of Reconstruction laws were based—can be shown untruthful by answering the following questions: "Was the alleged horrible mistreatment of slaves in the South true, and was slavery as practiced in the South based upon racial hatred?"

Two internationally recognized social scientists shocked and enraged the left when, in 1974, they declared the issue of slavery was used to poison race relations in the United States.[253] Their recognition of race used as a political tool brought down upon them the left's unrestrained wrath. The left is well known for substituting emotions for facts when facts demonstrate their social and political failures. Below are a few examples of the treatment of slaves in the South:

---

250 Bradford, M.E., *A Better Guide Than Reason: Federalists & Anti-Federalists* (1979, New Brunswick & London: Transaction Publishers, 1994), 55, footnote 31.

251 *Ibid.*, 51.

252 "The Slave Trade" National Archives (archives.gov), n.d. (Accessed 15 July 2023). www.bit.ly/xSlaveTrade.

253 Fogel & Engerman, *Time on the Cross: The Economics of American Negro Slavery* (New York: W.W. Norton & Co., 1974), 8-9.

- Post childbirth maternal death rate was lower for Southern slaves than for white Southern women[254]
- Southern slaves had a longer life expectancy than urban workers in the US or Europe[255]
- The diet of Southern slaves exceeded by 10% the energy value of the 1879 diet of free men[256]
- The slaves' diet exceeded the Federal Government's 1964 recommended diet[257]
- Housing for Southern slaves was more spacious than that of New York workers in 1893[258]
- Upwards of 25% of Southern male slaves were managers or craftsmen[259]
- Free blacks were better off in the South than in the North[260]

These "facts" were not newly discovered by Fogel and Engerman. Similar "facts" were noted by a foreign visitor to the United States in the 1840s:

> There is a great difference between white and black mortality rates in the States in which slavery has been abolished: from 1820 to 1831 only 1 white in 42 died, whereas the figure for blacks was 1 in 20. The mortality rate is not nearly so high among Negro slaves.[261]

One of the most poignant facts described by Fogel and Engerman was the comparison of the condition of Southern blacks before and after emancipation. They noted that sickness

---

254 Ibid., 123.
255 Ibid., 126.
256 Ibid., 113.
257 Ibid., 115.
258 Ibid., 116.
259 Ibid., 40.
260 Ibid., 244.
261 Tocqueville, Alexis de, *Democracy in America* Vol. 1, 351, fn. 41.

for post-War black sharecroppers was 20% higher than for slaves before emancipation.[262] These facts stand in sharp contrast to the anti-South slanderous lies put forth by South-hating Northern propagandists before and after the War for Southern Independence. And remember that sharecropping, established post-War, was known as a new form of slavery for eight and a half million Southerners—sixty percent of whom were white.[263]

THE NORTH'S ATTITUDE TOWARD BLACKS—FREE OR SLAVE

Northern propagandists strive to portray Northerners as paragons of virtue, racial brotherhood, and men willing to spill their blood and sacrifice their lives to free Southern slaves. Misguided conservatives often parrot the line that Americans should take pride because: "We fought a war to end slavery." Wrong! But like all other Yankee lies, it remains basically unanswered in the greater public domain of the news, academia, Hollywood, and the digital jungle. A major fact remains unappreciated by Americans when considering the so-called "Civil War." In all wars, the victor not only writes the history of the war, but the victor also uses his political, military, and financial power to enforce his version of the war while censoring the invaded and conquered peoples' history of the war. Of course, this situation is only possible if the invaded people remain pacified and subservient to the conquering "one nation indivisible." This lesson could be learned by looking at the almost seven centuries of English conquest and occupation of Ireland before they finally won their independence. The Irish refused to be pacified!

The reality is that Northerners disliked blacks in general and wanted to rid their lily-white society of blacks. Alexis de Tocqueville, a French visitor to America in the 1840s, noted the difference between race relations in the North and South:

> In that part of the Union [the North] where the Negroes are no longer slaves, have they come closer

---
262 Fogel & Engerman, *Time on the Cross*, 261.
263 Kennedy & Kennedy, *Punished with Poverty-The Suffering South*, 209-34.

to the whites? Everyone who has lived in the United States will have noticed just the opposite. Race prejudice seems stronger in those States that have abolished slavery than in those where it still exists, and nowhere is it more intolerant than in those States where slavery was never known.... In the South, where slavery still exists, less trouble is taken to keep the Negro apart: they sometimes share the labors and the pleasures of the white men; people are prepared to mix with them to some extent; legislation is more harsh against them, but customs are more tolerant and gentle.[264]

Tocqueville's observation that "customs are more tolerant and gentle" than the stricter state laws governing blacks was a common occurrence across the South. In Louisiana, "some of the statewide restrictions were simply not enforced by local authorities."[265] Tocqueville's keen insight and observations are generally ignored by modern-era "intellectuals" and "talking heads" in the mainline and digital media. He even noted that racial prejudice increased with emancipation.[266] He wrote that "In the United States people abolish slavery for the sake not of the Negroes but of the white man."[267] The point that the North sought to abolish slavery due to a general hatred of blacks was noted by John Adams of Massachusetts, a Founding Father and a President of the United States. He declared that the desire to end slavery in New England was **not** based upon a moral desire to expand freedom for blacks. Moral values:

> ...might have some weight in the abolition of slavery in Massachusetts, but the real cause was the multiplication of laboring white people, who would no longer suffer the rich to employ these sable rivals

---

264 Tocqueville, Alexis de, *Democracy in America* Vol. 1, 343.

265 Mills, Gary B. *The Forgotten People: Cane River's Creoles of Color* (Baton Rouge, LA: Louisiana State University Press, 1977), 107.

266 Tocqueville, Alexis de, *Democracy in America* Vol. 1, 344.

267 Ibid.

so much to their injury. The common people would not suffer labor, by which alone they could obtain a subsistence, to be done by slaves.[268]

Adams commented that if slavery were not abolished in New England, the common people would have revolted *en masse* and killed not only the slave but the white slave owner as well. Another Massachusetts citizen, Ralph Waldo Emerson, proclaimed that Northern abolitionists' ultimate desire was "to abolish the black man."[269] Tocqueville described how the North managed to rid their society not only of slavery but of blacks as well:

> We have pointed out how the Northern States managed to transition from slavery to freedom. They keep the present generation in chains, emancipating those of the future; by this means Negroes are introduced only slowly into society....[270]

> In the North, as I have said, as soon as slavery is abolished, and even from the moment when it begins to look likely that abolition is coming sometime, a double movement sets-in: the slaves quit [removed from] the country, being transported South; whites from the North and immigrants from Europe flow in to replace them.[271]

In his 1931 book *Lincoln the Man*, Edgar Lee Masters, a Northerner, noted that "New England had relieved herself of the presence of negroes by sending them South; so now would Lincoln free America of the evil of race antagonism by shipping the

---

268 Adams cited in Kennedy & Kennedy, *Punished With Poverty: The Suffering South*, 46. Authors cite Lorenzo, Green, Jr., *The Negro in Colonial New England, 1620-1776* (Port Washington, NY:Kennikat Press, 1966), 113, 322.

269 Emerson cited in Melish, Joanne P., *Disowning Slavery: Gradual Emancipation and "Race" in New England, 1780-1860* (Ithaca, NY: Cornell University Press, 1998), 164.

270 Tocqueville, Alexis de, *Democracy in America* Vol. 1, 354.

271 Ibid.

negroes to Central America or Liberia."²⁷² This almost universal Yankee aversion to living among blacks did not change during the War. Shepherd Pike, a correspondent for the *New York Tribune*, demonstrated his hatred for blacks in an article he wrote for the February 1861 issue of the *Atlantic Monthly*. He cruelly declared his desire to see blacks permanently segregated and kept away from white America:

> We say the Free States should say, confine the Negro to the smallest possible area. Hem him in. Coop him up. Slough him off. Preserve just so much of North America as is possible for the white man, and to free institutions.²⁷³

Pike's suggestion or desire to "Slough him off" [remove or get rid of blacks] aligns with the attitude of many Northern officials and military leaders during the War. Many Northern leaders believed blacks would die off and become extinct once slavery was abolished! This "extinction theory" is documented by Dr. Jim Downs, a liberal Northern scholar of the modern era.²⁷⁴ Another scholar, Dr. Joanne P. Melish, in her study of slavery in New England noted the condition of former slaves in New England thusly, "freed slaves perhaps, but free people, never... the grim truth of mounting hostility, ridicule, and escalating efforts to control and even eliminate their presence."²⁷⁵ President Grant, in 1881, endorsed the idea of keeping blacks out of the North by encouraging them to stay in the South:

---

272 Masters, Edgar Lee, *Lincoln the Man* (1931, Columbia, SC: The Foundation for American Education, 437-8.

273 Pike cited in Donald W. Livingston's "Confederate Emancipation Without War," *To Live or Die in Dixie*, ed., Frank Powell, III (Columbia, TN: Sons of Confederate Veterans, 2014), 463-4.

274 Downs, Jim, *Sick from Freedom: African-American Illness and Suffering during the Civil War and Reconstruction* (New York: Oxford University Press, 2012), 97,113.

275 Joanne P. Melish, *Disowning Slavery: Gradual Emancipation and "Race" in New England*, 238.

> I think the South is better suited [for blacks] than any other place...I want him to have the right to stay where the climate suits him.[276]

This is the same US President who wanted to acquire Santo Domingo as a place for freed slaves.[277]

This short review documents the fake history of the North's self-righteously claimed brotherly love for blacks. America's leftist propagandists in the media, Hollywood, and academia brazenly promote this self-righteous claim. But what was the condition of blacks, slave or free, down South? Was it as reprehensible as claimed by Northern propagandists before and especially after the War? As will be seen in upcoming chapters, these slanderous, anti-South lies were an essential justification for inflicting Reconstruction on the conquered and occupied South.

Race Relations Down South Before Lincoln's War

Slavery and race relations were not a uniquely Southern problem—they were an American problem. The pre-War North chose to resolve the question of race by removing blacks via gradual emancipation and selling their slaves to the South—as noted by Tocqueville in a previous paragraph. Before the Northern slave reached the age at which he was by law to be set free, his Yankee owner would take the slave to the Ohio River area and sell the slave to a slave merchant. The slave merchant would then transport the slave down the Ohio and Mississippi Rivers and sell the slave to Southern plantation owners. Thus, the origin of the critical term of being "sold down the river." Not only did Northerners cash in on their investment in slave property, but they also removed as many blacks as possible from their lily-white States. After that, they passed exclusion laws prohibiting "free people of color" from immigrating into their state. Illinois, Lincoln's home state, had an exclusion law on the books when Lincoln was a member of the state

---

276 Grant cited in Hair, William Ivy, *Bourbonism and Agrarian Protest: Louisiana Politics 1877-1900* (Baton Rouge, LA: Louisiana University Press, 1969), 174.

277 Leigh, Philip, *Southern Reconstruction* (Yardley, PA: Westholme Publishing, 2017), 82.

legislature—there is no record of Lincoln ever objecting to these laws. During the War, Northern leaders brought their concerns to Lincoln about free blacks immigrating to Northern States because of Emancipation. Lincoln replied that the States could pass exclusion laws. Tocqueville observed that "Ohio not only refuses to allow slaves but also prohibits the entry of free Negroes into its territory and forbids them from owning anything there."[278] While the North was taking the low road to emancipation, the South attempted to ameliorate the harsh conditions of slavery while seeking the high road to emancipation—a social experiment cut short by radical Yankee abolitionists and Lincoln's war.

Human slavery is not a matter of race, as portrayed by the Yankee Empire's modern-era propagandists. Slavery is not something unique to blacks. As a matter of historical record, more whites suffered under slavery than blacks. Black conservative scholar Dr. Thomas Sowell "triggered" many liberals when, in one of his many interviews available on YouTube, he said as much. He also informed his audience that around 75% of the people in early Rome were held in bondage.[279] St. Patrick was once held as a slave in Ireland. The word slave is derived from the word Slavs or the Slavic people. Muslim Turks constantly raided their country, and the captured white inhabitants were sold into slavery.

Slavery, in ancient societies and some non-Western modern-day societies, is a condition in which the slave owner held the slave as property, and the owner could do with his property as he pleased. Under this system of slavery, the slave owner could abuse or kill the slave. In some slave-owning societies, slaves were purchased as human sacrifices to pagan gods. This was not the case in America, where the slave was considered an indentured servant for life. The owner owned the slave's labor for life. The slave owner could not legally abuse a slave any more than an individual holding an indentured servant could legally abuse the indentured person.

---

278   Tocqueville, Alexis de, *Democracy in America* Vol. 1, 345, footnote 35.

279   This was also reported by Fogel & Engerman in *Time on the Cross*, 13. According to their findings, three out of four people in the Roman Empire—some 21 million people—were held in bondage.

Every Southern State had specific laws to assure the well-being of slaves. French Louisiana's 1724 *Code Noir* Article XLIII stated:

> Husbands and wives shall not be seized and sold separately when belonging to the same master; and their children, when under fourteen years of age, shall not be separated from their parents, and such seizures and sales shall be null and void.[280]

In Mississippi, shortly before the War, a white man murdered a slave. A white sheriff arrested the murderer, a white judge tried him, and a white jury convicted him of murder. The execution was swiftly carried out.[281] His crime was not that he destroyed the slave owner's property or denied the slave owner's right to the full lifetime labor of the slave. His crime was the murder of another human.

It was not uncommon for free blacks to take their case against a white man to court and trust the outcome.[282] Free people of color were always in danger of kidnapping by nefarious individuals. These kidnappers would then transport the free blacks away from their local community, and the free blacks would be sold into slavery. In Louisiana, as in other States, a free man or woman of color enjoyed the presumption of freedom as opposed to the presumption of bondage. As early as 1810 the Supreme Court of Louisiana ruled: "Considering how much probability there is in favor of the liberty of these persons [blacks claiming to be free persons of color], they ought not to be deprived of it upon mere presumption."[283] On January 4, 1853, the legal system of Louisiana freed a free man of color from New York who was kidnapped and sold into slavery. Selling a free person into slavery was known as "man-stealing." The individual, Solomon Northup, was not only freed by Louisiana's legal system but was provided with legal papers to secure his passage back to his home. Freeing Solomon Northup by the

---

280 Mills, Dr. Gary B. *The Forgotten People: Cane River's Creoles of Color*, 5.
281 Bettersworth, John K., *Mississippi: A History*, 191.
282 Mills, Dr. Gary B. *The Forgotten People*, 217.
283 *Ibid.*, 197. Author cites *Adele v. Beauregard*, 1 Mart. La. 183 (1810).

judicial system of Louisiana was praised in a local newspaper article, which concluded by stating, "Well may the South boast of its justice and loyalty."[284] In his journal, *Twelve Years a Slave*, published in 1853 Northup acknowledged how well he was treated: "It is but justice to say, that the authorities at Marksville [a town in Avoyelles Parish, Louisiana], cheerfully rendered all the assistance in their power."[285] In 1818 the [Mississippi] state supreme court actually freed two slaves sold by an Indiana resident in Mississippi, because slavery was not legal in the former state [Indiana].[286]

Were mistakes made? Without a doubt. People will make mistakes in any system of government created by fallible men. But it is evident that early in Southern history and continuing to the time of the War, Southerners attempted to solve the problems that naturally arise in a biracial society. Unlike their Northern brethren, white Southerners did not desire to rid themselves of a people they had become accustomed to and a people they trusted. A Northerner looking at the close relations between the races down South would be repelled and could not explain or accept it. Southerners, on the other hand, did not try to explain it but merely accepted it. The close relations between white and black Southerners during the age of slavery was a paradox of Southern society. But instead of wasting time explaining or analyzing this paradox, Southerners were satisfied with slowly progressing down the high road to emancipation. It was a slow progression, but such is how mutually acceptable social traditions develop. This slow pace was repugnant to the Yankee full of missionary social zeal eager to use the pulpit, propaganda, politics, or bayonets to enforce his latest trendy isms on the "others" of the world. Southerners took a different view of their world. "What better guide might a people have than abstract Reason? Why, Experience as a guide, the historic experience of a people, expressed in their legal institutions, the general frame of

---

284 *Marksville Villager,* 13 January 1853 quoted in the *New Orleans Bee,* 22 January 1853.

285 Northup, Solomon, *Twelve Years A Slave*, eds. Sue Eakin and Joseph Logsdon (1853: Baton Rouge: Louisiana State University Press, 1996), 234.

286 Bettersworth, John K., *Mississippi: A History*, 191.

government, customs, and conventions."[287] Yankee society was (and still is) in a constant state of trendy revolutions demanding the immediate adoption of some newly discovered ism. Southern society was satisfied with a slow almost imperceptible evolution of social change without a man-made deadline.

FREE OR SLAVE—THE SOUTH WAS THEIR HOME

When Southerners attempt to explain the living and working conditions of slaves in the South, they are typically cut short by a liberal indoctrinated individual who asserts that the Southerner is attempting to justify the inhuman system of slavery. With the typical leftist resort to emotions, all civil and factual discussion of the issue ends. The 1974 publication of *Time on the Cross* by Fogel and Engerman was met with strident cries of racism, pro-South bias, and attacks on their academic standing and intellectual scholarship. But the truth is most slave owners were decent folks who, due to their Christian upbringing and social pressure from within the community, tried to treat their slaves fairly. As Fogel and Engerman point out, the motivation to treat their slaves fairly came not only from a moral motive but also from an economic motive. Slaves who are treated fairly work more productively than disgruntled slaves who are mistreated.

Fredrick Law Olmsted is best known as the Father of Landscaping and the designer of Central Park in New York. He toured the pre-War South. He wrote several articles about what he saw down South. As a Yankee schooled in the abolitionist propaganda of the day, he could not be considered a friend of the South. He was surprised to find slaves working with great enthusiasm and seemingly happy with their condition. In a Louisiana sugar plantation, he found slaves who labored "with greater cheerfulness" during the sugar cane harvest season, even though their workday would last as long as eighteen hours. He discovered the reason was that during the harvest season, the slaves were "better paid." This was not something unique to Louisiana sugar plantations. In the Carolinas, he found similar conditions. He discovered that the master

---

[287] Russell Kirk in Bradford, M.E., *A Better Guide Than Reason*, xi.

gave them extra pay for "skill" and "perseverance." On a Georgia rice plantation, Olmsted met a slave engineer whose rewards for his work were "considerably higher wages, in fact, higher than the white overseer."[288] Mr. John Patterson of Virginia served under Washington during the Revolutionary War. He established a shipping company running to England and the West Indies. His ships' company included many of Mr. Patterson's slaves. He ordered the captain of his ships to pay his negroes "British seamen's wages."[289]

Southern slave owners often commented, half joking and half sincere, that they did not know if they owned the slaves, or the slaves owned them. Southern slave owners lived close to their slaves, which was vastly different from the absentee landlord system used in other parts of the world. One former slave declared, "We just went on peaceful and happy 'til the war came and rooted every blessed thing up by the roots."[290] When asked about their experiences during the war, former slaves often referred to the plantation as "home" and the plantation owners as "my white folks." The following examples were gathered from *The Slave Narratives: A Folk History of Slavery in the United States*, collected in 1931:

- When the Yankees come, they seemed to have a special vengeance for my white folks[291]
- I remember the Yankees come there to my white folks' plantation[292]
- As the Army pass, we all stand by the side of the road and cry and ask them not to burn our white folks' home[293]

---

288 Fogel & Engerman, *Time on the Cross*, 241.

289 *Confederate Veteran* Vol. VI, No. 10, Oct. 1898. Republished in *The Confederate Veteran Magazine* Vol. VI (Harrisburg, PA: The National Historical Society, 1987), 480.

290 Former slave Charles Stewart cited in Kennedy & Kennedy's *The South Was Right!*, 117.

291 Graham, Paul C., *When the Yankees Come: Former South Carolina Slaves Remember Sherman's Invasion* (Columbia, SC: Shotwell Publishing, 2016), 3.

292 *Ibid*, 7.

293 *Ibid.*, 40.

- When the Yankees come...one stuck a sword to my breast and said for me to come with him...(they) turned me loose.... I went fast and found my way back home[294]

The respect that white Southerners held for their black friends and neighbors was demonstrated in 1893 when the unofficial journal of the United Confederate Veterans published a plea for the Federal Government to grant to every former slave enough money to establish their own home and small farm. These Confederate Veterans understood the sad condition that Lincoln's low road to emancipation foisted upon slaves who were unprepared for their freedom. "His freedom was thrust upon him, and with it came many a sorrow that he knew not of in a state of servitude. Besides, there is a cruel disposition upon the part of some strangers to keep him disquieted and restless; for men, who are merciless and mercenary, tempt him into ill-starred expeditions...and laugh at his discomfiture...."[295] While the Federal Government gave millions of acres away to rich railroads, it refused to act upon this call from the South to help impoverished former slaves.

Slavery, even under the best of conditions and the best of masters, is NOT a good or ethical social system. Most Southerners understood this and knew the slave labor system would eventually end. The question was not if but how. When one honestly compares the way the North "solved" its race/slavery problem with the way the South attempted to handle its race/slavery problem, one sees that the South took a much more humane pathway. But the North's anti-South slanderous lies worked their evil magic on the thinking of the Northern population. It prepared them for a carnival of revenge, impoverishment, and dictatorial rule that they endorsed and imposed upon "We the People" of Dixie during Active, Passive, and Modern Era Reconstruction.

---

294   Ibid., 46.

295   *Confederate Veteran* Vol. I, No. 3, 1893. Republished in *The Confederate Veteran Magazine* Vol. I (Harrisburg, PA: The National Historical Society, 1987), 80-2.

Chapter 8:

DIVIDE & RULE—REPUBLICANS USE RACIAL HATRED TO GAIN POLITICAL POWER

"I tell you lady, if the rough element from the North had stayed out of the South the trouble of reconstruction would not have happened... they tried to excite the colored against their white friends.... I always say that if the South could have been left to adjust itself both white and colored would have been better off." —Cora Gillam - former slave[296]

BEFORE THE WAR, many key Southern leaders sought the high road to emancipation. The South's slow but evolving high road to emancipation stands in sharp contrast to Lincoln's violently implemented low road to emancipation. When Lincoln was asked what would become of the slaves after they were freed, with no preparation for freedom, he replied, "Let them root hog or die."[297] Lincoln's calloused attitude toward blacks merely reflected the notion held by many in the North who believed that, shortly after blacks gained their freedom, they would go extinct! [298]

---

296 Cora Gillam cited in Kennedy & Kennedy, *The South Was Right!* 3rd ed. (Columbia, SC: Shotwell Publishing, 135. The authors cite the *Slave Narratives*: The Arkansas Narratives, Vol. III, 27-33.

297 Lincoln cited by Alexander H. Stephens, *Constitutional View of the Late War Between the States* (1870, Harrisonburg, VA: Sprinkle Publications, 1994), Vol. II, 615.

298 Downs, Jim, *Sick From Freedom: African-American Illness and Suffering During the Civil War and Reconstruction* (New York: Oxford University Press: 2012), 97, 113.

Isaiah T. Montgomery Former Slave and Lifelong Friend of Jefferson Davis

"Feeling assured that you would take active interest in any enterprise tending to the welfare and development of the Colored people of Mississippi....If convenient for you to be in this locality about that time, we would be highly pleased to have you visit the Fair." From a letter dated 1886 by Mr. Montgomery to former President Davis inviting him to address a gathering of "Colored" Mississippians.

White Southerners had generations of experience living and working side-by-side with black Southerners. This relationship, though paternalistic, was based upon a sincere desire to protect a race of people who never in their entire history developed and *maintained* a democratic society. Jefferson Davis explained the South's willingness to prepare black Southerners for the day they would be a free and successful part of Southern society. "For its end the preparation of that race for civil liberty and social enjoyment [must be made]. When the time shall arrive at which emancipation is proper, those interested will be most anxious to effect it."[299] This was the high road to emancipation that would prepare Southern slaves for participation as free men in a free society. It would prevent the false claim that the War was necessary to free the slaves. It was the high road that would prevent Reconstruction and the eventual enslavement of black Americans on Uncle Sam's Plantation:

> The liberal establishment is involved in the slave trade, as surely as if they had put the chains on the people themselves. We work the ghettos instead of the fields, dutifully putting "massa" back in the Senate or House of Representatives.[300]

The high road to emancipation would prevent the Republican Party from using the technique of divide-and-rule to create racial hatred between the races in the South. It would allow the development of a society without the need for the 1964 and 1965 Civil Rights Acts, forced busing, affirmative action, racial hiring quotas, etc. It was a society that *could have been* if not for the Yankee invasion, conquest, occupation, and exploitation of both black and white Southerners. Post-War accounts provide ample evidence of what *could have been* if the North had allowed the South to naturally evolve into a just, bi-racial society acceptable to all the South's people.

---

299 Davis cited in McElroy, Robert, *Jefferson Davis, the Unreal and the Real* (New York: Harper Brothers Publishers, 1937), Vol. I, 104.

300 Parker, Star, *Uncle Sam's Plantation* (Nashville, TN: WND Books, 2003), 52-3.

Shortly after the close of the War, Union General and Republican politician Carl Schurz made a tour of the South and reported his findings back to his fellow Republicans in Congress. He noted that it was common to see the sincerest expressions of friendship and concern expressed openly in the streets between former slaves and their former masters. He was shocked to find out that "Centuries of slavery have not been sufficient to make them the enemies of the white man."[301] The Yankee Empire's propagandists labored diligently to convince the world that white Southerners were intrinsically evil and full of racial hatred toward black Southerners. But the facts are just the opposite—although little understood due to the South being an occupied country with no official means to respond to the Yankee Empire's propagandists. But the truth remains for those willing to see. In the 1890s, a black Republican Mississippi state representative bravely declared the truth about race relations in Mississippi:

> I was born in Mississippi but raised in a Northern State; associations there led me to regard Southern white men as dire foes to the Negroes but receiving such cordial and unprejudiced association upon this floor.... these suspicions have been eliminated from the bosoms of these...six and for them I am authorized to speak. You are our best friends.... you have shown to be our friends, not our enemies.[302]

Such friendly relations between men of different races and opposing political parties were not unusual in the South, even after Active Reconstruction. Yet, slanderous, anti-South propagandists are constantly presenting a different view. Slanderous, anti-South propaganda was necessary to allow the Yankee Empire to enact its strategy of divide-and-rule during Active Reconstruction. Today,

---

301 Kennedy & Kennedy, *Punished With Poverty* 2nd ed. (Columbia, SC: Shotwell Publishing, 2019. The authors cite Carl Schultz's, "Report of Carl Schurz," *A Just and Lasting Peace* (New York: Signet Classics, 2013), 140.

302 Representative Moore in Kennedy & Kennedy, *Punished With Poverty* 2nd ed., 68. The authors cite the *Daily Clarion-Ledger,* Jackson, MS, February 23, 1890.

the leftist ruling elite must continue their slander to ensure the continuation of racial hatred that the left-of-center establishment can use to maintain their control of the current political *status quo*. But even some post-War Northerners were impressed with the good race relations down South.

Edward King of Middlefield, Massachusetts, traveled the South during the post-War period. In his book, *The Southern States of North America*, he wrote: "the same negro who will bitterly oppose his old master politically, will implicitly follow his advice in matters of labor and investment."[303] If this much social and economic goodwill was present during the bad times of Active Reconstruction, one can only imagine what *could have been* accomplished had the North allowed the South to follow the high road to emancipation.

Foreign observers noted the general good relations between the races in the South as opposed to the less than friendly relations between the races in the North. James S. Buckingham, a British abolitionist, made the following observation about race relations in the pre-War South:

> The prejudice of color is not nearly so strong in the South as in the North. [In the South] it is not at all uncommon to see the black slaves of both sexes, shake hands with white people when they meet, and interchange friendly personal inquires; but at the North I do not remember to have witnessed this once; and neither in Boston, New York, or Philadelphia would a white person generally like to be seen shaking hands and talking familiarly with blacks in the streets.[304]

---

[303] Henry, Robert Selph, *The Story of Reconstruction*, 365.

[304] Kennedy & Kennedy, *Punished With Poverty* 2nd ed., 68-9. The authors cite J.S. Buckingham's *The Slave States of America* (New York: Negro University Press, 1968), II, 112.

After the War and before the Republican Party initiated its efforts to divide the races in the South and create a barrier of mistrust and hatred between the two races, numerous former Confederate officers encouraged black and white Southerners to work together to create a new and prosperous South. General P.G.T. Beauregard declared:

> The Negro is Southern born; with a little education and some property qualifications he can be made to take sufficient interest in the affairs and prosperity of the South to insure an intelligent vote."[305]

No one could question that the one Confederate General most slandered as an evil racist is General Nathan Bedford Forrest. In a post-War speech to a group of black voters, General Forrest reflected the goodwill existing before the Republican initiated racial hatred between the races in the South. Forrest openly declared:

> We were born on the same soil, breathe the same air, live in the same land, and why should we not be brothers and sisters.... I want you to do as I do—go to the polls and select the best men to vote for.... Although we differ in color, we should not differ in sentiment.... Do your duty as citizens, and if any are oppressed, I will be your friend.[306]

Notice the claim of Forrest that he "will be your *friend*," and reconsider the words of black Representative Moore from Mississippi speaking to his white associates, "you are our best friends."

When former Confederate Senator Benjamin Harvey Hill of Georgia returned to his home, the LaGrange plantation, he found

---

[305] P.G.T. Beauregard cited in Williams, T. Harry, *Napoleon in Gray*, (Baton Rouge: Louisiana State University Press, 1995), 266-67.

[306] Forrest cited by Seabrook, Lochlainn, *A Rebel Born; A Defense of Nathan Bedford Forrest* (Franklin, TN : Sea Raven Press, 2010), 483-4.

that not one of his slaves deserted or betrayed him even though Georgia was full of Yankees. In a speech delivered in Atlanta denouncing Republican Reconstruction, he paid particular attention to the evil perpetrated upon freedmen by those claiming to be their new friends:

> Oh, I pity the colored people who have never been taught what an oath is or what the Constitution means. They are drawn up by a selfish conclave of traitors to inflict a death-blow on the Republic by swearing them into a falsehood. They are to begin their political life with perjury to accomplish treason.... They are neither legally nor morally responsible—it is you, educated, designing white men, who thus devote yourselves to the unholy work, who are the guilty parties.... Ye hypocrites! Ye whited sepulchers! Ye mean in your hearts to deceive him and buy up the negro vote for your own benefit.[307]

Anti-South propagandists in the media and academia claim that the South's resistance movement during Active Reconstruction was a campaign of racial hatred. They claim that the efforts to remove the dictatorial Republican Reconstruction state governments were an effort to deny blacks the opportunity to vote and hold office. Facts present a different version of the South's struggle to regain at least some semblance of self-government. In Louisiana, the entire summer of 1872 was spent with five different groups hammering out a compromise between the various elements that wanted to reform the state government. They aimed to place Louisiana's government in a less corrupt and more stable economic condition. These five groups were reduced to two groups, both recognizing black voters, and they had black candidates in their list of candidates.[308] Not exactly the actions of "white supremacists...an

---

307 Bowers, Claude, *The Tragic Era*, 211.

308 Henry, Robert Selph, *The Story of Reconstruction*, 478.

episode in the long and bloody white supremacist resistance to black freedom," as claimed by postmodern leftist propagandists.[309]

During Wade Hampton's campaign for governor of South Carolina, the conservatives worked to mend the racial antagonism brought about by the Republican Party's Divide-and-Rule Reconstruction policy. Hampton declared, "I am in this fight to save South Carolina.... to bring the two races in friendly relations together with equal and impartial justice."[310] At a time when there was no "equal and impartial justice" for white Southerners who were ruled by carpetbaggers and scallywags and condemned as a conquered people by Congressional Republicans, at such a low time in Southern history, the leader of South Carolina's resistance movement called for equal and impartial justice for all races. "Equal and impartial justice for all races" was denied by law in most post-War Northern States!

Benjamin H. Hill advised the white people of Georgia to vote for candidates to the legislature "members whom lobbyists cannot buy. A black man who cannot be bought is better than a white man who can and a Republican who cannot be bought is better than a Democrat who can."[311] Strange words if what the Republican propagandists claimed was true about white Southerners hating black Southerners. But the truth of history tells a far different story than what Yankee propaganda tells.

Black Republicans and white Democrats in the Mississippi House of Representatives joined in presenting a watch to John R. Lynch, black Republican. The white Democrats offered a resolution praising Representative Lynch for his "ability, courtesy, and impartiality" as speaker of the Mississippi House of Representatives.[312] What Southern state has suffered more abuse and slander from arrogant, self-righteous Yankee propagandists than the

---

309   Lane, Charles, *The Day Freedom Died-The Colfax Massacre-The Supreme Court and The Betrayal of Reconstruction* (New York: Holt Paperbacks, 2008), 262.

310   Henry, Robert Selph, *The Story of Reconstruction*, 566.

311   Ibid., 438.

312   Ibid., 456-7.

state of Mississippi? In *Profiles in Courage*, future United States President John F. Kennedy noted, "No state suffered from 'reconstruction' and carpetbag rule more than Mississippi.... Vast areas of Mississippi lay in ruins. Taxes were increased to a level fourteen times higher than normal to support the reconstruction government." Kennedy noted that the state government was put in place by a "majority of freed slaves and radical Republicans, sustained and nourished by Federal bayonets."[313] The social evil produced by the Republican Party's effort to divide the races down South to allow the Republicans to control the defeated Southern States lives on today in the sad legacy of racial bitterness and mistrust.

Hiram Revels was the first black person elected to the United States Senate. Senator Revels was a Republican Senator from Mississippi. When elected to the Senate, many Northerners expected Revels to assist the Radical Republicans in their efforts to punish the South, but they were soon disappointed. Revels understood that by punishing the white South, the black South was also punished, i.e., economically and socially harmed. Revels resigned from the Republican Party after his efforts to improve the social and political well-being of the people of Mississippi. He often found that he was opposed by Congressional Republicans whose primary desire was to use black voters to advance the Republican Party's agenda. In a letter to President Grant, Senator Revels exposed the misuse of his people (black Southerners) by the Republican Party:

> A great portion of them [black voters] have learned that they were *being used as mere tools,* and, as in the late election, not being able to correct existing evils among themselves, they determined by casting their ballots against those unprincipled adventurers, to overthrow them.... My people have been told by these schemers [Republican carpetbaggers], when men have been placed on the ticket who

---

313   John F. Kennedy cited in Hoar, Jay S., *The South's Last Boys in Gray* (Bowling Green, OH: Bowling Green State University Press, 1986), 1.

were notoriously corrupt and dishonest, that they must vote for them; that the salvation of the party depended upon it; that the man who scratched a ticket was not a Republican. This is only one of the many means these unprincipled demagogues have devised to *perpetuate the intellectual bondage* of my people. To defeat this policy, at the late election men, irrespective of race, color, or party affiliation, united, and voted together against men known to be incompetent and dishonest."[314] [Emphasis added.]

As Senator Revels's letter to Grant resigning from the Republican Party demonstrates, it was not evil white Southerners who were using the newly freed black citizens as "mere tools," nor was it the "evil" white Democrats who were engaged in maintaining "the intellectual bondage" of these newly freed black citizens—it was the Republican Party and the ruling elite in Washington, DC.

In the Mississippi elections of 1875, many property-owning blacks voted for the Democratic ticket even though this brought upon them severe social ostracism among their fellow blacks. But their votes, just like the votes of whites, were not based on race but on the need to remedy the oppressive tax load created by the Republican Party that controlled the state legislature. Senator Revels, in his letter to President Grant decrying the corruption in the Radical Republican Party, States plainly that "At the late election men, irrespective of race, color, or party affiliation, united and voted together against men known to be incompetent and dishonest...."[315]

What Could Have Been—But Was Denied

After the close of the War, the South was presented with a complex problem of establishing a fair and just social system in which mostly illiterate, former slaves and whites would live

---

314 Hiram Revels cited in Garner, James, *Reconstruction in Mississippi*, (New York: The Macmillan Co., 1901), 399-400.

315 Henry, Robert Selph, *The Story of Reconstruction*, 549.

together in harmony. It was a challenge never faced in history by any conquered and occupied people. It was the monumental challenge of incorporating former slaves of African descent into the political process with former (before the surrender in 1865) self-governing whites. The black population was not prepared for the task of self-governing. They represented a large group of mostly illiterate citizens who lacked experience in the art of maintaining a democratic government. The Southern white population was encumbered with being ruled by a conqueror full of hatred, seeking revenge, and dictatorial political power. In addition, the conquerors of the South intended to use, as in exploit, the newly freed slaves by turning them into tools for the Republican Party. Illiterate Southern blacks would be the key to Republican domination of the South and Washington, DC. The opportunity for establishing a Southern society where the races could work in harmony was nullified by slanderous anti-South Yankee propaganda before the War and destroyed by the Yankee Empire's tactic of divide-and-rule during Active Reconstruction. The white South was under an alien government established and enforced by bloody bayonets, while the black South became pawns to be moved about on the Yankee Empire's political chess board—first by Republicans and today by Democrats.

The excuse used by the Republican Party to justify Active Reconstruction was that it was an act of treason for the South to leave their (the North's) Union and declare its independence as a sovereign nation, the Confederate States of America. The allegation of treason is still made and endorsed by America's postmodern, neo-Marxist propagandists and politicians of both national parties.[316] But if secession is an act of treason, then it must be punished. But if it was not an act of treason, then the

---

316   Office of US House Clerk, "House Republicans Vote to Remove Confederate Statutes from Capitol," clerk.house.gov. (Accessed 07 July 2021) www.bit.ly/Vote29Jun2021; Hoyt, Gregory "GOP Support "Transgenders as Federally Protected Class," Voice Media (redvoicemedia.com) 23 November 2021 (Accessed 25 November 2021) www.bit.ly/TransRepublicans; "GOP McConnell's China financial connection," National File (national.file.com) 15 December 2020 (Accessed 17 December 2020) www.bit.ly/xConChi;"McConnell's sister-in-law named to Bank of China," World Tribune (worldtribune.com) 24 April 2018 (Accessed 17 December 2020) www.bit.ly/ChiBankMcCon.

War and Reconstruction were an unconstitutional act of tyranny! The criminal was not "We the People" of the South who sought to establish a government based upon the American principle of government founded upon the "consent of the governed." Lincoln and the Republican Party are the criminals! They committed the crime by waging an unconstitutional, aggressive war against a people who asked only to be left alone. The Republican Party during Active Reconstruction used the hate-centered political technique of divide-and-rule to give them the political control of Congress and, thereby, the ability to hide their war crimes while enjoying the foul fruits of an aggressive war.

The Republican Party, during the War and Active Reconstruction, treated black Southerners with calloused disregard. Northerners reserved a special hatred for those black Southerners who maintained friendly relations with white Southerners. The pure hatred of Yankees toward blacks who refused to abandon their white Southern friends can be seen in the treatment of a black servant who chose to remain with his master in Johnson's Island POW camp. The Federal officers offered all kinds of inducements to get Captain Hewett's servant, Dick, to join the Union Army. Dick resolutely refused, preferring to remain in prison and share the hardships with his master. The Yankees were outraged and refused to supply Dick with his share of meager prison food. Dick's fellow Southerners divided their meager supply, giving him a portion equal to that of his fellow Confederates.[317]

Divide-and-Rule[318] as a political technique to gain power remains with us today in Modern Era Reconstruction. It has become a vital part of America's so-called "two-party" system of

---

317 *Confederate Veteran* Vol. XIII, No. 3, March 1905. Republished in *The Confederate Veteran Magazine* Vol. XIII (The National Historical Society, Harrisburg, PA: 1987), 111.

318 Divide and Rule is explained in greater detail in Kennedy & Kennedy's *Yankee Empire: Aggressive Abroad and Despotic at Home* (Columbia, SC: Shotwell Publishing, 2018), 115, 124-5, 195, 345.

governance.[319] Both political parties rely upon divide-and-rule to motivate their voter base. Democrats gain black and liberal voters by promoting racial hostility, while Republicans gain voters from gullible conservatives who wishfully expect the Republican Party to stand up for traditional American moral and political values—the same values destroyed by Lincoln and the Republican Party.

---

319   America's so-called two-party system is a uniparty system in which both national political parties are dedicated to maintaining the political *status quo* that provides the ruling elites of both parties with almost unlimited perks, privileges, and power. See Zimmer, Ben, "The Strange History of the Uniparty," Politico Magazine (politico.com) 17 November 2017, www.politi.co/3TcfT8p (Accessed 23 December 2023).

Chapter 9:

THE SOUTHERN PEOPLE'S RIGHT OF SELF-DETERMINATION

"The object was to sustain a principle—the broad principle of constitutional liberty, the right of self-government." —Jefferson Davis[320]

ONE OF THE REASONS used by the victorious North (the emerging Yankee Empire) to justify its aggressive invasion and conquest of the sovereign nation, the Confederate States of America, and its subsequent oppressive Active Reconstruction Plan was that secession is treason. Therefore, it is punishable by death or any other punishment the victor desires to inflict on the vanquished. The post-War punishment of poverty intentionally inflicted upon the South by the Yankee Empire resulted in the death of upwards of a million black and white Southerners during Passive Reconstruction.[321] As one self-righteous Yankee elaborated, "Every secessionist has received as the penalty of defeat only poverty. It is the mildest punishment ever inflicted after an unsuccessful civil war."[322]

The recent (2023) efforts of the United States Woke military to rename US military bases named for Southern heroes and the announced intention to destroy the Confederate, i.e.,

---

320   Davis, Jefferson, *Rise and Fall of the Confederate Government*, Vol. 1 (1881, Nashville, TN: William Mayes Coats, c.1980), 300.

321   Kennedy & Kennedy, *Punished With Poverty* 2nd ed., 119-24.

322   Rev. Thomas Higgins, Unitarian minister from New England, cited in Kennedy & Kennedy, *Punished With Poverty* 2nd ed., 7.

Reconciliation monument in Arlington National Cemetery is justified by claiming such things honor men who were traitors to the good ole USA. One of the leftists' talking points in their demand to tear down local monuments honoring Confederate veterans is that these monuments glorify treason. If secession is treason, then Reconstruction inflicted upon the South by the Republican Party was a legitimate political reaction. It also means the 21st-century destruction of traditional Southern symbols and monuments to Southern heritage is necessary and proper. But is secession treason? Can essential American political principles, as outlined in the Declaration of Independence be legitimately adjudicated by massed bloody bayonets? Does might make right?

If a state is sovereign, it has the right to withdraw authority it previously delegated to an agent.[323] If the States were sovereign, the States had the right to withdraw from the Union. Therefore, the Federal Government did not have a constitutional right to use force against the sovereign state(s). As High Federalist Alexander Hamilton in the Constitutional Convention admitted, "To coerce the States was one of the maddest projects ever devised."[324] Therefore, if the Southern States were sovereign, then their secession was a legal act of a sovereign withdrawing authority it previously delegated to the Union or Federal Government. In May of 1860 Senator Jefferson Davis of Mississippi offered a resolution in the Senate. Davis's resolution declared that "in the adoption of the Federal Constitution, the States adopting the same acted severally as free and independent sovereigns." The resolution passed 36 in favor and 19 opposed. Even Lincoln's future Vice President Andrew Johnson, voted in favor of the resolution.[325] Here, we see that less than a year before the lower South voted to secede from an abusive Union, the Union's Senate

---

323 Note: "delegate" not surrendered or renounced. The same authority that has the right to delegate retains the right to withdraw that delegation.

324 Hamilton cited in *Confederate Military History*, Vol. 1, Part 1 (1899, Harrisburg, PA: The Archives Society, 1994), 50; This cites the *Madison Papers*, and 2nd edition, *Elliot's Debates*.

325 Masters, Edgar Lee, *Lincoln the Man* (1931, Columbia, SC: The Foundation for American Education, 419.

acknowledged the sovereignty of the States that made up the Union. A Sovereign freely exercising its sovereign authority cannot be legitimately accused of treason!

Modern-day constitutional scholars have admitted that the North and South had uniquely different views of legitimate government. Each side viewed the same constitution from different perspectives.

> Each had evolved a fully-developed body of constitutional doctrine, and each section was able to justify its actions in the light of its interpretation of the Constitution.[326]

This raises the question: "Is it ethically logical that differences in constitutional interpretation should be resolved via trial by combat?" The fact that each side held virtually opposite views of the Constitution should argue in favor of peaceful secession. After so many years of failed efforts to coexist, would it not be more humane for each party to separate amicably? Without exception, trial by combat decides which side is the strongest, not which is morally or legally correct.

The South's "legal" right to establish its own government is discussed at length in other places and will not be repeated here.[327] But it is important to demonstrate why the South fought—they fought for their natural right of freedom. The Southern people's determination to defend their natural right to self-government is demonstrated in a letter written on August 5, 1863, by Major Robert Donnell of the Twenty-Second Alabama infantry in which he writes, "Our rations are very short indeed, but I am willing to live on acorns for seven years or longer to gain my freedom and independence....

---

[326] Bauer, Elizabeth Kelley, *Commentaries on the Constitution 1790-1860* (New York: Columbia University Press, 1952), 30.

[327] See Kennedy & Kennedy, Chapter 9, "A Legal Right to be Free," *The South Was Right!* 3rd ed., 219-233.

We adopt for our motto an old saying of one of the Revolutionary fathers of 1776, 'Resistance to tyrants is obedience to God.'"[328] Yet, Yankee propagandists claim he was fighting for slavery!

It has often been said that the South was right in 1861 because the American colonies were right in 1776. In both cases, a people who were being oppressed by a far-away central government decided to exercise their God-given right to "abolish" one government and to "institute" a new government that would protect their rights and liberty—as declared in the 1776 Declaration of Independence. In both cases, the States (in 1861) and the colonies (in 1776) were populated by slave owners. In 1776 slavery was legal and practiced in all thirteen colonies. Leftists often complain that the South did not deserve freedom because it denied freedom to slaves.[329] If that is true, then the thirteen American colonies did not deserve freedom—the claim currently made by neo-Marxists promoting neo-Marxist ideas such as Project 1619. The ultimate goal of America's neo-Marxists is not merely to destroy Southern symbols and monuments but to destroy (as in deconstruct or debunk) what remains of America's Constitution.

The Federal Government Taught the Right of Secession at West Point!

One of the most embarrassing historical facts for the Yankee Empire and its propagandists when attempting to pronounce secession as treason is that the right of a state to secede from the Union was taught at the West Point Military Academy. The first textbook on the Constitution used at West Point Military Academy was Rawle's *View of the Constitution*. It was replaced with Kent's *Commentaries on American Law*, but nowhere in Kent's *Commentaries* did he reject Rawle's view. Kent concluded that the way the Union would be held together was based on the

---

[328] *Confederate Veteran* Vol. VII, No. 1, Jan. 1898. Republished in *The Confederate Veteran Magazine* Vol. VII (Harrisburg, PA: The National Historical Society, 1987), 37.

[329] See Kennedy & Kennedy, Chapter 14, "Do Slave-owners or Their Descendants Deserve Freedom?" *Yankee Empire: Aggressive Abroad and Despotic at Home* (Columbia, SC: Shotwell Publishing, 2018), 311-21.

mutual benefits and responsibilities of the parties. Kent wrote, "...for on the concurrence and goodwill of the parts, the stability of the whole depends."[330] The Union would remain stable if "goodwill" between the parties remained. Northern "goodwill" had fled the Union by 1860. The official *rejection* of Rawle's view on the right of state secession was not published in a textbook for West Point until after the War! One constitutional scholar noted that "it is probable that if he [Jefferson Davis] had been brought to trial after the War between the States he would have sought to vindicate the constitutionality of secession by reference to the use of Rawle at West Point."[331] This is one of reasons the Federal Government hesitated and eventually refused to give Davis his "day in court" even though he repeatedly petitioned for a trial on the charge of treason.[332]

In Chapter 32 of his book, Rawle describes the procedure by which a sovereign state could secede from the Union. In Chapter 11, "Of Treason Against the United States," he does not mention the act of secession and, therefore, does not label it as an act of treason. An entire chapter on treason—the charge so often flung against traditional Southerners—yet secession is never mentioned! The injustice of it all is enough to drive one mad!

Judge Rawle was an abolitionist from Pennsylvania and a friend of George Washington and Benjamin Franklin. Boston's *North American Review* evaluated his textbook in 1826. The *Review* recommended, "To those, who are desirous of studying the noblest monument of human wisdom, the Constitution of the United States, we recommend the treatise of Mr. Rawle as a safe and intelligent guide."[333] It was a "safe and intelligent guide" until

---

330 Kent, cited in Rawle, William, A *View of the Constitution of the United* States, edited and annotated by Kennedy & Kennedy with subtitle *Secession as Taught at West Point Military Academy*, (1829, Wake Forest, NC: The Scuppernong Press, 2020), xvi.

331 Bauer, Elizabeth Kelley, *Commentaries on the Constitution, 1790-1860* (Lawbook Exchange, Ltd., Union, NJ: 1999), 339.

332 Kennedy & Kennedy, *Jefferson Davis: High Road to Emancipation and Constitutional Government* (Columbia, SC: Shotwell Publishing, 2022), 139-41.

333 Rawle, William, A *View of the Constitution of the United* States, vi.

Lincoln and the Republican Party were faced with their Southern "cash cow" fleeing their grasp and thereby ending years of Yankee exploitation of Southern resources for the benefit of Northern commerce. No wonder Mr. Lincoln, when asked, "Why not let the South go?" replied, "Let the South go! Where then shall we get our revenue?"[334]

President Jefferson Davis noted that if secession of the sovereign States is denied, coercion would replace consent as the primary principle of American government.[335] Early in 1861 many Northerners supported the idea espoused by Judge Rawle—this was before the Northern commercial elites realized their loss if the South left "their" Union. For instance, The *New York Tribune*—the leading organ of the party that triumphed in the election of 1860 declared: "We hold, with [Thomas] Jefferson, to the inalienable right of communities to alter or abolish forms of government that have become oppressive or injurious; and, if the cotton States shall decide that they can do better out of the Union than in it, we insist on letting them go in peace...whenever a considerable section of the Union shall deliberately resolve to go out, *we shall resist all coercive measures designed to keep her in. We hope never to live in a republic whereof one section is pinned to the residue by bayonets.*"[336] The *New York Herald* also stated: "Each State is organized as a complete government, holding the purse and wielding the sword, possessing the right to break the tie of the confederation as a nation might break a treaty, and to repel coercion as a nation might repel invasion.... Coercion, if it were possible, is out of the question."[337] Whether the South had the right to secede quickly changed into how the North would economically survive if they let the South secede.

---

334   Lincoln cited in Semmes, Admiral Raphael, *Memoirs of Service Afloat* (1868, Secaucus, NJ: The Blue & Grey Press, 1987), 59.

335   Davis, Jefferson, *Rise and Fall of the Confederate Government*, Vol. 1 (1881, Nashville, TN: William Mayes Coats, c.1980), 177.

336   *Ibid.*, 252; The author cites the *New York Tribune*, Nov. 9, 1860.

337   *Ibid.*, 254.

As in all things when dealing with the ruling elite of the North, emotions trump truth, and profits trump principles.

The March 30, 1861, issue of *The New York Times* contained a lengthy article warning about the potential loss of Northern revenue if they allowed the South to secede. They openly admitted the real reason for an aggressive and unconstitutional war upon the South: "We were divided and confused till our pockets were touched." An editorial in the Manchester, New Hampshire, *Union Democrat* was even more explicit:

> The Southern Confederacy will not employ our ships or buy our goods. What is our shipping without it? Literally nothing. The transportation of cotton and its fabrics employs more ships than all other trade. It is very clear that the South gains by this process, and we lose, No—we MUST NOT "let the South go."[338]

The South sought independence because it was viciously slandered and financially exploited by the Northern majority—something Patrick Henry and other Anti-Federalists predicted during the debates on the ratification of the proposed Constitution. Senator Thomas H. Benton of Missouri pointed out in a speech made in 1826 that the Southern States of Virginia, Georgia, and North and South Carolina provided 75% of the Federal Government's revenue. "This is the reason why wealth disappears from the South and rises-up in the North. Federal legislation does all this."[339] President James Buchanan warned that "The South had not had her share of money from the treasury, and unjust discrimination had been made against her."[340] The North's slander and oppressive legislation targeted against the South was far worse than anything the English King and Parliament did to the thirteen American colonies. If the slave-holding American colonies had

---

338 Kennedy & Kennedy, *The South Was Right!* 3rd ed., 64.

339 *Ibid.*, 60.

340 *Ibid.*, 61.

a right to self-determination in 1776, then so did the sovereign States of the South in 1861!

Seeking freedom from an oppressive government is not treason, but meekly and cowardly accepting tyranny is treason—treason to the very principle of self-determination, self-government, and liberty. As Thomas Jefferson said, "Rebellion to tyrants is obedience to God." For Southerners suffering under Republican Active Reconstruction, their motto could have been "Resistance to Republican-imposed tyranny is obedience to God." In the next chapter, we will review the social and economic conditions in the post-War South that compelled them to form a Southern resistance movement.

Chapter 10:

THE SOUTH'S POST-WAR SOCIAL, ECONOMIC, AND POLITICAL SITUATION

"The post-War Southern resistance movement was an historical development caused by the unnatural conditions of invasion, occupation, and the invader's intentional destruction of normal civil authorities. The breakdown of law and order fostered the development of secret vigilante groups to maintain order. It was not that dissimilar from the French Resistance Movement in WW-2." —James Ronald Kennedy

AFTER THE WAR, Billy Yank came home to a thriving economy. It was an economy bolstered by massive government spending. He returned to cities untouched by the horrors and social destruction of war. He arrived home to self-governing communities enjoying American liberty. He returned to his state, in which the Constitution protected his rights. He came home to his state with a functioning and reliable judicial system that he could appeal to if someone violated his civil rights. He also looked forward to the rich rewards promised by Union Army pensions that would eventually cost the Federal Government more than the cost of conducting its illegal invasion of the Confederate States of America.[341] Billy Yank came

---

[341] The last Union pension payment was made in May 2020. See Miller, Ryan W. & McCarthy, John, "Last person to receive pension from Civil War, $73.13 monthly, dies at age 90," *USA Today* (usatoday.com), 10 June 2020 (Accessed 26 July 2023). www.bit.ly/xYankeePensioner.

home to his part of a nation at the threshold of the Gilded Age. It was an age of unparalleled Northern industrial expansion and Northern public and private opulence. He returned to a nation prepared for the continuing conquest of the Western Plains Indians' homeland and, eventually, the invasion and conquest of Hawaii, Cuba, and the Philippines.[342] Billy Yank's future was bright as a citizen in the newly established Yankee Empire. Billy Yank came home to an exciting future of the promise of profits. But not so for war-weary Johnny Reb. As noted by Southern scholars:

> Northern soldiers returning home after the war would find prosperous communities and jobs awaiting them. But Southern soldiers found impoverished and exhausted communities with no employment to offer.[343]

One Northern traveler described the conditions in the war-torn South that the civilian population was enduring:

> By the roadside, here and there, might be seen... a poor, half-starved, half-naked white woman, gathering her little children about her, and cowering in the gray dawn over the dull embers by which... she had watched them through the wretched night.[344]

The post-War condition of the South was described in a letter from General Zebulon B. Vance of North Carolina to a friend in Australia written shortly after Vance was paroled and released from confinement. Although paroled he noted that, "I am here, a prisoner still," not being allowed to engage in any professional activities. He noted that "Murder and outrage are frequent, and the absence of civil law encourages the wickedly inclined." He described the Southern States, "...have been reduced to the con-

---

[342] See, Kennedy & Kennedy, *Yankee Empire*, 41-73, 90-109.

[343] Clark & Kirwan, *The South Since Appomattox* (New York: Oxford University Press, 1967), 22.

[344] *Ibid.*, 23.

dition of territories...denied all law except that of the military. Our currency, of course, is gone, and with it went the banks and bonds of the State, and with them went to ruin thousands of widows, orphans, and helpless persons whose funds were invested therein. Their railroads destroyed, towns and villages burned to ashes, fields and farms laid desolate, homes and cabins only marked by blackened chimneys...livestock driven off and destroyed, mills and agricultural implements specially ruined." He noted a ray of hope because due to a "fair crop" made in the fall [1865] which will hopefully relieve some of the suffering "except among the negroes, who...flocked into town in search of their freedom, where they are dying and will die by the thousands."[345]

This was the social condition facing the returning Confederate veteran. It was a cruel condition intentionally forced upon Americans by other Americans as punishment for claiming the rights clearly announced in 1776 in the Joint Declaration of Independence. According to the Declaration, they had the right to remove themselves from a bad government and create a new one based upon the free and unfettered consent of the governed. However, such American principles were not allowed for Southerners. Expecting Yankees to live by such honorable principles would be like expecting pity from a stone. *Vae Victis*—woe to the vanquished—became the *modus operandi* of the Yankee Empire. Successful invaders rule while the defeated must meekly hear and obey.

Confederate General P.G.T. Beauregard noted that "...the actual fact on the battlefield, in the face of cannon and musket, was that the Federal troops came as invaders, and the Southern troops stood as defenders of their homes."[346] This simple fact is little known and completely unacknowledged by the Yankee Empire's academic, media, Hollywood, and political propagandists. The reason they insist on repeating their magical incantations of

---

345 General Vance, cited in, *Confederate Veteran* Vol. XXXVII, No. 6, June 1931. Republished in *The Confederate Veteran Magazine* Vol. XXXIX` (Harrisburg, PA: The National Historical Society, 1987),215-7.

346 Beauregard cited in Weaver, Richard, *The Southern Tradition at Bay* (New Rochelle, NY: Arlington House, 1968), 192.

slavery, treason, and racism is that they know their unfounded but emotionally charged incantations will cover the sins of their Yankee fathers. As already pointed out, in modern America's mass democracy, emotions trump truth, facts, and logic. The Yankee Empire's emotionally charged incantations provided the Northern invaders and oppressors of the South an efficient smoke-screen behind which they could continue their Woke, politically correct destruction of all traditional conservative American values. As Professor Jay S. Hoar of Maine said, "I have lived long enough to see the Confederate soldiers' worse nightmare come to pass—a Federal Government completely out of control."[347] The valor and dedication of Confederate soldiers, sailors, officials, and citizens to the cause of liberty and self-government is unparalleled in American history.

At the beginning of the War, the North's population of military age stood at 3,954,776, and the South's was 1,064,193.[348] Like the Patriots of 1776, Southerners of 1861 did not let the odds deter them from standing up for their right to self-determination. This almost 4 to 1 disadvantage was evident during the War. During the 1861 to 1865 period, nearly three million men served in the Union Army. During the same period, 800,000 to 850,000 men served in the Confederate military. In addition, the North had the advantage of recruiting 489,920 foreign mercenaries to replace their ranks, constantly thinned by disease and Confederate marksmanship. Germans (210,000) and Irish (150,000) made up most of these foreigners from fifteen different nations.[349] As one modern-day Southern scholar noted, "Given the odds against it, it is not surprising the Confederacy lost. What is amazing is it held out for more than four years and came as close to winning as it did."[350] But the conditions awaiting these brave veterans returning home were worse than anything they endured during

---

347   From a conversation between Professor Hoar and the Kennedy Twins, 1986.

348   Mitcham, Jr, Dr. Samuel W., "War By The Numbers," *Confederate Veteran* Frank Powell ed., Vol. 80, No. 1, Jan/Feb 2022, 16.

349   *Ibid.*, 16-17.

350   *Ibid.*, 59.

the War.³⁵¹ They faced the total extinction of their families due to starvation, disease, and the complete breakdown of law and order. They faced barbarism championed and imposed upon a defeated people by the Federal Government—a barbarism gleefully turned loose upon their families and their kith and kin. Survival was at stake.

The returning Confederate veterans faced conditions at home never before or since faced by any group of Americans. (Yet, Southerners are the only group in America who are castigated and officially prohibited from publicly celebrating their heritage.) One author described the returning Confederate veterans as "Penniless, sick at heart and in body, and humiliated by defeat, they found their families in poverty and despair."³⁵² A Northern correspondent, upon seeing for himself the deplorable circumstances facing the post-War people of the South, declared that it was "A degree of destitution that would draw pity from a stone."³⁵³ The untold and well-hidden (censored) history of the Republican Party's Active Reconstruction demonstrates that it would be easier to obtain "pity" from a stone than from the Northern public eager for revenge and the Republican Party seeking to exploit their newly conquered territory and people for political and economic gain.³⁵⁴

One post-War Northern observer reported that "Never was there greater nakedness and destitution in a civilized community."³⁵⁵ For many returning soldiers, their only coat was their gray Confederate battle jacket. Upon returning home, they discovered that it was now a crime to wear the Confederate coat that had CS

---

351 "They limped home but were soon fighting the greater battle of Reconstruction." From article "Inside Looking Out" by Winnie Estes Sowell. Published in *The Maury Democrat* Columbia, Tennessee, n.d. She was the granddaughter of a Confederate veteran.

352 Bowers, Claude, *The Tragic Era* (New York: Halcyon House, 1929), 45.

353 *Ibid.*, author cites *Annual Encyclopedia*, 1865, 392.

354 The South became a colonial appendage to industrial and grain-growing sections of the country. See Clark & Kirwan, *The South Since Appomattox*, 91.

355 Henry, Robert Selph, *The Story of Reconstruction* (New York: Konecky & Konecky, 1938), 18.

buttons for the world to see.[356] Travel across the South was difficult everywhere and impossible in some places. There were no river bridges at the Rappahannock, none at the James, and none at the Appomattox. Railroads were out in all directions from trench-ringed Petersburg.[357] Even General Grant recognized the deplorable conditions facing the returning veterans and their families. He wrote his wife in May of 1865, "The suffering that must exist in the South the next year... will be beyond conception."[358] In Columbia, South Carolina, the mayor reported that the destitution was such that hundreds of people lived on loose grain picked up where the Yankee Army horses were fed.[359] During the war, the invading Yankee armies intentionally destroyed cattle, draft horses, and mules to create starvation among the South's *civilian* population—a violation of the rules of civilized warfare. By the spring of 1865, most of the livestock was gone.[360]

Arkansas scalawag Governor Murphy reported that citizens of his state were living in open brush shelters in the woods, begging for food. Some thirty miles from Atlanta, Georgia, over thirty-five people were without the necessities of life to the point of starvation. "A grandmother walked nineteen miles to Guntersville, Alabama, where she had heard that she might get food for her five orphaned grandchildren. Rations were issued to her, but on the way home she died of starvation and exhaustion."[361] God only knows what became of the starving orphans—*Vae Victis*, woe to the vanquished.

---

356 *Ibid.*, 19.

357 *Ibid.*, 19.

358 *Ibid.*, 20.

359 *Ibid.*, 20.

360 Clark & Kirwan, *The South Since Appomattox*, 22, 104. See also Henry's *The Story of Reconstruction*, 21.

361 Henry, Robert Selph, *The Story of Reconstruction*, 61.

The South's Post-War Social, Economic, and Political Situation

The Dixie Division's Color Guard—Circa 1955

The United States government, its puppet state, and local governments have viciously slandered the blood shed by Southerners in every American war by denying Southerners the right to honor their unique heritage. When the Federal Government forcibly expelled the Nez Perce from their ancestorial land, Chief Joseph asserted something that Southerners intuitively understand. He said, "A man who would not love his father's grave is worse than a wild animal."[362] For a spiritual people land, memory, ancestors, and heritage are the prime determinants of their society—destroy these values and you exterminate an entire people. The Yankee Empire, as an alien occupying power, understands this simple principle. Southern monuments and heritage matter!

---

362 Chief Joseph cited in Kennedy & Kennedy, *Yankee Empire*, 108.

Not only must the returning veterans find some way to rebuild ruined homes, public buildings, roads, and bridges, but a whole new labor system had to be created. New channels of business and economic intercourse had to be developed. These defeated and exhausted veterans had to develop a whole new manner of life.[363] The labor problem was a direct result of Lincoln's low road to emancipation—declaring slaves free without any preparations for freedom. The South's high road to emancipation would have produced a much better long-term solution for black and white Southerners.[364]

Bands of deserters and skulkers, guerrillas, and bushwhackers infested the country, preying on any potential victim, white or black, Union or Confederate. By the spring of 1865, there was no longer a government in the South which could make good its authority beyond the occupying Yankee Army garrisons. It was to meet this condition, in a measure, that Union General Sherman and Confederate General Johnston proposed the immediate restoration of the old state governments, upon taking the oath of future allegiance.[365] However, the Radical Republicans in Congress rejected such reasonable plans because such plans did not further their political and economic agenda.

Desolation and hopelessness were widespread among all classes of Southerners. Some efforts were made to reestablish stores and other businesses in destroyed Southern towns and cities. But all such efforts depended primarily on speculators from the North. Northern speculators were a key part of the North's commercial exploitation of the conquered South. White and black Southerners were virtually cashless—they were forced to depend upon "outside" sources for investment capital.[366] A returning Confederate veteran

---

363   Ibid., 22.
364   Kennedy & Kennedy, *Jefferson Davis: Highroad to Emancipation and Constitutional Government* (Columbia, SC: Shotwell Publishing, 2022), 5-14.
365   Henry, Robert Selph, *The Story of Reconstruction*, 22.
366   Kennedy & Kennedy, *Punished With Poverty-The Suffering South* 2nd ed., 107-10.

and owner of a large plantation in Mississippi found only a few mules and one cow when he finally made it back home.[367] The Northern political elites were remaking the South. They were turning the South into their political and economic colony ruled by Northern elites. The North forced a change from Southern chattel slavery to Southern political slavery and, soon to be added, a new form of slavery under the system of sharecropping. Sharecropping would bind large numbers of black and white Southerners for generations.[368]

It was routine for returning veterans to find houses of the most prosperous planters denuded of almost every article of furniture, and, in some parts of the South, women and children accustomed to luxury were seen begging from door to door.[369] In 1865, over 500,000 Southerners in Alabama, Georgia, and Mississippi were without the basic necessities of life (food, water, clothing, and shelter), and many died of starvation or diseases that overwhelmed their malnourished bodies.[370]

The lawlessness that reigned during Lincoln's illegitimate invasion and the Republican Party's Active Reconstruction is something that Yankee propagandists attempt to ignore, minimize, or distract by blaming "racist" Southerners for the lawlessness. The men of the South were in constant apprehension for not only their safety but for the safety of their wives, families, and what little private property was left to them after the visit of Yankee "Bummers." General Andrews Garnett described his anxiety, "I have never suffered such an amount of anguish and alarm in all my

---

367 Bowers, Claude, *The Tragic Era*, 46-7.

368 Kennedy & Kennedy, *Punished With Poverty*.

369 Bowers, Claude, *The Tragic Era*, 46.

370 Fleming, Walter Lynwood, *The Sequel of Appomattox* (1919, Yale University Press, 1970), 14.

life... I expected, and honestly anticipated, and thought it highly probable, that I might be assassinated, and my house set on fire at any time."[371]

The civil liberty of white Southerners was completely at the mercy of the occupying Yankee military—white Southerners had no rights the North was required to honor. As far as the occupying Yankee military and their scallywag/carpetbag co-conspirators were concerned, all "rebels" were actively plotting against the new Federal Government (the Yankee Empire). Yankee officials occupying the South would often allege that if a white Southerner was sober and meditating, he was planning treason, and if he was smiling, he was guilty of committing some undisclosed form of treason. For example, a Southern editor who jokingly wrote an amusing editorial about taking the required "loyalty oath" was condemned by the local military commander, arrested, charged with a high crime, his office seized, and the newspaper suppressed. Another white Southerner who was required to take the loyalty oath (something Confederate soldiers referred to as "swallowing the dog") made a joke and asked if his dog was also required to take the oath. He was arrested and thrown into jail.[372]

The white South lived in a state of constant fear in the early years of the Republican Party-imposed Active Reconstruction. An Englishman, Robert Somers, who visited the South during the beginning of Reconstruction, noted the large number of outside "agitators of the loosest type" that descended upon the South. He observed that these outsiders were "in all circumstances anti-social and destructive," and their efforts produced "a real reign of terror among the whites."[373] An English lady living in Georgia noticed the change in the attitudes of her hired black servants after the Union League was organized in her community. She acknowledged that,

---

[371] General Garnett Andrews cited in Fleming, Walter Lynwood, *The Sequel of Appomattox*, 278. Fleming labels Andrews as "General" but he is not found in authoritative listings of Confederate Generals. Perhaps it was a state militia or an honorary title.

[372] Bowers, Claude, *The Tragic Era*, 52. The author cites the *Macon Journal*.

[373] Bowers, Claude, *The Tragic Era*, 308. The author cites Somers, Robert, *The Southern States Since the War*, published in London, England, 1871.

throughout 1869, she never slept at night without a loaded pistol under her pillow.[374]

Worldwide, it is a common occurrence for some form of active and/or passive resistance to arise when a formerly free people are forced to accept a foreign power's illegitimate and oppressive rule. This is a natural human reaction, an action based upon one of man's most primitive motives—the struggle for survival. In the post-War South, an underground and, of necessity, a secret resistance to Yankee occupation emerged. It should be noted that the Southern resistance movement was directed at the Yankee Empire's occupation and oppression, not toward black Southerners. Black Southerners became the cannon fodder of the scallywag/carpetbag Republican regimes in the occupied South. The Republican Party exploited blacks during Active Reconstruction and then abandoned them when they were no longer useful to the Republican Party.[375] Similarly, the modern Democrat Party exploits blacks today during post-1965 Modern Era Reconstruction.

REPUBLICAN CONTROLLED RECONSTRUCTION SOUTHERN LEGISLATURES

Charles Nordhoff gave an insightful account of the Louisiana legislature under Republican control. Nordhoff was born in Erwitte, Germany (then Prussia), moved with his family to America and was educated in Cincinnati, Ohio. From 1861 to 1871, he was a journalist for several Northern papers, including the *New York Evening Post* and the New York *Tribune*. His observations are in line with conservative Southerners whose commentary is often discounted by postmodern "scholars" for the simple reason that they are Southerners. Upon viewing Louisiana's Republican Party-controlled Reconstruction legislature, he was amazed "not because they were black, but because they were transparently

---

374 Bowers, Claude, *The Tragic Era*, 308. The author cites Leigh, Frances Butler, *Ten Years on a Georgia Plantation*, published in London, England, 1883.

375 Johnson, Dr. Ludwell H., *The North Against the South: The American Iliad 1848-1877* (1978, Columbia, SC: The Foundation for American Education, 1993), 206, 267.

ignorant and unfit."[376] These ignorant and unfit "lawmakers," under the control of Republican scallywags and carpetbaggers and enforced by Yankee bayonets, were the political masters of black and white conservatives in Louisiana. Such scenes occurred not only in Louisiana but across the occupied South.

The breakdown in law and order was a direct result of the destruction of "normal" Southern civil governments and their replacement with Republican-controlled state governments. Scenes in the Republican Party-controlled Reconstruction Constitutional Conventions in Florida, Mississippi, and Virginia were typical across the South—some worse than others. In Florida, illiterate, newly freed black state legislators shouted, "pint ob orter" and loudly complained that "de pages and messgers" failed to put some "jinal" (papers?) on the desks, while other members smoked cigars with their feet on their desk; in Mississippi, pistols and knives were as necessary as "jinals," and there were frequent physical fights; in Virginia, arguments were frequently settled via fists fights. In the Republican-led Southern State Constitutional Conventions, the delegates, who had little land or property and therefore little or no taxes to pay (they had no skin in the taxation game), were spending money—the taxpayers' money—like drunken sailors[377] (with apologies to all sailors). Those with little or no "skin in the taxation game" were the ones setting the tax rates on the impoverished white and black population.

The oppressive social and political conditions throughout the South compelled white conservatives to join or support the resistance movement. Bowers gives an example of the conditions in Vicksburg, Mississippi, during Republican Reconstruction:

> With enormous taxes, mounting debts, and brazen stealing, the chancery clerk was refusing citizens ac-

---

376 Bowers, Claude, *The Tragic Era*, 437. The author cites Nordhoff, Charles, *The Cotton States in the Spring and Summer of 1875*, New York, 1875, 49.

377 Bowers, Claude, *The Tragic Era*, 217. The author cites Wallace, John, 1888, *Carpetbag Rule in Florida* 54, 56, and Eckenrode, H.J., *A Political History of Virginia During Reconstruction*, 1904, 97.

cess to his books, court clerks putting out fraudulent witness certificates and county warrants; and with tax-collecting time at hand, it was found that the bond of Peter Crosby, sheriff and tax-collector was defective....Ten taxpayers, led by a captain in the Union Army, were instructed, in a mass meeting, to call on the officials at the court-house and demand their resignations.[378]

Such circumstances were the rule, not the exception, across the Reconstruction South. In Mississippi, the tax assessments in 1871 were four times larger than in 1869; eight times greater in 1872; twelve and a half times greater in 1873; and fourteen times greater in 1874. In Greenville, Mississippi, 80% of the town was offered for sale to cover unpaid taxes! In one month in Mississippi, over 500,000 acres were put on the Sheriff's tax auction due to unpaid taxes.[379]

If similar social and political conditions were forced upon the people of Massachusetts or any other Yankee state, would the people of these fine Yankee States meekly accept it? If they were denied a just and lawful political system of their choosing, would they docilely accept their political enslavement? If a people of an alien culture came into their States and overpowered the military forces of their state, would they meekly accept the resulting dysfunctional political and social system imposed upon them by the invaders? No, of course not! But somehow, it is held up as evil when the people of the South reacted and formed a resistance movement against the post-War Federally enforced tyranny. No, as all freedom-loving people would react, the people of the South resisted. And for that resistance, the Yankee Empire's propagandists attempt to shame conservative Southerners and silence (censor) any attempt to tell "the other side of the story."

---

[378] Bowers, Claude, *The Tragic Era*, 450.

[379] Bowers, Claude, *The Tragic Era*, 452. The author cites McNeilly, J.S., *Climax and Collapse of Reconstruction in Mississippi*, Vol. xii of the Publications of the Mississippi Historical Society, 338-40, 334.

Northern Attitude Toward Its Newly Conquered Southern Territories

According to the *New York World,* on May 13, 1865, during a meeting at Cooper Union in New York, a speaker declared that Southerners were rebels guilty of treason and "the punishment for treason is death...."[380] The crowd of Northerners roared their approval. The speaker, Theodore Tilton, declared that they should hang Jefferson Davis and, to the cheering crowd, announced his special form of bigotry by declaring that negros are better voters than white Irishmen. Obviously, the Republican Party was shifting the argument over what type of Reconstruction policy the nation should follow: President Johnson's relatively conciliatory efforts to follow Lincoln's Ten Percent Reconstruction Plan or the Congressional Republican policy of radical and oppressive Reconstruction. Volumes of anti-South propaganda began pouring out from Republican-affiliated media and speakers such as Tilton. When President Johnson made his North Carolina Proclamation, in which he affirmed he intended to follow Lincoln's Ten Percent Reconstruction Plan, the Radical Republicans immediately demonstrated their hatred for the new President. President Johnson's conciliatory North Carolina Proclamation opened the floodgates of Radical Republican hatred directed against Lincoln's successor. Vicious and virtually unanswered slander against the new President (Andrew Johnson) and the powerless South would be the primary weapon used by the Republican Party in their eventually successful efforts to control Reconstruction.

Thaddeus Stevens (R-Pennsylvania), the great nemesis of the South and enemy of the Founding Fathers' Constitution, in a speech in Lancaster, proudly proclaimed his intentions. The tone and tenor of his speech was tyrannical. In essence, he declared that the people of the South should be treated as conquered alien enemies. Under the rules of imperial conquest, then, their property could be confiscated, and, as non-citizens of the United States, the conquered people of the South had no civil rights that

---

[380] Bowers, Claude, *The Tragic Era,* 11. The author cites *New York World,* May 13, 1865.

the Yankee needed to respect—*Vae Victis*.[381] He admitted that the Southern States had "severed from the Union and had been an independent government *de facto*." And as an alien enemy, the South was treated as a conquered province. He asserted his desire to see the "very foundations of their institutions ...broken up and replaced.... But by treating them as an outsider, conquered people, they can be refused admission to the Union unless they voluntarily *do what we demand.*"[382] Can a people who are forced at the point of bloody bayonets to submit to their conquerors be said to have "voluntarily done as we demand?" The emphasis being on the word "voluntarily." This is a thumbnail sketch of Active Reconstruction imposed upon "We the People" of the South by the Republican Party. Lincoln and the Republican Party denied "We the People" of the South the right of self-government. They denied Southerners the right pronounced in the Declaration of Independence to remove themselves from a bad government (the anti-South Northern-controlled Union) and establish a new government (the Confederate States of America) based upon the free and unfettered "consent of the governed." Without self-government, "We the People" of the South became (and remain) subjects of the Yankee Empire. Post-War, Southerners became political slaves in the country their ancestors helped to establish.

The push by Thaddeus Stevens and other Republicans for confiscating Southern property was seen by Northern Democrats, such as the Democratic *New Your World*, as a scheme to control the defeated South for political purposes. "The real leaders...see that unless the South can be trodden down and kept underfoot for long years, or unless they can give the negroes the ballot, and control it in their hands, their present political supremacy is gone forever.[383] In reviewing the words and actions of leaders and spokesmen of the North during Active Reconstruction, it is difficult at times to

---

381 *Vae Victis* the unofficial motto of the Roman Empire: *Woe to the vanquished*; those conquered should not ask and will not receive mercy. Such was the tyranny unleashed upon the Southern people by the Republican Party.

382 Bowers, Claude, *The Tragic Era*, 18. The author cites Stevens's speech reported in the *Lancaster Intelligencer*, September 13, 1865.

383 Bowers, Claude, *The Tragic Era*, 20.

determine if they were motivated more by a desire for political power or pure hatred for the people of the South. Yankee abolitionist Wendell Phillips never ceased in his hatred of the South. When efforts were made in the 1875 House of Representatives to pass an amnesty bill (approximately a decade after Appomattox!), Phillips denounced the trend toward reconciliation. He sent a note to a Republican who spoke against the spirit of reconciliation, thanking him for "the check you have given to this ridiculous gush which threatens to wash away half the hallmarks of the war."[384]

ONCE FREE PEOPLE OF THE SOUTH RULED BY REPUBLICAN TYRANNY AND BARBARISM

Charles Nordhoff toured Mississippi during the last days of Governor Ames's carpetbag rule. Nordhoff described Ames's associates: "his personal adherents are among the worst public thieves.... He has corrupted the courts, has protected criminals, and has played even with the lives of the blacks in a manner that, if this fall a good Legislature should be elected, ought to procure his impeachment and removal."[385] Mississippi was not unique. Every Southern State suffered under the rule of the Republican Party in Congress and the Republican Party's co-conspirators in the South. Even the outspoken abolitionist Horace Greeley recognized the Republican Party's efforts to exploit the uneducated and mostly illiterate freedmen. He accused carpetbaggers of preying on the credulity (gullibility or naivety) of the negroes.[386]

The once free people of the South—a people whose ancestors signed the Joint Declaration of Independence in 1776—would now be compelled by the Federal Government to accept bayonet constitutions at the state and federal levels. These bayonet constitutions were imposed by military force. They were and

---

384   Ibid., 464. The author cites Gail Hamilton, *Biography of James G. Blaine*, Norwich, 1895, 381.

385   Bowers, Claude, *The Tragic Era*, 457. The author cites Nordhoff, Charles, *The Cotton States in the Spring and Summer of 1875*, New York, 1875, 79.

386   Bowers, Claude, *The Tragic Era*, 357. The author cites the *New York Tribune*, July 19 & August 14, 1871.

continue to be illegitimate constitutions enacted without the consent of the governed. Thaddeus Stevens and his fellow Radical Republicans were openly proud of it, while the more moderate Republicans simply "went along to get along." Efforts to "get along" in the current political *status quo* have been the Republican Party's counterfeit conservatives *modus operandi* ever since. These new bayonet constitutions would, in principle and practice, violate the Southern people's right—as declared in the Declaration of Independence—to live under a government based upon the free and unfettered consent of the governed. The Federally established Southern state *puppet governments* would see the South reduced to an economic colony of the North,[387] suffer an intentionally imposed impoverishment, malnutrition, diseases unheard of in the North, and 8,500,000 black and white Southerners trapped in sharecropping—a new form of slavery. "This is not only economic slavery but human slavery, just as bad, just as dark, and just as unjust as ever existed on any continent of this earth."[388] And a point that Yankee propagandists—especially postmodern historians—prefer to ignore is that sixty percent of sharecroppers were white. The War did not end slavery—it merely changed its form into one more advantageous for America's ruling elites.[389] All Southerners became, and remain, the Yankee Empire's political slaves—unfortunately, too many Southern "conservatives" have learned to love their "one nation indivisible" chains!

---

387 "The revolution wrought by the Civil War" "...unprocessed products were shipped away from the region to yield bigger returns from non-Southern processors...an intra-national colonialism which subordinated both people and resources to the bidding of outside capitalism and management." Clark & Kirwan, *The South Since Appomattox*, 92, 12.

388 Senator James Eastland cited in Kennedy & Kennedy, *Punished With Poverty*, 198.

389 *Ibid.*, 113-32, 209-34.

Reconstruction—
The Disastrous Environmental Impact

The Ivory-billed woodpecker, America's largest woodpecker, became a victim of post-War Southern poverty and malnutrition. The Ivory-Billed woodpecker is most likely extinct. Post-War it became one of the many natural sources of protein for poor Southern farmers. Its population was destroyed by over-hunting and the destruction of its habitat via the loss of the South's virgin forest. The South's virgin forest was cut down and sold to the North during the Northern economic boom known as the Gilded Age. Over farming the land by sharecroppers caused a major loss of topsoil due to erosion.

Chapter 11:

LINCOLN'S TEN PERCENT RECONSTRUCTION PLAN

"Lincoln in 1856 told a Southerner that if the South tried to secede 'we won't let you. With the purse and sword, the army and navy and treasury in our hands and at our command, you couldn't do it.'" —Dr. Ludwell H. Johnson[390]

LINCOLN ISSUED his "Proclamation of Amnesty and Reconstruction," better known as Lincoln's Ten Percent Reconstruction Plan, on December 8, 1863. His plan allowed a former Confederate state to reenter the Union when voters, representing at least 10% of the 1860 vote count in the state, took an oath of allegiance to the United States and accepted the immediate and uncompensated emancipation of all slaves within the state. The state's voters were then allowed to elect delegates to the state's constitutional convention and draft a new state constitution. All Confederates except high-ranking Confederate military officers and government officials were granted a full pardon and allowed to vote.

Arkansas, Louisiana, and Tennessee (or portions thereof) established a functioning pro-Union government by 1864. Like the Nazi Quisling government of Norway and the Vichy government of Nazi-controlled France, these so-called "state governments" represented the will of the invader and not the will of the people. Lincoln planned to have these rogue, puppet state governments

---

[390] Lincoln cited in Johnson, Ludwell H., *The North Against the South: The American Iliad 1848-1877* (1978, Columbia, SC: The Foundation for American Education, 1993), 76-7.

ready to vote Republican in the November 8, 1864, presidential election, where Lincoln faced a serious challenge from the pro-peace Democrat candidate General George B. McClellan. With Sherman's successful march on Atlanta and other Union victories, the new rogue States would guarantee a Republican victory in the 1864 election. Both Lincoln and the Republicans in Congress saw the rogue-restored Southern States as a key to maintaining Republican control of the national government. The Republicans and native Unionists—most of whom became Unionists late in the War—firmly held control in Lincoln's three "restored" Southern States.

Lincoln also wanted to add Florida to the list of States he could count on in the 1864 election. In February of 1864 Lincoln sent an invading Yankee Army into Florida. He counted on a quick victory, allowing the Yankees to occupy the state capitol at Tallahassee, set-up a puppet state government, and declare that Florida was "back in the Union." He knew that since his military would manage the vote, Florida's electoral votes would go to him. This would be the fourth invasion of Florida and was designed to bring the state into the Union under the leadership of Lincoln's private secretary, who was sent to Florida to manage the political part of their invasion scheme. The Yankee invaders had around six thousand troops plus eighteen transport ships. The Confederate state of Florida was under the protection of General P.G.T. Beauregard, who sent approximately five thousand troops to defend the state. The battle was a resounding Confederate victory! In the first two hours, the Confederates pushed the enemy back and captured five artillery pieces. The invaders left 350 dead on the battlefield and abandoned a great number of their severely wounded. The Confederates lost eighty killed and 650 wounded. The *New York Herald* denounced the affair as something that grew out of "political jugglery," (manipulation or trickery especially to achieve a desired end) anticipating the upcoming US presidential election. The *Herald* branded the whole affair as a scheme by Lincoln to seize Florida's electoral votes and decried that "a thousand lives were lost in the attempt to get three electoral votes."³⁹¹ Lincoln's Florida expedition demonstrates the purely political nature of the man most Americans would select as America's best president. Lincoln destroyed the Union while proclaiming he was fighting to preserve the Union. He enslaved the white South while claiming to be fighting to limit or destroy slavery. He began Reconstruction using fraud and political corruption before the War was over. He knew he was destroying the civilization in the South but had no idea how to rebuild a new Southern society.

Lincoln was unsure how the South should be reconstructed and brought back into the Union, from which he and the Republican Party claimed they could not secede. "Nor is it a small additional embarrassment that we, the loyal people, differ among ourselves as to the mode, manner, and measure of reconstruction."³⁹² *Neither Lincoln's Ten Percent Reconstruction Plan nor the Republican Party's Congressional Reconstruction Plan had any expressed constitutional authority.* But as far as the Yankee Empire is concerned, "Might makes right," which is the only justification they needed for Reconstruction. This "might makes right" attitude was repeated numerous times during the post-War growth of the Yankee Empire. For instance, no constitutional authority existed for the Yankee Empire's 1893 invasion and occupation of the Kingdom of Hawaii, but "Might makes right." Queen Lili'uokalani of Hawaii denounced the new Constitution forced upon her Kingdom by the invading Yankees as a "bayonet" Constitution. Lincoln began forcing "bayonet" constitutions upon the once free people of the South, and the post-War Yankee Empire continued his tyrannical tradition.³⁹³

---

391   Kennedy, James Ronald, *Uncle Seth Fought the Yankees* (Gretna, LA: Pelican Publishing Co., 2015), 270-3. There was also a strategic military component to the invasion. The Union wanted to block Florida's large contribution of cattle from going to the Confederate Army.

392   Lincoln cited in Henry, Robert Selph, *The Story of Reconstruction* (New York: Konecky & Konecky, 1938), 8.

393   Kennedy & Kennedy, *Yankee Empire: Aggressive Abroad and Despotic at Home* (Columbia, SC: Shotwell Publishing, 2018), 51-73.

Lincoln's Ten Percent Reconstruction Plan Faced Radical Republican Opposition

Lincoln's Ten Percent Reconstruction Plan was an effort aimed at the restoration of conquered Southern States as Republican members of the *new Union*.[394] The Radical Republican's Reconstruction Plan was a scheme aimed at removing power from the States and centralizing power in the Federal Government that would henceforth be under the control of Northern ruling elites. Throughout the closing years of the War, the Republican-controlled Congress actively attempted to assert its control over the War and especially the post-War "Reconstruction" era. This conflict became obvious after Lincoln's assassination and the open political warfare between Lincoln's successor, President Andrew Johnson, and the Republican-controlled Congress. The struggle over controlling how Reconstruction would be administered became a vicious political struggle that the Republican-controlled Congress would eventually win. The Republican Party's goal was not only to win the War but to ensure continued Republican Party control of the United States' new and supreme Federal Government.

The Republican Party became anxious for its political future when it saw pre-War Union men sent to Congress by the post-War conservative South. They foresaw the possible combining of old-line Southern Unionists (many were former Whigs) with National Democrats. Such a combination would spell an end to the Republican Party's control of Congress and its vision of a greater American Empire controlled by Republican friendly Northern ruling elites. Republicans in Congress and their military in the occupied South began their efforts to sabotage Lincoln's Ten Percent Reconstruction Plan and the provisional Southern state governments established under Lincoln's Plan. They aimed to convince the Northern population that Lincoln's Plan was not sufficient and needed to be replaced with a more radical form of

---

[394] "New Union" because the US government that came after the War and Reconstruction was no longer the government outlined by the Founding Fathers and given its authority when ratified by the Sovereign States under the original Constitution. A coup d'état occurred in which the original constitutionally limited Republic of Sovereign States was replaced with an all-powerful, supreme Federal Government controlled by Northern ruling elites.

Reconstruction—a vindictive and punitive Reconstruction plan designed and controlled by a Republican-dominated Congress.

The Ten Percent Plan state governments also had difficulty maintaining law and order. The state governments' authority was permitted only until it was challenged by the military governor (dictator) assigned to the state. It became a common practice for criminals caught by the provisional state authorities to claim that they, the criminals, were being discriminated against by the state because they, the criminals, had a history of being loyal Unionist citizens. Thus, the case was removed from state jurisdiction to the occupying military jurisdiction and usually dismissed.

By the time the second session of the Thirty-ninth Congress (December 2, 1866, to March 3, 1867) assembled, Radical Republicans not only controlled the Republican Party but Congress as well. Southern States' representatives, who were unwilling to act as puppet representatives, were excluded from Congress. During the closing days of the War, Congress struggled with Lincoln over his Ten Percent Reconstruction Plan and the President's right to control Reconstruction. But thanks to the efforts of Radical propagandists in the mainline media, President Andrew Johnson's prestige suffered major blows. President Johnson's authority was in doubt. With the success of Radical Republicans in the 1866 Congressional elections, President Johnson was reduced to a figurehead when it came to matters touching on Reconstruction. Representative Shelby Moore Cullom (R-Illinois) clearly stated the intentions of the North: "The people of the rebel States by their pretended legislatures [conservative Southern State legislatures elected under Lincoln's Ten Percent Reconstruction Plan] are treating it [the proposed Fourteenth Amendment] with scorn and contempt…. It is time, sir, that the people of the [Southern] States were informed in language not to be misunderstood that the people who saved this country are going to reconstruct it in their own way, the opposition of rebels to the contrary notwithstanding."[395] Note his admission that the Republicans intended to reconstruct the

---

395 Rep. Cullom cited in Henry, Robert Selph, *The Story of* Reconstruction, 1938), 209.

country in a manner that would please the North. Senator Charles Sumner (R-MA) pronounced the people of the occupied Southern States as "hostile populations."[396] The South, which in 1861 asked only to be left alone, was once again under attack from Northern extremists. The Federal Government gave its full support to these extremists who were viciously attacking the South. This same Federal Government continues to use its slanderous attack against the South during Modern Era Reconstruction. In America's political *status quo*—nothing changes.

The Republican Party understood that its control of Congress relied upon preventing the election of Southern conservative Democrats and their eventual taking their seats in Congress. They knew a combination of National Democrats and Southern Democrats would out vote the Republican Party in Congress and thereby reduce the Republican Party to an insignificant minor party with a doubtful future in a post-War *reconciled* America. Republicans understood that there was little chance that white conservative Southerners who held a small government States' Rights view of the Constitution would vote *en masse* for Republican candidates. The only alternative for the Republicans was to disfranchise a large portion of white conservative Southerners while enfranchising the newly freed and mostly illiterate slaves. Republicans were pushing black voting rights in the South while these same rights for blacks in the North were minimal if not totally denied. For those Northern States that allowed blacks to vote, significant restrictions, such as education and property ownership, limited black voting rights. In those Northern States, the number of black voters was so small that it would have little, if any, impact on election results. This was not the case in the South. But this Yankee hypocrisy and insistence on illiterate and barbaric rule in the South made little moral or ethical impact on a Republican Party eager for unlimited control of *their* Federal Government.

The Republican Party in Congress refused to seat Southern representatives and senators elected under Lincoln's Ten Percent

---

396 Henry, Robert Selph, *The Story of Reconstruction*, 209.

Reconstruction Plan. These men held certificates of election from provisional state governments already recognized by the executive branch of the government and Congress when it accepted these States ratification of the Thirteenth Amendment.

The Republican-controlled Congress refused to seat even the loyal Unionists elected from the Southern States under the Ten Percent Plan. Horace Maynard, a longtime resident of Tennessee, was elected to represent Tennessee. He was a native of Massachusetts, a graduate of Amherst, who maintained his avowed loyalty to the Union during the war. In wartime, he served in the United States Congress representing occupied Tennessee. Yet, he was now unacceptable to the Republicans in Congress because he came from the South! The whole sham makes a mockery of the idea of "Liberty and Justice for all." Liberty and justice for all except Southerners yesterday and today!

Under President Johnson's executive direction, by December of 1865 the Southern States, except Texas and Florida, whose reentry work was almost complete, were recognized. Johnson described the population of these States as "yielding obedience to the laws and government of the United States with more willingness and greater promptitude than, under all the circumstances, could reasonably have been anticipated."[397] These neophyte States organized a government under Lincoln's Ten Percent Reconstruction Plan and, as States, ratified the Thirteenth Amendment to the United States Constitution. These States were implicitly recognized by the Republican-controlled Federal Congress when Congress accepted their acts of ratification and counted the Southern States in the number required for the passage of the Thirteenth Amendment outlawing slavery in the United States.

In the fall election of 1866, Kentucky voted overwhelmingly for the Democrats and against the Republicans. The act of engaging in the democratic process of electing state leaders, in which Democrats were elected, was falsely interpreted by the Northern media and Radical Republican politicians as evidence proving that

---

[397] Ibid., 139.

the South was still in rebellion. The Cincinnati *Gazette* bemoaned the fact that it appeared that the "rebel gray has whipped the Union blue at the polls."[398] The outcome was similar in Arkansas, where most elected offices were won by conservative Union men. Arkansas Scallywag Governor Murphy, to generate support for maintaining Federal military occupation in Arkansas, warned his fellows in the North that "Union men were being hunted down and shot by rebels."[399] He offered no evidence, but the emotional allegations were all that was needed. Truth, facts, and evidence are unimportant in America's mass democracy.

While Southerners, operating under Lincoln's Ten Percent Reconstruction Plan, were electing loyal, conservative Union men, the North was busy electing Radical Republicans. Maine voted by a large majority to enter the Radical Republican camp, as did New York, Pennsylvania, Ohio, and Indiana. After the elections in the fall of 1866 the prospects for local self-government in the South were bleak. The Radical Republican Party became and remains today the Republican Party. By March of 1867 the new Congress consisted of one hundred and forty-three Republicans and forty-nine Democrats. In the Senate, the Republican Party held control by a margin of forty-two Republicans to eleven Democrats. South-hating Republicans held a veto-proof House and Senate.[400] It was a Congress dedicated to the destruction of America's original Constitution and the extermination of the South's political power in the United States. Henceforth, Southern representatives would be the humble servants of the new political *status quo*—an all-powerful supreme Federal Government and its bureaucratic "Deep State." Many hot speeches would be made for home consumption, but the South's political leadership would never again rise to question the legitimacy of the Yankee Empire and its political *status quo*. Henceforth, States' Rights became nothing more than privileges an all-powerful, indivisible,

---

398 *Ibid.*, 197.

399 *Ibid.*, 197.

400 *Ibid.*, 198.

Federal Government might *allow* "We the People" of the States to exercise. Post-War, States' Rights became States' privileges.

Operating under Lincoln's Ten Percent Reconstruction Plan, the Arkansas state legislature authorized ten percent of the state's tax revenue for "the relief of the destitute, wounded, or disabled soldiers not otherwise provided for." The state also set aside another $10,000.00 to purchase artificial limbs for Arkansas' wounded veterans. In Mississippi, its legislature set aside 20% of its budget for the purchase of artificial arms and legs. Arkansas's Governor Murphy even recommended a tax reduction. This indicates what could have been if the Southern States were allowed to develop under Lincoln's less radical Ten Percent Reconstruction Plan.[401] However, the Southern States refused to participate in the ultimate destruction of the original Constitution by giving their ratification (consent) to the Republican's Fourteenth Amendment. This Southern refusal was the warning bell signaling a full-court press by the Republican Party to exterminate Southern political power. Republican and future president James A. Garfield surmised the attitude of his fellow Republicans upon learning of the South's rejection of the Fourteenth Amendment as "...with contempt and scorn (they) flung back into our teeth the magnanimous offer of a generous nation. It is now time to act."[402] And act they did!

President Andrew Johnson vs the Republican Party's Congress

President Johnson trod a fine line to complete Lincoln's Ten Percent Reconstruction Plan. As a native of the South (Tennessee), he realized the importance of instituting a more conciliatory Reconstruction policy. Radical Republicans were troubled about the sympathetic tone the new president took toward the South. But others were more reasonable. The *New York World* declared that Johnson's efforts would make him a historic figure due to his attempt to "strictly adhere to the letter and spirit of the

---

401 Ibid., 205.

402 Garfield cited in Henry, Robert Selph, *The Story of Reconstruction*, 207.

Constitution and by a wise and conciliatory course toward the masses of the Southern people."[403] Republicans understood that such conciliatory considerations toward the South would result in the return to Washington of numerous conservative Southern Democrat Representatives, Senators, and eventually, during the Presidential election, conservative electoral votes. To prevent that from happening, the Republican Party played its trump-card—the race-card. The Republican Party, the founding party of the Yankee Empire, used slander (the bloody shirt) to set in motion the age-old technique of empires—Divide-and-Rule the conquered population.[404] Their political strategy was to turn the white and black populations into political enemies (divide) and use the black population as a manipulatable bloc of Republican votes (rule). Henceforth, elections would be decided on racial fear and hatred with no room for compromise and mutual respect. Exploiting black voters today is commonly used by the Democratic Party, but it was the Republican Party that began this practice.

When President Johnson made his North Carolina Proclamation, in which he affirmed that he intended to follow Lincoln's Ten Percent Reconstruction Plan, Radical Republicans immediately exposed their hatred for the new President. President Johnson's conciliatory North Carolina Proclamation opened the floodgates of Radical Republican hatred directed against Lincoln's successor. Vicious and virtually unanswered slander against the new President and the powerless South was the primary weapon used by the Republican Party in their eventually successful efforts to seize control of Reconstruction.

Shortly after President Johnson took office, Congressional Republicans realized that the new President opposed Republican Reconstruction Plans. Although President Johnson opposed secession, he still held to the most rudimentary principles of the original Constitution. By 1865, the Radicals in the North rejected old-fashioned ideas, such as limited federalism and Sovereign

---

403   Bowers, Claude, *The Tragic Era*, 10. The author cites *New York World*, April 19, 1865.

404   Kennedy & Kennedy, *Yankee Empire*, 115, 124, 345.

States. The Northern public's mind embraced the Hamiltonian ideal of an all-powerful central government that would use its powers to advance Northern commercial and financial interests. President Johnson's veto of the Republican-sponsored Congressional Reconstruction Act exemplifies his effort to maintain the Constitutional authority of the Federal Government's executive branch. He was right on principle but wrong on his understanding of the ongoing, Republican-sponsored political revolution. He never realized he was in the middle of a political revolution, and revolutionaries make no compromises and take no prisoners. Admiral Raphael Semmes, CSN clearly understood what had happened to America. In the final words of his book penned in 1868, he declared, "But this is the second act of the drama, the first act of which was the secession of the Southern States. The form of government having been changed by the revolution, there are still other acts of the drama to be performed."[405] Unlike Admiral Semmes, President Johnson did not understand that,

> Old things had passed away, and new things had come to take their place. A violent, revolutionary faction had possessed itself of the once honored Government of the United States, and as is the case in all revolutions, coarse and vulgar men had risen to the surface, thrusting the more gentle classes into the background.[406]

Initially, President Johnson was a loyal Democrat and then Lincoln's VP nominee on the National Union Party in the 1864 election, but he was never a Republican. The Republican leadership in Congress targeted him because he refused to accept Radical principles. The House of Representatives created a special committee to find grounds to impeach the President. Representative James M. Ashley of Ohio chaired the Committee. Meanwhile, the House and Senate passed the Tenure of Office Act, designed to

---

[405] Semmes, Raphael, *Memoirs of Service Afloat* (1868, Secaucus, NJ: The Blue & Grey Press, 1987), 833.

[406] *Ibid.*, 335.

restrict the power of the President to remove certain appointed office-holders. The law was passed on March 2, 1867, and remained in force until 1887. President Johnson vetoed it, but his veto was overridden. Note the act remained in force during Active Reconstruction (1866-1877) but was no longer needed during Passive Reconstruction (1877-1965).

It would only be a matter of time before Johnson became the first American President to have his authority challenged and virtually destroyed by the act of partisan Congressional impeachment. But he would not be the last under America's new unconstitutional system of government. Weaponizing the Federal Government against domestic political enemies would become an art form in Modern Era Reconstruction (post-1965). Republicans in Modern Era Reconstruction may rightfully complain about "weaponizing the Federal Government," but it was the Republican Party that created this concept. As Shakespeare would say, the Republican Party was "hoisted with his own petard."[407]

Post-War, many Northerners viewed even local Democrats as traitors. Republican Lincoln and Democrat Andrew Johnson ran on the National Union Party[408] ticket to gain and maintain support for the war of Northern Democrats. The short-lived National Union Party supported Lincoln's restoration plan, much to the anger of Radical elements in the Republican Party. Southerners residing in States reorganized under Lincoln's Ten Percent Reconstruction Plan were enthusiastic in their support of President Johnson's effort to continue Lincoln's restoration efforts. The Southern enthusiasm hurt Johnson politically because Radical Republicans and their propagandists in the press told the Northern public that the Johnson administration was "pleasing

---

407 In the play *Hamlet*, Shakespeare used the term "Hoist with his own petard" to point out the irony of someone harmed by a device or plan meant for others but causing damage to himself. A bombmaker who is killed by his own bomb is an example of being "hoisted with his own petard." Ironic reversal or poetic justice.

408 The National Union Party was the name used by the Republican Party and elements of other parties for the national ticket in the 1864 presidential election during the Civil War. Most state Republican parties did not change their name. See "National Union Party" Wikipedia (wikipedia.org). wwwbit.ly/xNUParty.

to rebels and therefore, Johnson's efforts should be despised by all loyal Northerners.[409] Again, they demonstrated the impact that emotions have over facts in America's mass democracy. The fight against reconciliation began during the Lincoln administration and became dominant during Active Reconstruction. The effort to destroy North/South reconciliation continues via emotionally charged anti-South slander.[410]

The Republican-controlled Congress' hatred for Lincoln—because of his Ten Percent Reconstruction Plan—is demonstrated by the fact that, in June of 1870, a bill to provide a pension for Mrs. Lincoln was "shunted aside." The *New York Herald*, in its June 18, 1870, edition, declared this failure of Republican-controlled Congress to be "the most remarkable instance of petty malice ever evinced in any national legislature." Such was the evil mindset/attitude of the Republican-controlled Congress. Is there any wonder that they would be even harsher on "rebels" down South? But early in the Johnson administration, some still hoped for reconciliation between the North and the South. But the Radical Republicans had other ideas—ideas that sharply conflicted with Lincoln's Plan.

Under the Radical Republican's Reconstruction Plan, a Southern state could re-enter the Union only if the state government was elected by "loyal" men who took the *iron-clad oath affirming loyalty, past and future.* This would disfranchise virtually every white person in the South! The iron-clad oath looked to the past as well as to the future:

> I have never voluntarily borne arms against the United States...I have voluntarily given no aid, countenance, counsel or encouragement to persons engaged in armed hostility thereto; I have not yielded a voluntary support to any pretended government,

---

409 Henry, Robert Selph, *The Story of Reconstruction*, 182.

410 The Federal Government's destruction of the "Reconciliation Monument" in Arlington National Cemetery and its renaming of military bases named for Confederate heroes demonstrates that the Yankee Empire is not interested in reconciling North/South difference. Might makes right in the Yankee Empire—*Vae Victis*!

authority, power, or constitution within the United States, hostile or inimical thereto.[411]

The Lincoln Oath of December 8, 1863, looked to the future. Its most essential word was "henceforth." The Radical Davis-Wade iron-clad oath looked backward to the past. Under the plan voted by the Republican-controlled Congress, only those who could and would swear to the iron-clad oath could take part in the restored government of a state. Christian Roselius, German-born and Louisiana's outstanding authority on civil law was its most distinguished member of the Lincoln-ordained state government until he withdrew because of the iron-clad oath requirement.[412] The Republican Party was determined to deny the right to vote to most conservative whites as well as excluding the most intelligent and experienced members of the population from participating in state government. Many Southerners refused to swear allegiance to the new Union or ask for a "pardon" because they detested the idea of taking an oath to the government that denied them the right of self-determination. For example, Captain Levi Charles Harby, a Jewish Confederate from Galveston, Texas, died in 1870, "having never sought a pardon from the United States for his role in the war."[413] Joseph Benjamin, Judah P. Benjamin's brother, fled to Mexico and then to Spanish Honduras after the war. He was a Confederate veteran who refused to live under the new Union. When asked why he left the United States, he answered, "I wouldn't take the oath of allegiance to the United States."[414]

Mr. Lincoln pocket-vetoed the Davis-Wade bill and, on July 8, 1864, promptly issued a proclamation telling why. He declared that he did not intend to force the undoing of the start already made in Arkansas and Louisiana under his proclamation of the previous December.[415] Representatives Wade and Davis published

---

411   Henry, Robert Selph, *The Story of Reconstruction*, 10.

412   *Ibid.*, 40.

413   Rosen, Robert N., *The Jewish Confederates* (Columbia, SC: University of South Carolina Press, 2000), 141.

414   Evans, Eli N., *Judah P. Benjamin The Jewish Confederate*, 381.

415   Henry, Robert Selph, *The Story of Reconstruction*, 11.

their Manifesto denouncing Lincoln's pocket-veto. It was published in the New York *Tribune* on August 5, 1864. They charged that Mr. Lincoln was bent on holding the "electoral votes of the rebel States at the dictation of his personal ambitions."[416] After Lincoln's assassination, the revolt against the president's authority to control reconstruction became vicious.

While President Johnson and the Republican-controlled Congress engaged in a political struggle over who would control Reconstruction, other national political acts were playing out. The Senate, followed by the House, passed the Fourteenth Amendment on June 8, and 13,1866. The proposed amendment was then submitted to the States for ratification. The Constitution requires three-fourths of the States to ratify an amendment for it to be added to the US Constitution. The Constitution, in the same Article, also establishes "...that no State, without its Consent, shall be deprived of its equal Suffrage in the Senate."[417] This presented the Radical Republicans with a constitutional hurdle. In 1865, Republicans in Congress accepted and counted the ratification of the Thirteenth Amendment by Southern States organized under Lincoln's Ten Percent Reconstruction Plan.[418] Because only States can participate in the ratification of an amendment to the US Constitution, the Republican-controlled Congress' acceptance of the ratification by the Ten Percent States was a *de facto* acknowledgment that these States were, in fact, a legitimate member of their new Union. Yet, when it came to the Fourteenth Amendment and after the initial Southern States refused to ratify the Fourteenth Amendment, the Republican-controlled Congress *required* Southern States to

---

416 *Ibid.*, 11.

417 Article 5, US Constitution.

418 All Ten Percent Plan States except Mississippi. Mississippi refused to ratify, declaring that it was superfluous to do so because Mississippi's legislature already outlawed slavery within the state. While they were correct in principle, they did not comprehend the political situation they were in. The anti-South Radical press and politicians used Mississippi's refusal as an example of continuing rebellion down South. Northern emotional anti-South propaganda trumped firm constitutional principles. The more things change, the more they remain the same.

ratify the Fourteenth as a *prerequisite* for readmission to their Union.

The Republican-controlled Congress treated the Southern States as States within their Union for the ratification of the Thirteenth Amendment, but for the purpose of the Fourteenth Amendment, these same States were treated as mere conquered provinces of an empire. Their conquering masters ordered these occupied Southern non-state provinces to act as a state by ratifying the Fourteenth Amendment. These non-States were forcefully compelled to act as States while they were NOT a state, according to the Republican-controlled Congress. Only after performing the function of a state would the Republican-controlled Congress allow these conquered Southern provinces admission as a state in the newly created Republican Union. Republicans in Congress viewed the Ten Percent States as illegal bodies but not so illegal as to be prevented from voting for the Thirteenth Amendment. The South's initial rejection of the Fourteenth Amendment enraged the Republicans in Congress. Recall that the initial rejection by the Southern States of the Fourteenth Amendment was done by state legislatures organized under Lincoln's Ten Percent Reconstruction Plan.

It was generally felt by those pushing the Fourteenth Amendment that the Amendment's third section was "inserted for the expressed purpose of preventing the adoption...of any amendment." The Radical Republican plan was to make it appear that the Southern state governments organized under Lincoln's Ten Percent Reconstruction Plan were still in rebellion and refusing to yield to the national will. This would give Congressional Republicans the opportunity, or more exactly, an excuse, to take full control of their conquered Southern provinces.[419]

It soon became obvious that the Ten Percent Plan States would not voluntarily sign the death warrant of self-government as a Sovereign State by ratifying the Fourteenth Amendment. Even under military dictatorship, with their state government under the

---

419   Henry J. Raymond cited in Henry, Robert Selph, *The Story of Reconstruction*, 168.

point of Yankee bayonets, they refused to ratify and, by so doing, demonstrated that they preferred military dictatorship over state suicide. By rejecting the Fourteenth Amendment, Southern States declared to the world that they did not wish to be "re-made" at the hands of their Republican masters. By rejecting the Fourteenth Amendment, the Southern States defended the Union created by America's Founding Fathers. Defending the Union created by America's Founding Fathers was not something looked upon with favor by the Republican Party in 1866.

Unable to get their amendment ratified by the Ten Percent Plan States, Republicans in Congress on March 23, 1866, passed the first Supplemental Reconstruction Act, compelling the military commanders to carry out the work of Reconstruction within their districts without regard to local civil authorities. The vaunted ideal of "consent of the governed," so proudly proclaimed by the Founding Fathers in the Declaration of Independence, was unceremoniously replaced with the authoritarian practice of military dictatorship. Consent in the American government was replaced with compulsion. Their act was no big deal because Republicans in Congress were merely following Lincoln, who used force to deny the South's right to self-government. As President Jefferson Davis declared, "The alternative to secession is coercion."[420] An indispensable American political principle is that for a government to be legitimate, it must be based upon the free and unfettered consent of the governed. Silence obtained from a conquered people under the threat of bayonets is not legal consent. Silence and the passage of time do not bestow legitimacy upon a government formed without the consent of the governed. A government created via military or political force fails the test of consent and is, therefore, an illegitimate government regardless of how long it may exist. If Hitler's Third Reich had ruled occupied Europe for a thousand years, it would still have been an illegitimate government. The mere passage of time does not bestow legitimacy upon an illegitimate government.

---

420 Davis, Jefferson, *Rise and Fall of the Confederate Government*, Vol. 1 (1881, Nashville, TN: William Mayes Coats, c.1980), 177.

Southern States created under Lincoln's Ten Percent Plan became a "thorn in the side" of the Republican Party's leaders. The Republican leaders looked to their propagandists in the media to wave the "bloody shirt" and fill the Northern population with emotionally charged hatred for the Southern people. When the Mississippi legislature, a creature of Lincoln's Ten Percent Plan, passed laws like those in effect in Northern States regarding vagrancy, Northern politicians, the press, and the public rose to denounce such laws as an effort of white Southerners to re-enslave the freedmen.[421] The *Chicago Tribune* made it clear what they thought of Southern self-government: "The men of the North will convert...Mississippi into a frog pond before they will allow any such law to disgrace one foot of soil."[422] This widely heralded declaration is evidence that the North considered the very "soil" as well as the people of Dixie to be their personal property to do with as they pleased.

THE NATIONAL UNION PARTY—
THE FORLORN HOPE OF RECONCILIATION

Senator James R. Doolittle, a Republican from Wisconsin and a staunch supporter of Lincoln's Ten Percent Reconstruction Plan, issued a call for loyal Northern and Southern men to meet in a convention of the National Union Party in August 1866. They aimed to prepare for the upcoming elections. He wanted to ensure that men were elected who would be favorable to the readmission of loyal Southern States—organized according to the Ten Percent Plan. He labeled the attempt to keep loyal Southern States from rejoining the Union as another form of secession—one imposed on the South by Radicals in Congress, "no right anywhere to dissolve the Union...neither by secession nor exclusion....war measures should cease."[423]

---

[421] These same Northerners never denounced the actual re-enslavement of blacks and the enslavement of poor whites in sharecropping, yet they rose *en masse* to denounce Southern vagrancy laws as an effort to re-establish slavery. Such is the hypocrisy of Yankeedom!

[422] Bowers, Claude, *The Tragic Era*, 63; The author cites the *Chicago Tribune*, December 1, 1865.

[423] Doolittle cited in Henry, Robert Selph, *The Story of Reconstruction*, 182.

The call for a convention of the National Union Party did not include an announcement about the proposed Fourteenth Amendment. This caused great concern among Radical Republicans. They designed the Fourteenth Amendment with such harsh penalties against "rebels" that it was well understood that even the Ten Percent Plan States would not ratify the Fourteenth Amendment. That being the case, the Amendment may not muster enough state ratifications to pass. As such, it would prove to the emotionally charged Northern public that the white South was still in rebellion against the United States. This would allow the Republican Party and its propagandists to "Cry havoc and let slip the dogs of war."

President Johnson supported the efforts of the National Union Party, but his Cabinet did not. Three of the four Cabinet members resigned their posts in protest. Attorney General Speed, Postmaster General Dennison, and Secretary of the Interior Harlan left Johnson's Cabinet and joined with the Radical Republicans. Secretary of War and Radical Republican Stanton stayed in the Cabinet to serve as a Radical Republican spy and saboteur within President Johnson's Cabinet. Radical Republican propagandists in the Northern media slowly moved the Northern population into the Radical camp. Radical Republicans expertly positioned themselves for the eventual Republican Party's constitutional coup d'état.

Despite the nefarious efforts of Radical politicians and their propagandists in the media, there was still hope that national reconciliation and political harmony could be restored. Plans were made for the National Union Party's convention in August of 1866. The National Union Party was the party on which Lincoln (Republican) and Vice President Johnson (Democrat) were elected in 1864. It would be a convention of all Union Party members, consisting of Northern and Southern Democrats, who supported the Ten Percent Reconstruction Plan. Radical Republicans were excluded. Radical Republicans saw this as an imminent threat. It threatened not only their control of Congress, but it represented a threat to the survival of the Republican Party. They launched a campaign accusing President Johnson of planning to turn the United States government over to rebels and traitors. The conservatives countered that they were trying to admit every Southern State that, according to Senator James Dixon, "to its share in public legislation whenever it presents itself, not only in an attitude of loyalty and harmony but in the persons of representatives whose loyalty cannot be questioned under any constitutional or legal test."[424] But, typical of conservative thinking they could not comprehend the reality that they were dealing with a revolution, not a democratic process.

Moderate Northern Republicans and conservative Democrats from the North and the South never realized they were attempting the impossible. They tried to create a "democratic" government in a political system based upon war and utter disdain for constitutional principles on which the original Republic of Sovereign States was built. They were attempting to build a government based upon the firm foundation of the original Constitution but, thanks to Lincoln and the Radical Republicans, that old foundation was replaced with the quicksand of pragmatic radicalism. It was a structure doomed to tyranny from its beginning. It was destined to become the very type of government our Colonial and Confederate ancestors fought to prevent. It was the origins of Washington, DC's bureaucratic Leviathan and Deep State that "We the People" now suffer under in Modern Era Reconstruction.

The Republican Party destroyed efforts of the National Union Party to formalize North/South reconciliation. The Republican-controlled Congress passed the Reconstruction Act of March 2, 1867, over President Johnson's veto. Republicans in Congress and their lackeys in the South would create new Southern puppet States within the Yankee Empire's conquered and militarily occupied Southern territory. Republicans in Congress acted immediately before the Ten Percent Plan could be finalized and to prevent the people of the South from formalizing self-government under the Ten Percent Plan within their former "free, independent, and sovereign" States. Republican propagandists both in Congress and the Northern media worked vigorously to portray Southerners

---

424 Henry, Robert Selph, *The Story of Reconstruction*, 183.

as in a state of continuing rebellion against the "lawful" orders of the Federal Government. Their efforts to promote slanderous anti-South propaganda were merely a continuation of a long-established Yankee tradition of vilifying the South and her people.[425] Consequently, Lincoln's Ten Percent Reconstruction Plan died.

In July of 1861, shortly after the Yankee disaster at the First Battle of Manassas, the United States Congress declared that the war was being fought to "preserve the Union with all the dignity, equality, and rights of the several States unimpaired...."[426] The Republican Party's attitude after the war was radically different. No longer were the States of the South to be treated with "dignity, equality, and rights unimpaired." The States of the South were treated as conquered territory. The people of the South were treated as mere subjects of the Yankee Empire. Southern subjects could expect no rights other than those reluctantly extended to them by their conquerors—*Vae Victis*: Woe to the conquered. The conquered have no rights their master is required to respect.

The radical dichotomy between the Yankee Congress' stated claim for invading the South in 1861, as opposed to its actions in 1866, plainly demonstrates that preserving the original Union was not the primary motive for waging aggressive war against a sovereign nation, the Confederate States of America. The North's primary goal was and always had been, to create a centralized, all-powerful, *indivisible* Federal Government controlled by Northern ruling elites. The Northern elites would then have a free hand to exploit the resources and people of the South. Aggressive, genocidal war and Republican-managed Active Reconstruction were the primary tools used to complete their Hamiltonian plans for a glorious commercial empire—an America of "imperial glory."[427]

---

425 Kennedy & Kennedy, *Punished With Poverty* 2nd ed., 55-74.

426 Henry, Robert Selph, *The Story of Reconstruction*, 219.

427 Hamilton cited in DiLorenzo, Dr. Thomas J., *Hamilton's Curse* (New York: Crown Forum, 2008), 2, 129.

Chapter 12:

REPUBLICANS RECONSTRUCT THE CONSTITUTION—REPUBLIC TO EMPIRE

"The American people, North and South, went into the war as citizens of their respective States, they came out subjects of the United States."
—H.L. Mencken[428]

WHAT WAS THE PRIMARY AIM of Lincoln, the Republican Party, and their cronies who championed an aggressive war against their former countrymen?

> The war was not a war of slavery versus freedom; it was a war between those who preferred a federated nation to those who preferred a confederation of sovereign States. Slavery was the ink thrown into the pool to confuse the issue...it was necessary to make the Lincoln myth to cover the growing centralization which would make it possible for the trusts and corporations to gobble up the substance and liberties of the people.[429]

If slavery was the "ink thrown into the pool to confuse the issue," then the need for a powerful, centralized Federal Government to prevent evil, racist Southerners from harming the newly freed

---
428 Mencken, H.L., "The Birth of Order," *New York Herald Tribune*, February 8, 1931.
429 Lytle, Andrew Nelson, "The Lincoln Myth," *The Virginia Quarterly Review*, October 1931.

slaves was the "ink thrown into the pool" to confuse the issue of the creation of a new post-War Federal Government. This new all-powerful Federal Government is the Republican Party's handiwork. Republicans in the post-War Congress would create a new, centralized, all-powerful, supreme, and indivisible Federal Government while destroying the original, Constitutionally limited Republic of Sovereign States. Their political work would be done illegally and unconstitutionally. The Republican-controlled post-War Congress established the blueprint for all future Federal action against the once sovereign States—a fact conveniently ignored by modern-day, neo-conservative talk-show hosts. Thus, in Modern Era Reconstruction, when the people of California voted in a statewide ballot initiative to prohibit the use of taxpayer dollars to fund welfare for illegal aliens, the will of "We the People" meant nothing. The supreme Federal Government stepped in and overturned the will of the people of the once sovereign state.[430]

Active Reconstruction (1866-77) allowed the advocates of centralized federalism to complete their dream of a Federal Government that would do the bidding of the North's financial, commercial, and political elites. At first, as High Federalists, they began their efforts in 1787 and continued for the next 80 years before they finally overthrew the original constitutional limitations on the Federal Government's powers. Their efforts during Active Reconstruction produced a political coup d'état that overthrew the Founding Fathers' legitimate Federal Government and installed the Republican Party's new illegitimate system of oppressive Federalism. During Passive Reconstruction both national political parties embraced this new system of supreme Federalism. That embrace is as tight today as it was then, representing one of the South's major strategic failures.

The Federalist Party was the first political party to advocate for a strong, centralized Federal Government—a government that would have the power to correct, sanction, or discipline the States. John Jay, the first Chief Justice of the Federal Supreme Court,

---

430 "1994: California's Proposition 187", Library of Congress (loc.gov), n.d. (Accessed 17 September 2023). wwwbit.ly/x187prop

was a High Federalist. He "became a vocal advocate of a coercive, departmentalized federal government with vigorous executive and judicial branches."[431] Ironically, the Supreme Court held its first session in the New York Stock Exchange. Chief Justice Jay desired a strong Federal Court that could be used to exploit centralized power to compel the "supremacy of Federal law and to force state compliance."[432] He was a member of the Federalist Party, a political party that followed the ideas of High Federalist Alexander Hamilton.

Alexander Hamilton, one of the three writers of the *Federalist Papers*, was such a fervent believer in a strong, supreme Federal Government that his critics, including Thomas Jefferson, described Hamilton as a monarchist. Jefferson wrote that "Hamilton was not only a monarchist, but for a monarchy bottom on corruption."[433] During the Constitutional Convention on September 10, 1787, Hamilton "avowed himself a friend to a vigorous Government."[434]

Hamilton was the Godfather of the Federalist Party. The Federalist Party became so politically odious that in 1800, it was driven out of power at the expiration of John Adams's single term as president. But the dream of a supreme Federal Government did not die with the death of the Federalist Party. It lived on in the Whig Party. Whigs, like Hamilton and the Federalist Party, wanted to use the Federal Government to support business, commerce, and financial institutions via protective tariffs, national banks, and massive internal improvements. The followers of the defunct Federalist Party helped to form the Whig Party. Henry Clay was the chief proponent and ideological leader of the pro-protective tariff Whig Party. It is ironic that Lincoln's political idol, Henry Clay, was

---

431 *The Oxford Companion to the Supreme Court*, ed., Kermit L. Hall (New York: Oxford University Press, 1992), 446.

432 Ibid., 446-7.

433 Jefferson quoted by C.C. Burr in the Introduction of, Upshur, Abel P., *The Federal Government: Its True Nature and Character* (1868, Houston, TX: St. Thomas Press, 1977), v, 21.

434 Madison, James, *The Debates in the Federal Convention of 1787 Which Framed the Constitution of the United States of America* (New Jersey: The Lawbook Exchange, Union, 1999), 538.

a rich Southern slave-holder.[435] Influential members of the Whig Party, in addition to Henry Clay, included Daniel Webster, William Seward, John Quincy Adams, and Abraham Lincoln. Lincoln was elected to Congress as a Whig in 1846[436] and gave one of the eulogies at Clay's funeral.[437] The Whig Party included both slave owners and non-slave owners. In Louisiana, it was difficult for any candidate to win if the Whig Party opposed him.[438] However, with the rise of New England's radical abolitionists in the 1830s, it became difficult to hold together this alliance of slave owners and non-slave owners. Nat Turner's 1831 slave revolt and the resultant massacre of innocent whites in Virginia and the reported horrors of the Haitian slave revolt created, in most Southerners, a sense of fear and the perception of being betrayed by their "fellow" Americans in the North. This was especially true in the Deep South, where blacks made up as much as 50% of the population. When people are concerned about their survival, all other social issues fade into the background. As one modern scholar noted, "The slavery issue trumped all social, ethnic, and party creeds."[439] New England's radical abolitionists were the major roadblock to the South's attempt to travel the high road to emancipation.[440] New England's abolitionists were the major factor pushing the lower South toward secession—survival, not slavery, was the issue.

Eventually the Whig Party suffered the same fate as its predecessor, the Federalist Party. The Republican Party replaced the Whig Party. The founders of the Republican Party were determined to avoid repeating the mistakes made by the Federalists and Whigs. They were willing to use whatever methods were necessary

---

435   Kennedy, Walter D., *ReKilling Lincoln* (Gretna, La: Pelican Publishing Co., 2015), 59.

436   Office of the Illinois Secretary of State, (lsos.gov). (Accessed 29 July 2023).

437   Lincoln's Eulogy on Henry Clay (abrahamlincolnonline.org)_

438   Robertson, Henry O., *The Emergence of the Whig Party in Louisiana, 1828-1840* (Lafayette, LA: Centers for Louisiana Studies, 2007), 23-4.

439   Ibid., 43-5.

440   Kennedy & Kennedy, *Jefferson Davis: Highroad to Emancipation and Constitutional Government* (Columbia, SC: Shotwell Publishing, 2022), 5-14, and Kennedy & Kennedy, *Punished With Poverty*, 48-9.

to establish the dominance of a party dedicated to building a commercial/financial empire controlled by Northern elites. History, mostly hidden from the public by the Yankee Empire's censors, demonstrates that the new Republican Party was willing to use vicious slander, unconstitutional war, and dictatorial military rule against their Southern conservative opponents. But such immoral tactics gave the champions of a supreme Federal Government almost unlimited political power over "We the People" of the South and, eventually in Modern Era Reconstruction, all of America. As former Confederate Vice President Alexander Stephens declared after the War, "The Cause of the South is now the cause of all."[441]

Republicans Make War Against States' Rights

In 1867, Republican Congressman George W. Julian of Indiana declared his vision of Reconstruction and the government that would arise from Republican Reconstruction when he said, "What these regions [the defeated and occupied Southern States] need above all things is not an easy and quick return to their forfeited rights in the Union but government, the strong arm of power, outstretched from the central authority here in Washington."[442] Note his desire for "the strong arm of government" and all authority originating, not with "We the People" within our Sovereign States, but "the central authority here in Washington." The Republican Party put in motion the sinister political process that would eventually see the establishment of the military-industrial complex and the unelected, bureaucratic Deep State in Washington, DC. Eventually, Northern and Globalist ruling elites would control America to the detriment of "We the People," who are today disparagingly referred to as the bitter clingers and deplorables. Lincoln's War destroyed the spirit of America's legitimate Constitutional Republic, and the Republican Party's Active Reconstruction destroyed the very letter of America's legitimate Constitutional law.

---

441 Stephens, Alexander H., *The War Between the States* (1870, Harrisonburg, VA: Sprinkle Publications, 1994), Vol. II, 666.

442 Julian cited in DiLorenzo, Thomas J., *The Real Lincoln* (New York: Three Rivers Press, 2002), 162.

Radical Republican Robert G. Ingersoll, former Union Army Officer and outspoken agnostic, clearly stated the main reasons for the War when he declared, "The great stumbling block, the great obstruction in Lincoln's way and in the way of thousands, was the old doctrine of States' Rights."[443] Illinois wartime governor, Richard Yates boastfully proclaimed that:

> The war...has tended, more than any other event in the history of the country to militate against the Jeffersonian idea, that 'the best government is that which governs least.' The war has not only, of necessity, given more power to, but has led to a more intimate prevision of the government over every material interest of society.[444]

A former professor at Harvard University also noted the radical change in American government due to Lincoln's war:

> The civil war of '61 has made a great gulf between what happened before it in our century and what has happened since, or what is likely to happen hereafter. *It does not seem to me as if I were living in the country in which I was born,* or in which I received whatever I got of political education and principles.[445] [Emphasis added by author].

The words "It does not seem to me as if I were living in the country in which I was born" should be a wake-up call to all so-called Constitutional conservatives who continue to worship before Lincoln's icon. President Woodrow Wilson happily acknowledged the radical change Lincoln's war and the Republican Party's Active

---

443   Ingersoll cited in Kennedy & Kennedy, *Punished With Poverty-The Suffering South* 2nd ed., 4.

444   Yates cited in Hummel, Jeffrey Rogers, Emancipating Slaves, Enslaving Free Men (Peru, IL: Open Court Publishing Co., 1996), 332.

445   George Ticknor cited in Hummel, Jeffrey Rogers, Emancipating Slaves, Enslaving Free Men, 333.

Reconstruction produced. Before he was elected President and while a professor at Princeton University, he wrote, "The War between the States established ...this principle, that the federal government is, through its courts, the final judge of its own powers."[446] These three previous quotes demonstrate what any conservative "having ears to hear with and eyes to see with" should readily admit: The legitimate American Constitutional government was overthrown and replaced with an illegitimate government. A fundamental correction to this grievous and tyrannical usurpation of the original and legitimate Constitutional government will never be achieved until pacified conservatives (especially in the South) awaken from their slumber and demand a radical restoration of America's legitimate government. Unfortunately, too many have grown to love their "one nation indivisible" chains.

Modern-era leftist scholars agree that the strict construction of the Constitution—which depends upon real States' Rights—was "buried at Gettysburg and Appomattox."[447] In the original and, therefore, legitimate, American government, the Sovereign State stood as a barrier between "We the People" and an oppressive and potentially tyrannical Federal Government. This fact was (reluctantly) recognized by High Federalist Alexander Hamilton in *The Federalist Papers* Number 28 when he admitted:

> It may safely be received as an axiom in our political system, that the State governments will, in all possible contingencies, afford complete security against invasions of the public liberty by the national authority.

The necessity of and the Constitutional authority for the doctrine of States' Rights was declared by both High and Moderate Federalists in their arguments in favor of the ratification of the

---

446 Woodrow Wilson cited in DiLorenzo, Dr. Thomas J., *Hamilton's Curse* (New York: Crown Forum, 2008), 84.

447 Harold M. Hyman and William M. Wiecek cited in Bradford, M.E., *Original Intentions: On the making and ratification of the United States Constitution* (University of Georgia Press: 1993), 157, footnote 18.

proposed Constitution circa 1787. If Moderate and High Federalists had not taken such a stand, the States would have refused to ratify the Constitution. As modern-day scholar Dr. M.E. Bradford wrote, "a majority of the States would never have agreed to the meeting [the Constitutional Convention] had the idea of a total change been mentioned as its probable consequence."[448] These arguments favoring States' Rights were made in 1787-8 at the Constitutional Convention and the debates on ratification in the state conventions, well before the definitive defense of States' Rights was published in the Kentucky and Virginia Resolutions of 1798. Thomas Jefferson and James Madison authored these almost forgotten Resolutions of 1798. Why do you think postmodern, neo-Marxist "intellectuals" want us to forget about the Resolves of 1798?

The American political principle of States' Rights was the major barrier to the establishment of a federal banking system,[449] protective tariffs, and internal improvements that mainly benefited the North. But arguing dollars and cents is not as good of a political campaign tactic in America's mass democracy as using an emotional issue. The Republican Party seized upon the emotional issue of slavery and used it against those defending the Constitution and States' Rights. The Republican Party's victory on the battlefield gave them a golden opportunity to use their political power to reconstruct America's original, constitutionally limited Republic of Sovereign States and replace it with an all-powerful, supreme Federal Government. Recall that the Founding Fathers expressly and emphatically rejected a supreme Federal Government at the Constitutional Convention![450] The Republican Party's political attack on the original Constitution was based upon the forced enactment—as opposed to the constitutional process of voluntary, consensual ratification of Sovereign States—

---

448 *Ibid.*, 3.

449 Kilpatrick, James Jackson, The Sovereign States (Chicago: Henry Regnery Co., 1957), 144-58.

450 Bradford, M.E., Original Intentions, 6-7.

of several new amendments that would eviscerate the concept of real States' Rights.[451]

Modern-era Constitutional scholars freely admit that the enactment of the Fourteenth and Fifteenth Amendments, plus other Congressional Reconstruction enforcement legislation, was key to changing the original Constitution into its modern form. The "modern" form established an all-powerful Federal Government. One scholar noted that these "Constitutional amendment(s)... consolidated the North's victory."[452] America's legitimate Republic of Sovereign States was destroyed by a uniquely Yankee constitutional practice of might makes right. During the Progressive Era, the Federal Supreme Court, out of thin air and ideological passion for an all-powerful Federal Government, created the doctrine of "incorporation." This new constitutional theory allowed the Court to use the fraudulent Fourteenth Amendment to apply all the prohibitions against the Federal Government in the Bill of Rights to the once-sovereign States. According to some modern-era Constitutional scholars:

> The incorporation doctrine has a curious and controversial history. Until 1866 the rule, established by the Supreme Court in 1833 in the case of *Barron v. Baltimore*, was that guarantees of the federal Bill of Rights limited only the federal government, not the state governments.[453]

Note that this major change occurred after the forced, and therefore illegitimate, enactment of the Fourteenth Amendment—a bayonet amendment that created a bayonet Constitution. By the simple process of Judicial decree that began in earnest in 1937 *Palko v. Connecticut,* the Federal Government assumed complete

---

451   Real States' Rights includes the rights of State nullification and secession. Otherwise, States' Rights morphs into States' privileges exercised only when or if allowed by the supreme Federal Government.

452   Orth, John V., in *The Oxford Companion to the Supreme Court*, ed., Kermit L. Hall (New York: Oxford University Press, 361.

453   *Ibid.*, 181, 426.

control of what the Constitution meant and to whom its limitations would apply. Active Reconstruction created a federal tyrant that is now in charge of deciding what powers it will allow itself to exercise over "We the People."

In the textbook *Constitutional Law and Politics,* the author observed that it has become customary for the Supreme Court to "create out of whole constitutional cloth" rights they feel (note the emotional word "feel") necessary for society and then, using the Fourteenth Amendment, make these newly discovered "rights" "applicable to the States." The textbook author quoted Justice Black, who warned that whenever the Court's Justices substitute their own interpretative language for that of the Constitution, they threaten to become "a day-to-day constitutional convention."[454] The excesses now routinely practiced by the President, Congress, the Supreme Court, and unnumbered and virtually uncontrolled federal regulatory agencies and departments were made possible by enacting the Republican Party's Fourteenth and Fifteenth Amendments.

REPUBLICANS ENACT FRAUDULENT AMENDMENTS TO THE CONSTITUTION

David Lawrence (1888-1973) published a two-page editorial titled "The Worst Scandal In Our History" in the September 27, 1957, issue of the *US News and World Report.* He outlined the fraudulent methods used to enact the Fourteenth Amendment. He pointed out that the only way the post-War Republican Party could gain even the façade of ratification—and therefore the façade of legitimacy—was to:

> 1. Expel the South from Congress, which was a flagrant violation of Section V of the US Constitution, that guarantees that no state shall be denied representation in the Senate. Remember, these Ten Percent Lincoln Reconstruction Plan Southern States had already ratified the Thirteenth

---

[454] O'Brien, David M., *Constitutional Law and Politics* Vol. 2, 2nd ed, 308.

Amendment. The Republican-controlled Congress accepted and counted their ratification.

2. Illegally use military forces to occupy peaceful States that were recognized and functioning under Lincoln's Ten Percent Reconstruction Plan.

3. Disfranchise white "rebel" Southerners who had supported the Confederate States of America. This was a violation of the constitutional prohibition against *ex post facto* laws.

4. Declare that no Southern state would be allowed to take a seat in Congress until the state had ratified the Fourteenth Amendment. Forced consent is not legitimate consent in a free society.

5. Count as a vote for ratification the States of Ohio, New Jersey, and Oregon, which had reascended their ratifications upon learning about the methods used by the Republicans to gain their state's ratification.

David Lawrence wrote that the history of the forced "ratification" of the Fourteenth Amendment "is a disgrace to free government," but he reminded his readers (to no avail, unfortunately), "It is never too late to correct injustice."[455] The "injustice" forced upon the Southern people by the Republican Party during Active Reconstruction continues to have its evil impact upon conservative Southerners and all Americans today. The fraudulent way the Republican Party enacted the Fourteenth Amendment is justification to question the legitimacy of the current leftist political *status quo* created after Lincoln's war (1861-1865) and the Republican Party's Active Reconstruction (1866-77).

The post-War actions of the Republican-controlled Congress destroyed the concept of the state as an equal partner in the

---

455 See "New Jersey Rescinds Its Ratification of the Fourteenth Amendment," Addendum VI, and "Was The Fourteenth Amendment Constitutionally Adopted?" Addendum VIII in Kennedy & Kennedy, *The South Was Right!* 3rd ed. (Columbia, SC: Shotwell Publishing, 2020), 457,461.

Union originally created by the Sovereign States' ratification of the Constitution. Gone was the concept of a government in which authority arose voluntarily from the people and extended to their agent, the sovereign state. Gone was the concept of the sovereign States as the creators of the Federal Government and the Federal Government as the agent of the States. And for "We the People" of the South, gone was the concept of "government by the consent of the governed." "We the People" of the South became and remain the Yankee Empire's political slaves.

Republican Congressman Thaddeus Stevens (R-Pennsylvania) declared, "We shall treat the South as a defeated enemy." The Republican Party fulfilled this promise of Federal tyranny during Active Reconstruction. They used fraudulent, unconstitutional, and criminal methods to "enact" their Reconstruction Amendments to the Constitution. "Enact" as opposed to the Constitutional process of voluntary ratification by the Sovereign States.

When the Fourteenth Amendment was introduced, thirty-seven States were in the Union. These States, the Southern States were part of that number, ratified the Thirteenth Amendment ending slavery. But obtaining ratification of the Fourteenth Amendment was a problem for the Republicans. They needed the ratification of 28 States to ratify their Fourteenth Amendment. By mid-1867, the federal Secretary of State received official documents from the legislatures of thirty-three of the States giving their answer to the proposed Fourteenth Amendment. The result was a rejection of the Republican-sponsored Fourteenth Amendment. The vote total was as follows:

- States in the Union—37
- Votes needed to ratify the Amendment—28
- States voting to ratify the Amendment—22
- States voting to reject the Amendment—12
- States not voting—3

The Republican Party's effort to constitutionally ratify their Amendment was a failure! But if they could not pass it as required by the Constitution, then they would pass it by using more radical methods. After all, the Constitution did not stop Lincoln from waging an aggressive war upon the formerly free people of the South, and it certainly would not prove to be a barrier to the Republican Party in its efforts to reconstruct the original Constitution.

Republicans in Congress realized their attempt to secure passage by legal and constitutional methods failed. Thus, the letter of America's constitutional law survived its initial post-War assault. But Republicans in Congress were determined to complete the radical change in the American government they initiated. Frivolous technicalities, such as constitutional limitations, ethics, and morality, proved no obstacle in Lincoln's illegal invasion of a sovereign nation, the Confederate States of America, and such petty barriers would prove no obstacle in a Washington controlled by the Republican Party. To secure enactment of their Amendment, Republicans in Congress had to accomplish the following:

> 1. Deny the existence of all Southern States organized under Lincoln's Ten Percent Reconstruction Plan. They simply pretended those States never existed.

> 2. Declare the States that composed the Confederate States of America outside the former indivisible Union.

> 3. Deny majority rule in the Southern States by disfranchising most of the white Southern population.

> 4. Require these non-States to perform the function of a state by ratifying the Fourteenth Amendment. This was the price for getting back into the Union from which, heretofore, they were violently denied the right to secede.

They accomplished this by passing the Reconstruction Act of March 2, 1867. President Johnson vetoed the Act, but the Republican-controlled Congress overrode the President's veto. This was the Republican Party's final rejection of Lincoln's Ten Percent Reconstruction Plan. This and previous unethical Republican acts did not go unchallenged in Congress.

Representative Daniel W. Voorhees (D-IN) called to question the duplicity of Thaddeus Stevens and the Republican Party's "war to save the Union." In a speech in Congress on January 12, 1866, he declared that Representative Stevens's assertion that the Southern States were now conquered territory to be dealt with by the law of war and conquest meant that the claim of a war to save the Union was a lie. Voorhees blasted Stevens and this Republican theory. Voorhees warned, "It is a notice that the war to restore the Union was an utter failure—that the war is over, and yet the Union is rent in twain."[456] Historian Kenneth Stampp described Representative Voorhees as a man who had great:

> ...suspicion of the eastern Yankee, his [Voorhees] devotion to personal liberty, his defense of the Constitution and state rights faithfully reflected the views of his constituents.... He believed that whites temporary loss of total political control in places where they were not in the majority made them 'as very a slave in the hands of a brutal overseer as any negro ever driven in a cotton-field, and that he had no more power under existing laws to protect his personal freedom than an African bondsman on the auction-block before the war...the liberation of one race had been followed by the enslavement of another.[457]

The London *Times* recognized the Republican Party's tendency toward political slavery in their September 13, 1862, edition, "Republicans put empire above liberty, and resorted to political

---

456   Bowers, Claude, *The Tragic Era*, 96. The author cites the *Congressional Globe*, January 9, 1866.

457   "Daniel W. Voorhees," Wikipedia (Wikipedia.org) www.bit.ly/DanVoorhees (Accessed 10 May 2023) *(1897). Forty Years of Oratory: Daniel Wolsey Voorhees Lectures, Addresses and Speeches.* Bobbs-Merrill Company. (Accessed 27 January 2022).

oppression and war rather than suffer any abatement of national power... [national power] was upheld, like any other Empire, by force of arms." A scholar of the modern-era noted one of the many negative results of the War: "At the war's close the United States could boast higher taxation per capita than any other nation."[458] Colonial Americans fought a war to prevent political slavery,[459] but the Republican Party overthrew that victory and instituted political slavery to an all-powerful Yankee Empire.[460] Without realizing it, Representative Voorhees was America's Nineteenth century Jeremiah,[461] a "weeping prophet" agonizing over a dark future he saw for his country.

Representative Voorhees blasted the workings of the Republican Party as they used every means of fraud, corruption, and military dictatorship to assure Republican control of the conquered South. In a speech titled "Plunder of the Eleven States," delivered on March 23, 1872, in the House of Representatives, he outlined the Republican strategy:

> You not only said who should be elected to rule over these States, but you said who should elect them. You fixed the quality... of the voters. You purged the ballot box of intelligence and virtue, and in their stead, you placed the most ignorant and unqualified...in the world to rule over these people.... You clung to her throat; you battered her features out of shape and recognition, determined that your party should have undisputed possession and enjoyment of her offices, her honors, and her substance. Then bound hand and foot you handed her over to the rapacity of robbers.... I challenge

---

458 Hummel, Jeffrey Rogers, *Emancipating Slaves, Enslaving Free Men* (Illinois: Open Court, Chicago, 1996), 223.

459 Kennedy & Kennedy, *Jefferson Davis: High Road to Emancipation and Constitutional Government* (Columbia, SC: Shotwell Publishing, 2022), 15-24.

460 Kennedy & Kennedy, *Yankee Empire: Aggressive Abroad and Despotic at Home* (Columbia, SC: Shotwell Publishing, 2018), 109-18.

461 Jeremiah 5: 26-31, *The Holy Bible*, King James version.

the darkest annals of the human race for a parallel to the robberies which have been perpetrated on these eleven American States... you planted in hate and nurtured in corruption so have been the fruits which you have gathered.[462]

It was evident that, regardless of calls for reconciliation and pleas for harmony, the Republican Party was on a mission to punish the South and remake America's original Constitutional Republic of Sovereign States. The Republican Party's Reconstruction Act of 1867 dealt a death blow to America's original Republic and destroyed the once-vaunted American principle of government based upon the free and unfettered consent of the governed. Thanks to Lincoln and the Republican Party, consent was replaced with coercion.

The Reconstruction Act of 1867 divided the occupied Southern States into five military districts. All civil governments within these former States were placed under the complete control of the United States military. It was an officially sanctioned United States policy of military dictatorship of a conquered people. A Union general was placed in command of each military district. Below is a list of the five military districts and the States ruled by the military in that district:

1. Military District One; General John M. Schofield; Virginia

2. Military District Two; General Daniel E. Sickles; North and South Carolina

3. Military District Three; General John Pope; Georgia, Alabama, and Florida

---

462 "Daniel W. Voorhees," Wikipedia (Wikipedia.org) www.bit.ly/DanVoorhees (Accessed 10 May 2023). The entry cites *Voorhees, Daniel Wolsey, (1897). Forty Years of Oratory: Daniel Wolsey Voorhees Lectures, Addresses and Speeches.* Bobbs-Merrill Company. (Accessed 27 January 2022).

4. Military District Four; General O.C. Ord; Mississippi and Arkansas

5. Military District Five; General Philip Sheridan; Louisiana and Texas

These Generals took over the provisional (puppet or bogus) state governments established under Lincoln's Ten Percent Reconstruction Plan. "We the People" of the defeated South were allowed to pretend they had a form of self-government, but the concept of self-government for "We the People" of the South died at Appomattox. Any state or local law, regulation, or state court decision could be abolished, changed, or nullified by the United States military.[463] Scallywags, Carpetbaggers, and the Union League took full advantage of this new military "authority" available to promote Republican schemes of government.

The Republican-controlled Congress ordered the military to begin voter registration within its districts. All males twenty-one years or older would be registered, except those who participated in the "rebellion." This meant that, for the first time in world history, a newly freed, mostly illiterate black population would be given political control of the white race. Of course, there was no shortage of white Northern Carpetbaggers and Southern Scallywags willing to take advantage of the politically and socially unprepared freemen. This was something that Southerners who favored the high road to emancipation wanted to avoid. Men such as Jefferson Davis wanted to educate and prepare slaves for the day when they would be ready to stand in society on an equal footing with other free people. Davis did not view slavery as a permanent institution but saw it as an "institution for the preparation of that race for civil liberty and social enjoyment." Davis encouraged the people of the North to "leave natural causes to their full effect, and when the time shall arrive at which emancipation is proper, those most

---

463 The same holds true today in Modern Era Reconstruction, except the United States Military stands ready in the background while the Federal Courts now decide which local law, regulation, or court decision may be enforced within any of the Yankee Empire's provinces. Same song, different verse.

interested will be most anxious to effect it."⁴⁶⁴ These words were spoken well before the war. Davis did more than talk about the future freedom of slaves; he spent his own money promoting the idea of preparing "that race for civil liberty and social enjoyment." His former slaves left testimony about the education and training Jefferson Davis provided for his slaves on his plantations.⁴⁶⁵

THE CONSEQUENCE OF REPUBLICAN RECONSTRUCTION

America's unelected rulers, a political class of arrogant, moneyed elites, and leftist political power brokers destroyed government by the consent of the governed.⁴⁶⁶ This political fact was acknowledged in 2010 when Representative Peter Stark (D-CA) boasted, "The Federal Government can do most anything in this country."⁴⁶⁷ This tyrannical opinion was not a new expression of federal power. In 1942, the Federal Government prosecuted a simple farmer because he dared to raise wheat for his personal use on his own farm in violation of the rules established by a federal agency.⁴⁶⁸ Early in the 21st century, the Federal President declared America's children belonged to the government! "One nation under God?" Whose God promotes transgenderism and child grooming? "With liberty and justice for all?" But only if you accept and abide by the current postmodern, leftist, Woke ideology.

Republican-sponsored Reconstruction Amendments and enforcement legislation paved the way for an unlimited expansion of Federal authority over "We the People" at the local, state, and national level. This expansion included the right of the Federal Government to prohibit Southerners in the military from displaying symbols of their Southern heritage. In a 1990 case, the Supreme Court upheld the "right" of a federal judge to order the Kansas

---

464   Davis cited in Evans, Eli N., *Judah P. Benjamin-The Jewish Confederate* (New York: The Free Press, 1988), 72.

465   Kennedy & Kennedy, *Jefferson Davis*, 5-14.

466   *Rethinking the American Union for the Twenty-First Century*, Ed., Donald Livingston (Gretna, LA: Pelican Publishing Co., 2013), 86.

467   Pete Stark cited in *Rethinking the American Union for the Twenty-First Century*, 32.

468   *Wickard v. Filburn*, 317 US 111 (1942).

City, Missouri, school board to raise taxes to pay for a wide-ranging magnet school plan designed to achieve racial integration.[469] During the China COVID scare, the Federal Government engaged in flagrant violations of the Constitutional rights of freedom of assembly, freedom of speech, and freedom of religion. Yet, America's political slaves (with few exceptions) accepted Federal authority and meekly obeyed. During Active Reconstruction—1866-77 and Passive Reconstruction—1878-1965, America's Republic of Sovereign States was dissolved and unconstitutionally merged into one nation indivisible. The Republican Party, during Active Reconstruction, engineered this radical and unconstitutional perversion of America's original government. During Passive Reconstruction, both national political parties endorsed this unconstitutional change and used their political and social power to enforce these changes. The reason is simple: the traditionally conservative South became the timid and pacified South, offering no real resistance to this radical change. Politicians in both national political parties began to enjoy the perks, privileges, and power available to those working with the political *status quo*. The decentralized, Constitutionally limited Republic of Sovereign States morphed into the Hamiltonian dream of a centralized, supreme Federal Government controlled by Northern and eventually Globalist ruling elites.

The next to last stage of any society, leading directly to its final stage of collapse, is "its forcible political unification in a centralized state."[470]

---

469 *Missouri v. Jenkins*, 495 US 33 (1990).

470 Arnold Toynbee cited in *Rethinking the American Union for the Twenty-First Century*, 172.

THE VICTORIOUS NORTH BECOMES A HEARTLESS TASK-MASTER FOR THE DEFEATED SOUTH

The South was intentionally punished with poverty. Most of the South's mules, horses, and farm implements were destroyed. Returning Confederate veterans faced the daunting task of remaking their lives in their devastated homeland. Five years after the end of World War II Germany and Japan regained their pre-war economic status but after 150 years the South, once the richest section of the nation, is now the poorest section in the United States. There was no Marshal Plan for the South.

The Yankee Empire called it "Reconstruction", but it was not the South that was being reconstructed. The victorious North reconstructed America's original Constitutional Republic of Sovereign States and turned it into a supreme Federal Government controlled by Northern ruling elites. [Artwork by Jerry McWilliams, SCV member].

Chapter 13:

ACTIVE RECONSTRUCTION—1866-77

"In the postmodern era, the evil of slanderous anti-South lies is unconsciously accepted as truth when they masquerade as humanitarian idealism. In postmodern America, emotions trump facts and truth." —James Ronald Kennedy

RECONSTRUCTION WAS NOT an effort of post-War North/South reconciliation! It was a successful effort of the Republican Party to remake America's original Republic into a centralized nation/state controlled by Northern ruling elites. Part of that effort was to turn the South into an economic and political colony of the victorious North.[471] The North covered their evil intent in both the War and Reconstruction by creating a smokescreen of lies about their humanitarian idealism. Their propaganda asserted that they were fighting the War "to free the slaves" and they were conducting Reconstruction to achieve civil rights for newly freed slaves. Both assertions are lies, but the conquered and occupied South cannot effectively challenge the invader's falsehoods. With its tyrannical power, the Yankee Empire suppressed the South's counter-argument and the North's propaganda became accepted as true. Joseph Goebbels, Hitler's propaganda minister, followed the same tactic—if you repeat a big lie often enough while suppressing counter-arguments, the public will accept the "big lie" as the truth. This is possible only in a society where the opposing

---

471 Clark & Kirwan, *The South Since Appomattox* (New York: Oxford University Press, 1967), 91.

view is censored, banned, or extremely limited by the government or private groups (media, entertainment industry, and academia) working cooperatively with the government to promote a common "big lie" or ideology. The Yankee Empire and its sycophants created and enforced the accepted story of Reconstruction, which is a false narrative. But the truth, like the South, though crushed to the earth, shall rise again, though it is in another time and a different manner. President Davis declared, "The principles for which we contended is bound to reassert itself, though it may be at another time and in another form."[472]

Shortly after Appomattox, greedy Federal Treasury agents spread over the conquered South, devouring what little resources remained. The federally sanctioned plundering of the Southern people was done with no concern about the impoverished conditions of white and black Southerners. Some compared these Federal tax agents to the plagues of locusts mentioned in the Old Testament. In Alabama, a Federal agent stole $80,000.00 worth of cotton in one month.[473] That would equal $1,569,000.00 in 2023 dollars.[474] When Federal Treasury agents in Texas were caught "red-handed" stealing cotton property from white citizens, they were arrested by local officials but immediately released by the Federal military.[475]

In many cases, the evidence was so overwhelming that even Republican local and Federal judges could not ignore the crimes. When the evidence began to lead back to Federal officials, the trials were suddenly dismissed.[476] It was obvious to the local Southern population that the Federal agents were actively stealing private property under the protection of Yankee bayonets. Meanwhile,

---

472   Davis cited in Pollard, E.A., *Southern History of the War*, Vol. II (1866, Crown Publishers Inc., 1977), 582.

473   Bowers, Claude, *The Tragic Era* (New York: 1929), 61.

474   $1.00 in 1866 would be equal to $19.61 in the purchasing power of 2023. "Purchasing Power Today of a US Dollar Transaction in the Past," Measuring Worth, 2024. www.measuringworth.com/ppowerus/ (Accessed 07 May 2023.

475   Bowers, Claude, *The Tragic Era*, 61.

476   *Ibid.*, 61.

in the North, Republican politicians and anti-South Yankee newspapers were only interested in demagoguing the South. The Northern journal, *The Nation*, attacked Lee by declaring, "We protest against the notion that he (General Lee) is fit to be put at the head of a college in a country situated as Virginia."[477] The revengeful anti-South press and politicians were busy demanding to know why Jeff Davis, Lee, and other leaders of the "rebellion" had not been hung or shot. The despoliation of what remained of the South was of no consideration. Her people were simply targets for vengeful slander and dark humor directed toward "rebels" and other "white-trash" down South. Thus, began the Republican Party's Active Reconstruction.

Active Reconstruction (1866-77) was an era in US history in which the Federal Government, under the control of the Republican Party, used its political power, backed by military force, to impose social, economic, and political chaos upon "We the People" of the occupied South while a carnival of corruption played out in Washington, DC. Toward the end of the War, Lincoln found himself beset by numerous Republican critics who were upset with Lincoln's more lenient Ten Percent Reconstruction Plan. The Radicals in the Republican Party were taking advantage of the chaotic conditions in Washington during the last year of the War to gain control of the fledgling Republican Party. The corruption and political intrigue caused by the War had turned Washington, DC into a political jungle.

The prevailing attitude of the Radical Republican "leaders" is typified by Fredrick Law Olmsted of New York, who declared that the North should wage aggressive War to *exterminate* the South even if it "took seven years" and even if it required putting up "gallows in every town."[478] Olmsted was not restricting the use of gallows for towns only in the South. He wanted to intimidate Northern Democrats so they would passively submit to the

---

477   Ibid., 62; The author cites *The Nation*, September 14, 1865.

478   Olmsted cited in Chodes, John, *Washington's KKK: The Union League During Southern Reconstruction* (Columbia, SC: Shotwell Publishing, 2016), 6.

Republican Party's unconstitutional rule over the North as well as the occupied South. The War's end did not change such Northern attitudes.

Lincoln, as the leader of the Republican Party, was opposed by the Radicals in his party. Lincoln's desire for a quick return to local state governments in the South was based upon his desire to gain electoral votes from reasonably friendly, "reconstructed" *puppet* Southern States. The radicals had other ideas. They were motivated by hatred of the South and sought to punish the "rebels." They also saw an excellent opportunity to exploit illiterate black voters to gain a solid Republican South. Radicals within the Republican Party opposed Lincoln's nomination for a second term in 1864. They shocked many in the North when they issued their Wade-Davis Manifesto on August 4, 1864, blasting Lincoln's conciliatory stance toward the South. The Radicals offered a vastly more radical plan for Republican Reconstruction.[479] Today, in the Modern Era Reconstruction (Post-1965), Republicans and Democrats have rejected the spirit of Lincoln's more conciliatory approach to the South. They have adopted, in spirit and in fact, the Radical's view of revenge, hatred, slander, and punishment toward the South and its honorable heritage.

While his worshipers often praised Lincoln's conciliatory stance, he was not motivated by a sense of compassion for Southerners but by practical political consideration. Lincoln's only guiding principle was political pragmatism. It worked well for his entire political career, but it failed him toward the close of the War. He failed to correctly gauge the political ambitions and determination of the South-hating, revenge-seeking radicals in the Republican Party. According to Representative George W. Julian (R-Indiana) in 1864, you would be hard-pressed to find ten Republicans in Congress who supported Lincoln's re-nomination for the presidency. Representative Julian, like most Americans, North and South, was horrified at the news of Lincoln's assassination. Still, he felt that "the accession of [Vice President] Johnson would prove

---

479 Bowers, Claude, *The Tragic Era*, 244.

a Godsend to our cause."⁴⁸⁰ Julian, like all Radical Republicans, favored a harsher approach to the conquered South. Thus, the "cause" he spoke about was the cause of punishment, revenge, and total domination of the conquered and occupied South. This "cause" would see the maturing of the Yankee Empire, and it would see the once-free people of the South turned into the Yankee Empire's political slaves. The South's political slavery continues today, even though many conservative Southerners learned to love their "one nation indivisible" chains.

Lincoln was assassinated on a Friday, and by the following Sunday night, Radical Republicans met to plan for Republican control of Reconstruction. One of the main topics was how to use negro suffrage to control the conquered South.⁴⁸¹ A few days after Lincoln's death, former Union General Ben Butler—known in New Orleans as Beast Butler—proclaimed that "the time has not come for holding any relations with her [Virginia] but that of the conqueror to the conquered."⁴⁸² On April 21, 1865, the *New York World* ridiculed Butler as "an unscrupulous general whose cowardice and incapacity always left his enemies unharmed upon the field."⁴⁸³ His political crusade against the devastated South bore more foul fruit than any of his military campaigns. We will see him appear numerous times spouting his hatred of the South.

The *New York World*, on June 6, 1865, described Washington, DC, in the summer of 1865 as a place where a "crowd of bristling short-haired Puritans" replaced its one-time aristocratic elegance. Former Confederate General Richard Taylor, son of past President Taylor, noted the degradation trickling into the nation's capital. He observed that women of ill-repute who were common among the camp followers of the Yankee Army had "begun their march

---

480 *Ibid.*, 255.

481 *Ibid.*, 7. The author cites *Gideon Welles Diary*, II, Boston, 1911, 291.

482 *Ibid.*, The author cites *New York World*, 21 April 1865.

483 *Ibid.*, The author cites *New York World*, 22 April 1865.

upon the town with much swishing of skirts."⁴⁸⁴ This is a thumbnail sketch of the people and government that assumed dictatorial control over "We the People" of the South. By the end of the War, the Radicals were already plotting how they could manipulate and exploit the uneducated former slaves to ensure Republican ascendancy. Radical Republicans were opposed to Lincoln because he did not support the massive enfranchisement of illiterate freedmen in the South (something they refused to allow in the North). This is why Representative Julian (R-Indiana) celebrated the fact that he (incorrectly) thought President Johnson was in favor of negro suffrage down South "which is entirely different from his predecessor's."⁴⁸⁵ He meant that Lincoln resisted their urging to use presidential powers to bestow voting rights on all male blacks *in the South,* but Lincoln refused.

Northern Attitude Regarding Blacks

The reluctance of white Northerners to accept blacks on an equal basis, even though they were actively demanding such of whites down South, is demonstrated by the way they treated the first black appointed to West Point during Active Reconstruction. Senator Hiram Revels (R-Mississippi) appointed the young black man. *The Nation* called the appointment "A very foolish and cruel thing as far as the boy and his family is concerned, and a very injudicious thing as far as the colored race is concerned."⁴⁸⁶ The only result was a trip to West Point, breakfast at the Couzzen's Hotel, and then they sent the hopeful cadet home. The way the Republican Party exploited black Southerners for votes prompted Senator Revels to resign from the Republican Party.⁴⁸⁷

This Northern aversion to blacks was well known and was politically and socially accepted during the War and Active Reconstruction. Senator Trumbull (R-Illinois) admitted, "There is

---

484 Bowers, Claude, , 9. The author cites Richard Taylor, *Destruction and Reconstruction*, New York, 1879, 241.

485 Julian cited in *Ibid.*, 10; Here the author presents letter to Pierce Scheiden, iv, 242.

486 Bowers, Claude, , 296, The author cites *The Nation*, 09 June 1870.

487 Kennedy & Kennedy, *Punished With Poverty: the Suffering South* 2ⁿᵈ ed., 55-7.

a very great aversion...against having free negroes come among us. Our people want nothing to do with the negro."[488] Lincoln's own state of Illinois passed, by a 2 to 1 margin, a new state constitution in 1862 that prohibited free blacks from entering the state. While attempting to calm Northerners about their concerns that Lincoln's Emancipation Proclamation would send blacks northward, Salmon P. Chase of Ohio, a member of Lincoln's cabinet declared, "The blacks of the North will slide southward and leave no question to quarrel about."[489] Oregon entered the Union in 1859. The state's constitution had a provision that prohibited free blacks from entering the state. Proponents stated that they were anti-slavery, but that did not mean they intended to allow blacks to "be placed on an equal footing in the States with white citizens."[490] A black Louisianan observed that white Northerners would shed copious tears over the wrongs done to black Southerners, but "when we dare to leave this section...we are then only 'niggers' and nothing more."[491] The history of Northern racial hatred is conveniently hidden from the public by postmodern Yankee propagandists, while these same propagandists unjustly and viciously slander the South as the seat of racial hatred in America.

Carpetbaggers and other missionaries of the New England gospel came South after the War, claiming they intended to help blacks. But it did not take long for local whites to see that just because a man came from the North did not ensure any greater degree of kindness toward blacks at his hands. Union Chaplain Conway, in charge of the Labor Bureau created by General Banks, reported on July 1 (1865) that men from free States (Northerners) were "as ready to whip the freedman...as they are to condemn the same conduct on the part of the men who formerly owned the

---

488 Trumbull cited by Clyde N. Wilson in "Defeat and Occupation: The Cold War Known as "Reconstruction," *To Live and Die In Dixie*, ed., Frank Powell, III (Columbia, TN: Sons of Confederate Veterans), 448.

489 Chase is cited in *Ibid*.

490 Donald Livingston, "Confederate Emancipation Without War," *To Live and Die In Dixie*, ed., Frank Powell, III (Columbia, TN: Sons of Confederate Veterans, 2014), 463.

491 Hair, William Ivy, *Bourbonism and Agrarian Protest: Louisiana Politics 1877-1900* (Baton Rouge, LA: LSU Press, 1969), 99.

freedmen."[492] Yet, little is known today about the evil inflicted upon white and black Southerners by these unprincipled Yankee political speculators. The Yankee Empire's false narrative can live and dominate only in the darkness of censorship. For well over 150 years, the Yankee Empire and its sycophants have controlled the narrative about the War and Reconstruction. *Vae victis*—woe to the vanquished.

Postmodernist historians, true to their calling to "debunk" or "deconstruct"[493] Western Christian civilization, eagerly denounce post-War Southerners for their reluctance to accept the newly freed slaves as their social and political equals. Yet, these same "historians" fail to explain that this was a typical social evaluation in the nineteenth and early twentieth centuries. Representative George Boutwell (R-Massachusetts) suggested that the States of South Carolina and Florida be reserved exclusively for former slaves. He advocated a permanent separation of blacks from white America. President Grant considered the acquisition of Santo Domingo for the twofold purpose of a Naval coaling station in the Caribbean and a place to send America's blacks.[494] Numerous examples of Northern hatred of blacks are documented. During the Yankee Empire's invasion of the South, deliberate efforts were made to exploit and exterminate black Southerners.[495] Yet, this part of American history is not allowed to be taught for fear of calling into question the legitimacy of the War and the existing political *status quo* that arose and continues today due to Lincoln's War and the Republican Party's Reconstruction policies.

---

492   Henry, Robert Selph, *The Story of Reconstruction*, 30.

493   "Debunk traditional values" is a term used by C.S. Lewis in his book *The Abolition of Man*, and "deconstruct" is a term used by Stephen R.C. Hicks in his book *Explaining Postmodernism*.

494   Leigh, Philip, *U.S. Grant's Failed Presidency* (Columbia, SC: Shotwell Publishing, 2019), 63.

495   Kennedy & Kennedy, *Punished With Poverty: the Suffering South* 2nd ed., 88-94.

Northern Attitude Toward Granting Voting Rights To Blacks

In the nineteenth and up to the mid-twentieth century, voting was regarded in its historical light as a privilege to be earned rather than a right universally bestowed by the government. During the Constitutional Convention, on August 7, 1787, Oliver Ellsworth from Connecticut spoke about the importance of the States controlling voting qualifications:

> Mr. Ellsworth thought the qualifications of the electors stood on the most proper footing. The right of suffrage was a tender point, and strongly guarded by most of the State Constitutions. The people will not readily subscribe to the National Constitution if it should subject them to be disfranchised. The States are the best Judges of the circumstances and temper of their own people.[496]

During the War and Active Reconstruction, the franchise was the strict domain of each sovereign state. "In sixteen of the 'loyal' [Northern] States Negroes were not allowed to vote at all; in most of the other six only those blacks who could meet property or educational tests *more stringent than those applied to whites* were allowed to vote."[497] In those States that allowed blacks to vote, the percentage of blacks was so small that black voters had little if any impact on elections.

Representative Thaddeus Stevens (R-Pennsylvania) in 1865 made an initial effort to pass legislation enforcing black suffrage *in the South*. His initial effort failed because it received only eight votes in the Senate! Even his fellow Republicans could not bring themselves to vote for a bill forcing black enfranchisement upon the South "at this time." The reason was that they were facing a

---

[496] Oliver Ellsworth cited in Madison, James, *The Debates in the Federal Convention of 1787 Which Framed the Constitution of the United States of America* (Union, New Jersey: The Lawbook Exchange, 1999), 351.

[497] Henry, Robert Selph, *The Story of Reconstruction*, 45.

challenging 1866 election cycle. Republicans knew the Northern view on black suffrage and decided to wait until after the 1866 election to pursue their plan to corral and exploit black Republican voters in the South.[498] Republicans have always been, and remain to this day, pragmatic politicians. They follow the popular will only when it benefits the ruling elite, otherwise they carefully (cunningly) avoid the popular will by making hot speeches for home consumption while voting with the elites.

In the North, a strong current of opposition existed against granting voting rights to negroes. President Johnson's refusal to endorse Republican efforts, for using the Federal Government to force the enfranchisement of negroes upon the Southern States, is an example of President Johnson following the public will while upholding what was left of States' Rights under the original Constitution. President Johnson, in his December 1867 message to Congress, affirmed the general attitude of whites in nineteenth-century America and Europe regarding blacks:

> [Blacks had] shown less capacity for government than any other race of people. No independent government of any form has ever been successful in their hands. On the contrary, wherever they have been left to their own devices, they have shown a constant tendency to relapse into barbarism.[499]

Propagandists of the left point to the former President's statement as evidence of rampant racism in America. Others, looking at contemporary headlines and social data, point to the post-colonial conditions in Zimbabwe, South Africa, and in post-1965 American cities such as Chicago, Detroit, Memphis, and New Orleans, as evidence that President Johnson predicted the future. It would be a future under a political system catering to blacks who demand a socialist solution to "their" problems. Note: the

---

498 *Ibid.*, 141.

499 President Johnson cited in Cruden, Robert, *The Negro in Reconstruction* (Englewood Cliffs, NJ: Prentice-Hall, Inc., 1969), 5.

issue is not the color of the skin, but the postmodern, neo-Marxist political ideology followed by voters in those predominantly black dysfunctional societies. Yesterday's prophecy became today's reality but in politically correct Woke America no one is allowed to recognize this reality.

General Sherman wrote to his brother, Senator John Sherman (R-Ohio), expressing his views regarding forcing the conquered South to accept the enfranchisement of the newly freed and mostly illiterate blacks: "My belief is that to force the enfranchised negroes as 'loyal' voters on the South will produce new riot and war…My Army will not fight in that war." Senator John Sherman, a Radical but pragmatic Republican, replied, "The negroes are not intelligent enough to vote, albeit [although] we shall soon find him bowing to the party lash."[500] Blacks in America have been "bowing to the party lash" ever since their so-called emancipation. First, they bowed to the Republican Party's lash, and today, they bow to the Democrat Party's lash. The only interest either political party has in the black vote is to exploit it to capture and maintain their party's political power. The "influence" of blacks in either party has not produced an economic advancement for blacks equal to that of the mostly white ruling elites. The rich get richer while the poor get poorer. The same is true for white Southerners. Regardless of which party white Southerners support, their heritage is viciously slandered, and they remain at the bottom of America's economy.[501] This would not have been the situation for black and white Southerners had the North allowed the South to follow the high road to emancipation.

Former Indiana Governor Morton, in 1865, was a vocal opponent of black suffrage. He declared it would be unthinkable to allow the freedmen the right to vote without "a period of probation and preparation."[502] This is precisely what the South would have done had the North allowed the South to follow the high road

---

500   Bowers, Claude, *The Tragic Era*. Author cites Sherman, *Letters*, 248.

501   Kennedy & Kennedy, *Punish With Poverty: The Suffering South* 2nd ed., 169-74.

502   Bowers, Claude, , 16. The author cites the *New York World*, 03 October 1865.

to emancipation.[503] Morton continued to denounce the idea of forcing black suffrage upon the South by observing that among the newly freed slaves, "not one in a thousand could read...impossible to conceive of instantly admitting this mass of ignorance to the ballot." He then pointed to the hypocrisy of the North regarding black suffrage: "Indiana with twenty-five thousand negroes who can read and write, and who are refused the ballot....With what face can Indiana go to Congress and insist upon the right of suffrage to the negroes of the South?"[504] Morton was a pragmatic politician, and as such, he was merely expressing the popular opinion of Northern voters. Within less than three years, he changed his opinion when it became obvious the Republican Party would lose power in Washington without black voters from the South that the Republican Party could control and exploit. While the North made plans to impose illiterate black voters upon the South, how did Northerners feel about allowing blacks to vote in their elections?

Northerners Reject Black Voting Rights

Washington, DC, was governed essentially by Congressional appointees. Yet, the fine Yankees living in Washington, DC, in a popular vote on December 1867 rejected black suffrage! The vote was not even close: 7,369 against and 36 in favor![505] However, such attitude among Northerners was not limited to Washington, DC. Only six Northern States allowed blacks to vote in 1866. In New York, the right to vote for blacks was restricted by property ownership, which was not the case for whites. Connecticut, Wisconsin, and Minnesota voted against black enfranchisement in 1865; Kansas voted against it in 1867; Michigan, and Missouri in 1868; and New York in 1869.[506]

Harriet Beecher Stowe, who did more than any other woman to bring on the War as the author of *Uncle Tom's Cabin*, purchased

---

503   Kennedy & Kennedy *Jefferson Davis*, 5-24, 57-9.

504   Bowers, Claude, *The Tragic Era*, 16; The author again cites the *New York World*, 03 October 1865.

505   *Ibid.*, 99.

506   Henry, Robert Selph, *The Story of Reconstruction*, 211.

a plantation near Orange Park, Florida after the War—such irony! From there she wrote to her brother complaining that local "Corrupt politicians are already beginning to speculate on [the negroes] as a possible capital for their schemes, and to fill their poor heads with all sorts of vagaries." In a letter to the Duchess of Argyll, she wrote: "My brother Henry...takes the ground that it is unwise and impolitic to endeavor to force negro suffrage on the South at the point of the bayonet."[507]

Lincoln shared the same attitude toward black suffrage as most other Northerners. When asked by one of his Ten Percent Southern States' officials whether Lincoln would support black suffrage, he gave his usual cryptic answer to such questions: "I barely suggest, for your private consideration, whether some of the colored people may not be let in—as, for instance, the very intelligent....But this is only a suggestion, not to the public but to you alone."[508] Lincoln's mild—some would say reasonable—approach to allowing newly freed slaves access to the ballot was the main reason Radical Republicans opposed Lincoln.[509]

Republicans promoting the imposition of immediate suffrage for blacks in the Southern States were more than willing to leave the question of black voting rights to the individual Northern States. These were the same Northern States where Negroes were few and would have little if any impact on local and state elections. Yet, these Radical Republicans insisted the President of the United States, by executive proclamation, make voters of the great numbers of mostly illiterate freedmen in the South.[510] Thaddeus Stevens in his usual strident and hateful manner proclaimed that "...universal manhood suffrage be imposed in each Southern state..." (Note "imposed.") Thaddeus Stevens admitted that the

---

507 Bowers, Claude, *The Tragic Era*, 205. The author cites *Life of Mrs. Stowe*, 395.

508 Lincoln cited in Henry, Robert Selph, *The Story of Reconstruction*, 40.

509 Lincoln publicly declared that the western lands once populated by Native Americans would be preserved "as an outlet for free white people." Lincoln had no intentions of providing land for free black people. See Lincoln cited in Kennedy & Kennedy, *Yankee Empire: Aggressive Abroad and Despotic at Home*, 262-3.

510 Henry, Robert Selph, *The Story of Reconstruction*, 46.

reason Republicans must insist upon granting voting rights to illiterate former slaves was to assure the "perpetual ascendancy of the Party of the Union."[511] By "Party of the Union" he meant the Republican Party.

General Sherman saw through the Republican Party's Reconstruction Plan and declared it a plot "whereby politicians may manufacture just so much more pliable electioneering material." Scallywag Governor Brownlow of Tennessee admitted to a Northern audience: "I find here at the North you do not need, and many of you do not want, Negro suffrage. We are not so. We want the loyal Negroes to help us vote down the disloyal traitors and white people."[512] The Republican Party's strategy was based on the removal of the South's natural leaders, disfranchising the remaining whites, and using pliable (exploitable) mostly illiterate black voters to replace conservative leaders with local scallywags and Northern carpetbaggers. Such new Southern leaders would dance to the tune called by the ruling elite in Washington, DC. The more things change, the more they remain the same!

Once the new system of a supreme Federal Government controlled by Northern elites was established, it entrenched itself and remains in place today regardless of which national political party controls the Federal Government. Illegitimately obtained power breeds tyranny. As Christian moral philosopher C.S. Lewis declared, "I am very doubtful whether history shows us one example of a man who, having stepped outside traditional morality and attained power, has used that power benevolently."[513]

The reasons why Republicans enacted their various Reconstruction Amendments, and "Force Bills" were explained in the *National Republican*. The editors clearly understood that Republicans could not maintain their hold on national power if the South were allowed to adopt franchise laws like the franchise laws then in use in Northern States. They knew Republican political power

---

511   Stevens cited in Henry, Robert Selph, *The Story of Reconstruction*, 46.
512   Brownlow cited in *Ibid.*, 141.
513   Lewis, C.S., *The Abolition of Man* (1944, New York: Harper Collins, 2001), 66.

rested on disfranchising most white Southerners while giving the ballot to mostly illiterate freedmen. Republicans in Congress understood that the illiterate and uneducated black voters in the South could be controlled (exploited) by the North's ruling elite. Before the passage of one of the Force Bills, the *National Republican* boldly proclaimed:

> [The Bill] ...is required to preserve to the Republican Party the electoral votes of the Southern States. Remember that if the Democrats carry all the Southern States...it will require only fifty Democratic electoral votes from Northern States to elect a Democratic President.[514]

Reconstruction was a purely partisan Republican effort to maintain control of the emerging Yankee Empire. Of course, they hid their desire for political power behind a smoke-screen of slanderous anti-South lies. Lincoln's illegal War murdered the old American virtues of statesmanship and ushered in the new era of partisan political patronage and the rule of Northern (and in the Modern Era Reconstruction, Globalists) elites.

Former General Ben "Beast" Butler declared to the Union League Club of New York that negro suffrage must be *forced* upon the white people "in the late rebellious States." Note that he limits forcing black voting rights to only the "rebellious States." The more moderate Gideon Wells, Secretary of the Navy under Lincoln and Johnson, observed that "prominent men are trying to establish a party on the basis of equality of races in the Rebel States for which the people are not prepared."[515] Again, note that the Republican effort to impose black voting rights is limited to the "Rebel States." Why not Northern States? The reason was that the Northern States were, at that time but no longer, still operating as free, independent, and sovereign States. The Southern States were then and remain conquered provinces of the Yankee Empire.

---

514   Henry, Robert Selph, *The Story of Reconstruction*, 541.

515   Bowers, Claude, *The Tragic Era*, 15. The author cites Welles's *Diary* Vol. II, 369.

The Republican-controlled Congress passed the First Reconstruction Enforcement Act on May 31, 1870, but it did not bring forth the complete Republican success down South they sought. On February 28, 1871, the Republican Congress passed the Second Reconstruction Enforcement Act. This should be a familiar pattern to modern-day Americans. When the ruling elite in Washington do not get the political results they want, they simply pass yet another "Enforcement Act." At the beginning of the Modern Era Reconstruction (1965), the ruling elite passed the Civil Rights Act of 1964 and the Voting Rights Act of 1965 to break up the Solid South and foster the elections of left-of-center Southern Democrat Representatives and Senators.[516] Both Acts were passed to solve social/political problems created by the North's refusal to allow the South to follow the high road to emancipation. These "Civil Rights" Acts continued the imperialistic tactic of Divide-and-Rule by intensifying racial distrust and hatred not only down South but nationwide.

THADDEUS STEVENS, THE MAN WHO MADE THE REPUBLICAN PARTY OF TODAY

The elephant logo of the Republican Party today should be replaced with a photo of Thaddeus Stevens. He, more than any other Republican, including the "sainted" Lincoln, represents the origins and current conduct of the ruling elite of the Republican Party. Just like old Thad's photograph, the origins and current conduct of the Republican Party are almost too ugly to look upon.

Neither the Constitution nor a sense of compassion for innocent white Southerners would motivate Stevens to stifle his hatred of the South. His guiding principle regarding the people of the South was

---

516 It was reported to the author by an individual having indirect knowledge that in 1965 President Lyndon Baines Johnson met with influential Southern Democrats in New Orleans, seeking their support for the 1965 Voting Rights Bill. He told them that if they help him pass the Voting Rights Bill "I'll have these (n-word) voting Democrat for the next 200 years." There is good evidence that LBJ held prejudicial beliefs about African Americans. See Serwer, Adam, "Lyndon Johnson was a civil rights hero. But also a racist." MSNBC (msnbc.com) 11 April 2014 (Accessed 02 August 2023). www.on.msnbc.com/48Jzdyr.

simply his adherence to "The laws of war, not the Constitution." He chastised his moderate Republican colleagues in the House by asking them to consider, "Who pleads the Constitution? It is the advocates of rebels."[517] Stevens viewed the original Constitution as a political hindrance. He had no respect for the Constitution drafted by the Founding Fathers and given its legitimate authority by the ratifications of America's Sovereign States. He was a Free Thinker who rejected the fundamental principles of Christianity. Neither the Holy Bible nor the Constitution found favor in his worldview. Having nothing to bridle his political greed and hatred for the South, he was free to give vent to his darkest emotions.

When Stevens and other radical abolitionists advocated a slave uprising in the South, he made it clear that neither he nor the abolitionists cared about the Constitution. He shocked moderates when he openly stated his support for a slave revolt down South like the slave revolt in Haiti. In the Haitian slave revolt, innocent whites—men, women, and children, both slave owners and non-slave owners, were massacred. He and his Radical comrades understood that a Northern-instigated slave revolt down South would result in the massacre of innocent men, women, and children of slave owners and non-slave-holding whites. He stated, "I for one shall be ready to go for it—arming the blacks—horrifying to gentlemen as it may appear."[518] His plan for the execution of the War was simple: hang the leaders—crush the South—arm the negroes—confiscate the land. He famously declared in the House, "Our generals have a sword in one hand and shackles in the other."[519] The Yankee invaders' "swords" would be used to conquer a free people, and Republican-created political "shackles" would be used to politically enslave the conquered people of the South. Southerners would be made into political slaves to the emerging Yankee Empire. Thaddeus Stevens became America's first advocate of political slavery for white people the Federal Government considered to be of less value than America's dominant Yankee

---

517 Bowers, Claude, *The Tragic Era*, 1882, 111.

518 *Ibid.*, 72.

519 *Ibid.*, Author cites *Congressional Globe*, 22 January 1862.

majority. He never knew, or if he did, he did not care, that America's Founding Fathers' major concern was that the British Empire was attempting to make Americans into the mother country's political slaves. The American Revolution was a revolt against political slavery.[520] In 1776, "Taxation without representation" was merely a symptom of political slavery. During Active Reconstruction and under Thaddeus Stevens's leadership, the Republican Party in Congress would impose confiscatory taxation without representation upon the devastated people of the South.

A naive Southerner from Alabama traveled to Lancaster, Pennsylvania, and obtained an audience with Representative Thaddeus Stevens. The Southerner asked Stevens if he intended to confiscate private property of "rich" Southerners. Stevens replied that he would do everything according to the law. The Southerner replied that taking private property by the government without compensation violated the Constitution—silly Southerner. He still thought the Constitution meant what it said in this new Yankee-created America. Stevens answered harshly, "The Constitution... has nothing to do with it. I propose to deal with you entirely by the laws of war." The shocked Southerner responded, "And be satisfied with nothing less than confiscation?" Stevens caustically answered, "...anything less would be unjust to those wronged by your crime." The eternally hopeful Southerner then asked if Alabama gave blacks the vote, provided for their education, assured their legal rights, and sent to Washington Senators and Representatives who would take the oath of allegiance—would Stevens allow them to take their seats? Stevens replied, "No," and immediately closed the interview.[521] Naïve Southerners of today are still going "hat in hand," pleading with Stevens's Republican Party, expecting a better outcome. When will they ever learn?

---

520 Kennedy & Kennedy, *Jefferson Davis: High Road to Emancipation*, 15-24.

521 Bowers, Claude, *The Tragic Era*, 160. Author cites the *New York World*, 20 June 1867.

Divide-And-Rule—The Yankee Empire's Tool To Control Its Southern Captives

When an empire makes a successful conquest of a formerly free people, the empire is faced with the problem of either exterminating or controlling the occupied people. Invading and conquering formerly free people is just the first stage of the conquest. The empire must create a mode of occupation that will prevent future uprisings—after all, empires are indivisible.[522] It has always been the custom of ancient empires to either exterminate or use locals as part of their occupation forces. This is true in the twentieth century as well. Germany used Vichy French police and military to help control occupied France during World War II. Shortly after its successful invasion, conquest, and occupation of the South, the US military turned its attention to Native Americans in the West. The US military in the Western Plains used native Indian scouts in its successful effort to exterminate the Plains Indians.[523] As one modern-day scholar noted, "Setting one indigenous ethnic or religious group against another have often made the policing of a subordinate people easier and less expensive."[524] The Yankee Empire used the ancient technique of Divide-and-Rule to destroy the naturally friendly relations between most of the South's black and white population.[525] One of the primary efforts of the Union League was to teach black Southerners to fear, distrust, envy, and hate their white neighbors. The Union League then encouraged illiterate blacks to cling to their new friends from the North—who just happened to be activist members of the Republican Party.

Union General Swayne, head of the Republican Party's Freedmen's Bureau in Alabama, believed that, in time, the white people of Alabama would have provided the right to vote to qualified blacks if it was not for the alienation of the white and black races that arose from the extremes of Reconstruction. Union General

---

522 Kennedy & Kennedy, *The South Was Right!* 3rd ed., 259-65.

523 Kennedy & Kennedy, *Punished With Poverty-The Suffering South* 2nd ed., 142-3.

524 Johnson, Chalmers, *The Sorrow of Empire* (New York: Henry Holt & Co., 2004), 131.

525 Refer to Chapter 1 "What Could Have Been."

George H. Thomas testified, "Alabama has attempted to pass laws as judicious as they could at the time to regulate the affairs of the freemen."[526] The potential of black and white Southerners working together to create an acceptable and just social order in the defeated South was real and the leaders of the Republican Party knew it. A political unity between white and black Southerners posed a significant challenge to the national dominance of the Republican Party. A wedge of suspicion, mistrust, and eventually hatred had to be driven between the races in the South if the Republican Party was to survive.

A vital part of the Republican Party's divide-and-rule strategy was to disarm and disfranchise white Southerners and then place insolent (Union League) black militias over white Southern communities. They hoped to push whites to the point of open rebellion to federal authority. This, of course, would give the Republican-controlled Congress the perfect excuse to maintain the military occupation of the South for years to come. One technique was to station undisciplined armed blacks throughout the South near the homes of widows and crippled veterans.

Chapters 14-28 provide an overview of the South's resistance movement during Active Reconstruction within fifteen Southern States. When discussing the South's resistance movement, numerous references are mentioned of the insults and outrages performed by black militias during Active Reconstruction. Postmodern (neo-Marxist) historians and other apologists for the Yankee Empire often claim that Southern antagonism toward black militias was based on Southern racism. This is yet another Yankee fallacy used to detract from their tyrannical oppression of the conservative South. In a letter from Lincoln's Vice President, Andrew Johnson, one sees an example of the unruly and dangerous activities of newly freed, mostly illiterate, armed blacks. Andrew Johnson was from Tennessee. While serving as Lincoln's Vice President, he wrote a letter to the Yankee officer in command in

---

526 Henry, Robert Selph, *The Story of Reconstruction*, 153.

Tennessee. Johnson was complaining about his home that was taken over by black troops and turned into a house of prostitution!

> Negro troops stationed at Greenville, Tennessee are under little or no restraint, and are committing depredations through-out the country, domineering over, and in fact running the white people out of the neighborhood. Much of this is said to be attributable to the officers, whose countenance and rather encourage the negroes in their insolence and in their disorderly conduct.
>
> The negro soldiery take possession of and occupy property in the town at discretion and have even gone so far as to have taken my own house and converted it into a rendezvous for male and female negroes, who have been congregated there, in fact making it a common negro brothel.
>
> It was bad enough to be taken by traitors [Confederates] and converted into a rebel hospital, but a negro whore house is infinitely worse.[527]

This is dramatic evidence of why white Southerners were fearful of undisciplined black militias. Lawlessness was the rule, not the exception. "I know somewhat of the inferno of Reconstruction. I saw my people suffer, my father's house vandalized, my mother's tomb desecrated, I saw the South desolate!"[528] It is evidence as to why the peaceful, post-War South was forced to seek a means of self-defense in the form of the Southern resistance movement.[529]

---

[527] Vice President Johnson, Cited in Keys, Thomas Bland, *The Uncivil War: Union Army and Navy Excesses In The Official Records* (Biloxi, MS: The Beauvoir Press, 1991), 141.

[528] Johnstone, H.W., *Truth of the War Conspiracy of 1861*, 3.

[529] The Southern resistance movement was not a unified, South wide, campaign. Each state had its own unique resistance movement using various tactics to restore law and order and gain conservative control of state government. The official resistance movement lasted only until conservatives gained control of the state government. The movement's goals were to restore law and order, regain the right to vote for white Southerners, and restore reasonable taxation.

The danger was faced by all conservatives, black as well as white. Blacks who were loyal to their white friends exposed themselves to the hatred of blacks under the influence of Federal agents. During Reconstruction in South Carolina a former slave, Dave, was a friend of a white man accused of being a Klansman. Dave helped to hide his accused white friend. Dave was arrested by Federal agents and hung up by his thumbs for an extended time, but Dave refused to divulge the whereabouts of his white friend. He later told his friend's family, "I was jes agwine to die hung up before I would tell on him."[530]

Yankee soldiers occupying the South, as well as the Union League, were largely responsible for generating hatred in the hearts of blacks for their white Southern neighbors. This hatred remained long after the white, blue-coated soldiers left the South. The Yankee journal, *The Nation*, blamed the race and labor troubles between black and white Southerners on the influence on black Southerners by their purportedly "Northern friends, particularly soldiers."[531] Intentionally or not, the occupying troops were helping to establish the ancient technique of divide-and-rule in the South. Divide-and-rule was a political necessity for the Yankee Empire. As an alien occupier, they could not corral enough white Southerners to assure Republican dominance. Political necessity overruled traditional American Constitutional values in the War and Reconstruction.

Northern Republicans saw the political necessity of separating black Southerners from their white neighbors by creating an atmosphere of racial distrust and hatred. This, of course, is the primary aim of the divide-and-rule strategy of all empires. An integral part of the successful Republican Active Reconstruction was using the ancient imperial policy of divide-and-rule to control the population of the Yankee Empire's newly conquered territory. And today—same song but different verse. The ruling elite benefit while "We the People," both black and white, suffer.

---

530   *Confederate Veteran* Vol. VI, No. 11, Nov. 1898. Republished in *The Confederate Veteran Magazine* Vol. VI (Harrisburg, PA: The National Historical Society, 1987), 520.

531   Bowers, Claude, *The Tragic Era*, 51.

Dysfunctional and Tyrannical Federal Government

Some of the baby-boomer generations still remember when the corruption or sexual immorality of a politician in Washington, DC, was exposed, it produced public outrage and the end of that politician's career. But today things have changed. Today, in Modern Era Reconstruction, there is almost a total loss of public outrage at corruption or sexual impropriety in Washington. Cocaine found in the White House, no problem. National Senators and Representatives entangled and compromised by money from the Chinese Communist Party, no problem. The weaponization of the FBI, no problem—move along, nothing to see here. Republican Reconstruction set the stage for the dysfunctional system of government we live under today. The record of fraud and corruption that developed in Washington, DC, during Republican Active Reconstruction is generally ignored today. It is impossible to understand how we got where we are today as a nation without first understanding how the Republican Party was instrumental in setting low standards for American governance. America's *loss of outrage* is an indirect result of Republican-imposed Active Reconstruction.

James S. Pike of Maine, associate editor of the *New York Tribune*, observed that the national legislature during Reconstruction was just as likely to be influenced by fraud and corruption as the puppet state governments that the Republican-controlled Congress installed in the South.[532] While the Republican-controlled Congress was busy using racial tactics of divide-and-rule to implement Reconstruction in the conquered South, the North was also going through its form of Reconstruction. Reconstruction for the North meant gaining the economic profits available to the victors. Agents of various Northern commercial enterprises, especially railroads, were busy seeking governmental favors. The lobbies of the most prestigious hotels in Washington swarmed with such men waiting in the hotel lobby to catch the attention of a key Senator or Representative. The term "Lobbyist" became the common description for these agents. The term was first used in the United States in the 1830s. It was popularized in the United States during

---

532 Henry, Robert Selph, *The Story of Reconstruction*, 497.

President Grant's administration. The term has historical roots in Great Britain.[533]

While the South was impoverished and under dictatorial bayonet rule, the North began to feel the flush of the Gilded Age. The spirit of the age dominating the victorious North was a determination to use governmental influence for the rapid accumulation of fortunes by means fair or foul. Republican newspapers kept the public's mind distracted with slanderous anti-South hatred by waving the bloody shirt. In the meantime, politicians were busy cutting favorable deals with the well-connected business interests (today known as crony-capitalists and lobbyists). Senator James W. Grimes (R-Iowa), who would break with the Radicals by voting for acquittal in President Johnson's impeachment trial, was shocked by the corruption he witnessed. He complained, "Nearly all the grants of lands to railroads and wagon roads find their way into the hands of rich [crony] capitalists, and in eighteen months or two years after this grant is made, the script will be in the hands of the wealthy of the country."[534]

The power of the railroads in the post-War Congress is like the power of digital companies, financial houses, and the military-industrial complex in Congress today. A common complaint voiced by the average Northern citizen of the day was that railroads were involved in looting the public via their connections with key politicians in Congress. The accumulation of wealth and political power, not the "outrages" down South, was the Northern politician's primary political interest. The *New York Herald*, in its April 19, 1870, edition, complained that "All our railroad legislation is procured by corrupt practices and is formed in the interest of jobbery." The Republican Party found it necessary to wave the bloody shirt to distract the public from Congressional

---

533   The term "Lobbyist" originated in London, England. It referred to the lobbies outside the chambers of Parliament where influential individuals cut deals with members of Parliament. The term "Lobbyist" was in common usage in Britain in the 1840s. See Mapes, Joe, "What is a Lobbyist?," Mapes & Mapes, Inc. (mapesandmapes.com) wwwbit.ly/Mapes-Lobbyist (Accessed 30 October 2023).

534   Bowers, Claude, *The Tragic Era*, 116. Author cites the *Congressional Globe*, 07 February 1866.

corruption. In addition to distracting Northern voters from public corruption in Washington, it also provided the Republican Party with vengeful anti-South Northern votes.

Reconstruction in the North produced a radical change in America's commercial society. Senator Grimes's concern about the corruption and radical change in Washington was recognized by Southern historian and author Andrew Nelson Lytle, in the late 1920s:

> Since 1865 an agrarian Union has been changed into an industrial empire bent on conquest of the earth's goods and ports to sell them in. This means warfare, a struggle over markets, leading, in the end, to actual military conflict between nations.[535]

An example of the corruption in the Active Reconstruction era in Washington is The Five-Twenty Bonds scandal. The Five-Twenty Bonds[536]scandal demonstrates the unabashed willingness of political appointees to bend the law and violate ethical standards in the pursuit of financial gain. Jay Cooke, a "functionary" of the Department of the Treasury, decided on his own authority to redeem war-era bonds in gold. These bonds were purchased during the War with greenbacks. This was a boon to the banks and financial houses holding any of the Five-Twenty Bonds. These bonds were sold to banks at a discount of sixty to seventy percent. This was too much for even Representative "Beast" Butler, who declared it "an enormous robbery of the people for the benefit of the bankers."[537] Butler was joined by John Sherman (General Sherman's brother), who blasted the whole affair because "soldiers and sailors who shed their blood and saved the Union were paid with greenbacks… that our people were forced by law to accept greenbacks," and he could not understand why moneylenders who profited during the

---

535   Lytle, Andrew Nelson, "The Hind Tit," *I'll Take My Stand* (1930, Baton Rouge, LA: LSU Press, 1983), 202.

536   The bonds were known as "five-twenty bonds" because they were redeemable after five years but not payable until twenty years after July 1, 1865. See "Morgan v. United States (1885)" Wikipedia (wikipedia.org), n.d. (Accessed 22 May 2023). www.bit.ly/MorganvUS.

537   Bowers, Claude, *The Tragic Era*, 225. The author cites *Butler's Book*, 931.

war should be paid in gold.[538] Across the North, the general public began to question why, in the post-War nation (the emerging Yankee Empire), the rich were getting richer and the poor were getting poorer. It was the dawn of the Gilded Age, the age of rich and powerful financiers, and industrial monopolists. It was the precursor to the age of the military-industrial complex, corporate lobbyists, and Globalists. It was all made possible by Lincoln and the Republican Party's war on America's original constitutionally limited Republic of Sovereign States.

President Eisenhower in his 1961 Farewell Address as President also warned about the corrupting influence of what he termed the military-industrial complex. In his original draft, he used the term military-industrial-congressional-complex, but his managers thought it was too strong, so they struck "congressional" from the speech.[539]

Reconstruction did not end in 1877. It continued during Passive Reconstruction, in which the "Progressives" destroyed what was left of the original Constitution. Today—Modern Era Reconstruction—we endure the results of the Republican Party's Active Reconstruction. It was a plan that had a disastrous impact not only on the South but on the entire country. The ultimate impact of the Republican Party's Active Reconstruction was that it reconstructed America's original constitutionally limited Republic of Sovereign States and turned it into the supreme Federal Government. This supreme Federal Government, under the control of Northern ruling elites, produced the bureaucratic Deep State. The Deep State is an unelected bureaucratic state that owes its allegiance not to "We the People" but to America's ruling elite.[540]

---

538   Ibid., 225-6.

539   Eisenhower cited in Kennedy & Kennedy, *Yankee Empire*, 139.

540   Kennedy, James Ronald, *Nullification: Why and How*, 17-22, 31-2. Download a free copy at www.bit.ly/Kennedys_freePDF.

Dysfunctional Republican Carpetbag State Governments

The state governments that seceded from the Union and joined the Confederacy were destroyed by the end of May 1865. Most of the high-ranking elected officials, such as state governors and local government leaders were in prison with the civil leaders of the Confederate States national government. All the Confederate Cabinet members were held prisoner by the invaders, except Secretaries Benjamin and Breckinridge, who made their separate escapes to Europe. Military arrests were numerous, and military prisons held most of the South's leaders. Many, such as Jefferson Davis, eagerly awaited their trial for treason. For some reason, the Yankee Empire decided to forgo public trials for treason and allow its hate-filled propagandists to convict Davis and the entire South in the court of public opinion. In the Yankee Empire's court of public opinion, the accused would not be allowed a defense. The Yankee Empire's court of public opinion allows only the Empire's side to be heard while censoring, banning, and stigmatizing anyone attempting to defend "We the People" of the invaded nation. This was true during Active Reconstruction and remains true today during Modern Era Reconstruction.

While politicians in Washington held a high carnival with lobbyists and other special interests, similar dysfunctional state governments ruled the conquered people of the South. The Louisiana Republican Party's official publication the *Republican*, lamenting the circus in the 1876 state house, provided an example of a Reconstruction Republican state legislature in action:

> Nothing was done all day but howl, raise silly points of order, bully the chair, and each other, and listen to two or three windy orations from as many demagogues.[541]

Can any sensible, fair-minded American deny that there would be a logical reason and incentive for a popular resistance movement

---
541   Henry, Robert Selph, *The Story of Reconstruction*, 558.

to arise under the notorious and near-criminal rule of such a government? Did the Southern resistance movement do things that perhaps should not have been done? Yes! Did unprincipled men claiming to be part of the resistance but who merely used it as an excuse to extract revenge for prior conflicts, said conflicts having nothing to do with the resistance? Yes! But who drew "first blood?" Who created the situation in which a resistance movement would naturally arise? As international law explains—it is not the one who fired the first shot in a war, but it is the one who made firing the first shot in self-defense necessary who is responsible for the war. But as we shall see later, it was not the South that fired the first shot in the Southern resistance movement—it was the Federal Government's sponsored Union League!

The occupied Southern state governments Lincoln established under his Ten Percent Reconstruction Plan and, after Lincoln's assassination, by President Johnson, were mere puppet governments. All these puppet States had governors and legislatures. Yet, despite their titles, the state's governor and its legislature were subordinates of the President in his capacity as commander-in-chief of the Army.[542] The Army remained the real power and used its power to advance the interests of the Republican Party. Under Republican puppet governments, the tax load inflicted upon the devastated people of the South became unbearable. Exorbitant taxation established by Republican state legislators who had little property and, therefore, were not required to pay large tax assessments was a major reason for the development of the Southern underground resistance movement. As one taxpayer in New Orleans declared, "we are all ruined here and to hold property is to be taxed to death by our African communists."[543] In addition to unbearable taxation the people of the South had no judicial system they could look to for a fair adjudication of their legal claims.

---

[542] This is the reason the Republicans in Congress wanted to and eventually did remove control of Reconstruction from the President and gave it to Congress controlled by the Republican Party.

[543] Bowers, Claude, *The Tragic Era*, 438. The author cites the *New York Word*, 08 January 1873.

Former South Carolina Governor Chamberlain, born in Massachusetts, writing in the *Atlantic Monthly* in 1901, described the sad state of the judicial system in South Carolina during Reconstruction. He admitted that "Justice in the lower and higher courts was bought and sold or rather those who sat in the seats nominally of justice made traffic of their judicial powers."[544] This was not an isolated incident in South Carolina but was common across the entire South. Not only were many of the Reconstruction judges untrustworthy, but the jurors would be selected from a list of registered voters containing a few whites and many illiterate blacks. Under such circumstances, is there any wonder that an underground resistance movement would arise?

Taxation Without Representation

Yankee propagandists try to picture the South's resistance to Reconstruction as being motivated by racial hatred. They do this because such emotional claims obscure the tyrannical system of taxation Republicans imposed upon primarily white Southerners. Edward King, a Northern journalist, wrote a series of articles for *Scribner's* magazine that were collected and published in 1874 titled *The Southern States of North America*. He observed that many Northerners, including such notables as Harriet Beecher Stowe, moved to Florida, and after residing in the South for a while, they slowly moved toward the conservative side. Their move to conservatism was motivated by a personal desire to protect themselves from the ravages of ignorant politicians, corruption, and high taxation.[545]

Taxation was a major issue for white and black property owners during Reconstruction. Even Carpetbag Governor Kellogg of Louisiana—from Vermont—complained to his legislature that their rate of taxation imposed upon the people of Louisiana was "not far removed from confiscation." But in addition to the high rate of taxation that conservative whites and blacks complained about was the fact that they were taxed without representation.

---

544   Henry, Robert Selph, *The Story of Reconstruction*, 495.

545   *Ibid.*, 500.

Upwards of 85% of white Southerners were barred from voting under Republican Reconstruction.[546] Northern journalist Edward King noted:

> It is not taxation, not even an increase in taxation, that the white people of South Carolina object to; but it is *taxation without representation and unjust, tyrannical, arbitrary, overwhelming taxation*, producing revenues which never get any further than the already bursting pockets of knaves and dupes.[547] [Emphasis added].

The Federal Government successfully extracted the remaining wealth from its conquered Southern provinces via Acts of Congress and Presidential regulations such as:

- A charge of 25% of its value on all cotton grown by slave labor
- A revenue tax of 2.5 cents per pound of cotton regardless of who raised the cotton (A bale of cotton in 1865 typically weighed 500 pounds.)
- A shipping fee of $0.04 per pound for the privilege of moving it to market[548]

By Federal law, all Confederate cotton was forfeited to the Federal Government. The South was re-invaded by a swarm of Federal cotton agents. Unfortunately, the South had no army to resist this Yankee invasion.

There was often doubt as to whether the cotton was Confederate or if it belonged to private individuals. Such doubts were invariably resolved against private owners unless the private individual made special "arrangements" with the federal agent. The payoff to one federal agent did not guarantee that the cotton would not be seized

---

546   Wilson, Clyde N., "Defeat and Occupation: The Cold War Know as 'Reconstruction,"' *To Live and Die In Dixie*, 439.

547   Henry, Robert Selph, *The Story of Reconstruction*, 501.

548   *Ibid.*, 63.

by another agent down the line.[549] If the private individual took his case to court his case would be adjudicated by a military court. For all practical purposes, only scalawags and freedmen had "status" in these federal military courts. Patriotic Southerners, as a defeated and occupied people, had no standing in the federal military court. *Vae Victis*—Woe to the vanquished! Under such an unjust system of taxation, courts, and government, is there any wonder that a resistance movement would arise in the occupied South?

Yankee plundering of the defeated South was not reserved just for cotton. Secretary of the Treasury McCulloch, in his report to Congress, referred to the actions of his agents as "general plunder; every species of intrigue and speculation and theft."[550] An Ohio Republican politician and newspaper editor, Whitelaw Reid, described more particularly:

> ... the practice of regarding everything left in the country [the occupied South] as the legitimate prize of the first officer who discovered it. What shall be thought of the officer who finding a fine law library, straightway packed it up and sent it to his office in the North? Or what shall be said of the taste of the other officer who, finding in an old country residence a series of family portraits, imagined that they would form very pretty parlor ornaments anywhere, and sent the entire set, embracing the ancestors of the haughty old South Carolinian for generations back, to look down from the walls of his Yankee residence? ... In general, our people seem to go upon the theory that, having conquered the country, they are entitled to the best it has, and in duty bound to use as much of it as possible.[551]

---

549 *Ibid.*

550 *Ibid.*, 64.

551 Reid cited in Henry, Robert Selph, *The Story of Reconstruction*, 65.

Resentment at being ruled over by incompetent and corrupt politicians and the fact that whites were not allowed appropriate representation in the ruling governing bodies was a major factor in the rise of a South-wide secret resistance movement. "No taxation without representation" was the battle cry of their colonial forefathers in 1776. Almost a century later, their Southern descendants were echoing the same sentiment. According to a South Carolina taxpayers' convention meeting in the spring of 1871, "They who lay the taxes do not pay them."[552] This meant that many "taxpayers" were forced to liquidate their real estate and landholdings to pay their tax assessments. This was a boon for the politicians who had no taxes to pay and could purchase great estates, for pennies on the dollar. *Vae victis*—Woe to the vanquished.

A Federal revenue officer testified that he used United States troops to promote the idea of outrages conducted by the Klan by shooting a hole in his hat and then rushing to the troops to tell them he was set upon by the Klan. He stated that the troops would immediately form a skirmish-line and "advance upon the supposed KKKs with an intrepidity which reflected credit upon the troops, who knew no better than that there was a real foe before them."[553] Northern newspapers would then report this incident as proof of ongoing "rebel" outrages justifying strict bayonet rule over such dangerous and evil "rebels."

The Union League Draws First Blood

The Union League Clubs of New York and Philadelphia were organized to bolster the sagging support for the War in the North. By the summer of 1866 it became a partisan, Radical Republican organization with emissaries organizing the occupied South for the Republican Party. The occupying Yankees understood that there were not enough scallywag white Southerners to control the conquered territories and keep the South safely in the Republican Party. This was not possible even with former Confederates

---

552 *Ibid.*, 448.

553 *Ibid.*, 473.

disfranchised. They also understood that the only way they could hold the South in the Republican camp was by making voters out of the newly freed slaves. Allowing blacks to vote was something that whites in most Northern States would not allow. But the Radicals understood that, before the Republican Party could gain black votes in the South, they first had to separate black and white Southerners. Perhaps without realizing it, they were using the ancient technique of divide-and-rule used by empires to control the people in their newly conquered territory. It was imperative that Republicans teach black Southerners to hate their white neighbors. The Northern Union League ensured that there was an endless supply of teachers of hate rushing to the occupied South. Aided by the Federal Government's Freedmen's Bureau, these Union League agents of hatred began their efforts to organize the South. They claimed they were organizing the Union League to help blacks, but, for all practical purposes, they were organizing for the Republican Party. Federal agents of the Freedmen's Bureau informed freedmen that the government required them to enroll in pro-Republican political clubs and secret "loyal" societies. They were not beyond using coercion and actual violence to compel blacks to become members in "loyal" clubs and societies.

The Freedman's Bureau, with total disregard for the Constitution's Fourth Amendment protection of private citizens' property,[554] confiscated millions of acres of property owned by subjugated Southerners. In a report issued in 1896 by the Federal Secretary of Agriculture, the Federal Government admitted that "nearly two million of the farms had been given away by the government."[555] One wonders if the Federal Government will apologize and offer reparations to the descendants of the original owners whose property was unconstitutionally seized by the victorious Yankee Empire.

---

554 Amendment IV: The right of the people to be secure in their persons, houses, papers, and effects, against unreasonable searches and seizures, shall not be violated....

555 Chodes, John, *Washington's KKK: The Union League During Southern Reconstruction*, 15; The author cites the Annual Report of the Secretary of Agriculture, 1896, xlvi.

The Republican Party in Congress knew that it would take a large military force to occupy the defeated South and maintain control over the people. To allay the cost of such a large military force, they encouraged local state carpetbag and scallywag officials to raise a large militia of freedmen and pay for the expense by the sale of captured property. According to the *Congressional Globe*:

> ...all proceeds of the sale of contraband and captured property seized or captured by the militia will constitute a part of the fund out of which they will be paid, thus inciting the volunteers to harass the people in time of peace by unlawful seizure to provide the means of paying themselves.[556]

One "Colonel" James Sinclair held meetings with freedmen promising them a share of the land and property owned by local white "rebels" if they voted Republican. He urged them to hate their former masters and mistresses and treat them with insolence and contempt.[557] A South Carolina scalawag, James W. Hunnicutt, promised "the damnedest revolution" if Congress failed to pass universal franchise. Whites on remote plantations began to fear for their lives. They all knew about the Haitian slave revolt and the massacre of innocent whites and feared such violence would break out in their communities. An English woman living in Georgia was fearful of the coming race war caused by those now in power who were "exciting the negroes to every kind of insolent lawlessness."[558] The conquered South endured visiting Yankee Senators and Representatives who came down South to view their newly conquered territory while joyfully feasting their eyes on the distress and misery of the surviving "rebels." Senator Henry Wilson from Massachusetts and later Vice President under Grant came down "stirring up the blacks, irritating and insulting the whites."[559] Representative William D. (Pig-Iron) Kelly from Pennsylvania

---

556   *The Congressional Globe*, 40th Congress, 2nd Session, 510.

557   Bowers, Claude, *The Tragic Era*, 199.

558   *Ibid.*, 200. Author cites Leigh, Frances Butler, *Ten Years on a Georgia Plantation*, 67.

559   *Ibid.*, 201, Author cites Welles, Gideon, *Diary*, Vol. III, 87.

made a hateful anti-white South speech in Mobile, Alabama. He was successful in inflaming both black and white Southerners—which may well have been his "divide-and-rule" aim. A riot broke out which was attributed to "a recreant Northerner."[560]

Claude Bowers, a well-known Southern historian and well-respected until the beginning of Modern Era Reconstruction, described the Union League's mysticism designed to play upon the superstitions of the newly freed slaves:

> Night meetings, impressive, flamboyant ceremonies, solemn oaths, passwords, every possible appeal to the emotions and senses, with negroes on guard down the road to challenge prowlers, much marching and drilling—all mystery. And the incendiary speeches from Northern politicians promising the confiscation of the white man's land. Discipline, too—iron discipline. Intimidation, likewise—death penalty for voting the Democratic ticket. Strangers arriving mysteriously in the night with warnings that the native whites were deadly enemies. Promises of arms, too—soon to be fulfilled. And the negroes moved as a race into the clubs. And woe to the negro who held back or asked advice of an old master. This, they were taught, was treason to race, to party.[561]

Across the South upward of 90 percent of freedmen enrolled in the Union League. The Union League was a front for the Republican Party and an acknowledged enemy of white "rebel" Southerners. The Union League was an oath-bound grouping of mostly illiterate newly freed slaves who, through no fault of their own, were impervious to civil discourse, reason, and logic. They were a pliable group of Republican voters who would be controlled by emotions of hatred and greed stirred up by the worst of the

---

560   Ibid., Author cites *McMinnville Enterprise*, 22 June 1867.

561   Ibid., 202-3.

North—carpetbaggers. Northern carpetbaggers were aided by the even more despicable group of white Southerners—scallywags. In short order, the carpetbag state governments began arming the Union League members and preparing them to defend the Republican Revolution.

Charles Nordhoff, a Republican journalist and author of *The Cotton States* published in 1875, observed that Republicans in the South were well-versed in the use of intimidation as a technique to keep black voters "in line." He wrote that "the lowest Federal officer was a very powerful being, armed with the whole strength of the Federal government." But Mr. Nordhoff noted that "the most savage intimidators of all" were the black activists usually under the influence of the Union League or Freedman's Bureau. He wrote that "In their political relations among each other, they are as intolerant and unscrupulous as ignorant men suddenly possessed of political rights are sure to be."[562]

The Republican Party relied upon the Union League to control manipulable black voters. The *New York Herald* described how the Union League managed black votes: "The voter got his ticket from the captain, the captain had it from the colonel, and he from the general, and the general of course had it from the owners and managers in Washington of the grand scheme to secure political supremacy."[563] And all of this was done while most white Southerners were denied the right to vote. To secure its political dominance in Washington, the Republican Party placed the South under military dictatorship enforced by bayonet rule—most of those bayonets were in the hands of illiterate and insolent black militia.

The Federal Government's sponsored Union League appeared before the emergence of the Klan and other secret Southern resistance groups. As some would say today, "They drew first blood." After the appearance of the Union League in an area, the local white women were in constant danger when they ventured

---

562   Henry, Robert Selph, *The Story of Reconstruction*, 523-4.

563   Bowers, Claude, *The Tragic Era*, 219. Author cites Fleming, Walter F., *Documentary History of Reconstruction*, 514-16.

out of their houses or when they were left alone at home. This was especially true in areas where blacks outnumbered whites. As former Confederal General and post-War attorney James H. Clanton noted: "We are in the hands of camp followers, horse-holders, cooks, and bottle-washers and thieves." It was not unusual to see armed black militia or police leading white girls off to jail[564] on some trumped-up charge—something that would NEVER have been allowed to happen in the lily-white North of the day! The Southern plain folk, who were not part of the plantation system, were reduced to utter poverty by the War. Plain folk white women, when taking their farm products to market, traveled in groups to lessen the possibility of rape.[565]

The Federal Government's Freedman's Bureau served to protect blacks charged with crimes against white women. When black attackers were tried and convicted, they were shortly released after serving only a few days of incarceration.[566] Under such circumstances, is there any wonder that some form of white resistance would arise? For white Southerners, the most rudimentary form of safety and security for persons and property did not arise until the formation of secret resistance groups. The Southern resistance movement went by different names, the most well-known was the original Klan. Initially, these secret resistance groups were under the strict leadership of men like General James H. Clanton and General John T. Morgan of Alabama, General James Z. George in Mississippi, General Albert Pike in Arkansas, and General John B. Gordon in Georgia.[567] The early resistance movement was under the control of men who were accustomed to organizing and controlling large bodies of men. These resistance leaders were men of high moral character who would not countenance vengeance and criminality within their ranks.

---

564 Ibid., 308. Author cites Fleming, Walter F., *Documentary History of Reconstruction*, Vol. II, 269, 1906.

565 Ibid., 308. Author cites Fleming, Walter F., *Documentary History of Reconstruction*, Vol. II, 333-4, 1906.

566 Ibid.

567 Ibid., 310.

Unfortunately, as with all secret societies, it is easy for secret societies to come under the influence and eventual control of lesser-minded men. Once it became evident that unbridled black control of society was coming to an end, the original resistance movement leaders understood that the work of the resistance movement was over. Peaceful efforts on the political front were necessary. The leadership of the resistance movement realized that slanderous charges of "rebel outrages against blacks down South" were needed by the Republican Party to keep their power in Washington. However, the lawless element within the resistance movement refused the order to disband and used the resistance movement as an excuse to carry out attacks against personal enemies or to fulfill their personal hatred against local blacks. This was a God-send to the Northern propagandists.

The Republican Party depended on its Northern newspaper propagandists to provide the Northern public with continuing reports of real or imagined "rebel outrages." There were cases, never reported in the North, in which the Union League conducted acts of outrage against one of their own who was straying from the League and blamed the outrage on the Klan or other white resistance organizations. There were incidents in which white Union League members attempted to infiltrate the Klan but were found out to be agents of the Tennessee scallywag Governor Brownlow.[568] In 1869, General N.B. Forrest issued a stinging denunciation of the lawless elements that seized portions of the resistance movement. Forrest demanded that the secret mask be removed, but the lawless elements within the movement ignored this demand from such a well-respected former Confederate General.[569]

The Freedmen's Bureau was a Congressionally authorized federal agency. Its commissioners came from the Union Army. Having spent their careers destroying the white South, it was not unusual that these commissioners would hold a distinct bias favoring blacks and a strong prejudice against white Southerners,

---

568 Ibid., 311. Author cites Davis, S.L., *Authentic History of the Ku-Klux-Klan* , (New York, 1924), 109.

569 Ibid., 311. Author cites Davis, S.L., *Authentic History of the Ku-Klux-Klan*, 125-8.

both former slave owners as well as whites who never owned slaves.[570] As one Southern historian noted:

> [The Freedmen's Bureau] ...local officers...the greatest difficulties appeared. The work of a local Bureau agent was trying and exacting. His powers were great and ill-defined, touching the intimacies of everyday work and life of the people, white and black. The conditions and situations which confronted him from day to day were unprecedented.[571]

Representative Joseph Powell (D-Pennsylvania) warned Congress that the attraction of plunder down South would draw men of the lowest order to fill the ranks of the Freedmen's Bureau agents. He said such a situation will attract:

> ...a class of agents...fulfilled the prophetic description given in Congress during the debate on the passage of the bill creating the Bureau. The men who are to go down there, will be your broken-down politicians and your dilapidated preachers; that description of men who are too lazy to work...."[572]

The Freedmen's Bureau agents were described by Dr. W.E.B. DuBois as "varied all the way from unselfish philanthropists to narrow-minded busybodies and thieves...."[573] He also said that "the average was better than the worst," but that is true of any mathematical ranking. It was also equally true that the average was worse than the best. Yankee propagandists attempted to praise the occupying Union Army and the Freedmen's Bureau's work in combatting starvation and relief for destitute people. But the Yankee Empire's propagandists failed to acknowledge

---

570 *Ibid.*, 60.

571 Henry, Robert Selph, *The Story of Reconstruction*, 61.

572 Rep. Joseph Powell (D-Penn.) cited in Henry, Robert Selph, *The Story of Reconstruction*, 61.

573 DuBois cited in Henry, Robert Selph, *The Story of Reconstruction*, 61.

who caused the deplorable condition the people of the occupied South were suffering under. The invading Yankee Army, following Lincoln's vigorous war policy, caused conditions of starvation and homelessness in the South. The occupiers' primary aim was to prevent an open rebellion against their harsh rule which would have occurred if some effort to ameliorate starvation among both black and white Southerners was not accomplished. Once again, we see that Republican action was motivated not by "charity for all" but by pragmatic partisan politics.

The very existence of the Freedmen's Bureau with its condescending catering to the newly freed slaves increased the tendency of restlessness of certain elements among the freedmen. Many freedmen left the rural areas and flocked to towns and cities. The Bureau's offices in towns and cities became centers for the distribution of free government rations. Soon, large gatherings of unemployed freedmen gathered around these centers to hear Bureau officials promise "forty acres and a mule" for every man by Christmas time. With the promise of such government windfall awaiting them, the newly freed slaves saw no need to be actively engaged in work in the fields. In their defense, from their uneducated view, this was a rational choice. Unfortunately for them and Southern society, it was not an educated choice rationally made but a choice based upon Yankee falsehoods. Congress was busy giving away millions of acres of "free" land to railroads with the right connections in Washington, but not a single acre of Western land would be reserved for newly freed landless slaves.

Some Northerners recognized the unprincipled nature of the Republican's Freedmen's Bill. David Dudley Field, speaking at a mass meeting in New York, described the Bill as "the curious feature of the Freedmen's bill...that it took the blacks under the protection of the Federal Government as if they were not able to take care of themselves, while the same persons [Republicans] who urged...the measure are the most clamorous to give the same dependent population [blacks] a large share in the government of the country."[574] But Mr. Field overlooked that, in the emerging Yankee Empire, logical consistency with constitutional and ethical principles always took a back seat to the political aggrandizement of the Republican Party and its cronies.

The Occupied South's Resistance Movement

The general attitude of post-War Southerners is demonstrated by Confederate officer Martin Gary on his way home from the surrender at Appomattox. He declared that even though he served honorably in the Confederate Army, now as a private citizen, "I'm for the Union; we are licked but I'm glad it is all over." His attitude radically changed not by defeat but by eleven years of tyrannical rule of his homeland. Martin Gary was to be one of the organizers of the South Carolina Red Shirts raised and inspired by a sense of intolerable injustice, but in the first summer, there was "almost perfect tranquility" as reported by a correspondent of the *Nation*.[575]

The post-War Southern resistance movement had its origins not in race hatred or treason, as postmodern Yankee propagandists would have you believe, but in the tyrannical acts of the Yankee Empire's national Republicans. The Radical Republican Party controlled Congress and they controlled local Republican agents such as Treasury agents, the Freedman's Bureau, and indirectly, the Union League, Carpetbaggers, and Scallywags. The Republican Party stationed its military and insolent black militia in the conquered South to assure the "dominance of the Party of Union." The necessity for a Southern Resistance movement was forced upon Southern whites by the Republican Party which controlled the Federal Government's political and military forces.

Most Southerners, exhausted from war, were resigned to make the best out of a bad situation.[576] Even a scallywag such as John Minor Botts, a strong and uncompromising Union man admitted that "...at the time of the surrender of General Lee's Army and the

---

574   Ibid., 160.
575   Ibid., 66.
576   Ibid., 67.

restoration of peace there was not only a general, but an almost universal, acquiescence and congratulation among the people that the war had terminated, and a large majority of them were at least contented." [577] This state of mind quickly changed in 1866 when the North under Republican rule began to show their intentions to complete the economic exploitation and *political extermination* of the South. Southerners were destined to become political slaves of the North's ruling elite and the once prosperous South would become an economic colony of the industrialized and affluent North. But this was yet to play out. Late in 1865 and early in 1866 there was a general sense of relief that the War was over and a determination to make the best out of a bad situation.

The future president of the United States Rutherford B. Hayes wrote home from Memphis: "The Rebel officers are particularly interesting. I get on with them famously. I talk negro suffrage and our [extreme] radicalism to all of them. They dissent but are polite and cordial."[578] The willingness to work with Northerners was evident in late 1865 and early 1866. Union Major Truman wrote, "Large numbers of ex-Federal and ex-Confederate officers are engaged together in mercantile pursuits and in cotton planting."[579] Included in the cotton plantations on the Mississippi River was one jointly operated by General Nathan Bedford Forrest, CSA, and Union Major Diffenbach of Minnesota.[580]

Nor was the mutual respect between former enemies reserved just for business ventures. In Chattanooga, Tennessee, twelve young Union soldiers and twelve young Confederates worked together to form a fishing club that lasted for 70 years.[581] Touring the South in the summer of 1865, General Grant stated that:

---

577   *Ibid.*, 67.
578   *Ibid.*, 69.
579   *Ibid.*, 70.
580   *Ibid.*, 70.
581   *Ibid.*, 70.

> My observations lead me to the conclusion...that they are in earnest in wishing to do what they think is required by the government, not humiliating to them as citizens.... It is to be regretted that there cannot be a greater commingling [mingling—to combine into a more or less uniform whole] at this time between the citizens of the two sections, and particularly of those entrusted with the law-making power.[582]

Those "entrusted with the lawmaking power" were not interested in reconciliation between the North and the South—they were interested in erecting a political and economic empire controlled by Northern ruling elites.

Evil men such as General Ben "Beast" Butler were a constant worry to the new President, Andrew Johnson. Butler continually urged the President to execute Jefferson Davis and Robert E. Lee as well as urging severe punishment of the whole people of the former Confederate States of America.[583] Butler was one of the leading Radical Republicans taking control of the Republican Party and eventually Congress. With that control and political power, they were able to initiate the Republican Party's vengeful Reconstruction policies. "We the People" of the South were first oppressed by aggressive invading Yankee soldiers and then by aggressive Yankee politicians.

Union Colonel Henry A. Morrow described the social and political conditions in the South during Reconstruction in a report to General W.H. Emory. After a tour of Louisiana in late 1874 he reported that corruption:

> ...is manifest in almost every department of business...uncultivated fields, unrepaired fences, roofless and dilapidated dwellings, and abandoned houses...schools were closed for want of money to

---

582 General Grant cited in Henry, Robert Selph, *The Story of Reconstruction*, 70-1.

583 Bowers, Claude, *The Tragic Era*, 22.

pay the teachers...school funds had been stolen by State officials...money and not justice, is charged with turning the judicial scales...exorbitant taxes... ruined credit...depleted treasury...enormous debts... multiplication of officers...[584]

This unbiased report from a Union officer is a good explanation of the social and political situation faced not just in Louisiana but across the South. But even this description does not take into consideration the psychological impact that defeat and occupation by an alien power had upon a defeated, defenseless, impoverished, and occupied people. American postmodern "intellectuals" and "historians" have refused to consider this impact when slandering the South for its, sometimes inappropriate, efforts of resistance to federal tyranny. No doubt certain things were done by the French Resistance during Nazi occupation that were not justified but such things do occur when a once free people are invaded and occupied by an evil power. Cultural distortion is an automatic outcome of defeat and occupation.[585]

General Clanton of Alabama explained the reason for the development of popular resistance to Yankee-imposed Reconstruction state governments:

> So far as our state government is concerned, we are in the hands of camp-followers, horse-holders, cooks, bottle-washers, and thieves.... We have passed out from the hands of the brave soldiers who overcame us and are turned to the tender mercies of squaws for torture.[586]

South Carolina's Harvard-educated Carpetbag Governor, Daniel H. Chamberlain of Massachusetts, honestly admitted the corrupt nature of South Carolina's Republican Reconstruction

---

584 Henry, Robert Selph, *The Story of Reconstruction*, 532.

585 Kennedy & Kennedy, *Punished With Poverty-The Suffering South* 2nd ed., 140-6.

586 Henry, Robert Selph, *The Story of Reconstruction*, 443.

government, "Incompetency, dishonesty, corruption in all its forms...rule the party which rules the state."[587] South Carolina State Senator Beverly Nash, a black state senator and former barber, testified that he sold his vote for a particular bill for five thousand dollars and five thousand dollars worth of Railroad script.[588] Under such social and political conditions, it would be unreasonable to expect a popular resistance not to arise.

Ireland is an excellent example of how a people will seek ways to resist the occupation of their homeland. But when such conditions produce secret resistance organizations, the secret underground nature of the resistance greatly hampers the ability to control said resistance movements. Unrestrained violence emerges, often motivated by revenge for past offenses not necessarily associated with the resistance movement, and sometimes by opponents masquerading as part of the resistance to damage the reputation of legitimate resistance efforts. The intrinsic dangers of a resistance movement can be avoided only by avoiding the creation of the situation in which a resistance movement is needed. It is the invader, not the invaded people, who is responsible for the rise of a resistance movement. The French Resistance would not have developed if Germany had not invaded, conquered, occupied, and established their puppet government in Vichy France during World War II.

As the Southern resistance movement began to emerge, federal authorities responded with a massive campaign of oppression directed at the local population. The occupied South was governed by a military dictatorship that used tyrannical police-state tactics to fight the resistance movement. For example, Federal authorities rounded up and arrested more than six hundred individuals in Mississippi in 1871 on charges of violating the rights of the newly freed slaves. All were released under bond. In Georgia, Federal trials were held for twenty-three out of eighteen hundred whites arrested in 1871. Of the eighteen tried in Federal court, only one

---

587   *Ibid.*, 446.

588   *Ibid.*, 446.

was convicted![589] And remember, these courts were Republican courts using jurors selected from local voter rolls consisting of mainly newly freed slaves.

THE BLOODY SHIRT—YANKEE JUSTIFICATION FOR MILITARY DICTATORSHIP DOWN SOUTH

The phrase "Waving the bloody shirt" had its American origin in the post-War Active Reconstruction era. It was used to mock Radical Republicans who claimed that voting for conservative democrats was an insult to the blood shed by Union soldiers during the War. The phrase is commonly used today to rebuke an individual who attempts to stir up partisan animosity. As previously stated, the use of emotions in a mass democracy such as the modern-day USA is a leftist propaganda technique used to distract the public from facts, truth, or logic. Why? Because facts, truth, and logic are fatal to the cause espoused by the individual waving the bloody shirt. The Republican Party had a massive network of newspapers and public speakers (rabble-rousers) who would fire-up the emotions of Northerners with vicious anti-South propaganda while encouraging Northerners to demand strict application of Reconstruction. The bloody shirt was necessary because most folks in the North were ready to move past the War and "get on with their lives."

The Republican Party had to deal with a Northern population grown weary of war and entering what would become known as the Gilded Age of Northern economic growth. To counter-act growing public disinterest in affairs down South, Republicans, and their propagandists began waving the "bloody shirt." Republicans in Congress had the expert assistance of professional rabble-rousers leftover from the radical abolitionist movement.[590]

The campaign for president of 1866 had a promising beginning for those seeking an early end to Reconstruction and a return to "normalcy." Over fifteen thousand people attended the National

---

589   Ibid., 449.

590   Ibid., 136.

Union Convention that opened in Philadelphia on August 14, 1866. National reconciliation was the underlying theme of the convention. Union and Confederate veterans attended and made plain their newly acquired friendship. Delegates from Massachusetts and South Carolina, former Union and Confederate officers entered the convention arm-in-arm, a visual sign of their unabashed support for North/South reconciliation. President Johnson's supporters saw the National Union Convention as an indicator that moderates and conservatives would replace the current Republican-controlled Congress with a Congress controlled by moderates and conservatives. President Johnson and his supporters pinned their hopes on the upcoming election in which Representatives and Senators more friendly to the President would hopefully be elected. They did not consider the emotional power that would be generated by Republicans waving the bloody shirt. It is as true today as it was back then that, in a mass democracy, emotions generate more votes than truth, facts, and logic.

The bloody shirt was an essential emotional tool used by the Republicans during the 1866 elections. Albion W. Tourgee, a former Union Army officer and North Carolina carpetbagger, was a major Yankee propagandist who supplied Republican newspapers in the North with vivid though questionable accounts of rebel uprisings and violence in North Carolina. He told the press about an alleged recent discovery of a pond in which were found fifteen murdered blacks and that over twelve hundred former Union soldiers who were attempting to settle in North Carolina were forced to flee the state due to threats of violence. When challenged to produce the names of the twelve hundred former Union soldiers and the fifteen blacks, he maintained his silence. The harm was already done: the hysterical Yankee press picked up the story and published it as gospel to a Yankee public eager to devour anything that confirmed their bias toward "We the People" of the South.

Conservative citizens of North Carolina became restless and determined to use any effective means to unseat political corruption and remove North Carolinians from the annals of direct political slavery. The Republican masters of the state understood this and knew their only hope of keeping the state under Republican control was to use their armed black militia backed by Union troops to terrorize white and black conservatives. All such terroristic acts would be done under the pretext of the law. If the Republicans were lucky, some hot-tempered white could be lured into some act of violence toward a black Republican. Such "rebel" outrages were needed to keep the bloody shirt waving up North. If a legitimate "outrage" did not occur, the Republicans could count on anti-South Northern papers to print numerous manufactured incidents. The bloody shirt was used against President Johnson because he rejected the Radical Republican Reconstruction Plan, and it was also used against General Grant, who, shortly after the War issued a positive report about the people in the post-War South.

Republicans such as Senator Sumner rebuked President Johnson's slow approach and General Grant's positive report by declaring it to be a "white-washing affair." Republican and socialist General Carl Schurz, under the instructions of the Republican Party, issued a report to counter General Grant's report on the conditions down South. Schurz's report gave great support to those waving the "bloody shirt." He reported that "treason did not appear odious" to the defeated Southerners. His report concluded that, as soon as Federal authority was removed from the South, a new wave of oppression would arise. "Submission [was] the only means by which [Southerners] could rid themselves of the Federal soldiers and obtain once more control of their own affairs."[591] In other words, if the conquered people refused to repent for their sin of desiring self-government and acknowledge their former actions as being "odious," then they should be ruled as a conquered people. Self-government, the consent of the governed, in the view of the Republican Party, was odious if the conquered people refused to submit to Republican rule.

The Republican Party resorted to "waving the bloody shirt" because many folks in the North in the summer and fall of 1865 and early on into 1866 wanted an end to political hostilities. For

---

591   *Ibid.*, 139-40.

example, Governor John A. Andrew (R-Massachusetts) urged "vigorous prosecution of the Peace" and asserted:

> The Southern people...fought, toiled, endured, and persevered, with a courage, an unanimity and a persistency, not outdone by any people in any Revolution...They whose courage, talents, and will entitle them to lead, will lead.... We ought to demand, and to secure, the cooperation of the strongest and ablest minds and the natural leaders of opinion in the South. If we cannot gain their support of the just measures needful for the work of safe re-organization, re-organization will be delusive and full of danger....[592]

He clearly saw the danger of future Southern risings [as in, "The South Shall Rise Again!"] if the defeated but courageous people of the South were not treated as equals within a union now free of slavery. Unlike the radical element that controlled the Republican Party, he wanted to "extend our hands with cordial goodwill to meet the proffered hands of the South."[593] Governor Andres died in October of 1867, foreshadowing the death of men of goodwill in the Republican Party. Men of unlimited hatred for the South and its conservative, constitution-loving, political traditions stood at the helm of the Party of Reconstruction. They schemed to use their control of Congress to vastly expand the Federal Government's power. Their efforts would make Alexander Hamilton's dream of an imperial Federal Government permanent while assuring the death of Thomas Jefferson's dream of a limited Republic composed of Sovereign States.[594] Thus, the genesis of the so-called "Deep State."

---

592   Ibid., 142.

593   Ibid., 142.

594   DiLorenzo, Dr. Thomas J., *Hamilton's Curse: How Jefferson's Archenemy Betrayed the American Revolution—and What It Means for America Today* (New York: Crown Publishing Group), 12.

Just like the Deep State of the modern era, the Radical's Reconstruction Plan needed fake news and slander to confuse the issue and provide them a smoke-screen behind which they could hide while conducting their campaign of destruction and tyranny. Fake news was used to justify the Federal Government's tyrannical approach to "We the People" of the once-free South. The waving of the bloody shirt inflamed Northern hatred for the people of the conquered South. Fake news was the staple of the Republican Party's campaign against the South. For example, Union General Fisk declared that:

> ...only the day before yesterday, in Lexington, thirteen discharged colored soldiers stood in the streets, in full sight of the Henry Clay monument, with their bodies lacerated, their backs bleeding from the cruel lash, their heads cut to the scalp, and one or two of them with their eyes put out! And what for, do you suppose? Simply for going to their former masters and asking for their wives and children."[595]

No proof was provided, no accounts of arrests were made, and no accused were brought to trial. All that was needed was the accusation and the harm was done. As Southern comedian Lewis Grizzard (1946-1994) pointed out, the more extravagant and outrageous a claim about the South is, the more likely Yankees are to believe it. Northern newspapers were eager to obtain any reports of Southern "outrages" against the newly freed slaves or Northern occupation troops. No journalistic efforts were made to verify or to print corrections when an alleged "outrage" was demonstrated to be false. The purpose of the bloody shirt was not to obtain truth but to obtain votes for the Republican Party. One pragmatic Yankee politician openly declared that he believed that outrages down South reported in Northern newspapers were necessary to keep the Republican Party in power. It was boldly proclaimed that "A kilt nigger

---
595 Henry, Robert Selph, *The Story of Reconstruction*, 156.

is worth twenty thousand votes...north of the Potomac."[596] The Republican Governor of Alabama wrote a letter in 1870 explaining why the Union League and other Republicans promoted false outrages across the South:

> The Republicans are earnest in their efforts to deceive the people of the North in relation to the conditions of the South...to furnish an excuse for President Grant, who has ordered United States troops to North Carolina to aid Governor Holden.[597]

A letter to the editor to all pro-Republican papers in Indiana declared: "I desire to call your attention to the horrible scenes of violence and bloodshed transpiring throughout the South and suggest that you give them as great prominence as possible in your paper from this time until after the election." The letter was signed by Thomas J. Brady, State Chairman of the Indiana Republican Party. It was charged that the author of the letter was Senator Morton.[598]

One of the best examples of waving the bloody shirt is in a speech that Senator Robert G. Ingersoll gave to a Union Sailors and Soldiers convention held in September 1876 in Indianapolis, Indiana:

> Every man that shot Union soldiers was a Democrat. Every man that starved Union soldiers and refused them a crust in the extremity of death was a Democrat. Every man that loved slavery better than liberty was a Democrat. The man that assassinated Abraham Lincoln was a Democrat. Every man that sympathized with the assassin—every man glad that the noblest President ever elected was assassinated—was a Democrat.... Every man that helped to burn

---

596   Ibid., 564.

597   Chodes, John, *Washington's KKK: The Union League During Southern Reconstruction*, 50.

598   Bowers, Claude, *The Tragic Era* (Halcyon House, New York: 1929), 427. Author cites the *New York World*, 14 October 1874.

orphan asylums in New York was a Democrat.... Every man that tried to spread smallpox and yellow fever in the North...was a Democrat. Soldiers, every scar you have got on your heroic bodies was given you by a Democrat.[599]

Such pure hatred directed at the conquered, occupied, and defenseless people of the South is evidence that as far as the Republican Party was concerned, the War was not over. Ingersoll even admitted that the election was "simply a prolongation of the war."[600] As far as America's ruling elite were (and still are) concerned, the War never ends. Most occupied people understand this simple fact. The Irish understood this and maintained their dream of self-government during centuries of English occupation of their homeland. Unfortunately, most Southerners (and American conservatives nationwide) live in a fantasy world where "their" country provides "liberty and justice for all." In reality, the current political *status quo* provides the ruling elite with virtually unlimited perks, privileges, and power paid for by a dumbed-down electorate who learned to love their chains.[601]

Even in the era of the "bloody shirt" and vicious anti-South Northern propaganda, a few men in the Republican Party saw through the political maneuvering of their peers. Representative Frederick E. Woodbridge (R-Vermont) noted that impeachment "must be for some offense known to the law, and not created by the fancy of the members of the House." He then, unknowingly, warned that this effort (The February 1868 effort of Republicans to impeach President Johnson) was a political effort that would set an evil example for future American government.

> ...the day of political impeachments would be a sad one for this country. Political unfitness and

---

599   Henry, Robert Selph, *The Story of Reconstruction*, 555-6.

600   *Ibid.*, 556.

601   See Kennedy, James Ronald, *Nullification: Why and How* .Free download at wwwbit.ly/Kennedys_freePDF.

incapacity must be tried at the ballot box, not in the high court of impeachment.[602]

Modern Era Reconstruction has seen its share of weaponized impeachments used as a political tool. The Republican Party established the practice, and progressives, liberals, and neo-Marxists have followed it ever since.

The Republican Party's convention held in Chicago on May 20-21, 1868, nominated General Grant on a unanimous first ballot vote. The presidential campaign would be an emotional affair with the bloody shirt waving in the background. Unfortunately, presidential elections in a mass democracy are not won on a debate over principles, issues, and policies but on emotions. The Republican Party's 1868 Platform is demonstrative of the Republican Party's hypocrisy and general hatred for the Southern people. When it came to allowing blacks to vote in their (Northern) States, the attitude was radically different from what they were imposing, at bayonet point, upon the people of the South. The Republican Platform declared that "The guaranty by Congress of equal suffrage to all the loyal men of the South...must be maintained; while the question of suffrage in all the loyal States properly belongs to the people of those States."[603] Disfranchised whites in the former Confederacy would be forced at bayonet point to accept the rule of mostly illiterate blacks while Northern States would be allowed to continue their policy of reserving the franchise to whites only. Even in those few Northern States that allowed blacks to vote, the number of blacks in those States was so small as to have virtually no impact on local or state elections. Even after the end of the War, some of the Northern States were reluctant to remove their "exclusion" laws that prohibited blacks from coming into their lily-white States!

The Democrat Platform took the high road of constitutional principle in the 1868 presidential campaign. They attempted

---

602   Henry, Robert Selph, *The Story of Reconstruction*, 271.

603   *Ibid.*, 331.

to demonstrate that the Republican Party established military despotism in a time of peace and that, instead of restoring America's original Union, the Republicans destroyed the Founding Fathers' original Union. The Democrats platform insisted upon immediate restoration of all States, amnesty for past political offenses, and the regulation of the franchise by the States. They nominated Governor Horatio Seymour of New York as their presidential candidate. On principle, Seymour was a good choice, but from a practical, emotional point-of-view, his nomination played into the hands of Republican, bloody shirt propagandists. Seymour was an outspoken critic of Lincoln's government and its unconstitutional usurpation of power. With the South under Republican control and Texas, Mississippi, and Virginia not recognized as States, Grant easily won the election. Grant received 214 electoral votes and Seymour received 80. Seymour did manage to carry Louisiana and Georgia, but the rest of the occupied South went with the Republican Party.[604] It was clear that if the people of the North were enjoying prosperity brought on by massive government spending during the War, they would not turn away from the Republican Party that was actively waving the bloody shirt.

Grant's election proved that while things were prosperous in the post-War North, the Northern population could be swayed to vote Republican by the simple technique of waving the bloody shirt. But the political capital purchased by the bloody shirt worked only during prosperous times. The economic Panic of 1873 caused many in the North to question Republican leadership. Meanwhile, in the South, the Panic of 1873 went mostly unnoticed because Southerners were already living through a Federal Government-imposed economic disaster.

The National Democrats saw their first real chance to elect the president in the 1876 election. They nominated Samuel J. Tilden, the governor of New York, who was well-known for fighting corruption due to his fight with the Tweed Ring in New York City and the Erie Canal grafters. The Republicans nominated Governor

---

604 See "1868 United States presidential election" Wikipedia (Wikipedia.org). www.bit.ly/1868Presidential.

Rutherford B. Hayes of Ohio. Hayes was known as a sensible politician who had strong views about the importance of honesty in government. Corruption in government emerged as a potent political issue due to the corruption of the Grant Administration and the corruption in the Republican Southern States. The Republican Party understood this and knew the only way they could win was to wave the bloody shirt—continue to stigmatize the South as rebels and traitors and claim that the Democratic Party was the party of the Confederacy.[605]

The Presidential election of 1876 marked the end of Active Reconstruction. The election was so close it had to be settled by Congress. While Republican Rutherford B. Hayes was declared the winner, the deciding votes came from the South with a promise from Hayes to remove the last troops from the South.

This prior overview of Active Reconstruction sets the stage for a review of Reconstruction in each of the Southern States. The States will be reviewed in separate chapters and in alphabetical order.

---

[605] Henry, Robert Selph, *The Story of Reconstruction*, 554.

SIDNEY CLOPTON LANIER

Sidney Clopton Lanier, while living in Alabama, described to a Northern friend the conditions in the post-War, Reconstruction South as, "Perhaps you know that with us of the young generation in the South, since the war, pretty much the whole of life has been merely not dying." Lanier was a Private in the 2nd Georgia Battalion. He and Father Ryan were known as the poets of the Confederacy. Below is one of Lanier's poems lamenting the defeated South ruled by cruel and arrogant invaders. This poem can best be summed up as, "Aid will not come from Northern tyrants who are enjoying the distress they imposed upon the conquered South."

Laughter in the Senate (1868)

In the South lies a lonesome, hungry Land;
He huddles his rags with a cripple's hand;
He mutters, prone on the barren sand,
What time his heart is breaking.

He lifts his bare head from the ground;
He listens through the gloom around:
The winds have brought him a strange sound
Of distant merrymaking.

Comes now the Peace so long delayed?
Is it the cheerful voice of Aid?
Begins the time his heart has prayed,
When men may reap and sow?

Ah, God! Back to the cold earth's breast!
The sages chuckle o'er their jest;
Must they, to give a people rest,
Their dainty wit forego?

The tyrants sit in a stately hall;
They jibe at a wretched people's fall;
The tyrants forget how fresh is the pall
Over their dead and ours.

Look how the senators ape the clown,
And don the motley and hide the gown,
But yonder a fast-rising frown
On the people's forehead lowers.*

---

* Lanier, Sidney, *in Poems of Sidney Lanier* Mary Day Lanier editor (1884, The University of Georgia Press, Athens, GA: 1981), 223.

Chapter 14:

ALABAMA ENDURES
REPUBLICAN RECONSTRUCTION[606]

"Emissaries from the North, arousing the negroes to arson, rapine, and murder, were being dispatched to the Southern States. Their partial success in the John Brown raid had caused widespread terror and alarm"
—*General Joseph Wheeler*[607]

THE FINANCIAL COST and the unconstitutional, dictatorial methods used by the Republican Party to impose reconstruction on the state of Alabama are seldom mentioned by postmodern (neo-Marxist) historians. During Active Reconstruction, the cost of running the state government of Alabama increased two hundred percent and the state's tax rate increased four hundred percent.[608] Legislators, who had little real estate property and therefore did not bear the tax burden, put this confiscatory taxation in place. The white and black taxpayers (landowners) were forced to bear the tax

---

606 This is an overview of one of the 15 Southern States that suffered under Republican-imposed Active Reconstruction. Each state deserves more than a chapter and it is hoped that a pro-South author will take the challenge of writing a book detailing their own state's extensive trials, tribulations, as well as its resistance movement during Active Reconstruction. The same, of course, applies to all the States to follow.

607 General Joseph Wheeler, Alabama, *Confederate Military History*, Vol. VII, Part 1 (1899, Harrisburg, PA: The Archives Society, 1994), 17.

608 Fleming, Walter Lynwood, *The Sequel of Appomattox* (1919, Yale University Press, 1970), 231.

burden voted for by these non-tax-paying legislators. The white taxpayers were disfranchised and, therefore, were taxed without representation in the legislature that passed the tax levies. The political burden of bearing taxes without representation was the primary incentive for the American Colonial resistance movement that resulted in the Declaration of Independence in 1776. It should not be surprising that some form of a resistance movement would arise among the Southern descendants of the generation of 1776. But in Alabama, as in other post-War Southern States, resistance to the occupying powers was not their first choice.

General James H. Clanton of Alabama called for a September 4, 1866, meeting of "conservatives" in Montgomery. Clanton, like many Southern Whigs, was opposed to secession, but once Alabama left the Union, he joined in the defense of Alabama and the Confederacy. His original anti-secession stance made him a spokesman who appealed to the old Whigs, Democrats, and property-owning blacks. Some conservative blacks attended the Montgomery meeting, even though they met potentially violent harassment from blacks under the influence of the Union League, the Freedmen's Bureau, and the Federal military. The chairman of a black "Special Committee on the Situation," J.L. Williams, addressed the gathering. Resolutions were passed calling for education for blacks, local control of suffrage, and peace.[609] In Alabama, as in other Southern States, the initial post-War aim of the white population was not resistance to the alien occupying powers but an effort to establish a mutually beneficial restoration of their state's civil society. However, restoration and reconciliation were not part of the Republican Party's strategy for achieving political control of the South and the nation.

In late 1866 and early 1867, the Republican Party was faced with the question of what to do with these wicked former States in the occupied South. The Republican Party's sycophants in the media pumped out great volumes of anti-South slander and hatred. While such anti-South, pro-radical reconstruction political

---

[609] Henry, Robert Selph, *The Story of Reconstruction* (New York: Konecky & Konecky, , 263.

issues possessed the minds of Northern people, in the South, such political matters were a third or fourth-level concern. The revengeful and greedy Republican-controlled Federal Government passed special taxes on cotton instituted to raise Federal revenue from the South as well as to punish "the rebels." The detrimental impact on impoverished Southerners, both black and white, was noted by the New York Chamber of Commerce: "...the imposition of a discriminating tax which tends to make the rich of the North richer and the poor of the South poorer..."[610] The Republican-imposed discriminatory tax fell hardest on poor black and white tenant farmers (sharecroppers). In 1866, Alabama Governor Patton said twenty thousand widows and sixty thousand orphans lived in his state, and 75% of this number lacked food, shelter, and other necessities. Most were malnourished, and a large number faced disease and starvation. It was noted that many had not eaten meat for months. The lack of protein in their diet continued during Passive Reconstruction, causing a South-only epidemic of Pellagra.[611] In response to the near famine in the South, Kentucky citizens sent ten thousand bushels of corn to help relieve the famine in several war-torn and devastated Southern States.[612] Despite the unprecedented hardship fate handed to "We the People" of the South, Southerners did not surrender their hope for a better future. The folks of Alabama and across the South attempted to make the best out of a bad situation.

Former Major General of the Confederate Army, Henry D. Clayton, was appointed judge in the post-War state of Alabama. In an address to a Grand Jury, he outlined the two things necessary for the newly freed slaves to enjoy their rights and receive justice in the post-War South: "First, a recognition of the fact that all blacks were now free men, the enactment of just and humane laws, and the willing enforcement of these just and humane laws. Secondly, by treating the newly freed blacks with perfect fairness

---

610   Ibid., 200.

611   Kennedy & Kennedy, *Punished With Poverty-the Suffering South*, 2nd ed., 119-21. Pellagra is caused by a deficiency in certain nutrients the body obtains by eating a protein rich diet.

612   Henry, Robert Selph, *The Story of Reconstruction*, 201.

and justice in our contracts and in every way in which we may be brought in contact with them."[613] Such words do not express the sentiment of an evil Southern racist seeking to oppress blacks. They represent a sincere attempt to come to terms with the radical and sudden change in Alabama's society and make the best out of a bad situation.

Some Federal officials in Alabama acknowledged this sincere attempt to come to terms with the new situation. Union General Swayne, head of the Freedmen's Bureau in Alabama, believed that, in time, the white people of Alabama would have provided the right to vote to qualified blacks if it was not for the alienation of the white and black races that arose from the extremes of Reconstruction—without realizing it, he was describing the impact of the Yankee policy of divide-and-rule. Union General George H. Thomas stated, "Alabama has attempted to pass laws as judicious as they could at the time to regulate the affairs of the freemen."[614] Alabama had a good start to recovery, but the Republicans who controlled Congress did everything they could to derail this promising start in Alabama and across the South.

The Federal Government made it almost impossible to restore mail service across the occupied South. The Federal Government would not allow anyone to manage a post office if he could not take the iron-clad loyalty oath. This oath required an affirmation that the individual never supported the Confederate States of America. The lack of loyal men who could take the iron-clad loyalty oath required by the Federal authorities kept most of the state's local and regional post offices closed. In many communities in Alabama and across the South, it was common for people to form a group to make weekly trips to the nearest open post office.[615] It is hard for the modern reader to comprehend the totality of economic loss endured by post-War Southerners. Add to the financial loss the extensive loss arising from the Union Army's implementation of

---

613   Ibid., 145.

614   Ibid., 153.

615   Ibid., 124.

Lincoln's vigorous war policy. The North's invasion of the South destroyed physical structures such as homes, wooden rail fencing, barns and implements for agricultural cultivation, mills, churches, schools, public libraries, post offices, courthouses, infrastructure such as railroad lines, railroad bridges, railroad depots, public roads, bridges over small streams and rivers, and levies poorly maintained. When these poorly maintained levies are breached, it causes untold destruction.

Surrounded by such utter destruction, the white South was faced with the sudden necessity of designing and implementing a new social, political, and economic system. This was a challenge unprecedented in world history. It required the designing and implementing of a mutually beneficial, fair, and just social, political, and economic system between newly freed black slaves, most of whom were illiterate, and formerly self-governing whites now under alien occupation. This challenge would have been difficult in the best of circumstances. Unfortunately, the white South faced this challenge in the worst of circumstances.

When Alabama's state government, operating immediately post-War under Lincoln's Ten Percent Plan, elected its Senators and Representatives and sent them to Washington to represent Alabama, they were unacceptable to the Republican-controlled Congress. The Senators and none of the Congressmen could take the iron-clad oath. Radical Republicans designed the iron-clad oath to prevent the acceptance of officials elected under Lincoln's Ten Percent Plan. Its wording required that the oath taker had no prior allegiance to the Confederacy and had given it no support. Such an oath made it unlikely that anyone elected would honestly be able to take the iron-clad oath.[616] The iron-clad test oath was a technique used by the Republican-controlled Congress to prevent the seating of men who represented the will of "We the People" in the Yankee Empire's newly conquered and occupied Southern colony—since Lincoln's War and Republican Reconstruction, the Southern States are no longer sovereign States. Representation

---

616   *Ibid.*, 113.

in the Yankee Empire's government was allowed only if those "elected" would likely support the continuing expansion of the newly created Yankee Empire. There were, after all, other nations and people the Yankee Empire wanted to conquer.[617]

In 1867, Alabama held its first Republican state constitutional convention elected under the Republican Party's Reconstruction Plan. This Republican state constitutional convention indicates how dysfunctional these bayonet, Southern governments were. Only four conservatives were in the entire convention of one hundred delegates. The other ninety-six were moderate to extreme radicals. Of this number, eighteen were Federal Freedmen's Bureau agents, thirty-seven were newly arrived men from the North, and eighteen were blacks. Nine of the eighteen blacks were illiterate, while seven could only sign their names and two could read. The white radicals included seven who had never been to the counties they were said to represent. Samuel A. Hale, an Alabama Unionist, described two of the delegates to the state's constitutional convention representing Hale's county as:

> The two whites were strangers here.... One of them, called Rolfe, is said to be a vagrant from the State of New York.... He had been here some three or four months prior to his election as a delegate, sometimes working as a carriage trimmer, sometimes drinking whisky and making drunken exhibitions of himself upon the streets.... Of the other white delegate, called Yordy...I had never heard until the day of his nomination.... Yordy claims to have been a captain in the Federal Army.[618]

Mr. Hale stated that the reason such inferior and dishonest men were elected was because the Federal Freedmen's Bureau controlled the election process and that on election day blacks were

---

617 See, Kennedy & Kennedy, *Yankee Empire: Aggressive Abroad and Despotic at Home* (Columbia, SC: Shotwell Publishing, 2018).

618 Henry, Robert Selph, *The Story of Reconstruction*, 278.

given marked ballots that they "knew nothing of what was on their bits of paper." He also observed that the Freedmen Bureau officials who control the balloting were also candidates. At the close of the convention, December 10, 1867, thirteen of the delegates issued a protest denouncing the new regime's "degradation and abasement of the white population."[619]

To the problems of the dysfunctional political situation were added the issues of forming a new labor system and maintaining local law and order. A newly freed slave in Alabama stated the concern of many in his situation, "they say if we make contracts now, we'll be branded and made slaves again." How to put land back into production was a major issue facing landowners after the War. "No one knew whether the field Negroes would really work in freedom."[620] The newly freed slaves feared that they would lose their freedom if they signed a work contract, which was a common belief, as we will see in many Southern States. Where did the blacks get this idea? Who would profit from spreading such fears among the newly freed slaves? Who would profit from spreading fear, mistrust, and hatred between the black and white races in the South? This is the situation created by Lincoln's low road to emancipation. Added to the worry about restarting the South's farms was the breakdown in law and order that followed the North's destruction of the last legitimate state governments across the South.[621]

The breakdown of law and order fostered the development of secret vigilante groups to maintain order. The most noteworthy of these vigilante groups was the Ku Klux Klan. William Garrot

---

619   Ibid., 280.

620   Ibid., 117.

621   "Last legitimate state governments" because every state government that was established after the destruction of the Confederacy was and today is the product of bayonet constitutions both state and national. Coercion replaced consent. A government based upon coercion is in violation of the American principle of "the consent of the governed." Such a government is an illegitimate government. The mere passage of time does not bestow legitimacy upon an illegitimate government. If the Nazi-installed Vichy France government lasted for a thousand years, it would still be illegitimate. Bayonet constitutions, whether state or national, are illegitimate.

Brown (1868-1913), born in Alabama and educated at Harvard, wrote that the appearance of the Klan "was neither an accident nor a mere scheme. It was no man's contrivance, but an historical development of a disordered society and a bewildered people."[622] The unnatural conditions of the time caused the development of the Southern resistance movement. The Radical Republicans, who worked to undermine and eventually destroy Lincoln's Ten Percent Reconstruction Plan, made the bad situation worse.

President Johnson, following Lincoln's Ten Percent Plan, appointed Lewis Eliphalet Parson as provisional governor of Alabama on June 21, 1865. Parson was born in New York and was the grandson of the Puritan divine Jonathan Edwards. As provisional governor, he tried to follow most of Alabama's pre-War laws except for those dealing with slavery. It was a promising beginning that was nullified by the Radicals in Congress. After 1866, for all practical purposes, Lincoln's Ten Percent Plan was a dead letter.

In 1874, the Democratic Party of Alabama made the following observation about the Republican Party's use of racial mistrust and hatred as a tool to capture and maintain its rule over the state:

> The Republican Party of Alabama, for years past, has distinctly made and tendered to the people of this State an open, square issue of race...at the instance of the thieving crew known as carpetbaggers, and the more contemptible and infamous gang known as scalawags...[the] issue of race thus defiantly tendered and forced upon us....[623]

As C. Vann Woodward said years later, Jim Crow came down South full grown from the North. In her treatise on New England's history of slavery and racism, Dr. Joanne Melish pointed out that New England's "trope of virtuous, historical whiteness" moved

---

622 William Garrot Brown cited Henry, Robert Selph, *The Story of Reconstruction*, 181.

623 Henry, Robert Selph, *The Story of Reconstruction*, 525.

from New England to embrace all Northern States by 1860. She noted that the "anti-South, anti-slavery, and anti-black impulses" spread like an infection from New England to encompass the North.[624] Northern abolitionist Thomas Branagan displayed his "anti-black" impulse thusly: "The sons of Africa in America, are the inveterate enemies of America."[625] This is the very essence of racial antagonism, mistrust, and hatred that was embraced by most Northerners. The Republican Party used Divide-and-Rule, the age-old technique of empires, to consolidate their domination of the South and their power in Washington. The Republican Party used racial antagonism (divide-and-rule) to control *their* newly captured territories down South. In so doing they created cultural distortion—the unnatural emergence of racial hatred in the South.[626] This was the exact opposite of "what could have been."

The use of slanderous lies encouraged hatred for the occupied South in the North. The local impact via gossip and rumor on black Southerners is seen in a report sent North by Union Captain W.A. Poillon. He was the assistant superintendent of freedmen in Mobile, Alabama. His report to the Northern papers claimed that, in his area of responsibility, twenty-one murders by hanging, shooting, drowning, and burning were committed within two months. Such outrageous reports from down South made for great headlines in Northern papers (in the internet age, we would call such headlines click-bait). Interestingly, he provided no names of the alleged victims, no account of arrest and criminal charges, and he did not even provide the name of the plantation owner who Poillon alleged, "about the last of May [the plantation owner] hung his servant, a woman, in presence of all the neighborhood."[627] As a modern-day Southern comedian said, "The more outrageous a thing is said about the South, the more likely a Yankee is to believe

---

624   Melish, Joanne Pope, *Disowning Slavery: Gradual Emancipation and "Race" in New England, 1780-1860* (Ithaca, NY: Cornell University Press, 1998), 224.

625   Thomas Branagan cited in Melish, Joanne Pope, *Disowning Slavery: Gradual Emancipation and "Race" in New England, 1780-1860*, 226.

626   See Kennedy & Kennedy, *Punished With Poverty: the Suffering South* 2nd ed., 140-46.

627   Henry, Robert Selph, *The Story of Reconstruction*, 85.

it." Such "reports" spread through the black community creating a sense of fear and hatred.

In June 1868 the Federal Congress "approved" Alabama's new Constitution. On July 13, 1868, Alabama ratified the Fourteenth Amendment—done under compulsion as a condition of readmission to the Union. To get back into the Union from which Alabama was denied the right to withdraw, the non-state of Alabama had to perform the function of a state by ratifying the Fourteenth Amendment before it was allowed to return to the Union from which it, as a state, was not allowed to withdraw! This is the tale of a puppet government. With its bayonet constitution in place, Alabama's puppet government's representatives and senators were allowed to take their seats in Congress. Alabama's two senators were Willard Warner from Ohio and George E. Spencer, a New Englander previously politically active in Nebraska and Iowa. He made his way to Alabama as a merchant plying goods to Yankee soldiers.[628] Alabama was technically a state within the Union. But, considering the current political reality, Alabama and her sister States were and remain provinces in the Yankee Empire with puppet governments subservient to the Empire's supreme Federal Government.[629] As one Southern historian lamented:

> In form they [the Southern States] were States...but neither the General of the Armies nor the Radical leaders in Congress were yet willing to withdraw the leading strings and leave them on their own.[630]

---

628 *Ibid.*, 320.

629 For example, Alabama, nor any other state, are not allowed to place a plaque containing the Ten Commandments in one of their state's court houses without permission from its master, the supreme Federal Government. Freedom for "We the People" of the South died at Appomattox; its corpse was unceremoniously buried by the Republican Party's Active Reconstruction. The once sovereign States became provinces of the supreme Federal Government, while citizens of a Republic became subjects of the Yankee Empire. *Vae Victis*: Woe to the vanquished.

630 Henry, Robert Selph, *The Story of Reconstruction*, 320.

What was true for Alabama was also true for every Southern state. The new, and current, national Constitution was crafted via military force and deserves the title of a bayonet constitution. In a country that supposedly honors freedom, compelled consent is a nullity. The Southern States did not freely consent to the newly created supreme Federal Government. Their "consent" was derived via bloody bayonets. Such "consent" is no more valid than an innocent woman's forced "consent" to the overpowering strength of a rapist.

Essentially, Active Reconstruction ended in Alabama in 1874 with the election of Democrat George S. Houston and the establishment of conservative control of the legislature.[631]

---

631 "Reconstruction in Alabama," Encyclopedia of Alabama (encyclopediaofalabama.org). www.bit.ly/AlabamaReconstruction (Accessed 24 September 2023).

Chapter 15:

ARKANSAS ENDURES REPUBLICAN RECONSTRUCTION

"Should the general government take any step to encroach upon the constitutional rights of the Southern States, then the State of Arkansas should place herself in the column with her sister States of the South and share their destiny."
—Gov. Henry M. Rector [632]

AS THE YANKEE ARMY occupied areas of Arkansas, they brought with them government agents who would, with the help of local scallywags, organize a puppet state government for Arkansas.[633] The desire to secure electoral votes and control of Congress motivated Lincoln to ensure that Arkansas and other occupied Southern States would cast their puppet States' electoral votes for the Lincoln ticket, assuring his reelection. Arkansas puppet state government was created under Lincoln's Ten Percent

---

632   From Governor Henry Massie Rector's inaugural address on November 15, 1860, Arkansas, *Confederate Military History*, Vol. X, Part 2 (1899, Harrisburg, PA: The Archives Society, 1994), 5.

633   Postmodern "intellectuals" would argue that not all Northerners who came down South (Carpetbaggers) were agents of the Federal Government. Postmodernist Yankee propagandists claim these Carpetbaggers were private individuals acting on their own. Regardless, they were doing the bidding of the powers-that-be in Washington, DC. These individual Federal agents are like the Modern Era Reconstruction digital media "individuals" who do the bidding of the Woke Federal Government by censoring conservative voices. Direct agents or indirect agents, it makes no difference. The result is the same.

Reconstruction Plan early in 1864.[634] Conditions in Arkansas were desperate. According to scalawag Governor Murphy, many of Arkansas' people were living in open brush shelters in the woods, begging for food.[635] But providing for innocent people who were made homeless by the invading Yankee Army was not the first concern of Lincoln or the Republican Party. The primary purpose of Lincoln's moderate Reconstruction Plan, the Ten Percent Plan, was to quickly create puppet state governments that would be "acceptable" not to the people of Arkansas but "acceptable" to the Republican-controlled Congress. Lincoln and the Radical members of Congress held vastly different views on how to govern their newly conquered territories. The rancorous struggle between Lincoln and Congress came to an end with Lincoln's death. After Lincoln's assassination the Radicals took control of the Republican Party, the Radical Republican Party took control of Congress, and Congress took control of Active Reconstruction.

Operating under Lincoln's Ten Percent Reconstruction Plan, Arkansas, in the fall elections of 1866, went overwhelmingly for the Democrats. Lincoln's Plan did not allow for black voting, and it allowed whites to vote if they took an oath to remain henceforth loyal to the Federal Government. Conservative Union men won most of the elected offices in Arkansas. Under the Ten Percent Plan puppet government, the Arkansas legislature authorized ten percent of the state's tax revenue for "the relief of the destitute, wounded, or disabled soldiers not otherwise provided for." The state also set aside another $10,000.00 to purchase artificial limbs for Arkansas soldiers. Murphey, the state's Scallywag provisional Governor, even recommended a tax reduction. This foreshadowed what could have been if the Southern States were allowed to develop under Lincoln's Ten Percent Plan.[636] But the Southern puppet States' refusal to pass the Republicans' Fourteenth Amendment was the warning bell signaling a full-court press by the Republican Party to *exterminate* Southern political power. Republican and

---

634   Henry, Robert Selph, *The Story of Reconstruction*, 39.

635   *Ibid.*, 61.

636   *Ibid.*, 205.

future President James A. Garfield surmised the attitude of his fellow Republicans upon learning of the South's initial rejection of the Fourteenth Amendment as "...with contempt and scorn (they) flung back into our teeth the magnanimous offer of a generous nation. It is now time to act."[637]

Arkansas' Scallywag Governor, Murphy warned his fellows in the North that "Union men were being hunted down and shot by rebels."[638] This false claim was typical of Carpetbaggers who needed the support of Federal troops to keep their positions of power. Engaging in the democratic process of electing state leaders was reinvented by the Northern media and Radical Republican politicians as evidence proving that the South was still in rebellion. The Cincinnati *Gazette* bemoaned the fact that it appeared that the "rebel gray has whipped the Union blue at the polls."[639]

While Southerners, operating under Lincoln's Ten Percent Plan, were electing loyal, conservative Union men, the North was busy electing Radical Republicans. Maine voted by a large majority to enter the Radical Republican camp, as did New York, Pennsylvania, Ohio, and Indiana. After the elections in the fall of 1866, the prospects for local self-government in the South were bleak. The Radical Republican Party became the Republican Party. By March of 1867, the new Congress consisted of one hundred and forty-three Republicans and forty-nine Democrats. In the Senate, the Republican Party held control by a margin of forty-two Republicans to eleven Democrats. It was a veto-proof House and Senate.[640] It did not take long for the Republican Party-controlled Congress to reject all Southern state puppet governments organized under Lincoln's Plan. The objection was not that they were puppet governments but that they were not Radical Republican puppet governments. The Republican-controlled Congress also refused to recognize and seat the Senators

---

637   Garfield cited in Henry, Robert Selph, *The Story of Reconstruction*, 207.
638   Henry, Robert Selph, *The Story of Reconstruction*, 197.
639   *Ibid.*, 197.
640   *Ibid.*, 198.

and Representatives elected to Congress from the Lincoln Plan puppet States. In 1867 and 1868, the Republican Party passed their Reconstruction Acts. They established the Republican-controlled Congress as the sole authority on matters relating to the occupied Southern territories. These tyrannical acts placed the Southern States under military governments, i.e., military dictatorship. The Army began the process of registering black males to vote. Imagine the Federal Government weaponizing the military for political purposes! Note: The universal manhood suffrage was only for the occupied South. The victorious and self-righteous Northern States were allowed to keep their restrictive laws regarding black voting rights. In many of these Northern States, blacks were completely prohibited from voting.

After the removal of Lincoln's Ten Percent Plan puppet state government, Arkansas fell into the hands of far more vicious Republican scallywags and carpetbaggers. Arkansas' Republican puppet state government received a state with $319,000.00 in the Treasury and the counties that were virtually debt-free. By the time the Republican Party's state and local governments finished picking the bones of the defeated and destitute state, the people of Arkansas were left with a state indebted to the tune of $15,700,000.00 ($457,027,000.00 in 2023 dollars).[641] In addition to state debt, most of Arkansas' counties were on the verge of bankruptcy.[642] Fraud and corruption in Arkansas' Reconstruction government went from the highest to the lowest positions in government. A black Republican politician used his insider connections to receive a contract to repair a bridge that originally cost the state $100.00. He submitted a bill to the state for $900.[643] This was petty theft compared to the fraud and corruption engineered by white carpetbaggers. Glory, glory, hallelujah: the

---

641 "The US dollar has lost 97% its value since 1877," CPI Inflation Calculator (in2013dollars.com). wwwbit.ly/1877v2024 (Accessed 13 August 2023)

642 Bowers, Claude, *The Tragic Era*, 430.

643 *Ibid.*, Author cites Nordhoff, Charles, *The Cotton States in the Spring and summer of 1875*, New York, 1875, 30.

Yankee Empire goes marching on, but "We the People" are handed the bill to cover the cost!

Arkansas' Carpetbag Governor Powell Clayton replaced Lincoln's appointed provisional governor, Murphy. Clayton moved to Kansas in 1855 from Pennsylvania. He was a Union officer who settled on an Arkansas plantation after the War—one obtained at a fraction of the price it would have brought before the War. He helped organize the newly freed slaves into an effective political machine for the Republican Party. He used his powers as governor to mold the office into an efficient dispenser of tyrannical power. One observer noted that:

> The distance between him and Washington, his friendliness to the [Washington] Government, the ease with which his acts could be concealed, made him bold and careless. He knew his game. Clayton's policy was extermination.

UNDISCIPLINED BLACK MILITIA USED TO TERRORIZE BLACK AND WHITE CONSERVATIVES

The fear of black militia and white Yankee troops among the occupied people of the South was real. It was based upon the cruel experiences of invasion by an alien power. Yankee outrages against innocent civilians during the War were numerous and no Southerner believed the enemy would change his character once the War was over. Yankee outrages during the War were directed toward all Southerners not just slave-holders. For example, in Tennessee, when a troop of Yankees passed the home of Champ Ferguson, a civilian, non-combatant, Champ's little three-year-old child came onto the porch waving a Confederate flag. One of the men in blue leveled his gun, shot, and killed the child! In typical Scots-Irish fashion, Champ swore vengeance on all Yankees. One hundred and twenty is believed to be the number he put to death in his numerous bushwacking adventures.[644] Fear

---

[644] *Confederate Veteran* Vol. VII, No. 10, Oct. 1899. Republished in *The Confederate Veteran Magazine* Volume VII (Harrisburg, PA: The National Historical Society, 1987), 442.

of undisciplined and mostly illiterate black militia in Southern communities was intentionally designed by the victors to provoke a Southern reaction.

Governor Clayton organized the state's black militia and involved it in voter registration and counting the returns. His militia was so efficient that many deemed it part of the state's Republican Party. With the backing of Federal troops and his black militia, he overturned the registration rolls of ten counties that had a majority in favor of the Democrats. The Arkansas *Daily Republican* warned all opponents that "of course, the militia was to be armed to enforce the policies of the party."[645] The Republican Congressional-Executive Committee assured Clayton that Federal troops would be at his disposal if he needed to declare martial law. The Republican-controlled Congress could openly continue its unconstitutional and dictatorial rule over "We the People" of the South while hiding behind a smoke-screen of lies pumped out by Northern newspaper accounts of alleged "rebel outrages." Fake news was not invented in the 21st century. Fake news of the 19th century is like the way modern-day white Southerners who honor their Southern heritage were blamed for the nefarious shooting done on June 17, 2015, by Dylan Roof in Charleston, South Carolina. The false charge is made and the innocent South, having no official means to respond, is left to wear the scarlet letter of racism while scallywag politicians such as Republican Nikki Haley use it for their political advancement.[646]

When Clayton declared martial law, he released over two thousand undisciplined black militiamen to prey upon innocent whites in ten Arkansas counties—Democrat counties. There were reports of black militiamen stealing, looting, arresting, and generally harassing the otherwise peaceful population. Clayton, an efficient dictator, "sent the officers lists of men to be arrested,

---

645 Bowers, Claude, *The Tragic Era*, 368-9., Author cites Henry Watterson in the *Louisville Courier-Journal*, 22 December 1869.

646 Kennedy & Kennedy, *Punished With Poverty-The Suffering South* 2nd ed., 157-8.

with the comment that many of them could be executed."[647] He declared, "[W]e'll make Arkansas Republican or a waste howling wilderness."[648] It cost the Arkansas taxpayers, most of whom were conservative democrats, $330,676.43 ($8,223,922.81 in 2023 dollars) to pay for Clayton's Army's war against these ten Democratic counties.[649] One Southern scholar noted, during this time:

> Chief Justice John McClure (Arkansas Supreme Court), a notorious carpetbagger, is boasting of his guilt of bribery, editing the *Daily Republican* from his chambers, and handling the slush funds for the debauchery of the Legislature.[650]

Such was the condition across the South during Active Reconstruction. Thanks to the Republican Party, the once free and self-governing people of the South were reduced by alien forces to the condition of political slavery. Under such extreme and oppressive conditions why would there be any surprise that some form of an underground resistance movement would arise? Had similar conditions been present in the Northern state of New York, would the whites of New York remain docile and meekly accept their political enslavement? Of course not! Like all freedom-loving people they would have used any means available to resist tyranny.

Arkansas was redeemed when, on October 13, 1874, the resistance movement successfully elected a Democrat as governor and conservatives captured a large majority in the legislature.

---

647   Bowers, Claude, *The Tragic Era*, 370, Author cites Staples, Thomas S., *Reconstruction in Arkansas*, 290.

648   Ibid., 370. Author cites Staples, Thomas S., *Reconstruction in Arkansas*, 302.

649   Ibid., Author cites Staples, Thomas S., *Reconstruction in Arkansas*, 305.

650   Ibid., Author cites Staples, Thomas S., *Reconstruction in Arkansas*, 365.

FLORIDA'S REPRESENTATIVE JOHN WALLACE

During Active Reconstruction and up to the early 1900s, there were many examples of black leaders who could have formed a solid base for a mutually beneficial biracial Southern society. Representative John Wallace of Florida is an example of such men. John Wallace wrote, "The Governor was forced to appoint men as county judges and solicitors, some of whom it was very doubtful as to whether they had ever seen the inside of a law book."

Chapter 16:

RECONSTRUCTION IN FLORIDA

"Inspired by their fathers of 1776 the people of Florida resolved to unite in the patriotic effort to secure for the South an independent government, because the Constitution framed by their forefathers had been violated." [651]
—Col. J.J. Dickison

THE END OF THE WAR brought an end to slavery in Florida as well as in the rest of the South. Even without any preparation for freedom, the move from slavery to freedom appeared to be a relatively smooth change. A New York correspondent verified this in his report from Florida. He wrote, "that emancipation of the slaves had been accomplished, that most ex-slaves were on the plantations working for wages."[652] Not the best solution, but at least it was a good beginning. President Johnson recognized the Ten Percent Reconstruction Plan States as part of the Union. Johnson described the population of these States as "yielding obedience to the laws and government of the United States with more willingness and greater promptitude than, under all the circumstances, could reasonably have been anticipated."[653] These puppet States organized a government under Lincoln's

---

[651] Col. J.J. Dickison, "Military History of Florida," *Confederate Military History*, Vol. XI (1899, Harrisburg, PA: The Archives Society, 1994), 5.

[652] Henry, Robert Selph, *The Story of Reconstruction* (New York: Konecky & Konecky, 1938), 67.

[653] *Ibid.*, 139.

Ten Percent Plan and, as (puppet) States, ratified the Thirteenth Amendment to the United States Constitution. These States were implicitly recognized by the Federal Congress when it accepted their acts of ratification and counted the Southern States in the number required to pass the Thirteenth Amendment. The fact that Florida and her sister Southern States were (and still are) puppet States, is demonstrated by the fact that they were acceptable to the Republican-controlled Congress only as long as they did the bidding of the Republican-controlled Congress—the ratification of the Thirteenth Amendment. But when they rejected the Republican Party's proposed Fourteenth Amendment, then they were no longer States. A puppet must do the bidding of the puppet's master or else! The attitude of Northerners toward black and white Southerners is best demonstrated by Representative George Boutwell's (R-Massachusetts) suggestion that the States of South Carolina and Florida should be reserved exclusively for former slaves. This, once again, demonstrates the evil attitude that Northern leaders had for black and white Southerners. This attitude was evident during Active Reconstruction (1866-1877): it was somewhat attenuated during Passive Reconstruction (1877-1965) (when the Yankee Empire's military needed our men to serve in *their* military) and has reemerged with a vengeance in Modern Era Reconstruction (post-1965).

In 1866, Florida rejected the Republican Party's Fourteenth Amendment. Florida's provisional governor and legislature were organized under Lincoln's puppet state government established via Lincoln's Ten Percent Reconstruction Plan. The state's legislature expressed the general sentiment of the people of Florida and most likely the entire South when it declared:

Beyond the postal service, our people derive no benefit from our existence as a State in the Union. We are denied representation even when we elect a man who has never in fact sympathized with armed resistance to the United States...We are at the same time subject to the most onerous taxation; the civil law of the State is enforced and obeyed only when it meets the approval of the local commanders of the troops of the United States.... We are, in fact, recognized as a State for the single and sole purpose of working out our destruction and dishonor.[654]

Walker, Florida's Ten Percent Plan provisional Governor, added his opinion of the Northern effort to humiliate the people of Florida:

> We will bear any ill before we will pronounce our own dishonor. We will be taxed without representation; we will quietly endure the government of the bayonet, but we will not bring as a peace offering the conclusive evidence of our own self-created degradation.[655]

The Florida election in the fall of 1867 was held under Republican Active Reconstruction rules. With most whites removed from the voting rolls and mostly illiterate blacks given the vote, the results produced the removal of the conservative state legislature elected under Lincoln's Ten Percent Plan. It produced, as was to be expected, a heavy majority of Republican Radicals elected to Florida's legislature. With the removal of white conservatives from the voting rolls and the enfranchisement of blacks, most of whom were illiterate, the election produced a puppet state government pleasing (acceptable) to the Republican-controlled Congress.

The new puppet state legislature called for a state constitutional convention held in Tallahassee on January 20, 1868. Only two of the forty-six delegates to the convention were white conservatives. The balance of delegates consisted of eighteen blacks, and the remainder were scallywags and carpetbaggers of equal numbers. Several of the scallywag members were deserters from the Confederate Army.

A passing glimpse of *what could have been* if the South was left alone to develop a mutually beneficial bi-racial society can be seen in the black delegate, Jonathan Gibbs. Gibbs was a well-educated minister (Dartmouth and Princeton Theological Seminary) noted

---

654   *Ibid.*, 206.

655   *Ibid.*, 206.

as "a man of character and ability, was an outstanding-colored member of the convention, although he was eclipsed during its noisy sessions by the more vocal and more radical."[656] The Florida constitutional convention broke into two warring groups, one in Tallahassee and the other re-convening in Monticello. The Tallahassee group completed its constitution first and sent it to Atlanta, Georgia, for General Meade's approval and went into recess for two weeks. In the meantime, the Monticello convention completed its constitution, moved back to Tallahassee, took possession of the convention chambers, and had two members of the other group seized and forcefully brought into the chamber to gain a quorum. General Meade ordered the local military officer to settle the matter, and eventually, the Monticello group was recognized.[657]

Florida was declared a part of the Union after its puppet legislature ratified the Fourteenth Amendment as a requirement for re-entry into the Union. It then elected state officials acceptable to the Republican-controlled Congress. For governor, the state elected Harrison Reed, a former newspaperman from Wisconsin who came to Florida shortly after the end of the War to serve as the United States mail agent. William M. Gleason, also from Wisconsin, who was a lumberman in Wisconsin, was elected Lt. Governor. Gleason came to Florida as a speculator in Florida's pine and turpentine products. Florida's two new US Senators were Adonijah S. Welch from Michigan, who was engaged in teaching blacks in Florida, and Thomas W. Osborn of New Jersey, who was a Freedmen's Bureau agent. Such were the men elected to represent the interests of the people of Florida in the US Senate.[658]

The new Governor had great difficulty finding men both qualified and acceptable to the state and the national Republican Party to fill local appointed offices. As a black representative, John Wallace wrote:

---

656   *Ibid.*, 294.

657   *Ibid.*, 295.

658   *Ibid.*, 318-9.

The Governor was forced to appoint men as county judges and solicitors, some of whom it was very doubtful as to whether they had ever seen the inside of a law book. Many of the carpetbag office-holders, anterior to their advent in the South, had been blatant Democrats at the North, but not even respectable cross-politicians, yet who now claimed to be great men and proper leaders of the colored people of the State.[659]

Representative John Wallace is one of numerous fair-minded black Southerners who could have played a major role in establishing a mutually beneficial and equally respectful Southern society had the South been allowed to follow the high road to emancipation. It is an example of "what could have been."

The Southern resistance movement began to gain ground in Florida and across the South due mainly to the Republican general disinterest in ethical government. Under Republican-imposed Active Reconstruction, fraud, corruption, high taxation, and general breakdown of law and order were the daily burdens of the conservative white and black communities.

During Active Reconstruction, Florida was plagued not only by Republican-sanctioned fraud and corruption but also by widespread violence and lawlessness. The inability of local officials to maintain law and order became a pressing issue for both black and white citizens. Men such as George W. Swepson defrauded the state. He came to the state "with more than a million dollars of first-mortgage bonds...purchased by him at thirty to thirty-five cents on the dollar." He gave a check to cover the cost of the county bonds. The US Supreme Court later declared his check worthless. The same court declared that Swepson and Milton S. Littlefield embezzled funds from a North Carolina railroad. Their embezzlement scheme was accomplished via the "aid and

---

659   *Ibid.*, 319.

compliance" of that state's Radical legislature at its 1868 session.[660] Such were the men, and such were the Republican legislatures, who enjoyed the happy time of fraud and corruption forced upon the conservative people of Florida and the entire South.

In the Presidential election of 1868 Florida cast its electoral votes for Grant, but the people of the state did not participate in the election. The people were denied the right to vote in the presidential election by the simple tactic of the puppet state's legislature anointing three electors for the Grant-Colfax ticket, who then cast their votes without receiving the sanction of the people's vote.[661] In the same session, the legislature voted itself additional salary. Governor Reed vetoed the bill, and the legislature promptly overrode the Governor's veto. Shortly thereafter the legislature passed a bill of impeachment against the Governor by a vote of twenty-five to six. A political brawl ensued involving the Governor, both houses of the legislature, and the state's supreme court. When the legislature reconvened in January 1869 the tide turned against the Radicals, and on January 26 a committee of the Florida House decided to recommend dropping the impeachment. The House accepted the recommendation by a vote of forty-three to five.

By 1873 it was becoming impossible for the state's Republican Party to maintain unity. As is often seen in criminal enterprises, thieves often fall out with each other and begin to self-destruct their criminal organization. The reconstruction government in Florida was beginning its slow march to self-destruction.[662]

BLACK CODES IN FLORIDA

Across the devastated South, the so-called Black Codes passed were never in wide operation or rigorously enforced. They were passed to calm white fears of a mass uprising of blacks like what happened in several Caribbean nations. Most of these Codes were never fully enforced. John Wallace (1842-1908) was a self-

---

660   Ibid., 373.
661   Ibid., 345.
662   Ibid., 494.

educated former slave residing in Tallahassee, Florida. He was a lawyer elected to the Florida House of Representatives and later to the Florida Senate. At his death, he had held elected office longer than any other black elected official. He served terms in both Houses of the Florida legislature and one in the state Senate. He authored a book, *Carpet-Bag Rule in Florida*, in which he demonstrated that the errors, excesses, and miscalculations of the era were **not** caused by the enfranchised, newly freed slaves but by the fraud and corruption instigated by white men who came from the outside, claiming to be the saviors of the black man but they actually came to enrich themselves by taking advantage of the black folks of the South. Wallace declared that:[663]

> Many of these laws, of 1865-66, we know, of our own knowledge, were passed only to deter the freedmen from committing crime...the law prohibiting colored people handling arms without a license was a dead letter, except in some cases where some of the freedmen would go around plantations hunting, with apparently no other occupation, such a person would be suspected of hunting something that did not belong to him.... We have often passed through the streets of Tallahassee with our gun upon our shoulder, without a license, and were never disturbed.[664]

This was the general rule across the South. In Louisiana, one scholar described these types of restrictions on blacks before the war by noting that "...some of these restrictions were simply not enforced by local authorities."[665]

Reconstruction did not end in Florida until after the 1876 presidential election, in which Republican Rutherford B. Hayes

---

[663] Ibid., 152.

[664] Ibid., 152-3.

[665] Mills, Gary B., *The Forgotten People: Cane River's Creoles of Color* (Baton Rouge, LA: LSU Press, 1977), 107.

won after agreeing to remove the remaining Federal troops from the South. In that election, Democrats in Florida gained control of most of the state's offices.[666] Florida's resistance movement successfully redeemed the state. Active Reconstruction was at an end, but the state and the entire South entered the new era of Passive Reconstruction (1877-1965).

---

666 "Civil War and Reconstruction," Florida Department of State (dos.fl.gov). www.bit.ly/FL-Reconstruction (Accessed 24 September 2023).

Chapter 17:

GEORGIA UNDER REPUBLICAN RECONSTRUCTION

"Having resumed its original position as a sovereign, independent republic, Georgia began preparing for the maintenance of independence by force of arms." —Joseph T. Derry, A.M. [667]

JAMES JOHNSON was appointed governor of Georgia by President Johnson on June 17, 1865. The President's appointment was not well received by many of the more "loyal" or radical Unionist folks in Georgia, but the rank-and-file white population accepted him. He was a citizen of Georgia who, before the War, opposed secession and maintained a low profile during the War.[668] Governor James Johnson was aided by the strong support of Georgia's "war governor," Joseph E. Brown, who returned to the state urging Georgia's citizens to make the best out of a bad situation.[669] The people, after a long struggle to maintain their country's independence, were exhausted by war. Day-to-day survival was their primary concern. They faced the difficult task of providing their families with food and shelter and regaining a sense of civil normalcy. Peace came to Georgia, but it was the peace of a concentration camp or prison in which the inmates were hungry,

---

667 Joseph T. Derry cited in "Georgia," *Confederate Military History*, Vol. VI (1899, Harrisburg, PA: The Archives Society, 1994), 10.

668 "James Johnson (Georgia politician)," Wikipedia (wikioedia.org) www.bit.ly/xJames-Johnson (Accessed 15 August 2023)

669 Henry, Robert Selph, *The Story of Reconstruction* (New York: Konecky & Konecky,1938), 53.

ragged, impoverished, and facing a fearful future. In the summer of 1865, a citizen of Madison, Georgia, wrote to General Sherman, "True, there is no war upon us but then it is not peace."[670] General Sherman assured his brother, Senator John Sherman of Ohio, "You may look for outbreaks [of violence] in Ohio quicker than in Georgia or Mississippi."[671]

An English lady living in Georgia noticed the change in the attitudes of her hired black servants after the Union League began organizing in her community. She was fearful of a coming race war caused by those now in power who were "exciting the Negroes to every kind of insolent lawlessness."[672] She admitted that, throughout 1869, she never slept at night without a loaded pistol under her pillow.[673] It is a common occurrence for some form of active and/or passive resistance to arise when a formerly free people are forced to accept a foreign power's illegal, unfair, and oppressive rule. This is a natural human reaction, an action based upon one of man's primary motives—the struggle for survival. In the post-War South, an underground and, of necessity a secret, resistance to Yankee occupation emerged.[674] But the Southern resistance movement arose after it became apparent just how tyrannical and unjust the Yankee occupation of these once free and self-governing States would be. Unlike the resistance in other occupied nations, such as Ireland, it was not a resistance movement based upon a desire to rid themselves of foreign occupation and domination and return to their independent nation. This was a major Southern strategic failure.

The devastation faced by the returning soldiers of the South is evidenced by the fact that the railroads so necessary for the

---

670   Ibid., 66.

671   Ibid., 66.

672   Bowers, Claude, *The Tragic Era* (New York: Halcyon House, 200. Author cites Leigh, Frances Butler, *Ten Years on a Georgia Plantation*, 67.

673   Bowers, Claude, *The Tragic Era*, 308. Author cites Leigh, Frances Butler, *Ten Years on a Georgia Plantation*, published in London, England, 1883.

674   It should be noted that the resistance was directed at Yankee occupation and oppression not toward black Southerners.

movement of commerce in the South were inoperable. In 1865, a Georgia Railroad posted a notice warning passengers that "the cars are very likely to run off their tracks, in which case the danger to passengers is much increased."[675] In Georgia, over one hundred miles of bent rails and burned bridges testified to the Yankee Empire's invading armies' work of public and private destruction—carrying out Lincoln's vigorous war policy.[676] Recall that, during the latter phases of the War, many citizens faced starvation, so President Davis recommended rats be used as a possible food source.[677] The specter of starvation did not disappear with the ending of the War. Within a radius of fifteen miles of Atlanta, Georgia, thirty-five citizens were destitute and at the point of starvation.[678] In December of 1865, in Alabama, Georgia, and Mississippi, 500,000 white people suffered from malnutrition, and many died from starvation.[679] Similar situations could be found in the other Southern States. "We the People" of the South, within a short four-year period, witnessed the tragic economic decline of their homeland. Before the War, the South was the country's most prosperous section; after the War, it was reduced to the poorest section, and it remains so today.[680]

There was some hope that the victor would treat the vanquished white South with at least a form of fairness. There were a few signs that this might be the case. In the early days of the Freedmen's Bureau, when it was non-political, it acted fairly as it sought to help the freedmen. The Freedmen's Bureau agents in Georgia hired two hundred and forty-four agents from the *local population*. It was openly acknowledged that "they did not encounter the prejudice felt against officers of the Army, or agents for the North, and were

---

675   Henry, Robert Selph, *The Story of Reconstruction*, 72.

676   Again, it should be noted that the resistance was directed at Yankee occupation and oppression not toward black Southerners.

677   Hummel, Jeffrey Rogers, *Emancipating Slaves, Enslaving Free Men*, 279.

678   Henry, Robert Selph, *The Story of Reconstruction*, 61.

679   Fleming, Walter Lynwood, *The Sequel of Appomattox* (Yale University Press, 1919), 14.

680   Kennedy & Kennedy, *Punished With Poverty-the Suffering South* 2nd ed. (Columbia, SC: Shotwell Publishing, 2020).

thereby enabled more readily to secure justice to the freedmen, and to build up and foster a healthy public opinion."[681] But as soon as the Radical Republicans of the Thaddeus Stevens school took control of Congress, this magnanimous treatment of the conquered South vanished. Georgia and the rest of the South would be governed not by the old (original) US Constitution but by the laws of war and conquest. Union Secretary Wells asked Senator Sumner of Massachusetts, "Do you really think that Massachusetts could govern Georgia better than Georgia could govern herself?" Senator Sumner's reply was, "That is Massachusetts' mission!"[682] The Republican Party aimed to set up puppet state governments in the South—States that would henceforth be subservient to a supreme Federal Government controlled by Northern ruling elites.

The Republican Party in Congress used the ironclad oath to prevent "unfriendly" elected Southerners from taking their seats in Congress. Of the seven congressmen elected in Georgia, only one could take the ironclad oath. Of those excluded by Congressional Republicans, all were original Union men, and only two supported secession.[683] The Republicans were not looking for men loyal to the old Union, they were looking for men who could be controlled by the Northern elites in their new Union!

The 1866 elections in Georgia resulted in a landslide for the Republican radicals. The election was to determine if the state should hold a constitutional convention in which a new state constitution would be written that was acceptable to the Republican-controlled Congress. Most of the conservative whites refused to participate in the election. Over 100,000 votes were in favor, and only 4,127 were against.[684] Georgia would soon get a bayonet constitution to serve as political window dressing for its puppet state government.

---

681 Henry, Robert Selph, *The Story of Reconstruction*, 148.

682 Ibid., 133.

683 Ibid., 113.

684 Ibid., 266.

Georgia's experience with its first Republican Reconstruction legislature lasted for slightly over ten months. It produced results like Republican-controlled legislatures in other Southern States. Fraud, corruption, and profligate spending cost the state's impoverished taxpayers almost one million dollars for travel and other member expenses. The Republican state legislature found the funds to pay for their expenses by raiding the funds set aside to pay teachers in newly established state schools.[685]

THE FAÇADE OF SELF-GOVERNMENT— GEORGIA'S POST-WAR CONSTITUTIONAL CONVENTION

The effort to establish a state government in Georgia acceptable to the Republican-controlled Congress began on December 9, 1867, in Atlanta. The fact that the delegates were establishing not a government of a Sovereign State, but the government of a puppet state is evidenced by one of the first messages issued by the Convention. The first resolution was addressed to Union General Pope, declaring in a most subservient and kowtowing manner that, "In obedience to your orders this convention is now assembled and organized and invites your presence in the convention at your pleasure."[686] General Pope was the military dictator appointed by the Republican-controlled Congress to rule over Military District Three, consisting of the former Sovereign States of Georgia, Alabama, and Florida. In late 1867, General Meade replaced General Pope as military commander of Military District Three. He was ordered to enforce Republican Active Reconstruction.[687]

Georgia's 1867 Constitutional Convention consisted of one hundred and sixty-nine delegates. Of that number, only twelve were white conservatives, even though white conservatives represented the largest group in the state. Nine of the delegates were whites from outside the state. The rest of the white delegates

---

685   Ibid., 438.

686   Ibid., 284.

687   Sauers, Richard A., "George Gordon Meade," Essential Civil War Curriculum (essential-civilwarcurriculum.com) www.bit.ly/George-Mead (Accessed 03 August 2023).

were scallywags who were held in low esteem by white Georgians.[688] As was true in all the occupied Southern States, the cost of the Convention was well above the cost of prior conventions. The state treasury was embarrassed by its lack of funds. As such, the Convention had difficulty convincing the State Treasurer to pay the delegates' fees and other expenses generated by the Convention. The State Treasurer refused to pay an invoice from the Convention of $40,000.00. General Meade, who replaced General Pope as the Federal military dictator for District Three ordered the Treasurer to pay the Convention's request for funds. The State Treasurer again refused, and General Meade removed him from office. On January 13, 1868, Meade also removed the state's Comptroller and the Secretary of State. Meade then replaced these civilian office-holders with junior officers of the occupying Yankee Army.[689] Anywhere in the world, except in postmodern American history books, such acts would be described as military dictatorship!

The years 1866-7 brought no good news to white Southerners. The victorious Yankee Empire's Republican-controlled Congress was busy seeking ways to leverage the newly freed slaves into a manipulable Southern Republican voting bloc. Every effort was made by men such as Thaddeus Stevens to punish and exploit their newly conquered Southern provinces. Many conservatives were approaching the point where they were losing hope of regaining even a small sense of normalcy. Representative Bill Hill (D-Georgia), responding to an attack on Jefferson Davis and the South, assured the North "Go on and pass your qualifying acts, trample upon the Constitution...for all your iniquities the South will never again seek a remedy in the madness of another secession."[690] While such statements regarding the South never again seeking independence may have been necessary at the time, it unfortunately became the mantra of all future Southern officials, both State and National. With no fear of a second Southern move for Home Rule (as in Ireland during the English occupation of Ireland) or as in Quebec's

---

688 Henry, Robert Selph, *The Story of Reconstruction*, 284.

689 *Ibid.*, 285.

690 Bowers, Claude, *The Tragic Era*, 463. Author cites *Life of Hill*, 71.

call for a vote to separate from the Federal government of Canada, America's ruling elite were confident in their efforts to destroy traditional American constitutional, moral, and political values.[691] The North's ruling elite could do anything it wanted without fear of risking a Southern independence movement.[692] Under such defeatist leadership, Southerners became docile political slaves to the "one nation indivisible," supreme Federal Government—the Yankee Empire. The disastrous results of this Southern strategic failure are evident in the headlines and news reports today during Modern Era Reconstruction (post-1965).

ESTABLISHING A NEW LABOR SYSTEM

It was obvious to fair-minded Union Army officers that it was necessary to get the South's labor force back to work. Unfortunately, and through no fault of their own, the newly freed slaves were not properly prepared for their freedom. Many of them assumed that the Day of Jubilee had arrived when work was no longer necessary. Many looked first to the victorious Army and then to the Freedmen's Bureau for their welfare. Across the South, Army officers were faced with controlling thousands of unemployed blacks. The Army officers began efforts to relieve themselves of the burden of the ever-increasing criminal activity. In Georgia, Union General Davis Tilson issued an order in October 1865 that "all Negroes should be aided to get work, and that the able-bodied who refused it when offered should no longer draw government rations."[693] If you don't work, you don't eat. What a novel idea!

Many former leaders of the Confederacy recognized the need to establish a new society and labor system for the South. They understood that civil contract arrangements were unknown to

---

691 Quebec is an example of how a people, outnumbered in the total population of Canada, used the threat of separation (secession) to compel the Federal Government of Canada to respect Quebec's claim to local self-government. See Kennedy, James Ronald, *Dixie Rising-Rules for Rebels* 2nd ed. (Columbia, SC: Shotwell Publishing, 2021), 108-10.

692 The valid threat of a possible secession movement is often sufficient to force an oppressive government to relent or compromise with an occupied people. You can't put your foot on a man's neck when he is standing up!

693 Henry, Robert Selph, *The Story of Reconstruction*, 117.

most of the freedmen. They understood that a new labor system must be established based not on the compulsion of slavery, but on mutual respect and understanding. Former Vice President of the Confederacy, Alexander Stephens, addressed the Georgia legislature and lamented the fact that the Negroes were, through no fault of their own, "poor, untutored, uninformed, liable to be imposed upon..." and urged the legislature to secure for the freedmen "ample and full protection...so that they may stand equal before the law in the possession and enjoyment of all the rights of person, liberty, and property."[694] He also recommended that "such members of the black race as could come up to some proper standard of mental and moral culture, with the possession of a specified amount of property" should be allowed to vote.[695] This represented the attitude of most white Southerners. It was motivated by generations of experience working with black Southerners. Mississippi's black representative Moore later declared of the white South, "You are our best friends."

When the War ended in the spring of 1865, it was well into the planting season, but no labor system was previously designed to replace slave labor with self-employed contract labor. By the fall of 1865, it was evident that the harvest would be poor mainly because of the deficiencies of the labor system. Many newly freed slaves looked to their new "friends" from the North for advice, but these Northerners did not understand agriculture, particularly Southern agriculture. They often advised against freedmen signing a labor contract that covered the extended period from planting to harvesting. The landowner had to assure himself that he had a labor force sufficient to regain his investment in labor and material. He could not rely on "day" labor. He needed a labor force sufficient for planting in the spring, cultivating the crop during the summer, and harvesting the crop in the fall. A work contract that lasted only a few days or weeks made it too risky to invest limited dollars in planting. Added to that was that money to pay laborers

---

694 Ibid., 149. Author cites Alexander Stephens.

695 Ibid., 153.

daily or weekly was practically non-existent.⁶⁹⁶ Telling Southern landowners to pay workers when all forms of money, silver, gold, and other valuables were stolen or destroyed by the invading Yankee is akin to the Egyptians telling the Israelites to make bricks without straw!

The South's post-War, unreliable labor force had a negative impact on industry as well as agriculture. The Atlantic and Gulf Railroad attempted to build a line through southern Georgia, but it reported that when they hired blacks, they would not stay the whole month to collect their pay. This is another example of why individuals in the South attempted to take the high road to emancipation. Southerners, who were personally knowledgeable about slavery, understood the need for a slow but steady advancement of an entire race from slavery and illiteracy to self-sufficiency. The South could have evolved into a bi-racial society that would be mutually beneficial for all its citizens. This desire among white Southerners remained in many places even after emancipation. In Georgia and other States, plantation owners established schools for their tenants' children.⁶⁹⁷ But these post-War efforts were limited not by racial antagonism on the part of white Southerners but by the extreme lack of financial resources. Benjamin H. Hill, who served as one of Georgia's Senators in the Confederate Congress, explained the labor situation in the devastated South as: "How to make the negro observe his contract on the one hand, and how to make the bad white man fulfill his contract on the other."⁶⁹⁸ The problems facing the defeated, occupied, and impoverished South were not limited by race.

CULTURAL DISTORTION CAUSED SOME SOUTHERNERS TO BETRAY THEIR KITH AND KIN

Why would an individual betray his own people by helping the invader defeat and control his own people? Betrayal is common anytime an outside power can overwhelm the local population.

---

696 Kennedy & Kennedy, *Punished With Poverty-the Suffering South* 2ⁿᵈ ed., 107.

697 Henry, Robert Selph, *The Story of Reconstruction*, 128.

698 Senator Hill cited in Henry, Robert Selph, *The Story of Reconstruction*, 202.

Invasion and occupation always produce cultural distortion in the invaded society—an alienation of the natural feelings of kinship and community. Cultural distortion encourages individuals to seek ways to survive or to seek a way to gain power and material betterment that was unavailable under prior circumstances. Some Native Americans betrayed their people by becoming scouts for the Army, some Jews became unarmed prison guards working with the Nazi SS, and some Irish worked with the occupying English. Under Nazi rule, France had its Vichymen, Norway had its Quislings, and the South, under Yankee rule, had and still has its Scallywags.[699] Georgia was no exception.

Former Confederate General Longstreet was not the only former Confederate officer who betrayed his kinsmen and embraced Radical Republican ideology. Joseph E. Brown was the War Governor of Georgia. Sherman's Army captured the governor who was imprisoned in Washington until the end of the War. He became enamored with President Andrew Johnson and renounced all opposition to Reconstruction. His hopelessness became clear toward the end of the War when he advised an early surrender. He asked, "Why continue the fight?" He reasoned that the Jeffersonian idea of the State was dead and that real States' Rights were gone forever. His critics claimed that he rivaled Thaddeus Stevens in his denunciations of the Northern Democratic Party. He was received with great enthusiasm in the 1868 Republican Convention, where he proudly proclaimed the end of a limited Jeffersonian Constitution and the dawn of a new age of a supreme, centralized Federal Government. To the rapturous applause of the gathered Republicans, he declared, "the Hamiltonian and Websterian construction of the Constitution has been established by the sword."[700] Note "established by the sword." A people may win their freedom by the sword, but a free government can never be imposed upon a people "by the sword." He and Longstreet were

---

[699] Kennedy & Kennedy, *Punished With Poverty-The Suffering South* 2nd ed., 140-46.

[700] Bowers, Claude, *The Tragic Era*, 208-9, 225.

precursors of Vichymen and Quislings in Nazi-occupied France and Norway and, of course, the South's current "inept Southern politicians" who render the South such "pitiful service."[701]

THE SOUTHERN RESISTANCE MOVEMENT IN GEORGIA

The Southern Resistance Movement was mainly an effort to end confiscatory taxation, to gain representation in the state legislature for conservative property owners, and to enforce local law and order. The Klan is the only aspect of the resistance movement that postmodern "intellectuals" focus on—and they do so for political reasons of advancing their leftist agenda. The truth about the vigilantism of the original Klan is not part of modern history texts. What did the original participants have to say about the original Klan?

Former Confederate General Gordon from Georgia testified about the emergence of the Ku Klux Klan:

> The instinct of self-protection prompted that organization, the sense of insecurity and danger, particularly in those neighborhoods where the negro population largely predominated...The first and reason was the organization of the Union League....
>
> Apprehension took possession of the entire public mind of the State. Men were in many instances afraid to go away from their homes and leave their wives and children, for fear of outrage. Rapes were already being committed in the country. There was this general organization of the black race on the one hand, and an entire disorganization of the white race on the other hand.
>
> We were afraid to have a public organization; because we supposed it would be construed at once, by the authorities at Washington, as an organiza-

---

701 John Crowe Ransom, "Reconstructed But Unregenerate," *I'll Take My Stand* (1930, Baton Rouge, LA: LSU Press, 1983), 26.

tion antagonistic to the government of the United States.⁷⁰²

This is the same General Gordon who, in 1866, made substantial contributions of money and materials to aid the building of black churches and schools. He advised blacks to:

> ...educate themselves and their children, to be industrious, save money and purchase houses, and thus make themselves respectable as property holders, and intelligent people. With submission to the laws, industry and economy, with union among yourselves, and courtesy and confidence toward the whites, you will reach these ends, and constitute an important element in the community.⁷⁰³

General Gordon's record of the dread and anxiety of white Southerners during the era of Active Reconstruction was noted by other Georgians. Miss Eliza Frances Andrews of Georgia was quoted in the New York World on January 9, 1870, describing how the name of the Klan was used by less than honorable men:

> Whenever a set of low, disorderly fellows feel inclined to commit rascality, they put on masks and call themselves Ku Klux. A true statement of the case is not that the Ku Klux are an organized band of licensed criminals, but that men who commit crimes call themselves Ku Klux.⁷⁰⁴

Maintaining control of a secret society is almost impossible. If a crime is committed in the name of a publicly known organization that organization can bring the culprit to court, but this is impossible for a secret organization. It is easy to imitate the actions of a secret

---

702 General Gordon cited in Henry, Robert Selph, *The Story of Reconstruction*, 322-3.

703 "John B. Gordon," Wikipedia (wikipedia.org) www.bit.ly/John-B-Gordon (Accessed 02 April 2023).

704 Henry, Robert Selph, *The Story of Reconstruction*, 388-9.

organization or to blame it for crimes it did not commit. This, of course, worked to the great advantage of the Republican Party in Washington and locally. Yankee newspapers picked up accounts of real or imagined outrages and gleefully reported to the North that the Klan's outrages were continuing down South. Senator Lyman Trumbull (Ill.)[705] declared that he believed many of the so-called "outrages" were inspired by stories in Northern newspapers. The accounts of these "outrages," according to Senator Trumbull, came from stories created by "telegrams emanating from this city [Washington, DC]. The telegraph is used to create a public sentiment to operate upon Congress."[706] The Federal authorities then acted on these reports of "rebel outrages" by a string of mass arrests. In Georgia, Federal trials were held for twenty-three out of eighteen hundred whites arrested in 1871. Of the eighteen tried in Federal court, only one was convicted![707] Yankee propagandists masquerading as journalists provided the Republican Party with a smoke screen behind which they could do their work of dominating the South and destroying the original Constitution. This form of "Yellow Journalism" was not new to the North. Admiral Semmes, *CSS Alabama*, described it thusly:

> The war had been a godsend for newspaperdom. The more extraordinary were the stories that were told by the venal and corrupt newspapers, the more greedily they were devoured by the craving and prurient multitude. The consequence was, a race between the newspaper reporters after the sensational, without the least regard to the truth.... Such is the stuff out of which a good deal of the Yankee histories of the late war will be made.[708]

---

705 Senator Lyman Trumbull's political party association spanned the political spectrum of the time: Democrat, Republican, Liberal Republican, and Populist. "Lyman Trumbull," Wikipedia (wikipedia.org) www.bit.ly/Lyman-Trumbull (Accessed 08 April 2023).

706 Henry, Robert Selph, *The Story of Reconstruction*, 395-6.

707 *Ibid.*, 449.

708 Semmes, Raphael, *Memoirs of Service Afloat*, 235-6.

Southern comedian Lewis Grizzard (1946-1994) summed up this Yankee trait when he said that the more outlandish a story about the South is, the more likely the Yankees will believe it. E.A. Pollard, editor of the *Richmond Examiner* during the War, noted that "No human creature is more ingenious and industrious in misrepresentation than the Yankee."[709] Recall the words of John Taylor, a noted American Founding Father: "Tyranny is wonderfully ingenious in the art of inventing specious phrases to spread over its nefarious designs."[710]

REPUBLICAN RECONSTRUCTION GOVERNMENT LEAVES GEORGIA

The year 1871 turned out to be a good year for Georgia. Just two days before the state's newly elected conservative legislature was to be seated, the state's Carpetbag Governor, Rufus B. Bullock, fled the state. Bullock was from New York and moved to Georgia in 1857. He supported secession and served in the Confederate Army as Lieutenant Colonel.[711] Bullock, now a loyal Republican, arranged to have Benjamin F. Conley, Secretary of the Senate, born in New Jersey but moved to Georgia in his youth to take the office of Governor. Bullock explained his actions as necessary to prevent the conservative legislature from replacing Republicans holding state-appointed offices via removal or impeachment. Governor Conley issued proclamations of pardons for his friends and associates before their trials. Most of the pardons went to individuals indicted for fraud and corruption. The conservative state legislature appointed a committee to investigate. General Robert Toombs, formerly of the Confederate States Army, was named special attorney for the committee and served in that capacity without fee. The committee's report was over one hundred and sixty pages, charging Bullock and his associates with

---

709 Pollard, E.A., *Southern History of the War* (1866, Crown Publishers, Inc., 1977), Vol. 2, 392-3.

710 Taylor, John, *Tyranny Unmasked* (1822, Indianapolis, Indiana: Liberty Fund, 1992), 78.

711 "Rufus Bullock," Wikipedia (wikipedia.org) www.bit.ly/Rufus-Bullock (Accessed 17 August 2023).

corruption. A Grand Jury in Atlanta also investigated Bullock but could not find evidence to convict.[712]

Active Reconstruction ended in Georgia, but Georgia and the rest of the South now entered the era of Passive Reconstruction. Passive Reconstruction (1877-1965) set the stage for a return to conditions very similar to Active Reconstruction—Modern Era Reconstruction (post-1965). Reconstruction was not an effort to rebuild the devastated South; it was an effort to establish the Yankee Empire under which "We the People" of America now suffer.[713] As Georgian and former Confederate Vice President Stephens declared after the War, "The cause of the South is now the cause of all."[714]

---

712   Henry, Robert Selph, *The Story of Reconstruction* (Konecky & Konecky, New York: 1938), 452.

713   Kennedy & Kennedy, *Yankee Empire: Aggressive Abroad and Despotic at Home*, 273-82.

714   Stephens, Alexander H., *Constitutional View of the Late War Between the States* (1870, Harrisonburg, VA: Sprinkle Publications, 1994), Vol. II, 666.

Chapter 18:

KENTUCKY PUNISHED WITH RECONSTRUCTION

"The Southern States...were making a heroic defense of the principle of community independence and the right to regulate their own domestic affairs, which is inseparable from the idea of true republican and federal liberty."
—Col. J. Stoddard Johnston [715]

THE INVADING YANKEE Army ensured the people of Kentucky would remain a part of Lincoln's Union. The threat of military dictatorship would keep Kentucky in a Union that no longer respected the American principle of government based on the consent of the governed. Even though Kentucky remained in Lincoln's Union, the state was not treated equally as other "loyal" States.[716] The Yankee military that came into the state "assumed the airs and attitudes of conquerors toward a population subjected by force of their [Union Army] victorious arms."[717] Union President Lincoln was so concerned about Kentucky leaving his Union that he put the state under martial law and the state remained

---

715   Colonel Johnston, "Kentucky" in *Confederate Military History*, Vol. IX (1899, The Archives Society, Harrisburg, PA: 1994), 14.

716   Border States such as Kentucky did send delegates to the Confederate Congress. They never had a chance to use the formal process as was done by the other 11 States, but they did form "conventions" of the people and declared secession and sent many of their men to fight for Southern independence.

717   Henry, Robert Selph, *The Story of Reconstruction* (Konecky & Konecky, New York: 1938), 82-3.

under martial law until October 12, 1865, a full six months after Appomattox.[718] The ancient *writ of habeas corpus* inherited from America's English ancestors and adopted by the United States was not restored to Kentucky for a year after the end of the War—a war during which Kentucky remained a part of Lincoln's Union.[719]

Kentucky was numbered among the Southern States that were reluctant to join the Deep South States' secession from the old— as in Constitutional—Union. The people of the state never had a chance to freely express their will after Lincoln announced his unconstitutional invasion of Kentucky's sister States of the Deep South. Kentucky was occupied before the state legislature could call for a constitutional convention to consider secession. Lincoln placed Kentucky under martial law, but the state was not under a provisional government formed under Lincoln's Ten Percent Reconstruction Plan. Why? Because the state never left the Union. The state had Senators and Representatives in Washington, DC, during the War. Yet, post-War Kentucky was treated the same as her sister States of the South. As such, Kentucky was to endure the work of the Freedmen's Bureau and other quasi-official groups working with Kentucky's relatively small number of blacks.

The Republican-controlled Congress imposed Reconstruction on States that never seceded from the Union, such as Kentucky, Maryland, Missouri, and West Virginia. Kentucky was a primary target of Republican wrath. On May 4, 1866, the state dared to vote overwhelmingly for a straight Democratic ticket. The citizens of Kentucky voted to send nine representatives to the Fortieth Congress which began March 1867.[720] This represented a major fear of the Republicans. If Southern Democrats joined with Northern Democrats, then the Republicans would not control Congress, override Presidential vetoes, nor gain electoral votes from the Southern States. This was made even clearer when Northern States that, in 1866, voted with the Radical Republicans began to

---

718 *Ibid.*, 83.
719 *Ibid.*, 83.
720 *Ibid.*, 251.

go Democrat in the 1867 elections. The Radical Republican Party understood that they would go the way of the big government Federalist and Whig Parties of the past if something radical was not done.

The pure hatred toward folks who refused to accept the Republican Party's philosophy of Radical Reconstruction was demonstrated by the Cincinnati *Commercial* when it wrote that Kentucky had "gone overwhelmingly for the rebels.... Kentucky is today as effectively in the hands of the rebels as if they had every town and city garrisoned by their troops."[721] The free and unfettered consent of the governed means nothing to the Yankee Empire's ruling elite or their media sycophants. To demonstrate this point, look to the Congressional Record. On July 3, 1867, the Republican-controlled House of Representatives refused to allow the duly elected representatives from Kentucky to take their seats. The Republicans claimed that the Kentucky elections were not valid because "loyal voters...had been overawed and prevented from a true expression of their will and choice at the polls by those who have sympathized with or actually participated in the late rebellion." The message was simple—vote as we demand or else. Senator Summer declared that "nothing can be more certain than that Kentucky, at this time, is without a republican form of government." He implied that, according to the Constitution, Article IV, Section 4, Congress is responsible for assuring that every state has a "Republican form of government." In a speech in the United States Senate, he boldly announced that "Kentucky needs reconstruction, and it is our duty to provide it. Put her on an equality with Rebel States."[722] "We the People" of Kentucky answered the Republican Congress by electing John L. Helm (Democrat) as governor by a majority double the votes received by his Radical Republican and moderate Republican opponents. Kentucky was unrepresented in Congress during the summer session of 1867. In December, six Democrats were allowed to take their seats but Sam McKee, a Republican who had been defeated

---

721 Ibid., 251.

722 Ibid., 252.

by over 1,500 votes, was seated nonetheless, while John Young Brown (Democrat), who won by over 6,000 votes, was denied his seat because he gave aid and support to the Confederacy.[723]

Late in 1865, Southern States such as Kentucky were leaning Democrat. Fearful for their hold on power, Republicans saw an end to their control of the Federal Government. Something had to be done! The Republicans barely managed to gain the ratification of a new constitution in Missouri. But they failed to do so in Kentucky or Tennessee. By June of 1865, Representative Thaddeus Stevens began to fear that the Republican Plan for Reconstruction would be derailed by Southern white conservatives.[724] The 1865 elections were held in Southern States reorganized under Lincoln's Ten Percent Reconstruction Plan. Lincoln's Reconstruction Plan was hated by Republicans in Congress. The propagandists of the North convinced the Northern people that Southern whites would not "... repudiate at the ballot box, the treason they have supported at the mouth of the canon."[725] What they meant was that white Southern votes were meaningless if those conquered people did not parrot, vote, and fully embrace Northern ideas—especially the idea that America now belongs to the Northern ruling elite. Because the North was the conqueror, it would use its military and political power to force the conquered people of the South to bend a knee to the victor's will.

During the fall elections in Kentucky, the military rulers of the state stationed soldiers at the polls. The military and other unknown parties provided lists of those who were deemed not loyal enough to vote. As far as the military was concerned, the first and primary qualification of the franchise was that the individual was sympathetic to the Radical government and the Radical military command in the state.[726] As one Southern historian noted, the corruption of Kentucky politics reached all the way to Washington.

---

723   Ibid., 253-4.
724   Ibid., 84.
725   Ibid., 82.
726   Ibid., 83.

Kentucky Senator Garret Davis, zealous Unionist, sought to have his colleague, Lazarus Powell, expelled from the United States Senate.... Before the war ended, Senator Davis had become so outdone with the treatment of his state at the hands of the Union military...he publicly withdrew his attack on Senator Powell, declaring that the event had proved his colleague right and himself wrong.[727]

Even with the aid of the Yankee Empire's military, with most Confederates disfranchised and with only loyal Union men voting, the conservatives managed to elect five of eight congressmen and obtained a majority in the state's new legislature.[728]

Kentucky's post-War policy was, according to the Louisville, Kentucky, *Courier*, a sincere effort of healing and reconciliation. But Republicans saw it in a political, not social, light. They declared to the North that this was a "renewed rebellion." The Cincinnati *Gazette* condemned the efforts of the 1866 Kentucky legislature as being "...disloyal in spirit as any that ever met in Richmond or South Carolina."[729]

In the fall election of 1866, Kentucky went overwhelmingly for the Democrats and against the Republicans. Engaging in the democratic process of electing state leaders was reinvented by the Northern media and the Radical Republican politicians as evidence proving that the South was still in rebellion. The Cincinnati *Gazette* bemoaned the fact that it appeared that the "rebel gray has whipped the Union blue at the polls."[730] While Southerners, operating under Lincoln's Ten Percent Plan, were electing loyal, conservative, Union men, the North was busy electing Radical Republicans. Maine voted by a large majority to enter the Radical Republican camp, as did New York, Pennsylvania, Ohio, and

---

727 Ibid., 83.
728 Ibid., 83.
729 Ibid., 155.
730 Ibid., 197.

Indiana. After the elections in the fall of 1866, the prospects for local self-government in the South were bleak. The Radical Republican Party became the Republican Party. By March of 1867, the new Congress consisted of one hundred forty-three Republicans and forty-nine Democrats. In the Senate, the Republican Party held control by a margin of forty-two Republicans to eleven Democrats. It was a veto-proof House and Senate.[731]

On the first of May 1866, conservative Kentucky voters held an organizing convention in Louisville. Conservative delegates represented eighty-five of the state's counties. The so-called "loyal" or Union conservatives refused to attend and held their own meeting on May 30. The state's radicals, seeing a possible split in the white conservative ranks, offered to create an alliance between the radicals and the "loyal Unionists." Kentucky's "loyal Unionists" rejected the offer.[732]

During the 1868 campaign season, the folks of Kentucky elected Democrat, J.W. Stevenson as their governor by a four-to-one margin! The Republicans lost all except one judgeship race. Republican newspapers in the North blasted the election as if it were an act of treason to elect a Democrat in a Southern State. The editor of the *Courier-Journal* in Louisville, Kentucky, compared the one-sided election results in Kentucky with those in Massachusetts. He asked why Kentucky voters should be chastised for voting their convictions that resulted in a landslide victory similar to the election in Massachusetts, which resulted in a landslide victory for candidates who supported the views of Massachusetts voters. The editor questioned why Kentuckians:

> ...are denounced as traitors to our country and a despotism is sought to be placed over us by those who claim that we ought to be forced to vote for Republican candidates and Republican measures,

---

731   *Ibid.*, 198.

732   *Ibid.*, 173.

and who declare that if we do not, we are guilty of rebellion and should be punished therefor.[733]

The editor of the *Courier-Journal* wrote with courage in a time when men were seized by the Yankee military and imprisoned for speaking such truths. The editor, Henry Watterson, would win a Pulitzer Prize for journalism in 1918.

Fake news was used in Kentucky as in other Southern States. Its purpose was to give Yankee propagandists an excuse to wave the bloody shirt and create hatred toward the people of the conquered South. For example, Union General Clinton Bowen Fisk declared:

> ...only the day before yesterday, in Lexington, thirteen discharged colored soldiers stood in the streets, in full sight of the Henry Clay monument, with their bodies lacerated, their backs bleeding from the cruel lash, their heads cut to the scalp, and one or two of them with their eyes put out! And what for, do you suppose? Simply for going to their former masters and asking for their wives and children."[734]

As Southern comedian Lewis Grizzard (1946-1994) pointed out, the more extravagant and outrageous a claim about the South is, the more likely Yankees are to believe it.

The Kentucky legislature invited General Fisk to come and provide testimony or evidence supporting his allegations, but he refused the invitation. His final response gives ample evidence of the Republican Party's uncharitable attitude toward Southerners in general. He branded Kentuckians as "...the meanest, unsubjugated and unreconstructed rascally rebellious revolutionists that curse the soil of the country."[735]

---

[733] *Ibid.*, 344-5.

[734] *Ibid.*, 156.

[735] *Ibid.*, 156.

The recollection of an incident that occurred during the War by R.M.J. Arnette is indicative of Kentucky's loyalty to the Cause of Southern Independence:

> In the fall of 1864, after I made my escape from Camp Douglas, Chicago, and was in Kentucky...I met with "Sue Munday" and a squad of his men in Anderson County. He said that he was not going to leave Kentucky as long as he could find a good horse to ride, get plenty to eat, and find ammunition with which to kill Yankees.[736]

Lincoln's military forced Kentucky to accept a *puppet state government* well before such puppet state governments were foisted upon States in the Lower South.[737] These puppet governments, all dedicated to maintaining the political *status quo*, remain in place doing the will of the Yankee Empire's ruling elite. Today, these puppet state governments continue to supplicate before their one true Federal master. Modern Era Reconstruction (post-1965) is a continuation of the spirit of Active Reconstruction.

---

736 *Confederate Veteran*, Vol. V, No. 5, May 1897. Republished in *The Confederate Veteran Magazine*, (Harrisburg, PA: The National Historical Society, 1987), Vol. V, 200.

737 Some Southern conservatives may object to labeling the South's state governments as "puppet governments." General Stephen D. Lee writing in 1899, labeled States "organized and sustained by the military forces of the United States, not by the free will of its citizens," as "bogus governments." *Confederate Military History*, Vol. XII (1899, Harrisburg, PA: The Archives Society, 1994), 277.

Chapter 19:

LOUISIANA—
YANKEE TYRANNY IN THE BAYOU STATE

"The war was over, and Louisiana entered a new era. Reconstruction was just beginning."
—Dr. John D. Winters[738]

THE PEOPLE OF LOUISIANA, like folks in other Southern States, faced a bleak future after the War ended in April 1865. One out of every five Louisiana Confederate soldiers died during the War, and many of the surviving veterans lost arms and legs and were physically scarred and mentally exhausted. The immediate and uncompensated emancipation of slaves—as opposed to the efficient and economically profitable way Yankees removed slavery and blacks from their States—cost the state of Louisiana around $170,000,000.00 in lost investment capital ($3,188,000,000.00 in 2023 dollars).[739] Over half the state's horses, mules, hogs, and cattle were destroyed. Two-thirds of the farm implements necessary to produce crops were destroyed. The state's once flourishing sugar mills, numbering 1,200 before the War, were reduced to only 180 after the Yankee invasion, conquest, and occupation. The once world-renowned Bank of New Orleans that issued the famous Dix

---

738 Winters, John D., *The Civil War in Louisiana* (Baton Rouge, LA: LSU Press, 1963), 429.

739 "Value of $1 from 1865 to 2024," CPI Inflation Calculator (in2013dollars.com) www.bit.ly/dollar-1865 (Accessed 18 August 2023).

GENERAL PIERRE GUSTAVE TOUTANT-BEAUREGARD, CSA

BEAUREGARD THE REALIST:

"The Negro is Southern born; with a little education and some property qualifications he can be made to take sufficient interest in the affairs and prosperity of the South to insure an intelligent vote."

BEAUREGARD THE REVOLUTIONARY:

"Would that I could have said to [my soldiers], resist, and hang out our banners on the outer wall, etc., **but the day of retribution has not yet come** *when we shall be able to satiate our spirit of revenge on those fanatics and radicals of the North. Whenever it does, we shall make them drink of the poisoned chalice to the very dregs!"**[Emphasis added by author.]

*   Williams, T. Harry, *P.G.T. Beauregard: Napoleon in Gray* (Baton Rouge, LA: LSU Press, 1955), 266-7.

Notes[740] was destroyed. The only folks with money to loan, and that at extremely high interest rates, were Northern speculators, Union officials, and carpetbaggers. The war was over. Louisiana was entering a new era of social destruction far worse than Lincoln's War—the Republican Party's Active Reconstruction.

As bad as the destruction caused by Lincoln's unconstitutional war was, it was nothing compared to the damage done to Southern society by years of Republican-imposed Active Reconstruction. The racial bitterness, mistrust, and hatred thus generated worked well for the Yankee Empire's divide-and-rule strategy, but it left an angry wound that may never heal. "What could have been" was prevented, and what was created is America's current hate-filled, angry, and uncompromising leftist society where every offense or social inequality is viewed through the tainted lens of race.

Reconstruction Begins

The Republican-controlled Congress was willing to accept Louisiana's and other Southern States' post-War ratification of the Thirteenth Amendment that removed chattel slavery from America.[741] If the conquered Southern States performed in total submission to the political will of America's new rulers in Washington, then the Southern States were ignored. But when Louisiana and other Southern States refused to ratify the Republican Party's Fourteenth Amendment, then political war was declared on a prostrate South. To obtain total control of the South and gain passage of its Fourteenth Amendment, the Republican-controlled Congress passed the first of its numerous

---

740 Men from the Ohio Valley would float their wares downriver to New Orleans and return with their "pockets full of Dixies." Thus, the Bank of New Orleans $10.00 Dix note was the origin of Dixie as a popular term for the South.

741 Chattel slavery was removed, but shortly thereafter, it was replaced by what political, religious, and academic leaders described as a "new form of slavery"—sharecropping. This form of slavery was harsher than chattel slavery and bound twice as many people—around eight and a half million—for almost a century. Sixty percent were poor whites. Kennedy & Kennedy, *Punished With Poverty-The Suffering South* 2nd ed.

Reconstruction Acts on March 2, 1867.[742] It divided the Yankee Empire's conquered territories down South into five military districts. In effect, it created a military dictatorship to rule over the States of the former sovereign nation, the Confederate States of America. The reaction of Louisiana's conservatives to the Republican-controlled Congress' Military Bill, which put the Southern States under military dictatorship, was expressed by the *New Orleans Crescent*:

> The people of the South, if wise and prudent, can live for a time under such *damnable tyranny* as this, but if they consent, they deserve it.[743] (Emphasis added.)

After the end of Active Reconstruction, the "*damnable tyranny*" relented only slightly. During Active Reconstruction, the Yankee Empire's politicians and Federal Courts successfully transformed the original Constitution into one that allowed for an all-powerful Federal Government controlled by Northern elites. Then, during Passive Reconstruction, its puppet state governments (also referred to as bayonet governments and bogus governments) became normalized and accepted as legitimate state governments by the conquered people of the South. During Passive Reconstruction, Southern conservatives *subconsciously* learned to love their chains. All pacified slaves eventually learn to love (normalize) their chains. If you do not move around much, you will not notice your chains! This is the story of pacified Southerners since the end of Active Reconstruction. But the love of "one nation indivisible" chains is a one-way love-fest. The chains of federal tyranny grew heavier and tighter, especially after 1965. In the Modern Era Reconstruction (post-1965), the "*damnable tyranny*" began anew and with a slanderous vengeance. The Southern people made a strategic failure after the end of Active Reconstruction. They failed to keep the dream of freedom, self-government, and Constitutional liberty alive by initiating a vocal national and international movement to

---

742 "Primary Source: Military Reconstruction Act," Anchor | NCpedia (ncpedia.org) www.bit.ly/Reconstruction-Act (Accessed 18 August 2023).

743 Bowers, Claude, *The Tragic Era*, 209.

reclaim America's original and legitimate Republic of Sovereign States. This strategic failure gave the Yankee Empire a free hand during the so-called Progressive Era[744] to consolidate its powers in their *new* "one nation indivisible."

Louisiana and Texas were part of Military District 5, commanded by General Sheridan. He established his headquarters in New Orleans. Sheridan never relented in his hatred for the white South. While in command in New Orleans, he issued his infamous *banditti* request in a telegram to the Secretary of War in Washington. Sheridan proposed to label all whites who opposed his Reconstruction policies as "rebels" and "bandits" to be arrested and tried by his military courts. He promised that all who protested his rule would be seized and "no further action need be taken except that which would devolve upon me."[745] It was a late effort by one of the South's most infamous enemies to save Republican Active Reconstruction and, thereby, maintain the South under military rule. Such was the mindset of the South's "benevolent, with malice toward none and charity for all" rulers. Is there any wonder that a Southern resistance movement would arise under such tyranny? As Thomas Jefferson said, "Resistance to tyranny is obedience to God."[746]

A CARNIVAL OF IGNORANCE, INCOMPETENCE, AND THEFT—REPUBLICAN STATE GOVERNMENT

Louisiana's Republican-controlled Reconstruction Legislature is an example of what all Southern States, to one degree or another, were forced to contend with during Republican rule. It also demonstrates why a post-War Southern resistance movement

---

744 Some date the Progressive Era from 1896 to 1917. It continues today but by different terms, all promoting leftist/postmodernist ideology in one form or another. America's current "Woke," politically correct, social justice warrior culture is a natural outgrowth of Progressive ideology.

745 Bowers, Claude, *The Tragic Era*, 444.

746 Jefferson suggested it as the motto for the United States. He may have borrowed it from Benjamin Franklin. Jefferson used it as his personal motto, which is slightly different from the popular mis-quote: "Rebellion to tyrants is obedience to God." See www.bit.ly/xJefferson-Seal.

developed across the South. Outside the South, not a single American state has ever been forced, by the Federal Government, to tolerate for up to ten years a state government ruled by ignorance, incompetence, fraud, corruption, and unabashed tyranny, all backed by Yankee bayonets. Instead of being criticized for its Reconstruction resistance movement, Southerners should be praised for their ceaseless post-Active Reconstruction patriotic support for the country that invaded, impoverished, and continually slanders their Southern homeland. After Active Reconstruction—beginning circa 1877—Southern soldiers, sailors, and airmen shed rivers of blood in America's wars. Yet, this blood sacrifice has purchased no national respect for the traditionally conservative South. As Republican Thaddeus Stevens explained, the South is not ruled by the original Constitution but by the "rules of war and conquest."

When foreign visitors came to New Orleans during Active Reconstruction and asked to be directed to some of the more interesting sites in the city—New Orleans was then the state's capitol—the foreigner would be told to go to Mechanics Hall and watch the carnival of ignorance being played out there. Mechanics Hall was where the state legislature met. Ignorance and incompetence were there on public display. There, illiterate black legislators would offer amendments that were too vulgar to print but were received with gales of laughter. "The vulgarity of the speeches increases; members stagger from the basement bar to their seats."[747] Northern visitors to the city would organize "slumming parties" to go to the legislature as if viewing the animals at the zoo or athletes at a sports event. The business of corruption was conducted openly without fear of legal scrutiny. As a Southern historian noted:

> Measures involving millions...passed without examination, and members vote vast sums into their pockets openly, defiantly. The mileage and *per diem*

---

747 Bowers, Claude, *The Tragic Era* (Halcyon House, New York: 1929), 364.

for members and clerks leap from a quarter of a million in 1869 to half a million the next year.[748]

As bad as the fraud and corruption were, it could have been corrected at the next election if the Northern rulers allowed former Confederates to vote and the election was held honestly. But honesty in elections was the problem! Fraudulent elections were enforced by Federal and Republican Reconstruction state government tyranny.

Louisiana's carpetbag governor, Henry Clay Warmoth, was Louisiana's first Republican governor. He was a carpetbagger originally from Illinois and a former Union Army officer. He pushed several bills through the Reconstruction legislature that made him a virtual dictator. The Registration Bill gave the governor control of every parish (county) voter registration office and gave these offices the authority to accept or reject vote counts without interference from the courts; his Election Bill prohibited the courts from interfering with election results. It also gave the governor the right to reject the winning candidate's certificates of election and authorized the creation of a Returning Board to issue or certify the final "correct" vote count. The bill specified who would be on the Board, all of whom were part of Warmoth's political machine; the Constabulary Bill allowed the governor to name one of his cronies as chief constable in each parish (county); and the Militia Bill authorized the governor to organize and equip what amounted to his personal military force. Over one hundred thousand dollars was authorized to equip the militia. Of course, the militia would be composed of blacks with a few Republican whites as officers. The conservative, primarily white people held mass meetings to protest these undemocratic and tyrannical laws:

But behind the Legislature was Warmoth; behind him his militia and constables; and behind them Federal bayonets—and the laws went into operation.[749]

---

748   Ibid., 364.

749   Ibid., 365.

The cost of a Louisiana legislative session before Republican Reconstruction was $100,000.00, but during Republican Reconstruction, the cost in 1871 was $958,956.50.[750] The 1871 cost would be equal to approximately $23,849,248.20 in 2023.[751] By 1872, the productive citizens of Louisiana were under a tax system that amounted to government confiscation of private property. Impoverished property owners suffered under confiscatory taxation, and in many parishes (counties), tax collectors seized large tracts of rich land. These rich tracts of land were purchased at a dollar an acre—and typically purchased by "loyal" men or Northern "investors." In many cases, there was no one with money enough to purchase the land even at a dollar an acre.[752]

THE FIRST EFFORT TO REDEEM LOUISIANA GOVERNMENT

Six years after the beginning of Reconstruction and despite Republican propagandists vigorously waving the bloody shirt, the people of the North were beginning to tire of the Southern problem. Reports of fraud and corruption in the South's Republican Reconstruction governments were making their rounds among the more educated classes in the North. That and the reports of fraud in the Grant Administration and an economic downturn all made for an excellent opportunity to overturn ActiveReconstruction. Historian Claude Bowers described the general attitude of Northerners of the time:

All over the North, thinking men were beginning to resent the policy of imposing ignorant and criminally corrupt government on the Southern people. The scandalous contest over the Louisiana election of the previous year was still on, and many were shaking their heads in disapproval of the part played in Washington. It was the year Andrew D. White, visiting the South, was disgusted

---

750   Ibid., 366. Author cites Lonn, Ella, *Reconstruction in Louisiana after 1868*, New York, 1918, 86.

751   "Value of $1 from 1871 to 2024," CPI Inflation Calculator (in2013dollars.com) www.bit.ly/1871-UDS (Accessed 05 June 2023).

752   Bowers, Claude, *The Tragic Era*, 366. Author cites Lonn, Ella, *Reconstruction in Louisiana after 1868*, New York, 1918, 367,

Gov. John McEnery ejected via Yankee bayonets.

by what he saw "for the first time began to feel sympathy with the South" after seeing personally how he had been deceived by partisan prejudice and dishonest propaganda.⁷⁵³

Louisiana conservatives' resistance efforts appeared to be working in the election of 1872. Conservatives elected John McEnery as Governor thus unseating the carpetbag Reconstruction Governor William Pitt Kellogg. But as current history demonstrated, it is possible to artificially change the vote count in a highly

---

753   *Ibid.*, 414. Author cites White, Andrew, *Autobiography*, Two volumes, New York, 1905, Vol. I, 176.

contested election.⁷⁵⁴ And so, it was with McEnery's conservative victory. The people of Louisiana spoke, but the Republican political *status quo* had the final word. The Republican-controlled retuning board had the final say as to which votes were legitimate and would be counted and which were illegitimate and would be thrown out. Without even counting the votes or checking them for legitimacy, the returning board gave the election to the Republican carpetbag Governor Kellogg.

The state and nation were shocked by the audacious and tyrannical actions of the returning board. After the election, more than fifty-two hundred false voter registrations were found in New Orleans. In north Louisiana, an effort to impanel a jury had to be stopped because three-fourths of the names drawn from the voter registration list were found to be fabricated.⁷⁵⁵ According to a Congressional investigation, McEnery had a majority of up to ten thousand votes, and the state's conservatives won the majority in the state legislature with 39 conservatives elected to Louisiana's House of Representatives and 11 conservatives elected to the State Senate. The actions of the carpetbag Republican returning board were declared to be "Reprehensible and erroneous in point of law and wholly void for want of jurisdiction." This harsh criticism was pronounced by a Congressional investigation that included a majority of Republicans!⁷⁵⁶ Louisiana had two governors, one the legitimately elected conservative and the other a carpetbag Republican installed by a corrupt and tyrannical ruling establishment. The state Republicans played their trump card by appealing to Washington for support. President Grant issued an order for the "turbulent" people (meaning the McEnery government and supporters) "to disperse within five days" and accept the Republican carpetbag governor's government. To make sure the people obeyed his imperial order, President Grant sent three men-of-war

---

754 Furr, Amy, "Box of uncounted ballots found in storage unit in a local 2019 election decided by 19 votes," Breitbart News (breitbart.com) 10 June 2023, www.bit.ly/MI-Ballot-2020 (Accessed 11 June 2023).

755 Bowers, Claude, *The Tragic Era*, 442. Author cites Nordhoff, Charles, *The Cotton States in the Spring and Summer of 1875*, New York, 1875, 43.

756 *Ibid.*, 436. Author cites Senate Report 91, 42nd Cong., 3rd Sess.

and Federal troops to the state's capitol then in New Orleans.[757] Yankee Gunboat diplomacy began in the South long before it became an international norm in Hawaii, the Philippines, and Latin America.[758] In Louisiana, the Yankee Empire had once again dealt a blow to the concept of government based upon the consent of the governed.

Relief from direct Federal tyranny for Louisiana and South Carolina would have to wait until the Presidential election of 1876 between Republican Rutherford B. Hayes from Ohio and Democrat Samuel J. Tilden from New York. That election produced a deadlocked presidential electoral result which allowed the delegates and representatives from Louisiana and South Carolina to work out a "deal" with Hayes. These two States would support the Republican Hayes if he agreed to remove the last Yankee troops stationed in the South. The final act of the horror show known as Active Reconstruction was conducted in a smoke-filled room. It did not necessarily represent the will of the people, but such is the government produced by Lincoln's war and Republican Active Reconstruction. The next phase would be Passive Reconstruction (1877-1965) and its "Progressive" ideology that paved the way for Modern Era Reconstruction (post-1965).

---

757   Ibid., 441.

758   Kennedy & Kennedy, *Yankee Empire: Aggressive Abroad and Despotic at Home* (Columbia, SC: Shotwell Publishing., 2018).

Chapter 20:

MARYLAND RECONSTRUCTED SINCE 1861

*"The time will come when all the world will
realize that the failure of the Confederacy was
a great misfortune to humanity and will be the
source of unnumbered woes to liberty,"*
—General Bradley T. Johnson, CSA[759]

Maryland is a unique Southern state. Being close to the US capital, it was the first Southern state to feel the iron rod of Yankee Reconstruction—before the concept of Reconstruction was conceived in the evil hearts of the emerging Yankee Empire's political tyrants. Northern troops planned to use the sovereign state of Maryland as a thoroughfare as they marched to invade Maryland's Southern sister States. Although most of the state's citizens at the time held strong attachments to the "old Union," they did not approve of Lincoln's plan of armed invasion and coercion against the sovereign States of the South. Lincoln and his co-conspirators understood the strategic importance of Maryland. It could pose a point of invasion of the Yankee Empire's capital. If Maryland seceded and joined her sister States of the South, the Confederacy would surround the US capital in Washington, DC![760]

---

759 Maryland's General Bradley Johnson's speech, *Southern Historical Papers*, Vol. 23, 368-70.

760 Johnson, Dr. Ludwell H., *The North Against the South: The American Iliad 1848-1877* (1978, Columbia, SC: The Foundation for American Education, 1993), 84.

Something had to be done and as with all tyrants, the appeal was made not to logic and civil discourse but to the bayonet. Bayonet rule came early to the Southern state of Maryland.

To prevent "We the People" of Maryland from exercising their right to determine their political future—an essential element of sovereignty—Lincoln and his co-conspirators resorted to the tyrant's plea of the sword and shackles. They sent troops into the state and engineered replacing the legitimate state and city (Baltimore) officials with pro-Lincoln men. Lincoln's secretary of war, Simon Cameron, instructed Yankee General Banks (later to be known as "cotton thief Banks" in Louisiana): "If necessary, all or any part of the members of the legislature must be arrested."[761] It is worth noting that these "replacements" were pro-Lincoln not pro-Union men. Lincoln's puppets were not in favor of the old Union created by the Founding Fathers via the original Constitution, they were effecting a radical change from a voluntary Union to an empire created by conquest. Remember, if you can't leave, you are not free.

Most of Maryland's elected officials were already pro-Union men, but their disqualifying sin was that they were pro-original Union men. They were men who still honored the original Constitution and the original Federal Government of limited powers created by that Constitution. Lincoln and his co-conspirators had no use for such an "outdated" Constitution and eventually would destroy both the spirit and the letter of that old Constitution. They destroyed (debunked or deconstructed) America's Republic of Sovereign States and replaced it with the emerging all-powerful Yankee Empire.

To establish a new Maryland, which would be the South's first puppet state established by Yankee bayonets, the Federal Government arrested Baltimore's mayor, George William Brown, several of the outspoken city councilmen, and the city's Chief of Police, George Proctor Kane. They were imprisoned at Fort Warren in Boston Harbor. The enforcers of Lincoln's tyranny arrested

---

761 DiLorenzo, Thomas J., *The Real Lincoln* (New York: Three Rivers Press, 2002), 142.

twenty-one key Maryland officials and newspaper editors.[762] They received no hearing, no arrest warrant, and were afforded no opportunity to plead their case before a fair and unbiased court. The fact that Lincoln and the emerging Yankee Empire had no respect for the Constitution is demonstrated by the fact that these conservative Marylanders were arrested and imprisoned under a tyrannical order of the newly emerging Yankee Empire. They were seized by Federal authorities without the benefit of a court hearing or trial. They were incarcerated for a year and four months for the crime of posing a threat to the emerging Yankee Empire. Military forces from Massachusetts, led by General Ben (Beast) Butler and others, backed their arrests and illegal imprisonment. The fact that the Northern state of Massachusetts would allow its troops to be used to suppress liberty in a sister state is even more insulting when one understands that Maryland had on numerous occasions sent her sons to protect and defend Massachusetts.

The patriotic character of Maryland's citizens was demonstrated in 1774 when news came that the people of Boston, Massachusetts, were shot by the English tyrant's troops. Within two weeks the people of Maryland "rose as one man" and mustered in militia companies and battalions. They collected and sent money and provisions to the people of Boston. Marylanders pledged themselves to refuse to purchase any English goods until Boston Harbor was opened and free trade was resumed. This was not the first time they rallied to support Massachusetts people. Ten years earlier, they refused alone with the people of Massachusetts to honor the English Parliament's Stamp Act. Maryland blood was shed to protect the interests of their fellow Americans of Massachusetts.

When the farmers of New England met and drove the British regulars at Breed's Hill, the prompt response of Maryland was a battalion of riflemen which marched from Frederick to Boston, 550 miles, to reinforce their brethren. Maryland had no interest in this fight. She enjoyed a just and liberal government. Her people made their own laws, levied their own taxes, and expended them

---

762   Ibid., 142.

for their own benefit, and there was no friction between them and the government... But when word went out that Boston needed assistance, every country committee, every court, every provincial assembly proclaimed with one voice, "The cause of Boston is the cause of all."[763]

Maryland's repayment for its efforts and blood spent in the defense of Massachusetts were bloody bayonets in the hands of the sons of Massachusetts led by the soon-to-be infamous Yankee General "Beast" Butler. As the Romans declared, "**Carthaginian** faith."[764]

By the late 1850s, it was evident that the North's aggressive and slanderous attacks against the South were trending more and more toward actual physical violence. Although most Marylanders were opposed to secession, they were even more concerned about the violent threats coming from the North directed at their Southern neighbors. In 1860, the Maryland legislature appropriated $70,000.00 to arm the state's militia.[765] After the Presidential elections of 1860, with an anti-South sectional party winning the presidency, it was clear to the young men of the state that secession and war were likely on the horizon. But the old men who controlled the state urged caution. Their long-term tenure in public office and their defeated efforts to prevent dis-union exhausted their enthusiasm for resistance. They were like the "old and wise men" of Arabia who counseled against a revolt against the Turks who ruled Arabia. As T.E. Lawrence noted in *Seven Pillars of Wisdom*, "They were not old and wise, they were tired and defeated."

Governor Hicks of Maryland was a cunning politician. He witnessed what happened to those who opposed the new regime in Washington. He was never a devoted Constitutionalist. More of

---

763 Gen. Bradley Johnson, "Maryland," *Confederate Military History* (1899, Harrisburg, PA: The Archive Society, 1994), Vol. II, 8.

764 The phrase "Punic faith" or "Carthaginian faith" denotes perfidy, treachery, and bad faith. It translates classical Latin *Pūnica fidēs*, of the same meaning. "The Roman Origin Of 'Punic Faith'" World Histories (worldhistories.net) www.bit.ly/Punic-Faith (Accessed 26 August 2023).

765 Gen. Bradley Johnson, "Maryland," *Confederate Military History*, Vol. II, 11.

a man of pragmatism than principle, he sought the best results for Hicks. As General Bradley Johnson noted:

> Governor Hicks was no fool. He was a shrewd, sharp, positive man. He knew what he wanted, and he took efficient means to procure it. He wanted to save Maryland to the Northern States. He believed the Union was gone. In the Southern Confederacy, Maryland must, in his opinion, play a subordinate part and he, himself, fall back into the political obscurity from which he had been recently raised. With the North, Maryland in possession of the national capital, protected by the Northern Navy through her bay and great rivers, would be a conspicuous power, and he, as her governor, would fill a distinguished role.[766]

Citizens protesting the use of their city as a route for an army intent on invading sovereign States met Northern troops in the streets of Baltimore. Yankee bayonets and bullets met their protests. The city council approved $500,000.00 to defend the city. The mayor called all able-bodied citizens to enroll for militia service to protect the city. Over fifteen thousand citizens volunteered their services. On Sunday, April 21, 1861, while folks were at church, a rider galloped through the streets, shouting, "The Yankees are coming, the Yankees are coming!" Church services were dismissed, and folks went home or to their organized defense units. Lincoln, in his usual cryptic manner, declared that Maryland would not be attacked "if the people of Maryland would permit it and would not molest the troops."[767] Otherwise, Federal troops would subdue Maryland. The meaning of Lincoln's cryptic declaration was simple—the state of Maryland must surrender its sovereignty and submit to Federal authorities. Lincoln and his co-conspirators intended to make Maryland their first Southern puppet state. Another example of Lincoln's doublespeak was when, on May 6th, he told peace commissioners from Maryland that, as long as Maryland did not array itself against the Federal Government, the state, "would not be molested or interfered with, except so

---

766   *Ibid.*, Vol. II, 16.

767   *Ibid.*, Vol. II, 24.

far as it was necessary for the preservation of the Union."[768] In other words, the state could not maintain its neutrality but had to choose a side. The choice of neutrality was viewed by Lincoln and his co-conspirators as a choice against their new Union. As General Bradley Johnson described the situation:

> The President had declared war on her sister States. Was Maryland to support that war, or was she to stand by with hands folded and see the friends and kindred beyond the Potomac put to the sword and the torch? War on a State was against the common right. The cause of each was the cause of all; and precisely as Maryland had responded in 1775 to the cry of Massachusetts for assistance, so now did the people of Maryland, over governor, over general assembly, over peace commissioners, respond to the call of Virginia.[769]

The resolve of the people of Maryland to maintain the original Constitutional Republic of Sovereign States was expressed in two Resolutions passed by Maryland's legislature.

On the 10th of May 1861, with the once-sovereign state of Maryland in the grip of Federal troops, the state's legislature passed a clear statement declaring that the Federal Government was waging an unconstitutional and aggressive war against the people of the South. The following are pertinent parts of that resolution:

> Whereas, in the judgment of the General Assembly of Maryland, the war now waged by the government of the United States upon the people of the Confederate States is unconstitutional in its origin, purposes, and conduct; repugnant to civilization and sound policy; subversive of the free principles upon

---

768 *Ibid.*, Vol. II, 26. Author cites Lincoln.

769 *Ibid.*, Vol. II, 27.

which the Federal Union was founded, and certain to result in the hopeless and bloody overthrow of our existing institutions; and

Whereas the people of Maryland...do reverence...the great American principle of self-government, and sympathize deeply with their Southern brethren in their noble and manly determination to uphold and defend the same;...

Now, therefore, it is hereby resolved by the General Assembly of Maryland, that the State of Maryland owes it to her own self-respect and her respect for the Constitution, not less than her deepest and most honorable sympathies, to register this, her solemn protest, against the war which the Federal government has declared against the Confederate States...

Resolved, That the State of Maryland earnestly and anxiously desires the restoration of peace...the [Southern] President, authorities and people of the Confederate States having over and over, officially and unofficially, declared that they seek only peace and self-defense, and to be let alone...

The senators and delegates of Maryland do beseech and implore the President of the United States to accept the olive branch which is thus held out to him, and in the name of God and humanity to cease this unholy and most wretched and unprofitable strife...

Resolved, That the State of Maryland desires the peaceful and immediate recognition of the independence of the Confederate States...

Resolved, That the present military occupation of Maryland being for purpose which in the opinion of the legislature are in flagrant violation of the Constitution...⁷⁷⁰

General "Beast" Butler issued the Yankee Empire's response to the legitimately elected representatives of Maryland's people by sending Yankee troops into Baltimore and seizing the city the very night these resolutions were passed by the state's General Assembly. The votes in the General Assembly were, in the Senate:11 in favor and 3 opposed; in the House: 43 in favor and 12 opposed.

The state legislature passed a second resolution on June 22, 1861. It was to be their final protest against the tyrannical powers then occupying the once-sovereign state of Maryland.

> Now, therefore, be it resolved, ...[the] delegates of Maryland, in the name and on behalf of the good people of the State, do accordingly register this their earnest and unqualified protest against the oppressive and tyrannical assertion and exercise of military jurisdiction within the limits of Maryland... by the government of the United States, and do solemnly declare the same to be subversive of the most sacred guarantees of the Constitution and in flagrant violation of the fundamental and most cherished principles of American free government.⁷⁷¹

"We the People" of Maryland, through their legitimately elected representatives, had spoken. While the conservative old men passed resolutions, an aggressive Yankee Empire acted!

Maryland's legislature was composed of conservative old men who earnestly attempted to maintain a Constitution and a Union that no longer existed. Perhaps it was too painful for them to admit that all they struggled to maintain was now gone. Perhaps it was too painful to admit their total failure. They maintained their self-

---

770   *Ibid.*, Vol. II,30-2.

771   *Ibid.*, Vol. II, 35.

delusion and fantasy that the old Union and its Constitution still existed and could be appealed to for redress of their grievances until it was too late. As General Bradley Johnson noted, "The conservatives never could, never did understand that they were in the midst of a revolution." They stood by their honestly held opinion that their rights were protected by the Constitution, and they held firmly to this false assumption until it "landed them in Fort Lafayette or the military prisons in New York and Boston."[772] Even Francis Key Howard, grandson of "Star Spangled Banner" author Francis Scott Key was imprisoned for exercising his Constitutional right of supporting government by consent of the governed. Ironically, he was imprisoned at Fort McHenry, the very site where the flag which had inspired his grandfather had flown in defiance of tyranny. Conservatives in Modern Era Reconstruction should not scoff at the impractical and unproductive assumptions of Maryland's *self-deluded* conservative old men. Conservatives of the Modern Era are continuously repeating the same errors of judgment.

In principle, modern-era conservatives are doing the same thing. They refuse to accept that the original Constitution with its limitations on the Federal Government and reservation of rights to the Sovereign States is dead.[773] The original Constitutional concepts of real States' Rights, including the rights of nullification and secession, as described by Thomas Jefferson and James Madison in their Kentucky and Virginia Resolutions of 1798,[774] no longer exist. Today, "We the People" are ruled by a supreme, all-powerful Federal Government. Under the original Constitution, if the Federal Government ordered the closing of churches during a pandemic, a Sovereign State could nullify such unconstitutional Federal orders; under the original Constitution, a Sovereign State could use its militia to defend its borders against invasion or to

---

772   Ibid., Vol. II, 35.

773   Modern day conservatives meet the definition of "self-delusion: "Allowing oneself to believe something that is not true." Cambridge Dictionary (dictionary.cambridge.org).

774   See "Kentucky and Virginia Resolutions" in Kennedy & Kennedy, *Jefferson Davis: Highroad to Emancipation and Constitutional Government* (Columbia, SC: Shotwell Publishing), 371-6.

deport illegals; under the original Constitution, the sovereign state determined the definition of marriage; under the original Constitution, a Sovereign State could determine if sexual perverts would be allowed to teach in its schools—those days are over! Modern-day counterfeit conservatives in the Republican Party are repelled by the very idea of challenging the political *status quo*. They are instrumental in maintaining the political *status quo*. Their only disagreement with their political rivals in the Democrat Party is whether or when they will have the opportunity to hold the reigns of federal power. A *fundamental* change is the only way to restore America's once-great Republic. But a fundamental change is the last thing they want. Counterfeit conservatives in Washington make hot speeches for home consumption, but they would never lead a movement to restore America's original and legitimate Republic of Sovereign States. There is no hope for true liberty in America without a *fundamental* change in the current political *status quo*.[775] The uniparty[776] composed of Republican and Democrat political ruling elites, their cronies in the media, and their financial donors will use any means necessary to protect the political *status quo* that provides them with unlimited perks, privileges, and power. The Republican Party's Active Reconstruction made the creation of what is today referred to as the Deep State possible. Maryland was the first Southern State to feel the iron rod of Yankee domination. Her sister States of the South would soon be held in the clutches of the Yankee Empire's new Union—a Union typified by a hawk's bloody talons grasping a dove's breast.

Maryland—The Yankee Empire's First Puppet State

During Active Reconstruction, all the former Confederate States were reorganized under the duress of Yankee bayonets and forced to accept puppet state governments. Maryland was one of the first, if not the first, ruled by a Federally imposed puppet state government. "The governor and State authority were thus

---

775 Kennedy, James Ronald, *Dixie Rising-Rules for Rebels* 2nd ed., vii, xi, 7.

776 Zimmer, Ben, "The Strange History of the Uniparty," Politico Magazine (politico.com) www.politi.co/3TcfT8p (Accessed 28 August 2023).

superseded by the Federal government, as the legislature was shortly afterward dispersed, imprisoned, and disbanded, the judges ignored, and the courts trampled underfoot."[777] Under Lincoln and the Republican Party the once sovereign States of the South became puppet States or, as General Stephen Dill Lee branded them, "bogus States."[778] It soon became evident that the Constitution of the United States no longer held any meaning unless it would provide cover or illegitimate justification for the workings of tyranny. In times of war, paper guarantees, and written agreements have no force. As far as Lincoln and his co-conspirators were concerned, the Constitution was valid only so long as it did not interfere with their aggressive war and their efforts to create an economic and political empire controlled by Northern ruling elites.

Before the close of 1861, Maryland was under the rule of Lincoln's military. Over 40,000 Yankee troops were in the state to ensure it would remain "loyal" to the Union. This loyalty was obtained at the point of Yankee bayonets. Voices in protest would be threatened with arrest, and newspaper editors would be removed if they dared to print editorials against Maryland's military occupation. Maryland's scallywag governor Hicks was greatly alarmed at the potential of a pro-Southern vote in the upcoming November 1861 elections. He asked General Banks (of Massachusetts) to use his military to ensure "a killing majority shall be rolled up against secessionism."[779] General McClellan ordered Banks to post troops at the polling sites and to arrest anyone who recently returned from Virginia who attempted to vote. In other words, those Marylanders who traveled to Virginia were so tainted with secessionism that it negated their right to cast their ballots in their home state. "General Dix, governing in Baltimore, directed the United States marshal and the provost marshal to arrest all

---

777   Gen. Bradley Johnson, "Maryland," *Confederate Military History*, Vol. II, 93.

778   General Stephen D. Lee writing in 1899 labeled States, "organized and sustained by the military forces of the United States, not by the free will of its citizens," as "bogus governments." See *Confederate Military History*, Vol. XII, 277.

779   *Ibid.*, Vol. II, 93. Author cites Hicks.

disloyal persons and to hold them securely."[780] Where is the law that establishes "disloyalty" as a crime? Who is to determine that an individual is "disloyal?" Lincoln and the Republican Party eagerly used this tyrannical and unconstitutional power. It was reported that Union troops took part in the elections even though they were not citizens of Maryland. They were reported to have voted "freely without hindrance" and as often as they wanted.[781] A report to General Bank's headquarters dated November 8, 1861, bragged of the success of the Yankee Army's election interference:

> Previous to the election a number of enemies to the Union in this State...I had several of the most prominent actors in this, among whom was a candidate for senator, arrested before election and held until today. I had details from various companies of my regiment...places where the polls were held. Owing to the presence of the troops everything progressed quietly and I am happy to report a Union victory in every place in my jurisdiction.[782]

Maryland provides an excellent example of political ruling elites using their power to arrest a political candidate who opposed Washington's political establishment (a political establishment that was the forerunner of the Deep State), a political ruling elite that used arrest and intimidation to silence or censor their opponents, and a political ruling elite that orchestrated election interference to assure their side got enough votes to win the election—all brought to America by Lincoln and his Republican Party, a gift that keeps on giving today during Modern Era Reconstruction.

The Yankee Empire's massive arrest of "disloyal" subjects was successful, but in the massive sweep, the Empire's agents arrested several citizens of Great Britain residing in Baltimore. On November 4th, Lord Lyons, the English minister in Washington,

---

780 *Ibid.*, Vol. II, 94.

781 *Ibid.*, Vol. II, 95.

782 *Ibid.*, Vol. II, 94.

sent a letter of protest to the Secretary of State for the United States, William H. Seward, complaining about the treatment of British citizens in Maryland. Seward replied:

> The recent arrests had all been made in view of the Maryland elections, that those elections would be over in a week's time, and that he hoped then to be able to set at liberty all the British subjects now under military arrest.[783]

This is perhaps an unintentional admission of one of Lincoln's co-conspirators that they did indeed interfere with the election—not that anyone could doubt it at the time. In the Modern Era Reconstruction, postmodern propagandists such as Eric Foner and General James Tyrus Seidule, are used to excuse the actions of past and present Yankee tyrants.[784]

The British minister in Washington reported the actions of the United States government in Maryland as it impacted British interests. In his September 16, 1861, communication he wrote:

> A war has been made in Baltimore upon particular articles of dress, particular colors, portraits of Southern leaders and other supposed symptoms of supposed disaffection. The violent measures which have been resorted to have gone far to establish the fact that Maryland is retained in the Union only by military force.[785]

The war made upon Baltimore and Maryland was ultimately successful. Pro-Unionist Augustus W. Bradford was elected

---

783 Ibid., Vol. II, 95. Author cites Seward.

784 Eric Foner and General James Tyrus Seidule, are examples of postmodernist historians or more appropriate neo-Marxists propagandists advocating on behalf of the Yankee Empire. They write in defense of the political *status quo* proven to be highly profitable for them both professionally and economically.

785 Gen. Bradley Johnson, "Maryland," in *Confederate Military History*, Vol. II, 95. Author cites Lord Lyons.

governor, and the state's legislature was filled with pro-Union men who would meekly obey their masters in Washington. Judge Robert B. Carmichael was seized and forcefully removed from his state judicial position in Talbot County. During the assault upon the judge, a pistol was used to knock him unconscious. He was then "incarcerated in the negro jail in Baltimore, and thence sent to Fort Lafayette." Another state judge, James L. Bartol, was seized and imprisoned in Fort McHenry. General Robert E. Lee would summarize the treatment of the once-free citizens of Maryland thusly: "Words have been declared offenses, by an arbitrary decree of the Federal executive, and citizens ordered to be tried by a military commission for what they may dare to speak."[786] Thus, Maryland, a Southern State, was the first to feel the iron rod of Yankee tyranny—her sister States would soon follow.

Peace, But Without Freedom, Comes To The South

Peace at last came to Maryland and her sister States to the South. But it was the peace of the reservation. It was the peace obtained by accepting the rule of puppet States that were no longer sovereign States. Maryland, as with all other States, was reduced to nothing more than mere provincial governments doing the bidding of the all-powerful central government in Washington. During Passive Reconstruction, Maryland slowly became an adjunct to the Federal Government as more and more of its citizens took jobs in Washington. The loss of Maryland as a state populated by self-sufficient people employed in the private sector became apparent after the beginning of Modern Era Reconstruction in 1965. Today, Maryland and the northern counties of Virginia have been repopulated with a large block of liberal voting Federal bureaucrats who owe their allegiance not to "We the People," America's taxpaying citizens, but to the Yankee Empire's *status quo* which employs them. Their job is to grow big government at the expense of the liberties and property of the little people, the bitter clingers and deplorables in fly-over country. Expecting Federal employees to vote for a conservative, fiscally responsible candidate

---

[786] *Ibid.*, Vol. II, 96. Author cites Robert E. Lee.

campaigning on limited government and low taxes would be like expecting a welfare recipient to vote for a candidate pledged to reduce taxes by reducing welfare. In Modern Era Reconstruction, "We the People" are the political slaves of America's ruling elites and the elites' Globalist masters.

Once peace and some semblance of normalcy were established, Southern churches began their work of revival. The first efforts of Southern churches were to recover their church property that was confiscated by the invading Yankee Army. The Yankee Army "gave" confiscated church property to Yankee civilian representatives of Yankee churches or Yankee missionary societies that followed the Yankee Army as it plundered its way through the South. These fine Yankee Christians held the belief that their superior doctrine, blessed with the wisdom of Yankeedom, granted them ownership rights to any Southern church property that fell into Yankee hands. These "Christians" looked upon the Yankee Army's military conquest as a grant of ecclesiastical authority. After the War and Reconstruction, conventions of these "Northern" churches in the border States of Maryland and Kentucky began to break away and enter the Southern church bodies.[787] This is more evidence that the people of the border States of Maryland and Kentucky maintained their free and unfettered allegiance to their Southern kith and kin.

---

787   Henry, Robert Selph, *The Story of Reconstruction*, 126.

SENATOR HIRAM REVELS (R-MISSISSIPPI)

Senator Revels, the first black member of the US Senate, is an example of what could have been even after the War—a Southern society composed of black and white citizens working together to create a prosperous and peaceful South. He rejected the efforts of Northern radicals to divide the South along racial lines. He boldly proclaimed, "The bitterness and hate created by the late civil strife...would have long since been obliterated in this state, were it not for some unprincipled men who would keep alive the bitterness of the past, and inculcate a hatred between the races, in order that they may aggrandize themselves by office and the emoluments, to control my people, the effect of which is to degrade them.... A great portion of them [black voters] have learned that they were being used as mere tools.... To defeat this policy, at the late election men, irrespective of race, color, or party affiliation, united, and voted together against men known to be incompetent and dishonest."

Chapter 21:

MISSISSIPPI SUFFERS THE WRATH OF RECONSTRUCTION

"Mississippi will regard it [the election of Lincoln] as a declaration of hostility and will hold herself in readiness to co-operate with her sister States of the South in whatever measures they may deem necessary for the maintenance of their rights."
—Governor McWillie[788]

MISSISSIPPI JOINED South Carolina in a matter of a few days after South Carolina seceded from the Union. It was a matter of kith and kin. When a family member is under attack or in distress, honor demands that all family members come to aid their "kin." As General Beauregard declared, "The Federal troops came as invaders, and the Southern troops stood as defenders of their homes."[789] But great disaster fell upon Mississippi since the heady days in which the Bonnie Blue Flag was sung in Jackson, Mississippi. It was first heard in a Jackson theater on the joyous evening of the day when the state of Mississippi seceded.[790] The days in which Mississippi was listed as one of the richest States in

---

788 From a resolution presented to the Mississippi Legislature by Governor McWillie in 1859. *Confederate Military History*, Vol. VII, Part 2 (1899, Harrisburg, PA: The Archives Society, 1994), 6.

789 Weaver, Richard, *The Southern Tradition at Bay* (New Rochelle, NY: Arlington House, 1968), 192.

790 Henry, Robert Selph, *The Story of Reconstruction* (New York: Konecky & Konecky), 25.

the Union were gone. Poverty and political slavery were to be her inheritance from the Yankee Empire. In late 1865, starvation was looming in Mississippi and the entire South. In December of 1865 in Alabama, Georgia, and Mississippi 500,000 white people were suffering from malnutrition, and many died from starvation.[791] The Yankee Empire had but one response—*Vae Victis*, Woe to the vanquished.

President Andrew Johnson appointed William L. Sharkey as Mississippi's provisional governor on June 13, 1865. Sharkey served in that capacity from June to October of 1865. His term as provisional governor ended with the election of Benjamin G. Humphreys as governor. Sharkey was then chosen to represent Mississippi as a US Senator, but the Republican-dominated Senate refused to seat him.[792] Once again, they demonstrated to the people of Mississippi that their voice in the new government created by the Republican Party was permitted *only* if it pleased the powers that be in Washington. Subjects must obey the will of their master.

According to Johnson's Reconstruction Plan, Sharkey was entitled to draw pay for himself from the Federal War Department. But even though he was a "Union man," he still held to the old and now out-of-date belief of States' Rights. He held to his old-fashioned constitutional idea of the self-reliance and independence of a state in the Union. Because he was the governor of a Sovereign State, he was not a Federal employee, and, therefore, it would be improper for him to accept payment from the Federal Government. Out of a sense of honor and principle, he refused to draw government pay.[793] His was an act based upon traditional constitutional values, but such values would find little support in the emerging Yankee Empire.

---

791 Fleming, Walter Lynwood, *The Sequel of Appomattox* (Yale University Press, 1919), 14.

792 "Gov. William Lewis Sharkey," National Governors Association (nga.org) www.bit.ly/Gov-Sharkey (Accessed 21 August 2923).

793 Henry, Robert Selph, *The Story of Reconstruction*, 53.

Mississippi

In October of 1865, the people of Mississippi, operating under Lincoln's (and now Johnson's) Ten Percent Reconstruction Plan, elected former Confederate General Benjamin G. Humphreys as governor. He was an old-line Whig who stood for the Union if his state remained in the Union. He, like most Southerners at the time, did not understand the depth of hatred for the South that existed in the North. He made statements about limiting the civil rights of the newly freed slaves. His statements were based on the fact that most of the newly freed slaves were illiterate and unprepared for full participation in civil society. Northern propagandists took these remarks and used them as evidence that the Southern people were still in revolt against the Federal Government. But Governor Humphreys believed that blacks should be allowed to exercise certain civil rights such as testifying in court. [794] He and other Southerners did not see any inconsistency in their stand on black civil rights because, in most respects, it reflected the same attitudes held by whites in the North and enforced by state law in the North. Unlike Northern States, Mississippi's black population was almost equal to the white population. Humphreys expressed the general feeling of most Southerners when he declared his concern about the sudden release of a large body of uneducated and unprepared people into communities. He noted, "...the other great question of guarding them [blacks] and the State against the evils that may arise from their sudden emancipation."[795] There was great anxiety among the white population regarding the unprecedented social experiment of instantaneously giving an unprepared people of another race equal standing with the white race. This was something the people of the North never considered doing in their society even with a small number of blacks, but they were imposing it upon the exhausted and defeated South. Unlike the North, the South had a very large population of mostly illiterate blacks.

---

794   *Ibid.*, 99.

795   *Ibid.*, 99.

Mississippi Rejects The Thirteenth Amendment Abolishing Slavery

Leftist haters of Mississippi who are eager to slander the state will often point out that, even after the end of the War, Mississippi refused to give its assent to the ratification of the Thirteenth Amendment abolishing slavery in the United States. On December 4, 1865, the Mississippi legislature rejected the proposed Thirteenth Amendment. While this is true, it is not the whole and, therefore, it is not the correct story.

The people of Mississippi already adopted a state constitutional amendment abolishing chattel slavery in the state of Mississippi. They intended to comply with their amendment and, in good faith follow, the will of the American public regarding the ending of chattel slavery within the United States. Their rationale was that ratifying the Federal amendment would be meaningless for Mississippi because they already passed a state constitutional amendment prohibiting chattel slavery in the state.[796] But a far more important principle was at issue, a constitutional principle. The second clause of the Thirteenth Amendment gave Congress the power to enforce the Amendment. This was a power to compel, via the threat of Federal bayonets, a Sovereign State. It was a power never envisioned by the Founding Fathers. Mississippi's legislature saw how dangerous this provision was, but, unfortunately, they did not comprehend that the old Constitution that established a Republic of Sovereign States died at Appomattox. They were laboring under the misconception that post-War everything was back to "normal" with the exception that secession would not be tolerated, and chattel slavery must come to an immediate end. They, like most modern-day conservatives, did not understand that a revolutionary faction had seized the Federal Government[797] and turned it into a supreme Federal Government controlled by Northern elites. The old Federal Government was gone, it no longer existed. It was unceremoniously replaced with

---

796 *Ibid.*, 106.

797 Semmes, Admiral Raphael, *Memories of Service Afloat* (1868, Secaucus, NJ: The Blue & Grey Press, 1987), 335, 833.

a supreme all-powerful government that could do anything it wanted to do in the service and interests of the controlling elites. The change in the American government was unconstitutional and therefore illegitimate. But the illegitimate change in American government was *fait accompli*.[798] It continues today in Modern Era Reconstruction, for example: The supreme Federal Government can now open the nation's borders and allow anyone from an alien culture to come into the nation and dispossess the native population because an open border serves the interests of the elites or the elites' commercial and global cronies. The same Republican Party that imposed this form of government upon "We the People" of Dixie during Active Reconstruction continues today. Its supporters used the Federal Government's unconstitutional (illegitimate) powers during Modern Era Reconstruction for the benefit of the political class and their cronies.[799]

The Republican Party's propagandists used Mississippi's rejection of the Thirteenth Amendment as evidence that the South was still in a state of rebellion. The legislators in Mississippi also opposed ratification of the 13th Amendment on grounds of constitutional principle. They thought, as most conservatives think today, that they were a self-governing people when they were and remain mere subjects of the Yankee Empire. They stood on sound constitutional principles but never realized that principles mean nothing to propagandists who play on emotions. As already noted, in America's mass democracy—what the Founders referred to as a mobocracy—emotions always trump facts, logic, truth, and principles.

---

798 *Fait accompli*: A thing that has already happened or been decided before those affected hear about it. As a completed act, it leaves them with no option but to accept it.

799 See King, D.A., "Georgia's GOP Governor Helps Illegals By Giving Them Drivers' Licenses," Breitbart News (breitbart.com) 10 August 2015, www.bit.ly/GA-Illegal-DLs (Accessed 10 August 2016); Munro, Neil, "Republican Nikki Haley Immigration 'Makes Us Great,'" Breitbart News (breitbart.com) 09 May 2019, www.bit.ly/NHaley-on-Immigration (Accessed 10 May 2019); Carl, Jeremy, "Joe Kent's Big Win Prompts Establishment Backlash Against Anthony Sabatini," The National Pulse (thenationalpulse.com) 09 August 2022, www.bit.ly/xRINO-Backlash (Accessed 12 August 2022).

MISSISSIPPI'S BLACK CODES—
EMOTIONS TRUMP COMMON SENSE

The only American precedent or example of how a white society should treat blacks was the treatment afforded blacks in Northern States. The Northern attitude toward blacks was far less than a positive view. The masses of Northerners did not view blacks as equal to whites. Black Codes or laws specifically designed to place restrictions on blacks were not considered unusual by Northerners. During the War, Union General Banks of Massachusetts established a form of Black Codes while occupying lower Louisiana during the War. The task of feeding and controlling the large numbers of blacks who followed the Army after they were "freed" became so great that Banks had to establish a quasi-black code. His "code' was designed to prevent the idle congregation of freedmen, which was causing an increase in lawlessness. The answer was simple—force black men back to work on government plantations. There was a shortage of labor in the government plantations—plantations seized and operated by the Yankee Army. He ordered blacks capable of working to move to the government or other plantations.

> The Negro could choose the plantation on which he wished to work, but once he had made his choice he must remain for a year. If he ran away, he would be returned by force... Officers and enlisted men would be detailed to see that the Negro behaved himself and carried out his duties.[800]

The whites of the South looked to the North and the Yankee Army's experience with newly freed slaves as a guide for establishing their Black Codes.

Mississippi's as well as the other Southern States' Black Codes were broadly based upon laws then on the books of Northern States. These Northern laws were enacted to control contracted

---

800 Winters, Dr. John D. *The Civil War in Louisiana* (Baton Rouge, LA: LSU Press, 1963), 208.

apprenticeship and laws enacted to control vagrancy.[801] It was a time in which white Southern leaders were urging a time of "apprenticeship" before granting full civil rights to the mostly illiterate and ill-prepared newly freed slaves. "The need for some sort of legal tutelage for the freedmen, designed to establish and regulate society and labor, was felt acutely."[802] The Mississippi law passed by its new legislature, before the Republican carpetbaggers and scallywags took over the state, required every black to have a lawful home or employment by the second Monday in January 1866. Governor Humphreys and his legislature did not anticipate the fury and hatred these laws produced in the North. They relied on the fact that these laws were very similar to laws then in effect in many Northern States. In the December 1 issue of the Chicago *Tribune*, Mississippi's Black Code was denounced, and a promise was made that the men of the North "will convert Mississippi into a frog pond"[803] before they allow such laws to stand.

The threat to turn Mississippi into a frog pond because of these laws came from a paper published in a state that previously passed laws prohibiting free blacks from entering their lily-white state! Before the War, Illinois enacted a law that required free blacks entering Illinois without a certificate of freedom to keep a bond of one thousand dollars on file at the county courthouse. If he failed in this obligation, he would be arrested and "hired out" for a year. Illinois did not allow blacks to "give evidence in favor of or against any white person." Illinois did not repeal its exclusion law that required a free black entering the state to pay a fine of fifty dollars until after the end of the War. If the free black did not have sufficient funds to pay the fine, he would be sold (hired out under enforceable contract) to a man who would pay the fine on behalf of the free black.[804] Illinois law on apprentices

---

801 Henry, Robert Selph, *The Story of Reconstruction*, 98.

802 *Ibid.*, 102.

803 *Ibid.*, 104.

804 *Ibid.*, 104.

stated that blacks need not be "taught to write, or the knowledge of arithmetic." But Mississippi's law required all apprentices to be taught to read and write. [805]

Illinois was not the only Northern state to treat their blacks in such a discriminatory fashion. Most of the elements of restriction against free blacks written into Mississippi's Black Code could be found in many Northern States. Some of the Northern restrictions were even harsher than those in Mississippi. [806]

> In the New England States, in New York, Indiana, and Wisconsin the definition of vagrancy was as broad and inclusive as that in the Southern legislation; the penalty, more severe. "Servants" or "apprentices" departing from the service of the master, or neglecting their duty, were subject to fine and imprisonment at hard labor...In one, at least, any citizen was permitted of his own authority and without process: to arrest such [vagrants] wanders.[807]

The illogical rage produced by Northern propagandists caused even the educated classes in the North to reject logic and embrace anti-South emotionalism. Northern lawyers holding official positions or as public speakers zeroed in on the words "master" and servant" and treated them as evidence of Southern efforts to put the newly freed blacks back into the "chains of slavery." With logic and rationality suspended, Northerners treated these words in Southern statutes as if they were something new in America, something never seen in the good-ole USA. But many of their own States had similar laws! These words were part of our English Common Law tradition. They were used for generations before the USA became an independent nation. They were used to describe well-understood legal and contractual relations. "Master" and "servant" were in full and frequent use in the laws and decisions

---

805 *Ibid.*, 104.
806 *Ibid.*, 104.
807 *Ibid.*, 104-5.

of every Northern state.⁸⁰⁸ Yet when used in the occupied South, it brought forth emotional cries to restart the War and complete the destruction of the once-free people of the South. Such was the thinking and actions of those blinded by emotionalism ginned up by prejudice and hatred toward the conquered, impoverished, and occupied people of Dixie. *Vae Victis*—Woe to the vanquished.

The use of the bloody shirt was an emotional appeal to the Northern population designed to cause them to suspend rational thinking and encourage the adoption of immediate drastic social and political action against the South. The technique of using an emotional appeal to dispense with logic, facts, and truth is used today in Modern Era Reconstruction. If an individual uses documented facts to demonstrate that thirteen percent of the population commits over fifty percent of the crimes, the facts are not disputed, but the individual is silenced by the emotional charge of the individual being a racist. If you explain that America's gun violence would be reduced to the level of most European nations if you remove the gun violence data from black-dominated cities, the facts will not be challenged, but the individual will be silenced by the usual charge of racism. Under the current political *status quo*, the more things change, the more they remain the same.

Slanderous, anti-South fake news is not new. It was a primary weapon used by the Republican Party to gain and maintain control over the conquered and occupied South. In 1866, Republican Thaddeus Stevens was busy giving speeches in the House of Representatives, proclaiming that evil rebels in the South were nothing less than "...barbarians who are daily murdering [blacks and loyal Union men]...putting into secret graves not only hundreds but thousands of the colored people." Republican sycophants in the mainline media took these claims as facts and published them to a Northern populace already convinced that Southerners were capable of any amount of evil. Representative Stevens had no direct knowledge of the situation down South, nor did he care to find out.

---

808   *Ibid.*, 105.

Few if any in the North would hear the truth as detailed by Union General T.J. Wood, commander at Vicksburg, Mississippi:

> I think it is not going too far to say that substantial justice is now administered throughout the state by local judicial tribunals to all classes of persons, irrespective of race or color, or antecedent political opinions...It should not, perhaps, be a matter of surprise that so many outrages and crimes occur and go unpunished, but rather a matter of marvel that so few occur.[809]

Despite such unbiased reports from Northern officials and visitors, the Republican Party's propagandists were able to convince the Northern population that Southern Black Codes were an attempt to put blacks "back in chains." Republican politicians were then able to push through their harsh Active Reconstruction amendments, laws, and regulations. Emotionalism was used to convert the Constitution from an instrument to limit the powers of the Federal Government into a document that made the Federal Government the sole judge of the extent of its power.

A MISSISSIPPI FEDERAL SUPREME COURT CASE THREATENS TO UNDO RECONSTRUCTION

Leaders of the Republican Party in Congress became alarmed over the possibility that the Federal Supreme Court might strip Congress of its presumed right to have the final word as to how to conduct Reconstruction. The Court fired a warning shot across the bow of Congress in *Ex parte Milligan*, 71 US 2 (1866), declaring the use of military courts against civilians in areas where civil authority was functioning unconstitutional. Milligan and others were citizens of Ohio, arrested by the military in Ohio, and charged with acts of disloyalty and treason committed in Ohio. These Ohio citizens were convicted by a Yankee military court and sentenced to death! The Supreme Court ruled the military court's

---

[809] *Ibid.*, 204.

actions unconstitutional. However, it left unclear whether military courts were constitutional in the post-War Reconstruction South. Great anxiety arose among Congressional Republicans when they learned that the Supreme Court agreed to hear *Ex parte McCardle*. The *McCardle* case arose from Mississippi then under Yankee military occupation. This case was like the Ohio *Milligan* case, but it came from the South under military dictatorship. It had the potential to destroy the Republican Party's Reconstruction Plan. As one historian of the modern era noted:

> Fearful that the Court would declare such military tribunals unconstitutional and thus sweep away the whole enforcement apparatus of congressional Reconstruction, the Republican majority deprived the Court of its appellate jurisdiction in such cases.[810]

W.H. McCardle was the editor of the Vicksburg, Mississippi, *Times* and a former colonel in the Confederate Army. His newspaper's criticism of Reconstruction earned him the wrath of the Republican leaders in the city and state. On November 13, 1867, General Ord, the military commander of the conquered territory of Mississippi, had Mr. McCardle arrested on charges of encouraging whites to resist Reconstruction and held for trial by a military court. The local Federal Court upheld General Ord's authority to arrest McCardle and sent the case back to the local military court. McCardle's attorneys appealed the case directly to the Federal Supreme Court.

The *McCardle* case was a clear case defending the civil rights of citizens living in an area where the civil courts are open vs the right of the Federal military to establish its courts superior to the civil courts in areas where civil courts are open. If the Reconstruction Acts were constitutional, then the military would have the authority to adjudicate the *McCardle* case. But if the Reconstruction Acts were unconstitutional, then McCardle had a constitutional right

---

810   Johnson, Ludwell H., *The North Against the South: The American Iliad 1848-1877* (1978, Columbia, SC: The Foundation for American Education, 1993), 229.

to a trial in the local civil court.[811] If the Court made such a ruling, the power of the Republican Party in Congress to control Reconstruction would be in grave danger if not destroyed.

Republicans in Congress saw that the *McCardle* case posed a clear danger and threat to their rule of the South and eventually Congress. "Republican leaders in Congress feared that the Court might strike down the [Reconstruction] act and destroy the party's Reconstruction program."[812] While the Court was hearing the case, but before it could issue its findings, Republicans in Congress passed an act limiting the Supreme Court's jurisdiction and thereby preventing the court from issuing its decision in the *McCardle* case. It was then, as it is today, foolish to think Southerners would get a fair hearing in our conqueror's courts—state or federal. This sad fact demonstrates why Southerners today should actively campaign in the court of public opinion instead of spending millions of dollars filing lawsuits to protect our Southern heritage. If the population is *actively* supporting traditional American and Southern values and heritage, the attack would be stopped politically before it becomes necessary to file a lawsuit.

Republicans in Congress used their power under Article III, Section 2 of the Constitution to bar the Supreme Court from hearing cases dealing with military courts operating in the conquered South. In other words, conservative Southerners had no civil rights while under Active Reconstruction. With the Supreme Court judicially "neutered" and no longer a threat, the Republicans then set their sights on impeaching and removing President Johnson who refused to agree with the Republican Party's Reconstruction Plan.

THE SOUTHERN RESISTANCE MOVEMENT IN MISSISSIPPI

The heavy cost of state government during Active Reconstruction was a major incentive for the rise of a resistance movement in all Southern States. Fraud and corruption were the hallmarks

---

811 Henry, Robert Selph, *The Story of Reconstruction*, 260.

812 *The Oxford Companion to the Supreme Court of the United States*, ed., Kermit L. Hall (New York: Oxford University Press, 1992), 534.

of Republican governments during Active Reconstruction. Mississippi's post-War, Republican-controlled Constitutional Convention cost $250,000.00. That would equal $5,125,000.00 in 2023 dollars.[813] Republican newspapers supporting the Republican Party were paid $28,515.75 for publishing the proceedings. That would equal $584,572.88 in 2023 dollars.[814] And remember that the people who spent the taxpayers' dollars had no "skin in the game." This was before the income tax when most of the state's revenue was raised by taxes on land and permanent property. Why would there be any amazement that some form of resistance would develop under such an oppressive and tyrannical system? Yankee politicians and their postmodern, neo-Marxist, propagandists portray white resistance to Republican Reconstruction as a vicious race war directed toward the newly freed slaves. Such assertions are slanderous lies set forward to protect and promote the Yankee Empire. It is a successful leftwing propaganda maneuver to direct attention away from the Yankee Empire's dictatorial oppression of the South. The Southern resistance that arose during Active Reconstruction was essentially a tax revolt and a revolt against the breakdown of law and order.

Tax revolts are common in human societies. The first tax revolt occurred in 2400 B.C. led by a man named Urukagina. He accused religious leaders and government administrators of acting in their self-interests by seizing the property of citizens. His revolt resulted in prohibiting the government from taking property from common citizens, removing most tax collectors, and limiting the power of judges to rule in favor of the rich at the expense of the poor.[815] If ancient people who never knew constitutional liberty could mount a tax revolt, how much more would Southerners whose grandfathers helped to establish America's Republic of Sovereign States? Their grandfathers were leaders in a revolt

---

813   $1.00 in 1867 would be equal to $20.50 in 2023. See "Value of $1 from 1867 to 2024," CPI Inflation Calculator (officialdata.org) www.bit.ly/1867USD (Accessed 15 August 2023).

814   *Ibid.*

815   Llosa, Alvaro Vargas, Chapter 7: "The Case of Latin America," *Making Poor Nations Rich*, ed., Benjamin Powell (Stanford, CA: Stanford University Press, 2008), 189.

against centralized tyranny. They were inspired by the slogan "No taxation without representation."

The resistance movement began in Mississippi with a taxpayer meeting in Jackson, the state's capital city. The resistance movement in Mississippi was labeled "The Mississippi Plan." Its main effort was to organize taxpayer leagues in every county. The league was open to all taxpayers regardless of color. As with other Southern resistance movements, it was primarily motivated by the unconscionable and oppressive taxation imposed upon white and black property owners by the Republican state legislature. Mississippi's legislature was a carpetbag, scallywag, and black legislature in which the taxpayers had virtually no representation. It was a revolt that could be described by the 1776 patriotic cry of "No taxation without representation." The taxpayer league issued a memorial or white paper decrying the heavy tax load borne by the people and comparing the 1869 tax levies (enacted by a Republican Reconstruction legislature) with the increased tax levies of 1871, 2, 3, & 4.

> For the year 1871, it [tax levies] was four times as great. For 1872 it was eight and a half times as great. For the year 1873, it was twelve and a half times as great. For the year 1874, it was fourteen times as great.[816]

Desperate times called for desperate solutions—thus, the resistance movement in Mississippi went into action. The people had borne all they could bear. The tax situation grew to the point where half a million acres across the state and four-fifths of Greenville, Mississippi, was up for sale due to default tax payments. The taxpayers' league put General J.Z. George in charge of the upcoming battle at the polls. As the *Aberdeen Examiner* noted, "It is the rebellion, if you see fit to apply that term, of a downtrodden people against an absolutism imposed by their own hirelings, and

---

816 Bowers, Claude, *The Tragic Era* (New York: Halcyon House, 1929), 452. Author cites McNeilly, J.S., *Climax and Collapse of Reconstruction in Mississippi* (Publications of the Mississippi Historical Society, n.d.), Vol. XII, 338-40.

by the grace of God we will cast it off."[817] The fraud, corruption, and general lawlessness began to turn black Mississippians away from their new carpetbagger "friends" as they once again looked to their white friends and neighbors. This was lamented by the Republican *Columbus Press* which complained of the attitude among many blacks who wanted to rid themselves of the carpetbaggers.[818]

Fearful of losing power in Mississippi, the Republican Party under carpetbag Governor Ames commissioned William Gray to organize a black militia to help maintain Republican control of Mississippi. Gray was a black senator known best for his drunkenness and hatred for whites. Gray boasted that Governor Ames was sending him all the arms and ammunition necessary to equip his black militia. He declared that he would win the election if he had to kill every white man, woman, and child.[819] White Mississippians did not view Gray's declaration as an idle threat. Recall the words of Mississippi's General Garnett Andrews who declared, "I have never suffered such an amount of anguish and alarm in all my life... I expected, and honestly anticipated, and thought it highly probable, that I might be assassinated, and my house set on fire at any time."[820]

General J.Z. George's iron discipline helped to maintain order and prevented "outrages" that could be used by Northern propagandists to justify continued Federal troops in Mississippi. Great public meetings were held where conservative candidates spoke. Old men were joined by young men who pledged themselves to the battle to redeem Mississippi's honorable government. It was a resistance movement against political slavery, against tyranny, and a battle for constitutional liberty. As one attendee exclaimed,

---

817   Ibid., 453. Author cites Fleming, Walter F., *Documented History of Reconstruction*, Cleveland, 1906, Vol. II, 394.

818   Ibid., 453. Author again cites Fleming, Walter F., *Documented History of Reconstruction*, Cleveland, 1906, Vol. II, 396.

819   Ibid., 453. Author cites McNeilly, J.S., *Climax and Collapse of Reconstruction in Mississippi*, (Publications of the Mississippi Historical Society, n.d.), Vol. XII, 377.

820   General Andrews cited in Fleming, Walter Lynwood, *The Sequel of Appomattox* (1919, Yale University Press, 1970), 278.

"What a marvelous uprising!" To which another replied "Uprising? It is no uprising; it is an insurrection."[821] The movement continued to gain enthusiasm and additional supporters. The State Republican Committee was greatly alarmed. So much so that they sent a committee to Washington to meet with President Grant and plea for more troops. Mississippi's Republicans desperately needed Federal troops to help control the defeated rebels who refused to accept their federally assigned position on "the stools of everlasting repentance."[822] Ames knew his only hope was to incite violence and arrest those conservatives "responsible" for inciting violence. He knew he could count on his black militia and other Union League types to stir up certain elements in the black and white communities and thereby incite violence.

The conservatives of Mississippi took control of the Mississippi government in 1876, which essentially ended Active Reconstruction in the state. The following year, Republican Rutherford B. Hayes was selected as President by a "back room" agreement with Southern conservatives in which he agreed to remove the remaining Federal troops from the South. In 1877, Active Reconstruction was officially terminated across the South.

The Second Battle of Vicksburg, Mississippi

The oppressive social and political conditions throughout the South compelled white conservatives to join and support the resistance movement. Bowers gives an example of the conditions in Vicksburg, Mississippi, during Republican Reconstruction:

> With enormous taxes, mounting debts, and brazen stealing, the chancery clerk was refusing citizens access to his books, court clerks putting out fraudulent witness certificates and county warrants; and with tax-collecting time at hand, it was found that the bond of Peter Crosby, sheriff and tax-collector was defective.... Ten taxpayers, led by a captain in

---

821 Bowers, Claude, *The Tragic Era*, 455.

822 Frank Lawerence Owsley, "The Irrepressible Conflict," *I'll Take My Stand*, 63.

the Union Army, were instructed, in a mass meeting, to call on the officials at the courthouse and demand their resignations.[823]

If similar political conditions were forced upon the people of Massachusetts, would they meekly accept it? If they were denied a just and lawful political system of their choosing, would they docilely accept their political enslavement? Of course not! But somehow, such natural resistance to tyranny is declared as evil when the people of Mississippi and the South resisted the Yankee Empire's enforced tyranny. No, as all freedom-loving people would react, the people of Mississippi and the South resisted tyranny.

The white conservatives in Vicksburg marched to the courthouse, entered it, demanded, and received Sheriff Cosby's resignation. Cosby quickly fled to Jackson and met with carpetbag Governor Ames's administration seeking help in regaining his office. Instead of sending state militia, it was suggested that he call for blacks to arm themselves and march on Vicksburg, defeat the white conservatives, and restore the carpetbag government. When news reached Vicksburg of the impending invasion of the city, watchmen were placed in the courthouse tower. At daybreak, the watchmen saw a large procession of blacks marching on the town. A battle of sorts ensued in which the black "Army" was routed. It is noteworthy that the "white" Army included whites from both political parties and included a hundred former Federal soldiers. "It was necessary with the courts in possession of the tyrants and with no recourse from ruin in the law."[824]

Some folks in the North were beginning to understand the dire conditions under which the Republican Congressional Reconstruction had placed the white South. Colonel Gordan Adams, a Republican, commented in the *Cincinnati Commercial*, "My God! The whites have borne and borne until forbearance ceased to be a

---

823   Bowers, Claude, *The Tragic Era*, 450.

824   *Ibid.*, 451.

virtue and almost became a crime."[825] The resistance movement during Active Reconstruction in Vicksburg saved the city from destruction under the governance of carpetbag and scallywag tyrants. In Modern Era Reconstruction (post-1965) numerous cities in the South and nationwide have been reduced to crime-ridden bastons of fraud and corruption. These woke liberal cities have driven the white and black middle class out and are now seeing their tax base dwindling and are forever seeking Federal dollars to prop up their broken cities. Once again, the more things change, the more they remain the same—at least if "We the People" choose to meekly remain subjects to this "one nation indivisible."[826]

THE KLAN AND THE RISE OF THE SOUTHERN RESISTANCE MOVEMENT

Race is always the knee-jerk response of anti-South leftist propagandists. Race was not the reason post-War white Southerners objected to granting the privilege[827] of voting to the newly freed slaves. Post-war whites objected because the freedmen, through no fault of their own, lacked the necessary social and political skills necessary to be informed voters. Their civil and political deficiency made them easy tools for unscrupulous men (carpetbaggers, scallywags, and national Republicans) seeking to use illiterate voters for their personal gain. This could have been avoided if the South were allowed to follow the high road to emancipation. However, allowing black and white Southerners to work out the mutually beneficial parameters of a new and free Southern society would have cost the Republican Party and its financial and commercial elites their position of power and control in Washington, DC. Instead, the black and white people of the South were forced, at bayonet point, down Lincoln's and the Republican Party's low road to emancipation. The evil thus done carried through Active

---

825   *Ibid.*, 452. Author cites McNeilly, J.S., *Climax and Collapse of Reconstruction in Mississippi* (Publications of the Mississippi Historical Society, n.d.) 323.

826   For a peaceful way to remove America's bayonet governments, see Kennedy, James Ronald, *Dixie Rising-Rules for Rebels*, 2nd ed. (Columbia, SC: Shotwell Publishing, 2021).

827   Voting in a democratic republic is a privilege earned via meeting non-arbitrary qualifications. Voting is not a universal, unqualified right to be granted by government.

Reconstruction (1867-1877), into Passive Reconstruction (1877-1990), and continues with a vengeance today during Modern Era Reconstruction (post-1965).

What were the social conditions that fostered the development of the *original* Klan? The major reason for the development of the Klan was fear among an essentially disarmed white population faced with armed, hostile black militias and Union League-sponsored, or encouraged, violence against whites. Add to that the corruption and lack of fair representation, and the rise of the Southern resistance movement was inevitable. Garnett Andrews, living in Mississippi at the time, recorded the widespread fear he and other whites had at the time:

> I have never suffered such an amount of anguish and alarm in all my life. I have served through the whole war as a soldier in the Army of Northern Virginia and saw all of it, but I never did experience...the fear and alarm and sense of danger which I felt that time. And this was the universal feeling among the population, among the white people...It showed itself upon the countenance of the people; it made many of them sick. Men looked haggard and pale, after undergoing this sort of thing...I have felt when I lay down neither myself, nor my wife and children were in safety. I expected, and honestly anticipated, and thought it highly probable, that I might be assassinated, and my house set on fire at any time.[828]

In 1881, Garnett Andrews moved to Chattanooga, Tennessee, where he served as mayor from 1891 to 1893.

Thomas W. Gregory, from Mississippi, who became the Attorney General of the United States from 1914 to 1919 under President Woodrow Wilson, pronounced the original Klan as

---

[828] Gen. Garnett Andrews cited in Fleming, *The Sequel of Appomattox*, 278. Fleming described Andrews as "General", but he is not recorded in books on Confederate Generals. He may have held a state militia commission or perhaps it was an honorary title.

"the most thoroughly organized, extensive and effective vigilance committee the world has ever seen or is likely to see."[829] Mrs. Myrta Lockett Avary (1857-1946) of Virginia and author of *A Virginia Girl in the Civil War* and other books explained the rise of the Klan, "Northerners and Southerners who did not live in that day and black belts can form no conception of the conditions which gave rise to the white secret societies of which the most widely celebrated is the Ku Klux."[830] Once law and order were restored, the *original* Klan was no longer needed and was dispersed. Unfortunately, there were and still are many counterfeit Klans that emerged at different times falsely claiming to be a continuation of the *original* Klan.

The creed and purpose of the *original* Klan was published in its "Revised and Amended Prescript." It demonstrates that it was a survival movement, a resistance movement, not a revolutionary movement. It admonished its members to accept and uphold "the United States government, the supremacy of Constitutional Laws thereof, and the Union of the States thereunder." Its first Prescript addressed the lawlessness and inability or refusal of local "officials" to maintain law and order:

> First: To protect the weak, the innocent, and the defenseless, from the indignities, wrongs, and outrages of the lawless, the violent, and the brutal; to relieve the injured and oppressed; to succor the suffering and unfortunate, and especially the widows and orphans of Confederate soldiers.

The second "Prescript" spoke of the members' loyalty to the United States:

> Second: To protect and defend the Constitution of the United States, and all laws passed in conformity

---

829 Gregory cited in Henry, *The Story of Reconstruction*, 234.

830 Avary cited in *Ibid.*, 234.

thereto; and to protect the States and the people thereof from all invasions from any source whatever.

The third "Prescript" addressed their intention to prevent unlawful arrests of innocent citizens by corrupt officials:

> Third: To aid and assist in the execution of all constitutional laws, and to protect the people from unlawful seizure, and from trial except by their peers in conformity to the laws of the land.[831]

The *original* Klan and similar movements in the South were attempts of a conquered and occupied people to regain some control of their society and to make the best out of a bad situation. They were forced at bayonet point to accept a new government to rule over them, a government controlled by foreign enemies (Yankees) and mostly illiterate former slaves, a government that showed little concern for the safety and security of the white and conservative black population, and a government that was not based upon the American political principle of "the consent of the governed." A French resistance movement sprang up when France was invaded, conquered, and occupied by Nazi Germany, and a pro-German French government was imposed, at the point of bloody bayonets, upon the French people. The French Resistance's aim was revolutionary. The French were determined to overthrow the illegitimate Vichy government and replace it with a legitimate French government. The Reconstruction era Klan resistance movement sought only to make the best out of a bad situation. They accepted the new, illegitimate, supreme Federal Government and pledged themselves to uphold it **if** they were allowed the mere semblance of local self-government;—real States' Rights were replaced with mere state privileges enjoyed at the sufferance of a supreme Federal Government. The Southern resistance movement's primary aim was to establish local law and order while redeeming state governments from the hands of

---

831 Henry, Robert Selph, *The Story of Reconstruction*, 230-1.

thieves and corrupt politicians. Once this was done, the *original* Klan and similar resistance movements were ordered to disband.

What Could Have Been—
Black And White Citizens Working Together

The social and political conditions under which black and white Mississippians suffered during Active Reconstruction demonstrate the conditions across the South at that time. They also demonstrate "what could have been." By 1874, the Republican city government of Vicksburg, Mississippi, had virtually sent the city into bankruptcy. The city's debt grew from $13,000.00 to $1,400,000.00 in just five years of Republican rule! The city officials were elected by the mass votes of non-taxpaying freedmen. In the election of 1874, the city Republicans nominated a white man with twenty-three indictments against him for mayor and one illiterate white and seven illiterate or of "low moral standards" freedmen for alderman. An uprising began to brew among the white and around fifty black taxpayers. Included in the uprising were two Republicans, Union General C.E. Furlong,[832] and George McKee who represented the district in Congress. The peaceful "uprising" was a success and on August 4, 1874, the old city government was replaced with a new one that represented the interests of the taxpayers—both black and white.[833]

The Republican efforts to divide and rule Mississippians are seen in a Republican newspaper. The Republican *Columbus Press*, perhaps unintentionally, described the Republican technique of "Divide and Rule" when it warned black Mississippians:

> They will tell you to vote for your own color or die in the attempt...They will have you rush upon an issue of race against race and plunge the country into strife and bloodshed if they perchance might ride

---

[832] Garner, James Wilford, *Reconstruction in Mississippi* (Google Books), 334, footnote 2. General Furlong served in Sherman's Army during the War.

[833] Henry, Robert Selph, *The Story of Reconstruction*, 530.

safely upon the surging waves over the dead bodies of their countrymen to positions of profit.[834]

Here, we see a Mississippi newspaper echoing the words of black Senator Revels who complained about the unscrupulous people who used black voters for personal aggrandizement. But despite its harsh treatment by the North, Mississippi was able to demonstrate the fact that they could have erected a better society if they had been given the opportunity. Despite the Republican Party's effort to divide and rule by creating racial hatred in the state, men of goodwill of both races were able to rise above the temptation of hatred.

In the Mississippi elections of 1875, many property-owning blacks voted for the Democratic ticket even though this brought upon them severe social ostracism among their fellow blacks. But their votes, just like the votes of whites, were not based on race but on the need to remedy the oppressive tax load created by the Republican Party that controlled the state legislature. Hiram Revels (R-Mississippi), the first black man to serve as a US Senator, wrote to President Grant explaining the 1875 vote rejecting Republican rule in Mississippi. He explained that "At the late election men, irrespective of race, color, or party affiliation, united and voted together against men known to be incompetent and dishonest...."[835]

Another example of men of goodwill rising above the temptation of racial animosity was seen when Mississippi's black Lt. Governor, Alexander Kelso Davis, was impeached by the state's House of Representatives and tried in the state's Senate. The vote in the state legislature was overwhelmingly in favor of conviction. The vote in favor of conviction included one black Republican voting for conviction. Despite what Yankee propagandists claim, not everything is about race.[836]

---

834   Ibid., 545.

835   Ibid., 549.

836   Ibid., 553.

Republicans (mostly black) and Democrats (mostly white) in Mississippi's legislature joined in presenting a watch to John R. Lynch, a black Republican. In addition, the Democrats offered a resolution praising Representative Lynch for his "ability, courtesy, and impartiality" as speaker of the Mississippi House of Representatives.[837] The paradox of Southern race relations was recognized by John R. Lynch when he stated that the "...bond of sympathy between the two races at the South—a bond that the institution of slavery with all its horrors could not destroy, the Rebellion could not wipe out, Reconstruction could not efface, and subsequent events have been unable to change."[838] This paradox of race relations in the South was something Yankees could not explain; while Southerners did not attempt to explain it, they simply accepted it.

Friendly and mutually respectable relations between black and white political leaders existed long after the close of Active Reconstruction. John F. Harris, a black Republican representative from Washington County, Mississippi, left his sick bed to return to the state legislature to vote in favor of funding the erection of a monument to Confederate veterans. Speaking in the State House chamber, he declared:

> When the news came that the South had been invaded, those men went forth to fight for what they believed, and they made no requests of monuments...But they died, and their virtues should be remembered. Sir, I went with them. I too wore the gray, the same color my master wore. We stayed four long years, and if that war had gone on till now, I would have been there yet...I want to honor those brave men who died for their convictions...I want it known to all the world that my vote is given in

---

837 *Ibid.*, 456-7.

838 John R. Lynch cited in *Ibid.*, 120.

favor of the bill to erect a monument in honor of the Confederate dead.[839]

All six black members of the Mississippi House voted in favor of the bill to fund the erection of the Confederate monument. This stands in stark contrast to the Modern Era Reconstruction's woke mob in the US military who want to remove all mention of Southern heroes on military bases and warships, the politically correct Democrats demanding the removal of all symbols of Southern heroes from the nation's capital, and cowardly Republicans docilely submitting to these leftists demands. The political *status quo* understands that the truth will destroy their hateful and slanderous lies and possibly encourage "We the People" to initiate a Modern Era resistance movement.

Representative Moore, another black member of the Mississippi House of Representatives, described the close working relations between racially different people with opposing political beliefs:

> I was born in Mississippi but raised in a Northern State; associations there led me to regard the Southern white men as dire foes to the Negroes but receiving such cordial and unprejudiced association upon this floor [Mississippi House of Representatives]...these suspicions have been eliminated...you have shown to be our friends, not our enemies.[840]

Such acts and unsolicited testimonies can be found in every Southern state of the era. But such facts, and the truth itself, are carefully censored and replaced with slanderous, emotionally charged lies. Tyranny thrives in the darkness of ignorance—a darkness intentionally created and enforced by America's political *status quo*.

---

839   Kennedy & Kennedy, *The South Was Right!* 3rd ed. (Columbia, SC: Shotwell Publishing, 2020), 146.

840   *Ibid.*, 147.

Active Reconstruction Ends In Mississippi

By 1876, Active Reconstruction ended in Mississippi. The conservatives organized as a political movement in the state Democrat Party began taking control of the judicial branch of state government and the legislature. Active Reconstruction ended when Rutherford B. Hayes gained the presidency by promising to remove the remaining Yankee troops from the South. Mississippi and her sister Southern States were allowed to control their *puppet* state government *if* they did not challenge the newly established supreme Federal Government.[841] Mississippi and the South entered the era of Passive Reconstruction as a politically defenseless conquered people. The absence of an effective resistance movement to reclaim America's original constitutionally limited Republic of Sovereign States set the stage for the eventual implementation of a new form of Reconstruction. Modern Era Reconstruction (post-1965) would be even harsher than Active Reconstruction. *Vae Victis*—Woe to the vanquished!

---

841 Some Southern conservatives may object to labeling the South's state governments as "puppet governments." General Stephen D. Lee writing in 1899, labeled States, "organized and sustained by the military forces of the United States, not by the free will of its citizens," as "bogus governments." See *Confederate Military History*, Vol. XII (1899, Harrisburg, PA: The Archives Society, 1994), 277.

Chapter 22:

RECONSTRUCTION IN MISSOURI

"As a result of this agitation the Missouri legislature adopted resolutions affirming the rights of the States as interpreted by Southern statesmen, and instructing its senators in Congress to co-operate with the senators of the other Southern States in any measures they might adopt as a defense against the encroachments and aggressions of the North."
—Colonel John C. Moore [842]

MISSOURI AND OTHER BORDER STATES are often overlooked when it comes to recounting the story of Republican-imposed Active Reconstruction. But the people of Missouri, just like the rest of the South, suffered in Lincoln's war and the Republican Party's Active Reconstruction. The fact that Missouri made a significant contribution to helping end Active Reconstruction is also often overlooked. With war approaching, Missouri attempted to stay out of the coming war. She planned to remain in the Union while remaining militarily neutral. The state refused to send soldiers or material support to either side and pledged to fight any troops entering the sovereign state whether the troops be Northern or Southern. Missouri's outgoing Governor, Robert Marcellus Stewart, was known to have Northern sympathies, nevertheless, he was the first to recommend this plan of neutrality. The incoming

---
842   Colonel John C. Moore, "Missouri," *Confederate Military History* (1899, Harrisburg, PA: The Archives Society, 1994), Vol. IX, 5.

governor, Claiborne Fox Jackson, who sympathized with the South, agreed but warned that if the Federal Government attempted to invade the South, he would support "her sister Southern States."[843] Future Confederate General Sterling Price presided over the Missouri constitutional convention that addressed the question of secession. The convention voted to stay in the Union if the state's neutrality policy was honored.

The 1860 Presidential election demonstrates the attitude of Missouri's citizens toward the emerging Yankee Empire. Lincoln received only ten percent of Missouri's votes, while the candidates who wanted to maintain peace, John Bell of Tennessee, a member of the Constitutional Union Party, and Stephen A. Douglas of Illinois, a member of the Democratic Party, received seventy-one percent of the state's presidential votes. The remaining nineteen percent of the vote went to John C. Breckinridge of Kentucky, the 14th US Vice President, who ran as a Southern Democrat. Lincoln's call for state troops to invade the South ended the hope of state neutrality in the border States. It also gave Lincoln the excuse to send Federal troops into the border States to prevent them from expressing their desire for a government based upon the consent of the governed. Instead of self-government based upon the American political principle of the consent of the governed, Lincoln gave them military rule and a government based upon coercion via bloody bayonets.

Understanding the imminent threat to liberty posed by Lincoln and the new power exerted by the aggressively anti-South Republican Party in Congress, Governor Claiborne Jackson, the legitimate governor of Missouri, and the state's legitimate representatives voted, in October 1861, to secede from the Union. The legitimate will of "We the People" of Missouri was completely ignored by Lincoln and his war-hungry Republican supporters. A pro-Lincoln state constitutional convention—controlled by Union forces both military and civilian—appointed a provisional governor for the state. Lincoln's puppet state would have a puppet

---

843 "Missouri in the American Civil War," Wikipedia (wikipedia.org) www.bit.ly/MO-TheWar (Accessed 20 August 2023).

governor—Hamilton Gamble. Governor Gamble was assisted in the effort to control the people of Missouri by Radical Republican Charles D. Drake who managed to make himself a powerful politician in the state. He authored an ironclad oath which required, in essence, a citizen to affirm, under the pain of perjury, that he never supported or gave aid to the Confederacy. Failing to take this oath would prevent one from voting, holding a public office, and holding professional licenses such as lawyers, teachers, clergy, and other influential positions.[844]

At the close of the War, Radical Republicans, enforcing the ironclad oath, gained complete control of the state's government. Thomas C. Fletcher was elected Missouri's first post-War governor. The new "Drake" constitution was adopted on June 6, 1865, with its ironclad oath that barred from voting anyone who gave aid in any manner to the Confederacy. It also prohibited them from holding a public office or engaging in a state-licensed profession including the clergy. The new constitution had a unique provision in it that allowed only those who could fulfill its ironclad oath to vote on the constitution. The new constitution's provision for an ironclad oath was enforced *before* the new constitution received a positive vote from the state's citizens. Even with such strictures in place, the new constitution received only a small majority of the votes. It received a majority of less than two thousand votes out of a total vote of nearly eighty-five thousand.[845] If a fair vote was allowed, the puppet constitution would have failed! This type of constitution, one enacted under the duress of Yankee bayonets, is what Queen Lili'uokalani of Hawaii labeled as a "bayonet constitution."[846]

Late in 1865, Southern States were leaning Democrat. In June of 1865, the Radicals were barely holding Missouri. Added to this horror for Republicans was that they failed to carry either Kentucky or Tennessee. Fearful, power-hungry Republicans saw the possible

---

[844] "Reconstruction in Missouri," Conflict & Community: The Impact of the Civil War on the Ozarks (ozarkscivilwar.org) www.bit.ly/MO-Reconstruction (Accessed 20 August 2023).

[845] Henry, Robert Selph, *The Story of Reconstruction*, 56.

[846] Kennedy & Kennedy, *Yankee Empire: Aggressive Abroad and Despotic at Home* (Columbia, SC: Shotwell Publishing, 2018), 57.

end to their control of the Federal Government. These early post-War results gave Representative Thaddeus Stevens and his fellow Radical Republicans reasons to worry about the possible failure of their harsh, revengeful Reconstruction plans. Added to these early elections was the fact that the Federal Supreme Court seemed to be moving toward declaring unconstitutional the Republican Party's Reconstruction Plans. The Republican Party knew that something radical had to be done!

The April 1866, publication of the *Milligan*[847] decision created an outburst of rage from Northern politicians, the mainline media, and a vengeful Northern public. On January 14, 1867, the Supreme Court issued another decision that would again enrage Republicans. The "loyal" state of Missouri enacted a state constitutional requirement that all ministers of the Gospel and schoolteachers must take a loyalty oath—the ironclad oath—affirming never they gave aid or comfort to the Confederacy. The Court overturned the state's constitutional requirement that ministers and schoolteachers must pass the "Oath Test" before being allowed to preach or teach in the state. The Court correctly reasoned that these "Oath Tests" were designed to prevent former "rebels" from practicing their occupations. They were, therefore, a violation of the Constitution's prohibition against bills of attainder and ex post facto laws. They were punishments for crimes committed when the acts committed were not crimes. It was a 5 to 4 decision. In a dissenting opinion on behalf of the four Republicans on the Court, Justice Samuel Miller claimed that these Oaths were merely "...regulations to assure that practitioners in various professions possessed the qualifications—including moral character—essential to serve the public."[848] And of course, Republicans would be the ones to determine if the individual "possessed the qualifications—including moral character essential to serve the public." The tide of political opinion seemed to be moving against the Republican Party.

---

847   *Milligan, Ex parte*, 71 US 2 (1866).

848   *The Oxford Companion to the Supreme Court of the United* States, Kermit L. Hall, ed. (Oxford University Press, 1992), 210.

Republicans understood that if Southern Democrats joined with Northern Democrats, then the Republicans would not be able to control Congress, override Presidential vetoes, nor capture electoral votes from the Southern States. This was made even clearer when Northern States in 1866 voted with the Radical Republicans, but in the 1867 elections, they began to go Democrat. The leaders of the Republican Party understood that the Republican Party would suffer the same fate as the big government Federalist and Whig Parties of the past if something radical was not done. The Republican Party's solution was the Radical Reconstruction of the former Confederate States and to maintain an ironclad grip on the border States.

MISSOURI SLIPS OUT OF RECONSTRUCTION AND AIDS ENDING ACTIVE RECONSTRUCTION

In the elections of 1870, it was evident that the people of Missouri, both conservative Democrats and moderate Republicans, were becoming weary of the tyrannical rule of those elected under the restrictive 1865 State constitution. Among the Republicans were men such as General Carl Schurz, a German socialist from Wisconsin, Samuel T. Glover, a Unionist attorney who was fined by Missouri's puppet government for practicing law without first taking the ironclad oath, and Union Democrats under the leadership of Union General Frank P. Blair. The alliance of moderate Republicans, Union Democrats, and other conservatives swept the state in the 1870 election. The new legislature repealed the more onerous parts of the Drake Constitution such as the requirement for the ironclad oath to hold office or practice a profession. The legislature elected General Blair to replace the infamous Radical Charles D. Drake as US Senator.[849] The elections of 1870 marked the end of Active Reconstruction in Missouri.

---

849 Before the passage of the Seventeenth Amendment as part of the Progressive agenda, state legislatures elected Senators. Under the original Constitution, Senators were supposed to represent/protect the interests of their Sovereign States, while the House represented/protected the interests of the people within their state. By "democratizing" the Senate, the Progressives destroyed a key element of what was left of States' Rights. The Senate now marches to the tune of the woke mob. This is the type of mass democracy the Founding Fathers wanted to avoid.

The end of Reconstruction in Missouri did not end Missouri's contribution to the fight against fraud and corruption in Washington or the Deep South puppet States. Senator Schurz and moderate Missouri Republicans organized a convention of moderate Republicans, Unionist Democrats, and Southern Democrats. Initially, the convention was planned at a meeting in Jefferson City, Missouri. The national convention was held on May 1, 1872, in Cincinnati. The convention's purpose was to nominate a Presidential candidate to run against Grant seeking a second term. The candidate had to be acceptable to moderate Republicans, Northern Democrats, and Southern Democrats. The primary unifying points were opposition to the sleaze slowly becoming public knowledge in the Grant Administration, such as nepotism and political corruption;[850] a reform of the Federal civil service system; reducing the high tariffs that punished not only Southerners but Mid-Western farmers; and "the immediate and absolute removal of all disabilities imposed on account of the rebellion."[851] Their first choice for a Presidential candidate was Charles Francis Adams, but eventually, they settled on former radical abolitionist Horace Greeley. Greeley's nomination was problematic. Even though he was one of the Northern individuals who signed Jefferson Davis's bond that allowed the former Confederate President to regain his freedom, Greeley was still held in low regard throughout the South. In addition, he also was a vocal proponent of high protective tariffs. Greeley's vice president running mate was Governor B. Gratz Brown of Missouri. Of the two, Brown was the better selection and was a major contender for the presidential slot, which eventually went to Greeley. The Greeley-Brown ticket ran as candidates for the Liberal Republican Party and the Democratic Party. Grant was reelected by a landslide. It was Greeley's last hurrah. He died on November 29, 1872. However, the joint efforts of moderates and conservatives from

---

850   See Leigh, Philip, *U.S. Grant's Failed Presidency* (Columbia, SC: Shotwell Publishing, 2019).

851   Henry, Robert Selph, *The Story of Reconstruction*, 466. "It was not until June 6, 1898, after the United States was at war with Spain, that Congress passed a general act granting full amnesty to all who had supported the Confederacy," Henry, 469.

both the North and the South demonstrated that there were folks in the North looking for a way to reconcile the North and the South.

After six years of the Republican Party's Active Reconstruction efforts down South, many Americans in the North became disenchanted with the "South problem." Even Missouri's socialist carpetbagger Senator Carl Schurz recognized that it was unwise to continue forcing the South to accept bayonet rule. He supported civil rights for black Southerners—as did Southerners such as Confederate Generals Beauregard, Forrest, Hampton, and Confederate Vice President Alexander Stephens. The reality of the evil imposed upon the South post-War convinced Schurz that it was wrong to give unprepared blacks full voting rights, while at the same time disfranchising most of the white South. He wrote:

> The stubborn fact remains that the negroes were ignorant and inexperienced; that the public business was an unknown world to them and that in spite of the best intentions they were easily misled not unfrequently by the most reckless rascality... In other words, when universal suffrage was granted to secure equal rights for all, universal amnesty ought to have been granted to make all the resources of political intelligence and experience available for the promotion of the welfare of all.[852]

Here, we see a former European socialist, former Union General, and carpetbagger, who finally realized what Jefferson Davis and prior generations of Southerners knew, that blacks must first be prepared for freedom, self-sufficiency, and, eventually, full participation in civil society. It was what "could have been," but the potential of a fair and just bi-racial society was violently denied. *Vae Victis*—Woe to the vanquished!

---

852 Senator Schurz (R-MO) cited in Henry, Robert Selph, *The Story of Reconstruction*, 468.

Chapter 23:

NORTH CAROLINA-RECONSTRUCTION
AND THE KLAN-KIRK WAR

"First at Bethel, Last at Appomattox—This terse sentence epitomizes North Carolina's devotion to the Confederacy." —D.H. Hill, Jr.[853]

"WE THE PEOPLE" of the Old North State demonstrated their dedication to Southern independence by an outpouring of blood on the battlefield during the War.[854] They were offered peace if they would leave the Confederacy, but they rejected the blood-soaked tyrant's offer. During a meeting at Grant's headquarters, Lincoln told Sherman to inform Confederate Governor Vance of North Carolina that if their armies surrendered, the people of North Carolina "would at once be guaranteed all their rights as citizens of a common country."[855] They refused the offer. Another example of their desire for freedom in a country of their own was displayed when in the 1863 North Carolina governor's

---

853 D.H. Hill, Jr., "North Carolina," *Confederate Military History* (1899, Harrisburg, PA: The Archives Society, 1994), Vol. IV, 5.

854 North Carolina has always been a defender of liberty. She was the first Colony to declare independence from Great Britain in May of 1776 and demonstrated her fidelity to her Northern brethren by sending food to Boston, then suffering from the British. Massachusetts repaid North Carolina by sending an Army of invasion and plunder into the once Sovereign State. See *Confederate Veteran* Vol. V, No. 5, May 1897. Republished in *The Confederate Veteran Magazine* (Harrisburg, PA: The National Historical Society, 1987), Vol. V, 201.

855 Henry, Robert Selph, *The Story of Reconstruction* (New York: Konecky & Konecky, 1938), 15.

election the "peace candidate," Mr. Holden, was most ingloriously defeated by Governor Vance.[856] Governor Vance was a proponent of the continued fight to retain Southern independence and self-government. But despite her best efforts, freedom and self-determination were denied and the state fell under the rule of her alien enemies (carpetbaggers) and local scallywag traitors.

North Carolina, through no acts of her own, had a major impact on the vengeful intensity of Reconstruction. President Johnson intended to follow a less radical reconstruction policy than the one demanded by the Radical Republicans. He made this known by a public announcement regarding his intentions for North Carolina's Reconstruction. Essentially President Johnson planned to follow Lincoln's Ten Percent Reconstruction Plan. Under this plan, the citizens of a state could call for a constitutional convention to draft a new state constitution when 10% of the 1860 voters swore allegiance to the Federal Government.

According to the *New York World*, on May 13, 1865, during a meeting at Cooper Union, in New York, a speaker declared that Southerners were rebels guilty of treason and "the punishment for treason is death..."[857] and the crowd of Northerners roared their approval. The speaker, Theodore Tilton, declared that they should hang Jefferson Davis and to the cheering crowd announced his special form of bigotry by declaring that negroes are better voters than white Irishmen. It was obvious that the Republican Party was beginning to openly challenge the President regarding what type of Reconstruction policy the nation should follow. Radical Republicans in Congress insisted on abandoning President Johnson, who assumed office after the April 15, 1865, assassination of Lincoln. President Johnson intended to follow Lincoln's relatively conciliatory Reconstruction efforts. Radical Republicans insisted on their Congressional Republican policy of radical and oppressive Reconstruction. Volumes of anti-South propaganda began pouring out from Republican-affiliated media and speakers

---

856 Henry, Robert Selph, *The Story of Reconstruction*, 52.

857 Bowers, Claude, *The Tragic Era* (New York: Halcyon House, 1929), 11.

such as Tilton. When President Johnson made his somewhat conciliatory North Carolina Proclamation in which he affirmed he intended to follow Lincoln's Ten Percent Reconstruction Plan, the Radical Republicans immediately opened the floodgates of hatred directed against Lincoln's successor. Vicious and virtually unanswered slander against the new President and the powerless South was the primary weapon used by the Republican Party in their eventually successful efforts to control Reconstruction.

Even before the War, North Carolina had dealings with Thaddeus Stevens (R-Pennsylvania) who would become the leading Radical Republican and archenemy of the South. Thaddeus Stevens was known as an anti-Christian Free Thinker and an outspoken opponent of slavery. But his anti-slavery stance was secondary to his yearning for financial profit. That he was outspoken on the issue of slavery is true as far as it goes, but it goes only to the point of political and economic pragmatism. As an opponent of slavery in the United States House of Representatives he nonetheless supported a North Carolina slave owner for the speakership of the US House of Representatives. The reason he would support a slaveowner for House Speaker was purely economic. The North Carolina slaveowner was, just like Stevens, a proponent of high-protective tariffs. And Stevens was personally invested in the iron industry which craved high protective tariffs.[858] Throughout his political career, he would demonstrate his lust for protective tariffs. He even declared that tariffs were more important than slavery.[859] Greed, fraud, using government connections for personal gain, and vicious anti-South slander became the hallmarks of the Federal Government created by Lincoln's war and the Republican Party's Active Reconstruction. And it remains the same in Modern Era Reconstruction (post-1965), but today the Republican Party's anti-South mantra has been embraced by an even more cruel and harsher anti-South Democrat Party.

---

858   *Ibid.*, 71.

859   Leonard M. Scruggs, "The Morrill Tariff: Northern Provocation to Southern Secession," *To Live and Die In Dixie*, ed., Frank Powell, III (Columbia, TN: Sons of Confederate Veterans, 2014), 142.

The Republican-controlled Congress's hatred for Lincoln—because of his Ten Percent Reconstruction Plan—is demonstrated by the fact that in June of 1870, a bill to provide a pension for Mrs. Lincoln was "shunted aside." The *New York Herald*, in its June 18, 1870, edition declared this failure of the Republican-controlled Congress to be "the most remarkable instance of petty malice ever evinced in any national legislature." Such were the evil mindset/attitudes of the Republican-controlled Congress. Is there any wonder they would be even harsher on "rebels" down South?

During the closing months of Active Reconstruction, President Grant met with two Republican Senators from North Carolina—one a carpetbagger and the other a scallywag. They were concerned that the prospects of holding North Carolina under Republican control were dim. To prevent the loss of North Carolina they proposed a plan to terrorize the white "rebels" into submission. Their plan included using United States military forces to openly occupy, and thereby terrorize whites in, "disloyal" sections of the state. They would justify the use of military force by claiming it was necessary to protect "loyal" men. These carpetbag and scallywag Senators wanted the Federal Government to furnish them with guns and uniforms—obviously for arming and equipping their black militia. Recall that the Union League used insolent and untrained black militia to intimidate white and black conservative voters. President Grant agreed to the plan. Going over to his desk the President "with his own hand he wrote a page and a half letter to the acting Secretary of War, General Sherman, saying that, though the application was irregular, he would sign any paper to validate it."[860] This was the beginning of the infamous Klan-Kirk War in North Carolina.

---

860 Bowers, Claude, *The Tragic Era*, 305. Author cites *Holden Papers*, W.J. Clark to Governor Holden, June 18, 1870.

The Bloody Shirt in North Carolina

The bloody shirt[861] was an essential emotional tool used by the Republicans during Active Reconstruction and especially during the 1866 elections. Albion W. Tourgee, a former Union Army officer and North Carolina carpetbagger was a major Yankee propagandist who supplied Republican newspapers with vivid, though of questionable truthfulness, accounts of rebel uprisings and violence in North Carolina. He stated that no one loyal to the United States was safe in North Carolina. He told the Northern press about an alleged—though he reported it as fact—recent discovery of a pond in which there were found fifteen murdered blacks. He also declared that over twelve hundred former Union soldiers who attempted to settle in North Carolina were forced to flee the state due to threats of violence. When challenged to produce the names of the twelve hundred former Union soldiers and the fifteen blacks he maintained his silence. The harm was already done; the hysterical Yankee press picked up the story and published it as gospel to a Yankee public eager to devour anything that confirmed their bias toward "We the People" of Dixie.

In his 1879 novel, *A Fool's Errand by One of the Fools*, Tourgee wrote that the drive for Radical Republican Reconstruction did not come from the people of the North but "from its politicians." And, echoing Thaddeus Stevens, he noted that the purpose of Reconstruction was to assure Republican "political victory and party ascendency."[862]

The bloody shirt was an effective technique playing upon unreasoned emotions to convince the Northern population that Southern whites devoted themselves to killing inoffensive and innocent blacks. It was a form of confirmation bias in which the Northern

---

861 The phrase "Waving the bloody shirt" had its origins in the post-War Active Reconstruction era. It was used to mock Radical Republicans who claimed that voting for conservative democrats was an insult to the blood shed by Union soldiers during the War. The phrase is commonly used today to rebuke an individual who is attempting to stir up partisan animosity.

862 Tourgee, Albion W., *A Fool's Errand* (1879, Cambridge, Massachusetts: The Belknap Press, 1961), 237-8.

people saw the confirmation of generations of slanderous anti-South propaganda so eagerly consumed by Northerners for years before the War. The more outlandish the slanderous anti-South stories became, the more likely Northerners were to believe the stories. Unsubstantiated emotional stories of Southern outrages always trump facts in the Yankee Empire's mass democracy. Bowers, in his book *The Tragic Era*, wrote:

> As part of the propaganda, petitions were sent... complaining of an alleged persecution and indictment of Union men for acts committed in the Union cause, and these were featured in the Northern press; the fact that an investigation disclosed but two indictments out of the fifty-six mentioned, and one of these for illegally selling liquor, was not permitted to reach the Northern people.[863]

Such slanderous anti-South propaganda became so common, widespread, and accepted by the Northern people that even Union General Swayne (R-Ohio), who served as the military governor of Alabama from March 2, 1867, to July 14, 1868, was moved to denounce such stories. He wrote: "A man may travel in North Carolina with as much security as in any State of the Union. Cases of disturbance save in the chief towns are almost unheard of, and in the chief towns, they are much less frequent than in your cities."[864] Despite such brave words from their fellow Yankees, it did nothing to quell the Northern population's thirst for vengeance against what they perceived to be an evil and violent South. Once the emotional allegation is made, it spreads like wildfire but when the truth is announced by some brave soul, the truth is ignored, and the truth-speaker is slandered and harassed for challenging the emotional narrative. The more things change, the more they remain the same.

---

863 Bowers, Claude, *The Tragic Era*, 141. Author cites *The Correspondence of Jonathan Worth*, vol. I, 498.

864 *Ibid.*, 141, Author cites *The Correspondence of Jonathan Worth*, Vol. I, 498.

The Economic Condition of Post-War North Carolina

Yankee invasion, conquest, and occupation created a vast number of former slaves who were now "free" but for the most part, they were in pitiful poverty made free without land, workstock, implements, or any of the ordinary tools of production and living.[865] Without admitting it, the Yankee Empire destroyed chattel slavery and replaced it with a new form of slavery—tenant farming or sharecropping. It was a system of peonage that entrapped eight and a half million black and white Southerners for almost a century. Over 60% of these penniless serfs (sharecroppers) were white.[866]

In May of 1865 Union General John M. Schofield, commanding in North Carolina, ordered "All able-bodied persons of suitable age were warned that they were not to be supported by the government or their former masters unless they would work. As to the terms of work (work contracts), it was suggested that for the present season, they ought to expect only moderate wages or *a fair share of the crops to be raised.*"[867] Sharecropping or tenant farming was suggested by this Yankee General as a possible economic system for freed slaves. Unfortunately, sharecropping was not and is not recognized as a new form of slavery for impoverished black and white Southerners. With the end of the War, it was becoming obvious that a new system of labor was necessary if the South was to recover. But a new system of labor needs a stable state and local government to ensure that all parties are treated fairly, and labor contracts honored by both parties. But the arduous task of creating a completely new government and a new labor system required the talent of the South's most educated and talented citizens—most of whom had served honorably in the Confederate Army. However, as Confederate veterans they were prohibited, via the iron-clad oath, from participating in the civil task of creating a new Southern government. The task was eagerly taken up by

---

[865] Henry, Robert Selph, *The Story of Reconstruction*, 29.

[866] Kennedy & Kennedy, *Punished With Poverty: the Suffering South* 2nd ed. (Columbia, SC: Shotwell Publishing, 2020.)

[867] Henry, Robert Selph, *The Story of Reconstruction*, 29.

carpetbaggers, scallywags, and mostly illiterate blacks. These new "leaders" proceeded to do to the South what African leader Robert Mugabe and his followers did to Zimbabwe—formerly Rhodesia.[868]

The Republican-controlled Congress used the ironclad oath to prevent any Southerner who supported the Confederacy from taking his elected office. In North Carolina, only one of the seven successful candidates for Congress could take the iron-clad oath required since 1862. It was almost impossible to find men of high standing and education in the state who could honestly take the ironclad oath.[869] The invaders had not only destroyed the physical structures of state government, but they also barred the human resources necessary to rebuild an honest and efficient state government from participation in the political affairs of the state destroyed by the Yankee invasion.

Modern-day conservative economists documented the importance of a stable government that provides a just application of the law. This was impossible in the South during Active Reconstruction. Prosperity can only be produced and maintained within a society where the rule of law is honored. When the rule of law is ignored, as it was during Active Reconstruction, the result is organized criminal gangs or mobsters, public corruption, fraud, and elected officials engaged in self-dealing and inside trading. A prosperous society cannot exist under such conditions. It may benefit the ruling elite, but the people suffer.

> After over a decade of research, the empirical evidence is overwhelmingly clear: Societies that organize themselves with private property, *rule of law*, and free markets outperform, on almost every measurable

---

868   Under Mugabe's rule, the yearly inflation rate for Zimbabwe in 2008 was 89.7 sextillion percent. "Hyperinflation in Zimbabwe," Wikipedia (wikipedia.org) www.bit.ly/2008-Zimbabwe-Inflation (Accessed 30 August 2023).

869   Henry, Robert Selph, *The Story of Reconstruction*, 112.

margin, societies that are less economically free.⁸⁷⁰ [Emphasis added by the author.]

Another economist described the conditions that cause national poverty. These conditions were all present in the South under the puppet state governments imposed on the South during Republican Active Reconstruction.

> They do not have the institutions that enforce contracts impartially...They do not have institutions that make property rights secure over the long run... Production and trade in these societies are further handicapped by misguided economic policies and by private and public predation.⁸⁷¹

Republican-imposed, dysfunctional, puppet state governments were a major hindrance to the economic recovery of the devastated South. Railroad service was not restored in North Carolina until 1870—five years after the end of the War. However, many important bridges over large rivers were still unsafe, unusable, or destroyed.⁸⁷² Note that 1870 was five years after the end of the War, and still the South was struggling to recover. But five years after the end of World War 2, both Germany and Japan were well on their way to complete economic recovery—not so for the intentionally punished and impoverished South. "With liberty and justice for all?" *Vae Victis*—Woe to the vanquished, especially if you are a Southerner!

Many of the North Carolina Railroads had hoped that cotton stored by their railroad in South Carolina would provide the investment capital necessary to rebuild their railroads destroyed by the invading Yankee Army. One North Carolina railroad had

---

870 Benjamin Powell, "Introduction," *Making Poor Nations Rich*, ed., Powell, Benjamin (Stanford University Press, 2008), 10.

871 Olson Jr., Mancur, "Why Some Nations Are Rich and Others Poor," *Making Poor Nations Rich*, 48.

872 Henry, Robert Selph, *The Story of Reconstruction*, 123.

eight hundred bales of cotton stored in South Carolina. The cotton at 1865 market value would have provided enough investment capital to pay off the railroad's obligations and begin restoring the railroad. "But most of the cotton bales were ...stolen in the days of licensed and unlicensed cotton theft."[873] Recall how Federal cotton agents used the backing of Yankee bayonets to plunder millions of dollars in privately owned cotton after the War. According to Thaddeus Stevens and his Republican comrades, the spoils of war belong to the conqueror. Conquered Southerners have no rights that the Northern conquerors need respect. This is just as true today as it was then.

Many Northerners were astonished by the change in America's political, moral, and ethical standards that became evident during Active Reconstruction. Even the Reconstruction Governor of North Carolina, Jonathan Worth who was by all estimates a friend of conservatives, was troubled by the rule of Mammon.[874] Following the 1868 elections, a dispirited Worth wrote, "Money has become the goddess of the country, and otherwise good men are almost compelled to worship at her shrine. The proof was manifest in the fact that legislators, State and National are bribed by money or controlled by corrupt rings."[875] When Jay Gould (Yankee financier and gold speculator with connections to President Grant and key Republicans) was accused of using a bribe to get Governor Reuben E. Fenton (1865-1868), Republican of New York, to sign the Erie Bill, no one dared to investigate because "too many Radicals in place here are tarred by this or a similar stick."[876] Fraud became the standard in Washington. As Representative Julian (R-Indiana) noted, "The saddest part is that the public officials, both State and Federal, are in league with the capitalists in making the rich richer,

---

873   Ibid., 123.

874   Mammon is the symbol of ill-gotten wealth in the Bible. He is regarded as a demon, an evil influencer who turns men away from God and toward the love of money—the love of which is the root of so much evil.

875   Bowers, Claude, *The Tragic Era*, 267. Author cites *To William Clark*, Worth, II, 1259.

876   Ibid., 268. Author cites *New York World*, 27 March 1869.

and the poor poorer."[877] This is the government created by Lincoln and the Republican Party. It is a government that continues today. In America's political *status quo,* the more things change the more they remain the same.

UNION LEAGUE
PROMOTES VIOLENCE AS A POLITICAL WEAPON

The Reconstruction Scallywag Governor of North Carolina, Holden, had over eighty thousand Union League members who were loyal to Holden and his state Republican Party. Holden would eventually convert them into "militia" armed and constantly drilling in the streets—as a warning to the whites. Whites lived in constant fear for their lives.[878] Barn burnings became a favorite tactic of the Union League operatives to intimidate whites. The loss of a barn was more than the loss of an outbuilding. The barn was the storehouse for hay and grain to feed the family's livestock as well as the storage of farm implements and tools necessary to cultivate gardens and fields. The loss of a barn meant the loss of expensive farm equipment at a time when few Southern families had any disposable income. Under such conditions, the loss of a barn meant possible starvation for the family. In Gaston County, nine barn burnings occurred in one week.[879] The offending parties were arrested. They confessed and claimed that the Union League encouraged them to take such actions against white conservatives. In two months during 1869, there were numerous burnings of churches, cotton gins, barns, and homes. The arsonists were blacks acting out the instructions from the Union League. Some of the burnings were done on the orders of Scallywag Governor Holden.[880] One of Governor Holden's rabid followers, State Senator John W. Stephens, while addressing blacks at a Union League meeting, gave them a book of matches. He told the impressionable and

---

877 Ibid., 268. Author cites George W. Julian.

878 Ibid., 203. Author cites *The Correspondence of Jonathan Worth*, Vol. II, 963.

879 Chodes, John, *Washington's KKK: The Union League During Southern Reconstruction* (Columbia, SC: Shotwell Publishing, 2016), 39. Author cites Senate Report No. 1, 42nd Congress, 1st Session, 365.

880 Ibid., 40; Author cites Senate Report No. 1, 42nd Congress, 1st Session, 191.

mostly illiterate blacks that the matches given to them by an officer of the state would be useful in burning the homes of whites.[881] When the government is actively promoting acts of violence against defenseless people, is there any wonder that some form of resistance would arise? It was reported that Senator Stephens was eventually executed by the Klan.[882] General Stephen Dill Lee, in 1899 wrote, "The Ku Klux Klan was the perilous effect of which the odious league [the Union League] was the unhealthy cause."[883]

Governor William W. Holden tactically endorsed the use of violence when he declared, "Traitors must take back seats and keep silent...The issue is Union or Disunion. He who is not for the Union deserves to have his property confiscated and to suffer death by the law."[884] "By the law?" By what law was the Sovereign Nation the Confederate States of America invaded? By what law was the conquered South turned into an impoverished colony of the industrial North?[885] By what law was the right to establish their government based upon their free and unfettered consent denied "We the People" of the South? Modern-day conservatives should remember that in Russia and Germany, folks were sent to the Communist Gulags and the Nazi concentration camps according to the "law." The "law" in the defeated and occupied South, then and now, means whatever the ruling elites decide it means. Under the current political *status quo*, the "law" is interpreted and enforced in a manner that benefits America's ruling elites, their cronies, sycophants, and their neo-Marxist propagandists.

---

881   *Ibid.*, 40.

882   *Ibid.*, 40, Author cites Horn, Stanley, *The Invisible Empire: The Story of the Ku Klux Klan*, 1866-1871 (Cos Cob, CT: John E. Edwards, 1969) 17.

883   Gen. Stephen D. Lee, :The South Since The War," *Confederate Military History* (1899, Harrisburg, PA: The Archives Society, 1994), Vol. XII, 310.

884   Holden cited in Selph, *The Story of Reconstruction*, 224.

885   Josephson, Matthew, *The Robber Barons* (New York: Harcourt & Brace, 1934), 125-33; Clark & Kirwan, *The South Since Appomattox* (New York: Oxford University Press, 1967), 12, 61, 91-2, 97.

Peace Reigned In Post-War North Carolina

In the last months of 1865 after the end of the War and well into 1866 the people of the South lived in peace. It was an unsure peace due to the radical change in the Federal and State governments. However, violence in North Carolina was not a major problem even during the 1868 election. Despite the relatively calm nature during the campaign season, the Republican Governor repeatedly threatened to call out the state's black militia—a black military force disparagingly referred to as the Governor's "Carpetbagger Scalawag Militia." The relative calm does not mean that there was no violence, but it was highly questionable as to which side initiated the violence or if the violence was political or merely common criminality. General J.C. Abbott, a Northern man living in Wilmington (declared) "...that a Northern man is just as safe anywhere in the State of North Carolina as he is anywhere in the North...a man who comes here and attends to his own business and does not take some pains to make himself odious, I think, is as safe here as anywhere else."[886] Yet Northern newspapers were full of reports of "rebel outrages." Republicans pushing for a radical and punitive approach to Reconstruction eagerly repeated these mostly fake claims of "rebel outrages." For political purposes, they had to portray the South as a place of violence, hatred, racism, and treason. In 1867 Republican Representative Julian declared:

> What these regions need above all things is not an easy and quick return to their forfeited rights in the Union, but government, the strong arm of power, outstretched from the central authority here in Washington.[887]

---

886   Henry, Robert Selph, *The Story of Reconstruction*, 69.

887   Julian cited in DiLorenzo, Thomas J., *The Real Lincoln* (New York: Three Rivers Press, 2002), 162. Author cites Randall, James G., *Constitutional Problems under Lincoln* (1926, Urbana, Illinois: University of Illinois Press, 1964), 131.

"We the People" of North Carolina and the entire South wanted to be left alone[888] to reclaim some form of normalcy and restore state and local government that could maintain law and order. But the Republican Party had other ideas. Peace down South would spell doom for their Reconstruction Plan. Peace would prevent the establishment of Republican-controlled puppet Southern state governments that would do the bidding of the Republican Party in Washington.[889] Republican political necessity resulted in the infliction of Divide and Rule in the South. Racial mistrust and hatred became the Republican order of the day. It was the only way that the Republican Party could hope to maintain its position of power in Washington, DC. Divide and Rule may not have been the term the Republicans used to describe their efforts, but regardless of what it was called, it was the only way to separate black and white Southerners and turn them into political enemies. Empires never shun the use of racial or religious hatred if its use serves the empire, and the Yankee Empire is no exception to this rule!

THE RISE OF THE RESISTANCE MOVEMENT

Reconstruction Carpetbag North Carolina Judge and former Union officer, Albion Tourgee, saw the rise of resistance movements such as the Klan as a natural result of a defeated people ruled by outsiders from an alien culture.

> It [the resistance movement] was a daring conception for a conquered people. Only a race of warlike instincts and regal pride could have conceived or executed it... It differed from all other attempts

---

888   Clark & Kirwan, *The South Since Appomattox* (New York: Oxford University Press, 1967), 43. This has been an eternal plea from the South, a plea ignored by the arrogant Yankee, "All we want is to be left alone." Jefferson Davis cited in Evans, Eli N., *Judah P. Benjamin-The Jewish Confederate* (New York: The Free Press, 1988), 118.

889   In the Modern-Era these puppet state governments either actively do the bidding of the political *status quo* or passively accepts the Federal Government's infringements on the rights of its citizens. They are no longer sovereign States, but are mere provinces of the supreme Federal Government. These emasculated provinces are not even allowed to protect their borders from alien invasion—as per the last paragraph of Article 1, Section 9, US Constitution.

at revolution—for revolution it was in effect—in the caution and skill with which it required to be conducted. It was a movement made in the face of the enemy, and an enemy, too, of overwhelming strength...Should it succeed, it would be the most brilliant revolution ever accomplished. Should it fail—well, those who engaged in it felt they had nothing more to lose.[890]

"Nothing more to lose" is what faced white Southerners under the rule of an evil and oppressive alien power. The white South was forced to live under social, political, and economic circumstances that Northern citizens would not have tolerated. Under such circumstances, the frustrations and aggravations of the moment would eventually lead to violence. It is absurd to think otherwise. It is equally absurd for the Yankee Empire's sycophants and propagandists to refuse to acknowledge the fact that their illegitimate invasion and occupation of a formerly free and self-governing people was **the** causative factor. It was the reason the Southern resistance movement arose. The Yankee Empire's quest for control over the Sovereign States that had formed a Sovereign Nation, the Confederate States of America, is the proximate cause[891] for all the resulting violence during Reconstruction (Active, Passive, and Modern Era Reconstruction).

Riots in the post-War South occurred in places such as Norfolk, Virginia, on April 16, 1866, when blacks celebrating the passage of a Civil Rights Bill were involved in a riot in which two whites and two blacks were killed. An investigation by the occupying Yankee military concluded that both blacks and whites were at fault. In the same year on April 30th a riot of sorts occurred in Memphis between black soldiers and Irish policemen. The riot devolved into a general race riot in which forty or more blacks were killed. Many Northern observers, including General Grant, noted that

---

890 Tourgee cited in Henry, Robert Selph, *The Story of Reconstruction*, 229.

891 The term "proximate cause" means a cause which in a direct sequence produced the injury complained of and without which such injury would not have happened.

the presence of armed black soldiers was the focal point, if not the instigators, of many public disturbances. Governor Perry of South Carolina wrote to President Johnson declaring that "The only disturbance we have is from the garrisons. They are behaving badly both to whites and blacks." Governor Sharkey of Mississippi made a similar report declaring "the great amount of complaint originates from the localities where Negro soldiers are." The entire town of Brenham, Texas was burned down in 1866 by the local black garrison who were seeking revenge against local whites. The local whites had protected friendly blacks from a group of drunken black soldiers who broke into a ball being held by local blacks and a fight between the two groups of blacks broke out. These black soldiers were led by officers who were indicted by the local authorities. But the garrison's military would not allow the officers to face "civil" charges. In Beaufort, North Carolina a group of black soldiers from Fort Macon were arrested and charged with rape and attempted rape. The soldiers were released when the authorities at Fort Macon threatened to turn the guns of the fort on the town. Both black and white undisciplined Yankee soldiers were at fault for the various disturbances occurring across the post-war South. The problem was the lack of good officers rather than a matter of race. It was reported that undisciplined white Yankee soldiers caused as much disorder and damage in Asheville, North Carolina as did black soldiers. It was generally felt that well-disciplined garrisons led by competent officers were viewed by local citizens as friends and were valuable in upholding law and order. Yankee General John Tarbell declared that in areas where well-disciplined and well-led garrisons were located and where the Freedmen's Bureau was "upright, intelligent and impartial" the local civilians accepted both the military and the Freedmen's Bureau as an asset to peace and harmony.[892]

Before the War, Southerners had established and maintained just and well-regulated state and local governments. Southerners living through Active Reconstruction could remember a time when their local and state governments were competent to maintain law

---

892 Henry, Robert Selph, *The Story of Reconstruction*, 180-1.

and order. The people longed for a return to the peace and security for which all just governments are established. Vigilantism was not the South's first choice. It was forced upon the South by the evil and oppressive alien powers that had seized their state and local governments. As soon as some form of normality was restored the people no longer needed the resistance movement. The Raleigh *Telegram* urged the end of secret societies on both sides, "The Leagues of the Republicans and the Klans of the Conservatives have already damaged the material interests of North Carolina... They are a nuisance...if continued, will undermine our liberties and subvert the government."[893]

A Scottish journalist and visitor to the South in 1870 described the downfall of the Klan:

> It is the deep vice of all such secret leagues to survive, in a more degenerate form, the circumstances which could give even a (somewhat) justification to their existence, and to pass finally into the hands of utter scoundrels, with no good motive, and with foul passions of revenge, or plunder, or lust of dread, and mysterious power alone in their hearts.[894]

But before the Klan and other resistance efforts could be removed from North Carolina a final battle had to be fought.

THE KLAN-KIRK WAR

By the spring of 1870 the good people of North Carolina, black and white, were tired of Governor Holden's reign over railroad swindlers and the general looting of the public treasury for the private benefit of those with close connections with the ruling Republican Party. Governor Holden and his co-conspirators were aware of the anti-Holden popular attitude that was rampant among the people. The state's Republicans had already arranged with President Grant for a private army to "protect"

---

893   *Ibid.*, 442.

894   *Ibid.*, 448-9.

Republican rule in North Carolina. The Republican rulers in the North Carolina legislature rationalized their actions by telling each other that if a law was passed to blackmail an out-of-state insurance company, it was acceptable because the money would end up in the Republican Party's campaign fund; if thousands were given to subsidize local state newspapers, it was fine because they were "loyal" newspapers; and if furnishings for the State House were made at well above market prices, it was fine because they were purchased from loyal Union men. Who would dare to complain about the legislature spending $37,718.83 (equal to $904,545.25 in 2023[895]) in two years on stationery?[896] Added to this brazen corruption was the ignorance in some of the most important appointed positions in state and local government. Under such circumstances, the once free and self-governing people of the once sovereign state of North Carolina became restless and determined to use any effective means to unseat political corruption and remove North Carolinians from the annals of political slaves. The Republican masters of the state understood this. They knew that their only hope of keeping the state under Republican control was to use their armed black militia backed by Union troops to terrorize white and black conservatives. All such terroristic acts would be done under the pretext of the law. And if the Republicans were lucky, some hot-tempered white could be lured into some act of violence toward a black Republican. Such "rebel" outrages were needed to keep the bloody shirt waving up North. A pragmatic Yankee politician openly declared that outrages down South reported throughout the North were essential in keeping the Republican Party in power. One stated that "A kilt nigger is worth twenty thousand votes north of the Potomac."[897] If a legitimate "outrage" did not occur the Republicans could count on anti-South Northern papers printing numerous manufactured incidents.

---

895   "The Relative Worth of $145,001,890 in 1870," Measuring Worth (measuringworth.com) www.bit.ly/145m1870 (Accessed 02 June 2023).

896   Bowers, Claude, *The Tragic Era*, 316-7. Author cites Hamilton, J.G. de Roulhac, *Reconstruction in North Carolina*, 427-51, 403, 407, 411.

897   Henry, Robert Selph, *The Story of Reconstruction*, 564.

One moderate Republican wrote that agitators were urging Negroes to burn houses and barns and that some (houses and barns) were given to the flames. He complained that "Two wrongs cannot make a right and such advice to negroes and bad white men will be ruinous to us."[898] But moderation was not on the table for Republican consideration. One of Holden's advisors, John Pool, was busy pushing Holden to quickly form his army. With this army he planned to arrest Holden's conservative rivals, have them tried in military courts by the troops, and put conservative counties under military rule. This was agreed to by President Grant according to Pool and others. If an arrested disloyal individual appeals for a *writ of habeas corpus* and is released the military would immediately re-arrest him on different charges. If an individual in a country under military rule resisted, he would be killed, "lost and never heard of again." Pool knew just the man that Holden should put in charge of their army—George W. Kirk.[899]

George Washington Kirk was from Tennessee. He joined the Confederate Army but left to join the Union Army. He rose to the rank of colonel in the service of the invader's Army. When appointed by Holden, Kirk was only thirty-three years old. He had a reputation for being notorious while conducting Union raids during the War and was known as a man accustomed to brutality. One correspondent wrote of Colonel Kirk, "Such men as Colonel Kirk do not do a political party any good. He is universally detested by the people as a military man. They fear and hate him."[900] Colonel Kirk's audacious leadership during the Kirk and Klan war led to his arrest, and the impeachment of Governor Holden. A United States Marshal helped Kirk to escape from a North Carolina jail. Kirk was later given a position as a

---

898 Bowers, Claude, *The Tragic Era*, 318. Author cites N.A. Ramsey, Haywood, May 4, 1870, Holden MSS.

899 *Ibid.*, 319. Author cites Badger's testimony in Impeachment Trial of Holden; Holden, *Memoirs*, 187-99; Hamilton, 497-8.

900 *Ibid.*, 320. Author cites Dowell, Holden MSS.

police officer with the Capital Force in Washington, D.C.[901] Even back then, the Deep State looked after its own!

With an Army and commander in place, Pool rushed back to Washington to initiate, with the aid of Northern newspapers, a campaign of anti-South lies and slander. Pool brazenly informed the *New York Tribune* that "we intend to use the military in the election and must get these statements [manufactured cases of rebel outrages against loyal blacks and whites] disseminated through the North."[902] With the anti-South Northern newspapers spreading accounts about rebel "outrages" in North Carolina, it was easy to get President Grant on board with the Holden/Pool plan. Holden was warmly received by Grant in the White House. The President assured him of his support: "Let those men resist you, Governor, and I will move with all my power against them."[903]

Northern Democrats, although at the time in the minority, understood that President Grant and Governor Holden were using unconstitutional, tyrannical powers to intimidate Democratic voters in North Carolina. It was slowly becoming apparent to some in the North that the Constitution meant nothing if it stood in the way of Republican ambitions. The *New York World* in its June 9, 1870, edition implied as much. It bemoaned the fact that the South was being treated as a conquered province where the once free people were being held under the oppressive control of "a government not of their choice, administered by men in whom they have no confidence, and supported by Federal bayonets instead of the public opinion of free men." Even some moderate North Carolina Republicans understood the dangers posed by using the military against their Democratic opponents. One declared, "For God's sake, don't send troops here. The town is quiet, and all works well. Avoid strife."[904] Another moderate Republican stated "The

---

901   "George Washington Kirk," Wikipedia (wikipedia.org) www.bit.ly/GWKirk (Accessed 01 June 2023).

902   Bowers, Claude, *The Tragic Era*, 319. Author cites Hamilton, J.G. de Roulhac, *Reconstruction in North Carolina*, New York, 1914, 503.

903   *Ibid.*, 320. Author cites Holden, *Memoirs*, 187-99.

904   *Ibid.*, 320. Author cites T.C. Evans, Holden MSS.

Republicans do not want troops in this section, Governor. It will kill us in the next election...We have no outrages of consequence here and I have not heard of any for two months."[905] But other Republicans had different views: "This is the only way to carry the State in the next election." The Republican Party had to rely on "fear" to win the election.[906]

Fear and cruelty were Colonel Kirk's primary weapons used against white and black conservatives. Kirk's Army was composed of the lowest order of whites and ignorant blacks. One witness later described Kirk's Army as, "The most ignorant and stupid creatures I ever talked with."[907] Another testified of Kirk's Army, "They were uniformed like an army, but their actions were more like a mob."[908] They carried their Federally supplied guns haphazardly in an unmilitary fashion, they pointed pistols at innocent civilians, and threatened to burn towns—this was not an idle threat. The threat was given to folks who had lived through Yankee armies burning towns. Aside from the threats and bullying, the major issue was that they indiscriminately arrested innocent folks on trumped-up charges. Kirk's men seldom gave a reason for the arrest and bragged that the individual would be tried by their military court and executed.[909]

Historian Claude Bowers gave the following example of Reconstruction evil when Kirk's soldiers tried to force a confession from an innocent civilian:

> [They] crowded in upon him in the night...Four pistols were aimed at his breast. "Now, will you confess?" Then putting a rope around his neck, they drew him up until he lost consciousness. On recovering, he was again told to confess. Meeting

---

905   *Ibid.*, 320. Author cites Albert H. Dowell, Asheville, Holden, MSS.

906   *Ibid.*, 320. Author cites W.F. Henderson, Salisbury, Holden MSS.

907   *Ibid.*, 321. Author cites Holden Impeachment Trial, Jesse Grant, I, 488.

908   *Ibid.*, 322. Author cites Holden Impeachment Trial, Thomas H. Holt, I, 629.

909   *Ibid.*, 322. Author cites Holden Impeachment Trial, J.S. Scott, I, 605.

dumb silence, the officer went into a rage. "Then hang him on that limb till eight o'clock tomorrow morning and then cut him down and bury him under that tree on which you hang him." Thankfully the officer changed his mind.[910]

In another incident, Colonel Kirk marched his troops into a Democratic meeting in the town of Yanceyville. He intended to terrorize the assembled citizens. He arrested the Democratic leaders and sternly informed the crowd that he would meet any resistance by shooting women and children.[911] The anti-South Yankee press was insistent in its defense of Governor Holden, claiming that such methods were necessary to defeat the rebel outrages committed by the Klan. The *New York Tribune* August 3, 1870, edition stood firm in its endorsement of Holden and Kirk. But other Northern media were giving their readers the "rest of the story." *The Nation* was appalled by the raising of a "specially levied body of men, mostly black" commanded by "a wandering adventurer, trained to command by bushwhacking in Tennessee." *The Nation* realized that the entire adventure was "an electioneering dodge."[912]

In the August 1870, North Carolina election, the conservative people of North Carolina swept the Republican Party out of power and elected a conservative Democratic legislature. The new Democratic legislature pledged to launch an investigation of Holden and his co-conspirators. This resulted in Holden's impeachment. So ended the Kirk-Klan War. The elections of 1870 were a dire warning to the Republican Party. North Carolina and Georgia had Democratic legislatures. Republican Governor Holden was impeached, and Republican Governor Bullock of Georgia fled the state. The prospects for the 1872 presidential election looked grim for the Republicans, but they were experts in waving the bloody shirt and cutting special deals. There was hope yet for the Grand Ole Party.

---

910   *Ibid.*, 323. Author cites Holden Impeachment Trial, L.H. Murray, I, 660-63.

911   *Ibid.*, 323. Author cites Holden Impeachment Trial, H.F. Brandon, I, 749, 764.

912   *Ibid.*, 324. Author cites *The Nation*, August 4, 1870.

North Carolina's resistance movement continued to gain political victories and by 1877, Active Reconstruction was officially ended in the South. As Federal troops left the South, Southern States gained the *appearance* of self-government. But the Southern States were no longer Sovereign States—the Federal Government was now supreme, and the States were reduced to mere provinces of the Yankee Empire. Pretending otherwise only demonstrates how foolish a conquered, dispirited, and pacified people can be. After the end of Active Reconstruction, the puppet state governments of the South would dutifully perform their assigned task of helping the North's ruling elite to maintain the new and unconstitutional system of supreme Federalism while giving it the façade of legitimacy. Eventually, a new form of anti-South Reconstruction would emerge during the Modern Era Reconstruction (post-1965). It would be a form of Reconstruction that "inept Southern politicians" would be either unable or unwilling to challenge.[913]

---

913 John Crowe Ransom, "Reconstructed But Unregenerate," *I'll Take My Stand*, 23.

Chapter 24:

SOUTH CAROLINA—
RECONSTRUCTION IN THE CRADLE OF SECESSION

"South Carolina did not finish paying off the fraudulent [Reconstruction era] bonds until 1955." —Dr. Clyde N. Wilson[914]

PRESIDENT ANDREW JOHNSON appointed Benjamin Franklin Perry as the provisional Governor of South Carolina on June 30, 1865. Perry held strong Unionist views before the secession of South Carolina. He served the state from June 30, 1865, to November 29, 1865. Pre-War he was a leading state figure promoting a pro-Union sentiment. He loved the old Union and therefore resisted the movement toward secession. "His great failing...was a legalistic rigidity of mind cast in the old constitutional molds."[915] Even though he was a pre-War pro-Union man, Radical Republicans in Congress opposed his appointment. He left office after the state adopted its 1865 post-War constitution. In 1866 South Carolina's legislature was elected under Lincoln's and later Johnson's Ten Percent Reconstruction Plan. The state elected Perry to represent South Carolina in the US Senate. The Republican-controlled Congress however refused to allow him to take his seat

---

[914] Dr. Clyde N. Wilson, "Defeat and Occupation: The Cold War Known as 'Reconstruction,'" *To Live and Die In Dixie*, ed., Frank Powell, III (Columbia, TN: Sons of Confederate Veterans, 2014), 444.

[915] Henry, Robert Selph, *The Story of Reconstruction*, 54.

in the Senate.⁹¹⁶ This was a blatant violation of Article V of the Constitution, "no state shall be deprived of its equal Suffrage in the Senate." However, the Republican Party had already demonstrated that it would only honor the Constitution when it benefits the Republican Party. Their hatred for South Carolina and black Southerners is evidenced by the fact that Representative George Boutwell (R-Mass.) suggested that the States of South Carolina and Florida be reserved exclusively for former slaves.⁹¹⁷ Boutwell planned to turn these two Southern States into contraband camps similar to the reservations the Federal Government used to corral Native Americans.⁹¹⁸ The Republicans who controlled America's post-War Congress hated the South, blacks, and the original Constitution.

Governor Perry, as with most Southerners then and now, did not comprehend the radical revolution that had occurred in America's government. Nor did they understand that this radical revolution changed the nature of the Constitution from one protecting liberty to one that fostered the oppression of individual liberty under the guise of "the law." Lincoln's war and the Republican control of Congress foisted a radical change in the Federal Government. Governor Perry (and modern-day conservatives), unlike Confederate Admiral Semmes, did not understand:

> A violent, revolutionary faction had possessed itself of the once-honored Government of the United States, and as is the case in all revolutions, coarse and vulgar men had risen to the surface, thrusting the gentler classes into the background.⁹¹⁹

---

916   "Gov. Benjamin Franklin Perry," National Governors Association (nga.org) www.bit.ly/BFPerry (Accessed 31 August 2023).

917   Leigh, Philip, *U.S. Grant's Failed Presidency* (Columbia, SC: Shotwell Publishing, 2019), 63.

918   Shepard Pike, writing for the *Atlantic Monthly* in February 1861, suggested that the North should "confine the Negro to the smallest possible area: "Hem him in. Coop him up." See Donald Livingston "Confederate Emancipation Without War," *To Live and Die In Dixie*, 463.

919   Semmes, Admiral Raphael, *Memories of Service Afloat* (1868, Secaucus, NJ: The Blue & Grey Press, 1987), 335.

Perry and his contemporaries did not recognize the political revolution that had occurred in Washington. Modern-day conservatives are no better because they operate on the false premise that the original Constitution still exists and that it is an efficient means to protect their rights. Perry's "provisional" government was a mere puppet government subservient to the power that created the provisional government—the unconstitutional, illegitimate, supreme Federal Government. Then as now, America's so-called States have no rights that the Federal Government is bound to honor.[920] Lincoln's unconstitutional war and post-War Republican political tyranny converted real States' Rights into States' privileges—privileges exercised only if they are approved by the supreme Federal Government. But Perry, as with most post-War Southerners, attempted to make the best out of a bad situation. Before he left office, he sent a message to the President declaring "The only disturbance we have is from the garrisons. They are behaving badly both to whites and blacks." The people wanted peace, law and order, and a government that would administer justice fairly while leaving the people alone to heal their wounds, grieve their dead, and restart their lives.

In the post-War South, most black and white folks were impoverished. Men who before the War had great possessions of land and money were reduced to working at menial tasks just to feed their families. They "accepted the discipline of poverty and made the best of their situation."[921] There was no underground movement to unseat the Federal Government, no desire to restart the War, no overflowing hatred directed toward the newly freed slaves, and in general a desire to be left alone as the Confederate veterans and their families attempted to start their lives anew. This is typified by the remarks of Martin Gary, a returning South

---

920 Recall that under the original Constitution the word "state" meant the same as "nation." Nations, also known as States, are sovereign. Strip them of their sovereignty and they become mere provinces subservient to the central authority. The American States came into the Union retaining their sovereignty, freedom, and independence. See Graham, John Remington, *Principles of Confederacy* (Salt Lake City, UT: Northwest Publishing, 1990), 33-4.

921 Fleming, Walter Lynwood, *The Sequel of Appomattox* (1919, Yale University Press, 1970), 16.

Carolina Confederate veteran on his way home, "I'm for the Union; we are licked but I'm glad it is all over." This was the attitude of a Confederate veteran on his way home from Appomattox. Eleven years later, the same Martin Gary was to be one of the organizers of South Carolina's resistance movement, the Red Shirts. But Martin Gary's attitude, as well as that of other Southerners, changed not out of some intrinsic hatred of the Federal Government or racial hatred directed toward the newly freed slaves but the change of attitude was caused and inspired by a sense of intolerable injustice inflicted upon "We the People" of his native state. But immediately after the War, there was "almost perfect tranquility" as reported by a correspondent of the *Nation*.[922] "We the People" of Dixie wanted peace but the Republican Party wanted power and would do whatever it took to achieve their hardhearted, revengeful, and greedy goal!

Yankee reporter Sidney Andrews came to South Carolina in the late summer of 1865. He sent reports back to Radical newspapers in Boston and Chicago. In one of his reports, he observed:

> ... the South is beaten; desiring nothing so much as long years of peace...mostly disposed to make the best they can of the freedman...I have not discovered much of a sullen spirit in the State. They exult in their war record...Shall we not, in other fashion, though it be, also exult in the heroism of her people?[923]

The answer to the question he posed to the Yankee nation has been answered with a resounding negative. His was an honorable statement of a Northern journalist in the form of a question, "Shall we not, in other fashion though it be, also exult in the heroism of her people?" The slanderous anti-South propaganda and violence promoted by or issued by Woke social justice activists or political leaders in Modern Era Reconstruction answered the question with

---

922 Henry, Robert Selph, *The Story of Reconstruction* (New York: Konecky & Konecky, 1938), 66.

923 *Ibid.*, 67.

the destruction of the South's ancient monuments to its heroes. America's neo-Marxist social justice warriors, leftists local, state, and national politicians in conjunction with counterfeit conservative political leaders have answered his honorable question with a resounding NO! The spirit of scallywags, carpetbaggers, and Radical politicians lives on in the modern era in **both** national political parties.[924]

Former South Carolina Governor Francis Wilkenson Pickens, who was governor when South Carolina seceded from the Union, described the intentions of the people in post-War South Carolina when he declared, "The work South Carolina begins today she begins in good faith. She was the first to secede, and she fought what she believed to be a good fight, with all her energies...She has seen enough of war; in God's name I demand that she shall not be made to appear as if she still coveted fire and sword."[925] In the 1865 South Carolina convention Pickens introduced the resolution rescinding the 1861 ordinance of secession. *The Nation* noted:

> The passage was received in silence – strikingly suggestive when one remembered with what dramatic applause the ordinance of secession was proclaimed passed.[926]

Regardless of what the post-War Southern people wanted, what really mattered was what the Republican Party wanted, and the Republican Party wanted power. A power that could only be achieved if it could drive a wedge of mistrust and hatred between black and white Southerners and use black bloc-voting as a tool for Republican dominance of the South and Congress.

---

924 See Chapter 11, "Political Poverty-The Death of Southern Statesmanship," in Kennedy & Kennedy, *Punished With Poverty-The Suffering South* 2nd ed. (Columbia, SC: Shotwell Publishing, 2020), 133-60.

925 Henry, Robert Selph, *The Story of Reconstruction*, 87.

926 "Francis Wilkinson Pickens," Wikipedia (wikipedia.org) www.bit.ly/FWPickens (Accessed 31 August 2023).

Carpetbag Rule Comes To South Carolina

South Carolina was destined to endure the dictatorial rule of a carpetbagger governor, Robert K. Scott, from Ohio. He became governor of the once sovereign state by the grace of Yankee bayonets. After his service on behalf of the Yankee Army, he entered South Carolina post-War politics by way of the Freedmen's Bureau. While serving in the Freedmen's Bureau he gained a large following by haranguing mostly illiterate former slaves. Another former Yankee military man, Niles G. Parker of Massachusetts, oversaw the state's Treasury. Parker left Massachusetts fleeing criminal prosecution and was now in charge of South Carolina's Treasury. What could go wrong with such wonderful specimens of Yankeedom in charge of the state? In South Carolina's Reconstruction-era House of Representatives, a small group of Democrats sat with solemn faces looking upon what was once an honored, educated, and principled assembly of a once sovereign state. Bowers described the scene:

> Mingling with the negroes we see ferret-faced carpetbaggers, eager for spoils; and in the rear, 'Honest' John Patterson, vulture-eyed, calculating the prices of members. Two years hence he will reassure his kind with his classic statement that 'there are five years more of good stealing in South Carolina.[927]

According to a report in the Yankee journal, *The Nation*, eighty percent of the South Carolina House could not read or write above the simplest level.[928] A room next to the office of the Senate's clerk was used by the House members as a bar! House members were consuming gallons of alcoholic beverages all paid for by South Carolina's impoverished taxpayers. And who were these taxpayers? They were the mostly white landowners whose taxes were approaching the level of government confiscation. Those legislators who passed the tax assessments had little real property

---

927 Bowers, Claude, *The Tragic Era* (New York: Halcyon House, 1929), 353. Author cites Renolds, John S., *Reconstruction in South Carolina* (Columbia, SC, 1905), 229.

928 Bowers, Claude, *The Tragic Era*, 354.

Gen. Wade Hampton, CSA, future redeemer and post-Reconstruction Governor of South Carolina.

and therefore paid little or no taxes. In modern parlance, we would say "They had on skin in the game." The taxpayers were not represented in the legislature that enacted the confiscatory taxation. It was South Carolina's second experience with "Taxation without representation." And like the original in 1776, in 1866 it would eventually produce a tax revolt—a Southern resistance movement. Dysfunctional governments will eventually face popular revolts and revolts, when they come, tend to be messy affairs that make it hard to control society after victory is achieved.[929] The state of dysfunction in South Carolina, and the entire South during Active Reconstruction, is typified by the answer given by a legislator when he was asked how he got his money. He replied, "I stole it."[930] Or as Louisiana's Carpetbag Governor Warmoth declared, "Corruption is the fashion. I do not pretend to be honest, but only as honest as anybody in politics."[931]

---

929 Hart, B.H. Liddell, *Strategy* (1954, New York: Frederick A. Praeger, 1968), 380-1.

930 Bowers, Claude, *The Tragic Era*, 356.

931 Warmoth cited in Fleming, Walter Lynwood, *The Sequel of Appomattox* (1919, Yale University Press, 1970), 225.

Wade Hampton and What Could Have Been

Former Confederate General Wade Hampton of South Carolina supported black suffrage and urged the state to take appropriate action declaring, "The negroes...have behaved admirably...and are in no wise responsible for the present condition of affairs...Deal with them with perfect justice, and thus show them that you wish to promote their advancement and enlightenment."[932] Hampton's views on the subject are similar to those expressed by General Beauregard of Louisiana, General Forrest of Tennessee, and former Vice President Alexander Stephens of Georgia. The potential was there but the potential was destroyed by the Republican Party, the Freedmen's Bureau, the Union League, Yankee carpetbaggers, and Southern scallywags.

W.H. Trescott of South Carolina in *DeBow's Review* wrote of the following year after emancipation: "...(there) was no impatience, no insubordination, no violence. They have received their freedom quietly and soberly. They remained pretty steadily on the farms of their (former) masters, a very general disposition being manifested to adjust the terms of compensation on a reasonable basis."[933] This reflects the potential that the high road to emancipation held in South Carolina the "Cradle of the Confederacy."

The Union League's Terror and Intimidation

The Union League encouraged blacks to ostracize, harass, and bully fellow blacks who dared to show support for conservative Democrat candidates. In Charleston, South Carolina a group of whites were escorting home a group of blacks who had attended a conservative rally held September 6, 1876. The white and black conservatives were set upon by a mob of black Republicans. The violent attack resulted in the death of one white man and numerous individuals, both black and white, were wounded.[934] While the Yankee press, then and now, happily report violence against black

---

[932] Hampton cited in Henry, Robert Selph, *The Story of Reconstruction*, 236.
[933] Henry, Robert Selph, *The Story of Reconstruction*, 29.
[934] *Ibid.*, 568.

supporters of the political *status quo*, they seldom report similar violence against white and black conservatives. The more things change, the more they remain the same.

Black Southerners who did not agree with the corruption and hatred inflicted upon society by the carpetbag/scallywag government and who supported Democrats during elections were constantly assaulted.[935] For example, in South Carolina, a black man, Stephen Riley, a former slave joined the Democrats in 1868. He was repeatedly attacked and beaten by fellow blacks who were supporters of the Union League and the Republican Party. Black supporters of the Republican Party amused themselves by chanting in the streets:

> Oh Riley, he am straight and tall,
>
> He hab no bone in de back,
>
> He bend and scrape to de white folks all,
>
> And forget dat he am black.[936]

This was "chanted' in the streets by blacks to intimidate any of their fellow blacks who might consider siding with the white conservatives.

South Carolina's Carpetbag Governor Scott was from Ohio and rose to the rank of Major General in the Union Army during the War.[937] As governor, he was confident in his ability to maintain Republican rule in South Carolina. He felt that the bayonet was the master of the ballot. To maintain Republican domination of the whites Scott acquired over seven thousand rifles that he used to

---

935 Bowers, Claude, *The Tragic Era*, 358. Author cites Reynolds, John S., *Reconstruction in South Carolina*, 105.

936 *Ibid.*, 358, Author cites *New York Herald*, 11 May 1871.

937 "Gov. Robert Kingston Scott," National Governors Association (nga.org) www.bit.ly/RKScott (Accessed 11 September 2023).

arm his black militia.[938] He had his militia stationed in areas that were more heavily conservative. They were reported to be "Rough, swaggering bullies, with badges and bayonets, they promised to overawe the whites. The negro militia drilled constantly, parading the streets with fixed bayonets, forcing citizens from the highway."[939]

DIVIDE AND RULE IN SOUTH CAROLINA

South Carolina's last Reconstruction Governor, Daniel H. Chamberlain, described the efforts of the Republican Party to separate white and black Southerners to help the Republican Party capture political control of the conquered South. Unknowingly, the former Scallywag Governor described the technique of Divide and Rule used by the Republican Party. Writing in the *Atlantic Monthly* some thirty years afterward he noted:

> It cannot be too confidently asserted that from 1867 to 1872 nothing would have been more unwelcome to the leaders of reconstruction at Washington than the knowledge that the whites of South Carolina were gaining influence over the blacks, or were helping to make laws, or were holding office...Seventy-eight thousand colored voters were distinctly and of design pitted against forty-six thousand whites...It was deliberately planned and eagerly welcomed at Washington.[940]

Empires very often use the ancient technique of Divide and Rule to facilitate the empire's subjugation and control of their newly conquered territories. The newly emerging Yankee Empire used Divide and Rule against the South, and, after its successful

---

938 Bowers, Claude, *The Tragic Era*, 360. Author cites Reynolds, John S., *Reconstruction in South Carolina*, 136.

939 *Ibid.*, 360.

940 Henry, Robert Selph, *The Story of Reconstruction*, 471.

colonial conquest of the Confederate States of America, the Yankee Empire would use divide and rule repeatedly around the world.[941]

Governor Chamberlain was from Massachusetts. He rose to the rank of Captain in the Union Army during the War. He ran for a second term as Governor, but his election was contested by the conservatives. The conservative candidate, Wade Hampton, set up a rival government, and for a short while South Carolina had two governors. As a result of the Compromise of 1877 which allowed Rutherford B. Hayes to be declared winner of the Presidential election, troops were withdrawn from the South. Without the backing of Federal troops, Chamberlain was powerless. He soon left the state. Chamberlain moved to New York to practice law and teach. He ultimately retired to Charlottesville, Virginia.[942]

SOUTH CAROLINA'S CUBAN FREEDOM FIGHTER AND CONFEDERATE COLONEL

Cuban Freedom Fighter, Colonel Ambrosio Jose Gonzales, served on Beauregard's staff during the War. He was paroled on May 1, 1865. He reunited with his family in Springville, South Carolina. He attempted to get his plantation back in production but had trouble finding reliable laborers. As his biographer noted:

> According to African American historian Alrutheus Ambush Taylor, when blacks "worked for white people for wages they found that by two or three days' work they could procure money enough to support them in idleness the next week."[943]

The development of a labor system suitable for the time demands of raising crops would have been accomplished had the

---

941   See Kennedy & Kennedy, *Yankee Empire: Aggressive Abroad and Despotic at Home* (Columbia, SC: Shotwell Publishing, 2018), 115, 124-5.

942   "Gov. Daniel Henry Chamberlain," National Governors Association (nga.org) www.bit.ly/DHChamberlain (Accessed 12 September 2023).

943   Taylor cited in De La Cova, Antonio Rafael, *Cuban Confederate Colonel-The Life of Ambrosio Jose Gonzales*, 270.

*Col. Ambrosio Jose Gonzales,
Cuban Freedom Fighter who served on Beaureguard's staff.*

North allowed the South to follow the high road to emancipation. The lust for empire destroyed *what could have been*. "The lust of empire impelled them [Yankees] to wage against their weaker neighbors [Southerners] a war of subjugation."[944]

Added to Colonel Gonzales's labor problems were the economic conditions and social unrest that South Carolina suffered during Active Reconstruction. These deplorable conditions made recovery difficult for all conservative South Carolinians. The stress, unstable government, crime, and general fear for personal and family safety were the most prominent aspects of the emotional state of men attempting to restart their lives and regain their fortune. Cuban Colonel Gonzales was attempting to regain his financial standing but "His commercial failures were the result of fateful circumstances that affected many other Carolinians."[945] A race riot

---

944 Davis, Jefferson, *Rise and Fall of the Confederate Government*, Vol. 1, 229.

945 De La Cova, Antonio Rafael, *Cuban Confederate Colonel-The Life of Ambrosio Jose Gonzales*, 285.

in Charleston destroyed one of his business ventures. Such were the conditions South Carolinians and other Southerners were laboring under during Republican-imposed Active Reconstruction. During this time Colonel Gonzales's wife, Hattie, wrote to him expressing her concern that their Cuba may fall into the clutches of the United States. She wrote that she hoped that Cuba could avoid "the clutches of the detested eagle!"[946] By 1898 Cuba would be made one of the Yankee Empire's economic colonies.[947]

REDEMPTION OF SOUTH CAROLINA

During Wade Hampton's campaign for governor of South Carolina, the conservatives worked to mend the racial antagonism brought about by the Republican Party's Divide and Rule Reconstruction policy. Hampton declared, "I am in this fight to save South Carolina...to bring the two races in friendly relations together with equal and impartial justice."[948] By 1870, the Southern resistance movement was gaining momentum across South Carolina. While South Carolina's Republicans were pleading their case in Washington seeking President Grant's support and promise of more Federal troops, the people of the state were on the move. They were determined and ready for the political struggle to redeem their once sovereign state. Bowers describes the situation in South Carolina as a "revolt."

> Strange scenes were being enacted in South Carolina. Day and night, men in flaming red shirts were dashing through the dust of country roads into villages, towns, and groves, singing, shouting, cheering—good natured, and yet grim. The State had risen in revolt and was moving to the polls.[949]

---

946 Ibid., 271.
947 Kennedy & Kennedy, *Yankee Empire: Aggressive Abroad and Despotic at Home*, 97-100.
948 Henry, Robert Selph, *The Story of Reconstruction*, 566.
949 Bowers, Claude, *The Tragic Era*, 499.

South Carolina's last Carpetbag Governor, Harvard educated, Daniel H. Chamberlain from Massachusetts, honestly admitted the corrupt nature of South Carolina's Republican Reconstruction government, "Incompetency, dishonesty, corruption in all its forms...rule the party which rules the state."[950] South Carolina State Senator Beverly Nash, a black state senator, and former barber, testified that he sold his vote for a bill for five thousand dollars and five thousand dollars worth of Railroad script.[951]

Former South Carolina carpetbag Governor Chamberlain, writing in the *Atlantic Monthly* in 1901, described the sad state of the judicial system in South Carolina during Reconstruction. He admitted that "Justice in the lower and higher courts was bought and sold or rather those who sat in the seats nominally of justice made traffic of their judicial powers."[952] Chamberlain admitted that "two hundred trial justices were holding office by executive appointment, who could neither read nor write."[953] Dysfunctional government and high, confiscatory, taxation were major drivers of the Southern resistance movement. But it was not so much the high level of taxation that whites complained about but that they were being taxed without representation. Northern journalist Edward King noted:

> It is not taxation, not even an increase in taxation, that the white people of South Carolina object to; but it is *taxation without representation and unjust, tyrannical, arbitrary, overwhelming taxation*, producing revenues which never get any further than the already bursting pockets of knaves and dupes.[954] [Emphasis added].

---

950 Henry, Robert Selph, *The Story of Reconstruction*, 446.

951 Ibid., 446.

952 Ibid., 495.

953 Chamberlain cited by General Stephen D. Lee, *Confederate Military History* (1899, Harrisburg, PA: The Archives Society, 1994), Vol. XII, 309.

954 Henry, Robert Selph, *The Story of Reconstruction*, 501.

Under such social and political conditions, it would be unreasonable to expect a -popular resistance not to arise. Ireland is an excellent example of how a people will seek ways to resist the occupation of their homeland. But when such conditions produce secret resistance organizations the ability to control said resistance movements is greatly hampered by the secret underground nature of the resistance. Unrestrained violence emerges, often motivated by revenge for past offenses not necessarily associated with the resistance movement. This would plague the Southern Resistance movement after the legitimate resistance movements were ordered to disband.

South Carolina was one of the last Southern States to throw off the carpetbag rule. The state's resistance movement was under the leadership of honorable men such as Wade Hampton and actively supported by brave men in red shirts. With the end of Active Reconstruction South Carolina and her sister Southern States entered another phase of Reconstruction—Passive Reconstruction (1877-1965). It would be a time known as the Progressive Era. During Passive Reconstruction, the Yankee Empire would establish itself as if it were the legitimate American government. Southerners would dutifully forget about the past, about America's legitimate government under the *original* Constitution, and dutifully remain upon their assigned position on the "stools of everlasting repentance."[955] Such is the lot of a conquered and meekly pacified people. *Vae victis*—Woe to the vanquished! And a double "woe" for those submissive individuals who insist on maintaining a "conquered" mindset within an indivisible Empire. Since the end of Active Reconstruction, Southerners have meekly accepted their assigned position as second-class citizens in the nation their Colonial ancestors helped to create. Southerners became slaves to the ruling elite's political *status quo*—Southerners, like good slaves, learned to love their chains! And if you remain silent and do not move around much, you will not notice your chains.

---

[955] Frank Lawrence Owsley, "The Irrepressible Conflict," *I'll Take My Stand*, 63.

Chapter 25:

TENNESSEE—
LINCOLN'S AND BROWNLOW'S RECONSTRUCTION

"The flags of the Confederacy represented the aspirations of a brave and resourceful people... Their desire to live under a government based upon 'the consent of the governed' should be respected." —Devereaux D. Cannon, Jr.[956]

TENNESSEE BECAME the sixteenth state in June 1796 when Congress accepted Tennessee into the Union. The act was approved by President George Washington. The first governor of the state was John Sevier, a hero of the Revolutionary War Battle of Kings Mountain. The victory of the "Over the Mountain Men" in the Battle of Kings Mountain was one of the American "Rebels'" victories that forced British Commander Cornwallis to eventually take refuge in the Virginia town of Yorktown. The people of Tennessee were primarily descendants of agrarian folks from North Carolina and Virginia. Future States of Arkansas, Mississippi, and Texas would receive many of their founding citizens from Tennessee. This network of kith and kin across the South played a key role in the desire of Southern States to protect their "kin" when they were threatened with invasion by an aggressive and unconstitutional Federal Government.

---

956   Cannon, Jr, Devereaux D., *Flags of the Confederacy* (Gretna, LA: Pelican Publishing Co., 1997), 73. Devereaux D. Cannon, Jr. (1954-2007) was from Nashville, Tennessee, an attorney at law, and member of the Sons of Confederate Veterans.

Tennessee citizens provide an excellent example of Southern civilians following the high road to emancipation. Under the constitution of 1796 free negroes were allowed to vote. In 1801 Tennessee enacted a law favoring voluntary emancipation. In 1824 The Moral and Religious Manumission Society of West Tennessee was formed at Columbia, Tennessee, and in 1827, of the one hundred and thirty-five anti-slavery societies in America, one hundred and six were in the South. Twenty-five of the Southern anti-slavery societies were in Tennessee. Three-fifths of the people of Tennessee were in favor of slave emancipation before it was thought of in Boston.[957]

Tennessee was part of the upper South that was initially reluctant to leave the "old Union." An initial popular vote to hold a "Secession Convention" was voted down by a large majority.

> The people of Tennessee wished to avoid war between the States and were anxious for a settlement of the questions of difference. Their old love for the Union of the States animated them and they believed that the conservative sentiment of all the States could devise an adjustment that would prevent a resort to arms.[958]

The state legislature elected twelve influential citizens to attend a peace conference in Washington. Ex-President John Tyler presided over the Peace Conference but despite the best efforts of those advocating peace, the Conference was a failure. Following the failure of the Peace Conference the state's general assembly passed a resolution declaring the state's cooperation with the Southern States if the Federal Government attempted to use military force to coerce Sovereign States. The resolution was a clear statement of support for their Southern kith and kin as announced by the state's governor:

---

957   *Confederate Veteran* Vol. XVI, No. 3, March 1908. Republished in *The Confederate Veteran Magazine* Volume (Harrisburg, PA: The National Historical Society, 1987), XVI,124.

958   Porter, James D., Tennessee," *Confederate Military History* (1899, Harrisburg, PA: The Archives Society, 1994), Vol. VIII, 4.

...whatever line of policy may be adopted by the people of Tennessee with regard to the present Federal relations of the State, I am sure that the swords of her brave and gallant sons will never be drawn for the purpose of coercing, subjugating, or holding as a conquered province any one of her sister States whose people may declare their independence of the Federal government.[959]

After Lincoln demanded that Tennessee provide 2,000 troops to help in his invasion and conquest of the lower South, the state legislature authorized the submission of an ordinance of secession to the voters of Tennessee. The vote was set for June 8, 1861. The vote count was officially announced on June 24, and the governor issued the following announcement:

...it appears from the official returns that the people of the State of Tennessee have, in their sovereign capacity, by an overwhelming majority, cast their votes for separation, dissolving all political connection with the United States, and adopted the provisional government of the Confederate States of America.[960]

By a vote of "We the People" of Tennessee it was decided to follow the spirit and letter of the Declaration of Independence which declares that "Governments are instituted among Men, deriving their just powers from the consent of the governed. That whenever any Form of Government becomes destructive of these ends, it is the Right of the People to alter or to abolish it, and to institute new Government." "We the People" of Tennessee spoke. America's founding document acknowledged their right to speak and act, but Lincoln and the Republican Party had long ago rejected such American principles. In Tennessee and across the South government by consent was abolished and government

---

959 Ibid., Vol. VIII, 5.

960 Ibid., Vol. VIII, 6.

by coercion was established. As President Jefferson Davis later noted when a free people's consent to the government under which they are to live is denied then tyranny abounds. "The alternative to secession is coercion."[961] The mere passage of time does not validate acts of tyranny. The passage of time does not legalize Lincoln's war, the Republican Party's imposition of puppet governments and constitutions on the post-War South, or the illegal perversion of America's original Republic of Sovereign States. An illegitimate government remains illegitimate regardless of how many generations of the conquered nation swear that it is "one nation indivisible with liberty and justice for all." Can the mere passage of time convert murder, rape, and pillaging of innocents into acceptable occupations or praise-worthy political acts?

RECONSTRUCTION IN BROWNLOW'S TENNESSEE

By 1867-68 bayonet constitutional conventions were held in ten Southern States—Tennessee being the exception. Tennessee was already tacitly recognized due to the efforts of President Johnson and the dictatorship of Governor Brownlow. The general attitude of Republicans in Congress and their sycophants in the Northern media was that the crises of the times produced the *necessity* of requiring Congress to act regardless of the limitations previously imposed by the original Constitution. It was *necessary*, they argued, to impose their form of Republican government on the United States. But as John Milton warned in *Paradise Lost* "Necessity (is) the tyrant's plea,"[962] and as William Pitt noted in a speech on the India Bill before Parliament in 1783 "Necessity is the argument of tyrants, it is the creed of slaves." Necessity was the talisman, magic wand, or smoke screen used by the Republican Party to justify its dictatorial rule of the invaded and now conquered Southern people. Necessity was the appeal of post-Active Reconstruction, conservative Southern political leaders. Southern leaders urged "We the People" of the South to accept

---

961 Davis, Jefferson, *Rise and Fall of the Confederate Government* (1881, Nashville, TN: William Mayes Coats, circa 1980), Vol. 1, 177.

962 Milton, John, *Paradise Lost, John Milton Complete Poems and Major Prose*, ed., Merritt Hughes (New York: The Odyssey Press, 1957), Chapter IV, Line 393.

the new, illegitimate, and unconstitutionally enacted Federal Constitution and the new Federal and State Governments. These new governments were forced—at the point of bayonets—upon a conquered and defenseless people. This raises the question of whether the mere passage of time can bestow legitimacy upon illegitimate, bayonet governments.

The Republican-controlled Congress used bayonet-enforced Southern state constitutional conventions under the control and leadership of the Yankee military, scalawags, carpetbaggers, and newly freed and mostly illiterate slaves to "remake" the former "free, independent, and sovereign" States[963] of the South. The Republican Party's goal was to turn the once sovereign States of the South into Federal puppet States that would henceforth obediently follow the dictates of the ruling elite in Washington, DC. The Republican Party in Congress and its sycophants in the national press acted as if they had a divine unction or mandate to remake the United States into one nation indivisible. As noted in the Foreword of John Taylor's *Tyranny Unmasked,* "Ideas such as "divine right" and "parliamentary supremacy" have been replaced by "general welfare" and "federal supremacy."[964] Such an attitude was the very essence of the emerging Yankee Empire. In their exalted state of mind, they assumed the right to determine the power and limitations of *their* new all-powerful government. The Fourteenth Amendment, which greatly enlarged the powers of the Federal Government, was viewed by the Republican Party as merely a way to complete the revolution initiated by Lincoln and the Republicans in 1861.[965]

President Johnson proclaimed on June 13, 1865, the rebellion in Tennessee to be over. Johnson's proclamation recognized the

---

963 As set forth in Article Two of the Articles of Confederation, ratified by each Sovereign State March 1, 1781.

964 F. Thornton Miller cited in Taylor, John, *Tyranny Unmasked* (1822: Indianapolis, IN: Liberty Fund, 1998), xix.

965 "...the constitutional amendments that consolidated the North's victory." *The Oxford Companion to the Supreme Court of the United States,* ed., Kermit L. Hall (New York: Oxford University Press, 1992), 361.

Brownlow government in Tennessee.[966] Governor William G. Brownlow, a Methodist minister, became Tennessee's first post-War governor. Brownlow was full of hatred for Confederates which was typical of the South's scallywag governors. But as a minister, he seemed to think he had a special unction from on High to execute the trampling out of the grapes of wrath. He was of the mind that it was his duty to fulfill the judgment of God on all those heathens who dared to support the Confederacy. As far as he was concerned all rebels, by which the Parson meant not only those who had actively or passively aided the Confederacy but also those who did not now support his regime, must be punished and prevented from participation in the new local, state, and national governments. Brownlow admitted to a Northern audience "I find here at the North you do not need, and many of you do not want, Negro suffrage. We are not so. We want the loyal Negroes to help us vote down the disloyal traitors and white people."[967]

Governor Brownlow confirmed his hatred for white Southerners when he boasted "I would rather be elected by loyal Negroes than by disloyal white men." Brownlow urged organizing the freedmen into a division "armed with pine torches and spirits of turpentine to do the burning...and with guns to do the killing."[968] These words coming from the governor of a "loyal" (Republican-controlled) Southern state caused no small amount of fear and distress throughout the white South. Governor Brownlow introduced laws to assure Republican rule in Tennessee and declared, "We want another war to put down the rebellion. After that is fought, reconstruction will be easy in the Confederacy. We will only want a surveyor-general and a land office, with a deputy in each county, and a large amount of hanging."[969] Now why would white Southerners be anxious about their safety under such a government? Do you think that this kind of rhetoric from a state governor backed by

---

966   Henry, Robert Selph, *The Story of Reconstruction*, 169.

967   Ibid., 141.

968   Ibid., 193.

969   Ibid., 328.

bloody Federal bayonets might prove to be a motivating factor for the establishment of a Southern resistance movement?

Brownlow's legislature enacted laws requiring all who could not take an oath like the ironclad oath would be disfranchised for five years and those who were leaders in the "Rebellion" would be disfranchised for fifteen years."[970] So much for the Constitutional provision against *ex post facto* law.[971] But that old, outdated document was but a mere historical artifact of no real importance to America's post-War ruling elites—then and now.

During Brownlow's dictatorial rule, Tennessee was blessed with numerous Northern speculators and carpetbaggers. Like buzzards, they came to pick the flesh of the dead body of the Confederacy. Even A.J. Fletcher, Reconstruction Secretary of State for Tennessee, agreed with the South's general distaste for Northern carpetbaggers:

> No one more gladly welcomes the Northern man who comes in all sincerity...but for the adventurer and office-seeker who comes among us with one dirty shirt and a pair of dirty socks, in an old rusty carpetbag, and before his washing is done becomes a candidate for office, I have no welcome.[972]

Because they had no connection with the people of the state and were generally men of low morals, the carpetbag government became an oppressive tyranny ruling an impoverished people. The Republican-controlled legislature of Tennessee proposed a bill that denied the right to vote for all persons who did not oppose secession in 1861 and who did not oppose the cause of the Confederacy during the War. The net effect of the bill would be to reduce Tennessee voters to only hardcore Union men. Tennessee was thereby made into a Republican state. A Tennessee Republican

---

970 Ibid., 55.
971 Article I, Section 9, paragraph 3, US Constitution.
972 Fletcher cited in Henry, Robert Selph, *The Story of Reconstruction*, 222.

celebrated the ultimate passage of a similar bill by declaring that "Any means must be resorted to, if necessary, to keep rebels from the polls and out of office."[973]

Tennessee's Republican-controlled legislature enacted laws infringing upon freedom of speech and press. These acts put "in the hands of the Governor an armed force in each county which could be used to carry out his political agenda."[974] This meant an end to freedom of speech and the beginning of armed Negro militia in each county to intimidate the defeated and impoverished white population. The legislature, as was common across the occupied South, passed laws to fine an individual upwards of $50.00 for wearing a "rebel uniform." This was at a time in which the only coat or trousers the returning Confederate veterans owned were the tattered remnants of the Confederate uniform he was wearing. The legislature also passed laws to forbid religious officials who were sympathetic to the Confederacy from performing marriages and to require couples getting married to take the oath (pledge) of allegiance before a marriage license would be issued.[975]

Under Brownlow's administration, Senators and Congressmen from Tennessee were sent to Washington but the Republican-controlled Congress refused to seat them. This is interesting because just like all the Lincoln Ten Percent Reconstruction Plan Southern States, Tennessee was considered a state in the Union and participated, on April 3, 1865, in the state action of ratifying the proposed Thirteenth Amendment. In other words, the Republican Party-controlled Congress recognized Southern elected officials when it benefited the Republican Party, otherwise "We the People" of the South must move to the back seat of America's political and social bus and should feel privileged that America's new rulers allow the South on the bus at all.[976] The only

---

973   Henry, Robert Selph, *The Story of Reconstruction*, 151-2.

974   Ibid., 55.

975   Ibid., 55-6.

976   This raises the question of why "We the People" are insisting that we must remain on the bus **if** we are not allowed equal rights. This question is posed to all conservatives not just Southern conservatives. We must either fix the bus or get a new one.

purpose of the South then, and now in modern America, was to remain permanently on the stools of everlasting repentance. "The South, confused, ill-informed because taught by an alien doctrine so long, unconsciously accepts portions of the Northern legend and philosophy."[977]

Governor Brownlow's Republican state government added approximately $5,000,000.00 to the state debt in 1866, almost as much in 1867, and by the time he left Tennessee for a new post as Senator in Washington, his administration added more than $16,000,000.00 (equal to $374,400,000.00 in 2023 dollars)[978] of new debt to the state government.[979] It was rumored that Tennessee's bonds were being sold in New York by unauthorized persons and the money collected was not going back to Tennessee. Such rumors "...finished the destruction of the state's credit, insofar as the postbellum bonds were concerned."[980] In 1869, Brownlow resigned as governor before the end of his term to assume the position of US Senator from Tennessee. Republican Dewitt Clinton Senter took office as governor for the remaining few months of Brownlow's term. Senter then ran for governor and served from 1869 to 1871. He was one of the better Reconstruction Southern governors. He worked to remove the restrictions on Confederates that Brownlow imposed.[981]

Reconstruction in Tennessee ended with the election of moderate Republican Dewitt Clinton Senter. One of Senter's pledges was to return the right to vote to former Confederates. The Radical Republicans opposed Senter because they knew that if they allowed Confederate veterans to vote, it would spell the doom of the Republican Party in the state. Senter's election was assured when the conservative Democrats wisely endorsed

---

977   Frank Lawrence Owsley, "The Irrepressible Conflict," *I'll Take My Stand*, 63, 67.

978   "Value of $1 from 1869 to 2024," CPI Inflation Calculator (in2013dollars.com) www.bit.ly/1869-USD (Accessed 03 September 2023).

979   Henry, Robert Selph, *The Story of Reconstruction*, 367.

980   Ibid., 368.

981   "Gov. DeWitt Clinton Senter," National Governors Association (nga.org) www. https://bit.ly/DCSenter (Accessed 14 September 2023).

the Republican, Senter, who defeated the Radical Republican candidate Colonel William B. Stokes. The vote tally was Senter – 120,333 and Stokes – 55,036.[982] The election resulted in the seating of a new conservative Democrat state legislature. The conservative legislature called for a state constitutional convention which was held in 1870. The new constitution was ratified by the voters on March 30, 1870. The new constitution put severe limitations on the use of the state militia as a political weapon.[983] (The first time in American history that an evil political *status quo* weaponized a department of government and used it against advocates of Constitutional liberty was during Active Reconstruction.) A new election was held in which Democrat John C. Brown was elected governor. Brown entered the Confederate Army as a private but was promoted during the War to Major General. He was wounded four times while leading his men.[984] With conservative Democratic victories in the legislature and governorship, Active Reconstruction in Tennessee ended.

Racial Hatred Encouraged By Scallywags, Carpetbaggers, and Other Republicans

The general hatred toward blacks held by most Northerners was reflected in the actions of local Unionists in the occupied South. An official of the Freedmen's Bureau stated that a Unionist in Tennessee told him that "If you take away the military from Tennessee, the buzzards can't eat up the niggers as fast as we'll kill them."[985] These are the words that reflect the attitude not of "evil, racists Klansmen" but of local scallywags, and other white Republicans. Another reported "...among the bitterest opponents of the negro in Tennessee are the intensely radical loyalists of the mountain district, the men who have been in our (Union)

---

982   Henry, Robert Selph, *The Story of Reconstruction*, 380.

983   *Ibid.*, 402.

984   Mitcham, Jr., Samuel W., *The Encyclopedia of Confederate Generals* (Washington, DC: Regnery Publishing, 2022), 71-2.

985   Henry, Robert Selph, *The Story of Reconstruction*, 77.

armies...⁹⁸⁶ Nor was this sentiment reserved for the uneducated, unsophisticated, poor whites. Such attitudes were held by those holding political power in Reconstruction Tennessee.

Brownlow's Reconstruction legislature demonstrated the almost universal dislike of blacks among "loyal Unionists." The legislature defeated a state civil rights bill in May of 1865. This defeat was the first serious refusal of civil rights to the newly freed slaves by any of the restored Southern States—of course Northern States did not have a better record. Its defeat was the act of the first "Brownlow" legislature, a body made up almost entirely of radical Southern Unionists. Mr. John T. Trowbridge, an observer from Massachusetts, noted that there was "more prejudice against color among the middle and poorer classes—the Union men of the South, who owned few or no slaves—than among the planters who owned them by scores and hundreds." Governor Brownlow summed up the general attitude of these "loyal Union men" when he remarked that "it is hard to tell which they hate the most, the Rebels or the Negroes."⁹⁸⁷

ELECTION FRAUD—THE MAINSTAY OF THE REPUBLICAN PARTY'S ACTIVE RECONSTRUCTION

In June of 1865, the Radicals barely carried Missouri's vote on the ratification of Missouri's new constitution; in August, they failed to carry either Kentucky or Tennessee. There was good reason for Mr. Thaddeus Stevens's fears of failure of the Radical plans. An election for congressmen was held in Tennessee on August 7, 1865. Under the strict disfranchisement laws of the state none but Union men of proven loyalty could vote. Confederate veterans and others who supported the Confederacy were disfranchised. But the conservative nature of the state was demonstrated when six of the eight men chosen for Congress were Conservative. Governor Brownlow, using typical Reconstruction-era election

---

986   Ibid.
987   Ibid.

fraud techniques, threw out the vote of twenty-nine counties.[988] On Brownlow's "authority" around one-third of the state's votes were discarded. These votes just happened to be from conservative counties. But even this additional disfranchisement by Brownlow changed the result in only one district. The general conservative mood of the few who were allowed to vote could not be nullified by the ruthless electoral methods of 1865.[989] The Republican Party needed a pliable (as in exploitable) black bloc vote to assure victory for the party of the Union. In Modern Era Reconstruction it is the same song but a different verse.

The 1865 elections in the reorganized Southern States convinced the North that Southern whites would not "repudiate at the ballot box, the treason they have supported at the mouth of the canon."[990] As far as the victorious North was concerned, white Southern votes were meaningless if said voters did not parrot and fully embrace Northern ideas. The Radical North was demanding a repentant South, a South firmly seated upon the stool of eternal repentance—but Southerners, then and now, have nothing for which they need to repent. Repentance belongs to those of the North who illegitimately destroyed America's original Republic of Sovereign States.

The desire of the Republican Party to begin exploiting the newly freed and mostly illiterate slaves by turning them into a reliable bloc of voters ran into a major problem early on in Active Reconstruction. Most Northern States either restricted or would not allow blacks to vote in their lily-white state. But since the South was being treated as nothing more than a conquered province, then the victor could establish his rule as to who was allowed to vote in these conquered provinces. At first, the Radicals wanted the president to use his "authority" to decree who would be allowed to vote down South. Secretary of War Stanton, Attorney

---

988 Recall the Returning Boards used by Republican officials in Louisiana to throw out enough conservative votes to give the election to the Republican candidate. Could things like that happen today in Modern Era Reconstruction?

989 Henry, Robert Selph, *The Story of Reconstruction*, 82.

990 Ibid., 82.

General Speed and Postmaster General Denison supported this position. They wanted to leave voting rights up North to be dealt with by each Northern state but the "rebel" States, now provinces, would be ordered to allow universal male franchise while refusing access to the franchise to most white Southerners.[991] To his credit, President Johnson, a native of Tennessee, stood on constitutional grounds and refused to follow the Republican plan. But soon the Republican Party would brush aside the President and push through the Fourteenth and Fifteenth Amendments thus shattering the letter of the law regarding the rights of Sovereign States. The Republic became an empire controlled by Northern ruling elites.

The Southern Resistance Movement in Tennessee

Brownlow attempted to use the activities of the Southern resistance movement as evidence that the state was in continuing rebellion against the Federal Government. In 1868, former Confederate leaders, including General Nathan Bedford Forrest, met in Nashville to allay the fear of white insurrection that Governor Brownlow claimed was imminent. They passed a resolution declaring:

> In as much as the supposed danger to the peace of the State is apprehended from that class of the community with which we are considered identified, as inducement and reason to your honorable body not to organize such military force (Black militia), we pledge ourselves to maintain the order and peace of the State with whatever of influence we possess.[992]

The appeal had little effect because Governor Brownlow was determined to put a large part of Tennessee under martial law enforced by his well-armed and ill-disciplined black militia.

Early in 1869, the Grand Wizard of the KKK ordered the dissolution of the order and to destroy all records and regalia. The

---

991 Ibid., 45.

992 Ibid., 329.

order was given because the KKK was no longer needed, especially in the upper South, where it was originally organized. Tennessee had elected a relatively conservative legislature, Brownlow had moved to Washington, and General Grant was now president. A former KKK member, J.C. Lester, in 1884 wrote a history of the Klan. This "history" was written some 15 years after the dissolution of the Klan and after all records had been destroyed. But even after the original Klan was dissolved many folks used the name of the Klan to pursue personal grudges against both black and white folks. Miss Eliza Frances Andrews of Georgia was quoted in the New York World, on January 9, 1870, describing how the name of the Klan was used by less than honorable men:

> Whenever a set of low, disorderly fellows feel inclined to commit rascality, they put on masks and call themselves Ku Klux. A true statement of the case is not that the Ku Klux are an organized band of licensed criminals, but that men who commit crimes call themselves Ku Klux.[993]

Maintaining control of a secret society is almost impossible. If a crime is committed in the name of a publicly known organization, that organization can bring the culprit to court, but this is impossible for a secret organization. It is easy for scoundrels to imitate the actions of a secret organization or to publicly blame it for crimes it did not commit. This of course worked to the great advantage of the Republican Party in Washington and locally. Yankee newspapers would pick up accounts of real or imagined outrages and gleefully report to the North that the Klan's outrages were continuing down South. Senator Lyman Trumbull (Ill.)[994] declared that he believed that many of the so-called "outrages" were inspired by stories in Northern newspapers. The accounts of these "outrages" according to Senator Trumbull came from stories

---

993   *Ibid.*, 388-9.

994   Senator Lyman Trumbull's political party association spanned the political spectrum of the time: Democrat, Republican, Liberal Republican, and Populist. "Lyman Trumbull," Wikipedia (wikipedia.org) www.bit.ly/Lyman-Trumbull (Accessed 08 April 2023).

created by "telegrams emanating from this city (Washington, DC). The telegraph is used to create a public sentiment to operate upon Congress."⁹⁹⁵ This form of "Yellow Journalism" was not new to the North. Admiral Semmes, *CSS Alabama*, described it thusly:

> The war had been a god-send for newspaperdom. The more extraordinary were the stories that were told by the venal and corrupt newspapers, the more greedily they were devoured by the craving and prurient multitude. The consequence was, a race between the newspaper reporters after the sensational, without the least regard to the truth... Such is the stuff out of which a good deal of the Yankee histories of the late war will be made.⁹⁹⁶

Southern comedian Lewis Grizzard (1946-1994) summed up this Yankee trait when he said that the more outlandish a story about the South is, the more likely the Yankees will believe it. E.A. Pollard, editor of the *Richmond Examiner* during the War noted that "No human creature is more ingenious and industrious in misrepresentation than the Yankee."⁹⁹⁷

There were incidents in which Union League members attempted to infiltrate the Klan but were found out to be agents of the Tennessee scallywag Governor Brownlow.⁹⁹⁸ In 1869 General N.B. Forrest issued a stinging denunciation of the lawless elements that had seized portions of the resistance movement. Forrest demanded that the secret mask be removed but this demand from such a well-respected former Confederate General was ignored by the lawless elements within the movement.⁹⁹⁹

---

995 Henry, Robert Selph, *The Story of Reconstruction*, 395-6.

996 Semmes, Raphael, *Memoirs of Service Afloat*, 235-6.

997 Pollard, E.A., *Southern History of the War* (1866, Crown Publishers, Inc., 1977), Vol. 2, 392-3.

998 Bowers, Claude, *The Tragic Era*, 311. Author cites Davis, S.L., *Authentic History of the Ku-Klux-Klan* (New York, 1924), 109.

999 *Ibid.*, 311.

The Klan was only one element of the Southern resistance movement. There were other organizations, some secret and others public. In Louisiana, the Knights of the White Camellia and in South Carolina the Red Shirts are two examples. But the greater part of the resistance movement was conducted by honorable men who insisted on a peaceful political approach to unseating Republican imposed tyranny. Because their story of peaceful political action does not fit the Yankee Empire's narrative of evil racist Southerners, their story is seldom told.

President Andrew Johnson's Final Victory Over His Washington Enemies

Thaddeus Stevens often referred to President Johnson as, "an alien enemy, a citizen of a foreign state...not legally President."[1000] President Johnson, a Tennessee Democrat, was only useful for a short while and then the Yankee Empire rejected him. Such treatment is not that dissimilar from the way the US Army disposed of its Indian scouts and guides once their usefulness was over. This is generally the fate of men who, due to mistaken faith or trust in another or for the sake of personal advantage, betray their people.[1001]

President Johnson, on February 19, 1866, vetoed a Republican bill that would increase the power of the Republican-controlled Freedmen's Bureau. His veto was based on firm constitutional grounds, but it provided Republican propagandists in Washington and across the North with tremendous emotional material for their anti-South propaganda mills. The President correctly reasoned that the bill would allow for punishment for vaguely defined crimes, and action could be taken against individuals without indictment, trial by jury, or right to appeal. The Republican Bill would also establish the Executive as the responsible party for over four million newly freed slaves, and thus he could potentially use his influence over this mass of people to create a partisan bloc of black voters. The current

---

1000   Henry, Robert Selph, *The Story of Reconstruction*, 159.

1001   Kennedy & Kennedy, *Punished With Poverty-the Suffering South*, (2016, Columbia, SC: Shotwell Publishing, 2020), 142-3.

or future Executive could use such control for political purposes. But President Johnson's greatest concern was that the Republican Bill was passed by only a part of Congress, the Southern States being denied equal representation in Congress.[1002] His veto was possibly the last veto cast by a president grounded on principles of the *original* Constitution that sought to limit the powers of the Federal Government. President Andrew Johnson did not realize that a new day and a new illegitimate Constitution had arrived. The Republican Party murdered the spirit and letter of America's original and legitimate Constitution. The meaning and purpose of the Constitution were destroyed by the illegal "enactment" of the Fourteenth and Fifteenth Amendments and subsequent Supreme Court decisions based upon these illegitimate amendments.[1003] The Republican Party imposed bayonet constitutions on its puppet States in the South and upon the American people via their new bayonet Constitution in Washington, DC.

Former President Andrew Johnson's ultimate personal political victory and what many perceived as his vindication occurred in the opening special session of the US Senate on March 5, 1875. That was the day that Brownlow's successor to the Senate took the oath of office. Former President Andrew Johnson, the first president to stand trial for impeachment in the Senate chambers, took the oath of office and replaced his archenemy as US Senator. He would serve for a short term of the special session before his death on July 27, 1875.[1004] So ended the life of a famous Tennessean. To his fellow Southerners, he was and to many, he remains, an enigma. He was a man loyal to the general principles of the old Constitution, but he was unable to leave the Union when it was captured by a revolutionary faction. This Republican revolutionary faction that captured the Federal Government became his undoing in Washington, DC. After his term as President, his fellow

---

1002 Henry, Robert Selph, *The Story of Reconstruction*, 159.

1003 Kennedy & Kennedy, *Yankee Empire: Aggressive Abroad and Despotic at Home*, 109-18; Kennedy & Kennedy, *The South Was Right!* 3rd ed. (Columbia, SC: Shotwell Publishing, 2020), 232-245,457-60,461-3.

1004 Henry, Robert Selph, *The Story of Reconstruction*, 542.

Tennesseans honored him by sending him back as their Senator to the very chamber where seven years prior he stood charged with "high crimes and misdemeanors." His was a story that could have been a Greek tragedy where our hero is undone by hubris.[1005] Overconfident that he was right and self-encouraged by his sense of importance to the struggle of saving the old Union, like Icarus of Greek Mythology, he became so intoxicated by his new sense of importance to the old Union that he blindly flew too close to the hot sun of Thaddeus Stevens's Republican Party.

If Thaddeus Stevens is the symbol of the Republican Party, then Andrew Johnson is the symbol of Modern Era conservatives. Modern Era conservatives, like Johnson, still believe that the Constitution is a valid instrument for the protection of their rights. Like Johnson, they cannot conceptualize the fact that the principles and spirit of the old flag, the old Union, and the old Constitution have been deconstructed, destroyed, and replaced. The political *status quo* owes its allegiance to America's ruling elites nationally and globally, while "We the People" are reduced to political slaves of the illegitimate political *status quo*.

1005 "Hubris" is a typical flaw in the personality of an individual who enjoys a powerful position; as a result of which, he overestimates his capabilities to such an extent that he loses contact with reality.

Chapter 26:

TEXAS—INDEPENDENT NATION TO SOVEREIGN STATE TO PUPPET STATE

"Since the war for thirty years, the national government has been administered in a way to result in promoting the commercial, manufacturing, and general moneyed interests of the Northern people, and as claimed by the Southern people, prejudicial to their agricultural interest, which makes them dissatisfied and causes a continued political contention." —Oran Milo Roberts, Chief Justice Texas Supreme Court. Written in 1899.[1006]

TEXAS AND HAWAII are the only States whose state flag was once the flag of an independent sovereign nation. The flag of Texas represents a former nation that gained its independence after it seceded from Mexico. The United States recognized the right of secession when it recognized Texas as an independent nation and then again when it accepted Texas into the Union as a free independent and sovereign state. Both Texas and Hawaii represent sovereign entities whose sovereignty was destroyed by Yankee invasions.[1007] But as a conquered and occupied people, they attempted to make the best out of a bad situation.

1006 Colonel Oran Milo Roberts, "Texas," *Confederate Military History*, Vol. XI, (1899, Harrisburg, PA: The Archives Society, 1994), 148.

1007 See Chapter 3, "Hawaii the Yankee Empire's First International Conquest" in Kennedy & Kennedy, *Yankee Empire: Aggressive Abroad and Despotic at Home* (Columbia, SC: Shotwell Publishing, 2018), 51-73.

Under President Johnson's executive direction by December of 1865 the Southern States except Texas and Florida, whose work of reentry was almost complete, were recognized and Johnson described the population of these States as "yielding obedience to the laws and government of the United States with more willingness and greater promptitude than, under all the circumstances, could reasonably have been anticipated."[1008] These puppet States[1009] organized a government under Lincoln's Ten Percent Reconstruction Plan and as puppet States, they ratified the Thirteenth Amendment to the United States Constitution. These puppet States were implicitly recognized by the Federal Congress when it accepted their acts of ratification and counted the Southern States in the number required for the passage of the Thirteenth Amendment.

Texas, as with most other Southern States immediately after the War, attempted to restore civilian authority. The former and legitimate government under the Confederacy was destroyed by Federal invasion and conquest. Post-War a new government was needed to keep public order and begin the arduous task of restoring the South's devastated economy. The Southern people and their natural leaders assumed that President Johnson's proclamation of peace was an authoritative declaration of the end of the War and the beginning of new state governments in the South.

The people of Texas elected James Webb Throckmorton as Texas's first post-War governor on June 25, 1866. He was a well-respected Texas citizen who had opposed secession but after Texas left the Union, he joined the Texas military and rose to the rank of Brigadier General of Texas troops. Texas's first post-War Constitution was adopted, and impressive efforts were made during Throckmorton's short administration to restart the Texas

---

1008 Henry, Robert Selph, *The Story of Reconstruction* (New York: Konecky & Konecky, 139.

1009 "Puppet States" because they were not organized based upon the free and unfettered consent of the people but based upon Federal coercion. They were (and still are) allowed to exist only as long as they did the bidding of their puppet masters in the Republican-controlled Congress. The ultimate allegiance or subservience of these puppet States is not to "We the People" but to the political *status quo* and its Northern (and today Globalists) ruling elites.

economy. During his term in office, the famous cattle drives northward from Texas began. These post-War overland cattle drives are best remembered in Western folklore as the Chisholm Trail which ran from ranches in Texas to railheads in Kansas. But once the Republican-controlled Congress enacted the first of its Reconstruction Acts, the Yankee military moved in and expelled Throckmorton from office. The Republican Party's military deemed Throckmorton to be "an impediment to reconstruction."[1010] Thus began the Yankee Military dictatorship in Texas. The will of "We the People" of Texas was discarded and replaced with Republican bayonet rule.

Under Throckmorton's administration civil authority was re-established. But Texas civil authority was rendered impotent as soon as the Yankee military took over. Any time an individual was charged with a crime in civil court the individual would appeal to the military claiming he was being persecuted due to his long-standing pro-Union stance. The military would then order the removal of the case from civil court and send the case to the military court. As one modern-day historian noted, "It became the fashion in the South for those charged with criminal offenses to lay their troubles to 'loyalty' during the war."[1011] The Federal interference with local law enforcement even went as high as the President of the United States. In a case in which a Yankee soldier was tried and convicted of rape by a Union military court, the guilty party was released from prison on order of President Johnson.[1012] While the Yankee Empire's sycophants renounce the idea of state nullification, they have no problem with the Yankee Empire's agents nullifying state law. Thanks to the Republican Party, the Constitutional concept of state nullification was removed from the once sovereign States and given over to the supreme Federal Government. For example, in Modern Era Reconstruction, when the state of Alabama wanted

---

1010 "Gov. James Webb Throckmorton," National Governors Association (nga.org) www.bit.ly/Gov-Throckmorton (Accessed 18 September 2023).

1011 Henry, *The Story of Reconstruction*, 203.

1012 Cisco, Walter Brian, *War Crimes Against Southern Civilians* (Gretna, LA: Pelican Publishing Co., 2008), 152-3.

to put a copy of the Ten Commandments in a state courthouse, the Federal Government nullified that act of the once sovereign but now puppet state.

Texas and Louisiana were under the dictatorial rule of South-hating General Philip Sheridan. Sheridan ordered troops to be stationed in large towns and cities in Texas. He claimed that he did it to prevent rebel outrages against loyal Union men. Governor Throckmorton complained that those "loyal Union men" became so only after the end of the war. And as with many such reports of "rebel outrages" most were manufactured by media and local Republicans seeking Union military support. Governor Throckmorton urged General Sheridan to send troops to the frontier area of Texas. The white citizens who lived on the frontier were experiencing deadly raids from hostile Indians. Sheridan refused to help Texas citizens living on the frontier. Texas, being an occupied state, had no state troops to send to protect the white settlements on the frontier. Comanche raids were notorious for their violence. Comanches, also known as the "Lords of the Plains," were regarded as the most dangerous Indian tribe of the Western Plains. It was common for white women and children to be kidnapped and young white children raised by the tribe.[1013] Sheridan had no sympathy for Southern men, women, or children and had no compunction about leaving white women and children to the mercies of the Comanches. His attitude demonstrated in Texas was in line with his attitude about Southern civilians during the War.

Sheridan sent a letter to General Grant during the War, in which he reported the determination of Southerners to resist Yankee invasion and occupation. He wrote, "I know of no way to exterminate them except to burn out the whole country."[1014] Note Sheridan's use of the word "exterminate." Sheridan's cruel nature exhibited during the War continued during Active Reconstruction in the 5th Military District consisting of Texas and Louisiana. After

---

1013 "Native American History in Fort Worth," Visit Fort Worth (fortworth.com) www.bit.ly/FW-NAHistory (Accessed 18 September 2023).

1014 Sheridan cited Keys, Thomas Bland, *The Uncivil War: Union Army and Navy Excesses In The Official Records* (Biloxi, MS: The Beauvoir Press, 1991), 107.

his tenure as military dictator of Texas and Louisiana, Sheridan visited Otto von Bismarck in Germany in 1870. Sheridan admitted his contempt for the concept of "civilized warfare" by announcing that as far as enemy civilians were concerned, they "must be left with nothing but their eyes to weep with over the war."[1015] Bismarck was shocked by the remark, but Sheridan's advice was followed by all participants in twentieth-century wars.

General Sheridan never relented in his hatred for the white South. While in command in New Orleans he issued his infamous request to the Secretary of War to label all whites who opposed his Reconstruction policies as "rebels" and "bandits" to be arrested and tried by his military courts.[1016] It was a late effort by one of the South's most infamous enemies to save Republican Reconstruction and thereby maintain the South under military rule.

Before General Grant removed General Sheridan from what amounted to his dictatorial rule of the 5th Military District of Texas and Louisiana, Sheridan had managed to remove from civil offices of Louisiana elected aldermen, levee commissioners of New Orleans, the Mayor of New Orleans, the state's Attorney General, and of course Governor Madison Wells.[1017] Sheridan appointed local Radical Republicans with little or no qualifications for the positions and unprepared, inexperienced, and often illiterate black politicians to replace these elected civil officials. His attitude toward the whites on the Texas frontier and his actions in Louisiana demonstrate his utter contempt for the defeated and impoverished white South. His and other Northern occupiers' disdain for the South was a major contributing factor in the rise of the Southern resistance movement. When lawlessness abounds and the government refuses to act, then people will of necessity act.

It was impossible to maintain law and order on the frontier for two years or more after the end of the War. The Texas frontier became an area controlled by outlaws and Indians. Neither

---

1015 Sheridan cited in Cisco, Walter Brian, *War Crimes Against Southern Civilians*, 17.

1016 Bowers, *The Tragic Era*, 444.

1017 Henry, *The Story of Reconstruction*, 257.

Indians nor outlaws had any interest in Texas or national politics. They plundered and raided all regardless of their past or current political allegiances. "But the outrages reported in the North were those whose victims claimed sympathy and redress on the ground of loyalty."[1018] Sheridan used the lawlessness on the Texas frontier as an excuse for maintaining his military rule over Texas.

Fraud and Public Corruption are The Hallmarks of Post-War America

Some of the political leaders in Texas, as with leaders in other Southern States, recognized the radical change that had occurred in the original American government. Some could see the emerging Yankee Empire was intentionally disguising itself as the continuation of the original Federal Government created by the Founding Fathers. The reliability of their political foresight is verified by the fact that the expanding Federal Government's annual expenses before the War never exceeded $80,000,000.00. But thirty-five years after the War it amounted to $400,000,000.00. As Texas's Supreme Court Justice Oran Milo Roberts noted this "is a fair test in determining the character of the government at the two periods."[1019] Unfortunately, after the end of Active Reconstruction, Southern political leaders' primary concern was to make sure that the Federal Government did not re-establish Active Reconstruction. Therefore, they did not dare initiate a radical challenge to the political *status quo*. It was a major strategic failure that would eventually lead to the re-establishment of a new form of Reconstruction during Modern Era Reconstruction—post-1965. The horrors of Active Reconstruction left an indelible mark on the psyche of Southerners in general and Southern political leaders in particular. This was noted in 1930 by a Southern historian who lamented "what pitiful service had the inept Southern politicians for many years rendered the cause!"[1020] and another in the 1960s

---

1018   Ibid., 86.

1019   Chief Justice Oran Milo Roberts Texas Supreme Court (1874-1879). See *Confederate Military History*, (1899, Harrisburg, PA: The Archives Society, 1994), Vol. XI, 148.

1020   John Crowe Ransom, "Reconstructed But Unregenerate" *I'll Take My Stand*, (1930, Batton Rouge, LA: LSU Press, 1983), 26.

who wrote the South "had to...accept the defensive where an offensive was indicated."[1021] The immediate government of post-War Texas was composed of men of high ethical standards who were attempting to negotiate with men of low moral standards. This dichotomy of moral virtue led to a problem that Southern mothers would often warn children "Good seldom pulls bad up, but bad will almost always pull good down."

According to Union Major General D.S. Stanley, Inspector General for the Freemen's Bureau "Texas was worse than any other state because she had never been whipped. One campaign of the United States Army through eastern Texas, such as Sherman's through South Carolina, would greatly improve the temper and generosity of the people."[1022] Such was the attitude of the South's conquering masters. They viewed the South as their playground to do with as they pleased, "We the People" be damned.

Post-War greedy Federal Treasury agents spread over the conquered South devouring what little resources remained with no concern about the impoverished conditions of white and black Southerners. Some compared them to the plagues of locusts mentioned in the Old Testament. A Federal agent stole $80,000.00 worth of cotton in one month in the state of Alabama.[1023] That would be equal to $1,569,000.00 in 2023 dollars.[1024] When Federal Treasury agents in Texas were caught "red-handed" stealing cotton property from white citizens, they were arrested but immediately released by the Federal military.[1025] In many cases, the evidence was so overwhelming that even Republican local and Federal judges could not ignore the crimes. When the evidence began to lead to Federal officials the trials were suddenly dismissed. Lincoln and the Republican Party introduced the unconstitutional system

---

1021   Weaver, Richard, *The Southern Tradition at Bay* (New Rochelle, NY: Arlington House, 1968), 389.

1022   Henry, *The Story of Reconstruction*, 86.

1023   Bowers, *The Tragic Era* (New York: Halcyon House, 1929), 61.

1024   "The Relative Worth of $1 in 1866," Measuring Worth (measuringworth.com) www.bit.ly/1866USD (Accessed 05 May 2023).

1025   Bowers, Claude, *The Tragic Era* (New York: Halcyon House, 1929), 61.

of two-tier justice to the United States.[1026] It was obvious to the local Southern population that the Federal agents were actively stealing private property under the protection of Yankee bayonets. Meanwhile, in the North, Republican politicians and anti-South Yankee newspapers were only interested in demagoguing the South. The Northern Journal *The Nation* attacked Lee by declaring "We protest against the notion that he (General Lee) is fit to be put at the head of a college in a country situated as Virginia."[1027] The revengeful anti-South press and politicians were busy demanding to know why Jeff Davis, Lee, and other leaders of the "rebellion" had not been hung or shot. The plundering and pillaging of what remained of the South and her people were of no consideration except as targets for vengeful slander and cruel humor.

BLACK CODES AND A NEW LABOR SYSTEM

White Southerners understood the necessity of putting the freed laborers back to work. As slaves, blacks did not worry about food, shelter, clothing, or healthcare; that was provided to them by their owners. White Southerners generally understood that the newly freed slaves did not have the proper training to easily transition from dependent slaves to independent self-sustaining free people. Their ignorance was not of their doing—it could have been avoided had the South been allowed to follow the high road to emancipation. The Houston, Texas *Telegraph* reported that the newly freed slaves were "visiting around" while the cotton crop suffered, but urged tolerance for them because they were "not responsible for their own emancipation."[1028] Union General J.B. Kiddoo reported from Texas that he believed, "The better class of planters, who were

---

1026 The concept of a two-tier justice system was not created in the early 21st century. America's two-tiered justice system is a creature of Active Reconstruction. In 2022, the Trafalgar Group in conjunction with the Convention of States Action polled potential American voters and discovered that almost 80% of polled voters believed that in the United States there existed "two tiers of justice: one set of laws for politicians and Washington D.C. insiders, vs one set of laws for everyday Americans." Justice, Tristan, "4 In 5 Americans See Two-Tiered Justice System: Poll," The Federalist (thefederalist.com), 09 August 2022, www.bit.ly/2-Tiered-Justice (Accessed 27 September 2023).

1027 Bowers, *The Tragic Era*, 62. Author cites *The Nation*, 14 September 1865.

1028 Henry, *The Story of Reconstruction*, 29-30.

former slaveholders, are, as a general thing, disposed to deal fairly with them (the newly freed slaves).[1029] Unfortunately, the work of carpetbaggers, scallywags, and the Yankee military planted in the minds of impressionable blacks that the government would soon be giving them free land. The false promise of forty acres and a mule caused many of the freedmen to maintain a persistent belief that the great division of land and mules was to take place during the 1865 Christmas holiday.[1030] Because of this unrealistic belief, a large portion of the uneducated and impressionable freedmen refused to sign work contracts. In Texas, General E.M. Gregory, the Freedmen's Bureau assistant commissioner, issued a warning to the freedmen in November that they would get nothing from the government at Christmas or any other time. General Gregory's warning had little impact on the idle freedmen.

The idleness of unemployed freedmen was the cause of a fair number of petty crimes and violence. Unemployed men roaming around in gangs is a danger to any society regardless of the skin color of the vagrants. Across the South, many States attempted to address this new social problem by passing the so-called Black Codes. These codes followed the pattern of vagrancy laws then on the books in Northern States, but the Southern laws were denounced by Northern propagandists as efforts to return blacks to slavery. Texas took advantage of the good and bad experiences of other Southern States and enacted Black Codes that tended toward more equal treatment of freedmen in the laws it passed in 1866. The right to own property, the right to appeal issues to the state and local courts, and the right to testify in court were all covered in these laws.[1031]

1029 Ibid., 77.

1030 Ibid., 118.

1031 Ibid., 153-4.

Governor Fletcher S Stockdale of Texas and The Sulphur Springs Letter

Evidence of the defeated South's determination to remain peaceful while seeking a return to local self-government is seen in the White Sulfur Letter signed by twenty-seven well-known former Confederates including Generals Lee, Beauregard, former Confederate Vice President Stephens, and former Confederate Governor of Texas Stockdale. Below are pertinent portions of that letter addressed to US General Rosecrans, then Minister to Mexico. The letter was submitted at General Rosecrans's request:

White Sulphur Letter
Signed By 27 Southern Leaders

> The idea that the Southern people are hostile to the negroes and would oppress them if it were in their power to do so, is entirely unfounded. They have grown up in our midst, and we have been accustomed from childhood to look upon them with kindness. The change in the relations of the two races has brought no change in our feeling towards them...

> Self-interest, even if there were no higher motive, would therefore prompt the whites of the South to extend to the negroes care and protection...

> The important fact that the two races are, under existing circumstances, necessary to each other is gradually becoming apparent to both, and we believe that but for the influences exerted to stir up the passions of the negroes that the two races would soon adjust themselves on a basis of mutual kindness and advantage...

> It is true that the people of the South, together with the people of the North and West, are, for obvious reasons, opposed to any system of laws that will place the political power of the country in the hands of the negro race. But this opposition springs

from no feelings of enmity, but from a deep-seated conviction that at present the negroes have neither the intelligence nor other qualifications which are necessary to make them safe depositories of political power. They would inevitably become the victims of demagogues, who for selfish purposes would mislead them, to the serious injury of the public...

The great want of the South is peace. The people earnestly desire tranquility and the restoration of the Union. They deprecate disorder and excitement as the most serious obstacle to their prosperity. They ask for a restoration of their rights under the Constitution. They desire relief from oppressive misrule. Above all, they would appeal to their countrymen for the re-establishment in the Southern States of that which has justly been the right of every American — the right of self-government.

R.E. Lee, of Va.,	F.S. Stockdale, Texas,
W.J. Green, N.C.,	T.P. Branch, Ga.,
P.G.T. Beauregard, La.,	Jos. R. Anderson, Va.,
Lewis E. Harvie, Va.,	Jeremiah Morton, Va.,
Alex. H. Stephens, Ga.,	W.T. Turner, W. Va.,
P.V. Daniel Jr., Va.,	John B. Baldwin, Va.,
C.M. Conrad, La.,	C.H. Suber, S.C.,
W.T. Sutherlin, Va.,	Geo. W. Bolling, Va.,
Linton Stephens, Ga.,	E. Fontaine, Va.,
A.B. James, La.,	Theo. Flourney, Va.,
A.T. Caperton, W. Va.,	John Letcher, Va.,
T. Beauregard, Texas,	James Lyons, Va.,
John Echols, Va.,	B.C. Adams, Miss.
M.O.H. Norton, La.,	

After the White Sulphur Springs meeting, as the group of fellow Confederates were leaving the meeting, General Lee closed the door before Governor Stockdale could leave. Lee spoke privately with Governor Stockdale of Texas and declared:

> Governor, if I had foreseen the use those people [General Lee's polite reference for Yankees] designed to make of their victory, there would have been no surrender at Appomattox Courthouse; no, sir, not by me. Had I foreseen these results of subjugation, I would have preferred to die at Appomattox with my brave men, my sword in this right hand.

This is the same General Lee who wrote to Lord Acton that with the loss of States' Rights, the Federal Government would become "aggressive abroad and despotic at home."

Texas Moves Slowly Away From Reconstruction State Government

President Grant proclaimed Reconstruction in Texas to be over on March 30, 1870.[1032] The other half of the 5th Military District (Louisiana) had another seven years of struggle before the end of direct military dictatorship would end. By 1870 many people in the North began to tire of the "Southern problem." Historian Claude Bowers described the general attitude of Northerners of the time:

> All over the North, thinking men were beginning to resent the policy of imposing ignorant and criminally corrupt government on the Southern people. The scandalous contest over the Louisiana election of the previous year was still on, and many were shaking their heads in disapproval of the part played in Washington. It was the year Andrew D. White, visiting the South, was disgusted by what he saw and "for the first time began to feel sympathy with the South" after seeing personally how he had been deceived by partisan prejudice and dishonest propaganda.[1033]

[1032] "The 1860s: Reconstruction," Texas State Library and Archive Commission (tsl.texas.gov) www.bit.ly/1860sRecon (Accessed 19 September 2023).

[1033] Bowers, *The Tragic Era*, 414. Author cites White, Andrew, *Autobiography*, Two volumes (New York, 1905), Vol. I, 176.

The bluster of Republican Reconstruction would end in a smoke-filled room as Republicans struck a deal with Southerners from South Carolina and Louisiana to remove the remaining troops from the South in exchange for their support for Republican Rutherford B. Hayes as President.

Reconstruction did not end in 1877, it merely morphed into its next form—Passive Reconstruction (1877-1965).[1034] During Passive Reconstruction the South's docile and unquestioning acceptance of the *illegitimate* Federal Government created by Lincoln's war and the Republican Party's Active Reconstruction allowed the Yankee Empire to claim legitimacy. Southerners would soon be taught to "swallow the dog" by taking the modern form of the ironclad oath by swearing allegiance to the Yankee Empire's "one nation indivisible." This represents a major strategic failure of the South which allowed for the eventual imposition of Modern Era Reconstruction post-1965. In Modern Era Reconstruction Americans would be victimized by an all-powerful Federal Government that would open the nation's borders in a deliberate effort to deprive conservative Americans of their country, a weaponization of the Federal government that would be used to silence conservative citizens, and a massive promotion of immoral standards that are Biblically defined as sexual perversion. All that is required for evil to win is for good people to do nothing.[1035]

1034 The time-period of 1877-1965 includes the eras known as the Gilded Age and the Progressive Era. The Gilded Age was an age of Northern opulence while the South was being punished with poverty and the Progressive Era was a political era in which centralized federalism became the *unconstitutional* norm for American politics. It was a time in which "We the People" became political slaves and learned to love our chains.

1035 Kennedy, James Ronald, Chapter 5, "Is America Still a Nation 'Under God?'" *Be Ye Separate: Bible-Belt Revival or Marxist Revolution*, 46-52. Free downloadable copy at www.kennedytwins.com.

Chapter 27:

Virginia—
Reconstruction in the Old Dominion

"The war was not fought by the South as a whole, and certainly not by Virginia, for the perpetuation of slavery, nor by the North...for its abolition."
—Major Jed Hotchkiss[1036]

WHEN THE CAUSE of American liberty was in its infancy, in the early days when New England was struggling against the tyranny of a centralized government in London, it was from Virginia that a clarion call was heard—"Give me liberty or give me death!" Such was the patriotic zeal that infused the sons and daughters of Virginia in 1776 and again in 1861. The love for liberty outweighed the allegiance to an abusive and self-proclaimed indivisible government. As Virginian Patrick Henry declared, "The first thing I have at heart is American *liberty*, the second is American *union*."[1037] [Italics in the original].

Virginia's love of liberty was expressed in war and peace. Virginia was the second Sovereign State to pass a law prohibiting the introduction of slaves from abroad.[1038] Virginia, remembering that the first ship trafficking in the international slave trade

---

[1036] Major Jed Hotchkiss, "Virginia," *Confederate Military History*, Vol. III, Part 1 (1899, Harrisburg, PA: The Archives Society, 1994), 17.

[1037] *Patrick Henry: Life, Correspondence and Speeches*, W.W. Henry, ed. (Harrisonburg, VA: Sprinkle Publishing, 1993), 449.

[1038] *Confederate Military History*, Vol. III, Part 1, 17.

arrived in Virginia in 1646, sought to end that nefarious trade in human flesh. It was also noted that the 1646 slave ship was from Boston, Massachusetts. It was a son of Virginia, St. George Tucker, who published the first authoritative analysis of the Constitution in 1803. This same Virginian openly declared the need to remove slavery from America.[1039] Virginians, at their own expense, freed more slaves than all the New England States combined. Virginia, the mother of Presidents, was an early advocate of limiting slavery in the United States. In 1787 Virginia gave to the United States, as common territory for the American people, the great Northwest Territory beyond the Ohio River. One of Virginia's key provisions in that generous grant was that "slavery should be forever prohibited from that region."[1040] Virginia's benevolence was repaid by massed bloody bayonets in the hands of blue-coated invaders, many from the States carved out of the Northwest Territory. Such is the Punic faith of a Union dominated by Yankees.[1041] Virginia with her sister Southern States was compelled to remove themselves from a Union that had become abusive and unwilling to let the South alone. The South was forced to leave a Union dominated by a people (Yankees) who refused to allow the South to solve its social problems in a manner acceptable to all Southerners black and white. "It was not the Union that our Southern forefathers seceded from, but the deadly combination of Yankee greed and righteousness."[1042]

1039 Tucker cited in Rawle, William, *A View of the Constitution*, 1825, edited and annotated by Kennedy & Kennedy, *A View of the Constitution: Secession as Taught at West Point* (Wake Forest, NC: The Scuppernong Press, 2020), 292, 293.

1040 *Confederate Military History*, Vol. III, Part 1, 18.

1041 Punic faith or Carthaginian faith is a Roman expression for treachery of dishonorable people or nations. "Punic," Oxford Reference (oxfordreference.org) (Accessed 18 September 2023).

1042 Wilson, Clyde N., *The Yankee Problem: An American Dilemma* (Columbia, SC: Shotwell Publishing, 2016), 11.

John Brown's Attack on Harper's Ferry and The South's Fear of a Slave Revolt

On the quiet Sunday morning of October 16, 1859, the radical abolitionist John Brown and upwards of twenty other men seized the United States arsenal in Harper's Ferry, Virginia. His admitted intention was to seize weapons, arm slaves, and initiate a slave uprising. The men who followed Brown were from the Northern States of Connecticut, New York, Ohio, Iowa, Pennsylvania, Maine, and Indiana, and one from Canada.[1043] Virginian Hayward Shepherd, a free man of color, was the first victim of Brown's raid.[1044] Shepherd was shot and killed after confronting the raiders. After a short battle Brown and most of his followers were captured, tried for treason against Virginia, and executed by hanging.

The incident at Harper's Ferry did more to galvanize the pro-secession attitude of Southerners in the lower South than any other act. It did not generate a similar pro-secession attitude in Virginia and other Upper South States. The reason is that the fear of a Haitian-style slave uprising—resulting in the massacre of innocent white men, women, and children both slave owners and non-slave owners alike—was greatest in the lower South in which many counties blacks made up 50% of the population. Even though Virginia had more slaveholders than other Southern States,[1045] the type of slavery was very different. In the lower South, most of the slaves worked on large plantations. However, the conditions were different in Virginia for most of her slaves.

> While Virginia had more slaveholders among her citizens than did any of her sister Southern States, she strikingly differed from them in the distribution of the ownership of her slaves, showing thereby that within her borders slavery was a peculiarly "domestic institution;" for while she had more

---

1043 *Confederate Military History*, Vol. III, Part 1, 26.

1044 In 1860 Virginia had 57,374 free blacks. *Confederate Military History*, Vol. III, Part 1, 22.

1045 *Confederate Military History*, Vol. III, Part 1, 21.

slaveholders than any other State, yet, as a rule, the holdings of the individual were smaller.[1046]

Under these "domestic" conditions there developed close personal relations between master and slave. This also occurred in the Lower South but not to the same degree as it did in the Upper South. Fear of a slave uprising was less in the Upper South than in the Lower South. Such fear was the major reason why the Lower South seceded after the election of Lincoln, an anti-South sectional president, in 1860.

It was not just the attempted slave uprising promoted by John Brown that caused so much concern, especially in the Lower South. Brown was not some *lone* lunatic. He was part of a massive New England conspiracy against the South. Brown was financed by men in Boston, Massachusetts—the so-called Secret Six. Southerners viewed the North's reaction to John Brown's attempted slave uprising as evidence that their fellow countrymen were now under the influence of an emotional, radical, hate-filled, anti-South ideology. Newspapers were filled with reports of church bells across the North being tolled on the day that John Brown was executed. Several of Brown's conspirators escaped to Northern States and the governors of these States refused to extradite these men to Virginia for trial. Republican governors of Ohio and Iowa gave safe-haven for John Brown's men who managed to escape capture in Virginia and make it to Ohio or Iowa. Southerners saw such acts by Northern governors as evidence that the North under Republican control would not honor the law or the Constitution. "Many Southern moderates started to believe the 'fire-eaters' had been right all along."[1047] The Lower South States of Texas, South Carolina, and Georgia mentioned in their secession document

---

1046   *Ibid.*, Vol. III, Part 1, 21.

1047   Mitcham Jr., Samuel W., *It Wasn't About Slavery: Exposing the Great Lie of the Civil War* (Washington, DC: Regnery History, 2020), 100-101. Like too many conservatives they waited too long to realize they were being placed into political slavery. By 1861 the truth was the Constitution was a mere parchment barricade that could not protect "We the People" from the onslaught of an emotionally charged Yankee aggressor. In America's mass democracy, emotions trump facts, logic, and Constitutional principles.

Northern refusal to extradite Brown's men. It was evident that the Union was no longer a Union of mutual benefits and obligations but had become a Union of the Northern majority against the Southern minority. The Lower South was becoming restless, but Virginia was determined to seek, in good faith, a solution short of secession and war.

VIRGINIA OFFERS THE NORTH AN OLIVE BRANCH

The Lower South saw the handwriting on the wall with the election of Lincoln. Virginia and the other Upper South States held out hope for reconciliation or at least the avoidance of a bloody war between fellow countrymen. But the evidence was mounting that no solution other than a total submission of the South would be acceptable to the Republicans who now controlled the Federal Government. This, of course, confirmed the Lower South's decision to secede. But hope springs eternal and Virginia continued its efforts to find common ground with the North.

The US House of Representatives elected a Republican from New Jersey as Speaker of the House on February 1, 1861. With the conservative elements of the Lower South no longer in the House, it became obvious that the new and aggressive Republican Party would be the primary power in Congress. During this time Virginia was not idle. In January of 1861, the Legislature of Virginia called for a special convention to discuss possible secession from the Union. The election for delegates to the convention was held on February 4, 1861, with a three-to-one split between those wanting to remain in the Union while working for a solution and those who wanted immediate secession. Virginia's "secession" convention remained in session waiting impatiently for Lincoln to put into practice his peace and union plan. Virginian John B. Baldwin, a Union man was selected by the pro-Union men of the convention to go to Washington and secretly meet with Lincoln. On April 4th Baldwin met with Lincoln and urged him to call a conference of the States and to issue a "peaceful union proclamation" in line with Lincoln's broadly (but unofficial) proclaimed, "yearning for peace." Lincoln responded to Baldwin by declaring "I fear you are too late." Lincoln, despite his assurances of his peaceful intentions, had already sent several invasion fleets toward Fort Sumter and Fort Pickens.[1048] When Lincoln initiated war and demanded Virginia and other States send troops to support his invasion of the South, Virginia's convention voted 88 to 55 to secede. Baldwin voted against secession but signed the ordinance of secession.[1049] The most notable pro-Union Virginian at that time was John Tyler, the 10th President of the United States. As part of Virginia's Peace Commission, he went to Washington attempting to prevent war, but his efforts were rejected. Returning home, this Unionist voted for secession.[1050] Tyler, like Patrick Henry, believed in *"liberty* first, *union* second."

LINCOLN AND THE REPUBLICAN PARTY IMPOSED A PUPPET GOVERNMENT IN VIRGINIA

On May 9, 1865, President Johnson's cabinet recognized the Alexandria government in Virginia. This puppet state government was tacitly recognized previously to allow Lincoln the façade of legitimacy when he created the state of West Virginia. Lincoln's Virginia puppet government was needed to register Virginia's "consent" to the separation and establishment of West Virginia. In 1863, Virginia's puppet government "consented" to Lincoln's directive to transfer Jefferson and Berkeley counties to the new state.[1051] Even before the end of the War the four "Lincoln puppet States" of Louisiana, Arkansas, Tennessee, and Virginia were established and functioning.[1052] The façade of local self-government was needed to assure Lincoln and the Republican Party the electoral votes from the puppet States as well as to assure that these puppet States would send Republican Representatives

---

1048   See timeline of Lincoln's secret conspiracy to initiate war by forcing the South to fire the first shot in Chapter 32.

1049   Johnstone, H.W., *Truth of the War Conspiracy of 1861* (Wake Forest, NC: The Scuppernong Press, 2012), 23-4.

1050   Kennedy and Benson, *Lincoln, Marx, and the GOP* (Columbia, SC: Shotwell Publishing, 2023), 279.

1051   Henry, *The Story of Reconstruction*, 39.

1052   *Ibid.*, 54.

and Senators to Washington. These provisional Lincoln governors had all the titles of governor, but they were, in reality, Lincoln's puppets. After Lincoln's assassination, these States became puppets of the Republican Party. Even before the surrender at Appomattox, it was clear that under the new American government created by the Republican Party in Congress, States were now subordinate to the supreme Federal Government. In the post-War South "the provisional governors, despite their titles, were but subordinates of the President in his capacity as commander-in-chief of the Army.... The Army remained the real power."[1053] Military dictatorship was necessary to assure the dominance of "the party of the Union."

Virginia's Reconstruction Governor Francis Harrison Pierpont took a more liberal stance toward allowing former Confederates to vote in the state's elections. Even though he was a dedicated Unionist before, during, and after the War he nonetheless diverged from the punitive stance taken by other scallywag and carpetbag governors. He noted that "It is folly to suppose that a State could be governed under a republican form of government, wherein a large portion of the State, nineteen-twentieths of the people, are disfranchised and cannot hold office."[1054] He was not an advocate of restrictions to the right to vote such as the ironclad oath. Republicans in Congress used the ironclad oath to prohibit state elected officials from taking their seats in Congress if they were not pleasing to the Republican majority. For example, several Virginians such as A.H.H. Stuart, "whose work for reconciliation was outstanding, could not take the iron-clad oath."[1055] Pierpont's past radical opposition to the Confederacy did not shield him from the assaults of Radical Republicans. Virginia Republicans attacked him suggesting that "he had fallen under the influence of 'slave aristocracy.' Republicans in Washington claimed that neither the governor nor his state government were legitimate!"[1056] Governor Pierpont's liberal attitude toward reconciliation between

---

1053 *Ibid.*, 58.

1054 Governor Pierpont cited in Henry, *The Story of Reconstruction*, 56.

1055 Henry, *The Story of Reconstruction*, 112.

1056 *Ibid.*, 57.

Virginians who supported the Confederacy and Virginia's Unionists was used by Republicans in Congress as one of their numerous reasons against permitting "We the People" of the South to govern themselves.[1057] The Republican Party in Congress as well as at the local level, was opposed to the political theory of local self-government if it did not produce a government submissive to the Republican Party. The old expression that "there is no honor among thieves" could be modified for Active Reconstruction to "there is no honor among those attempting to destroy the Republic and replace it with an empire.'

Lincoln's assassination provided the Radical Republicans a golden opportunity to jettison Lincoln's moderate Reconstruction Plan and impose the Radical Republican Reconstruction Plan. This meant that even those puppet Southern States created by Lincoln were now targeted for removal. A few days after Lincoln's death former Union General Ben Butler—known in New Orleans as Beast Butler—proclaimed that "the time has not come for holding any relations with her (Virginia) but that of the conqueror to the conquered.[1058] On April 21, 1865, the *New York World* ridiculed Butler as "an unscrupulous general whose cowardice and incapacity always left his enemies unharmed upon the field."[1059] Virginia who had fought to prevent the War, was destined to receive her share of Republican vengeance. Her honored legislature where the likes of George Mason, James Madison, and Patrick Henry once stood would be reduced to a carnival of ignorance and corruption. In short order, Active Reconstruction was taken over by the Republican-controlled Congress. Virginia was placed under military dictatorship and assigned to Military District One, General John M. Schofield in command.

In Virginia's post-War, Republican-controlled legislature, arguments were frequently settled via fists fights; and in the Republican-led Southern State Constitutional Conventions the

---

1057   Ibid., 112.

1058   Bowers, *The Tragic Era*, 7.

1059   Ibid., 7, Author cites the *New York World*, 22 April 1865.

delegates, who had little land or property and therefore had little or no taxes to pay, were spending money—the taxpayers' money—like drunken sailors[1060] (with apologies to all sailors).

Hope For an Early End to Reconstruction Shattered

There was great hope in the South for an early end of Republican Reconstruction when word reached the South about President Grant's response to the conservative delegation from Virginia. The Virginians came to Washington hoping to overturn Virginia's Radical Republican Underwood Constitution. The Radical Underwood Constitution was named for the Radical Republican Federal Judge John C. Underwood (R-NY), who served as President of Virginia's Constitutional Convention that adopted the Radical state Constitution. The Underwood Constitution disfranchised all who could not take the Ironclad Oath. This oath required that before being registered to vote the individual must swear, that they never assisted the Confederacy.[1061] Meanwhile, the Underwood Constitution enfranchised illiterates who had never participated in a democratic government. President Grant listened sympathetically to the Virginia conservatives and concurred with the Virginians that the Underwood Constitution was a monstrosity. He understood that the Underwood Constitution would create a society in Virginia where those most prepared to serve in the state government would be excluded while forcing them under the rule of freed slaves who were not prepared to administer a democratic society. Grant agreed that all citizens in Virginia should be allowed to vote on the various elements of the Underwood Constitution. During the election, the Democrats and moderate Republicans worked together to nominate C.G. Walker for Governor. During the campaign for governor, Union General E.R.S. Canby shocked all by declaring that he was using his authority under the Reconstruction Acts and as a military ruler to exclude anyone elected to a state office who could not take the iron-clad oath. Grant ordered the Radical military dictator of Virginia to rescind his "order." With Grant's sympathetic help, the conservatives

---

1060   *Ibid.*, 217.

1061   This is not the exact wording, but it does reflect the oath's intent.

in Virginia elected their candidate, Walker, as governor of Virginia. For a moment it seemed that President Grant would be able to modify and control the Radical Republicans in Congress. But that hope was soon dashed.

A similar set of circumstances was occurring in Mississippi. The conservatives in Mississippi sought to nominate Judge Louis Dent as their candidate for governor. Judge Dent was President Grant's brother-in-law. At that time Dent was living with the President in Washington, DC. Judge Dent previously lived in Mississippi and had a network of friends in the state. But Grant refused to endorse his brother-in-law's candidacy. It now became clear that Grant's sympathy toward the South as expressed in the Virginia case was a mere momentary break between Grant and the Radicals. Grant's Virginia decision led the Radicals to make a vigorous stand against the President's leniency toward the conquered South. Grant's friends and foes in the media took a dim view of the entire Dent affair. In its August 16, 1869, edition the *New York World* lamented President Grant's decision stating that Dent "... would have been a less deplorably bad President than his brother-in-law." The *New York Herald* of the same date noted that the whole Dent affair "...puts the President's support of the extreme Radicals in a clear light as a mischievous step." Many have noted that the Dent affair sealed the President's loyalty to the program of Radical Republican Congressional Reconstruction.[1062]

FEDERAL JUDGE UNDERWOOD REAPPEARS IN VIRGINIA'S HISTORY

Judge Underwood who labored so hard to install the ironclad oath in Virginia to disfranchise former Confederates reappeared presiding over a very important Federal case. Unfortunately for the South, it was a case that would never go to trial. Judge John C. Underwood was the presiding Federal Judge at President Davis's arraignment. It is ironic that the Federal Judge in the Davis case was from New York and came down South, like so many Yankees, to take advantage of the opportunities there after the

---

1062 Bowers, *The Tragic Era*, 282.

war. Underwood was no stranger to Virginia. He came down to teach in a girls' school in Virginia and after marrying one of his students, (a scandal then and now) moved back to New York. He was appointed to his office in the "restored" state of Virginia when Alexandria, Virginia was the "restored" state capitol. "Restored" is better understood to mean a puppet state doing the bidding of its Yankee masters. While there he managed to use his office to confiscate the handsome home of a Confederate, he ordered it sold at public auction and then purchased it for himself at a fraction of the true value of the home. The Federal Supreme Court ultimately reversed the sale and declared the entire event as "a blot upon our jurisprudence and civilization."[1063]

VIRGINIA BECOMES A REPUBLICAN STATE UNDER SCALLYWAG AND CARPETBAG RULE

In short order, Radicals replaced moderates and took over Virginia's Republican Party. The Reverend James W. Hunnicutt, originally from South Carolina, became the leader of the Radical element in Virginia's Republican Party. His ability to switch sides according to the possibilities presented at the moment is demonstrated by the fact that he was originally a slaveholder and a vocal secessionist. After the War, he was the editor of the *New Nation*, a radical newspaper in Richmond. He was a leading participant in a Radical Republican convention in Richmond held on April 17, 1866, that established the Virginia Republican Party. Two hundred and ten delegates attended, of which one hundred and sixty were black delegates. Hunnicutt's radical appeals to the black delegates provoked distress among white Republican leaders in the North,[1064] but the New York *Times* celebrated by declaring "...he (Hunnicutt) and such as he, are unceasing in their endeavors to organize the blacks as a party *which shall hereafter control Southern affairs.*"[1065] Outsiders, people with a cultural background alien to native Virginians soon became the masters of

---

1063 Henry, *The Story of Reconstruction*, 241.

1064 *Ibid.*, 223.

1065 *Ibid.*, 224.

a once-free people. And just like today, those with alien ideas are the ones who are quoted, embraced, and politically supported by the political *status quo*.

John T. Trowbridge from New England was very critical of Virginia's planters who, post-War, no longer supported their former slaves. He came from a New England society where worn-out mill workers had no social security once they were no longer able to contribute profitable labor. Workers in New England, once they could no longer labor, were consigned to the scrap heap just like any other worn-out machine of Yankee industry and commerce. Yet he was indignant that Virginia planters were no longer supporting "old worn-out niggers."[1066] Trowbridge, with typical Yankee arrogance, believed that the South must be "regenerated by Northern ideas." Northern ideas destroyed the South and the possibility of a fair and mutually beneficial Southern society that "could have been." In the antebellum South, it was part of the slaveholders' moral and legal responsibility to provide for slaves too young, too old, or too ill to be productive. It was a form of social security in which those unable to work were provided food, housing, and healthcare. As one former mistress in Virginia commenting on the emancipation of her slaves put it, "Freedom! It is we who are freed. We belonged to our Negroes."[1067]

If left alone the South could have developed a post-slavery society in which similar social security would be provided by a network of kith and kin enforced first and foremost by moral standards and then the law. This is part of *what could have been* had the South been allowed to follow the high road to emancipation. But such ideas died with the advent of Lincoln's war and the Union's low road to emancipation. It was such a social and economic disaster that it led to the post-War development of debt peonage better known as sharecropping. According to Senator

---

1066   Ibid., 72.

1067   Ibid., 30.

James Eastland (D-Mississippi) and others, sharecropping was a new form of slavery.[1068]

Republican Plot To Keep The South Under Military Dictatorship

As previously described, Republicans and their sycophants in the media used the emotional appeal to Northerners regarding the alleged need to control evil white Southerners who were routinely killing innocent blacks and white Unionists. Yes, under the circumstances of the day, some violence was committed on both sides. Riots in the post-war South occurred in places such as Norfolk, Virginia on April 16, 1866. The riot in Norfolk developed as blacks were celebrating the passage of a Civil Rights Bill. The riot resulted in the deaths of two blacks and two whites. The occupying Yankee military investigated the origins of the riot. The Yankee military determined that both black and white citizens were at fault.[1069] However, the Republican Party was determined to use these instances of social unrest as an excuse to keep the South under Republican military rule.

The Republican-controlled Congress created a committee to find evidence of a South that was still in rebellion against the supreme Federal Government. The Radical Republican Committee of Fifteen in Congress held hearings to gain "proof" of a South still in rebellion. The Committee heard from one hundred and forty-four witnesses. From this carefully selected gaggle of witnesses, only 30 could be considered even remotely unbiased toward the conquered Southern provinces. Many of those who testified against the South, accusing or implying a rebellious and un-loyal spirit running rampant across the South, were men whose political future depended on the continuation of Congressional control of the South. Of the twelve witnesses from North Carolina, testifying on the conditions in North Carolina, only one was a native of the state. General Robert E. Lee appeared and assured the Committee

---

1068 Senator Eastland cited in Kennedy & Kennedy, *Punished With Poverty-The Suffering South* 2nd ed. , 198.

1069 Henry, Robert Selph, *The Story of Reconstruction*, 180-1.

that "so far as I know the feelings of the people of Virginia, they want peace." His testimony was countered by Northerners who had come to Virginia after the war. These carpetbaggers claimed that Virginians were hostile toward the new Federal Government, blacks, and local Unionists. They claimed that retribution would be taken against the blacks and Unionists if the Federal Government removed troops from the state. The Republican Party needed emotional stories, real or imagined, about "rebel outrages" down South as an excuse to keep the South under Yankee military dictatorship. Without the use or threat of bloody Yankee bayonets, the Republican Party could not dominate the South and hold its political control of the newly established Yankee Empire in Washington.

Resistance Movement in Virginia

Postmodern academics and other "historians" typically look to the actual or alleged violence committed by the Klan as the South's reaction to Reconstruction. But in Virginia as we have noted in other Southern States the primary effort was in the realm of the political battle. In the political battle, it served the interest of the Southern resistance movement to keep tales of violence to a minimum. Vigilantes such as the Klan did have an impact on the efforts to redeem state governments but, at times, they were the source of problems for Southerners trying to peacefully gain political control of their state.

Mrs. Myrta Lockett Avary (1857-1946) of Virginia and author of *A Virginia Girl in the Civil War* and other books explained the rise of the Klan, "Northerners and Southerners who did not live in that day and in black belts can form no conception of the conditions which gave rise to the white secret societies of which the most widely celebrated is the Ku Klux."[1070] Once law and order was restored the original Klan was no longer needed and was ordered to disperse, its records and regalia destroyed. Unfortunately, there were, and still are, many counterfeit Klans that emerged at different times falsely claiming to be a continuation of the original Klan.

1070   Avary cited in Henry, *The Story of Reconstruction*, 234.

In Virginia, as in other Southern States, the resistance movement centered around gaining political influence and eventual control of their local and state governments. Active Reconstruction died a slow death in Virginia. Postmodern "intellectuals" and "historians" claim that Reconstruction ended in Virginia when President Grant signed an act readmitting Virginia to the post-War Union on January 26, 1870.[1071] But this assumes that the new Union was a legitimate government based upon the free and unfettered consent of the governed. This of course was not the case.

Virginia and the rest of the South would enter Passive Reconstruction with no political weapon sufficient to overthrow the radical change from a Republic of Sovereign States to an Empire—an Empire the Republican Party and Northern ruling elites so craftily engineered. Virginia's hallowed monuments so proudly erected during Passive Reconstruction would come tumbling down during Moder Era Reconstruction. This is the fate of liberty when a people are not psychologically equipped to mount an effective resistance movement. Virginia and the South suffered because they lacked audacious leaders willing to fearlessly challenge the Yankee Empire's illegitimate political *status quo*. By winking at the unconstitutional and illegitimate origins of the current political *status quo* the South allowed America's Federal Government to become a centralized tyranny that could do anything it wanted regardless of the wording in that parchment document known as the original Constitution. "We the People" of the South and the Nation are punished with Federal tyranny. "And I for winking at your discords too have lost a brace of kinsmen. All are punished."[1072] Evil wins when good men do nothing.

1071 "Reconstruction in Virginia," The Library of Virginia (lva-virginia.libguides.com) www.bit.ly/VA-Reconstruction (Accessed 25 September 2023).

1072 The Prince in Act 5, Scene 3, in Shakespeare's *The Tragedy of Romeo and Juliet*.

Chapter 28:

WEST VIRGINIA—THE HYPOCRISY OF RECONSTRUCTING A LOYAL STATE

"Those [Confederates veterans] from West Virginia...in time mainly accepted citizenship in the new State born in the throes of war, and after enduring the hardships and persecution which followed their home-coming, and the annoyances of adverse legislation, resumed the stations to which their worth entitled them."
—Colonel Robert White[1073]

WEST VIRGINIA is unique in its origin as a state. It was carved out of counties in the State of Virginia. It is not unusual in the United States's early history to have new States carved out of existing States. Alabama was once part of the Mississippi territory but when Mississippi became a state, it set the stage for the territory of Alabama to become a state. However, West Virginia emerged on the political stage because of secession and Lincoln's war.

"Forty western counties of Virginia agreed to secede and form a new state without the consent of the old one!"[1074] It was done with the aid of Lincoln and his Republican government but in direct violation of the Constitution. The Constitution was quickly being

---

1073 Colonel Robert White, "West Virginia," *Confederate Military History*, Vol. II, Part 2 (1899, Harrisburg, PA: The Archives Society, 1994), 104.

1074 "West Virginia," *Confederate Military History*, Vol. II, Part 2, 3.

relegated to an artifact of the past by Lincoln and his Republican Party. Republican Thaddeus Stevens was clear about it when he boastfully proclaimed, "We know it is not constitutional, but it is necessary."[1075] A large portion of the people of what was to become West Virginia threw their lot in with Lincoln and the Republican Party. But as we shall see they were never accepted as equals. They and their descendants suffered the poverty imposed upon the rest of the post-War South. There has always been a greater sense of "kith and kin" between the people of West Virginia and the rest of the South than ever existed between West Virginia's people and the people of the North. This is documented in the last pages of this chapter.

The forced division of Virginia was not endorsed by all of Lincoln's Cabinet. Lincoln's Attorney General, Bates objected. Edward Bates was born in Belmont, Virginia, in 1793. In 1814 he moved to Missouri where he practiced law and was eventually elected to represent Missouri in the US House of Representatives. He served as Lincoln's Attorney General from 1861 to 1864. After his resignation, he returned to Missouri.[1076] Perhaps his Southern roots had an impact on his attitude regarding the Constitution's requirements for forming a new state out of an existing state. Lincoln's Attorney General boldly declared:

> The formation of a new State out of western Virginia is an original, independent act of revolution. Any attempt to carry it out involves a plain breach of both the constitutions of Virginia and the nation.[1077]

The first vote for the division of Virginia and the creation of West Virginia was voted down in the Senate.[1078] Lincoln's

---

1075 Stevens cited in "West Virginia," *Confederate Military History*, Vol. II, Part 2, 3.

1076 "Attorney General: Edward Bates," The US Department of Justice (justice.gov) www.justice.gov/ag/bio/bates-edward (23 September 2023).

1077 Attorney General Bates cited "West Virginia," *Confederate Military History*, Vol. II, Part 2, 12.

1078 "West Virginia," *Confederate Military History*, Vol. II, Part 2, 12.

Administration kept the pressure on and eventually, they were successful. But regardless of its origins and as will be demonstrated by historical facts, West Virginia is Southern.

> The Old Dominion [Virginia] which had voluntarily donated the vast Northwest to the Union and dedicated it to the use of white labor, was cloven by the hand it had nurtured into strength. Yet Virginia and all the South hail West Virginia and rejoice in its progress as one of the States of the Union, notwithstanding the nature of its origin.[1079]

WEST VIRGINIA—
THE LAST SLAVE STATE ADMITTED TO THE UNION

In late May of 1861 General George B. McClellan commanding the Federal Department of Ohio proclaimed to the people of western Virginia that he was bringing Federal troops into their counties to protect public property from efforts of "rebels" to destroy property, especially rebel efforts to ruin "your magnificent railways." He ordered his troops into their counties but "He pledged...not only to non-interference with slaves, but an 'iron hand to crush' any servile [slave] insurrection."[1080]

From McClellan's proclamation we can conclude that (1) it was well known in the Lincoln Administration that these counties and future state would come into the Union as a slave state and (2) even in areas where slaves were less numerous than in the Lower South, there was still fear of a slave uprising. The first conclusion argues against the Yankee propagandist assertion that the War was fought by the North to free the slaves. Lincoln is recorded in history (a history well hidden by postmodern "intellectuals" i.e., the Yankee Empire's propagandists) as the last President whose administration worked to admit a slave state to the Union. The second conclusion is that the Lower South was justified in its fear

---

1079 Colonel Robert White cited in "West Virginia," *Confederate Military History*, Vol. II, Part 2, 3.

1080 "West Virginia," *Confederate Military History*, Vol. II, Part 2, 14.

of a massive slave revolt and was therefore justified in seceding from a Union in which the ruling political party's leadership and influencers were promoting a slave insurrection down South.

Slavery was a factor in West Virginia's society, but it was not the major concern of the people of the new state. George H. Moffett, Parkersburg, W. Virginia, relates a story illustrating the bond of friendship between black and white Southerners during the War. In late 1864 while Moffett was a POW in Fort Delaware a black civilian was brought into the POW prison. When asked why he was being imprisoned the black man explained that while walking near his home he was approached by Yankee cavalry. They demanded information about the position of Lee's Army. He refused to provide them with information, so they arrested him for non-compliance. One day he was taken to the Federal officer's office and offered his freedom if he would pledge allegiance to the United States. The slave refused because that was something his master would not do, and he would not bring shame upon the family. They sent him back to prison where, six weeks later, he died.[1081]

Lincoln wanted to create the new state of West Virginia because it would assure him of more electoral votes in his re-election bid. But the Republican-controlled Congress had a problem with bringing a slave state into *their* Union. Senator Charles Summer of Massachusetts insisted upon an emancipation clause in the Bill in Congress creating the state of West Virginia. Senator John S. Carlile from Virginia[1082] generally opposed the separation of the western counties from Virginia. He suggested that a popular vote be taken on the matter. Eventually, a compromise was established in which gradual emancipation would be allowed. "Therefore, West

---

1081 *Confederate Veteran* Vol. XIV , No. 12, Dec. 1906. Republished in *The Confederate Veteran Magazine* Vol. XIV (Harrisburg, PA: The National Historical Society, 1987), 547-8.

1082 Senator Carlile, a strong Unionist, "represented" the restored government of Virginia that was recognized by Lincoln as the puppet government. It was Lincoln's first effort to establish puppet governments in Southern States so that he and the Republican Party would then control.

Virginia became the last slave state to enter the union. In February 1865, Governor Arthur I. Boreman signed an act officially freeing all slaves."[1083]

The Lincoln administration jumped through several hoops to create the new Union-friendly state of West Virginia. On May 9, 1861, his cabinet recognized the puppet Virginia government with its capital at Alexandria, Virginia. It was necessary to have a puppet government in Virginia to "consent" to the secession of the western counties of Virginia and the formation of a new state. Approximately twenty-seven counties participated in a convention in Wheeling May 13-15, 1861. This 'rump' government claimed to represent all of Virginia. They drafted a new Virginia Constitution and sent delegates to the Congress in Washington.

A second Wheeling convention met in June 1861. Though more counties were represented at this convention, there were still many counties in the future state which were not represented. Before they began their official business all delegates were required to take "an oath of supreme allegiance to the United States."Before Lincoln's war Americans were citizens of their respective sovereign state and were never required to take an oath to the United States. As a citizen of one of the States of these United States, their loyalty was always to the compound Republic, these United States of America, of which their State was a member. Citizens owed their allegiance to that state and if that state remained in the Union, the state owed its allegiance to the United States. Extreme caution should be taken when swearing allegiance to any earthly authority or government. As Founding Father James Iredell of North Carolina warned, no oath of allegiance to a prince is binding if it is "not consistent with the safety and liberties of the people."The swearing of allegiance to the supreme Federal Government was never required before Lincoln's war and the Republican Party's Active Reconstruction. Yet Virginia's Convention began only after everyone swore allegiance to the Federal Government.

[1083] "A Brief History of African Americans in West Virginia," West Virginia Archives & History (archive.wvculture.org) www.bit.ly/WV_African-Americans (23 September 2023).

This convention unanimously elected Francis Harrison Pierpont provisional governor on June 20, 1861. Pierpont, as discussed in the previous chapter, made it known that he did not intend to divide Virginia. Many delegates, however, thought the people of the western counties should have a vote on secession. Congress and President Lincoln were quick to recognize this government as the legitimate government of Virginia and seat the two senators it sent to Washington. The convention adjourned on June 25, 1861.

The Convention reconvened on August 20 and called for a vote by the citizens on the question of forming a new state, making provision for a constitutional convention upon a favorable vote. The vote on statehood was not representative of the will of the people. Many counties did not vote at all. Turnout was low, and soldiers were stationed at polls to make sure only 'loyal citizens voted. These 'loyal' citizens included many of the soldiers. So much for government by 'consent of the governed.' The 'Panhandle' counties had the heaviest turnout. The 'majority' voted for the creation of a new state. The state Constitutional Convention met on November 26, 1861, and by February 1862 had a constitution which was submitted to the 'qualified' voters and passed in a special election on May 3, 1862.

At the election of May 3, 1862, Pierpont was also elected "governor of Virginia," to fill the "unexpired" term of Governor Letcher, and he continued to administer the affairs of the Trans-Alleghany until the new State was established, when he removed his "seat" of government to Alexandria, Virginia.

A bill to form West Virginia was introduced in the United States Senate in May 1862. Lincoln signed off on the new state on December 31, 1862, and the date for admission was set for June 20, 1863. In 1863, the puppet Virginia state government also "consented" to the transfer of Jefferson and Berkeley counties to West Virginia.

West Virginia's first elected governor was Republican Arthur Ingraham Boreman who served from 1863 to 1869. He was born in Pennsylvania but moved to Parkersburg, Virginia—now in West Virginia. As a pro-Union delegate to Virginia's Secession Convention, he voted with the majority to remain in the Union. After Virginia seceded from the Union, he maintained his anti-secession stance and worked with fellow believers in western Virginia. He was elected President of the Second Wheeling Convention in 1861 which voted to establish a separate state consisting of the counties of western Virginia.

Once the new state was created, Republicans in Congress and West Virginia insisted that a state constitutional amendment be submitted to the State's voters and passed to disenfranchise all those who had provided "voluntary aid or assistance to the rebellion." This new amendment was very controversial, and a direct violation of Article I, Section 9 prohibiting *ex post facto* laws, and the prohibition on creating new States out of existing States in Article IV, Section 3 of the US Constitution—but at that point the Constitution was meaningless unless it could be manipulated to advance the North's ruling elites' agenda. The Republicans were afraid that the disenfranchisement amendment would not pass the popular vote. In other words, Republicans were fearful that the people of West Virginia would not sign on to the Republican Party's punitive attitude toward their fellow Southerners. To assure their victory, they prohibited anyone from voting who would be disenfranchised by the amendment if it passed the election! As in Missouri, the disenfranchisement amendment became law before it was voted on! The disenfranchisement amendment passed by only seven thousand votes out of thirty-seven thousand votes cast. This was an early indication of the conservative nature of the majority of West Virginia's citizens.

Did The North Treat West Virginia as a Northern or Southern State Post-War?

Post-War the victors treated the occupied South as a colony.[1084] The victorious North actively exploited the South's natural resources while exploiting cheap Southern labor.[1085] The coal miners of West Virginia suffered impoverishment like the sharecroppers in the former Confederacy.

> Mining in the Appalachian Highlands...the miner became dependent upon the operators for everything he ate and wore, and for the shack in which he lived. In a majority of the communities, few miners ever saw much cash money from one year's end to the next.[1086]

Economically, it appears that post-War West Virginia was treated as a second-class state in the new Union. But what about today? Is West Virginia's economy closer to the victor's States up North or is it closer to the conquered States of the South? The two Southern States that have been stuck at the bottom of America's economy since the War are Mississippi and Arkansas. The National Mean (average) Family Income for 2020 was $126,500.00.[1087] The average household income for Arkansas in 2021 was $73,346, for Mississippi it was $68,636, and for West Virginia, it was $69,436.[1088] It would appear that West Virginia's natural resources and its "cheap" labor force have been exploited just like the rest of the Yankee Empire's Southern colony.

1084   Clark & Kirwan, *The South Since Appomattox*, 91.

1085   See Chapter 9, "Post-War Economic Exploitation of the South," in Kennedy & Kennedy, *Punished With Poverty-The Suffering South* 2nd edition (Columbia, SC: Shotwell Publishing, 2020), 103-112.

1086   Clark & Kirwan, *The South Since Appomattox*, 155.

1087   "Mean Family Income in the United States," Fred Economic Data (fred.stlouisfed.org) www.bit.ly/MeanFI-US (Accessed 23 September 2023).

1088   All state data from "Income By Zip Code," www.incomebyzipcode.com (Accessed 23 September 2023).

But the South has traditionally been more in-tune with enjoying family and spiritual matters as opposed to Northerners who tend to concentrate on material things. How does church attendance in West Virginia compare with church attendance in Northern and Southern States? Is church attendance in West Virginia closer to the attendance patterns of the North or South? Church attendance is not the only marker for spiritual people as opposed to materialist people, but it does serve as a good indicator. Modern scholars have noted that Northerners tend to be more materialistic than Southerners. "The values of Southerners and Yankees, like those of Celts and Englishmen, were not just different—they were antagonistic."[1089] The value assessment is very different between the two groups. It is not surprising that the term "Almighty dollar" originated from New England.

Percent of the population attending Church at least once a week:[1090]

State	Percent
Mississippi	49%
West Virginia	46%
Louisiana	46%
Texas	42%
Arkansas	41%
Florida	35%
Nationally	30%

Again, it appears that West Virginia is closer to her Southern sister States than to the national average. Note: the national average is as high as it is because of the high numbers for the Southern States plus Utah. If you remove the Southern States from the

---

1089 McWhiney, Dr. Grady, *Cracker Culture: Celtic Ways in the Old South* (Tuscaloosa, AL: The University of Alabama Press, 1988), 245.

1090 "Attendance at religious services by state," Pew Research Center (wresearch.org) https://pewrsr.ch/3TE3Gby (Accessed 23 September 2023); Jones, Jeffrey M., "US Church Attendance Still Lower Than Pre-Pandemic," Gallop (news.gallup.com), 26 June 2023, www.bit.ly/church-attendance_post-covid (Accessed 23 September 2023).

national average, then the national (Yankee States) average would be below 30%. The Southern Bible Belt is very important in maintaining America's Christian moral values.[1091]

While West Virginia did not secede from the Union and her people at that time were more Unionist than those in other Border States, they nonetheless were treated the same as the rest of the South post-War. West Virginia may have been spared the horrors of Active Reconstruction but she with her sister Southern States have been forced into enduring Passive Reconstruction and Modern Era Reconstruction. A poll commissioned by the National Sons of Confederate Veterans and conducted by Kaplan Strategies documented that West Virginians supported traditional American values including Southern values and heroes in numbers very similar to her Southern neighbors.

1091 As explained in Kennedy, James Ronald, *Be Ye Separate: Bible Belt Revival or Marxist Revolution*. Free downloadable copy available at: www.bit.ly/Free-Download_BYS.

Chapter 29:

PASSIVE RECONSTRUCTION, THE GILDED AGE, AND THE PROGRESSIVE ERA

"Louisianians [and all Southerners] were victims of the psychological retrogression into which the South lapsed after the Civil War: The South was poor, and in certain areas, such as education, Southerners simply had to be content with second or third best." —T. Harry Williams[1092]

WHILE THE SOUTH was forced into poverty during the era of Passive Reconstruction (1877-1965) the North was enjoying a time of opulence for the ruling elite and their cronies. The years from 1870 to 1900 were a time in the North known as the Gilded Age or the Age of Robber Barrons. This era of enormous Northern economic growth, 1870 to 1900, was also the time in which political policies and laws were enacted to increase the power of the central government. Politically it was known as the Progressive Era. While this was taking place in the North, the South was struggling to come to terms with the new form of federal and state governments and the economic and social conditions imposed upon "We the People" of the South by its conquering Northern masters.

When the last Yankee troops were removed from the South in 1877, they took with them their massed bloody bayonets, but they did *not* take away the heavy hand of Yankee control and

---

1092 Williams, Dr. T. Harry, *Huey Long* (1961, New York: Random House, 1981), 493.

domination. They left in place puppet state governments organized under bayonet constitutions. Both state and national constitutions were created under the threat of bloody Yankee bayonets—which voids the American principle of "the consent of the governed." As Yankee troops exited the South, they left "We the People" of Dixie under the rule of an unconstitutional, illegitimate supreme Federal Government. It was and is a national government created by Lincoln's war and the Republican Party's Active Reconstruction. This new American government was created in violation of America's founding principle that legitimate governments are based upon the free and unfettered consent of "We the People." Across the South, the joy of seeing Yankee troops leaving their States and being allowed the *semblance* of self-government clouded the understanding of what happened to America's once-free Republic of Sovereign States. Without realizing it Southerners exchanged Active Reconstruction for Passive Reconstruction. Unlike Active Reconstruction, no Southern resistance movement was active during Passive Reconstruction. Without protest, Southerners accepted the fact that America's once Sovereign States had become mere provinces of a central government controlled by Northern ruling elites. The South became a colonial appendage of the central government, and that central government, flush with victory in its imperialistic war against the South, slowly began to morph into an international imperialistic power.[1093] In the meantime, the South was mired in poverty. It was poverty intentionally inflicted upon "We the People" of the South by the North as punishment for daring to leave "their" Union.[1094] The North gave the world another example that empires are indivisible and once they begin forcefully acquiring new territory, they never cease their expansion. After a successful conquest, empires will immediately begin searching the globe for new territories to conquer or control. The post-War Yankee Empire was no different.

1093 See Kennedy & Kennedy, *Yankee Empire: Aggressive Abroad and Despotic at Home* (Columbia, SC: Shotwell Publishing, 2018).

1094 See Kennedy & Kennedy, *Punished With Poverty-The Suffering South* 2nd ed. (Columbia, SC: Shotwell Publishing, 2020).

OVER-EVALUATION OF THE SOUTH'S REDEEMED STATE GOVERNMENTS

When the Southern States seceded from the Union, they did so because they understood that they were merely exercising a right announced in the Declaration of Independence and ingrained in the original Constitution.[1095] In 1861 they were following the example of their 1776 grandfathers. Their grandfathers seceded from an oppressive central government in 1776 and acted "to institute new Government, laying its foundation on such principles and organizing its powers in such form, as to *them* shall seem most likely to affect *their* Safety and Happiness."[1096] Their failure to maintain the independence of their Confederate government against the overwhelming power of the Yankee Empire did not cause them to reconsider the righteousness of that Cause. (A fact that greatly angered many post-War Yankees and still angers Woke Yankees and Southern scallywags today). But psychologically their failure in war caused Southerners to over-emphasize their "victory" in the efforts to redeem their States during Active Reconstruction. The defeated people of the South knew that their cause was right and needed a victory of sorts to redeem their sense of honor and wipe away the shame of defeat. Thus, too many Southerners looked to the redemption of their States as a post-War victory and became patriotically attached to their new puppet state government and, therefore, patriotically attached to the puppet state's central governmental master in Washington, DC. For generations, they would swear allegiance to this new nation asserting in vain repetition that it was a nation "indivisible with liberty and justice for all." Yet, they never dared to acknowledge the evidence that "We the People" of the South were violently denied our "liberty" and post-War "justice" was

---

1095 Kennedy & Kennedy, *The South Was Right!* 3rd ed. (Columbia, SC: Shotwell Publishing Co., 2020), 209-232.

1096 From *The Declaration of Independence* as enacted by the Second Continental Congress on July 4, 1776. Note emphasis added to "them" and "their" in the quote. The thirteen American Colonies sought no permission from the central government but took action to secure *their* safety and happiness. All thirteen colonies were slave-holding colonies, but chattel slavery did not negate their right to establish free and independent governments. The South was right in 1861 because the American Colonies were right in 1776.

available only to those who agreed with and obeyed the North's ruling elites. Such refusal to acknowledge clear evidence remains today in Woke America and the pacified South.

This overestimation of the removal of carpetbag and scalawag rule during Active Reconstruction was a major factor in the South's fourth strategic failure—the failure to continue the struggle for Southern independence after the end of Active Reconstruction.[1097] The fighting South became the impoverished, meek, docile, and pacified South. The pacified South dutifully remained on its assigned "stools of everlasting repentance." As such it allowed the victor to exterminate the South's political power or influence in the new national government. It prevented the emergence of a resistance movement dedicated to reclaiming America's original Republic of Sovereign States in which real States' Rights, inclusive of the rights of state nullification and secession, were available to enforce the limitations on Federal authority enshrined in the original Constitution. This failure resulted in the twentieth-century failures of conservative efforts to defend the Constitution and limit Federalism, making Deep State Federal tyranny a reality.

SOUTHERN ECONOMIC AND POLITICAL POVERTY

The victorious North, seeking vengeance and economic gain, intentionally imposed poverty upon the South. President Johnson declared that Southerners who supported the Confederacy were traitors and "traitors must be impoverished."[1098] Unitarian minister Thomas W. Higginson from Rhode Island bluntly declared, "Every secessionist...has received as the penalty of defeat only

---

[1097] The mere threat of another secession movement, not only in the South but in other conservative States, could have been (and still could be) used as a bargaining lever to force the restoration of America's original and legitimate Republic of Sovereign States. The South needed men like the Irish freedom fighter Charles Stewart Parnell but all we got were compromisers and appeasers like Neville Chamberlain! Two things are certain if you are willing to accept a bad political situation: (1) The bad situation will never get better, and (2) over time the bad situation will become unbearable. *Welcome to Woke America!*

[1098] President Johnson cited Fleming, Walter Lynwood, *The Sequel of Appomattox* (1919, Yale University Press, 1970), 73.

poverty."[1099] From the Northern victor's point-of-view the defeated and defenseless South deserved poverty[1100] and its few remaining resources were free for the taking. As already pointed out, post-War the South became an economic colony of the North. The South could have overcome its economic poverty if it had strong and audacious political leadership, but such leadership—political and social—did not exist. The results are evident today. The South was once America's richest section but today more than a century and a half after the War, the South remains the poorest section in this "one nation indivisible with liberty and justice for all." But greater than the South's economic poverty was the South's lack of visionary political leaders. The post-War South needed a Charles Stewart Parnell (leader of the Irish Home Rule movement) or a Mahatma Gandhi (leader of India's struggle for independence) but what the South got was pacified, pragmatic, party politicians. As Southern author John Crowe Ransom lamented in the late 1920s:

> But what pitiful service have the inept Southern politicians for many years been rendering to the cause! Their Southern loyalty at Washington has rarely had any more imaginative manifestation than to scramble vigorously for a Southern share in the federal pie. They will have to be miraculously enlightened.[1101]

It is essential to point out that after the end of Active Reconstruction, the South did not need to start a new movement to secede, but it did need to keep the *option* of secession valid and available. "The South shall rise again" should have been more than a prayerful joke. Often the mere threat of a valid secession movement is enough to compel an oppressive central government to relent in

---

1099 Higginson, "Some War Scenes Revisited," *A Just and Lasting Peace: A Documentary History of Reconstruction*, ed., John David Smith (New York: Signet Classics, 2013), 527.

1100 The desire to punish the South with poverty was expressed at the beginning of the war. A Northern newspaper gave expression to this hatred of the South: "We mean to conquer them, Subjugate them… Never would traitors be permitted to 'return to peaceful and contented homes;' instead, they 'must find poverty at their firesides, and see privation in the anxious eyes of mothers and the rags of children.'" As cited in, Simkins, Francis Butler, *A History of the South* (New York: Alfred A. Knopf), 219.

1101 John Crowe Ransom, "Reconstructed But Unregenerate," *I'll Take My Stand*, (1930, Baton Rouge, LA: LSU Press, 1983), 26.

its oppression and compromise with the oppressed people who are boldly standing up for their rights. Keeping the option of secession open would encourage the occupied Southern people to develop an attitude that the political *status quo* established by Lincoln's war and Republican Active Reconstruction was an illegitimate government. Southerners would look upon the unconstitutional government as one that did not deserve their *unquestioned* allegiance. This attitude alone would assure the ultimate freedom and liberty for "We the People" of the South and all Americans.[1102] This attitude of peaceful non-acceptance of an oppressive government was explained by Mahatma Gandhi's biographer.

By 1930, automatic Indian obedience to British fiat was a thing of the past. Imperceptibly, in 1928, 1929, and 1930, unknown even to themselves, and scarcely noticed by outsiders, Indians became free men. The body still wore shackles; but the spirit had escaped from prison. Gandhi had turned the key. No general directing armies against an enemy ever moved with more consummate skill than the saint armed with righteousness as his shield and a moral cause as his spear.[1103]

The attitude of peaceful but unequivocal and unending resistance to tyranny was something that men such as Parnell, Gandhi, and the leaders of the Baltic States in the late twentieth century intuitively understood.[1104] Unfortunately, pacified Southern leaders never conceived of such an audacious strategy.

The South's post-War leaders were military men who viewed the struggle for Southern independence through the prism of a military struggle. They and the Southern people were exhausted by war and were determined, at all costs, to avoid a repeat of war and the re-imposition of Active Reconstruction. In their military thinking,

---

1102 "The cause of the South is now the cause of all," former Confederate Vice President Alexander Stephens.

1103 Fischer, Lewis, *The Life of Mahatma Gandhi* (New York: Harper & Row, Publishers, 1950), 252.

1104 See Chapter 9, "Lessons Learned: Successful Non-Violent Independence Movements" in Kennedy, James Ronald, *Dixie Rising-Rules for Rebels*, 2nd ed. (Columbia, SC: Shotwell Publishing, 2021), 103-15.

independence could only be obtained by war, and to them, that effort was a lost cause.[1105] The sons of those Confederate veterans suffered from the same political and social malady. They and their descendants were (and still are) unable to imagine any resistance movement that could peacefully reclaim America's lost Republic of Sovereign States. Therefore, they were (and are) satisfied with making the best out of a bad situation. This is the mental attitude of people trapped on reservations, in Gulags, or in concentration camps. It is the essence of the South's fourth strategic failure—the failure to continue the struggle for Southern independence after the end of Active Reconstruction. As President Davis said, "But the principle for which we contended is bound to reassert itself, though it may be at another time and in another form." [1106]

NORTHERN PROSPERITY—THE GILDED AGE AND ROBBER BARONS—THE RULE OF MONEY

Mark Twain, a Southerner from Missouri, coined the term "the Gilded Age" in his 1873 novel *The Gilded Age: A Tale of Today*. The Gilded Age,[1107] 1870 to 1900, covers the first third of the era of Passive Reconstruction. The Gilded Age was a time in American history in which Northern industrialists and financiers created vast fortunes for themselves and their families. While "We the People" of the South were enduring poverty the Northern elites and their cronies were enjoying an age of opulence. The so-called "Captains of Industry" or "Robber Barons" created, inflation-adjusted, wealth greater than the wealth of tech giants of today. The wealth

---

1105 Southern independence should be conceived as a return to America's original Republic of Sovereign States where the Constitution is enforced by "We the People" via state nullification or, if necessary, secession. Secession may not be necessary, but the valid threat of secession **is necessary** if you desire to meet the enemy and "negotiate a better deal."

1106 President Jefferson Davis cited in Pollard, E.A., *Southern History of the War* (1866, Crown Publishers Inc., 1977), Vol. II , 582.

1107 Mark Twain's labeling this era as being "gilded" is an expression of looking rich and important but lacking in refinement and riches. The "gilding" procedure is the act of placing gold over base metal. While looking very rich, i.e., gold, it is a thin veneer of richness over less valuable metal. This is a wonderful expression of what these United States became after the destruction of the Original Constitutionally limited Federal Government—a thin veneer of freedom that covers Federal tyranny.

of today's tech giants such as Gates, Musk, Zuckerberg, and Bezos are overshadowed by Robber Barons such as Rockefeller, Morgan, Vanderbilt, and Carnegie. Modern-day historians and economists brag about the economic advancement made during the Gilded Age as if the South did not exist. Yes, the North had a dynamic and growing economy, but the South was mired in an intentionally imposed poverty that continues to this day.

With wealth comes power, especially political power. The rich elites of the second half of the nineteenth century consisted of Northern industrialists and financiers. Lincoln's war and the Republican Party's Active Reconstruction created an American government that was greatly influenced and eventually controlled by monied interests.[1108] In this new American government lobbyists hired by monied interests would exert more influence on America's elected Representatives and Senators than "We the People." Plutocracy[1109] is a government in which money rules and during the Gilded Age America was becoming a nation in which "money talks and BS walks."

Robber Barons were experts in using questionable techniques to eliminate their actual or potential competitors. Free and open competition is the key to a free market economy—otherwise the economy will evolve into a form of national socialism. The elimination of potential competition hit the impoverished South the hardest. Elimination of competition increases the cost of goods and services for the consumer. Such increases hit the poor who have limited disposable income the hardest and "We the People" of the South were among America's poorest. It also makes it difficult for the development of local industries that tend to enrich the local population.

1108 For example, opinion polls demonstrate that most Americans want the Federal Government to control our open borders but politicians in Washington respond not to "We the People" but to the Chambers of Commerce and other business interests who want cheap labor. In America's plutocracy, money trumps "We the People."

1109 Plutocracy: An elite or ruling class of people whose power derives from their wealth.

An economic panic created by Wall Street in 1907 was used by Northern financiers and industrialists to acquire emerging Southern iron and steel industries in Tennessee and Alabama. On November 2, 1907 "Robber Baron" J.P. Morgan acquired the Tennessee Coal, Iron, and Railroad Company and later added the Moore and Schley Steel Company of Birmingham, Alabama. The otherwise "Trust Busting," President, Theodore Roosevelt, agreed to the purchase and instructed his Attorney General not to interfere with the purchase/merger.[1110] The purchase of struggling Southern iron and steel industries prevented the development of competition for Northern iron and steel industries and put Southern industries under eastern control.[1111] These Southern industries were "struggling" due to a chronic lack of investment capital—by 1907 the struggle was over and so was the opportunity to develop Southern iron and steel industries on a par with those in the North.

In a letter requesting a report on the economic conditions in the South dated July 5, 1938, President Franklin D. Roosevelt acknowledged the dire economic conditions then existing in the South. He noted,

> It is an *unbalance* that can and must be righted, for the sake of the South and of the Nation. Without going into the long history of how this situation came to be—the long and ironic *history of the despoiling* of this truly American section of the country's population—suffice it for the immediate purpose to get a clear perspective of the task that is presented to us...a population still holding the great *heritages of King's Mountain and Shiloh* — the problems presented by the South's capital resources and the *absentee ownership of those resources*, and

---

1110   Clark & Kirwan, *The South Since Appomattox* (New York: Oxford University Press, 1967), 159.

1111   *Ibid.*, 160.

problems growing out of the new industrial era and, again, of *absentee ownership of the new industries* [emphasis added by author].¹¹¹²

The Yankee Empire's President was unwilling to acknowledge that the reason for Southern poverty was not a lack of human capital or natural resources but a lack of self-government in the occupied States of the conquered Confederate States of America. Self-government would have prevented Northern exploitation of Southern resources and the "absentee ownership" of Southern resources and industry. The Federal Government even refused to release a report prepared in January 1935 by an attorney from the Federal Agricultural Adjustment Administration that documented the increased evictions of sharecropper families due to Federal legislation (Agricultural Adjustment Act).¹¹¹³ Roosevelt and the Yankee Empire's elites knew that Southern politicians could be easily bought off thereby providing Roosevelt and the Empire's ruling elite political "cover." Socialist Norman Thomas lamented the fact that:

> He [President Roosevelt] seems more interested in the labor problems of Pennsylvania where he needs their votes, than in the South, where he does not need the votes of the laboring man.¹¹¹⁴

The South's politicians assured the National Democrats that the Democrats would automatically get the votes from the "Solid South." During Passive Reconstruction, the Democratic Party received votes from the Solid South, but the South got nothing in return for this bloc of loyal Democratic votes. Today the Democratic Party does the same thing to black bloc voters. During Passive Reconstruction, no thought was given to negotiating for a better

---

1112 Report on Economic Conditions of the South, Prepared for The President by The National Emergency Council (1938), 1-2. PDF available at www.bit.ly/South-Economic-Conditions.

1113 Venkataramani, M.S., "Norman Thomas, Arkansas Sharecroppers, and the Roosevelt Agricultural Policies, 1933-1937," *The Mississippi Valley Historical Review*, (Sept. 1960), Vol. 47, No. 2, ,226. Downloaded from www.jstor.org 07 March 2016.

1114 *Ibid.*, 242.

deal for the South. As payment for abandoning legitimate self-government via real States' Rights, Southern politicians received advancement up the Federal Government's political ladder or, in the Modern Era Reconstruction, paid positions as consultants or board members of big corporations. With no real political leadership promoting a Southern resistance movement, the South's poor black and white folk continued to labor in poverty as peasants, serfs, and virtual slaves.[1115]

After the end of Active Reconstruction, the South's political leadership rejected any effort to reclaim *real* States' Rights inclusive of the rights of nullification and secession. Southern politicians in Washington made many hot speeches for home consumption, but no real efforts were ever made to reclaim the Republic of Sovereign States destroyed by Lincoln's war and the Republican Party's Active Reconstruction. By abandoning the initiative and passively accepting as legitimate the political *status quo,* Southern political and social leaders rejected the opportunity of facing the enemy and at least negotiating a better deal. The "pitiful service" provided by "the inept Southern politicians"[1116] failed the South because as author Richard Weaver noted they "surrendered the initiative," they "took the decision of 1865 too literally" and if the South is to survive, the South must "recover the initiative."[1117]

INTERNATIONAL YANKEE IMPERIALISM—
THE ORIGINS OF YANKEE GO HOME!

Modern Era progressives[1118] do not like to acknowledge that the Progressive Era established the United States as an imperialistic power. The American tendency toward world domination is

---

1115   *Ibid.,* 239, 237.

1116   John Crowe Ranson, "Reconstructed But Unregenerate," *I'll Take My Stand,* 26.

1117   Weaver, *The Southern Tradition at Bay,* 390-1.

1118   In Modern Era Reconstruction the word "progressive" is often claimed by those on the left who are much more radical leftist—essentially neo-Marxists—than the Progressive Era individuals who were satisfied with pushing America toward Prussian Socialism like the emerging national socialism promoted by Germany's Chancellor Otto von Bismarck. In 1881 Bismarck introduced the Western world's first system of government financed social security.

described as American "hubris" in which American leaders think that America is divinely anointed to remake the world "in what we imagine to be America's image."[1119] This has been the mission of the New England elite from the very beginning of these United States.[1120] The drive to become an international player in the game of imperialism is described as a time in which American politicians were driven by "boldness unburdened by excessive scruples."[1121] America's leaders sought to soften the charge that their policies were imperialistic by avoiding acquiring colonies in the traditional sense. However, the US did not hesitate to use its military to enforce monopolistic access to markets and resources of smaller nations, especially in the Caribbean and Latin America. Despite the façade of anti-imperialism, it was clear to any who investigated that "American purposes were intrinsically imperial.[1122]

The dream of an American empire was announced early in American history by Alexander Hamilton.[1123] After only a few years of the War, the New York *Herald* in an 1863 edition looked forward to the day when the Union would rule not only the South but a large share of the world:

> With a combined veteran Army of over a million of men, and a fleet more powerful than that of any European power, we could order France from Mexico, England from Canada, and Spain from Cuba, and enforce our orders if they do not obey. The American continent would then govern the New World. The President at Washington would govern the New World.[1124]

1119   Bacevich, Andrew J., *The Limits of Power: The end of American Exceptionalism* (New York: Henry Holt & Co., 2008), 7.

1120   Wilson, Clyde N., *From Union to Empire* (Columbia, SC: The Foundation for American Education, 2003), 171.

1121   Bacevich, The Limits of Power: The end of American Exceptionalism, 22.

1122   *Ibid.*, 142.

1123   DiLorenzo, Thomas J., *Hamilton's Curse* (New York: Crown Forum, 2008), 2.

1124   Pollard, Southern History of the War, Vol. II, 291-2.

It did not take long after its victory over the Confederate States of America for the Yankee Empire to begin conquering other people. The first move was against the Native Americans on the western plains, then to seize the Kingdom of Hawaii, the Philippines, and exercise control of Cuba and Latin American Republics.[1125] In 1898 Republican Senator Beveridge of Indiana proclaimed, "The Philippines are ours forever...and just beyond...China...the Pacific Ocean is ours."[1126]

The Yankee Empire has a worldwide reach. It has more foreign bases than any empire in history—and an unknown number of secret military bases around the world. When republics become empires the people at first support the expansion of the empire but eventually the empire begins to oppress its citizens/subjects. One modern-day scholar predicted that four things would happen as America moves from a Republic to an Empire:

1. Perpetual war, a rash of no-end wars,
2. Individual rights formerly protected by the Constitution will be openly violated,
3. Truth in government will be replaced with propaganda that glorifies leaders, wars, international power, the military, and
4. Eventually the country will become unable to satisfy its financial obligations—bankruptcy.[1127]

This same scholar warned "Having grown accustomed to our empire and having found it pleasing, we have come to take its institutions and its assumptions for granted."[1128] Too many Southerners have taken the Yankee Empire for granted and have learned to love being a second-class subject of the world's largest empire. These Southerners and conservatives in general need

---

1125   See, Kennedy & Kennedy, *Yankee Empire: Aggressive Abroad and Despotic at Home.*

1126   Senator Beveridge cited in Kennedy & Kennedy, *Yankee Empire: Aggressive Abroad and Despotic at Home*, 33.

1127   Johnson, Chalmers, *The Sorrows of Empire* (New York: Henry Holt & Co., 285).

1128   *Ibid.*, 65.

to review Founding Father John DeWitt's November 5, 1787, warning about the danger of an American empire under the guise of being a Constitutional Federal Government:

> They are presented as a Frame of Government purely Republican, and perfectly consistent with the individual governments in the Union. It is declared to be constructed for national purposes only, and not calculated to interfere with domestic concerns... Whereas the very contrary of all this doctrine appears to be true... In short, my fellow citizens, it can be said to be nothing less than a hasty stride to Universal Empire in the Western World, flattering, very flattering to young ambitious minds, but fatal to the liberties of the people.[1129]

The political, economic, and social conditions under which Southerners live today are evidence that empires do not invade, conquer, and occupy a formerly free people to improve the lot of the invaded people.

SOCIALISM REPLACES INDIVIDUAL RESPONSIBILITY— GOVERNMENT REPLACES KITH AND KIN

The Progressive Era was a time in which the idea of socialism became acceptable for the "intelligentsia," that class of people whose only output is ideological thoughts and political schemes. They were and still are self-appointed purveyors of leftwing social activism. Today, they are known as social justice warriors who support the destruction (deconstruction or debunking) of all traditional conservative values and replace those values with their utopian fantasy of a socialist system that enforces equality of outcome. But in the late nineteenth century, the idea of socialism was still bitterly opposed by most Americans. Progressives undermined this American attitude by a system of slowly advancing socialist ideas and programs. In England, this socialist strategy was known as Fa-

---

1129 John DeWitt cited in *The Anti-Federalist Papers and the Constitutional Convention Debates*, ed., Ralph Ketcham (New York: Penguin Books, 1986), 313.

bian Socialism.[1130] Fabian socialism emerged in England in 1884. Fabians rejected the revolutionary approach of Marxist socialism in favor of a gradual, almost imperceptible transition of societies originally based upon a free-market economy, slowly turning them into a governmentally enforced socialist society.[1131] Fabian socialism was akin to Prussian socialism promoted by German Chancellor Otto von Bismarck in the 1880s. President Woodrow Wilson was a key player in the ranks of the Progressives. It is no surprise that two of Wilson's heroes were Abraham Lincoln, the great centralizer of government power, and Otto von Bismarck, the great proponent of gradual socialism.[1132] By the late 1920s and early 1930s, many American university professors began to note that students returning from communist Russia, Nazi Germany, or Fascist Italy returned to the United States with an extreme hatred for traditional Western civilization.[1133] The work of the Progressives was progressing well!

A Nobel laureate economist wrote that he believed that the American Socialist Party exerted more influence in America regarding the normalizing of socialism than either of the national parties. He noted that virtually every plank in the Socialist Party's platform of 1928 was, by 1980, "enacted into law."[1134] Another economist described the rapid expansion of Socialism as being like the rapid expansion of Islam "which inspired the sons of the desert to lay waste ancient civilizations, cloaked their destructive fury with an ethical ideology and stiffened their courage with rigid fatalism."[1135] The rapid spread of socialist ideology during the Progressive Era was helped by the strong connection between

---

1130 "Fabianism," Britannica Money, www.britannica.com/money/topic/Fabianism (Accessed 03 October 2023).

1131 Hicks, Stephen R.C., *Explaining Postmodernism-Skepticism and Socialism from Rousseau to Foucault* 2nd edition (Ockham's Razor Publishing, 2011), 138-9.

1132 Goldberg, Jonah, *Liberal Fascism* (New York: Double Day, 2007), 84.

1133 Hayek, F.A., *The Road To Serfdom* (1944, The University of Chicago Press, 2007), 81.

1134 Friedman, Milton, *Free to Choose* (New York: Harcourt Brace Jovanovich, 1980), 286-7.

1135 Mises, Ludwig von, *Socialism: An Economic and Sociological Analysis* (1936, Indianapolis, IN: Liberty Fund, 1981), 417.

Lincoln, the Republican Party, and European socialists of the 1848 revolutionaries who came to the United States and became influential supporters of Lincoln's war and the Republican Party's effort to remake American government.[1136]

Progressives look upon socialism as a universal good. President Franklin D. Roosevelt viewed Soviet socialism as a pattern that could be adapted to the United States.[1137] But as international experience in the twentieth century has demonstrated, socialism is a universal evil. Why? Because the theory of socialism assumes that a self-anointed group of ruling elites know better than the individual how best to spend his money. The ruling elite will use the force of government to take, via taxation, inflation, and regulations, money from the productive element of society and give it to the unproductive element—which amounts to a legalized vote-buying scheme. The unproductive element will always vote in a bloc for any candidate who promises to give them more "free stuff." In such a society the heavy load of taxes and inflation compels married couples to limit the size of their family while encouraging non-productive individuals to increase the size of their families. In effect, the system of socialism compels the productive population to decrease while encouraging the non-productive portion of the population to increase. Socialism leads to the destruction of the family unit and the destruction of the age-old tradition of relying on kith and kin for help in times of distress. Socialism is a deceptive death warrant to any people who adopt it. American-style Fabian socialism has destroyed the once solid black family.[1138]

During Passive Reconstruction there developed a sharp divide between Northern Progressives such as Franklin D. Roosevelt and Southern Populists such as Huey Long. While both were promoting socialists' goals, they viewed it from differing social settings. The

---

1136   See, Kennedy and Benson, *Lincoln, Marx, and the GOP*, 9-14, 260.

1137   Lukacs, John, *Democracy and Populism: Fear and Hatred* (Yale University Press, 2005), 98-9.

1138   Sowell, Thomas, *Race and Culture: A World View* (New York: Harper Collins Publishers, 1994), 220. See also Sowell, Thomas, *Civil Rights: Rhetoric or Reality?* (New York: William Morrow & Co., 1984), 75.

South was agrarian with large numbers of impoverished farmers and field hands whereas the North was primarily industrial and relatively wealthy. The cultural distortion of Yankee invasion and domination caused many in the impoverished South to look to populism, a political ideology that advocated a form of socialism, as a possible solution to its post-War poverty. For example, before the War Louisiana's property value ranked second in the United States per capita but the census after Active Reconstructions ranked Louisiana's property value per capita as thirty-seventh out of 38 States.[1139] As one author noted, "There was, in fact, a direct connection between Populism and the whole Louisiana Socialist movement."[1140] But the South's leaning toward popularism should not be viewed as a natural endorsement of socialism. It was an unnatural response created by the cultural distortion caused by Yankee invasion, conquest, occupation, and exploitation. Cultural distortion always follows conquering armies.[1141]

THE POLITICAL PROGRESSIVE ERA—
THE CONSUMMATION OF CENTRALIZED FEDERALISM

During the first twenty-three years of Passive Reconstruction, while the South was mired in poverty, the North was enjoying a booming economy known as the Gilded Age, the Age of Robber Barons. During this period the Progressive movement ushered in the age of unlimited Federal power. As Progressive President Woodrow Wilson declared while he was still a professor at Princeton University, "The War Between the States established... this principle, that the federal government is, through its courts, the final judge of its own powers."[1142] With no real check on Federal powers, except that which the Supreme Court may from time to time issue, the Federal Government became America's ultimate judge on any social or economic issue that might impact the ruling

---

1139   Hair, William Ivy, *Bourbonism and Agrarian Protest: Louisiana Politics 1877-1900* (Baton Rouge, LA: LSU Press, 1969), 34.

1140   Williams, T. Harry, *Huey Long*, 44.

1141   For more on cultural distortions see, Kennedy & Kennedy, *Punished With Poverty-The Suffering South* 2nd ed., 140-6.

1142   Woodrow Wilson cited in DiLorenzo, *Hamilton's Curse*, 84.

elites or their cronies. The advocates for progressive political policies were successful in shaping the bureaucratic state that in Modern Age Reconstruction would be termed the "Deep State." Below is a list of a few of the major Progressive political victories from 1877 to 1940:

- In 1896 the Federal Supreme Court endorsed "separate but equal" Jim Crow segregation in *Plessy v. Ferguson*. The vote was seven to one, the negative vote coming from Justice Harlan the only Southerner on the bench. Justice Harlan's family, from Kentucky, owned slaves before the War. The majority decision was written by Justice Henry Billings Brown from Michigan and the decision was based upon a line of cases beginning with a case from Massachusetts.[1143] If the North had allowed the South to follow the high road to emancipation the question of segregation would have most likely never arisen. The social problems caused by Lincoln's war and the Republican Party's Active Reconstruction became an open wound that continues to bleed today in Modern Era Reconstruction.
- 1898 Fourteenth Amendment used to establish "Birthright citizenship" also known today as "Anchor Babies."[1144]
- In 1913 the Sixteenth Amendment was ratified giving the Federal Government the right to tax the income of its subjects—note, "subjects" not citizens.
- 1913 America's form of central banking was created when President Wilson signed the Federal Reserve Act into law. Progressives completed the old Hamiltonian dream of a Federally controlled central bank. This greatly enlarged the government's ability to artificially increase credit expansion. Governments "are inherently inflationary institutions" and the key

---

1143 *The Oxford Companion to the Supreme Court*, 638.

1144 *United States v. Wong Kim Ark*, 169 US 649 (1898).

to inflation in America today is the Federal Reserve working with the US Treasury.[1145] Inflation is an indirect tax that does not require politicians to go on the record with a vote to increase taxation.[1146]

- 1920 Nineteenth Amendment ratified prohibiting States from limiting voting to only males. Historically, the reason that voting was limited to qualified males was that only males were subject to the draft and military service during a war. Also, because men, even today, are the major holders of wealth and therefore pay the larger share of the taxes, they were the ones to elect men to control the government's system of taxation.
- 1925 US Supreme Court, in *Gitlow v. New York*, dealing with state restrictions on speech, used the Fourteenth Amendment to "incorporate" the "Bill of Rights" into a constitutional theory that allows the Federal Courts to apply the limitations in the "Bill of Rights" to the once sovereign States. "Until 1866 the rule, established by the Supreme Court in 1833 in *Barron v. Baltimore*, was the...Bill of Rights limited only the federal government, not the state governments."[1147] A prior ruling in 1897, *Chicago, Burlington, and Quincy Railroad Co. v. Chicago*, dealt similarly with the question of States taking private property. The original Constitution limited the power of the Federal Government but during Passive Reconstruction the South sat silently while the original Constitution was converted into an instrument of unlimited Federal power.

1145   Rothbard, Murray N., *America's Great Depression* (1963, Auburn, AL: The Ludwig von Mises Institute, 2000), 24-5.

1146   Kennedy, James Ronald, *Reclaiming Liberty* (Gretna, LA: Pelican Publishing Co., 2005), 174.

1147   *The Oxford Companion to the Supreme Court*, 181, 426.

- 1935 President Roosevelt signed into law the Social Security Act. This was a major progressive step toward American socialism. It was based on Otto von Bismarck's model of Prussian socialism. It would become a major means of organizing a large voting bloc of elderly folks who would respond to the emotional claim that conservatives wanted to take away or reduce old folks' Social Security payments. It became to the elderly what welfare is to minorities—a way for liberal politicians to use conservative taxpayers' dollars to buy votes for liberal politicians. Recall the description of Fabian or gradual socialism discussed previously.[1148]
- 1933-1939 FDR's New Deal was enacted which was essentially a Fabian socialist effort to solve the Great Depression that the Federal Reserve was unable to prevent. The New Deal saw the enactment of numerous federal agencies and agency-generated regulations dealing with banking, relief programs, public works programs, labor union protection, and of course the Social Security Act.

By the end of World War II Progressive ideology became the mantra of American politics. The last fifty years of the twentieth century became five decades of continuous conservative retreat and Southern politicians were a part of that retreat. The 1940-1960 Conservative Coalition between Republicans and mostly Southern conservative Democrats was formed as an unofficial opposition to the New Deal and subsequent liberal policies.[1149] However, they were unable to roll back any of the major gains enjoyed by the Progressives. This trend of conservative failure would continue

---

1148 Kennedy, James Ronald, *Reclaiming Liberty* (Gretna, LA: Pelican Publishing Co., 2005), 26-32.

1149 See Jenkins, Jeffery A. and Monroe, Nathan W., "Negative Agenda Control and the Conservative Coalition in the US House," The Journals of Politics (journals.uchicago.edu) www.bit.ly/NegAgenda-CCC; or "Conservative Coalition Remains Potent in Congress," Voting Studies, n.d. PDF available at www.bit.ly/ConsCoal-PDF (Both accessed 04 October 2023).

throughout the remainder of Passive Reconstruction and would only accelerate during Modern Era Reconstruction.

Passive Reconstruction's North/South Reconciliation Bargain

At the close of Active Reconstruction, a tacit or unwritten bargain was acknowledged between the North and the South. That "bargain" guaranteed the South's loyalty to the new Union while recognizing all veterans of the war as honorable Americans. When Confederate officers gave their last orders to their troops at the end of the War, they told their men to go home, live in peace, and rebuild their lives. Active Reconstruction made that difficult but by the end of Active Reconstruction, the men and women of the South set themselves to the task of rebuilding their lives, and their communities, and making the best out of a bad situation. They gave their word of honor to remain loyal to the new government and to repudiate the thought of initiating another Southern uprising. In exchange the people of the South expected the new government to leave them alone to bury their dead, memorialize the fallen, and teach their children about the valor of the men who wore the gray in the War for Southern Independence. Across the South and for generations you would hear Southerners laughingly proclaiming, "The South shall rise again!" But it was nothing more than a half-hearted prayer in the form of a joke. The post-War people of the South made a tacit agreement that the South would become a patriotic member of the nation if the North would allow the South the *semblance* of self-government, allow Southerners to honor Confederate veterans, and leave the Southern people alone. As an innumerable number of graves of Southern soldiers, sailors, and airmen who, post Active Reconstruction, died defending the United States proves, the South has kept its part of the unspoken bargain.

President McKinley, a Union Army veteran, addressing the Georgia legislature demonstrated his desire for North/South reconciliation by declaring, "And the time has now come in the evolution of sentiment and feeling, under the providence of God, when in the spirit of fraternity, we should share with you in the care of the graves of the Confederate soldiers."[1150] Today, this sense of "fraternity" is rejected by America's Woke political *status quo* in Modern Era Reconstruction. Instead of sharing in the care of Confederate graves the Federal Government and its military declared all things Southern as forbidden.

Despite the South's sincere efforts of reconciliation, the North's hatred for the South remained and continues. In early 1890 the Sons of the Grand Army Veterans (sons of Union veterans) denounced the proposed establishment of the Sons of Confederate Veterans. Numerous Northern newspapers used "ugly language... against the rearing of Confederate monuments."[1151] These insulting attacks against the South continue "on steroids" in Modern Era Reconstruction. What is the value of Southern blood that is shed in defense of a country that does not value Southern heroes?

With the outbreak of the Spanish-American War in 1898, many people in the North were unsure whether Southerners would support the nation's expansionist war against Spain in Cuba and the Philippines. There was fear that Southerners might support Spain. But the South upheld its end of the tacit North/South bargain. Former Confederate officers served in the US Army and thousands of sons of Confederate veterans joined the ranks of US soldiers headed to Cuba.

During the Spanish-American War (1898) the *Albany Journal* of New York acknowledged the patriotic contribution made by Southerners. The *Journal* observed that "...the honors of the war are being carried away by the sons of the South.... Sons of the South are showing the same acts of heroism that they have always shown

---

1150   Quoted in *Confederate Veteran* Vol. VI, No. 12, Dec. 1898. Republished in *The Confederate Veteran Magazine* Vol. VI (Harrisburg, PA: The National Historical Society, 1987), 546.

1151   *Confederate Veteran* Vol. III, No. 4, 1895. Republished in *The Confederate Veteran Magazine*, Vol. III, 112.

in time of war, and, unless the sons of the North bestir themselves the honors of this conflict may go to the Southland."[1152]

And so, it has been in every war since then. In World War I the highest decorated American soldier was Alvin York from Tennessee and in World War II the highest decorated American soldier was Audi Murphy from Texas. The Federal Government acknowledged this tacit agreement when its Post Office issued numerous stamps honoring Confederate veterans, officers, and political leaders, and when the 1925 Federal mint issued a 50-cent coin with the likeness of General Lee and General Jackson on one side and the other side with the words "Memorial to the valor of the soldier of the South." The US military named tanks for Confederate Generals Lee and Stuart and several ships were named for Confederate heroes. President Eisenhower, in office from 1953 to 1961, kept a framed photograph of General Lee in Confederate uniform in his office. President Eisenhower not only kept a framed photograph of General Lee in his presidential office, but he issued a proclamation celebrating the Centennial of the Civil War declaring "It was a demonstration of heroism and sacrifice by men and women of both sides who valued principle above life itself and whose devotion to duty is a part of our Nation's noblest tradition."[1153] All of this happened during Passive Reconstruction when both sides honored the tacit North/South agreement. "We the People" of the South have kept our end of the North/South bargain.

The South proved its dedication to the tacit agreement with the shedding of Southern blood in every American war since Appomattox. The *New York Times* published an article on January 12, 2020, documenting that Southerners are more likely to volunteer for the military than any other section of the United States. The article noted "The South...produces 20 percent more recruits than would be expected, based on its youth population.

1152 *Confederate Veteran* Vol. VI, No. 7, July. 1898. Republished in *The Confederate Veteran Magazine*, Vol. VI, 304.

1153 Eisenhower, Dwight D., "Proclamation 3382—Civil War Centennial," The American Presidency Project (presidency.ucsb.edu), 07 December 1960, www.bit.ly/3382—CWC (Accessed 05 October 2023).

The States in the Northeast...produce 20 percent fewer." The article noted that one city in North Carolina produced more recruits than Manhattan in New York even though Manhattan has more than eight times the population. Another article published on February 26, 2015, with the headline "Volunteer Force: Middle-Class US with a Southern Drawl" noted that "The military continues to recruit most heavily from Southern States."[1154]

Unfortunately, the Yankee Empire's neo-Marxist political and social leaders have broken the North/South bargain. They have initiated a campaign of cultural genocide against the very memory of the South. Both Republican and Democrat political leaders in Washington have endorsed this current campaign of slanderous anti-South cultural genocide.[1155] A bargain broken by one party relieves the other party from its obligations under that bargain. The key part of the tacit North/South bargain was that the South would renounce any effort to regain its independence. That bargain no longer exists! [1156]

Summary

Passive Reconstruction (1877-1965)

Northern hatred for the South did not die during Passive Reconstruction. It would often rear its ugly head during heated exchanges in Congress. In 1890 Representative Henry Cabot Lodge introduced a bill that would have the effect of reimposing

---

1154 Philpott, Tom, "Volunteer Force: Middle-Class US with a Southern Drawl," Fleet Reserve Association (fra.org), 26 February 2015, www.bit.ly/VolunteerForce (Accessed 05 October 2023).

1155 Pollak, Joel B., "Republican-led Committee Passes Elizabeth Warren's Amendment to Rename Military Bases," Breitbart News (breitbart.com) 11 June 2020, www.bit.ly/Republicans_Bases-Named (Accessed 12 June 2020).

Philpott, Tom, "Volunteer Force: Middle-Class US with a Southern Drawl," Fleet Reserve Association (fra.org), 26 February 2015, www.bit.ly/VolunteerForce (Accessed 05 October 2023).

1156 Southern independence should be conceived as a return to America's original Republic of Sovereign States where the Constitution is enforced by "We the People" via state nullification or, if necessary, secession. Secession is not necessary, but the valid threat of secession is necessary if you desire to "negotiate a better deal."

Active Reconstruction on the South.[1157] Senator Weldon Brinton Heyburn, (R-Idaho) July 12, 1911, denounced the South's proud defense of the "cause" and labeled it an "infamous" cause.[1158] The South's only political solution was to remain the Solid South loyal to the Democratic Party and hope to avoid the reimposition of Active Reconstruction. It was a hope that was ultimately unfulfilled—hope, after all, is not a plan! It is perhaps understandable that Southern politicians would avoid "radical" ideas such as Southern independence or initiating a social and political struggle to reclaim America's original Republic of Sovereign States. They likely did this out of fear of inciting the North's ruling elites and causing them to reimpose Active Reconstruction. Unfortunately, such a stance gave the Progressives (liberals, postmodernists, neo-Marxists, etc.) a virtually free hand in dealing with "We the People" of Dixie. It also set the stage for the reintroduction of a new form of Active Reconstruction not only in the South but in cities and States throughout America in post-1965 Modern Era Reconstruction.

1157   Clark & Kirwan, *The South Since Appomattox*, 71-2.

1158   Richardson, J.A., *A Historical and Constitutional Defense of The South* (1914, Harrisonburg, VA: Sprinkle Publications, 2010), 13.

SOUTHERNERS ARE FOOLS IF THEY EXPECT JUSTICE FROM THE YANKEE EMPIRE'S JUDICIAL SYSTEM

THE FEDERAL JURY EMPANELED FOR JEFFERSON DAVIS'S TRIAL ON CHARGES OF TREASON

The Yankee Empire empaneled a jury for their trial of President Jefferson Davis on the charge of treason. Of the twenty-four men selected, twelve were black. Even with a "select" jury empaneled, the Yankee Empire feared they could not convict Davis on the charge of treason. Davis repeatedly demanded his "day in court" but the Yankee Empire refused his request. Constitutional rights mean nothing to an empire—Vae Victis!

Southerners have raised over a million dollars in the Modern Era Reconstruction fighting to prevent the removal of monuments, the banning of Southern symbols, and the renaming of military bases but to no avail. Modern-day Southerners are in the same condition as President Jefferson Davis. He had "right" on his side, so much so that the Yankee Empire feared to give him his day in court. Today, too many Southerners think the only way to fight against the destruction of Southern heritage is to raise money, hire a lawyer, and "sue the bastards!" It would be better to spend the money in the one court in which Southerners can win—the court of public opinion.

Chapter 30:

MODERN ERA RECONSTRUCTION POST 1965

"Even 'good' conservatives once elected must work within the current political system; a system that is designed to favor the ruling elites; a system in which elected officials have a vested interest in maintaining the political status quo; a corrupt and corrupting system that quickly converts 'good' conservatives into loyal Democrats or Republicans." —the Kennedy Twins[1159]

THE ASSASSINATION of President Kennedy in 1963 and Lyndon Baines Johnson's landslide victory in the Presidential election of 1964 gave Johnson a mandate to carry on and greatly expand President Kennedy's efforts for an expanded Federal Government to enforce civil rights laws initially aimed at the South. Johnson's successful efforts to enact into law the 1964-5 Civil Rights Acts and his "Great Society" programs mark the end of Passive Reconstruction and the beginning of Modern Era Reconstruction.

Lyndon Baines Johnson (LBJ) was a pragmatic politician who would move from supporting the Solid South's anti-civil rights stance to embracing the Civil Rights movement.[1160] It was well

---

1159 Kennedy & Kennedy, *Nullifying Tyranny* (Pelican Publishing Co., Gretna, LA: 2010), 163-4.

1160 The so-called Civil Rights movement was an effort of the political *status quo* to lessen the impact of a system of racial division that the Northern ruling elite established during Active and Passive Construction. The ruling elite exploited the natural desire of blacks to

known that LBJ held strong racist views, but such views were overlooked by his followers.[1161] The hallmark of LBJ's presidency was the passage of the 1964 Civil Rights Act and the 1965 Voting Rights Act. These Acts would be greatly expanded and become the tools used by neo-Marxist agitators to initiate their attack against the traditionally conservative South and eventually against all traditional conservative American values. The first great steppingstone into Modern Era Reconstruction was LBJ's greatest political accomplishments—the 1964 and 1965 Civil Rights and Voting Rights Acts. He and his Democrat Party did to the South in a few months what it took the Republican Party and Thad Stevens years to accomplish. But in Modern Era Reconstruction, the horrors of Active Reconstruction (racial antagonism) are not limited to the South but are today shared by Northern cities and States.

LBJ's Great Society was a major victory for those Progressives promoting a socialist solution to leftist social issues such as civil rights, the environment, healthcare, housing, and poverty. His "war on poverty" resulted in the issuing of over 6,000 pages of federal rules and regulations governing welfare and poverty programs. Within twenty years the cost of these Great Society programs reached $132,000,000. In 1960 the cost for such programs was only $21,000,000. In education, the Great Society was an utter failure. The education level of students declined as measured by national exams while racial tensions in schools and the streets rose. But what was the conservative Republican Party doing during this time of expanding and oppressive Federalism?

The elites who controlled the GOP determined long ago that it was more important to win elections than to defend conservative

---

improve their social standing to garner black bloc votes with no regard for the long-term consequences of their public policies. It was a continuation of the divide-and-rule strategy initially used to gain black votes for the Republican Party. If the South had been allowed to follow the high road to emancipation there would not have been a need to enact such legislation.

1161 Serwer, Adam, "Lyndon Johnson was a civil rights hero. But also a racist," MSNBC (msnbc.com), 11 April 2014, www.on.msnbc.com/48Jzdyr (Accessed 05 October 2023).

principles. Thus, they made no efforts to roll back the essential elements of either Franklin Roosevelt's or Lyndon Johnson's socialist programs.[1162] Holding office became an end unto itself, after all, holding office provided the office holder and his cronies with unending perks, privileges, and power regardless of whether they were Democrats or Republicans. Thanks to the GOP's inaction or ineffective action liberals reaped the benefit of promising more payments to a huge bloc of welfare voters. Add to this the even larger group of aged Social Security recipients. The elderly were also easy to mobilize against conservative candidates because the liberal media would assure them that the conservatives were going to cut out Social Security payments. Again, it must be stressed that the left uses emotional allegations even when there is no evidence to support their false claims. In America's mass democracy emotions trump facts. With these two blocs of voters, bought off with conservative taxpayers' dollars, liberals became the key power in the predominantly socialized American economy.[1163]

By the end of the twentieth century, it became evident that the promises of the Great Society—just like all socialist promises—were empty promises that worked primarily for the benefit of social workers, government bureaucrats in the Deep State, liberal/neo-Marxist academics, neo-Marxist ideologues, and politicians. When LBJ left office in 1968, the poverty rate, according to the government, was around 16 percent. Twelve years and billions of tax dollars later, in 1980 the poverty level was 16 percent![1164] After the Great Society's programs, laws, rules, and regulations were put in place, there was a major breakdown in law and order. Five years after the passage of LBJ's Civil Rights Acts a researcher from the Massachusetts Institute of Technology completed a study of

---

1162 These and similar government programs are examples of Fabain or gradual socialism in action.

1163 The 2022 Cato Institute's "Human Freedom Index 2022" ranked the US as 23 out of 165 countries—below Austria. It represented a seven-point decline since 2019. Vasquez, Ian, et. al., *The Human Freedom Index 2022: A Global Measurement of Personal, Civil, and Economic Freedom*, Cato Institute (cato.org) wwww.bit.ly/2022-Cato-Index (Accessed 11 November 2023).

1164 Murray, Charles, *Losing Ground: American Social Policy 1950-1980*, 8.

violent crime in the United States and determined that in 1970 an individual living in a large city in the United States had a greater chance of being killed by violent crime than a World War II soldier being killed in combat.[1165] The greatest harm done was to the black family. According to black scholar Dr. Thomas Sowell, it was *normal* for black children to grow up in a two-parent home even during slavery and the Jim Crow era.[1166] But today it is *uncommon* to find intact two-parent black families, especially in the black areas of urban centers. According to an agency of the Federal Government, only 43% of black children live in a two-parent home.[1167] These "Great Society" socially destructive social programs were initiated at the beginning of Modern Era Reconstruction before the radical leftist demands of BLM, Antifa, and social justice warriors to "defund the police" or demands for "reparations." As the years rolled by things only got worse.

The passage of the 1964 Civil Rights Act in essence created a new Constitution even more radical than the one created by the Republican Party during Active Reconstruction. Thanks to this new emphasis on civil rights for the few (minorities of all flavors, many unimaginable in 1964), the majority would now be compelled to pay for bilingual education, pay for welfare for illegal aliens, businesses would be compelled to enforce political correctness in the workplace and readjust their hiring practice from one based on merit to one based on affirmative action and quotas. As one observer of this era noted "...in any conflict it was the new unofficial constitution, nurtured by elites in all walks of life, that tended to prevail."[1168] By the beginning of the 21st century, the mere threat of a Civil Rights claim had evolved to the point that it virtually repealed freedom of speech if a minority of any flavor

---

1165   Ibid., 117.

1166   Sowell, Thomas, *Civil Rights: Rhetoric or Reality?* (New York: William Morrow & Co., 1984), 75; Sowell, Thomas, *Race and Culture: A World View* (New York: Harper Collins Publishers, 1994), 220.

1167   "Living arrangements of children by race/ethnicity," Office of Juvenile Justice and Delinquency Prevention (ojjdp.gov) www.bit.ly/Living-Arrangements (Accessed 10 October 2023).

1168   Caldwell, Christopher, *The Age of Entitlement: America Since the Sixties* (New York: Simon & Schuster, 2020), 171.

claimed they were offended, or it created a "hostile environment." The worship of "civil rights" created a new era in which Wokeness was enforced by the Human Resources departments of private businesses. A leftist federally "protected" minority could rely on a civil rights claim to obtain court-ordered enforcement of gay marriages. The Equal Employment Opportunities Commission, created under the 1964 Civil Rights Act, began its leftist demands to recognize transgenders as a federally protected minority, and biological males claiming to "identify" as a female were given federal authority to use female restrooms and locker rooms in public schools.[1169] Such absurdities would become normal and begrudgingly accepted by America's "conservative" middle class.

The demand for universal franchise during Modern Era Reconstruction produced results like the results achieved during Active Reconstruction. The quality of elected leaders is something approaching the average "quality" of the electorate—the voting public. Put bluntly, the dumber the electorate the dumber (or more devious) will be those individuals who win the votes of the dumb electorate.[1170] After taking office such low-quality or devious political "leaders" use their office for self-aggrandizement and to push trendy, leftist social issues. With such leadership in place during Modern Era Reconstruction the push for more government spending created a national debt in 2016 of $20 trillion and government unfunded liabilities of over

---

1169 Knudsen, Hannah, "Federal Appeals Court Rules in Favor of Pro-Transgender Bathroom Policy" Breitbart News (breitbart.com) 10 August 2020, www.bit.ly/Fed-Trans-Policy (Accessed 10 August 2023).

1170 Being uneducated and unlearned about civic responsibilities is not something that need be a permanent disability in all but the rarest cases. Like the uneducated newly freed slaves, it was something that could be overcome with education, training, and experience. But to allow individuals to vote who do not possess specific educational qualifications is an open invitation for exploitation. John Stuart Mill, English classical liberal (1806-1873), recommended that to be allowed to vote, the individual should be educated and not be a recipient of public funded charity, i.e., welfare. Mill, John Stuart, "Representative Government," *American State Papers, Federalist*, ed., Robert Maynard Hutchins (London: Britannica Great Books, 1952), 382.

$100 trillion.[1171] The national debt as of October 5, 2023, is now $33,474,904,868,026.00.[1172] Recall the debt that was loaded onto the Southern States during Active Reconstruction. In Modern Era Reconstruction, the same thing is happening to the United States, and it is being done by elected officials with similar ethics or lack thereof. Modern Era Reconstruction is typified by high taxation, inflation (indirect taxation), excess spending, fraudulent or questionable elections, and the weaponization of the government against conservatives. Modern Era Reconstruction is Active Reconstruction applied to the entire United States.

A New Type of Reconstruction in The Modern Era

The unstoppable growth of governmental intrusion into the private life of "We the People" after the passage of the Great Society programs has been noted by modern-era political observers. One wrote that the "growth of imperial power of the White House," is today beyond the control of the people.[1173] He noted that America had become an "overextended empire."[1174] He pointed out that it makes no difference who is in the White House or which party controls Congress, the established "mode of thought" in the political *status quo* is one of endless war and the continuous "application of military force."[1175] This is something that President Eisenhower warned Americans about in his final address to the American people as President. He warned of the existence of something more powerful than "We the People" called the military-industrial complex. The coalition of big business, big financial institutions, and big government plus the ever-increasing

---

1171 Caldwell, Christopher, *The Age of Entitlement: America Since the Sixties* (Simon & Schuster, NY: 2020), 177.

1172 "What is the national debt?" US Treasury Fiscal Data (fiscaldata.treasury.gov) https://bit.ly/US-Nat-Debt (Accessed 05 October 2023).

1173 Englehardt, Tom, *Shadow Government: Surveillance, Secret Wars, and a Global Security State in a Single-Superpower World* (Chicago, Ill.: Haymarket Books, 2014), 25.

1174 Englehardt, *Shadow Government*, 118.

1175 *Ibid.*, 118.

welfare state has created an American government that is more national socialist than free market capitalism.[1176]

The government now tracks private citizens directly or indirectly through its connections with monopolistic tech giants. The Central Intelligence Agency (CIA), as originally organized, was prohibited from becoming involved in domestic politics. But recently it went around that prohibition by having its contacts in "friendly" foreign agencies investigate Americans and then hand the results over to the CIA.[1177] This is but one example of the invisible tentacles of the Deep State that control America regardless of which political party is supposedly in control of "our" government—indeed the political parties are a major supporter of the Deep States' *political status* quo.

The weaponization of the FBI in the 2016 Presidential campaign is another example of the Reconstruction era type of corruption that exists today in "our" Federal Government. FBI agent Linda Page expressed her concern about the possibility of Trump becoming president in an e-mail to her lover and fellow FBI agent Peter Strzok. Strzok was Chief of the Counterespionage Section of the FBI. Page texted her fellow FBI agent Peter Strzok, "[Trump] is not going to become president, right?" Strzok replied "No. No, he won't. We'll stop it."[1178] Here you see the depth to which our once-vaunted free government has sunken. The bureaucrats hold more power than "We the People!" The ruling elite have no respect for "We the People" in what they refer to as "fly-over country." They view "We the People" as being "irredeemables, deplorables, bitter clingers, and smelly Walmart shoppers." To prevent Trump from winning or to limit his ability to govern the elites:

1. Illegally spied on Trump when he was a candidate,
2. Developed fake data to justify criminal investigations into the Trump campaign,

---

1176 Lukacs, John, *Democracy and Populism: Fear and Hatred* (Yale University Press, 2005), 41, 139-40.

1177 McCarthy, Andrew C., *Ball of Collusion: The Plot to Rig an Election and Destroy a Presidency* (New York: Encounter Books, 2019), 24.

1178 Strzok and Page cited in McCarthy, Andrew C., *Ball of Collusion*, 195.

3. Used these criminal investigations to infer criminal activities that were promoted by the leftist mainline and digital media,
4. Initiated criminal investigations used to justify impeachment,
5. Impeachment used as a political tactic to harm Trump's reelection bid,
6. Entire efforts used to straight-jacket Trump's presidency and his re-election bid.[1179]

This is something more appropriate for a banana republic or a hostile dictatorship, not the once-free Republic of the United States. This is America's political *status quo*. It is a system of government that is the natural evolution of the government created by Lincoln's war and the Republican Party's Active Reconstruction. It is a system of government that both national political parties are dedicated to protecting and leaving in place. It is a system of oppressive government that will not change short of a *fundamental* change in the current illegitimate Constitution. Electing good conservatives will not change the political *status quo*—it requires an audacious strategic plan to restore America's original and legitimate Republic of Sovereign States.

Modern Era Anti-South Cultural Genocide

In the 1994 second edition of *The South Was Right!* the authors warned that a campaign of anti-South cultural genocide was approaching. We gave evidence of the intentions of the rising left to destroy Confederate monuments and viciously slander traditional Southern conservative values.[1180] Many leaders in the Southern Heritage movement denounced us as being too political, too radical, and un-American. Below are examples of the ongoing campaign of slanderous, anti-South campaign of cultural genocide being conducted at the national, state, and local level.

1179 McCarthy, Andrew C., *Ball of Collusion*, 350.

1180 See Chapter 17, "The Yankee Campaign of Cultural Genocide 1861- 2020," in Kennedy & Kennedy, *The South Was Right!* 3rd ed., 371-411.

- **Republican-led Committee Passes Elizabeth Warren's Amendment to Rename Military Bases.** These were bases named for Confederate military heroes.[1181]
- **House Votes to Remove Confederate Statues from Capitol**[1182] Republican Steve Scalise from the most conservative district in Louisiana voted in favor of removing all symbols of Confederate heroes.
- **Georgia's Republican Governor Gives Illegals Drivers' Licenses**[1183] It is not just the Democrats who are attempting to re-populate America with illegals from socialist countries. Traditional Americans are being dispossessed of the country their ancestors built and fought for via open borders and illegal immigration. There is a vast difference between legal and illegal immigration.
- **Poll Democrats say the Constitution is racist and sexist**[1184] The traditional conservative South has always stood for limited federalism enforced by real States' Rights according to the original Constitution. One of the main reasons the left attacks the South is because we still honor the original intentions of the Constitution.

1181   Pollak, Joel B., "Republican-led Committee Passes Elizabeth Warren's Amendment to Rename Military Bases," Breitbart News (breitbart.com) 11 June 2020, www.bit.ly/Republicans_Bases-Named (Accessed 12 June 2020).

1182   McCarthy, Reagan, "House Votes to Remove Confederate Statues from Capitol," Town Hall townhall.com) 30 June 2021, www. (accessed 06 July 2021).

1183   King, D.A., Georgia's GOP Governor Helps Illegals By Giving Them Drivers' Licenses," Breitbart News (breitbart.com) 10 August 2016, www.bit.ly/GA-GOP-Illegal-DLs (Accessed 10 August 2016).

1184   Knudsen, Hannah, "Most Democrats Believe the Constitution Is Racist and Sexist," Breitbart News (breitbart.com), 14 July 2022, www.bit.ly/Racist-Constitution (Accessed 15 July 2022).

- **Virginia's Kiggans Voted With Democrats on Trans School Bathrooms**[1185] This is an example of how local Republicans do not hesitate to betray traditional Southern conservative moral and political values.
- **NY city removes Thomas Jefferson statue**[1186] Anyone associated with the South is now deemed to be an evil racist and must be purged from Woke American society. The effort to deconstruct conservative American society began in earnest with the destruction of Confederate monuments.

The left aims to use political pressure to force "conservative" elected officials (national, state, and local) to vote with BLM, Antifa, and leftist politicians promoting the Democratic Party's genocidal efforts to remove all mention of traditional Southern conservative values and symbols. As the list above demonstrates, they have been successful despite many laws on the books which protect our historic American heritage. When laws are not enforced, you have tyranny by an elite which decides what laws it will enforce. The South's pacified political leaders will not defend traditional Southern conservative values unless "We the People" of Dixie apply political pressure. A modern-era Southern Resistance Movement is needed to create this political pressure.[1187]

1185 Stockes, Frankie, "VIRGINIA: Kiggans Voted With Dems On Trans School Bathrooms, But Now Campaigns On Parental Rights In Schools," National File (nationalfile.com), 21 December 2021, https://bit.ly/Trans-Toliets (Accessed 23 December 2021).

1186 Marsh, Julia, "Thomas Jefferson statue removed from City Hall after 187 years," *New York Post* (nyp.com), 22 November 2021, https://bit.ly/Jefferson-Removal-187 (Accessed 23 November 2021).

1187 See Kennedy, James Ronald, *Dixie Rising-Rules for Rebels*, 2nd ed.

Chapter 31:

MODERN ERA SOUTHERN RESISTANCE MOVEMENT

"It is useless to say Confederates were brave and skillful soldiers and then fail to understand and defend their cause, for then we are accomplices in the lie that they were brave in a bad cause."
—*Dr. Clyde N. Wilson*[1188]

IN 1787-8 the Southern States made their first strategic mistake (failure) when they elected to ratify the original Constitution while ignoring the dire warnings of men such as Patrick Henry; in 1850 at the Nashville Convention they made the second strategic mistake when they tied Southern rights to the issue of protecting slavery instead of demanding time to pursue the high road to emancipation; the third (primary military) strategic mistake was the failure to pursue the fleeing Yankees at the Battle of First Manassas; the South's fourth strategic mistake came after the end of Active Reconstruction during Passive Reconstruction when the South passively avoided efforts to undo the destruction of America's original Constitution caused by Lincoln's war and the Republican Party's Active Reconstruction. This failure gave rise to the South's fifth strategic mistake during Modern Era Reconstruction (post-1965), a failure that resulted in the infliction of Modern-Era Reconstruction upon all Americans. The fifth strategic failure is

---

1188 Clyde N. Wilson, "Our History and their Myth: Comparing the Confederacy and the Union," *To Live and Die In Dixie*, 413.

America's Woke Ruling Elite Destroyed Post-War North/South Reconciliation

The demonizing of all things Southern by America's politically correct Woke ruling elite destroyed the post-War North/South reconciliation. In Modern Era America, traditional Southern moral, social, and political values are censored, forbidden, and ridiculed. The traditional South provided America with military men such as Alvin York (Tennessee) and Audie Murphy (Texas) and the highest percentage of military recruits in the volunteer military. However, the recent (December 2023) removal of the Arlington National Cemetery Reconciliation Monument by the Federal Government and removing the names of Southern heroes from US military bases by the US military, demonstrates that the South is no longer allowed in America's Woke society and its military. The South is America's red-headed stepchild, with no hope of regaining its inheritance of freedom.

The time has come to establish a Modern Era Southern Resistance Movement and invite non-Southern conservatives to join us as we begin a peaceful revolution to restore America's original Constitutional Republic of Sovereign States—states possessing real States' Rights as described by Thomas Jefferson and James Madison in the Kentucky and Virginia Resolutions of 1798.

the South's unquestioned acceptance as legitimate the current indivisible political *status quo* that inflicts an American form of neo-Marxist political slavery upon "We the People."[1189] The question that begs to be asked is, "Will we meekly accept the results the Woke radicals have planned for us, or will 'We the People' initiate our own Modern Era Resistance Movement?"

It is hard for humans to admit failure especially when they know that their cause was right, and their intentions were honorable. This is true for all humanity not just for Southerners. As a winner of the Nobel Memorial Prize in Economics noted,

> We are ready to accept almost any explanation of the present crisis of our civilization except one: that the present state of the world may be the result of genuine error on our own part and that the pursuit of some of our most cherished ideals has apparently *produced results utterly different from those which we expected.*[1190] [Emphasis added by the author.]

When Southern leaders elected to forgo any radical attempts to restore America's original Constitution during Passive Reconstruction, they honestly thought the Northern ruling elites would keep their end of the tacit North/South bargain for reconciliation. Unfortunately, it *"produced results utterly different from those which we expected."* When the Democratic Solid South freely gave their support to the Democrat Party without extracting a *fundamental* change in the political *status quo* they must have thought that their loyalty to the party would purchase unending support for the South, but they were wrong. Today, conservative Southerners in particular and American conservatives in general place their hope on a political system that will "drain the swamp," "build the wall," balance the budget, cease "endless war," or promote

---

1189 The term "political *status quo*" means the supreme Federal Government, its massive "Deep State" bureaucracy, military, and financial/business interests with their well-financed lobbyists, all doing the bidding of national and global ruling elites to the detriment of the "forgotten man," America's "bitter clingers" and "deplorables."

1190 Hayek, F.A., *The Road To Serfdom* (1944, The University of Chicago Press, 2007), 65-6.

real Constitutional government but such hope is vain **if** "We the People" allow the neo-Marxist political *status quo* to remain in power. The current political system is designed to maintain itself and reward those who work within the corrupt system.[1191] As the Bible explains, Satan will not cast out Beelzebub. In the same manner, the current corrupt political system will not heal itself. If Americans are to reclaim the original and legitimate Constitution, it will be done by the revolutionary action of "We the People." But it must be a peaceful non-violent revolution. We must comply with the ancient advice "Beware the shedding of blood, for blood never sleeps."[1192] This is a moral imperative, but it is also pragmatic advice. As noted previously, even when a violent revolution is successful it is almost impossible to control revolutionaries who come to power via violence. The effort to secure independence for the Canadian province of Quebec was almost destroyed when certain elements within the Quebec separatist movement resorted to violence.[1193]

The consequences of the War and Reconstruction are not over. The deadly impact on American liberty lives with all Americans today. The South lost its first effort to gain independence, but that loss did not negate the right of "We the People" of the South and the rest of America to establish a government based upon the free and unfettered consent of the governed. The Yankee Empire's victory over the South assured the continuation of the struggle for constitutional liberty at another time and in another fashion. As one author wrote,

> [The South's] opponents pressed steadily on to win and in its aftermath sowed the seeds for a century

---

1191 Kennedy, James Ronald, *Nullification: Why and How*, 10-16. Free downloadable copy at www.bit.ly/Kennedys_FreePDF.

1192 "**Saladin**, Arabic in full **Ṣalā▪ al-Dīn Yūsuf ibn Ayyūb (Righteousness of the Faith, Joseph, Son of Job)**, also called **al-Malik al-Nāṣir Ṣalā▪ al-Dīn Yūsuf I**. Born 1137, Mesopotamia [now in Iraq], Died March 4, 1193." Britannica, www.britannica.com/biography/Saladin (Accessed 17 September 2023).

1193 Kennedy, James Ronald, *Dixie Rising-Rules for Rebels*, 2ⁿᵈ edition (Shotwell Publishing Co., Columbia, SC: 2021), 108-9.

of hatred and resistance, because in a sense they [Yankees] were so English that they thought victory on the battlefield was the equivalent of conquering a region—and, more important, a culture.[1194]

Americans have forgotten that "For our Fathers, liberty consisted in a negative upon government. It was not a boon bestowed by the government, but something that must be asserted against the government."[1195] Americans in Modern Era Reconstruction live in a time when the Federal Government is constantly expanding its powers due to some real or imagined "crisis." "We the People" are told to accept the invasion of our Fourth Amendment right to privacy by the National Security Agency (NSA) because it is necessary to protect us from terrorists, we are ordered to accept government-mandated injections of experimental drugs because it is necessary to prevent a modern-day plague, we are told to forget about freedom of religion and speech due to the necessity of fighting COVID—**necessity is the plea of tyrants!**[1196] But once the real, imagined, or manufactured crisis has passed, the government never relents in the power it has gained, nor renounces the precedent that was thus established.

> No matter what rhetoric they employ, politicians and the bureaucracies over which they preside love power, and power is never easily surrendered once the danger, if there ever was one, has passed.[1197]

Notice how emotional "reasoning" is used to stampede people into surrendering their rights. The use of emotional allegations backed by a virtually monopolistic, leftist, mainline, and digital media has reduced "We the People" to political slaves of the

---

1194 Webb, Jim, *Born Fighting: How Scots-Irish Shaped America* (New York: Broadway Books, 2004), 233.

1195 Wilson, Dr. Clyde N., *From Union to Empire*, 335.

1196 "So spake the Fiend, and with necessity, The Tyrant's plea, excused his devilish deeds." —John Milton, *Paradise Lost*.

1197 Bruce Caldwell in Introduction to Hayek, F.A., *The Road To Serfdom*, 32.

Yankee Empire's ruling elite. Overcoming the political *status quo* will require more than merely voting for the best candidate, electing good conservatives, or dutifully listening to conservative talking-heads who worship Lincoln, the Republican Party, and the corrupt unconstitutional government created by Lincoln and the Republican Party. Lincoln's and the Republican Party's illegitimate government was forced upon "We the People" of the South and the rest of America. It is now up to "We the People" to decide whether we remain obedient political slaves by accepting this unconstitutional and therefore illegitimate government or whether we elect to replace it with a legitimate government.

CREATING A MODERN-ERA SOUTHERN RESISTANCE MOVEMENT

Action speaks louder than words. Books can be written, and speeches made but nothing motivates the people better than action. That was one of the main reasons for the sudden appearance of the 2009 Tea Party movement. At a time of high conservative unrest, the action (rallies and speeches) of the Tea Party movement attracted great crowds and enthusiasm. But the movement died just as quickly when it failed to produce new action that promised to make a *fundamental* political difference—something that will not happen by simply electing "good" conservatives. In effect, it told the enthusiastic crowds to keep doing what we have always done and hope for better results. Successful revolutionaries of the past endorsed what has been termed "propaganda of the deed."[1198] If we wish to attract the mass of conservatives, the "deed" must be audacious but not beyond the possibility of being accomplished. It must provide an opportunity to make a *fundamental* change in the current political *status quo*. Politics as usual, as advocated by mainline conservatives, may provide an occasional tactical victory *but it will never provide a strategic victory*—a fundamental change back to America's original Republic of Sovereign States.

1198 Posobiec, Jack, *The ANTIFA: Stories from Inside the Bloc* (Washington, DC: The Calamo Press, 2021), 69.

Most conservatives do not understand the need to create a mass movement to restore America's legitimate Constitutional Republic of Sovereign States. It takes more than books, and rallies to create, in the mind of the public, an understanding of the need to remove the illegitimate political *status quo* and replace it with a legitimate Republic of Sovereign States. Convincing the public requires an ongoing, continuous public relations campaign. In the political world the old expression, "repetition is the mother of learning," holds true.

> Affirmation, however, has no real influence unless it be constantly repeated,.... The thing affirmed comes by repetition to fix itself in the mind in such a way that it is accepted in the end as a demonstrated truth.[1199]

A modern-day Southern resistance movement can be initiated by a dedicated few who work to establish an ongoing public relations campaign explaining the reasons why "We the People" must unite to make a fundamental change in the current political *status quo*.

Mr. Conservative Ronald Reagan served two terms as President. He promised to return power to the local communities and States, but it never happened![1200] Reagan wanted to reduce the size and impact of the Federal Government, but the political *status quo* was there to prevent any loss of its power. In 1994 Newt Gingrich's Contract With America produced a majority in the United States House of Representatives. President Bill Clinton declared that the day of big government was over. President Clinton's words were a joke played on gullible conservatives. Big Government has grown tremendously since President Clinton's "joke on America." Why? Because the instrument of big government was in place and never ceased its gradual seizure of tax dollars and rights from

---

1199 Le Bon, Gustave, *The Crowd: A Study of the Popular Mind* (1896, London: T. Fisher Unwin, 1910), 142.

1200 Caldwell, Christopher, *The Age of Entitlement: America Since the Sixties* (New York: Simon & Schuster, 2020), 95-6.

Reconstruction

'The "Strong" government 1869–1877 — The "weak" government 1877–1881.'
J.A. Wales, artist. c. 1880. Courtesy LOC.gov.

an unsuspecting, politically naive public. Change will not come without a strategic plan for *fundamental* change implemented by dedicated individuals.[1201] Otherwise, the deconstruction of rights and liberties once protected by the Constitution will continue unabated.

The visible bayonets are gone but their threat remains. The South, as well as all the rest of conservative America, remains today chained to the Yankee Empire's illegitimate, unconstitutional, supreme Federal Government—*Vae Victis*!

1201 See Kennedy, James Ronald, *Dixie Rising-Rules for Rebels*, 2nd ed.

Chapter 32:

TIMELINE FOR LINCOLN'S SECRET WAR CONSPIRACY

The secret treachery that caused the war will come to light and justify the South. Truth is deathless. —Admiral Raphael Semmes, C.S.N.[1202]

LINCOLN WAS PLANNING for war even before he was elected. During the 1856 campaign, he told a Southerner that if the South attempts to leave the Union "we won't let you. With the purse and sword, the army and navy and treasury in our hands and at our command, you couldn't do it."[1203] Four years later and before his inauguration he wrote to a friend from Illinois on December 21, 1860:

> Present my compliments to Lieutenant-General Scott, and tell him confidentially, I shall be obliged to him to be as well prepared as he can to either hold or retake the forts, as the case may require, at and after the inauguration.[1204]

1202 Admiral Semmes cited in Johnstone, H.W., *Truth of the War Conspiracy of 1861* (c. 1917, Wake Forest, NC: The Scuppernong Press, 2012), 2.

1203 Lincoln cited in Johnson, Ludwell H., *The North Against the South: The American Iliad 1848-1877* (1978, Columbia, SC: The Foundation for American Education, 1993), 76-7.

1204 Lincoln cited in *Confederate Military History*, Vol. X, Part 2, 11.

Notice how he instructed his friend to "tell him [General Scott] *confidentially*." Lincoln's war plan was a secret conspiracy among folks who desired war and were planning to force the South to "fire the first shot." The following timeline demonstrates that the War was indeed "Lincoln's war." The data is taken from a booklet written circa 1917 by Captain H.W. Johnstone, CSA.[1205]

Date	Southern Peace Efforts	Lincoln's Secret War Conspiracy
November 6, 1860, Lincoln wins the election		
December 6, 1860	Armistice arranged between US and S.C. An agreement to maintain *status quo* until peaceful negotiations can take place.	
December 20, 1861, S.C. Secedes		
December 26, 1860	South Carolina's Peace Commissioner arrives in Washington. [*If secession is an act of treason, why didn't Lincoln have these "traitors" arrested?*]	South Carolina's Peace Commissioner is met with official indifference from the US president and officials.
December 26, 1860		Maj. Anderson (US) violates an agreement between the US and SC by occupying Fort Sumter.
January 9, 1861		US sends *Star of the West* attempting to reinforce Fort Sumter in violation agreed to between S.C. and the US SC artillery halts Lincoln's effort to reinforce Fort Sumter.
January 9, 1861	Senator Jefferson Davis visits President Buchanan asking him to avoid steps toward war.	

1205 Johnstone, *Truth of the War Conspiracy of 1861*.

Timeline for Lincoln's Secret War Conspiracy

Date	Southern Peace Efforts	Lincoln's Secret War Conspiracy
January 10, 1861, Florida Secedes		
January 21, 1861	Senator Jefferson Davis Farwell Address to the Senate stating he hopes for peaceful relations with the US.	
January 29, 1861	Armistice between Florida and the US as it relates to Fort Pickens. Both parties agree to maintain the *status quo*.	
February 2, 1861	Captain Barron (US) makes a report that good faith is being observed by both parties at Fort Pickens.	
February 6, 1861		Lt. Fox (US) meets with Lt. Hall (US) who was sent from Ft. Sumter to discuss reinforcing the fort.
February 18, 1861, J. Davis becomes President C.S.A.		
On March 4, 1861, Lincoln became President USA		
March 12, 1861	C.S.A. Peace Commissioners present their request to the USA for peaceful relations. [*If secession is an act of treason, why didn't Lincoln have these "traitors" arrested?*]	USA refuses to deal directly with Peace Commissioners; appoints Federal Judge Campbell as go-between.
March 12, 1861	C.S.A. Peace Commissioners in Washington ready to negotiate peace with the USA.	US government orders Capt. I. Vogdes, 1st Artillery, US Army, on board *USS Brooklyn* to reinforce Ft. Pickens in FL.

Date	Southern Peace Efforts	Lincoln's Secret War Conspiracy
March 12, 1861	C.S.A. Peace Commissioners in Washington ready to negotiate peace with the USA.	M. Blair of Lincoln's Cabinet telegraphs Lt. Fox to prepare for the reinforcement of Ft. Sumter, S.C.
March 15, 1861	C.S.A. Peace Commissioners in Washington ready to negotiate peace with the USA.	Seward assures C.S.A. Peace Commissioners via Judge Campbell "Sumter will be evacuated in ten days…there is no intent to reinforce Ft. Sumter."
March 15, 1861	Sen. Douglas (D-Illinois) introduced a resolution calling for the withdrawal of all US forces in the seceded States.	
March 19, 1861	C.S.A. Peace Commissioners in Washington ready to negotiate peace with the USA. C.S.A. authorities allowed US Lt. Fox to enter Ft. Sumter because he falsely claimed he was on a peace mission.	Lt. Fox was sent from Washington, under the pretext of a peaceful mission, to Ft. Sumter and once there urged Maj. Anderson to hold out until April 15th. He then returned to Washington to report.
March 20, 1861	C.S.A. Peace Commissioners in Washington ready to negotiate peace with the USA.	Seward repeats his false assurances regarding no intention to reinforce Ft. Sumter.
March 1-28, 1861	C.S.A. Peace Commissioners in Washington ready to negotiate peace with the USA.	US Senate in executive session but receiving no information regarding Lincoln's secret plan to initiate war adjourned Mar. 28. (Only Congress has constitutional authority to declare war.)
March 29, 1861	C.S.A. Peace Commissioners in Washington ready to negotiate peace with the USA.	Lincoln's secret order to Sec. of Navy "I desire expedition…6th of April… cooperate with the Sec. of War."

Timeline for Lincoln's Secret War Conspiracy

Date	Southern Peace Efforts	Lincoln's Secret War Conspiracy
March 30, 1861	C.S.A. Peace Commissioners in Washington ready to negotiate peace with the USA.	Lincoln sends Lt. Fox to New York to prepare three warships to transport 200 troops to Ft. Sumter, ready to leave by April 6th, orders marked "private."
March 30, 1861	C.S.A. Peace Commissioners in Washington ready to negotiate peace with the USA.	Judge Campbell asked Seward about rumors that had reached the C.S.A. authorities regarding the pending US attack on Ft. Sumter. Seward denied the rumors.
March 31, 1861	C.S.A. Peace Commissioners in Washington ready to negotiate peace with the USA.	Capt. Vogdes of USS Brooklyn off Pensacola, FL receives orders to reinforce Ft. Pickens.
April 1, 1861		Capt. Adams (US) refuses to reinforce Ft. Pickens, stating "both sides are faithfully observing the agreement entered into by the US."
April 1, 1861	C.S.A. Peace Commissioners in Washington ready to negotiate peace with the USA.	Seward tells Judge Campbell that he, Campbell, would have notice of any change to "the existing status of Ft. Pickens" and there were "no designs to reinforce Ft. Sumter."
April 1, 1861	C.S.A. Peace Commissioners in Washington ready to negotiate peace with the USA.	US Army HQ issued orders to reinforce Ft. Pickens noting "The object and destination of this expedition will be communicated to no one."
April 1, 1861	C.S.A. Peace Commissioners in Washington ready to negotiate peace with the USA.	Lincoln issues orders to "All officers of the Army & Navy…to aid Col. Brown…resupply Ft. Pickens."
April 1, 1861	C.S.A. Peace Commissioners in Washington ready to negotiate peace with the USA.	Lincoln ordered Lt. D.D. Porter to "…go to New York without delay, assume command of any steamer available & proceed to Pensacola Harbor…This order would be communicated to no person."

Date	Southern Peace Efforts	Lincoln's Secret War Conspiracy
April 1, 1861	C.S.A. Peace Commissioners in Washington ready to negotiate peace with the USA.	Lincoln sent an order to the commandant of the Navy Yard in Brooklyn, NY to "… fit out the *Powhatan* without delay…[for] Lt. Porter…She [*Powhatan*] is bound on secret service; you will under no circumstances communicate to the Navy Department."
April 2, 1861	C.S.A. Peace Commissioners in Washington ready to negotiate peace with the USA.	Colonel Brown US Army received orders from Army HQ to reinforce Ft. Pickens.
April 4, 1861	John Baldwin, the pro-Union man from Virginia, met with Lincoln to urge him to issue a "peaceful Union proclamation."	Lincoln replied to John Baldwin's peace request by telling him "I fear you are too late."
April 4, 1861	John Baldwin, a pro-Union Virginian, leaves Lincoln's office. [Like most other pro-Union Southerners, he believed in the original Union in which the States were Sovereign, and the Federal Government was ultimately answerable to the States. He, like most other pro-Union Southerners, supported his state when she seceded from Lincoln's new Union of Force.]	As Baldwin was leaving his meeting with Lincoln he met and spoke with seven Northern governors—the War Governors. They were there to urge Lincoln to do whatever was necessary to keep the Southern States under Union [Northern] control. They were concerned about the economic loss their States would suffer if "we let the South go."
April 5, 1861	C.S.A. Peace Commissioners in Washington ready to negotiate peace with the USA.	Lincoln's Sec. of the Navy issued a confidential order for four US steamers that would compose "a naval force…to be sent to the vicinity of Charleston, SC."

TIMELINE FOR LINCOLN'S SECRET WAR CONSPIRACY

Date	Southern Peace Efforts	Lincoln's Secret War Conspiracy
April 6, 1861	C.S.A. Peace Commissioners in Washington ready to negotiate peace with the USA.	Sec. of Navy rebukes Capt. Adams and orders "...it being the wish & intention of the Navy Department to cooperate with the War Department in that objective." [This is the same Capt. Adams discussed in column for April 1, 1861.]
April 11, 1861	C.S.A. Peace Commissioners in Washington ready to negotiate peace with the USA.	Lt. J.L. Worden (US) was sent on a secret mission to Ft. Pickens; he told Gen. Bragg, CSA, that he (Lt. Worden) was there to deliver a *peaceful* message to Capt. Adams (US) but secretly brought orders from Washington to cooperate with efforts to reinforce Ft. Pickens.
April 11, 1861	C.S.A. Peace Commissioners in Washington ready to negotiate peace with the USA.	*USS Brooklyn*, in violation of the armistice agreed to by both parties, landed troops & supplies at Ft. Pickens; the original order was issued *March 12*, 1861.
April 12, 1861		With a Yankee invasion fleet off its coast, the C.S.A. is forced to fire on Ft. Sumter as an act of self-defense. *The first who renders force necessary to defend and protect a right is the aggressor in a war.*
April 13, 1861		Justice Campbell US Supreme Court sends letter to Seward "what is going on at Ft. Sumter ...Lincoln ...proximate cause..."

Numerous Northern newspapers recognized the affair at Ft. Sumter as Lincoln's effort to force the South to "fire the first shot." On April 5, the *New York Herald* wrote in an editorial:

> We have no doubt Mr. Lincoln wants the [Confederate] Cabinet at Montgomery to take the initiative by capturing...forts in its waters, for it would give him [Mr. Lincoln] the opportunity of throwing the responsibility of commencing hostilities.

Two days later, on April 7, the same paper noted:

> Unless Mr. Lincoln's administration makes the first demonstration and attack, President Davis says there will be no bloodshed. With Mr. Lincoln's administration, therefore, rests the responsibility of precipitating a collision, and the fearful events of protracted war.

The New Jersey *American Standard* wrote on April 12:

> The measure is a disingenuous feint...a mere decoy to draw the first fire from the people of the South, which act by the pre-determination of the government is to be the pretext for letting loose the horrors of war. It [Lincoln's government] dares not itself fire the first shot or draw the first blood and is now seeking by a mean artifice to transfer the odium of doing so to the Southern Confederacy.

The Providence Daily Post in its April 13 edition noted:

> We think the reader will perceive why Mr. Lincoln saw an opportunity to inaugurate civil war without appearing in the character of an aggressor.

Timeline for Lincoln's Secret War Conspiracy

The *Buffalo Daily Courier's* April 16 editorial declared:

> The affair at Fort Sumter, it seems to us, has been planned as a means by which the war feeling at the North should be intensified, and the [Lincoln] administration thus receive popular support for its policy.... War is inaugurated, and the design of the administration is accomplished.[1206]

The "secret" war conspiracy was recognized for what it was but the emotional claim that the South fired the first shot, that the nation's flag suffered an unpardonable insult aroused the appropriate amount of popular passion to give Lincoln the cover he needed to initiate an aggressive war against a sovereign nation—the Confederate States of America.

Lincoln was unmoved by the specter of the horrors of war. His callous attitude toward his own people is demonstrated by his secret efforts to initiate war. His hatred for the Southern people was demonstrated by his response to a speech by Senator Douglas (D-Illinois) in 1860. Senator Douglas speaking in the US Senate in December of 1860 introduced a resolution to protect the constitutional rights of the States and to punish individuals who were guilty of promoting slave insurrection. He aimed to calm the fears in the South—especially the Deep South—about the promotion of John Brown type of interstate slave insurrectionist activities. Lincoln speaking at Cooper Union, New York denounced Senator Douglas's resolution.[1207]

One modern-day scholar succinctly described Lincoln's intentions: "Lincoln's *union* was essentially a means to a public policy end, i.e., the economic subordination of the Southern States to the Republican Party's business constituents by all means necessary.

[1206] All quotes from Karen Stokes, "Fort Sumter and the Siege of Charleston," *To Live and Die In Dixie*, 165-7.

[1207] Johnstone, *Truth of the War Conspiracy of 1861*, 21.

In other words, a militaristic imperialism against an independent Southern confederacy was not off the table."[1208]

When a British journalist was asked why the North was fighting against the South he replied, "For empire, sir, for empire." The *Telegraph* of London, England observed that even though the post-War United States claimed to be a republic, "...some eight million of the people are subjects, not citizens." [1209] Lincoln's war and the Republican Party's Active Reconstruction destroyed America's legitimate Republic of Sovereign States and imposed an illegitimate, tyrannical, supreme Federal Government controlled by Northern, and today Global, ruling elites. "We the People" have been reduced to the Yankee Empire's political slaves. It awaits to be seen if there remains enough courage in the South to initiate a second resistance movement—or did the bloody ground of unnumbered Southern battlefields drink not only our fathers' blood but their children's courage as well?

Deo Vindice

1208 DeRosa, Dr. Marshall, "The Rationalization of American Militaristic Imperialism," *To Live and Die In Dixie*, 298.

1209 Bowers, *The Tragic Era*, 146.

Bibliography

A Just and Lasting Peace: A Documentary History of Reconstruction, John David Smith, editor (NY: Signet Classics, 2013).

Confederate Military History, Volumes I through XII (1899, Harrisburg, PA: The Archives Society, 1994).

The Confederate Veteran Magazine Volumes I – 40 (Harrisburg, PA: The National Historical Society, 1987).

I'll Take My Stand, (1930, Baton Rouge, LA: LSU Press, 1983).

John Milton Complete Poems and Major Prose Merritt, Hughes, editor (New York: The Odyssey Press, 1957).

Making Poor Nations Rich, Powell, Benjamin, editor (Stanford University Press, 2008).

Patrick Henry: Life, Correspondence and Speeches, Vol. III, W.W. Henry, editor (Harrisonburg, VA: Sprinkle Publishing, 1993).

Rethinking the American Union for the Twenty-First Century, Donald Livingston, editor (Gretna, LA: Pelican Publishing Co., 2013).

The Anti-Federalist Papers and the Constitutional Convention Debates Ralph Ketcham, editor (New York: Penguin Books, 1986),

The Oxford Companion to the Supreme Court, Kermit L. Hall, editor (New York: Oxford University Press, 1992).

To Live and Die In Dixie, Frank Powell, III, editor (Columbia, TN: Sons of Confederate Veterans, 2014).

Bacevich, Andrew J., *The Limits of Power: The End of American Exceptionalism* (New York: Henry Holt & Co., 2008).

Bauer, Elizabeth Kelley, *Commentaries on the Constitution 1790-1860* (New York: Columbia University Press, 1952).

Bettersworth, John K., *Mississippi: A History* (Austin, Texas: The Steck Company, 1959).

Bowers, Claude, *The Tragic Era* (New York: Halcyon House, 1929).

Bradford, Dr. M.E., *Founding Fathers: Brief Lives of the Framers of the United States Constitution* (New York: The University Press of Kansas, New York: 1981).

Bradford, Dr. M.E., *A Better Guide Than Reason: Federalists & Anti-Federalists* (1979, New Brunswick & London: Transaction Publishers, 1994).

Bradford, Dr. M.E., *Against the Barbarians and Other Reflections on Familiar Themes* (Columbia, MO: University of Missouri Press, 1992).

Bradford, Dr. M.E., *Original Intentions: On the Making and Ratification of the United States Constitution* (University of Georgia Press: 1993).

Cahn, Jonathan, *The Return of the Gods* (Lake Mary, FL: FrontLine, 2022).

Caldwell, Christopher, *The Age of Entitlement: America Since the Sixties* (New York: Simon & Schuster, 2020).

Calhoun, John C., *On the Constitution and Government*, in *The Works of John C. Calhoun*, Vol I. (New York: Appleton & Co., 1851).

Cannon, Jr., Devereaux D., *Flags of the Confederacy* (Gretna, LA: Pelican Publishing Co., 1997).

Chodes, John, *Washington's KKK: The Union League During Southern Reconstruction* (Columbia, SC: Shotwell Publishing, 2016).

Cisco, Walter Brian, *War Crimes Against Southern Civilians* (Gretna, LA: Pelican Publishing Co., 2008).

Clark & Kirwan, *The South Since Appomattox* (New York: Oxford University Press, 1967).

Colbourn, Trevor, *The Lamp of Experience* (1965, Indianapolis, IN: Liberty Fund, 1998).

Cruden, Robert, *The Negro in Reconstruction* (Englewood Cliffs, NJ: Prentice-Hall, Inc., 1969).

Davis, Jefferson, *Rise and Fall of the Confederate Government*, Vol. 1, (1881, Nashville, TN: William Mayes Coats, c.1980).

De La Cova, Antonio Rafael, *Cuban Confederate Colonel-The Life of Ambrosio Jose Gonzales* (University of South Carolina Press, 2003).

DeRosa, Dr. Marshall, "The Rationalization of American Militaristic Imperialism," *To Live and Die In Dixie*, Frank Powell, III, editor (Columbia, TN: Sons of Confederate Veterans, 2014).

De Tocqueville, Alexis de, *Democracy in America* Vol. 1 (1848, Garden City, NY: Doubleday & Co., 1966).

DiLorenzo, Dr. Thomas J., *The Real Lincoln* (New York: Three Rivers Press, 2002).

DiLorenzo, Dr. Thomas J., *Hamilton's Curse* (New York: Crown Forum, 2008).

Downs, Jim, *Sick from Freedom: African-American Illness and Suffering during the Civil War and Reconstruction* (New York: Oxford University Press, 2012).

Ellul, Jacques, *Propaganda: The Formation of Men's Attitudes* (New York: Alfred A. Knopf, 1965).

Englehardt, Tom, *Shadow Government: Surveillance, Secret Wars, and a Global Security State in a Single-Superpower World* (Chicago, IL: Haymarket Books, 2014).

Evans, Eli N., *Judah P. Benjamin-The Jewish Confederate* (New York: The Free Press, 1988).

Fleming, Walter Lynwood, *The Sequel of Appomattox* (1919, Yale University Press, 1970).

Floan, Howard R., *The South in Northern Eyes-1831 to 1861* (New York: McGraw-Hill Book Co., 1958).

Friedman, Milton, *Free to Choose* (New York: Harcourt Brace Jovanovich, 1980).

Goldberg, Jonah, *Liberal Fascism* (New York: Double Day, 2007).

Graham, John Remington, *Principles of Confederacy* (Salt Lake City, UT: Northwest Publishing, 1990).

Graham, Paul C., *When the Yankees Come: Former South Carolina Slaves Remember Sherman's Invasion* (Columbia, SC: Shotwell Publishing, 2016).

Hair, Dr. William Ivy, *Bourbonism and Agrarian Protest: Louisiana Politics 1877-1900* (Baton Rouge, LA: LSU Press, 1969).

Hart, B.H. Liddell, *Strategy* (1954, New York: Frederick A. Praeger, 1968).

Hayek, F.A., *The Road To Serfdom* (1944, The University of Chicago Press, 2007).

Henry, Robert Selph, *The Story of Reconstruction* (New York: Konecky & Konecky, 1938).

Henry, William Wirt, *Patrick Henry: Life, Correspondence and Speeches*, Vol. III (1891, Harrisonburg, VA: Sprinkle Publications, 1993).

Hicks, Dr. Stephen R.C., *Explaining Postmodernism-Skepticism and Socialism from Rousseau to Foucault,* 2nd edition (Ockham's Razor Publishing, 2011).

Hoar, Jay S., *The South's Last Boys in Gray* (Bowling Green, OH: Bowling Green State University Press, 1986).

Hummel, Jeffrey Rogers, *Emancipating Slaves, Enslaving Free Men* (Peru, IL: Open Court Publishing Co., 1996).

Johnson, Chalmers, *The Sorrows of Empire* (New York: Henry Holt & Co., 2004).

Johnson, Ludwell H., *The North Against the South: The American Iliad 1848-1877* (1978, Columbia, SC: The Foundation for American Education, 1993).

Josephson, Matthew, *The Robber Barons* (New York: Harcourt & Brace, 1934).

Johnstone, H.W., *Truth of the War Conspiracy of 1861* (circa 1917, Wake Forest, NC: The Scuppernong Press, 2012).

Kennedy & Kennedy, *Jefferson Davis: Highroad to Emancipation and Constitutional Government* (Columbia, SC: Shotwell Publishing, 2022).

Kennedy & Kennedy, *Nullifying Tyranny* (Gretna, LA: Pelican Publishing Co., 2010).

Kennedy & Kennedy, *Punished With Poverty-The Suffering South* 2nd edition (Columbia, SC: Shotwell Publishing, 2020).

Kennedy & Kennedy, *Yankee Empire: Aggressive Abroad and Despotic at Home* (Columbia, SC: Shotwell Publishing, 2018).

Kennedy & Kennedy, *The South Was Right!*, 3rd edition (Columbia, SC: Shotwell Publishing, 2020).

Kennedy, James Ronald, *Dixie Rising-Rules for Rebels*, 2nd edition (Columbia, SC: Shotwell Publishing, 2021).

Kennedy, James Ronald, *Nullification: Why and How*. Free downloadable copy (pdf) available at www.bit.ly/Kennedys_freePDF.

Kennedy, James Ronald, *Reclaiming Liberty* (Gretna, LA: Pelican Publishing Co., 2005).

Kennedy, James Ronald *Be Ye Separate: Bible Belt Revival or Marxist Revolution*. Free downloadable (pdf) copy available at www.bit.ly/Free-Download_BYS.

Kennedy, Walter D., *ReKilling Lincoln* (Gretna, LA: Pelican Publishing Co., 2015).

Kennedy and Benson, *Lincoln, Marx, and the GOP* (Columbia, SC: Shotwell Publishing, 2023).

Keys, Thomas Bland, *The Uncivil War: Union Army and Navy Excesses In The Official Records* (Biloxi, MS: The Beauvoir Press, 1991).

Kilpatrick, James Jackson, *The Sovereign States* (Chicago, IL: Henry Regnery Co., 1957).

Lane, Charles, *The Day Freedom Died-The Colfax Massacre-The Supreme Court and The Betrayal of Reconstruction* (New York: Holt Paperbacks, 2008).

Lanier, Sidney, in *Poems of Sidney Lanier* Mary Day Lanier editor (1884, Athens, GA: The University of Georgia Press, 1981).

Le Bon, Gustave, *The Crowd: A Study of the Popular Mind* (1896, London: T. Fisher Unwin, 1910).

Leigh, Philip, *Southern Reconstruction* (Yardley, PA: Westholme Publishing, 2017).

Leigh, Philip, *U.S. Grant's Failed Presidency* (Columbia, SC: Shotwell Publishing, 2019).

Lewis, C.S., *The Abolition of Man* (1944, New York: Harper Collins, 2001).

Lukacs, John, *Democracy and Populism: Fear and Hatred* (Yale University Press: 2005).

Lytle, Andrew Nelson, *Bedford Forrest and His Critter Company* (1931, Nashville, TN: J.S. Sanders & Company, 1992).

Madison, James, *The Debates in the Federal Convention of 1787 Which Framed the Constitution of the United States of America* (Union, NJ: The Lawbook Exchange, 1999).

Masters, Edgar Lee, *Lincoln the Man* (1931, Columbia, SC: The Foundation for American Education, 1997).

McCarthy, Andrew C., *Ball of Collusion: The Plot to Rig an Election and Destroy a Presidency* (New York: Encounter Books, 2019).

McDonald, Forrest & McWhiney, Grady, "The South from Self-Sufficiency to Peonage: An Interpretation," *The American Historical Review*, Vol. 85, No. 5 (Dec. 1980).

McDonald, Dr. Forrest, *A Constitutional History of the United States* (Malabar, FL: Robert E. Krieger Publishing Co., 1982).

McWhiney & Jamieson, *Attack and Die: Civil War Military Tactics and the Southern Heritage* (Tuscaloosa, AL: The University of Alabama Press, 1988).

McWhiney, Dr. Grady, *Cracker Culture: Celtic Ways in the Old South* (Tuscaloosa, AL: The University of Alabama Press, 1988).

Melish, Dr. Joanne P., *Disowning Slavery: Gradual Emancipation and "Race" in New England, 1780-1860* (Ithaca, NY: Cornell University Press, 1998).

Mills, Dr. Gary B., *The Forgotten People: Cane River's Creoles of Color* (Baton Rouge, LA: LSU Press, 1977).

Mill, John Stuart, "Representative Government," *American State Papers, Federalist, J.S. Mill* Vol. 43, Robert Maynard Hutchins, editor (London: Britannica Great Books, 1952).

Mises, Ludwig von, *Socialism: An Economic and Sociological Analysis* (1936, Indianapolis, IN: Liberty Fund, 1981),

Mitcham, Jr., Dr. Samuel W., *It Wasn't About Slavery: Exposing the Great Lie of the Civil War* (Washington, DC: Regnery History, 2020).

Mitcham, Jr, Dr. Samuel W., *The Encyclopedia of Confederate Generals* (Washington, DC: Regnery Publishing, 2022).

Murray, Charles, *Losing Ground: American Social Policy 1950-1980* (New York: Harper Collins Publishers, 1984).

Nicholson, James W., *Stories of Dixie* (1915, Toccoa, GA: The Confederate Reprint Co., 2015).

Northup, Solomon, *Twelve Years A Slave*, Sue Eakin and Joseph Logsdon editors (1853, Baton Rouge, LA: LSU Press, 1996).

O'Brien, David M., *Constitutional Law and Politics* Vol. 2, 2nd edition (New York: Norton & Company, 1991).

Pollard, E.A., *Southern History of the War* (1866, Crown Publishers Inc., 1977).

Posobiec, Jack, *The ANTIFA: Stories from Inside the Bloc* (Washington, DC: The Calamo Press, 2021).

Quirk & Bridwell, *Judicial Dictatorship* (New Brunswick & London: Transaction Publishers, 1995).

Rawle, William, *A View of the Constitution*, 1825, edited and annotated by Kennedy & Kennedy as *A View of the Constitution: Secession as Taught at West Point* (Wake Forest, NC: The Scuppernong Press, 2020).

Richardson, J.A., *A Historical and Constitutional Defense of The South* (1914, Harrisonburg, VA: Sprinkle Publications, 2010).

Robertson, Henry O., *The Emergence of the Whig Party in Louisiana, 1828-1840* (Lafayette, LA: Centers for Louisiana Studies, 2007).

Rosen, Robert N., *The Jewish Confederates* (Columbia, SC: University of South Carolina Press, 2000).

Rothbard, Murray N., *America's Great Depression* (1963, Auburn, AL: The Ludwig von Mises Institute, 2000).

Seabrook, Lochlainn, *A Rebel Born; A Defense of Nathan Bedford Forrest* (Franklin, TN: Sea Raven Press, 2010).

Semmes, Admiral Raphael, *Memories of Service Afloat* (1868, Secaucus, NJ: The Blue & Grey Press, 1987).

Simkins, Francis Butler, *A History of the South* (New York: Alfred A. Knopf, 1959).

Sowell, Thomas, *Civil Rights: Rhetoric or Reality?* (New York: William Morrow & Co., 1984).

Sowell, Thomas, *Race and Culture: A World View* (New York: Harper Collins Publishers, 1994).

Stephens, Alexander H., *Constitutional View of the Late War Between the States* (1870, Harrisonburg, VA: Sprinkle Publications, 1994), Vol. I.

Stokes, Karen, "Fort Sumter and the Siege of Charleston," *To Live and Die In Dixie*, Frank Powell, III, editor (Columbia, TN: Sons of Confederate Veterans, 2014).

Taylor, John, *News Views and An Inquiry into the Principles and Policy of the Government of the United States* (1814: New Haven, CT: Yale University Press: 1950).

Taylor, John, *Tyranny Unmasked* (1822: Indianapolis, IN: Liberty Fund, 1992).

Tourgee, Albion W., *A Fool's Errand* (1879, Cambridge, MA: The Belknap Press, 1961).

Upshur, Abel P., *The Federal Government: Its True Nature and Character* (1868, Houston, TX: St. Thomas Press, 1977).

Weaver, Dr. Richard, *The Southern Tradition at Bay* (New Rochelle, NY: Arlington House, 1968).

Webb, Senator Jim, *Born Fighting: How Scots-Irish Shaped America* (New York: Broadway Books, 2004).

Williams, T. Harry, *Huey Long* (1961, New York: Random House, 1981).

Williams, T. Harry, *P.G.T. Beauregard: Napoleon in Gray* (Baton Rouge, LA: LSU Press, 1955).

Wilson, Clyde N., *From Union to Empire* (Columbia, SC: The Foundation for American Education, 2003).

Wilson, Clyde N., *The Yankee Problem: An American Dilemma* (Columbia, SC: Shotwell Publishing, 2016).

Winters, Dr. John D., *The Civil War in Louisiana* (Baton Rouge, LA: LSU Press, 1963).

Index

This index consists of only a few key names and phrases. Researchers are encouraged to obtain an e-copy of this book which allows for the searching of the book by any name or topic desired.

Allen, James S., ix, xiii.

Articles of Confederation, 46, 53-56, 63, 109-111, 431.

Beauregard, P.G.T., 7, 13, 73-74, 88, 130, 140, 159, 176, 326, 351, 385, 418, 421, 454-455.

black militia, 32, 43, 45-46, 236-237, 252-253, 257, 264, 289-290, 366-367, 370, 390, 399, 404, 420, 439.

bloody shirt, 85, 87, 90, 94, 96-97, 184, 192, 240-241, 262-264, 266-271, 323, 332, 360, 391, 404, 408.

Brown, John, x, 16, 71, 91, 104, 273, 461-462, 537.

Corwin Amendment, 38.

Cultural Genocide, 22, 518.

Davis, Jefferson, 1-2, 6, 16, 18, 23, 37, 47, 56, 68, 72, 79-80, 89, 115, 118, 136-137, 149-150, 153-154, 164, 170, 191, 200, 211, 213-214, 228, 234, 243, 259, 306, 344, 384-385, 388, 400, 430, 491, 510, 530-531.

Deep State, x, xi, 20, 27, 39, 81, 182, 194, 201, 242, 265-266, 345, 347, 406, 488, 502, 513, 517, 523.

Divide-and-Rule, 42, 142, 146, 184, 232, 235, 281.

Forrest, Nathan Bedford, xvi, 7, 73, 140, 258, 439.

Fourteenth Amendment, 49, 179, 183, 189-191, 193, 205-209, 282, 286-287, 294, 296, 327, 431, 502-503.

Freedmen, 6, 235, 249, 254-256, 274, 276, 278-279, 296, 303, 307, 318, 402, 416, 418, 436, 442, 453.

French resistance movement, 33, 372.

Genocide, 22, 518.

Globalist, 19, 25, 31, 39, 81, 83, 201, 215, 231, 242, 349, 446.

Grant, President, 6, 12, 45, 116, 127-128, 143-144, 162, 224-225, 240, 250, 258-259, 264, 267, 269-271, 298, 332, 334, 367, 374, 384, 387, 390, 396, 401, 403, 405-407, 412, 423, 440, 448-449, 456, 467-468, 473.

Hamilton, Alexander, 29, 57, 62, 64, 105, 109, 112, 150, 199, 203, 265, 496.

Hampton, Wade, 14, 142, 417-418, 421, 423, 425.

Henry, Patrick, xiii, 2, 64-65, 67-68, 70-71, 96, 111-112, 116, 155, 459, 464, 466, 521.

Hill, Benjamin Harvey, 4, 140.

Ireland, 87, 124, 129, 261, 302, 306, 424.

Jefferson, Thomas, xiii, 27-28, 34, 47, 54, 58, 61, 65, 79, 96, 105, 108, 113, 118, 122, 156, 199, 204, 265, 329, 344, 520, 522.

Johnson, Andrew, 91, 150, 170, 178-179, 183, 186, 236, 259, 310, 353, 411, 442-444.

Johnson, Bradley T., 2-3, 42, 335.

Klan-Kirk War, vii, 387, 390, 403.

Ku Klux Klan, 32-33, 280, 311, 398.

Lanier, Sidney Clopton, 272, 543.

Lee, Robert E., 27-28, 89, 259, 349, 472.

Lee, Stephen Dill, 345, 398.

Madison, James, xi, xiii, 47, 58-60, 62, 65, 79, 106, 108-110, 113, 204, 344, 466, 522.

Nashville Convention, 69-71, 521.

Plessy v. Ferguson, 502.

Quebec, 77-78, 81, 306-307, 524.

Rawle, William, 16.

Red Shirts, 257, 414, 442.

Resolutions of 1798, 47-48, 79, 115, 118, 204, 344, 522.

Revels, Hiram, 12, 143-144, 222, 352, 374.

Semmes, Admiral Raphael, 88, 185, 529.

Southern Resistance Movement, viii, 19, 311, 363, 369, 439, 520-522, 526.

Spanish-American War, 77, 506.

Stephens, Alexander, 3, 8, 201, 308, 385, 418, 490.

Stevens, Thaddeus, 36, 40-41, 76, 170-171, 173, 208, 210, 225, 229, 232-234, 304, 306, 310, 320, 330, 360, 382, 389, 391, 396, 437, 442, 444, 476.

strategic failure, 34, 51-52, 67, 70, 74, 77, 80-83, 105, 118, 198, 302, 307, 328-329, 450, 457, 488, 491, 521.

Sumner, Charles, 40, 180.

Thirteenth Amendment, 48, 181, 189-190, 207-208, 294, 327, 355-356, 434, 446.

Turner, Nat, x, 200.

Union League, ix, 8, 17, 32-33, 43-45, 166, 213, 219, 231, 235-236, 238, 244, 248-249, 251-252, 254, 257, 267, 274, 302, 311, 367, 370, 390, 397-398, 418-419, 441.

Vallandigham, Rep. 6.

Vicksburg Mississippi, 12, 168, 361-362, 367-369, 373.

Vigilantism, 44, 403.

What could have been, xii, xvi, 2, 137, 139, 183, 281, 286, 295, 297, 352, 373, 422, 470.

About the Author

JAMES RONALD (RON) KENNEDY

RON KENNEDY was born and raised in south-central Mississippi. In 1974 he moved to Louisiana where he now resides.

Ron received a Master's in Health Administration (MHA) from Tulane University in New Orleans, a Master of Jurisprudence in Health Law (MJ) from Loyola University Chicago, and a Bachelor's degree from Northeast Louisiana University. He retired in April 2015 after serving over 20 years as Vice President of Risk Management for a Louisiana-based insurance company.

Ron and his twin brother Donnie are the authors of the bestselling book *The South Was Right!* with more than 150,000 copies sold—the third updated edition was released in November 2020. The Kennedy Twins have co-authored numerous other books including *Jefferson Davis: High Road to Emancipation and Constitutional Government; Punished with Poverty—the Suffering South*; and *Yankee Empire: Aggressive Abroad and Despotic at Home.*

Ron's most recent books are *Dixie Rising—Rules for Rebels, When Rebel Was Cool, Red State Red County Secession, Be Ye*

Separate-Bible Belt Revival or Marxist Revolution, and Nullifying Federal and State Gun Control.

Ron is the past Commander of the Louisiana Division Sons of Confederate Veterans. He is the former Chief of Heritage Operations for the National Sons of Confederate Veterans. He is a frequent speaker at Southern Heritage and political conservative meetings.

Author's website: www.kennedytwins.com

More By The Kennedy Twins

Over 90 Titles For You To Enjoy
ShotwellPublishing.com

JEFFERY ADDICOTT
Union Terror: Debunking the False Justifications for Union Terror

MARK ATKINS
Women in Combat: Feminism Goes to War

JOYCE BENNETT
Maryland, My Maryland: The Cultural Cleansing of a Small Southern State

GARRY BOWERS
Slavery and The Civil War: What Your History Teacher Didn't Tell You

Dixie Days: Reminiscences Of a Southern Boyhood

JERRY BREWER
Dismantling the Republic

ANDREW P. CALHOUN
My Own Darling Wife: Letters From A Confederate Volunteer

JOHN CHODES
Segregation: Federal Policy or Racism?

Washington's Kkk: The Union League During Southern Reconstruction

WALTER BRIAN CISCO
War Crimes Against Southern Civilians

JOHN DEVANNY
Continuities: The South in a Time of Revolution

JOSHUA DOGGRELL
Doxed: The Political Lynching of a Southern Cop

JAMES C. EDWARDS
What Really Happened?: Quantrill's Raid On Lawrence, Kansas

TED EHMANN
Boom & Bust In Bone Valley: Florida's Phosphate Mining History 1886-2021

JOHN AVERY EMISON
The Deep State Assassination of Martin Luther King Jr.

DON GORDON
Snowball's Chance: My Kidneys Failed, My Wife Left Me & My Dog Died...

JOHN R. GRAHAM
Constitutional History of Secession

PAUL C. GRAHAM
Confederaphobia

When The Yankees Come: Former Carolina Slaves Remember

Nonsense on Stilts: The Gettysburg Address & Lincoln's Imaginary Nation

JOE D. HAINES
The Diary of Col. John Henry Stover Funk of the Stonewall Brigade, 1861-1862

CHARLES HAYES
The REAL First Thanksgiving

V.P. HUGHES
Col. John Singleton Mosby: In the News 1862-19

TERRY HULSEY
25 Texas Heroes

The Constitution of Non-State Government: Field Guide to Texas Secession

JOSEPH JAY
Sacred Conviction: The South's Stand for Biblical Authority

SUZANNE JOHNSON
Maxcy Gregg's Sporting Journals 1842-1858

JAMES R. KENNEDY
Dixie Rising: Rules For Rebels

Nullifying Federal and State Gun Control: A How-To Guide For Gun Owners

When Rebel Was Cool: Growing Up In Dixie, 1950-1965

WALTER D. KENNEDY
The South's Struggle: America's Hope

Lincoln, The Non-Christian President: Exposing The Myth

Lincoln, Marx, and the GOP

J.R. & W.D. KENNEDY
Jefferson Davis: High Road to Emancipation and Constitutional Government

Yankee Empire: Aggressive Abroad and Despotic at Home

Punished With Poverty: The Suffering South

The South Was Right! 3rd Edition

LEWIS LIBERMAN
Snowflake Buddies; ABC Leftism For Kids!

PHILIP LEIGH
The Devil's Town: Hot Springs During The Gangster Era

U.S. Grant's Failed Presidency

The Causes of the Civil War

The Dreadful Frauds: Critical Race Theory And Identity Politics

JACK MARQUARDT
Around The World In 80 Years: Confessions of a Connecticut Confederate

MICHAEL MARTIN
Southern Grit: Sensing The Siege at Petersburg

SAMUEL MITCHAM
The Greatest Lynching In American History: New York, 1863

Confederate Patton: Richard Taylor and The Red River Campaign

CHARLES T. PACE
Lincoln As He Really Was

Southern Independence. Why War? The War To Prevent Southern Independence

JAMES R. ROESCH
From Founding Fathers To Fire Eaters

KIRKPATRICK SALE
Emancipation Hell: The Tragedy Wrought By Lincoln's Emancipation Proclamation

JOSEPH SCOTCHIE
The Asheville Connection: The Making of a Conservative

ANNE W. SMITH

Charlottesville Untold: Inside Unite The Right

Robert E. Lee: A History for Kids

KAREN STOKES

A Legion Of Devils: Sherman In South Carolina

The Burning of Columbia, S.C.: A Review of Northern Assertions and Southern Facts

Fortunes of War: The Adventures of a German Confederate

A Confederate in Paris: Letters of A. Dudley Mann 1867-1879

JACK TROTTER

Last Train to Dixie

JOHN THEURSAM

Key West's Civil War

H.V. TRAYWICK, JR.

Along The Shadow Line: A Road Trip through History and Memory on the Old Confederate Border

LESLIE TUCKER

Old Times There Should Not Be Forgotten: Cultural Genocide In Dixie

JOHN VINSON

Southerner Take Your Stand!

MARK R. WINCHELL

Confessions of a Copperhead: Culture and Politics in the Modern South

CLYDE N. WILSON

Calhoun: A Statesman for the 21st Century

Lies My Teacher Told Me: The True History of the War For Southern Independence

The Yankee Problem: An American Dilemma

Annals Of The Stupid Party: Republicans Before Trump

Nullification: Reclaiming The Consent of the Governed

The Old South: 50 Essential Books

The War Between The States: 60 Essential Books

Reconstruction and the New South, 1865-1913: 50 Essential Books

The South 20th Century And Beyond: 50 Essential Books

Southern Poets and Poems, 1606-1860: The Land They Loved, Volume 1

Looking For Mr. Jefferson

African American Slavery in Historical Perspective

JOE WOLVERTON

What Degree Of Madness?: Madison's Method To Make American States Again

WALTER KIRK WOOD

Beyond Slavery: The Northern Romantic Nationalist Origins of America's Civil War

Green Altar (Literary Imprint)

CATHARINE BROSMAN
An Aesthetic Education and Other Stories (2nd Ed)

Chained Tree, Chained Owls: Poems

Aerosols and Other Poems

RANDALL IVEY
A New England Romance: And Other Southern Stories

JAMES E. KIBBLER, JR.
Tiller : Clayback County Series, Vol. 4

THOMAS MOORE
A Fatal Mercy: The Man Who Lost The Civil War

PERRIN LOVETT
The Substitute, Tom Ironsides 1

KAREN STOKES
Belles

Carolina Love Letters

Carolina Twilight

Honor in the Dust

The Immortals

The Soldier's Ghost: A Tale of Charleston

WILLIAM THOMAS
Runaway Haley: An Imagined Family Saga

Gold-Bug
(Mystery & Suspense Imprint)

BRANDI PERRY
Splintered: A New Orleans Tale

MARTIN WILSON
To Jekyll and Hide

Free Book Offer

DON'T GET LEFT OUT, Y'ALL.
Sign-up and be the first to know about new releases, sales, and other goodies
—plus we'll send you TWO FREE EBOOKS!

Lies My Teacher Told Me:
The True History of the War for
Southern Independence
by Dr. Clyde N. Wilson

When The Yankees Come
Former Carolina Slaves Remember
Sherman's March From the Sea
by Paul C. Graham

FreeLiesBook.com

Southern Books. No Apologies.
We love the South — its history,
traditions, and culture — and are proud
of our inheritance as Southerners.
Our books are a reflection of this love.